CENTAUR CLASSICS

GENERAL EDITOR: J. M. COHEN

LITERARY ANECDOTES
OF THE EIGHTEENTH CENTURY

JOHN NICHOLS, ESQ. F.S.A.

Literary Anecdotes

of the

Eighteenth Century

by

JOHN NICHOLS F.S.A.

Edited by

COLIN CLAIR

SOUTHERN ILLINOIS UNIVERSITY PRESS
CARBONDALE   ILLINOIS

© *Centaur Press Ltd, 1967*

Published in the United States by
Southern Illinois University Press, Carbondale, Illinois.

Printed in Great Britain

CONTENTS

	Page
INTRODUCTION	9
AMES, JOSEPH	19
ASTLE, THOMAS	28
BAGFORD, JOHN	31
BASKERVILLE, JOHN	33
BATTIE, WILLIAM	38
BOSWELL, JAMES	45
BOWYER, WILLIAM	49
BOYDELL, JOHN	59
BRADLEY, RICHARD	63
BRAND, JOHN	66
BROWNE, SIR WILLIAM	68
CASLON, WILLIAM	72
CAVE, EDWARD	76
COLLINS, ARTHUR	89
DAVIES, THOMAS	94
DESGULIERS, JOHN THEOPHILUS	98
DODSLEY, JAMES	100
DUCAREL, ANDREW COLTEE	102
DUNTON, JOHN	114
ELSTOB, WILLIAM & ELIZABETH	125
FIELDING, HENRY	131
GAINSBOROUGH, THOMAS	145
GARRICK, DAVID	147
GED, WILLIAM	154
GOUGH, RICHARD	155
GUY, THOMAS	164
HERBERT, WILLIAM	166
HOLLIS, THOMAS	168
HOOLE, JOHN	173
ILIVE, JACOB	177
JACKSON, JOSEPH & COTTRELL, THOMAS	180
JAMES, FAMILY OF	184
LAW, WILLIAM	188
LEAKE, STEPHEN MARTIN	192
L'ESTRANGE, SIR ROGER	195
LINTOT, BERNARD & HENRY	199

LINTOT AND HIS AUTHORS   203
SWIFT ON LINTOT   215
LYTTELTON, GEORGE LORD   216
MARKLAND, JEREMIAH   220
MEAD, RICHARD   233
MIDDLETON, CONYERS   238
MORES, EDWARD ROWE   243
MUDGE, JOHN & ZACARIAH   249
MURRAY, JOHN   252
MYLNE, ROBERT   255
NICHOLS, JOHN, AND DR. JOHNSON   257
OSBORNE, THOMAS   264
PALMER, SAMUEL   267
PARSONS, JAMES   271
POPE, ALEXANDER   274
PRINCE, DANIEL   284
RAIKES, ROBERT   291
RATCLIFFE, JOHN   293
RICHARDSON, SAMUEL   296
RYMER, THOMAS   304
SELDEN, JOHN   305
SETTLE, ELKANAH   308
STACKHOUSE, THOMAS   312
STEEVENS, GEORGE   319
STRAHAN, WILLIAM   324
STRUTT, JOSEPH   329
TASSIE, JAMES   336
TAYLOR, JOHN   339
THICKNESSE, PHILIP   354
TOOKE FAMILY, THE   360
URRY, JOHN   374
VERTUE, GEORGE   376
WALPOLE, HORACE   382
WANLEY, HUMFREY, (ON BAGFORD'S COLLECTION)   388
WARBURTON, BISHOP   391
WEDGWOOD, JOSIAH   401
WESLEYS, THE   404
WHITEFIELD, GEORGE   430
WILKES, JOHN   437
WILLIS, BROWNE   446
WOODFALL, HENRY & WILLIAM   452
WORTLEY-MONTAGUE, EDWARD   457

THE SACRED TOUCH   471

HISTORY OF THE ORIGIN OF PAMPHLETS   478

ON THE FIRST PRINTED POLYGLOTTS   487

THE AUTHOR OF ΕΙΚΩΝ ΒΑΣΙΛΙΚΗ   490

REMARKS ON STEPHENS'S THESAURUS   496

THE BOOKSELLERS OF LITTLE BRITAIN   523

INTRODUCTION

JOHN NICHOLS was born at Islington on 2nd February, 1745, the eldest son of Edward Nichols (1719-1779), a master baker, and his wife Anne, daughter of Thomas Wilmot of Beckingham, Gainsborough. At Islington, still at that time a village, the boy received his education at the hands of John Shield, a graduate of Edinburgh University who ran an academy for boys. At this school, where Nichols remained for eight years, he received a grounding in Latin which became useful to him in the profession which he was destined to follow, although it was not the one originally conceived for him.

It had been arranged that he should join the Royal Navy, but this project was abandoned when his maternal grandfather's friend, Admiral Barrington, died in 1751. Instead, when Nichols was twelve his father apprenticed him to William Bowyer the Younger, a printer of White Friars, London, often referred to as "the last of the learned printers". This man's father, William Bowyer the Elder, was also an eminent printer, and his maternal grandfather, Thomas Dawks, had been employed on the famous Polyglot Bible of Bishop Walton, published in 1657. Edward Nichols paid a fee of £20 for his son's apprenticeship.

Bowyer was very concerned about the number of apprentices in the printing trade who were almost devoid of any education, and when he advertised for an apprentice he insisted that he required one "with some share of learning, the more the better." Moreover Bowyer took his obligations as master seriously and showed a keen interest in those he employed, particularly so in the case of the young John Nichols whose exceptional qualities he seems to have discerned from the first.

Nichols had not been long with Bowyer before the latter was entrusting him with many duties not normally expected from a young and inexperienced compositor. He found the young man not only honest and industrious, quick and receptive of ideas, but also — and this must have weighed in his favour with the "learned printer" — fairly well grounded in Latin. While still an apprentice, at the age of sixteen he translated some Latin epigrams for a pamphlet, *Verses on the Coronation of their late Majesties King George II and Queen Caroline,* which was published in 1761. Indeed Bowyer seems to have treated his young apprentice as a personal friend, for Nichols tells how he sometimes had the pleasure of attending the lectures of the astronomer James Ferguson in company with his master, who not infrequently consulted him on that subject.

In 1765 Nichols was sent to Cambridge to negotiate with the Vice-Chancellor of the University on behalf of his employer for the purchase of a lease of their exclusive privileges, since Bowyer felt at that time inclined to undertake the management of the University Press. In entrusting a young man of twenty with such a responsible mission it is clear that Bowyer had the highest regard for his protégé's capabilities. Although nothing came of these negotiations, apparently Bowyer had no particular regrets. Nichols writes in 1810:

"At the distance of 45 years I have great satisfaction in recollecting this pleasant journey. The world was then all fair before me; and I was looking forward to my future settlement in life. I had never before been above 20 miles from London; and my heart expanded when I mounted on the outside of the coach to undertake so long a journey as to Cambridge. The Colleges, the Libraries, the Public Walks, and the fertile Gardens, were a source of inexpressible delight; and, though drenched with rain on my lofty seat in returning, I enjoyed my few holidays to the last moment."

On 4th March, 1766, Nichols was made free of the Stationers' Company at the end of his apprenticeship, and Bowyer returned to Nichols's father half the apprenticeship fee, which he had promised to do on condition that the lad had "behaved suitable to his expectations." Indeed, Nichols, now twenty-one, must have exceeded those expectations, for in that same year Bowyer took him into partnership. He was probably disappointed that his only surviving son, Thomas Bowyer, showed no inclination to enter the business; moreover, a previous partnership between Bowyer and a relative of his named James Emonson, an overseer in the printing works, had been dissolved after a law-suit. The six years that had elapsed between this dispute and Nichols's termination of his apprenticeship made it clear to Bowyer, now an elderly man, that he must have someone to share the immediate labours of the business and eventually to succeed him, for his health was beginning to decline.

At all events the partnership was a successful one; a cordial union which lasted until Bowyer's death in 1777. Nichols later wrote : "His [i.e. Bowyer's] new Associate, whilst an Apprentice, had been intrusted with a considerable share of the management of the Printing-office; and the connexion was such as, I am proud to say, was highly satisfactory to Mr. BOWYER. To his Partner, it was all that a young man could possibly have hoped for; it was an introduction to a number of respectable Friends, whose patronage was equally honourable and advantageous." As Bowyer not only printed for some of the finest scholars of the age, but was also on terms of intimate friendship with them and at times took a hand in their labours, Nichols had frequent opportunities of meeting them and soon acquired their esteem and patronage, more especially as he was now looked upon as Bowyer's legitimate successor.

From 1766 Bowyer was able to divest himself of some of the business routine inseparable from a large printing and publishing business, and devote more of his time to literary pursuits, leaving his young partner to deal in ever increasing measure with the work in hand. This was growing to such an extent that the premises at Dogwell Court, White Friars, where Bowyer's father had worked for many years, were too restricted and a move became imperative, though not without reluctance on the part of Bowyer, unwilling now to depart from White Friars where he was born and had lived for more than 66 years.

Eventually, having consulted his old friend Jeremiah Markland, as he invariably did on matters of importance, he consented to the move. "Far from condemning you in what you have done as to the Printing-house," wrote Markland, "I agree with you entirely, provided you agree with yourself; for if a man does not know at our time of life what is proper for him to do, the condition of mortality is certainly on a worse footing than Providence designed it." And so, in 1767, Bowyer took new premises in Red Lion Passage, Fleet Street, where he styled himself *Architectus Verborum,* and placed over the door of his new printing-house a bust of Cicero, under which was an inscription *M. T. Cicero, a quo primordia preli.* In that same year Bowyer was appointed printer of the Rolls of Parliament and the Journals of the House of Lords, largely through the influence of the Earl of Marchmont.

The printing house in Red Lion Passage was among the most important in London at that time, for in addition to the normal printing of books, the firm was engaged in a considerable amount of parliamentary printing, as well as printing periodicals and the

transactions of learned societies. With the deterioration of Bowyer's health Nichols was more or less in sole charge of the
business, of which he became the head when his former master
died on 18th November 1777, at the age of seventy-seven.

In 1778 Nichols obtained a share in the *Gentleman's Magazine,* of which he became joint editor with David Henry, another
printer. Nichols became the guiding spirit, and under his care
and by his industry the magazine acquired a well-justified
reputation as the most informative and entertaining Miscellany
of the period. It outlived all its rivals largely because it was
independent of the ephemeral fashions of the time. For Nichols,
the acquisition of the *Gentleman's Magazine* held certain
advantages. Since the contributors to it were men of learning,
Nichols made many new friends, and acquired from them
information which laid the foundations for such compilations as
the *Literary Anecdotes* and *Illustrations.* In addition he had at
his disposal the means of publicising the works he was publishing.

It was in 1778 that Nichols printed a small pamphlet containing a short account of Mr. Bowyer, *which was later amplified
and published as *Anecdotes of Mr. Bowyer* and formed the basis
of the *Literary Anecdotes.* One of the books on which Bowyer
and Nichols had been engaged before the former's death was a
complete edition of *Domesday Book,* which was not finished until
1783. It had been undertaken as the result of a decision of the
House of Commons in March, 1767, to print "such Parliamentary and other Public Records as His Majesty shall see proper
and fit." The types for this facsimile were cut by Joseph Jackson
under the supervision of Abraham Farley. This was the book of
which Nichols said "On the correctness and the beauty of this
important work I am content to stake my typographical credit."
It took a good ten years in passing through the press.

So successful was Jackson with his facsimile letter for *Domesday Book* that he was commissioned by Nichols to cut the type
for Dr. Woide's facsimile of the New Testament of the *Alexandrian Codex* in the British Museum. The work came from
Nichols's press in 1786, and as a tribute to the punch-cutter his
name was mentioned on the title-page.

Like Bowyer before him Nichols printed a number of topographical works. In conjunction they had issued in 1774 John
Hutchin's *History and Antiquities of Dorset,* largely at the in-

---

*Reprinted in Vol. XLVIII of the *Gentleman's Magazine.*

stigation of Richard Gough, one of the most eminent antiquaries of his time, who considered that local history in Britain had been grossly neglected by competent historians. Nichols's friendship with Gough, which lasted until the latter's death in 1809, began, according to Chalmers,* about 1770, and was further cemented whilst Gough was superintending the printing of his friend Hutchin's history. The antiquary became the godfather of Nichols's grandson, who was named John Gough Nichols.

With Richard Gough as its chief contributor, Nichols's *Bibliotheca Topographica Britannica* appeared in fifty-two numbers between 1780 and 1790, and was followed by the *Miscellaneous Antiquities*. The numbers varied in size and price, and numbers 50 and 51 contained collections for a history of Leicestershire compiled by Nichols himself. These were subsequently enlarged and published between 1795 and 1815 as *The History and Antiquities of the County of Leicester,* in four volumes, each of two parts, the whole forming what the *Monthly Review* termed a work "of prodigious and almost inconceivable labour." Unfortunately a disastrous fire at Nichols's printing office in 1808 destroyed all the remaining copies of the six parts that had by then been published and Nichols told Bishop Percy that in respect of that one book alone he had incurred a loss of at least £5,000 as a result of the fire.

In 1780 Nichols published his own *Select Collection of Poems, with Notes, Biographical and Historical,* in 4 volumes, to which were added a further 4 volumes in 1782. In this publication Nichols revived a number of curious and valuable pieces which had long been forgotten as well as some which might with advantage have remained in obscurity. In the following year appeared the *Biographical Anecdotes of William Hogarth,* a book of 160 pages in which Nichols collaborated with the eminent Shakespearian critic George Steevens. In 1782 the book came out in a second edition, augmented to 482 pages; and this, in turn, was extended to form a three-volume production called *The Genuine Works of William Hogarth,* 1808-17.

Nichols was a great compiler, and since he was in the habit of printing material as soon as he came by it, his many historical compilations are often badly arranged. For instance the *Progresses and Public Processions of Queen Elizabeth* made its first

---

*Author of an obituary notice of Nichols in the *Gentleman's Magazine,* December, 1826.

appearance in two quarto volumes in 1788, to be followed seventeen years later by a third volume, and by the first part of a fourth volume thirty-three years later (the second part never appeared).

Nichols, "indefatigable in the pursuit of what is curious and antique" (to quote the *Monthly Review*), went to great pains to collect material for his *Royal and Noble Wills,* which included all those known to be extant from William the Conqueror to Henry VIII. The Collection was begun in 1780, and the Wills of Henry VII and Henry VIII were issued as separate publications,* the series being completed in 1794. In this project Nichols was assisted by Richard Gough and Andrew Ducarel, the keeper of manuscripts at Lambeth Palace, to whom the idea was due. These two gentlemen also assisted him in the editing of *The History of the Royal Abbey of Bec,* and *Some Account of the Alien Priories,* both published in 1779.

The year 1780 saw London life disrupted for a time by the Gordon Riots, and we find Richard Gough writing to Sir John Cullum (who was responsible for the Glossary to the *Royal Wills*):

"Poor Nichols being personally threatened, as well as the King's Printer, all business stopped there last week. The distress of his family affected me more than all the shocking scenes I saw in London last Thursday, or that my servant related to me on his return from the scene of action that morning."

Yet another historical compilation by Nichols was *Illustrations of the Manners and Expences of Antient Times in England* (1797). He was justifiably proud of this publication, which does indeed contain much curious and valuable information, and speaking of it he remarks: "I have been accused of prolixity; but, in this instance, *had I been as tedious again, I would have bestowed it all upon the Publicke.*"

Whilst still an apprentice Nichols had conceived an admiration for Swift, when he assisted in passing through the press his master's edition of the 13th and 14th octavo volumes of that author's works (1762). He later shared in the editing of two supplementary volumes to Dr. Hawkesworth's edition (1775). When he succeeded to the business Nichols was anxious to edit and print his own edition of Swift's works but ran into difficulties

---

*The Will of Henry VII was published with notes by Thomas Astle in 1775.

with the London booksellers who, despite the Copyright Act of 1710, still insisted on their Common Law rights to perpetual ownership of copyright. An edition edited by Thomas Sheridan had been produced in 1784 with the sanction of all the booksellers who held part of the copyright, and in 1801 Nichols was permitted to produce a new version of Sheridan's edition the printing of which he shared with three other firms. Two further editions of this version came out in 1803 and 1808.

In addition to the normal routine of book printing and a considerable amount of parliamentary printing, Nichols reprinted *The Spectator* and *The Tatler* in book form, as well as a number of other periodicals. From 1770 to 1798 he printed *Archaeologia*, the journal of the Society of Antiquaries, of which body he was himself elected a Fellow in 1810. On Bowyer's death Nichols had succeeded to the offices of Printer to the Royal Society and to the Society of Antiquaries. Towards the end of the century, however, he lost both the contracts, the former in 1791 and the latter in 1798. The reason was that his printing, although accurate, was no match in typographical style for that of his two great rivals, Bulmer and Bensley, whereas his charges were as high. As a result Thomas Bulmer obtained the contract for printing the transactions of the Royal Society, and Bensley was employed in place of Nichols by the Society of Antiquaries.*

At his best Nichols was a good printer; his *Domesday Book* proves it. But in later years the onerous duties of editor and compiler seem to have left him insufficient time effectively to supervise the printing, which lagged behind that of his principal competitors. The *Literary Anecdotes of the Eighteenth Century*, from which the extracts comprising the present volume have been taken, is a case in point. There are nine volumes in all, each of 700 pages or more, set in the dullest possible fashion, often with two lines of text suspended above 40 lines of notes in small type, and each page liberally bespattered with asterisks, daggers, and other reference marks. As Albert H. Smith remarks† "it is the quantity of worth-while books that Nichols printed which impresses rather than the printing itself."

A further example of Nichols's fruitful collaboration with

---

*In 1821 the firm of Nichols was, however, reappointed Printer to the Society.

†Albert H. Smith: *John Nichols, Printer & Publisher, in* "The Library," Sept., 1963.

Richard Gough is shown in *The Antiquaries Museum* by Jacob
Schnebbelie, a quarto volume with plates, published in 1800,
and prefaced by Gough's biographical memoir of the artist.
Schnebbelie, according to Gough, had by 1791 mastered the art
of aquatinting, and intended to publish a work illustrating
ancient architecture, painting and sculpture in Britain, but died
before it was finished. His drawings came into the hands of his
two friends, Gough and Nichols, who determined to complete it.

In 1804 Nichols, who had the previous year been appointed
a Warden of the Stationers' Company, achieved his lifelong
ambition in being elected Master of the Company. Although
shorn of the powers it once possessed the Stationers' Company
was still a very influential body.

In February, 1808, Nichols experienced a calamity similar
to that which had once overtaken his former partner's father,
the elder Bowyer, for his printing office and warehouses, together
with almost the whole of their contents, were destroyed by fire.
In this misfortune he was supported, as he expressed it, "by the
consolatory balm of friendship, and the offers of unlimited
pecuniary assistance," and in 1809 he was busy once again with
his literary labours.

In 1812 Nichols began the publication of the work by which
he is perhaps best known today — the *Literary Anecdotes of the
Eighteenth Century*. The six volumes which Nichols contem-
plated grew to nine, the final volume appearing in 1815. Paul
Maty, in his *New Review,* describes the work as "an account of
a very distinguished and very worthy Printer [William Bowyer]
. . . together with Anecdotes, some longer, some shorter, of the
Writers who printed at Mr. Bowyer's press: the Warburtons,
the Sherlocks, the Marklands, the Jortins, the Taylors, the De
Missys, the Gales, the Stukeleys, &c. &c. &c. The use of this
Work, which will grow more precious the older it grows, is, that
several memorials of Works and Authors will hereby be preserved, which otherwise would have sunk in oblivion." The Rev.
Joseph Robertson, writing in the *Critical Review,* states that
"this Work contains a copious treasure of biographical information; and may be said to form a valuable history of the progress
and advancement of Literature in this kingdom from the beginning of the eighteenth century to the end of the year 1777." This
was written before the series was completed and the whole may
be said to cover the eighteenth century in its entirety.

Writing to Nichols on 20th April, 1812, after the publication of the first six volumes, Isaac D'Israeli said : "I congratulate you in having accomplished this important work, which will now rank on our shelves with Wood's *Athenae* — a great favourite with me; yet you have the advantage of a more interesting period, from the superiority of the works and the authors."

It must be admitted that the *Literary Anecdotes* is an exasperating work to read in its original form. There are in all 6,580 pages, of which probably three-quarters is in small print, and there is a complete lack of any arrangement of the material. Nichols himself was well aware of this and excused it by saying that "such a book could not very easily have been otherwise produced." The main trouble with the book is that Nichols was incapable of condensing his material, with the result that the volumes are swollen with trifling details which might well have been omitted. Moreover he was far from discriminating in the material he printed. Many of the biographical notices are of the utmost value, but a large proportion are almost destitute of any reason for their preservation. "Country curates who have occupied their idle hours," says a writer in the *Monthly Review,* "in what they supposed to be literature, the composition of sermons, verses of which nobody beyond their own small circle had ever heard, essays upon subjects of local interest . . . think that their letters and the story of their lives must be supremely worthy of preservation, and forthwith they turn their eyes towards Mr. Nichols. He, good man, deems every scrap of their writings worthy of being printed." The writer concludes by saying : "We beg of him to condense his materials in future, to omit without mercy, and consign to the fire a ton or two of the stores which are yet far from being exhausted !"

In this present selection from the *Literary Anecdotes* an attempt has been made to retain the good grain after winnowing the chaff, for as Nichols truthfully remarks in his "advertisement" to Vol. 9 : "It is a Mine of literary materials, whence future Biographers and Historians will readily and unsparingly collect what may suit their several purposes." Indeed, since the compiler penned those lines writers have dipped freely into this literary treasure-chest, frequently without acknowledgment. In view of the fact that the work has never been reprinted *in extenso* and that a set of the original volumes is now almost impossible to obtain, even at a high price, this selection should meet a very present need.

Such were the almost inexhaustible stores which Nichols had

accumulated that he planned a sequel to the *Anecdotes,* which he called *Illustrations of the Eighteenth Century.* This appeared in eight volumes between 1817 and 1858. He himself left the fifth volume nearly completed at the time of his death, and the remaining volumes were compiled and printed by his son, John Bowyer Nichols.

In 1803 Nichols and his family moved from their house in Red Lion Passage to Highbury Place, Islington — at that period a fashionable residential district for business men — and there he died on 26th November, 1826. He was buried in the family grave at St. Mary's, Islington, within a few yards of the house in which he was born. His business remained in the capable hands of his son, John Bowyer Nichols.

COLIN CLAIR

NOTE.—In this edition a uniform size of type has been used throughout. Passages which in the original were embodied in the notes are distinguished by being enclosed in square brackets. The orthography of the original edition has in general been retained, although obvious printer's literals have been corrected.

JOSEPH AMES

JOSEPH AMES was descended from an antient family in Norfolk, where they are to be traced as far back as the middle of the 16th century. His great grandfather John Ames, son of Lancelot, was born at Norwich, March 3, 1576. He settled at Great Yarmouth, where his son Joseph was born March 5, 1619; who became a commander of some eminence in the Navy during the Protectorate; here mention should be made of the honorary medal that was given him for his public services. He died Dec. 1, 1695, æt. 76; leaving six children; of whom John, the sixth, settled in Wapping; where he had a small freehold of 40*l.* a year; and was a person of some curiosity; having made several collections for the town of Great Yarmouth, as well as other places which he had visited, particularly the sea-coast of England, Scotland, Norway, Holland, and France. He was the father of Joseph, the subject of this memoir; who was born at Yarmouth Jan. 23, 1688-9, and was about 12 years old at his father's death, and at a little grammar-school in Wapping. At 15, it is said, he was put apprentice to a plane-maker near Guild-hall, London; and, after serving out his time with reputation, settled near the Hermitage, in Wapping, in the business of a ship-chandler, or ironmonger, and continued there till his death. In 1712 he lost his mother, who was buried in Wapping-church near her husband; and in 1714 he married Mary, daughter of William Wrayford, merchant of London.

When Mr. Ames's father came to live in Wapping, Mr. John Russel, minister of Poole in Dorsetshire, was preacher at St. John's, and continued so till his death in 1723. During his residence at Poole he had received many marks of friendship from the family of the Rev. Mr. John Lewis, minister of Margate, afterwards vicar of Minster in the Isle of Thanet about 40 years; an eminent divine and antiquary, well known for his many learned publications. In return for this kindness, Mr. Russel invited Mr. Lewis, who then taught grammar at Poole, whither he returned after his early removal to Bristol, to live with him at Wapping. Being himself much favoured by Abp. Tenison, he introduced Mr. Lewis to that Prelate, which Mr. Lewis acknowledged to have laid the foundation of his preferment in the

19

Church. Mr. Russel was a worthy Divine, and took great notice of his neighbour, Mr. John Ames, and his infant son; and when Mr. Joseph Ames commenced housekeeper, Mr. Russel frequently visited him, and gave him his advice, which Mr. Ames ever after gratefully acknowledged. He introduced him to the acquaintance of Mr. Lewis, with whom he soon formed a friendship that continued as long as Mr. Lewis lived.

Mr. Ames very early discovered a taste for English history and antiquities, which was encouraged by his two friends. Some time before 1720, in attending Dr. Desaguliers' lectures, he formed an acquaintance with Mr. Peter Thompson, another native of Poole and with whom Mr. Ames continued on terms of the most friendly intercourse till his death. [Mr. Oldys, in his British Librarian, published in 1737, returns many thanks "to Mr. Joseph Ames, member of the Society of Antiquaries, for the use 'of one antient relick of the famous Wicliffe'." This was an illuminated MS. on vellum, called "Wicliffe's Pore Caitiff." Mr. Oldys goes on to acknowledge his obligations to Mr. Ames, whom he styles "a worthy preserver of antiquities," and to " his ingenious friend Mr. Peter Thompson, for the use of several printed books, which are more scarce than manuscripts; particularly some, set forth by our first printer in England; and others, which will rise, among the curious, in value, as, by the depredations of accidents or ignorance, they decrease in number."]

Some time before 1730, Mr. Lewis, who had himself collected materials for such a subject, suggested to Mr. Ames the idea of writing the History of Printing in England. Mr. Ames declined it at first, because Mr. Palmer, a printer, was engaged in a similar work, and because he thought himself by no means equal to an undertaking of so much extent. But, when Mr. Palmer's book came out, it by no means answered the expectations of Mr. Lewis or Mr. Ames, or those of the publick in general. Mr. Ames, therefore, at length consented to apply himself to the task; and after 25 years spent in collecting and arranging his materials, in which he was largely assisted by Mr. Lewis and other learned friends, and by the libraries of Lord Oxford, Sir Hans Sloane, Mr. Anstis, and many others, published in one volume, 4to, 1749, his "Typographical Antiquities, being an Historical Account of Printing in England, with some Memoirs of our antient Printers, and a Register of the Books printed by them, from the Year 1471 to the Year 1600; with an Appendix concerning Printing in Scotland and Ireland to the Same Time."

What was his own opinion of this work, may be seen by his words in the Preface:

"I do also ingenuously confess, that, in attempting this History of Printing, I have undertaken a task much too great for my abilities, the extent of which I did not so well perceive at first; but though it is not so perfect a work as I could wish, yet, such as it is, I now submit it to the publick; and hope, when they consider in what obscurity and confusion Printing in its infancy was involved, they will acknowledge that I have at least cleared away the rubbish, and furnished materials towards a more perfect structure." The opinions of others may be seen in the "Nova Acta Eruditorum," for 1754.

The work was inscribed to Philip Lord Hardwicke, Lord High Chancellor of Great Britain. Mr. Ames was then fellow of the Royal and Antiquarian Societies, and secretary to the latter of these learned bodies. He was elected F.S.A. March 3, 1736; and on the resignation of Alexander Gordon, previous to his going to settle in Carolina, 1741, was appointed secretary. In 1754, the Rev. William Norris was associated with him; and on his decease became sole secretary till 1784. The Minutes of the Society in the earlier periods of it were barely outlines of the proceedings of each meeting; for no secretary, before Mr. Norris, had an idea of giving abridgements of papers, however indispensably necessary, before the finances of the Society enabled them to print the memoirs themselves. This office gave Mr. Ames farther opportunities of gratifying his native curiosity by the communications as well as conversation of the Literati; and these opportunities were farther enlarged by his election into the Royal Society, and the particular friendship shewn to him by Sir Hans Sloane, then president, who nominated him one of the trustees in his will. The circumstances of Mr. Ames's death are thus related by his friend Sir Peter Thompson, in a short account of him, from whence the principal parts of this life are extracted: "After he had dined heartily with Sir Peter, Oct. 7, 1759, he went to Mr. Romelo's, in Basinghall-street, to see some curiosities, drank some coffee, and stayed there till past seven o'clock, when he and another friend, an ironmonger in St. Clement's-lane, whose name is not mentioned, departed to their respective homes. As they passed by the Royal Exchange, Mr. Ames was seized with a violent fit of coughing, which brought on a profuse perspiration, and lasted near a quarter of an hour. When he had recovered himself, his friend asked him to come into his house in Clement's-lane, and sup with him. Mr. Ames complied with his invitation, in order to rest himself, and sat himself down on the first thing which presented itself in the shop. His friend desired him to remove into a chair in the counting-house, which he had no sooner done, than he expired without a sigh or groan. He was immediately put into a warm bed, and medical assistance called in; but without effect. He was removed to his own house the next day; and from thence to the church-yard of St. George in the East, Oct. 14, 1759, where he was deposited, at the depth of eight feet, in virgin earth, in a stone coffin.

The following paragraph, inserted in the Public Advertiser the Tuesday after his decease, contains his real character:

"Last Sunday evening died, after a violent fit of coughing, Mr. Joseph Ames, author of the History of Printing in England, fellow of the Royal Society, and Secretary to the Society of Antiquaries, for which station he was eminently qualified by an inquisitive genius and assiduous application. His judicious taste in manuscripts, medals, and other curiosities, will be submitted to the public decision by the large and valuable collection he has left behind him. His amiable simplicity of manners, exemplary integrity, and benevolence in social life, greatly endeared him to all who had the pleasure of his acquaintance."

Much as we are indebted to the eccentric Mr. Mores for his account of our Founders, we cannot forbear noticing his harsh censure of Mr. Ames as an "arrant blunderer," supposed to have made English of the *Wetsteins,* and called them the *Westons.* Mr. Bagford committed a similar error in changing *Wenceslaus Hollar* into *William Hillier.* Mr. Mores adds more truly, Mr. Ames "was unlearned, yet useful; he collected antiquities, and particularly old title-pages and heads of authors, which he tore out, and maimed the books: for the first of these crimes he made some amends by his 'Typographical Antiquities'; for the second by his 'Catalogue of English Heads,' taken from the collection of Mr. Nickolls. This performance is not to be despised." Mr. Mores proceeds with a just invective against *portrait-fanciers,* compared with whom Mr. Ames was but one sinner among many.

Mr. Ames's collection of coins, natural curiosities, inscriptions, and antiquities, were sold by Mr. Langford, Feb. 20 and 21, 1760. His library of books and manuscripts and his prints, May 5-12, 1760, by the same auctioneer. Many of the books had notes by him; and among the MSS. besides a number of valuable historical and oriental transcripts, were:

Several Saxon Homilies, &c. by Mr. Elstob and his learned sister, purchased for a very small sum by the late James West, esq. and at his sale by John Maddison, esq.

A folio volume, handsomely bound in Turkey, inscribed "John Bull, doctor of musique, organiste and gentleman of her Majesty's most honourable chappell"; the ruled paper of which is marked in every sheet with T. E. the initials of Thomas East, who printed music under the patent granted to Thomas Tallis and William Birde, by Queen Elizabeth, 1575, for 21 years; few however of the tunes have the words put to them, or the name of the composer; and Dr. Bull's name is not there, but only those of other persons, so that it is probable he was only owner of the book.

A transcript of King Alfred's translation of Orosius's "Hormesta Mundi," purchased by Mr. Pegge, and published with a literal English translation by the Hon. Daines Barrington, 1773, 8vo.

Mr. Lewis's History and Antiquities of Feversham, with many MS notes by the author.

Mr. Lewis's History and Antiquities of the Isle of Thanet, with many MS notes and additions by the author, drawings, plans, &c. it having been Mr. Lewis's own copy, and by him left to Mr. Ames.

Both these were bought by James Beauclerk, Lord Bishop of Hereford, came afterwards into the hands of Mr. Gulston, and on the sale of his library became the property of Mr. Gough; as did also Gardiner's Antiquities of Dunwich, with MS notes by Mr. Ames; Coker's Survey of Dorsetshire, with MS additions by Mr. Ames and Mr. Lewis; Martin's Western Islands, 1716, with MS notes by Mr. Toland and Lord Viscount Molesworth; and Dugdale's View of the Troubles of England, with MS notes by the author.

Mr. Palmer's History of Printing, with a number of MS Notes by Mr. Ames, and Heads of the early Printers; and an Essay towards the History of Printing in England, by the Rev. Mr. Lewis, dated May 15, 1739.

The second volume of Mr. Palmer's work on the practical part of Printing, ready for press.

A variety of letters concerning Printing, from Mr. Lewis, Mr. Ballard, Mr. Rawlinson, Mr. North, Mr. Anstis, Mr. Thomas Baker, and others, purchased by Mr. Tutet. Some of these, which were given me by Mr. Gough with his interleaved copy of the former edition of these "Anecdotes," have been selected as a suitable illustration of the present publication, and shall be given in a future part of it.

Mr. Ames's History of Printing in two volumes, interleaved with a great number of MS additions and notes by himself. This copy, with the plates, blocks, and copy-right to the same, were purchased by his friend Sir Peter Thompson for nine pounds, and sold by him to Mr. Herbert, who, from his own valuable library, and the access he had to the Royal and others, the assistance of his friends, and his own unwearied assiduity, during a course of 25 years, might justly flatter himself that he had ascertained the rise and progress of the typographic art in these kingdoms, to as full an extent as any one man's life and application can attain; still however convinced, by continually recurring experience, that additions may be made even to this collection, as well as mistakes corrected in it.

Mr. Ames's collection of title-pages to books, from 1474 to 1700, in three volumes, folio, with several bundles more, and of title-pages alphabetically arranged according to the place where printed, in two more folio volumes; a written title-page with a curious border, containing some thousand letters cut in wood, a folio volume, bound in Russia, were purchased by Mr. Walpole; a collection of initial letters, from the beginning of Printing, with some notes by Mr. Ames; and a catalogue of Caxton's books, portraits, and devices of printers; making in the whole seven large portfolios, and three bundles, were purchased by Mr. West; and at his sale, 1773, by Mr. Bull.

Besides his great work, Mr. Ames printed,

"A Catalogue of English Printers, from 1471 to 1700," in 4to, intended to accompany the proposals for the former.

"An Index to Lord Pembroke's Coins."

"A Catalogue of English Heads, or an account of about 2000 Prints, describing what is peculiar on each, as the name, title, or office of the person, the habit, posture, age, or time when done, the name of the painter, graver, scraper, &c. and some remarkable particulars relating to their lives, 1748," 8vo. This was a kind of Index to the ten volumes of English Portraits, which had been collected by Mr. John Nickolls, F. R. and A. SS. of Ware, in Hertfordshire, in 4 volumes, folio, and 6 in 4to.; and after his death, in 1745, were purchased for 80 guineas by the late Dr. Fothergill. Mr. Ames dedicated his catalogue to Mr. West, "well knowing," as he says, "that if ever these increase to another volume, it must be from his valuable treasure." Mr. Granger resumed Mr. Ames's work about 20 years after; and we have only to regret, that the interval since the period which Mr. Granger assigned to himself has not been yet attended to, while the rapid improvement in the art of engraving daily multiplies its subjects to such an amount.

The last of Mr. Ames's literary labours was the drawing up the "Parentalia, or Memoirs of the Family of Wren," 1750, in one volume, folio, from the papers of Mr. Wren.

At Mr. Ames's expence was engraved, on a scale one third of the original, a Greek inscription, in honour of Crato, the musician of Pergamus, erected in the reign of Eumenes, King of Pergamus, 150 years before the Christian æra, brought from the village of Segucque, in Asia Minor, between Smyrna and Ephesus, by Captain Thomas Morley, 1732, and preserved at the house of Mr. Timothy Tennant, in Wapping; and at the sale of Mr. Ames's coins and antiquities purchased by General Campbell. The plate is dedicated to the Society of Antiquaries.

Mr. Ames was also possessed of the antient marble pillar from Alexandria, with the Cufic inscription, purchased since by the late Mr. West, and the late Gustavus Brander, esq. with all the letters from Dr. Hunt, Mr. Costard, and Mr. Bohun, illustrating it; and it was by him presented to the Society of Antiquaries, and engraved and published in their Archæologia, vol. VIII. pl. I. p. 1.

Mr. Ames (as has been observed) married April 12, 1714, Mary, daughter of Mr. Wrayford, merchant of London, who died Aug. 12, 1734; and by whom he had six children. Only one daughter, Mary, survived her mother. She was born Nov. 21, 1759; and married, after her father's decease, to Edward Dampier, late commander of the Sea-horse East Indiaman, which he quitted in 1772, and was appointed deputy surveyor of shipping to the East India Company.

[This memoir of Mr. Ames is taken principally from the biographical account of him by his highly valued friend Mr. Gough, prefixed to the "Typographical Antiquities."]

AN EXCHANGE OF LETTERS BETWEEN
GEORGE NORTH AND JOSEPH AMES

[On a visit to Cambridge in 1747, the antiquary George North came across an early printed book in Bene't College, which he fondly imagined had been printed in 1418, thus antedating Gutenberg by several decades. (*Ed.*)]

"DEAR SIR,   *Bene't College, April* 21, 1747.

"I should have been very glad could you have recovered my letter, in which were the memorandums concerning the papers relating to Printing, in Bene't-college library, because then I might possibly have had the pleasure of serving you. But, even without any such assistance, I have discovered a book, hitherto unknown and unheard-of by me, which puts back the use of Printing at Cambridge long before Serbert's or Sebroch's time.* The title is, *Fratris Laurentii Gulielmi de Saona Nova Rhetorica.* It is in folio, without the number of pages, without any catchwords or signatures: the types very much like Caxton's, or rather (as far as my memory can be trusted to) exactly like those of the book printed at Cologne in 1464, which you shewed me, and from which Caxton made a translation. At the end are these words: "Compilatum autem fuit hoc opus in almâ Universitate Cantabrigiæ, anno D'ni 1418, die et 6 Julii, quo die festum Sanctæ Marthæ recolitur, sub protectione serenissimi regis Anglorum Edwardi quarti." I have no doubt with myself of its being printed here, according to the date. Every particular is to me a proof. I will soon send you a fuller account and a correct specimen of the letter. The post is now going out, therefore can only desire to let me know if I can any ways promote your design in your History of Printing while I am here, where I design to continue till this day se'nnight. If this discovery proves new to you, I must bespeak its being inserted in your Book, that this University may not for the future be so triumphed over by her sister Oxford, on the false notion of being so very late before she had the useful art of Printing."

To this, and another letter on the same subject, Mr. Ames gave the following answer:

"To the Rev. Mr. George North, at Codicote, near Welwyn.

---

*Johann Laer of Siegburg, commonly known as John Siberch, the first printer at Cambridge. (*Ed.*)

"Dear Sir,   *London, 3d May,* 1748.

"I am exceedingly obliged to you for the favour of both your
letters, and your endeavours to serve me in my pleasant work of
the History of English Printing. Though I have been long about
it, yet I am not fatigued or weary. At first reading of your
letters, I rejoiced to find so early a specimen of Printing at
Cambridge as 1418; but, after remembering I had got such a
title down somewhere, I at last found I had transcribed from
Dr. Mead a book which I conceive the same; therefore desire
you would be more critical about it. It runs in the same words;
only the size is different. Thus:

"Rhetorica nova Fratris Laurentii Gulielmi de Saonâ ordinis
minorum. Compilatum autem fuit hoc opus in Almâ Vni-
versitate Cantabrigie, anno Domini 1418, die 6 Julii. Quo
die festum Sancte Marthe recolitur, sub protectione serenissimi Regis Anglorum Edwardi quarti. Impresum fuit hoc
presens opus Rhetoricæ facultatis apud villam Sancti Albani
anno Domini m'cccc'lxxx."

It is divided into three parts, or heads, as a quarto, and printed
in red and black ink, as you represent; only I fear your's wants
the later end; so I am yet in doubt what to do, till I have the
favour of another from you. If it should be a Cambridge book,
the same would be more admirable. But I meet with many
things I want to be better informed of, and should be very
thankful for information; as the ceasing of the Press at

Oxford from	1519	to the year			1585
Cambridge	1521	-	-	-	1524
St. Alban's	1481	-	-	-	1536
Tavistock	1525	-	-	-	1534
Scotland	1510	-	-	-	1540

I can hear of no Books printed between these years. I desire
my best respects to be returned to the Rev. Mr. Masters, whose
receipt I have signed, and sent inclosed to you, having by me
no other frank than this; and will thankfully send you down
some proposals at another opportunity. I am now waiting for
the sheet K of my History of Printing from the press; and have
discovered about 60 Books printed by Caxton; which I have
been more particular in, because of their scarceness. Upon the
whole, I please myself, it will be the best Catalogue of Old
English Books that ever appeared. I am, good Sir,

Your sincere friend and humble servant,   J. Ames."

"I received the two books, *Nicolson* and *Sharp,* very safe, and will take effectual care that they shall be returned to you as unhurt. As to what you mention of a plumb-pudding stone, I wish I could say positively when it may be in my power to oblige you : for the case is this : we have none in our neighbourhood whose grit or cement is hard enough to cut. What I have had were brought from the other side of the country, by a man who used to search for them to carry to London. The chief place for finding them is at Market-street, not far from Dunstable.

THOMAS ASTLE

A GENTLEMAN well known for his extensive and accurate acquaintance with the History and Antiquities of his Country; Keeper of the Records in the Tower, and one of the Keepers of the Paper-office; Trustee of the British Museum, where, when a young man, he had been employed to make an Index to the Harleian Catalogue of MSS.; F. A. S. 1763; F. R. S. 1766; F. R. S. Edinb. Reg. Scient. Soc. Island. Soc. Antiq. Cassel. et Soc. Volscorum Velitris sod. honorar. He was son of Mr. Daniel Astle, keeper of Needwood Forest in Staffordshire; who died 1774, and was buried in Yoxal church, where a neat mural monument is erected to his memory (see it in Shaw's History of Staffordshire, vol. I. p. 101); and who appears to have been descended from a family of that name, resident at, and lords of, the manor of Fauld, in Hanbury parish adjoining, the seat of Burton the Leicestershire Antiquary. Mr. Shaw had access to Mr. Astle's Library, and the use of several MSS. &c. for both volumes of his Staffordshire; his MS Library being accounted to exceed that of any private gentleman in England; and his liberal utility to men of science their acknowledgments abundantly testify. — Mr. Astle, about 1763, obtained the patronage of Mr. Grenville, then First Lord of the Treasury and Chancellor of the Exchequer, who employed him as well in his public as private affairs; and joined him in a commission with the late Sir Joseph Ayloffe, bart. and Dr. Ducarel, for superintending the regulation of the Public Records at Westminster. On the death of his Colleagues, Mr. Topham was substituted; and both were removed by Mr. Pitt during his administration. In 1765 he was appointed Receiver-general of six pence in the pound on the Civil List. In 1766 he was consulted by the Committee of the House of Lords concerning the printing of the antient Records of Parliament. To the superintendance of that Work he introduced his father-in-law, Mr. Morant; and, on his death, in 1770, was himself appointed by the House of Lords to carry on the Work; a service in which he was employed till its completion, five years afterwards. He was then appointed, on the death of Henry Rooke, esq. his Majesty's Chief Clerk in the Record-office in the Tower of London; and, on the decease of Sir John Shelley, he succeeded to the office of Keeper of the Records. Mr. Astle was several times on the Continent on literary pursuits; and died Dec. 1, 1803, in his 69th year, at Battersea Rise, Surrey, of a dropsical complaint to which he had been some time subject. He was buried at Battersea; and a neat tablet has been put up to his memory, at the East end of the church; the inscription on which records his titles and offices, with the date of his decease. His Library, including that of Mr. Morant, and many of the Books enriched by his own MS Notes, particularly on the subject of Biography, and a capital Collection of Antiquarian Tracts, in 5 quarto volumes, was purchased by the Royal Institution. See Mr. Harris's Preface to the judiciously-compiled Catalogue of the Library of the Royal Institution, 1809, 8vo. His MSS. (comprising those of Mr. Morant, the *Aspilogia,* and other rare articles, from the Libraries of Mr. Anstis and Dr. Ducarel), and from other valuable Collections, accumulated during a long series of years, are now deposited at Stowe, the seat of his noble Patron the Marquis of Buckingham, to whom the option of purchasing at a fixed price was given by the will of its owner.

In a letter dated July 17, 1781, Mr. Astle was thus handsomely noticed by Dr. Johnson : "Sir, I am ashamed that you have been forced to send so often for your books; but it has been by no fault on either side. They have never been out of my hands; nor have I been at home without seeing you; for to see a man so skilful in the Antiquities of my Country, is an opportunity of improvement not willingly to be missed. Your notes on *Alfred the Great* appear to me very judicious and accurate; but they are too few. Many things familiar to you are unknown to me, and to most others; and you must not think too favourably of your readers : by supposing them knowing, you will leave them ignorant. Measure of land, and value of money, it is of great importance to state with care. Had the Saxons any gold coin? I have much curiosity after the manners and transactions of the middle ages; but have wanted either diligence, or opportunity, or both. You, Sir, have great opportunity; and I wish *you both diligence and success.* I am, Sir, &c.

SAM. JOHNSON."

The Author of the "New Catalogue of English living Authors" thus delineates the literary character of Mr. Astle. "In order to treat his subject (the character and reign of Henry VII.) with advantage, he has exerted himself to view it on every side; and it must be allowed that he exhibits it in a very comprehensive survey. His learning, which is various, cannot escape observation; and his authorities in general are the best which could be found. His judgment, precision, and minuteness, are all to be highly commended. There is even a considerable spirit of philanthropy in his Work; and in so far he advances beyond the character of a mere Antiquary. He displays not, however, any splendour or brightness of genius. He is simple and judicious, but not original. He avails himself of the labours of others with an assiduity that could not be wearied; and his collection of facts, being numerous as well as exact, exhibits instructive openings into the important topics which he treats. His Work is chiefly for consultation, and serves to encourage rather than to supersede the inquiries of those who have a relish for the diplomatic science, and the study of Antiquity. We prize his labour more than his invention; and are more forcibly struck with his patience than his ingenuity. In his language he is clear; and it is difficult to misunderstand the sentiments he conveys; but he has nowhere the expression of a master. The dryness of his manner suffers no interruption; it is cold, nerveless, and insipid; and he advances through his performance without rising into any strain of animation, and without any approach towards elegance."

JOHN BAGFORD

J OHN BAGFORD was born in London, most probably some time in the year 1675; for in a volume of his "Collectanea," Harl. MSS. 5979, on a blank leaf, there is the following endorsement in Bagford's own hand-writing, with a black-lead pencil, "John, son of John and Elizabeth Bagford, was baptized Oct. 31, 1675, in the parish of St. Anne, Black Friars." He was bred, it seems, to the business of a shoe-maker; for he acknowledges that he practised, or had practised, "the gentle craft," as he calls it, in a little curious and entertaining tract on the fashions of shoes, &c. and the art of making them, which may be seen in the British Museum, Harl. MSS. 5911. It appears that he married, or at least that he was a father, pretty early in life; for there is, in the same Collection, a power of attorney from John Bagford junior to John Bagford senior, empowering him to claim and receive the wages of his son, as a seaman, in case of his death, dated in 1713, when the father could only have been of the age of 38 years. (See Harl. MSS. 5995.) He seems to have been led very early, by the turn of his mind, to enquire into the antiquities of his own country, and the origin and progress of its literature. By such enquiries he acquired a great knowledge of old English books, prints, and other literary curiosities, which he carefully picked up at low prices, and re-sold honestly on moderate profits. In this kind of curious but ungainly traffick, he seems to have spent much of his life; in the prosecution of it, he crossed the seas more than once, with abundance of commissions from intelligent booksellers, and curious people of learning and opulence, who, no doubt, contributed to his support; and there are very many of his bills among his papers in the British Museum, that vouch very strongly for his great skill in purchasing, and his great reasonableness in selling, various sorts of uncommon things. All this while he appears to have been a book-broker, rather than a book-seller, and a most proper and honest person to employ in the purchase of scarce and curious publications, prints, &c. on moderate terms. It is evident that he had been at very extraordinary pains to inform himself in the history of printing, and of all the arts immediately, or more remotely, connected with it. He published, in the Philosophical Transactions, in 1707, his "Proposals for a History of Printing, Printers, Illuminators, Chalcography, Paper-making, &c. &c. On subscription 10s.; and 10s. more on the delivery of a volume in folio, containing about 200 sheets." These Proposals were printed on a half-sheet, with a specimen on another, containing the life of William Caxton, first printer in the Abbey of Westminster, with a list of his books. There are several copies of these Proposals in the British Museum, Harl. MSS. 5995.

Whoever will take the trouble of examining the numerous volumes of Mr. Bagford's MSS. on this subject, now in the British Museum, will be thoroughly convinced that he was well qualified for his undertaking, though he wrote a bad hand, and spelt very ill. Destitute as he appears to have been of the benefit of a liberal education, by his great ingenuity and industry he seems to have acquired a degree of accurate knowledge, that, all things considered, is really wonderful. At his death these MSS. were purchased by Mr. Humphrey Wanley, lord Oxford's librarian, for his Lordship's library, and came in course with the Harleian MSS. into the British Museum. It has been said that there are more of this curious man's collections for the same purpose in the Public Library at Cambridge; and that they have never been opened since they came there. But we have the authority of the late worthy master of Emanuel College, to assert, that this is not a fact. It would, indeed, have been a reproach to so curious and inquisitive a man as Dr. Farmer, to have had such papers in his custody, without the curiosity to inspect them.

Mr. Bagford did not confine himself solely to the theory of printing: it appears, likewise, that he practised the art, by two cards, printed on the frozen river Thames, Jan. 18, 1715-16, among the Harl. MSS. 5936. In the first of these cards, he is styled "Dr. *John Bradford*, patron of printing, Jan. 2, 1715-16.* Printed at his Majesty's printing office in Black-Friars." Round this card are prints of the heads of Gottenburg and W. Caxton, with other devices, the royal arms, and the city of London below, &c. (Harl. MSS. 5936.) The second card is as follows: "The noble art and mystery of printing, being invented and practised by John Gottenburg, a soldier at Harlem in Holland, *anno* 1440, King Hen. VI. *anno* 1459, sent two private messengers, with 1500 marks, to procure one of the workmen. They

---

*Not so; the card reads "Dr. John Bagford, Patron of Printing, January the 2nd, 1717/18." (*Ed.*)

prevailed on one Frederick Corsellis* to leave the printing-office in disguise, who immediately came over with them, and first instructed the English in this famous art, at Oxford, the same year, 1459." In the area of the card, in capital letters, "Mr. John Bagford," and the four following lines:
  "All you that walk upon the Thames,
  Step in this booth, and print your names,
  And lay it by, that ages yet to come,
  May see what things upon the Thames were done.
      Printed upon the frozen River Thames,
          Jan. 18, 1715-16."
The very curious and well-written letter of this ingenious man to Mr. Hearne, printed in the first volume of the second edition of "Leland's Collectanea," p. 58, & seqq. relative to London, and the antiquities in its vicinity, does Mr. Bagford very great honour. He seems to have been much employed and respected by Lord Oxford, Dr. John Moore, first bishop of Norwich, afterwards of Ely, Sir Hans Sloane, Sir James Austins, Mr. Clavel, &c.; and it is said, that for having enriched the famous library of his patron Bishop Moore with many curiosities, his Lordship procured him an admission into the Charter-house, as a pensioner on that foundation, in the cemetery of which he was buried. He died at Islington, May 15, 1716, aged 65.

In 1728, a print of him was engraved, by Mr. George Vertue, from a picture by Mr. Howard.

JOHN BASKERVILLE

THIS celebrated Printer was born at Wolverley, in the county of Worcester, in 1706, heir to a paternal estate of 60*l.* *per annum*, which fifty years after, while in his own possession, had increased to 90*l.*; and this estate, with an exemplary filial

---

*The legend of Frederick Corsellis and his introduction of the art of printing into England was first put forward in a tract by a certain Richard Atkyns called *The Original and Growth of Printing*, 1664. The documents to which he referred for evidence have never been found, and his story is discredited. (*Ed.*)

piety and generosity, he allowed to his parents till their deaths, which happened at an advanced age.

He was trained to no occupation, but in 1726 became a writing-master at Birmingham.

In 1737, he taught at a school in the Bull-ring, and is said to have written an excellent hand.

As painting suited his talents, he entered into the lucrative branch of japanning, and resided at No. 22, in Moor-street; and in 1745 he took a building lease of eight acres and two furlongs, North-west of the town, to which he gave the name of *Easy Hill*, converted it into a little Eden, and built a house in the centre : but the town, daily increasing in magnitude and population, soon surrounded it with buildings. — Here he continued the business of a japanner for life : his carriage, each pannel of which was a distinct picture, might be considered the pattern-card of his trade, and was drawn by a beautiful pair of cream-coloured horses.

His inclination for letters induced him, in 1750, to turn his thoughts towards the press. He spent many years in the uncertain pursuit; sunk 600*l*. before he could produce one letter to please himself, and some thousands before the shallow stream of profit began to flow.

His first attempt was a quarto edition of Virgil, in 1756, price one guinea, now worth several. This he reprinted in octavo 1758; and in that year was employed by the University of Oxford on an entirely new-faced Greek type.

Soon after this he printed many other works, with more satisfaction to the literary world than emolument to himself; and obtained leave, from the University of Cambridge, to print a Bible in Royal Folio, and two Editions of the Common Prayer in three sizes; for the permission of doing which, he paid a great premium to that University.

The next in order of his works was "Dr. Newton's Edition of Milton's Poetical Works, 1759," 2 vols. 8vo.

In May 1760 he circulated Proposals for printing a Folio Bible; and in that year he printed "The Book of Common Prayer, 1760," in octavo.

"The Holy Bible, for the use of Churches, 1763," a beautiful Royal Folio.

He also printed editions of Terence, Catullus, Lucretius, Sallust, and Florus, in Royal Quarto.

These publications rank the name of Baskerville with those

persons who have the most contributed, at least in modern times, to the beauty and improvement of the art of Printing. Indeed, it is needless to say to what perfection he brought this excellent art. The paper, the type, and the whole execution of the works performed by him, are the best testimonies of his merit.

After the publication of the Folio Bible; Mr. Baskerville appears to have been weary of the profession of a Printer; or at least he declined to carry it on, except through the medium of a confidential agent.

[The following is a copy of a Letter from Mr. Baskerville.

"To the Hon'ble Horace Walpole, Esq. Member of Parliament, in Arlington-street, London, this.

"SIR,   *"Easy Hill, Birmingham,* 2d. *Nov.* 1762.

"As the Patron and Encourager of Arts, and particularly that of Printing, I have taken the liberty of sending you a specimen of mine, begun ten years ago at the age of forty-seven; and prosecuted ever since, with the utmost care and attention; on the strongest presumption, that if I could fairly excel in this divine art, it would make my affairs easy, or at least give me Bread. But, alas! in both I was mistaken. The Booksellers do not chuse to encourage me, though I have offered them as low terms as I could possibly live by; nor dare I attempt an old Copy till a Law-suit relating to that affair is determined.

"The University of Cambridge have given me a Grant to print their 8vo and 12mo Common Prayer Books; but under such shackles as greatly hurt me. I pay them for the former twenty, and for the latter twelve pounds ten shillings the thousand; and to the Stationers' Company thirty-two pounds for their permission to print one edition of the Psalms in Metre to the small Prayer-book; add to this, the great expence of double and treble carriage; and the inconvenience of a Printing-house an hundred miles off. All this summer I have had nothing to print at home. My Folio Bible is pretty far advanced at Cambridge, which will cost me 2000*l.* all hired at 5 *per Cent.* If this does not sell, I shall be obliged to sacrifice a small patrimony, which brings me in 74*l.* a year, to this business of Printing, which I am heartily tired of, and repent I ever attempted. It is surely a particular hardship, that I should not get bread in my own country (and it is too late to go abroad) after having acquired the reputation of excelling in the most useful art known to mankind; while every one who excels as a Player, Fiddler, Dancer,

&c. not only lives in affluence, but has it in their power to save a fortune. . . .]

In 1764, he had the honour of presenting to his Majesty, and to the Princess Dowager of Wales, his then newly printed Octavo Common Prayer book; which was most graciously received.

In 1765, he applied to his friend the eminent and excellent Dr. Franklin, then at Paris, and who had before in vain endeavoured to assist him in London, to sound the Literati respecting the purchase of his types; but received for answer, "That the French, reduced by the war of 1756, were so far from being able to pursue schemes of taste, that they were unable to repair their public buildings, and suffered the scaffolding to rot before them."

After this, we hear little or nothing of Mr. Baskerville as a Printer.

He died, without issue, Jan. 8, 1776; but it is painful to observe that, in the last solemn act of his life, he unblushingly avowed his total disbelief of Christianity. Agreeably to the singularity of his opinions, he was buried in a tomb of masonry, in the shape of a cone, under a windmill in his garden, belonging to a handsome house which he had built at the upper end of the town of Birmingham. On the top of the windmill, after it fell into disuse, he had erected an urn, for which he had prepared the following inscription :

"Stranger,
beneath this cone, in *unconsecrated* ground,
a friend to the liberties of mankind directed his
body to be inurn'd.
May the example contribute to emancipate thy mind
from the idle fears of *Superstition*,
and the wicked arts of Priesthood."

The principal part of his fortune, amounting to about 12,000*l.* he left to his widow; who sold the stock, and retired to the house which her husband had built.

That building was destroyed in the riots of 1791; but his remains continued undisturbed.

In regard to his private character, he was much of a humourist, idle in the extreme; but his invention was of the true Birmingham model, active. He could well design, but procured others to execute : wherever he found merit, he caressed it : he was remarkably polite to the stranger, fond of shew : a figure rather of the smaller size, and delighted to adorn that figure with gold lace. Although constructed with the light timbers of a frigate, his movement was stately as a ship of the line.

During the twenty-five last years of his life, though then in his decline, he retained the singular traces of a handsome man. If he exhibited a peevish temper, we may consider that good-nature and intense thinking are not always found together. Taste accompanied him through the different walks of agriculture, architecture, and the fine arts. Whatever passed through his fingers, bore the lively marks of John Baskerville.

In April 1775, Mrs. Baskerville wholly declined the Printing business; but continued that of a Letter Founder till February 1777.

Many efforts were used after his death, to dispose of the types; but, no purchaser could be found in the whole common-wealth of letters. The Universities rejected the offer.

The London Booksellers preferred the sterling types of Caslon and his apprentice Jackson. The valuable property lay a dead weight, till purchased by a literary society at Paris, in 1779, for 3700*l.*

It is an old remark, that no country abounds with genius so much as this Island; and it is a remark nearly as old, that genius is no where so little rewarded: how else came Dryden, Goldsmith, and Chatterton, to want bread? Is merit like a flower of the field, too common to attract notice? or is the use of money beneath the care of exalted talents?

Invention seldom pays the inventor. If you ask what fortune Baskerville ought to have been rewarded with? The most which can be comprised in five figures. If you farther ask what he possessed? the least; but none of it squeezed from the press. What will the shade of this great man think, if capable of thinking, that he has spent a fortune of opulence, and a life of genius, in carrying to perfection the greatest of all human inven-tions, and that his productions, slighted by his country, were hawked over Europe in quest of a bidder?

We must admire, if we do not imitate, the taste and œconomy of the French nation, who, brought by the British arms in 1762 to the verge of ruin, rising above distress, were able, in seventeen years, to purchase Baskerville's elegant types, refused by his own country, and to expend an hundred thousand pounds in poisoning the principles of mankind by printing the works of Voltaire."

Mrs. Baskerville died in March 1788.

DR. WILLIAM BATTIE

WILLIAM BATTIE, son of the Rev. Edward Battie, was born at Medbury in Devonshire, in 1704. He received his education at Eton, where his mother resided after her husband's death, in order to assist her son with those little necessary accommodations which the narrowness of her finances would not permit her to provide in any other form.

In the year 1722 he was sent to King's College, Cambridge; to which place also his mother accompanied him. He took the degree of A. B. 1726; M. A. 1730; M. D. 1737.

On a vacancy of the Craven scholarship, by the resignation of Mr. Titley of Trinity College, he offered himself as a candidate, and was successful. The circumstance of his getting the scholarship, as I have it from one of his Competitors on that occasion, is singular. [This Competitor was Dr. Morell; whose name in the former edition of these Anecdotes I did not think it right to mention. But, as there is now no reason for concealment, I shall give the Letter of Corrections with which he then favoured me, several of which were adopted at the time.

"DEAR SIR,   *Feb.* 1781.

"Yours received; and, having happily an hour to spare, shall endeavour, if not to serve you by correcting a few mistakes, at least to divert you with some additional Anecdotes. As to Dr. Battie, I shall begin with him *before* the Craven scholarship, and beg leave to acquaint you, that though there are seldom any changes (or winning of places) in the upper school, yet as he was so very diligent and laborious, I may well say of him, as Quin did of Garrick, *that he kick'd my — and kept me awake;* for he was next below me (there being only a cypher between us, one *Rodney Croxall,* the very reverse of his brother *Sam*); and his mother was so busy and anxious for his advancement, that she presumed to scold at Dr. Snape, for stopping a remove, as she thought, for two or three days, when I staid out with the tooth-ach and a swoln-face. However, we jogged on *in statu quo* till we came to the upper end of the school; when Dr. Bland introduced a new method of declaiming (and I think a very good one) instead of a theme. I was to make a motion as in the Athenian Council, — *Exulet Themistocles,* — and Battie was to defend himself as Themistocles. We were strictly charged to have no assistance in the composition; and as there was something in mine with regard to the argumentative part far above my reach,

Battie every where proclaimed that it was not mine; and even Dr. Bland suspected me, till I gave him an account of the plagiarism, from a weekly paper, in one of the Letters signed *Cato*, against affecting popularity, and very much to my purpose; for which Dr. Bland rather commended than blamed me. However, the dispute, or rather the quarrel, continued, till we had a fair set-to; when, finding him, as I thought, the stronger, I knocked his head against the Chapel, and this put an end to the affair for the present; and his mother paid me with a swinging slap on the face, two or three days afterwards, as I was going into the Chapel. — Now for King's College. We went thither about the same time; and during our scholarship his mother very kindly recommended to us a Chandler, at 4s. 6d. *per* dozen. But, as the candles proved very dear even at that price, we resented it; and one evening, getting into Battie's room before canonical hour, we locked him out, and stuck up all the candles we could find in his box, lighted, round the room; and, while I thrummed on the spinnet, the rest danced round me in their shirts. Upon Battie's coming, and finding what we were at, he fell to storming and swearing, till the old Vice-provost, Dr. Willymot, called out from above, 'Who is that swearing, like a common soldier?' 'It is I,' quoth Battie. 'Visit me,' quoth the Vice-provost. Which indeed we were all obliged to do, the next morning, with a distich, according to custom. Mine naturally turned upon, 'So fiddled Orpheus, and so danced the Brutes'; which having explained to the Vice-provost, he punished me and Sleech with a few lines in the Epsilon of Homer, and Battie with the whole Third Book of Milton, to get, as we say, by heart. — As to the Craven Scholarship (vacant upon the resignation of Mr. Titley of Trinity college, Envoy, I think, to Prussia), I know not how far Dr. Snape befriended Battie; but I know I should not have stood for it if Dr. Snape had not ordered me so to do. There were many candidates; who all, on the day of examination, dwindled away to six: Johnson and Bentley, of Trinity; myself, Battie, and Dale, of King's; and Broughton of Caius college. Our Provost examined us together, that, as he said, we might be witnesses ourselves to the successful Candidate. We were first examined in Sophocles; and the Servant was ordered to lay before us three of King's the old small folio edition, without a translation, while the other three had Johnson's edition. This, and Lucian on the Gout, &c. being over, the Provost dismissed us with a pleasing compliment: 'I believe, Gentlemen, I must trouble you to come again, as I am not yet determined in my choice.' I could fill the sheet with what relates to this trial of skill before Dr. Bentley and the other electors, who examined us separately. But, after all, as one of them (Dr. Pilgrim, the Greek Professor) was absent, the other six were so divided as (after a year and a day) to lapse it to the Donor's family; when Lord Craven gave it to Battie."]

His own inclination prompted him to the profession of the Law; but, feeling how unequal he was, independent of other assistance, to the expence attending that course of study, he made known his intention, and his inability to accomplish it, to two old bachelors, his cousins; both wealthy citizens, whose names were Colman. Of them he solicited the loan of a small allowance, that might qualify him to reside at one of the Inns of Court, where he was assured he could pursue his profession on a more contracted plan of expence than any other young man called to the bar; with a positive engagement to indemnify them for their kindness if ever his future success should furnish him with the means: but they declined interfering in any respect with his concerns.

This disappointment diverted his attention to physick, and he first entered upon the practice at Cambridge, where, in 1729, was printed, "Isocratis Orationes Septem et Epistolæ" . . .

It was about this time the Colmans, retiring from business, settled at Brent Elyhall, in the county of Suffolk, near enough to admit of the Doctor's accepting a general invitation to their house, which he was encouraged to make use of whenever the nature of his business allowed him the leisure; this he did with no small inconvenience to himself, without the least prospect of advantage; not to mention the wide disproportion between their political principles, the old gentlemen being genuine City Tories, and the Doctor a staunch Whig, though both parties afterwards reversed their opinions; and the Doctor was one whom no consideration of advantage in the greatest emergencies of life could ever prevail on to swerve from what he conscientiously believed to be truth.

A fair opening for a physician happening at Uxbridge, induced Dr. Battie to settle in that quarter.

His medical skill being attended with some fortunate events, he was quickly enabled to realize five hundred pounds. With his money in his pocket, he again paid a visit to his relations in the country, requesting their advice how to dispose of his wealth to the best advantage. This solid conviction of the young man's industry and discretion fired them with equal pleasure and astonishment, and from that hour they behaved towards him with the firmest friendship.

He then removed to London, where the established emoluments of his practice produced him 1000*l. per annum.*

In the year 1738 or 1739 he fulfilled by marriage a long attachment he had preserved for a daughter of Barnham Goode, several years under-master of Eton school, against whom the Colmans at all times expressed the most inveterate political antipathy; they however behaved to the wife with the utmost civility; and when they died they left the Doctor more than twenty thousand pounds.

In 1746 he published an Harveian Oration; and in 1749 (being then F. R. S.) he obliged the learned world with a correct edition of his favourite Isocrates, from Mr. Bowyer's press, in two volumes 8vo.

In the dispute which the College of Physicians had with Dr. Schomberg, about the year 1750, Dr. Battie, who was at that time one of the Censors, took a very active part against that gentleman; and in consequence of it was thus severely characterized in a Poem called "The Battiad*."

"First *Battus* came, deep read in worldly art,
Whose tongue ne'er knew the secrets of his heart :
In mischief mighty, though but mean of size,
And, like the Tempter, ever in disguise.
See him, with aspect grave, and gentle tread,
By slow degrees, approach the sickly bed :
Then at his club behold him alter'd soon,
The solemn Doctor turns a low Buffoon :
And he, who lately in a learned freak
Poach'd every Lexicon, and publish'd Greek,
Still madly emulous of vulgar praise,
From Punch's forehead wrings the dirty bays."

By successfully mimicking this character, however, Dr. Battie is said to have once saved a young patient's life. He was sent for to a gentleman, then only 14 or 15 (who was living in 1782), who was in extreme misery from a swelling in his throat; when the Doctor understood what the complaint was, he opened the

---

*Said to be written by Moses Mendez, Paul Whitehead, and Dr. Schomberg.

curtain, turned his wig, and acted Punch with so much humour and success, that the lad (thrown into convulsions almost from laughing) was so agitated as to occasion the tumour to break, and a complete cure was the instantaneous consequence. Had such a story been told of Hippocrates, it would probably have been considered as a great instance of his sagacity, good sense, and good nature: for, if the restoration to health be the physician's aim, how could this desirable effect be obtained sooner or more effectually?

In 1751 he delivered the Lumleian Lecture at the Royal College of Physicians; which he published that year, under the title of "De Principiis Animalibus Exercitationes in Collegio Reg. Medicorum, Lond. habitæ," in three parts; and which was followed next year by a fourth part.

About the year 1756, on application from an intimate friend to solve the appearance of certain consequences suggested by a passage in the beginning of Mr. Locke's "Reasonableness of Christianity," which implies the eternity of that death all the race of Adam were exposed to by his transgression until redeemed by Christ, which redemption depends upon the terms delivered by him to mankind in the dispensation of the Gospel; the Doctor applied himself closely to the illustration of this point. It was fourteen years before he communicated the result of his reflections, which he then read over to his friend in MS. before the concert at his own house in Russel-street, and then appointed a whole day to read it together. This tract, with certain others, was printed some time before his death; but, not having been published, will at present admit of no farther discussion.

In 1758, being then physician to St. Luke's Hospital, and superintendant of a private mad-house near Wood's Close in the road to Islington, he published, in 4to, "A Treatise on Madness"; in which, having thrown out some censures on the medical practice formerly used in Bethlem Hospital, he was replied to, and severely animadverted on, by Dr. John Monro, in a pamphlet called "Remarks on Dr. Battie's Treatise on Madness," published the next year. This Reply contained a defence of the author's father, who had been lightly spoken of in the fore-mentioned Treatise.

In 1762 he published "Aphorismi de cognoscendis et curandis Morbis nonnullis ad principia animalia accommodati."

In February 1763 he was examined before a Committee of the House of Commons, on the State of the Private Madhouses in this Kingdom; and received in their printed Report a testimony very honourable to his professional abilities.

In April 1764 he resigned the office of Physician to St. Luke's Hospital; and in 1767, when the disputes ran high between the College of Physicians and the Licentiates, Dr. Battie wrote several letters in the public papers in vindication of the College.

In 1776, he was seized with a paralytic stroke, which carried him off, June 13, in that year, in his 75th year. The night he expired, conversing with his servant, a lad who attended on him as a nurse, he said to him, "Young man, you have heard, no doubt, how great are the terrors of death. This night will probably afford you some experiment; but may you learn, and may you profit by the example, that a conscientious endeavour to perform his duty through life, will ever close a Christian's eyes with comfort and tranquillity." He soon departed without a struggle or a groan. He was buried, by his own direction, at Kingston in Surrey, "as near as possible to his wife, without any monument or memorial whatever."

To the other Anecdotes of Dr. Battie add the following letter, written in 1788 by his old friend and schoolfellow Ralph Thicknesse. "You mention the success with which the late Dr. Battie administered a *potion* of *mimickry* to some of his patients; nor can there be any doubt but that a *cordial laugh,* properly timed, may prove as beneficial in some cases as any cordial in the *Materia medica;* and I can assure you that Battie always carried that *cordial about with him,* though lately it was only here and there that he would administer it. In short, the Doctor was as good a *Punch* as he was a Physician. At School, or at College, he was always in pursuit of what we call *fun.* Now, Sir, as it is agreed that those that play at bowls must take rubbers, I cannot help relating a piece of *funnery,* which befell the Doctor himself at Uxbridge, the place where he first opened his *medical budget,* and when his Fellowship of King's College, Cambridge, and what little he could pick up in fees, were his whole support. Mr. Thicknesse, a Fellow of the same College, and a *fellow-funster* also, having rode from London one morning, to visit his old *chum,* arrived when the Doctor was out upon his visits, and, as a little rain had wetted his visitor's wig, he called upon *William* to bring him the Doctor's *old grizzle,* and to put a *dust of powder into his.* But, before that operation was compleated, the Doctor appeared in his well-dressed *tye.* As soon as the mutual civilities were over, "Zounds," said Battie, "Ralph, what a cursed wig you have got on!" "It is true," said Thicknesse (taking it off his head), "it is a bad one, and if you will, as I have another, I will burn it." "By all means," said the Doctor, "for, in truth, it is a very *caxon*." Accordingly, the *fry went into the fire*. Now, in *those days frugality was necessary*; and the Doctor constantly, upon returning home, uncovered his yarn under-stockings, and *edged* off his tye, that a *once-a-week* combing might do; and therefore, previous to his skinning his legs, "Here, William," said he, "bring me my old wig, and put up my tye." William informed the Doctor Mr. Thicknesse had got it. "And where is it, Ralph?" "Why, burnt, as you bid me." And thus it is throughout all mankind. We can see the shabby wig, and feel the pitiful tricks of our friends, and yet overlook the disorder in which our own wardrobes often are left during life.

"You may, if you please, close this account of an *innocent* piece of *fun,* unless the following additional anecdote may administer *health to your many readers*. There was at King's College, a very good-tempered, handsome, six-feet-high Parson, of the name of Lofft. He was one of the College Chaunters, and the constant butt at commons, in the hall as well as in the parlour. Harry dreaded so much the sight of a gun, or a case of pistols, that such of his friends as did not care for too much of his company, always kept fire-arms in their rooms. The relater of this article, then scarce a man, was encouraged by the *reverend the Fellows* to place himself at the corner of the Chapel, with a gun loaded only with powder, and, as Harry went to prayers, to shoot at him at the distance of about twenty yards. Unfortunately, the gun being loaded with coarse damp common powder, the whole of it did not burn; and poor Harry Lofft's face received a great many whole grains therein, and with such force as to remain in the skin. The fright, and little inflammation, put the poor Chaunter to bed. We were all much alarmed; and, lest the report should reach the Vice-chancellor's ears, the good-tempered Lofft was prevailed upon *to sink* the cause of his disorder, and to be *only ill*. Battie and Banks (the only two Fellow-students in Physic) happened not to be of the *shooting party,* and were, therefore, called to the assistance of the sick man. They found his face red, inflamed, and sprinkled with black spots! that his pulse was high, and his spirits low; and, after a serious consultation on his case, they prescribed : and then being examined by the impatient plotters of this wicked deed, they pronounced it to be the *black rash*. This was a never-to-be-forgotten *roast* for the two medical students. And if we may add to this, that, after the Doctor had justly established a high reputation as a Physician, he sent Mrs. Battie to Bath for a *dropsy*, and that she was cured by *dropping* a child at his door, it may give us a little insight into the *practice of Physic*, and induce us to say with the Poet,

> Better to search in fields for health unbought,
> Than fee the Doctor for a nauseous draught."

JAMES BOSWELL

JAMES BOSWELL, esq. eldest son of Alexander Boswell, Lord Auchinleck, one of the judges in the supreme courts of session and justiciary in Scotland. He was born at Edinburgh, Oct. 29, 1740; and received his first rudiments of education in that city. He afterwards studied Civil Law in the universities of Edinburgh and Glasgow. During his residence in these cities, he acquired, by the society of the English gentlemen who were students in the English colleges, that remarkable predilection for their manners, which neither the force of education, nor the *dulcedo* of his *natale solum,* could ever eradicate. But his most intimate acquaintance at this period was the Rev. Mr. Temple, a worthy, learned, and pious Divine, whose well-written character of Gray was inserted in Johnson's Life of that Poet. Mr. Boswell imbibed early the ambition of distinguishing himself by his literary talents, and had the good fortune to obtain the patronage of the late Lord Somerville. This Nobleman treated him with the most flattering kindness; and Mr. Boswell ever remembered with gratitude the friendship he so long enjoyed with this worthy peer. Having always entertained an exalted idea of the felicity of London, in the year 1760 he visited that capital; in the manners and amusements of which he found so much that was congenial to his own taste and feelings, that it became ever after his favourite residence, whither he always returned from his estate in Scotland, and from his various rambles in different parts of Europe, with increasing eagerness and delight; and we find him, nearly twenty years afterwards, condemning Scotland as too narrow a sphere, and wishing to

make his chief residence in London, which he calls the great
scene of ambition, instruction, and, comparatively, making his
heaven upon earth. He was, doubtless, confirmed in this attachment to the Metropolis by the strong predilection entertained
towards it by his friend Dr. Johnson, whose sentiments on this
subject Mr. Boswell details in various parts of his life of that
great man; and which are corroborated by every one, in pursuit
of literary and intellectual attainments, who has enjoyed but a
taste of the rich feast which the city spreads before him. — The
politeness, affability, and insinuating urbanity of manners, which
distinguished Mr. Boswell, introduced him into the company of
many eminent and learned men, whose acquaintance and
friendship he cultivated with the greatest assiduity. In truth, the
esteem and approbation of learned men seems to have been one
chief object of his literary ambition; and we find him so successful in pursuing his end, that he enumerated some of the greatest
men in Scotland among his friends even before he left it for the
first time. Notwithstanding Mr. Boswell by his education was
intended for the bar, yet he was himself earnestly bent at this
period upon obtaining a commission in the Guards, and solicited
Lord Auchinleck's acquiescence; but returned, however, by his
desire, into Scotland, where he received a regular course of
instruction in the Law, and passed his trials as a Civilian at
Edinburgh. Still, however, ambitious of displaying himself as one
of "the manly hearts who guard the fair," he re-visited London
a second time in 1762; and, various occurrences delaying the
purchase of a commission, he was at length persuaded by Lord
Auchinleck to relinquish his pursuit, and become an advocate at
the Scotch bar. In compliance, therefore, with his father's wishes,
he consented to go to Utrecht the ensuing winter, to hear the
lectures of an excellent Civilian in that University; after which
he had permission to make his grand tour of Europe. In 1762
Mr. Boswell published the little Poem which occasions this note;
and the next year may be considered the most important epocha
in his life, as he had the singular felicity to be introduced to Dr.
Johnson. This event, so auspicious for Mr. Boswell, and so
fortunate for the Literary World, happened on May 16, 1763.
Having afterwards continued one winter at Utrecht, during
which time he visited several parts of the Netherlands, he commenced his projected travels. Passing from Utrecht into
Germany, he pursued his route through Switzerland to Geneva;
whence he crossed the Alps into Italy: having visited on his

journey Voltaire at Ferney, and Rousseau in the wilds of Neuf-
chatel. Mr. Boswell continued some time in Italy, where he met
and associated with Lord Mountstuart, to whom he afterwards
dedicated his *Theses Juridicæ*. Having visited the most remarkable cities in Italy, Mr. Boswell sailed to Corsica, travelled over
every part of that island, and obtained the friendship of the
illustrious Pasquale de Paoli, in whose palace he resided during
his stay at Corsica. He afterwards went to Paris, whence he
returned to Scotland in 1766, and soon after became an advocate
at the Scotch bar. The celebrated Douglas cause was at that time
a subject of general discussion. Mr. Boswell published the
"Essence of the Douglas Cause"; a pamphlet which contributed
to procure Mr. Douglas the popularity which he at that time
possessed. — In 1768, Mr. Boswell obliged the world by his
"Account of Corsica, with Memoirs of General Paoli." Of this
printed performance Dr. Johnson thus expresses himself: "Your
Journal is curious and delightful. I know not whether I could
name any narrative by which curiosity is better excited or better
gratified." This book was received with extraordinary approbation, and has been translated into the German, Dutch, Italian,
and French languages. In the following winter, the theatre-royal
at Edinburgh, hitherto restrained by party-spirit, was opened.
On this occasion Mr. Boswell was solicited by David Ross, esq.
to write a prologue. The effect of this prologue upon the audience
was highly flattering to the author, and beneficial to the manager, as it secured to the latter, by the annihilation of the
opposition which had been till that time too successfully exerted
against him, the uninterrupted possession of his patent, which he
enjoyed till his death, which happened in September, 1790. Mr.
Boswell attended his funeral as chief mourner, and paid the last
honours to a man with whom he had spent many a pleasant
hour. — In 1769, was celebrated at Stratford-on-Avon the
Jubilee in honour of Shakespeare. Mr. Boswell, an enthusiastic
admirer of the writings of our immortal Bard, and ever ready to
partake of "the feast of reason and the flow of soul," repaired
thither, and appeared at the masquerade as an armed Corsican
chief; a character he was eminently qualified to support. This
year Mr. Boswell was married to Miss Margaret Montgomery,
a lady who, to the advantages of a polite education, united
admirable good sense and a brilliant understanding. She was
daughter of David Montgomery, esq. related to the illustrious
family of Eglintoune, and representative of the antient peerage

of Lyle. The death of this amiable woman is recorded in the Gentleman's Magazine for June 1790; and Mr. Boswell honoured her memory with an affectionate tribute. She left him two sons and three daughters; who, to use Mr. Boswell's own words, "if they inherit her good qualities, will have no reason to complain of their lot. *Dos magna parentûm virtus.* — In 1782, Lord Auchinleck died. — In 1783, Mr. Boswell published his celebrated "Letter to the People of Scotland"; which is thus praised by Johnson in a letter to the author: "I am very much of your opinion ****; your paper contains very considerable knowledge of History and the Constitution, very properly produced and applied." Mr. Pitt, to whom Mr. Boswell communicated the pamphlet, honoured it with his approbation. This first letter was followed by a second, in which Mr. Boswell displayed his usual energy and political abilities. In 1785, Mr. Boswell published "A Journal of a Tour to the Hebrides" with Dr. Johnson; which met a similar success to his entertaining account of Corsica. This year Mr. Boswell removed to London, and was soon after called to the English bar. But Mr. Boswell's professional business was interrupted by preparing his most celebrated work, "The Life of Samuel Johnson, LL. D." This was published in 1790, and was received by the world with most extraordinary avidity. It is a faithful history of Johnson's life, and exhibits a most interesting picture of the character of that illustrious moralist, delineated with a masterly hand. The preparation of a second edition of this work was almost the last literary performance of Mr. Boswell; though he was at the same time preparing a general answer to a letter from Dr. Samuel Parr, in Gent. Mag. vol. LXV. p. 179; in which he proposed also briefly to notice the attacks of his more puny antagonists. He had also a design, which was in some forwardness, of publishing a quarto volume, to be embellished with fine plates, on the subject of the controversy occasioned by the Beggar's Opera; and it is to be regretted that the publick were not gratified with a perusal of what so good a judge of human nature would say on so curious a subject. With this particular view he had paid frequent visits to the then truly humane "Governor of Newgate," as he ordinarily styled Mr. Kirby. His death, unexpected by his friends, was a subject of universal regret; and his remains were carried to Auchinleck; and the following inscription is engraved on his coffin-plate: "JAMES BOSWELL, esq. died 19 May, 1795, aged 55 years."

WILLIAM BOWYER

WILLIAM BOWYER, confessedly the most learned Printer of the Eighteenth Century, was born in Dogwell Court, in the extraparochial precinct of White Fryars, London, Dec. 19, 1699; and may be said to have been initiated from his infancy in the rudiments of the art in which he so eminently excelled.

His father, whose name was also WILLIAM, was the son of *John Bowyer,* citizen and grocer, by *Mary King.* He was born in 1663; bound apprentice to Miles Flesher in 1679; admitted to the freedom of the Company of Stationers Oct. 4, 1686; and very soon after became eminent in his profession.

He was twice married. By the first wife he had no issue. The second wife was *Dorothy* daughter of *Thomas Dawks,* a printer of some celebrity in his day, who in his youth, from 1652 to 1657, had been employed as a compositor on the celebrated Polyglott Bible of Bishop Walton.

The daughter of Mr. Dawks was born March 6, 1664-5; and was married, Oct. 10, 1685, to Mr. *Benjamin Allport,* of St. Botolph's, Bishopsgate, bookseller; by whom she had one son, *Benjamin* (who was born after his father's death, and died before he was a year old), and one daughter. She afterwards became the wife of Mr. Bowyer, who commenced his career as a printer by "A Defence of the Vindication of King Charles the Martyr; justifying his Majesty title to *ΕΙΚΩΝ ΒΑΣΙΛΙΚΗ,* in answer to a late Pamphlet, intituled 'Amyntor'; by the Author of the Vindication. *London; printed by W. Bowyer, at the White Horse in Little Britain;* and sold by most Booksellers in London and Westminster, 1699"; a very neat small quarto, containing ninety-six pages.

Before the close of the year 1699, Mr. Bowyer removed his printing-office into *White Fryars,* to a house which had formerly been the George tavern; and on the 6th of May 1700, was admitted a Liveryman of the Company of Stationers.

The earliest publications that we find from his new press were, "Two Sermons concerning Nature and Grace, preached at Whitehall, April 1699, by Edward Young, fellow of Winchester College, and Chaplain in ordinary to his Majesty, published in April 1700," 4to.

"A Sermon preached at the Triennial Visitation of the Right Rev. Father in God James [Gardiner] Lord Bishop of Lincoln,

held at Hartford, June 12, 1700. By *Philip Falle,* Rector of
Shenley in the County of Hartford, Prebendary of Durham, and
Chaplain in ordinary to his Majesty. Published by his Lordship's
Command. Text, Acts xviii. 3. London: Printed by W. Bowyer,
for John Newton, at the Three Pigeons, over-against the Inner
Temple Gate, in Fleet-street," 4to. This Sermon is beautifully
printed.

If any apology were necessary for the scanty records of the
typographical labours in this early period of our history, too
good an excuse will be found for it in the fatal fire which consumed the office where they were produced, by which all original
documents were lost.

After having for thirteen years pursued business with unremitted industry and unsullied reputation; and having amply
experienced the patronage and encouragement he well deserved;
on the fatal night of Jan. 29-30, 1712-13, he was reduced to a
state of almost absolute indigence by a calamitous fire, which
totally destroyed his printing-office, and many considerable
works at that time in his warehouse and under his press.

I have several different setts of newspapers of that period; but
do not find this dreadful accident mentioned in any of them,
except "The Weekly Packet, of Jan. 31," where it is thus slightly
noticed: "The night between Thursday and Friday a fire
happened in White Fryers; which burnt down the house of Mr.
Bowyer, a printer, and damaged the next to it."

Among the articles which perished by this sudden and aweful
visitation, was by far the greater number of Sir Robert Atkyns's
valuable "History of Gloucestershire"; a few copies only of it
having been snatched from the flames, of which they still retain
indelible marks.

A considerable part of the impression of Bp. Bull's "Important
Points of Primitive Christianity" was destroyed; and several
other works then printing.*

At this melancholy crisis the younger Bowyer was fortunately
absent; having been placed at Headley, near Leatherhead in
Surrey, under the care of the Rev. Ambrose Bonwicke, B. D. a
Nonjuring clergyman of great piety and learning, who had

---

*To indemnify the sufferer a royal brief was granted for a collection of
charity, which brought in £1,377, to which was soon added a further
£1,162 subscribed by his fellow printers and others of his friends. He
thus received £2,539 — about half of his estimated loss through the fire.
Ed.

succeeded Dr. Hartcliffe as master of Merchant Taylors School in 1686, and held it till 1691; when, refusing the oaths, he was ejected; and kept afterwards a private school at Headley.

At this excellent seminary young Bowyer made such advances in literature, as reflected the highest credit both upon himself and his preceptor; for whose memory, to his latest years, he entertained the sincerest respect; and to whose family he always remained an useful friend. The attachment, indeed, was mutual.

The Saxon types, which had been used in 1709 for printing St. Gregory's Homily, having been burnt with the rest of Mr. Bowyer's printing materials, Lord Chief Justice Parker was so munificently indulgent as to be at the expence of cutting a new sett of Saxon types for Mrs. Elizabeth Elstob's Saxon Grammar; the punches and matrices of which were afterwards presented to the University of Oxford, as will appear in the course of these memoirs.

Consoled by such unequivocal testimonies of respectful friendship, the energies of Mr. Bowyer were soon recalled into activity; and, in less than two months, we find him again beginning business, though he had no printing-office of his own, in the houses, and by the kind permission and assistance, of his friends Mr. Norton and Mr. Rawlins; where his first employment was the reprinting of the Fifteenth Volume of "Rymer's Fœdera," and "Goodman's Conference"; both which had been destroyed.

In June 1722, the younger Bowyer entered into the printing business with his father; and from this period, to prevent the repetition of the *elder* or the *younger* Bowyer, I shall in general speak of them as one person; the principal attention to the executive or mechanical part of their business devolving on the father, the correcting of the proofs almost exclusively to the son.

On the death of Mr. Bonwicke (Oct. 20, 1722), his grateful scholar had an opportunity of requiting in some measure the obligations he had received, by officiating for a time in the capacity of a schoolmaster, for the benefit of the family; and, after having discharged this act of kindness, he applied diligently to the management of the printing-office.

Through the friendship of the Right Honourable Arthur Onslow, Mr. Bowyer was appointed Printer of the Votes of the House of Commons in 1729; and continued in that employ, under three successive Speakers, for almost fifty years. Soon after his appointment, it was suggested to Mr. Onslow, that there was an impropriety in giving the Votes to be printed by a

Nonjuror: but the worthy Speaker treated the hint with the contempt it deserved, and said, "he was convinced he had employed *an honest man*."

Among other books printed in this year was:

"A brefe Chronycle concernynge the Examynacyon and Death of the blessed Martyr of Christ Syr Johan Oldecastell the Lorde Cobham. Collected togyther by Johan Bale. To which is added, an Appendix of Original Instruments. Beautifully and correctly printed on a royal paper, in 8vo, 250 copies only. There are *six copies* printed on a superfine writing vellum for the curious."

In 1730 several valuable books were produced from the press of Mr. Bowyer.

"Matthæi Parker Cantuariensis Archiepiscopi de Antiquitate Britannicæ Ecclesiæ et Privilegiis Ecclesiæ Cantuariensis, cum Archiepiscopis ejusdem LXX. E XXI, exemplarium 1572 excusorum, sibique mutuo sorte plane singulari discrepantium, Collatione integra nunc primum numerisque absoluta omnibus Historia.*

This very correct and beautiful volume may truly be said to vie with the most capital productions of the press at the period in which it appeared; and, though it possesses not the adventitious aids of *fine wove paper* and *hot-pressing*, will bear a comparison with the more splendid efforts of modern typography.†

It is dated in 1729; but the publication (after having been *nine years* in the press, was delayed till the beginning of the following year.

By the recommendation of Mr. Drake,‡ in May 1736, Mr. Bowyer was appointed Printer to the Society of Antiquaries; and began his work for them by a single sheet, in folio, under the title of "Collectanea Antiquitatum"; and by another, called "A Table of English Gold Coins from the Eighteenth Year of King Edward III. when Gold was first coined in England, with their several Weights, and present intrinsic Value, by Martin Folkes, Esquire."

Mr. Bowyer was elected into that respectable body on the 7th of July following; and soon shewed himself to be a very

---

*First printed, 1572, by John Day [*Ed.*]

†A reference to John Baskerville, q.v.: page 33 [*Ed.*]

‡Francis Drake, F.R.S.A., an eminent antiquary.

useful member. It appears from the Minute-books that he regularly attended their meetings; and frequently entertained them with valuable communications.

On the 27th of December, 1737, Mr. Bowyer lost his father, at the age of 74; and it is evident, from his scattered papers, that he severely felt the affliction; applying to himself the beautiful apostrophe of Æneas to Anchises:

> " Hic me, pater optime, fessum
>
> Deseris, heu ! tantis nequicquam erepte perîclis."

[In the July of the same year, he had lost his aunt Dawks (widow of the well-known printer of *Dawks's News-Letter*), who made him her executor.]

In 1754, with a view to exonerate himself from fatigue, he entered into a treaty for a partnership with Mr. James Emonson (a near relation) and Mr. C. Spens, at that time a corrector of the press, and afterwards editor of Lloyd's Evening Post. In consequence, however, of some disagreements not material to mention, this connexion was not of long subsistence.

The Saxon types, which were used in printing St. Gregory's Homily, having been destroyed by fire (as has been already mentioned) Lord Chief Justice Parker was at the expence of cutting a new Saxon type from *fac similes* prepared for Mrs. Elstob by Mr. Wanley; the punches and matrices of which Mr. Bowyer's son presented, by the hands of Edward-Rowe Mores, esq. to the University of Oxford, with the following letter:

"To Edward-Rowe Mores, esq. at Low Leyton.

"SIR,   Dec. 4, 1753.

"I make bold to transmit to Oxford, through your hands, the Saxon punches and matrices, which you were pleased to intimate would not be unacceptable to that learned Body. It would be a great satisfaction to me if I could by this means perpetuate the munificence of the noble Donor, to whom I am originally indebted for them, the late Lord Chief Justice Parker, afterwards Earl of Macclesfield, who, among the numerous Benefactors which my father met with, after his house was burnt in 1712-13, was so good as to procure those types to be cut, to enable him to print Mrs. Elstob's Saxon Grammar. England had not then the advantage of such an Artist in Letter-cutting as has since arisen: and it is to be lamented, that the execution of these is not equal to the intention of the noble Donor; I now add, to the place in which they are to be reposited. However, I esteem it a peculiar happiness, that as my father received them from a great Patron of Learning, his son consigns them to the greatest Seminary of it, and that he is, Sir, your most obliged friend, and humble servant,   W. BOWYER."

Among the specimens of the University types, these Saxon characters are preserved, under the following title : "Characteres Anglo-Saxonici per eruditam fœminam Eliz. Elstob ad fidem codd. mss. delineati : quorum tam instrumentis cusoriis quam matricibus Univ. donari curavit *E. R. M.* è Collegio *Regin.* 1753.

In consequence of overtures from a few respectable friends at Cambridge, Mr. Bowyer had some inclination, towards the latter end of 1765, to have undertaken the management of the University Press, by purchasing a lease of their exclusive privileges, by which for several years they had cleared a considerable sum. To accomplish this, he took a journey to Cambridge; and afterwards sent the Compiler of these Anecdotes to negotiate with the Vice-Chancellor. The treaty was fruitless; but he did not much regret the disappointment.

Mr. Clarke, Sept. 4, 1765, wrote thus upon this subject: "What to say about the University affair, I do not well know — it is certain that you have more business already than does you good; and such a fortune as will answer all the rational purposes of life, that you need not wish for more. If you were younger, and ambitious of raising a greater fortune, I could tell what to say. But there are certainly two objects in view in this proposal, which, if these objections did not lie in the way, would to me be great inducements. The thoughts of *governing the Booksellers,* either for gain or glory, would give me a greater pleasure, than any other object in trade. In that respect, I think just as you do. But *Tanti non est;* the laurel is scarce worth the labour. Happiness and ease are greater acquisitions than victory. — Besides, the honour of putting the University in a way to get something besides credit, would be a means of enrolling you among her Benefactors; and that not for a temporary, but a perpetual Donation. — But you had better relinquish all these honours, unless you quit business, and think of doing nothing else."

In the beginning of the year 1766, by engaging in a partnership with the Writer of these Memoirs, Mr. BOWYER was again enabled to withdraw, in some degree, from that close application which had begun to be prejudicial to his health. His new Associate, whilst an Apprentice, had been intrusted with a considerable share of the management of the Printing-office; and the connexion was such as, I am proud to say, was highly satisfactory to Mr. BOWYER. To his Partner, it was all that a young man could possibly have hoped for; it was an introduction to a number of respectable Friends, whose patronage was equally honourable and advantageous. The good-natured Reader will pardon the vanity of this paragraph; it is meant as a tribute of gratitude to a Benefactor, whose memory the Writer cannot but heartily revere.

In 1767 Mr. Bowyer was appointed to print the Rolls of Parliament and the Journals of the House of Lords. He was principally indebted for this appointment to his noble Friend Hugh Earl of Marchmont; and his gratitude to that worthy Peer is testified in the inscription placed in Stationers-hall.

The want of sufficient room now compelled him, though not without reluctance, to exchange White Fryars, where he was born, and had resided nearly 67 years, for Red Lion-passage, Fleet-street; where he styled himself "ARCHITECTUS VERBORUM." Over the door of the new printing-office he placed a bust of his favourite Cicero; under which was inscribed,

" M. T. CICERO, A QUO PRIMORDIA PRELI,"

in allusion to the well-known very early and valuable editions of Tully's Offices.

Early in 1768 Mr. Bowyer received from New England the following polite acknowledgement of his abilities and his bounty :

"SIR,   Cambridge, Dec. 1767.

"The President and Fellows of Harvard College in Cambridge beg leave to return you their grateful acknowledgements for the valuable donation you have been pleased to make to their library, through the hands of their most worthy friend and generous benefactor, Thomas Hollis, esq.

"We have not been strangers to your character as a learned Editor, a character by no means common in the present age; and the very accurate editions of many learned authors, which have come abroad into the world under your inspection, assure us of your great merit in that respect.

"It is a particular pleasure to us to mention your very curious edition of the Greek Testament, in two volumes, with critical notes, and many happy conjectures, especially as to punctuation, an affair of the utmost importance as to ascertaining the sense. This Work, though small in bulk, we esteem as a rich treasure of sacred learning, and of more intrinsic value than many huge volumes of the Commentators.

"We are greatly obliged to you for the favourable sentiments you have been pleased so elegantly to express of our Seminary, in the blank leaf of the New Testament; and we hope it will prove a powerful stimulus to our youth, more and more to deserve so good a character.

"This Society is as yet but in its infant state; but we trust that, by the generosity of the Benefactors whom the Divine Providence is raising up to us, and by the smiles of Heaven upon our endeavours to form the youth here to knowledge and virtue, it will every day more effectually answer the important ends of its foundation. We are, with great respect, your most obliged, and humble servants (at the direction and desire of the Corporation of Harvard College), EDW. HOLYOKE, President.

"Sir, inclosed you have our vote of thanks for your valuable present.

"At a meeting of the President and Fellows of
Harvard College, Dec. 10, 1767.

Present,
The President,
Mr. Appelton,
Mr. Winthorp,
Mr. Elliot,
Mr. Cooper,
Mr. Danforth,
Mr. Treasurer."

"VOTE IV. That the thanks of this Corporation be given to Mr. William Bowyer of London, for several valuable Books sent to Harvard College; particularly his late curious Edition of the Greek Testament, with learned Notes.

A true Copy, extr. de Lib. vii. p. 175.

Per EDW. HOLYOKE, President.

Our eminent Printer now drew to the end of his literary career; but he had first the satisfaction of completing in this year "The Rolls of Parliament," in six volumes folio; and THIRTY-ONE volumes of "The Journals of the House of Lords."

The last Publication in which Mr. Bowyer assumed the office of an Editor, was a new impression of the "Dissertation on the Epistles of Phalaris." Dr. Bentley was a writer whom he had always held in the highest estimation. In the re-publication of this great Critick's Dissertation, Mr. Bowyer inserted the remarks which had occurred to him, in the course of many years attention to the subjects there treated of; and he hath ascribed them to the respective Authors from whose books or personal communication they were selected.

Two large and very handsome folio volumes of the most invaluable as well as most antient Record in this or any other kingdom, known by the name of "DOMESDAY BOOK," and kept with very great safety and strictness in the old Chapter-house at Westminster, were begun in Mr. Bowyer's life-time, but not completed in 1783, under the proposed* title of "Domesday Book, seu Liber Censualis Willelmi Primi Regis Angliæ, inter Archivos Regni Domo Capitulari Westmonasterii asservatus, jubente Rege Augustissimo Georgio Tertio Prelo mandatus. Londini: Typis J. Nichols." On the correctness and the beauty of this important Work I am content to stake my typographical credit. It was full ten years in passing through the press; requiring a very considerable degree of manual nicety; and no ordinary share of attention in the revisal of the proof sheets; and the expence was comparatively small, the two volumes, on fine royal paper, having cost very little more than fifty shillings a sett.

Mr. Bowyer had always been subject to a bilious colic, and during the last ten years of his life was afflicted with palsy and the stone : but, notwithstanding these infirmities, he preserved, in general, a remarkable cheerfulness of disposition; and received great satisfaction from the conversation of some few literary friends, by whom he continued to be visited. In the Spring of 1776, he had a severe paralytic attack, which for several weeks severely affected him; but, through the great attention of Dr. Heberden, he in a good measure got the better of it. The faculties of his mind, though somewhat impaired, were strong enough to support the labour of almost incessant reading, which had ever been his principal amusement; and he regularly corrected the learned Works, and especially the Greek Books, which came from his press. This he did till within a very few weeks of his death; which happened on the 18th of November 1777, when he had nearly completed his 78th year.

For more than half a century he stood unrivalled as a learned

---

*I use the word *proposed,* as, after several communications of the Lords Committees of the House of Peers, with the Lords Commissioners of His Majesty's Treasury, and with the Council of the Society of Antiquaries, the Title not being finally adjusted, the Work was delivered to the Members of the Two Houses of Parliament without any Title.

Printer: and some of the most masterly productions of this kingdom have been described as appearing from his Press. Nor was his Pen unknown to the World of Letters. The Work, however, which stamps the highest honour on his name is the "Conjectures on the New Testament," a Book in which the profoundest erudition and the most candid criticism are happily united. And of the Sacred Text, there is not an edition which ever passed through his correction, but what has its peculiar value.

To his literary and professional abilities he added an excellent Moral Character. His regard to Religion was displayed in his Publications, and in the course of his Life and Studies; and he was particularly distinguished by his inflexible probity, and an uncommon alacrity in assisting the necessitous. His liberality in relieving every species of distress, and his endeavours to conceal his benefactions, reflect great honour on his memory. Though he was naturally fond of retirement, and seldom entered into company, excepting with men of letters, he was, perhaps, excelled by few in the talent of justly discriminating the real characters of mankind. He judged of the persons he saw by a sort of intuition; and his judgments were generally right. From a consciousness of literary superiority, he did not always pay that attention to the booksellers which was expedient in the way of his business. Being too proud to solicit the favours in that way which he believed to be his due, he was often disappointed in his expectations. On the other hand, he frequently experienced friendships in cases where he had much less reason to have hoped for them; so that, agreeably to an expression of his own, "in what he had received, and in what he had been denied, he thankfully acknowledged the will of Heaven." The two great objects he had in view, in the decline of life, were to repay the benefactions his Father had received, and to be himself a benefactor to the meritorious of his own profession. These purposes are fully displayed in his last Will.

Mr. Bowyer, agreeably to his own direction, was buried in the church-yard of Low-Leyton in Essex; near the South-west corner of the church, where an inscription is placed to the memory of himself and his Relations.

JOHN BOYDELL

THE history of this worthy Alderman affords an extraordinary instance of what a life of spirited exertions is able to accomplish. It appears almost impossible that an individual, who began the world in so humble circumstances, could have effected so much for the improvement of the Arts, and of the national taste. He was a native of Derbyshire,* and was originally intended for a Land Surveyor. When more than 20, he was put apprentice to a Mr. Tomms, an Engraver, at a time when there were no very eminent Engravers in England. He saw the necessity of forcing the art of Engraving, by stimulating men of genius with suitable rewards. He himself mentioned, that the first means which enabled him to encourage other Engravers, were the profits he derived from the sale of a book of 152 prints, engraved by himself; and he very modestly allowed, that he himself had not at that time arrived at any eminence in the art of Engraving, and that those prints are now principally valuable from the comparison of them with the improved state of the art within the last 60 years. With the profits of this book, however, he was able to pay very liberally the best Engravers then in the country, and presented the publick with English engravings of the works of the best Masters. The encouragement he experienced from the publick was equal to the spirit and patriotism of the undertaking, and soon laid the foundation of an ample fortune.

He was elected Alderman of Cheap Ward in 1782; Sheriff in 1785; Lord-mayor in 1790; and in the same year Master of the Stationers Company.

The Alderman had the satisfaction to see in his life-time the effect of his labours. Though he never himself made great progress as an Engraver, yet he was the greatest encourager of the art that this country ever saw. The English engravings, which were before considered much inferior to those of foreign nations, began from that time to be highly prized; and the exportation of them became a valuable article of commerce. Having done so much for the art of Engraving, he resolved to direct his efforts to encourage the art of Painting in this country. To this effect he undertook that superb edition of Shakspeare, the originals of which were for several years exhibited in the Shakspeare Gallery.

---

*Not so; he was born at Stanton, Shropshire, on 19 Jan. 1719 [Ed.]

The expence of these paintings was prodigious, and more, perhaps, than any individual had ever before embarked in for such
an object.

The effect which this produced on the fortune of the worthy
and patriotic Alderman will be best explained by the Letter
which he addressed to his friend Sir John Anderson; by whom
it was publicly read in the House of Commons, when applying
for leave to dispose of the Paintings, &c. by Lottery.

["DEAR SIR,   *Cheapside, Feb.* 4, 1804.

The kindness with which you have undertaken to represent
my case, calls upon me to lay open to you, with the utmost candour, the circumstances attending it, which I will now endeavour
to do as briefly as possible. It is above sixty years since I began
to study the Art of Engraving, in the course of which time,
besides employing that long period of life in my profession,
with an industry and assiduity that would be improper in me to
describe, I have laid out with my brethren, in promoting the
commerce of the Fine Arts in this country, above 350,000*l.*
When I first began business, the whole commerce of prints in
this country consisted in importing foreign prints, principally
from France, to supply the cabinets of the curious in this kingdom. Impressed with the idea that the genius of our own
countrymen, if properly encouraged, was equal to that of
Foreigners, I set about establishing a *School for Engraving in
England;* with what success the publick are well acquainted. It
is, perhaps, at present sufficient to say, that the whole course of
that commerce is changed; very few prints being now imported
into this country, while the foreign market is principally supplied
with prints from England. In effecting this favourite plan, I have
not only spent a long life, but have employed near 40 years of
the labour of my nephew, Josiah Boydell, who had been bred to
the business, and whose assistance during that period has been
greatly instrumental in promoting a School of Engraving in this
country. By the blessing of Providence, these exertions have been
very successful; not only in that respect, but in a commercial
point of view; for, the large sums I regularly received from the
Continent, previous to the French Revolution, for impressions
taken from the numerous plates engraved in England, encouraged me to attempt also an *English School of Historical
Painting.* I had observed with indignation, that the want of such
a School had been long made a favourite topic of opprobrium
against this country among foreign writers on national taste. No

subject, therefore, could be more appropriate for such a national attempt, than England's inspired Poet, and great Painter of Nature, Shakspeare; and I flatter myself, the most prejudiced Foreigner must allow that the Shakspeare Gallery will convince the world that Englishmen want nothing but the fostering hand of encouragement to bring forth their genius in this line of art. I might go further; and defy any of the Italian, Flemish, or French Schools, to shew, in so short a space of time, such an exertion as the Shakspeare Gallery; and if they could have made such an exertion, the pictures would have been marked with all that monotonous sameness which distinguishes those different Schools. Whereas in the Shakspeare Gallery every Artist, partaking of the freedom of his country, and endowed with that originality of thinking so peculiar to its natives, has chosen his own road to what he conceived to be excellence, unshackled by the slavish imitation and uniformity that pervade all the foreign Schools. This Gallery I once flattered myself with being able to have left to that generous publick, who have for so long a period encouraged my undertakings; but unfortunately for those connected with the Fine Arts, a Vandalic Revolution has arisen, which, in convulsing all Europe, has entirely extinguished, except in this happy Island, all those who had the taste or the power to promote those Arts; while the Tyrant that at present governs France, tells that believing and besotted nation, that, in the midst of all his robbery and rapine, he is a great patron and promoter of the Fine Arts; just as if those Arts that humanize and polish mankind could be promoted by such means, and by such a man. You will excuse, my dear Sir, I am sure, some warmth in an old man on this subject, when I inform you, that this unhappy Revolution has cut up by the roots that revenue from the Continent which enabled me to undertake such considerable works in this country. At the same time, as I am laying my case fairly before you, it should not be disguised, that my natural enthusiasm for promoting the Fine Arts (perhaps buoyed up by success) made me improvident. For, had I lain by but ten pounds out of every hundred pounds my plates produced, I should not now have had occasion to trouble my friends, or appeal to the Publick; but, on the contrary, I flew with impatience to employ some new Artist with the whole gains of my former undertakings. I see too late my error; for I have thereby decreased my ready money, and increased my stock of copperplates to such a size, that all the Printsellers in Europe could not purchase it, especially at these times so unfavourable to the Arts. Having thus candidly owned my error, I have but one word to say in extenuation. My receipts from abroad have been so large, and continued so regular, that I at all times found them fully adequate to support my undertakings at home — I could not calculate on the present crisis, which has totally annihilated them — I certainly calculated on some defalcation of these receipts, by a French and Spanish war, or both; but with France or Spain I carried on but little commerce — Flanders, Holland, and Germany, who, no doubt, supplied the rest of Europe, were the great Marts; but, alas! they are now no more. The convulsion that has disjointed and ruined the whole Continent, I did not foresee — I know no man that did. On that head, therefore, though it has nearly ruined me and mine, I can take but little blame to myself. In this state of things, I throw myself with confidence upon that publick, who has always been but too partial to my poor endeavours, for the disposal of that which, in happier days, I flattered myself to have presented to them. I know of no means by which that can be effected just now but by a Lottery; and if the Legislature will have the goodness to grant a permission for that purpose, they will at least have the assurance of the even tenour of a long life, that it will be fairly and honourably conducted. The objects of it are my Pictures, Galleries, Drawings, &c. &c. which, unconnected with my copper-plates and trade, are much more than sufficient to pay, if properly disposed of, all I owe in the world. I hope you, my dear Sir, and every honest man, at any age, will feel for my anxiety to discharge my debts; but at my advanced age of 85, I feel it becomes doubly desirable. I am, dear Sir, with great regard, your obedient and obliged servant,

JOHN BOYDELL."]

The good old man had the satisfaction of living to see the Act passed through both Houses of Parliament, and of being cheered in its progress by the elogium of several individual Members. After the passing of the Act, it became one of the principal employments of the Alderman's life to arrange with his own hands the several prizes. He did not, however, live to see the event of the scheme; being called from his labours, Dec. 12, 1804. He had attended his duty as Alderman at the Old Bailey Sessions on the 8th, when it is supposed he caught cold. On the 10th he found himself much indisposed; on the 11th he was pronounced by his physician to be in danger; and the next morning expired without a groan. It was rather singular, that he should have just lived long enough to see the Shakspeare Lottery disposed of; for, on the day he paid the debt of Nature, not a ticket remained unsold. Of his unbounded liberality let the Council-chamber of the City of London, the Court-room of the Stationers' Company, and the Dining-room at the Sessions House, loudly speak. To every benevolent institution he was a generous benefactor and attentive guardian. Witness, particularly, "The Royal Humane Society," and the "Literary Fund for the Relief of distressed Authors;" of both which he was for several years a most worthy Vice-president, and a frequent attender at their meetings. Of his private charities, were they to be brought before the publick, the list would be abundant. His remains were interred in great funeral state, in the afternoon of the 19th of December, in the church of St. Olave Jewry.

RICHARD BRADLEY

THOUGH the country had a great loss by the death of Evelyn, yet he was succeeded in about twenty years, by another of equal abilities, and as indefatigable in endeavouring to improve the art of gardening and agriculture, in the early part of the eighteenth century.

"Mr. Bradley possessed considerable knowledge, and was one of the first who treated those subjects in a philosophical manner. He first made himself known to the publick in 1713, by two papers, printed in the XXIXth volume of the Philosophical Transactions; one "on the Motion of the Sap in Vegetables;" the other, "Microscopical Observations on Vegetation, and on the quick Growth of Mouldiness on Melons." He was a Fellow of the Royal Society before 1721; and was chosen Professor of Botany in the University of Cambridge in 1724. — Mr. Bradley was not eminent for any discoveries relating to the indigenous plants in England; but exotic botany was indebted to him for an undertaking, which there is reason to regret he was not enabled to pursue and perfect : I mean, his book on Succulent Plants. As this tribe is incapable of being advantageously preserved in a

Hortus Siccus, there is no part of botany that calls more essentially for a separate publication. His work bears the following title: "Historia Plantarum Succulentarum, complectens hasce insequentes Plantas, Aloen scilicet, Ficoiden, Cercos, Melocardium, aliasque ejus generis quæ in Horto sicco coli non possunt, secundum Prototypum puta naturam in tabellis æneis insculptas, earumdem Descriptiones huc accedunt et Cultura," 4to, 1716, t. 50. It was published in decads, at different times, between the years 1716 and 1727; of which only five were completed. The whole was republished in 1734. The descriptions are in Latin and English, and the figures extremely well done in the style of the time. It preserves its value, as being cited by Linnæus, and as containing some plants not figured in any other publication. A species of Sedum is the only indigenous plant contained in it. Bradley gave a course of Lectures on the Materia Medica in London in 1729, which he published in 8vo, 1730. — Though Bradley's writings do not abound in new discoveries, yet they are not destitute of interesting knowledge, collected from contemporary gardeners, and from books. He was an advocate for the circulation of the sap, and made several new observations on the sexes of plants, in consequence of the production of hybrid species, by which he added strength to that doctrine. He wrote instructively on the germs of trees, on bulbs, on grafting, and particularly on the methods of producing variegated and double flowers; and, on the whole, his writings, coinciding with the growing taste for gardening, the introduction of exotics, and improvements in husbandry, contributed to excite a more philosophical view of these arts, and diffuse a general and popular knowledge of them throughout the kingdom. The industry and talents of Bradley were not mean; and, though unadorned by learning, were sufficient to have secured to him that reputable degree of respect from posterity, which it will ever justly withhold from him who fails to recommend such qualifications by integrity and propriety of conduct. In these, unhappily, Mr. Bradley was deficient. We learn from the account given of him by Mr. Martyn, that he procured the Professorship in a clandestine and fraudulent manner, and afterwards neglected to perform the duties of it. The University, nevertheless, allowed him to retain the nominal distinction of Professor, and appointed Dr. Martyn [who was in 1732 elected the regular Professor of Botany] to give the Lectures. Near the conclusion of his life, his conduct was so unbecoming, that it was in agitation to deprive him of this nominal title. He died on Sunday evening, Nov. 5, 1732."

[Among his numerous publications were: "A general Treatise of Husbandry and Gardening, containing such Observations and Experiments as are new, and useful for the Improvement of Land: with an Account of such extraordinary Inventions and Natural Productions as may help the Ingenious in their Studies, and promote universal Learning. With variety of curious Cuts. For the Months of June and July, the second Year," 8vo. and dedicated, in 1723, to Sir Nicholas Carew, of Beddington, Surrey, bart. "whose delightful gardens would alone be enough to draw upon him the admiration of that part of mankind who study the pleasures and tranquillity of life;" and whose "wonderful Orange-trees, first made familiar to an English climate by his noble ancestors, and the agreeable structure raised for their preservation," are honourably noticed. — The third and last part (for August, September, and the remaining part of the second year) is inscribed to the Earl of Burlington, "whose Palaces and Gardens give an Example of his distinguishing genius;" and has in it, among many other interesting articles, "Observations concerning Vineyards and their Produce, with some Account of the Vineyard near Bath." This celebrated Vineyard, it is stated, contains six acres of ground; and in 1718 produced 66 hogsheads of wine, which was then worth 660l. We are told also that in 1722 there were still superior vines at Mr. Fairchild's at Hoxton, and at Mr. Warner's at Rotherhithe. Mr. Peter Collinson, in his copy of this volume (now mine) has added this note: "The celebrated garden of Mr. John Warner, the Bacchus of his age, and planter of the first modern vineyard, contained about four or five acres. A long and broad canal ran through the length, which was some hundred yards. The earth out of the canal raised the quarters on each side, on which was planted a double and treble row, all the length, of the choicest Pears and Apples; in some places rows of Vines; and Vines round the four quarters of the Flower-garden. It was situate on the East side of East Lane, Rotherhithe; only a rope-walk interposed between the back gardens of the houses in East-lane, and this garden. His brother, Simeon Warner, had his house and garden last of the left-hand side of the way in East-lane."]

REV. JOHN BRAND

IN the "Literary History of the XVIIIth Century" the Rev.
John Brand is too striking a feature to be passed over unnoticed. This industrious Investigator of hidden curiosities was
born at Newcastle-upon-Tyne about 1743, and educated at
Lincoln College, Oxford, where he took his Bachelor's degree;
but left College in 1774, on being presented, by Matthew Ridley,
esq. to the Curacy of Cramlington, a Chapel of Ease to St.
Nicholas at Newcastle, from which it is distant about eight miles.
While at the University, he published a Poem "On illicit Love,
written among the Ruins of Godstow Nunnery, 1775," 4to. The
spot where this poem was written is the burial-place of the
celebrated Rosamond, mistress of Henry II. whose history has
afforded subject for various productions both of the amorous
and elegiac kind; but perhaps none in which the criminality of
an unlawful passion is more forcibly exposed, or chastity recommended in a warmer strain of poetry, than in this production by
Mr. Brand. The sentiments are glowing and just, the imagery
is animated, and the poem is in general beautiful, pathetic, and
moral. Mr. Brand, however, does not appear to have much
cultivated his poetical talent, and had already begun to devote
himself to researches into the Antiquities of his native Country.
In 1777 he evinced a general knowledge of antient manners and
customs by publishing "Observations on Popular Antiquities,
including the whole of Mr. Bourne's *Antiquitates Vulgares,* with
Addenda to every Chapter of that Work; as also an Appendix,
containing such Articles on the subject as have been omitted by
that Author," 8vo. This work is dated from Westgate-street,
Tyne, where the Author then resided. He afterwards continued
to augment his materials by subsequent and more extensive
researches; and left immense materials, which were purchased
by some spirited Booksellers, and have since been judiciously
incorporated by Mr. Ellis of the British Museum, and given to
the Publick in two handsome quarto volumes. — About the
time of the publication of his "Popular Antiquities," Mr. Brand
was admitted a Member of the Society of Antiquaries; and in
1784 was presented by the Duke of Northumberland, who, if
we mistake not, had been his earliest friend and patron, to the
Rectory of St. Mary-Hill. In the same year he was elected
Resident Secretary to the Society of Antiquaries, on the death of
Dr. Morell; the duties of which office he performed with

uncommon ability, and to the entire satisfaction of the Society, who continued to re-elect him annually until his death. In 1789 he published "The History and Antiquities of the Town and County of Newcastle-upon-Tyne," 2 vols. 4to, a very elaborate work, embellished with Views of the Public Buildings, engraved by Fittler at an expence of 500*l.* In the sale, however, from various circumstances, and particularly the death of his Bookseller, he was peculiarly unfortunate, notwithstanding its high merit as a piece of local history. Mr. Brand also communicated many Papers on subjects of Antiquity to the Society, the principal of which are printed in the *Archæologia,* vols. VIII. X. XIII. XIV. and XV. He was twice prosecuted by common informers for non-residence, having let his Parsonage-house when he went to reside in the Society's Apartments at Somerset-house, although none could exceed him in the punctual discharge of his parochial duties, both on Sundays and Week-days. After the late regulations respecting residence, he constantly slept in the Rectory-house. He always took much exercise; and on the day before his death had a long ramble with two much-valued Friends, with whom he parted in the evening, apparently in perfect health, Sept. 10, 1806. He rose next morning about seven o'clock, his usual hour, and went into his study, when his servant took him an egg, which he usually ate before he went to Somerset-house. The servant afterwards, wondering at his remaining so long in his study, went into the room, and found him lying on the floor lifeless. He died unmarried, and without leaving any relation except a very aged aunt. He was buried in the chancel of his church, Sept. 24. In him the Society of Antiquaries sustained a very great loss. Although his publications were few, his knowledge of Antiquities was very extensive; and he had accumulated a very numerous and curious Library, rich in old English Literature, which was sold by auction some time after his death. His manners, somewhat repulsive to a stranger, became easy on closer acquaintance; and he loved to communicate to men of literary and antiquarian taste the result of his researches on any subject in which they might require information. Many of his books were supplied with portraits drawn by himself in a style not inferior to the originals, of which they were at the same time perfect imitations. — The First Part of his extensive Collection, consisting of 8611 articles, or lots, of Printed Books, exclusive of 243 lots of Manuscripts, was sold by Mr. Stewart in May 1807. The Second Part, containing 4054

articles of Duplicates and Pamphlets, was sold in February 1808.
See an account of some of the rarer Tracts in the "Bibliomania,"
p. 605. — A small silhouette likeness of Mr. Brand is in the
Frontispiece to his "History of Newcastle."]

SIR WILLIAM BROWNE

THIS worthy old Knight was the son of a Physician. He
was born in 1692; and in 1707 was entered at Peter house,
Cambridge; where he describes himself, in 1711, as in his Soph's
year, and attentively studying the Articles of the Church of
England. He took the degree of B. A. 1710; M. A. 1714; and
M. D. 1721; soon after which he settled at Lynn, where he
practised with considerable success; though even then he shewed
some degree of eccentricity. Once, in particular, a pamphlet
having been written against him, he nailed it up against his
house-door.

In 1735 he commenced author, by publishing the third edition
of "Dr. Gregory's Elements of Catoptrics and Dioptrics. Translated from the Latin Original, by William Browne, M. D. at
Lynn Regis in Norfolk.

Having acquired a competency by his profession, he removed
to Queen's Square, Ormond Street, London, where he seems to
have cultivated his attachment for Apollo, as the Patron both
of Poetry and Physic; and a great number of lively essays, both
in prose and verse, the production of his pen, were printed and
circulated among his friends.

As a member of the Royal College of Physicians, he was
appointed in 1751 to deliver the Harveian Oration; and in 1765
had the honour of being chosen President of the College; an
office which he held for two years; and on quitting the chair,
delivered an Oration, in which he thus delineates his own
character:

"The manly age and inclination, with conformable studies, I
diligently applied to the practice of physic in the country: where,
as that age adviseth, I sought riches and friendships. But afterward, being satiated with friends, whom truth, not flattery, had

procured, satiated with riches, which Galen, not Fortune, had presented, I resorted immediately to this College : where, in farther obedience to the same adviser, I might totally addict myself to the service of honour. Conducted by your favour, instead of my own merit, I have been advanced through various degrees of honour, a most delightful climax indeed, even to the very highest of all which the whole profession of Physic hath to confer. In this chair therefore, twice received from the Elects, shewing their favour to himself, he confesseth, much more than to the College, your President

Acknowledges, that he has happy been,
And, now, content with acting this sweet scene,
Chuses to make his exit, like a guest
Retiring pamper'd from a plenteous feast :

in order to attach himself and the remainder of his life, no longer, as before, solely to the College, but, by turns, also to the medicinal springs of his own country; although, as a Physician, never unmindful of his duty, yet after his own manner, with hilarity rather than gravity : to enjoy liberty more valuable than silver and gold, as in his own right, because that of man-kind, not without pride, which ever ought to be its inseparable companion.

Now the free foot shall dance its favourite round. Behold an instance of human ambition! not to be satiated, but by the conquest of three, as it were, medical worlds; lucre in the country, honour in the College, pleasure at medicinal springs! I would, if it were possible, be delightful and useful to all : to myself even totally, and aequal : to old age, though old, diamet-rically opposite, not a censor and chastiser, but a commender and encourager, of youth. I would have mine such as, in the Satire,

Crispus's hoary entertaining age,
Whose wit and manners mild alike engage.

The age of praesiding, by the custom of our praedecessors, was generally a *lustrum,* five years; although our Sloane, now happy, like another Nestor, lived to see three ages, both as Praesident, and as man. But two years more than satisfy me : for, that each of the Elects may in his turn hold the sceptre of prudence, far more desirable than power, given by Caius, which the law of justice and aequity recommends,

No tenure pleases longer than a year.

But, in truth, among such endearing friendships with you, such delightful conversations, such useful communications, with which this amiable situation hath blessed me, one or two things, as is usual, have happened, not at all to my satisfaction. One, that, while, most studious of peace myself, I hoped to have praeserved the peace of the College secure and intire, I too soon found that it was not otherwise to be sought for than by war : but, even after our first adversary, because inconsiderable, was instantly overthrown, and his head completely cut off by the hand of the Law, yet from the same neck, as if Hydra had been our Enemy, so many other heads broke out, yea, and with inhuman violence broke into this very Senate, like monsters swimming in our medical sea, whom I beheld with unwilling indeed, but with dry or rather fixed eyes, because not suspecting the least mischief from thence to the College, and therefore laughing, so far from fearing. The other, in reality never enough to be lamented, that, while I flattered myself with having, by my whole power of pursuasion, in the room of Orphaean music, raised the Croonian Medical Lecture as it were from the shades into day, if there could be any faith in solemn promises; that faith being, to my very great wonder, violated, this Lecture, like another Eurydice, perhaps looked after by me too hastily, beloved by me too desperately, instantly slipped back again, and fled indignant to the shades below." He used to say he resigned the Presidentship because he would not stay to be beat :— alluding to the attack of the Licentiates.

As soon as he was out of office, he entered on his plan of visiting the medical springs. Whilst he was at Bath, he paid a visit to Bp. Warburton at Prior Park; and the learned Prelate has exhibited a most capital literary portrait of him; which every one who knew Sir William Browne will pronounce to be an excellent likeness. ["When you see Dr. Heberden, pray communicate to him an unexpected honour I have lately received. The other day, word was brought to me from below, that one Sir William Browne sent up his name, and should be glad to kiss my hand. I judged it to be the famous Physician, whom I had never seen, nor had the honour to know. When I came down into the drawing-room, I was accosted by a little, round, well-fed gentleman, with a large muff, in one hand, a small Horace, open, in the other, and a spying-glass dangling in a black ribbon at his button. After the first salutation, he informed me that his visit was indeed to me; but principally, and in the first place, to Prior-Park, which had so inviting a prospect from below; and he did not doubt but, on examination, it would sufficiently repay the trouble he had given himself of coming up to it on foot. We then took our chairs; and the first thing he did or said, was to propose a doubt to me concerning a passage in Horace, which all this time he had still open in his hand. Before I could answer, he gave me the solution of this long misunderstood passage, and, in support of his explanation, had the charity to repeat his own paraphrase of it in English verse, just come hot, as he said, from the brain. When this and chocolate were over, having seen all he wanted of me, he desired to see something more of *the seat*; and particularly what he called the *monument,* by which I understood him to mean, the Prior's tower, with your inscription. Accordingly I ordered a servant to attend him thither; and, when he had satisfied his curiosity, either to let him out from the park above into the Down, or from the garden below into the Road. Which he chose, I never asked; and so this honourable visit ended. Hereby you will understand that the design of all this was, to be *admired.* And, indeed, he had my *admiration* to the full; but for nothing so much, as for his being able, at past eighty, to perform this expedition on foot, in no good weather, and with all the alacrity of a boy, both in body and mind." *Letter to Dr. Hurd, Nov.* 18, 1767.]

Sir William Browne died at his house in Queen-square, Bloomsbury, March 10, 1774, at the age of 82. His lady died July 25, 1763, in her 64th year.

I shall subjoin a well-known Epigram*, by Sir William Browne, which the Critics have pronounced to be a good one:

"The King to Oxford sent a troop of horse,
For Tories own no argument but force;
With equal skill to Cambridge books he sent,
For Whigs admit no force but argument."

[*The following by an Oxonian, which gave rise to that by Sir William, is at least as good:
"The King, observing with judicious eyes,
The state of both his universities,
To Oxford sent a troop of horse; and why?
That learned body wanted loyalty:
To Cambridge books, as very well discerning
How much that loyal body wanted learning."]

WILLIAM CASLON

M R. WILLIAM CASLON, born in that part of the town of Hales Owen which is situated in Shropshire, in 1692, and who is justly styled by Mr. Rowe-Mores "the Coryphæus of Letter-founders," was not trained to that business; "which is a handy-work, so concealed among the artificers of it," that Mr. Moxon, in his indefatigable researches on that subject, "could not discover that any one had taught it any other; but every one that had used it learnt it of his own genuine inclination." [Dissertation upon English Typographical Founders and Founderies, p. 17.] — He served a regular apprenticeship to an engraver of ornaments on gun-barrels; and was taken from that instrument to an employment of a very different tendency, *the propagation of the Christian faith*. In the year 1720 (the year in which his eldest son was born) the Society for promoting Christian Knowledge, in consequence of a representation made by Mr. Salomon Negri, a native of Damascus in Syria, well skilled in the Oriental languages, who had been professor of Arabic in places of note for a great part of his life, deemed it expedient to print, for the use of the Eastern Churches, the New Testament and Psalter in the Arabic language, for the benefit of the poor Christians in Palestine, Syria, Mesopotamia, Arabia, and Egypt; the constitution of which countries allowed of no printing; and Mr. Caslon was pitched upon to cut the fount which in his specimens is distinguished by the name of *English Arabic*. Mr. Caslon, after he had finished his Arabic fount, cut the letters of his own name in Pica Roman, and placed the name at the bottom of a specimen of the Arabic; and Mr. Palmer (the reputed author of Psalmanazar's "History of Printing") seeing this name, advised Mr. Caslon to cut the whole fount of Pica. Mr. Caslon did so; and as the performance exceeded the letter of the other founders of the time, Mr. Palmer, whose circumstances required credit with those who, by this advice, were now obstructed, repented of having given the advice, and discouraged Mr. Caslon from any farther progress; a circumstance which was verified by the celebrated Dr. Franklin, who was at that time a journeyman under Mr. Watts, the first printer that employed Mr. Caslon. Mr. Caslon, disgusted, applied to Mr. Bowyer; under whose inspection he cut, in 1722, the beautiful fount of English which was used in printing Selden's Works, 1726; and the Coptic types which were used for Dr. Wilkin's edition of the Pentateuch (which letter, having accidentally escaped the conflagration of 1808, I still possess); Mr. Caslon was encouraged to proceed farther both by Mr. Bowyer and his brother-in-law, Mr. Bettenham; and had the candour to acknowledge Mr. Bowyer as his master, and that he had taught him an art, in which, by diligence and unwearied application, he arrived to that perfection, as not only to remove the necessity of importing types from Holland; but in the beauty and elegance of those made by him so far surpassed the best productions of foreign artificers, that his types have not unfrequently been exported to the Continent; and it may still with great justice and confidence be asserted, that a more beautiful specimen than his is not to be found in any part of the world. It appears by the Dissertation of Mr. Mores, p. 86, that Mr. Caslon had a brother named Samuel, who was his mould-maker, and afterwards lived with Mr. George Anderton, of Birmingham, in the same capacity. Mr. Caslon's first foundery was in a small house in Helmet Row in Old Street; he afterwards removed into Ironmonger Row; and about the year 1735 into Chiswell-street, where the foundery was carried on at first by himself, and afterwards in conjunction with William, his eldest son; whose name first appeared in the specimen of 1742. In or about the year 1750, Mr. Caslon was put into the commission of the peace for the county of Middlesex; and retired from the active part of business to a house opposite the Nag's Head, in the Hackney road; whence he removed to another house, in Water Gruel Row; and afterwards to Bethnal Green; where he died, Jan. 23, 1766, at the age of 74, and was buried in the church-yard of St. Luke, Middlesex; in which parish all his different founderies were situated. A monument, erected to his memory, is thus briefly inscribed:

"W. CASLON, esq. ob. 23 Jan. 1766, æt. 74.
Also, W. CASLON, esq. (son of the above)
ob. 17 Aug. 1778, æt. 58 years."

One particular in his character is thus excellently described by Sir John Hawkins (History of Music, vol. V. p. 127). "Mr. Caslon, meeting with encouragement suitable to his deserts, settled in Ironmonger row, in Old-street; and, being a great lover of music, had frequent concerts at his house, which were resorted to by many eminent masters; to these he used to invite his friends, and those of his old acquaintance, the companions of his youth. He afterwards removed to a large house in Chiswell-street, and had an organ in his concert-room; after that he had stated monthly concerts; which, for the convenience of his friends, and that they might walk home in safety when the performance was over, were on that Thursday in the month which was nearest the full moon; from which circumstance his guests were wont humorously to call themselves Lunatics. In the intervals of the performance the guests refreshed themselves at a sideboard, which was amply furnished; and when it was over, sitting down to a bottle of wine, and a decanter of excellent ale, of Mr. Caslon's own brewing, they concluded the evening's entertainment with a song or two of Purcell's, sung to the harpsichord, or a few catches; and about twelve retired." There is a good mezzotinto print of him by J. Faber, from a painting by F. Kyte, inscribed Gulielmus Caslon. His second son, Thomas, was for many years a bookseller of eminence in Stationer's court; where he died, March 29, 1783. — Of the modern state of this undoubtedly most capital foundery in the world, the particulars are given by Mr. Mores, with some attempts at pleasantry. His ridicule, however, before the publication of his book, had lost its sting by the death of the *second* of the Caslons, who, as an artist, had certainly great merit, though not equal to his father. He died in 1778; leaving a widow, whom, in the history of this celebrated foundery, it would be improper to pass unnoticed. She was the only child of Dr. Cartledge; and her mother marrying again imprudently, she was put to school by an uncle, who took care to provide for her. Her merit and abilities in conducting a capital business during the life of her husband, and afterwards till her son was capable of managing it, can only be known to those who had dealings with that manufactory. In quickness of understanding, and activity of execution, she has left few equals among her sex. On the death of her husband, and their eldest son's establishing himself in the magnificent building now occupied by Messrs. Lackington and Co. in Moorfields (the Temple of the Muses), she conducted the foundery herself, and continued to do so till disabled by an attack of the palsy; which she survived but a few months, dying Oct. 23, 1795, aged about 70. After the death of the mother, there were still two very large founderies carried on; one of them by a third *William Caslon,* who, having quitted Moorfields, had become the purchaser of the *Jackson* foundery in Dorset-street; since given up to his son, a fourth *William Caslon,* a young man of considerable abilities, to whom I cannot recommend a better model than his great grand-father, who was universally esteemed as a first-rate artist, a tender master, and an honest, friendly, and benevolent man. — The original foundery in Chiswell-street was purchased by Mr. Charles Catherwood, a distant relation, who died June 7, 1809, æt. 45; and is still carried on by Mr. Henry Caslon (another great-grandson of the first William) under the firm of Caslon and Catherwood.

It is but common justice to mention in this place the names of Cottrell and Jackson, as Letter-founders who were trained up under the auspices, and pursued with commendable industry the steps, of their excellent instructor. Mr. Mores says, "Mr. Thomas Cottrell is in order *à primo proximus*. He was in the late Mr. Caslon's house, an apprentice to *dressing,* but not to *cutting*. This part he learned, as Mr. Moxon terms it, 'of his own genuine inclination.' He began in the year 1757, with a fount of English Roman;" [and afterwards cut a fount of Norman, intended (but not used) for Domesday-book]. "He lives in Nevil's-court, in Fetter-lane; obliging, good-natured, and friendly; rejecting nothing because it is out of the common way, and is expeditious in his performances." — Mr. Cottrell died in 1785, I am sorry to add, not in affluent circumstances, though to his profession of a Letter-founder were superadded that of a Doctor for the Tooth-ache, which he cured by burning the ear; and had also the honour of serving in the Troop of his Majesty's Life-guards. — "Mr. Joseph Jackson was in Mr. Caslon's house too, an apprentice to the whole art, into which he launched out for himself upon the same principle as did Mr. Cottrell; for, actuated by the same motives, they both flew off together. Mr. Jackson lives in Salisbury-court, in Fleet-street; he is obliging, and communicative, and his specimen will, *adjuvante Numine,* have place amongst the literate specimens of English letter-cutters." — Of Mr. Jackson Mr. Mores would have said more, if he had lived to witness the progress of his diligent exertions. He too, after cutting a variety of types for the Rolls of Parliament (a work which will ever reflect honour on the good taste and munificence of the present Reign), employed his talents on Domesday, and in a manner more successful than his fellow-labourer. I have much gratification in stating, that the two beautiful volumes of that valuable record were finished at the press in 1783, on a plan which I had the honour of projecting, and Mr. Jackson the skill to execute, under the title of "Domesday Book; sive Liber Censualium Willielmi Regis Angliæ, inter Archivis Regiis in Domo Capitulari Westmonasterii asservatus :

Jubente Rege Augustissimo Georgio Tertio prelo mandatus. Londini, Typis J. Nichols, 1783." — To Mr. Jackson's Occidentals may also be added a beautiful Pica Greek, which he cut under the express direction of Mr. Bowyer.]

EDWARD CAVE

EDWARD CAVE was born at Newton in Warwickshire, Feb. 29, 1691. His father was the youngest son of Mr. Edward Cave, of Cave's in the Hole, a lone house, on the Street-road in the same county, which took its name from the occupier; but, having concurred with his elder brother in cutting off the intail of a small hereditary estate, by which act it was lost from the family, he was reduced to follow in Rugby the trade of a shoe-maker. He was a man of good reputation in his narrow circle, and remarkable for strength and rustic intrepidity. He lived to a great age, and was in his latter years supported by his son.

It was fortunate for Edward Cave, that, having a disposition to literary attainments, he was not cut off by the poverty of his parents from opportunities of cultivating his faculties. The school of Rugby, in which he had, by the rules of its foundation, a right to be instructed, was then in high reputation, under the Rev. Mr. Holyock, to whose care most of the neighbouring families, even of the highest rank, entrusted their sons. He had judgment to discover, and, for some time, generosity to encourage the genius of young Cave; and was so well pleased with his quick progress in the school, that he declared his resolution to breed him for the University, and recommend him as a servitor to some of his scholars of high rank. But prosperity which depends upon the caprice of others is of short duration. Cave's superiority in literature exalted him to an invidious familiarity with boys who were far above him in rank and expectations; and, as in unequal associations it always happens, whatever unlucky prank was played, was imputed to Cave. When any mischief, great or small, was done, though perhaps others boasted of the stratagem when it was successful, yet upon detection or miscarriage the fault was sure to fall upon poor Cave.

Under pretence that Cave obstructed the discipline of the school, by selling clandestine assistance, and supplying exercises to idlers, he was oppressed with unreasonable tasks, that there might be an opportunity of quarreling with his failure; and when his diligence had surmounted them, no regard was paid to the performance. Cave bore this persecution for a while; and then left the school, and the hope of a literary education, to seek some other means of gaining a livelihood.

He was first placed with a Collector of the Excise. He used to recount with some pleasure a journey or two which he rode with him as his clerk, and relate the victories that he gained over the Excisemen in grammatical disputations. But the insolence of his mistress, who employed him in servile drudgery, quickly disgusted him; and he went up to London in quest of more suitable employment.

He was recommended to a timber-merchant at the Bank side, and, while he was there on liking, is said to have given hopes of great mercantile abilities. But this place he soon left, I know not for what reason, and was bound apprentice to Mr. Collins, a printer of some reputation, and deputy alderman.

This was a trade for which men were formerly qualified by a literary education, and which was pleasing to Cave, because it furnished some employment for his scholastic attainments. Here therefore he resolved to settle, though his master and mistress lived in perpetual discord, and their house could be no comfortable habitation. From the inconveniences of these domestic tumults he was soon released, having in only two years attained so much skill in his art, and gained so much the confidence of his master, that he was sent without any superintendant to conduct a printing-house at Norwich, and publish a weekly paper. In this undertaking he met with some opposition, which produced a public controversy, and procured young Cave reputation as a writer.

His master died before his apprenticeship was expired; and, as he was not able to bear the perverseness of his mistress, he quitted her house upon a stipulated allowance, and married a young widow, with whom he lived at Bow. When his apprenticeship was over, he worked as a journeyman at the printing-house of Mr. Barber, a man much distinguished and employed by the Tories, whose principles had at that time so much prevalence with Cave, that he was for some years a writer in 'Mist's Journal,' which (though he afterwards obtained, by his wife's interest, a small place in the Post-office) he for some time con-tinued. But, as interest is powerful, and conversation, however mean, in time persuasive, he by degrees inclined to another party; in which, however, he was always moderate, though steady and determined.

When he was admitted into the Post-office, he still continued, at his intervals of attendance, to exercise his trade, or to employ himself with some typographical business. He corrected the "Gradus ad Parnassum," and was liberally rewarded by the Company of Stationers. He wrote an account of the Criminals, which had for some time a considerable sale; and published many little pamphlets that accident brought into his hands, of which it would be very difficult to recover the memory. By the correspondence which his place in the Post-office facilitated, he procured country news-papers, and sold their intelligence to a journalist of London for a guinea a week.

He was afterwards raised to the office of Clerk of the Franks, in which he acted with great spirit and firmness; and often stopped franks which were given by Members of Parliament to their friends, because he thought such extension of a peculiar right illegal. This raised many complaints; and having stopped, among others, a frank given to the old Duchess of Marlborough by Mr. Walter Plummer, he was cited before the House, as for breach of privilege, and accused, I suppose very unjustly, of opening letters to detect them. He was treated with great harsh-ness and severity : but, declining their questions by pleading his oath of secrecy, was at last dismissed. And it must be recorded to his honour, that when he was ejected from his office, he did not think himself discharged from his trust, but continued to refuse to his nearest friends any information about the manage-ment of the office.

By this constancy of diligence, and diversification of employ-ment, he in time collected a sum sufficient for the purchase of a small printing-office, and began *The Gentleman's Magazine,* a periodical pamphlet, of which the scheme is known wherever the English language is spoken. To this undertaking he owed the affluence in which he passed the last twenty years of his life, and the fortune which he left behind him, which, though large, had been yet larger, had he not rashly and wantonly impaired it by innumerable projects, of which I know not that ever one succeeded.

The Gentleman's Magazine, which has already subsisted three

and twenty years, and still continues equally to enjoy the favour of the world, is one of the most successful and lucrative pamphlets which literary history has upon record, and therefore deserves, in this narrative, particular notice.

Mr. Cave, when he formed the project, was far from expecting the success which he found; and others had so little prospect of its consequence, that, though he had for several years talked of his plan among printers and booksellers, none of them thought it worth the trial.* That they were not restrained by their virtue from the execution of another man's design, was sufficiently apparent as soon as that design began to be gainful; for in a few years a multitude of magazines arose, and perished: only *The London Magazine,* supported by a powerful association of booksellers, and circulated with all the art, and all the cunning of trade, exempted itself from the general fate of Cave's invaders, and obtained, though not an equal, yet a considerable sale.†

Cave now began to aspire to popularity; and, being a greater lover of poetry than any other art, he sometimes offered subjects for poems, and proposed prizes for the best performances. The first prize was fifty pounds, for which, being but newly acquainted with wealth, and thinking the influence of fifty pounds extremely great, he expected the first Authors of the kingdom to appear as competitors; and offered the allotment of the prize to the Universities. But, when the time came, no name was seen among the writers that had been ever seen before; the Universities and several private men rejectd the province of assigning the prize. At all this Mr. Cave wondered for a while; but his natural judgment, and a wider acquaintance with the world, soon cured him of his astonishment, as of many other prejudices and errors. Nor have many men been seen raised by accident or industry to sudden riches, that retained less of the meanness of their former state.

He continued to improve his Magazine, and had the satisfaction of seeing its success proportionate to his diligence, till in the year 1751 his wife died of an asthma; with which though he seemed not at first much affected, yet in a few days he lost his

---

*"The invention of this new species of publication may be considered as something of an epocha in the Literary History of this Country. The periodical publications before that time were almost wholly confined to political transactions, and to foreign and domestic occurrences.

†This was actually the case in 1754; but The London Magazine ceased to exist in 1785.

sleep and his appetite; and, lingering two years, fell, by drinking acid liquors, into a diarrhœa, and afterwards into a kind of lethargic insensibility, in which one of the last acts of reason he exerted, was fondly to press the hand that is now writing this little narrative. He died on January 10, 1754, æt. 63, having just concluded the twenty-third annual collection.

He was a man of large stature, not only tall but bulky, and was, when young, of remarkable strength and activity. He was generally healthful, and capable of much labour and long application; but in the latter years of his life was afflicted with the gout, which he endeavoured to cure or alleviate by a total abstinence both from strong liquors and animal food. From animal food he abstained about four years, and from strong liquors much longer; but the gout continued unconquered, perhaps unabated.

His resolution and perseverance were very uncommon; whatever he undertook, neither expence nor fatigue were able to repress him; but his constancy was calm, and, to those who did not know him, appeared faint and languid; but he always went forward, though he moved slowly.

The same chillness of mind was observable in his conversation; he was watching the minutest accent of those whom he disgusted by seeming inattention; and his visitant was surprized when he came a second time, by preparations to execute the scheme which he supposed never to have been heard.

He was, consistently with this general tranquillity of mind, a tenacious maintainer, though not a clamorous demander of his right. In his youth, having summoned his fellow-journeymen to concert measures against the oppression of their masters, he mounted a kind of rostrum, and harangued them so efficaciously, that they determined to resist all future invasions. And when the Stamp Officers demanded to stamp the last half sheet of the Magazines, Mr. Cave alone defeated their claim, to which the proprietors of the rival magazines would meanly have submitted.

He was a friend rather easy and constant, than zealous and active; yet many instances might be given, where both his money and his diligence were employed liberally for others. His enmity was in like manner cool and deliberate; but, though cool, it was not insidious, and though deliberate, not pertinacious.

His mental faculties were slow; he saw little at a time, but that little he saw with great exactness. He was long in finding

the right, but seldom failed to find it at last. His affections were
not easily gained, and his opinion not quickly discovered. His
reserve, as it might hide his faults, concealed his virtues; but
such he was, as they who best knew him have most lamented.*"

To the foregoing incomparable article I shall take the liberty
of making some additions.

From the time of Mr. Cave's first connexion with the News-
paper at Norwich, he had conceived a strong idea of the utility
of publishing the Parliamentary Debates; and had an opportunity, whilst engaged in a situation at the Post-office, not only,
as stated by Dr. Johnson, of supplying his London friends with
the Provincial Papers; but he also contrived to furnish the
Country Printers with those written Minutes of the Proceedings
in the Two Houses of Parliament, which within my own
remembrance were regularly circulated in the Coffee-houses,
before the Daily Papers were *tacitly permitted* to report the
Debates.

The Orders of the House were indeed regularly repeated, and
occasionally enforced; and under these, in April 1728, Mr. Cave
experienced some inconvenience and expence; having been
ordered into the custody of the Serjeant at Arms, for supplying
his friend Mr. Robert Raikes with the Minutes of the House, for
the use of the Gloucester Journal. After a confinement of several
days, on stating his sorrow for the offence, and pleading that he
had a wife and family who suffered much by his imprisonment,
he was discharged, with a reprimand, on paying the accustomed
fees."

In the following year Mr. Raikes again incurred the censure
of the House by repeating his offence; but Mr. Cave was at that
time out of the scrape.

The plan of inserting a regular series of the Parliamentary
Debates in the Gentleman's Magazine, was a project which Mr.
Cave had long in contemplation before he adventured to put it
into practice. At length, in July 1736, he boldly dared; and his
method of proceeding is thus related by Sir John Hawkins:

"Taking with him a friend or two, he found means to procure
for them and himself admission into the gallery of the House of
Commons, or to some concealed station in the other House; and

---

*Thus far this article is given in the words of Dr. Johnson, from Gent.
Mag. vol. XXV. p. 55—57; revised by its excellent Author, at my
particular request, in 1781.

then they privately took down notes of the several speeches, and the general tendency and substance of the arguments. Thus furnished, Cave and his associates would adjourn to a neighbouring tavern, and compare and adjust their notes; by means whereof, and the help of their memories, they became enabled to fix at least the substance of what they had so lately heard and remarked. The reducing this crude matter into form was the work of a future day and of an abler hand; Guthrie, the Historian, a writer for the booksellers, whom Cave retained for the purpose." But these Debates were not given till the Session was ended; and then only with the initial and final letters of each Speaker.

Thus far all went on smoothly for two years; till on the 13th of April 1738, a complaint being made to the House, that the publishers of several written and printed News-Letters and Papers had taken upon them to give accounts therein of the Proceedings of the House; it was Resolved, "That it is a high indignity to, and a notorious breach of, the Privilege of this House, for any News-writer, in Letters, or other Papers (as Minutes, or under any other denomination), or for any Printer or Publisher of any printed News-paper of any denomination, to presume to insert in the said Letters or Papers, or to give therein, any account of the Debates, or other Proceedings, of this House, or any Committee thereof, as well during the Recess, as the Sitting of Parliament; and that this House will proceed with the utmost severity against such offenders."

Some expedient was now become necessary; and the *caution* (not the *vanity*) of Cave suggesting to him a popular fiction; in June 1738 he prefaced the Debates by what he chose to call "An Appendix to Captain Lemuel Gulliver's Account of the famous Empire of Lilliput;" and the proceedings in Parliament were given under the title of "Debates in the Senate of Great Lilliput."

Not thinking himself, however, perfectly secure, even by this total concealment of the speakers, he did not venture to put his own name to the Title-pages of the Magazine; but published them under the name of one of his nephews, "Edward Cave, junior;" which was continued till 1752. In the following year he again used his own name; and gave the Debates, as at first, with the initial and final letters.

A new æra in politicks, occasioned by the motion to remove the Minister, Feb. 13, 1740-1, bringing on much warmer Debates, required "the pen of a more nervous writer than he who had hitherto conducted them;" and "Cave, dismissing Guthrie, committed the care of this part of his monthly publication to Johnson;" who had already given ample specimens of his ability. But the Lilliputian disguise was still continued, even beyond the period of Johnson's Debates; which, as has been authenticated by his own Diary, began Nov. 19, 1740, and ended Feb. 23, 1742-3. And these Debates, which, every competent judge must allow, exhibit a memorable specimen of the extent and promptitude of Johnson's faculties, and which have induced learned foreigners to compare British with Roman eloquence, were hastily sketched by Johnson while he was not yet 32, while he had little acquaintance with life, while he was struggling, not for distinction, but existence.

On the 3rd of April 1747, a complaint having been made in the House of Lords, against Edward Cave, and Thomas Astley, for printing in their respective Magazines (the Gentleman's and the London) an account of the Trial of Simon Lord Lovat; they were both ordered into the custody of the Gentleman Usher of the Black Rod. — On the 10th of April, Mr. Cave, in custody, petitioned the House; expressing his sorrow for his offence; begging pardon for the same; promising never to offend again in the like manner; and praying to be discharged.

Mr. Astley in regard of his lameness with the gout as not to be able to walk, was discharged out of custody, paying his fees; and Mr. Cave was ordered to be brought up for the same purpose on the following day; which was accordingly done, and he was also discharged, with a reprimand, on paying his fees.

On the morning of Dec. 7, 1784, only six days before his death, Dr. Johnson requested to see the Editor of these Anecdotes; from whom he had borrowed some of the early volumes of the Magazine, with a professed intention to point out the pieces which he had written in that collection. The books lay on the table, with many leaves doubled down, particularly those which contained his share in the Parliamentary Debates; and such was the goodness of Johnson's heart, that he solemnly declared, "that the only part of his writings which then gave him any compunction, was his account of the Debates in the Gentleman's Magazine; but that, at the time he wrote them, he did not think he was imposing on the world. The mode," he said, "was to fix upon a Speaker's name; then to make an argument for him; and to conjure up an answer. He wrote those Debates with more velocity than any other of his productions; often three columns of the Magazine within the hour. He once wrote *ten pages* in one day, and that not a long one, beginning perhaps at noon, and ending early in the evening. Of the Life of Savage he wrote forty-eight octavo pages in one day; but that day included the night, for he sat up all the night to do it."

His portion of the Parliamentary Debates was collected into two octavo volumes; to which the Editor has substituted the real for the fictitious speakers. "The illuminations of Johnson's Oratory," it is observed, "were obscured by the jargon which Cave thought it prudent to adopt, to avoid Parliamentary indignation. These Debates, like the Orations of Cicero and Demosthenes, ought to be studied by the British youth, as specimens of splendid eloquence, nervous argument, and Parliamentary decorum. Though few can hope to rival Johnson's performances, every youth, who from his birth or fortune expects to sit in Parliament, ought to aim, by studious perusal, at Johnson's perfection in oratory and reasoning. And those Debates may be usefully inspected by every public man, for felicities of expression, for the structure of sentences, happy at once for point, dignity, and elegance. [In the Preface to Johnson's Debates, 1787, we read:]

"It was the Revolution which finally unshackled the press. But it was still criminal, at least dangerous, to publish Parliamentary proceedings without Parliamentary permission. During King William's reign ,the Newspapers sometimes gave a detached speech of a particular speaker, who wished, by contributing the outlines, to gratify his vanity, or secure his seat.

"It was in the factious times which immediately succeeded, when Parliamentary Debates were first distributed through the land in monthly pamphlets. Then it was that Boyer's zeal propagated the Political State. This was succeeded, on the accession of George I. by the Historical Registers, which were published by soberer men, and may be supposed therefore to contain more satisfactory information.

"The Gentleman's Magazine soon after furnished the publick with still more finished Debates, which were first compiled by Guthrie, then by Johnson, and afterwards by Hawkesworth. The success of this far-famed Miscellany prompted many competitors for public favour, who all found an interest in propagating what the people read, however contrary to Parliamentary resolves. And these resolves have at length given way to the spirit of the people, who, as they enjoy the right of instructing their

Representatives, seem to have established the privilege of knowing what their Representatives say."

The Lilliputian names were continued in the Magazine till
1745; in which year, p. 135, Mr. Cave very fully announced
his plan of publishing Mr. Anchitell Grey's Debates, from 1669
to 1694; and gave the particular subject of each Debate. After
which no Debate occurs till November 1749, when they were
given in the form of a Letter from a Member of Parliament to
his Country Friend.

In 1752 the Proceedings in Parliament were reported briefly
in the Magazine, in the shape of a letter thus introduced: "The
following heads of Speeches in the H—— of C—— were given
me by a gentleman, who is of opinion, that Members of Parliament are accountable to their Constituents for what they say, as
well as what they do, in their Legislative capacity; that no
honest man, who is intrusted with the liberties and purses of the
people, will be ever unwilling to have his whole conduct laid
before those who so intrusted him, without disguise; that if every
gentleman acted upon this just, this honourable, this constitu-
tional principle, the Electors themselves only would be to blame,
if they re-elected a person guilty of a breach of so important a
trust. But let the arguments speak for themselves. Thus much
only may be necessary to premise, that as the state of public
affairs was, in a great measure, the same both last year and
this, I send you a speech, in the Committee of Supply, upon the
number of Standing Forces for the year 1751, and also another
in the lest Session of Parliament, for the year 1752. You may be
assured they are really genuine, and not such an imposition
upon the speakers and the publick, as some that have appeared
in other Monthly Collections."

From the above period, the Debates were regularly given as
formerly, with the initial letters of the several speakers, till the
end of 1782; subsequent to which, they have been printed
without the least affectation of disguise; and form, in the whole,
a complete and impartial report for more than seventy years.

I once possessed a paper, in Johnson's handwriting, which I
gave to Mr. Boswell, intituled, "Account between Mr. Edward
Cave and Sam. Johnson, in relation to a version of Father Paul,
&c. begun Aug. 2, 1738;" by which it appears, that from that
day to April 21, 1739, Johnson received for that work 49l. 7s.
in sums of one, two, three, and sometimes four guineas at a time,
most frequently two. And it is curious to observe the minute and

scrupulous accuracy with which Johnson has pasted upon it a slip of paper, which he has intituled "Small Account," and which contains one article, "Sept. 9, Mr. Cave laid down 2s. 6d." There is subjoined to this account a list of some subscribers to the work, partly in Johnson's handwriting, partly in that of another person; and there follows a leaf or two, on which are written a number of characters which have the appearance of a short-hand, which, perhaps, Johnson was then trying to learn.

In a conversation with Boswell, talking of Ghosts, Dr. Johnson said, "he knew one friend, who was an honest and a sensible man, who told him he had seen a Ghost — old Mr. Edward Cave, the printer at St. John's Gate." He said, "Mr. Cave did not like the talk of it, and seemed to be in great horrour whenever it was mentioned." — B. "Pray, Sir, what does he say was the appearance?" — J. "Why, Sir, something of a shadowy being*."

"His friend Edward Cave having been mentioned, he told us, Cave used to sell 10,000 of the Gentleman's Magazine; yet such was then his minute attention and anxiety that the sale should not suffer the smallest decrease, that he would name a particular person who he heard had talked of leaving off the Magazine, and would say, 'Let us have something good next month!'" — Mr. Cave's attention to the Magazine may indeed truly be termed unremitting; for, as Dr. Johnson once observed to me, "he scarcely ever looked out of the window, but with a view to its improvement."

In the latter part of Mr. Cave's life, having an extensive connexion in the line of his business; at Reading particularly, at Gloucester, and at Northampton, and several relations at Rugby; he was a frequent traveller; and, time being more an object to him than expence, and the luxury of turnpike-roads being then but little known, he generally used four horses. In one of these journeys, calling on an old school acquaintance, a man of great consequence, he directed the servant of the house to inform his master, "that Ned Cave the Cobler was come to visit him;" the name by which he was known to his quondam friends at Rugby-school, and of which in his more properous days he never was ashamed.

It is well remembered also that he was an ingenious mechanic; and, to the no small diminishing of his property, was continually

---

*Boswell's Life of Johnson, vol. II. p. 175.

devising plans for the improvement of mills, &c. &c.

That he was the publisher of some valuable books, may be seen by various advertisements in the early volumes of the Magazine.*

[Sir John Hawkins writes:] "Cave had no great relish for mirth, but he could bear it; and having been told by Johnson, that his friend had talents for the Theatre, and was come to London with a view to the profession of an Actor, expressed a wish to see him in some comic character. Garrick readily complied; and, as Cave himself told me, with a little preparation of the room over the great arch of St. John's Gate, and with the assistance of a few journeymen printers, who were called together for the purpose of reading the other parts, represented, with all the graces of comic humour, the principal character in Fielding's farce of the Mock Doctor.

"Cave's temper was phlegmatic: though he assumed, as the publisher of the Magazine, the name of *Sylvanus Urban*, he had few of those qualities that constitute the character of urbanity. Upon the first approach of a stranger, his practice was to continue sitting, a posture in which he was ever to be found, and, for a few minutes, to continue silent: if at any time he was inclined to begin the discourse, it was generally by putting a leaf of the Magazine then in the press into the hand of his visitor, and asking his opinion of it. I remember that, calling in on him once, he gave me to read the beautiful poem of Collins, written for Shakspeare's Cymbeline, 'To fair Fidele's grassy tomb,' which, though adapted to a particular circumstance in the play, Cave was for inserting in his Magazine, without any reference to the subject. I told him it would lose of its beauty if it were so published: this he could not see; nor could he be convinced of the propriety of the name *Fidele*: he thought *Pastora* a better, and so printed it.

"He was so incompetent a judge of Johnson's abilities, that, meaning at one time to dazzle him with the splendour of some of those luminaries in literature who favoured him with their correspondence, he told him that, if he would, in the evening, be at a certain alehouse in the neighbourhood of Clerkenwell, he might have a chance of seeing Mr. Browne and another or two of the persons mentioned in the preceding note: Johnson

---

*The best-known of the learned books printed by Cave are Du Halde's *History of China* (1736) and Dr. Newton's *Compleat Herbal* (1725) [Ed.]

accepted the invitation; and being introduced by Cave, dressed in a loose horse-man's coat, and such a great bushy uncombed wig as he constantly wore, to the sight of Mr. Browne, whom he found sitting at the upper end of a long table, in a cloud of tobacco-smoke, had his curiosity gratified.

"Johnson saw very clearly those offensive particulars that made a part of Cave's character; but, as he was one of the most quick-sighted men I ever knew in discovering the good and amiable qualities of others, a faculty which he has displayed, as well in the life of Cave, as in that of Savage, printed among his works, so was he ever inclined to palliate their defects; and, though he was above courting the patronage of a man whom, *for many reasons, he could not but hold cheap**, he disdained not to accept it, when tendered with any degree of complacency.

"Cave, who had no idea of the powers of eloquence over the human mind, became sensible of its effects in the profits it brought him. He had long thought that the success of his Magazine proceeded from those parts of it that were conducted by himself, which were, the abridgment of weekly papers written against the Ministry, such as the Craftsman, Fog's Journal, Common Sense, the Weekly Miscellany, the Westminster Journal, and others, and also marshaling the pastorals, the elegies, and the songs, the epigrams, and the rebuses, that were sent him by various correspondents; and was scarcely able to see the causes that at this time increased the sale of his pamphlet from ten to fifteen thousand copies a month. But, if he saw not, he felt them, and manifested his good fortune by buying an old coach and a pair of older horses; and, that he might avoid the suspicion of pride in setting up an equipage, he displayed to the world the source of his affluence, by a representation of St. John's gate, instead of his arms, on the door-pannel. This, he told me himself, was the reason of distinguishing his carriage from others, by what some might think a whimsical device, and also for causing it to be engraven on all his plate.

"It might seem that between men so different in their endowments and tempers as Johnson and Cave were, little of true friendship could subsist; but the contrary was the case: Cave, though a man of a saturnine disposition, had a sagacity which

---

*This phrase was, on my remonstrance, corrected in the second edition thus: "whom, in respect to mental endowments, he considered much inferior."

had long been exercised in the discrimination of men, in search-
ing into the recesses of their minds, and finding out what they
were fit for; and a liberality of sentiment and action, which,
under proper restrictions, inclined him not only to encourage
genius and merit, but to esteem and even to venerate the possessors of those qualities as often as he met with them : it cannot,
therefore, be supposed but that he entertained a high regard for
such a man as Johnson, and, having had a long experience of
his abilities and integrity, that he had improved this disposition
into friendship. Johnson, on his part, sought for other qualities
in those with whom he meant to form connexions; had he
determined to make only those his friends whose endowments
were equal to his own, his life would have been that of a
Carthusian; he was therefore more solicitous to contract friendships with men of probity and integrity, and endued with good
moral qualities, than with those whose intellectual powers, or
literary attainments, were the most conspicuous part of their
character; and of the former, Cave had a share, sufficient to
justify his choice. On this mutual regard for each other, as on a
solid basis, rested the friendship between Johnson and Cave. It
was therefore with a degree of sorrow proportioned to his feelings
towards his friends, which were ever tender, that Johnson
reflected on the loss he had to sustain, and became the narrator
of the most important incidents of his life.

ARTHUR COLLINS

ARTHUR COLLINS, the Historiographer of the "Baron-
age" and "Baronetage" of England, was born in 1682. He
was the son of William Collins, esq. gentleman-usher to Queen
Catharine in 1669, by his wife Elizabeth, daughter of Thomas
Blyth, daughter of John Horwood, esq. of Okely, in the county
of Southampton. Having received a liberal education, and being
from his youth much inclined to the cultivation of letters, particularly to the study of Antiquity, he conceived the arduous
design of digesting a compendious account of the Nobility of
these kingdoms, whose genealogies had till that time lain

mouldering in private cabinets. For the execution of this task he was certainly entitled to the gratitude of the Nobility, if we consider the great pains he took to investigate, and the perspicuous manner in which he has recorded, the illustrious deeds of their ancestors; tracing with a faithful and interesting pen the steps by which each family had risen to eminence. Neither was a work of this nature without a considerable claim upon his countrymen at large; inasmuch as a faithful picture of the rewards attendant on meritorious services and heroic actions, must necessarily prove the strongest incitement to the statesman, the soldier, and the citizen, to pursue the glorious career of virtue and honour. The merit of the before-mentioned works is unquestionable; and to the present day they have continued the great authorities to which all subsequent writers on the same subject have had recourse. But the fruits of them were not in proportion; nor did their author experience that liberal patronage to which the many midnight vigils he had passed in dry genealogical studies seemed to give him an indubitable claim. The other literary productions which bear his name are, the "Sydney State Papers;" some "Historical Collections of the noble Families of Cavendish, Holles, Vere, Harley, and Ogle;" and a "Life of Edward the Black Prince." Delighted with raking in the dust of the closet, with poring over MSS. scarcely legible, and rescuing half-devoured sentences from the combined attacks of Time and the moth, he lost many years which might have been employed much more profitably to himself. While unfolding the pedigrees of other families, he lost sight of the provision which was necessary for his own. Such were the laborious productions of Arthur Collins, and so inadequate his rewards! Whatever praise is due to biographical literature in general, certainly belongs to one who dipped even into the funereal urn to stamp his labours with authenticity; and such is the credit they have obtained, that, while there remains a spark of veneration for the ancestry and actions of our Peerage, the volumes which record them, and bear Collins's name, will be consulted as the faithful history of that splendid and necessary part (which has been so happily termed the Corinthian column) of the British Constitution. Mr Collins married about 1708; died in 1760; and was interred in the parish-church of Battersea, in Surrey. He had issue several children; of whom one son only survived him, viz. Arthur Tooker Collins, esq. who died Jan. 4, 1793 (a major-general in the service, and commandant of the Plymouth division of marines);

closing in London a life of honourable service, zeal, and integrity. David Collins, esq. who lately favoured the publick with an ample and interesting "Account of the English Settlement in New South Wales," is a son of Major-general Collins above mentioned. — I owe this note to my very accurate friend Mr. Stephen Jones.

Mr. Collins also wrote an Account of the Noble Family of Harley, inscribed to Edward Earl of Oxford, &c. London, printed 1741, 8vo, pp. 37, no printer's name. It appears to have been printed for the Earl (who died in that year) and his particular friends. — The following particulars of this able Genealogical Historian are extracted from his own unpublished Diary:

"*Jan.* 30, 1752. I breakfasted with their Graces the Duke and Duchess of Portland, with their two eldest daughters, Lady Elizabeth Cavendish Bentinck and Lady Henrietta Cavendish Bentinck, both very beautiful in their persons, of most agreeable sweet tempers, with a modest and affable behaviour. The discourse between us gave me an opportunity to say how I was descended, and the misfortunes that attended my family and myself; on which they seemed to pity me, but said nothing more. The Countess of Oxford had sent up pictures of her ancestors to be engraved by Mr. Vertue, one of the most eminent of his profession; but her Grace of Portland, thinking of the expence, determined to have only two engraved, that of Elizabeth Countess of Shrewsbury, who was the advancer of the noble Family of Cavendish, and of Horace Lord Vere of Tilbury, a person very famous, and from whom the Countess of Oxford was also descended. Her Grace desired me to call on Mr. Vertue, that he might have the pictures; which I did, and then returned to Highgate, where I employed myself in writing part of the Life of Denzil Lord Holles, and never stirred out of my house till February 5, that I came to London.

"About half an hour after 12 o'clock I took coach for St. James's, to attend the King's Levee, and to speak to some of the Lords to intercede for me; but principally in hopes of seeing the Duke of Newcastle, who had told me to wait on him soon after the meeting of the Parliament, which I had done at three several times; but his Grace was so taken up with business, as he said, he had not time to talk with me. I therefore wrote the following letter, with an intent to deliver it to him at St. James's before he went to the King:

'May it please your Grace,   *Feb.* 5, 1752.

'When I consider what your Grace has said to me, with what most of the Nobility have told me, and am yet kept in suspence, it fills me with amazement; but I have a heart and a spirit (with blood from my ancestors) not to be conquered by oppression, or I could not have wrote that which will make my name memorable to after-ages; celebrating the memory of eminent and extraordinary persons, and transmitting their virtues for the imitation of posterity, being one of the principal ends and duties of History.

'I am the son of Misfortune, my father having run through more than 30,000*l.* and, from my fruitless representations, am likely to die so; but I have left in manuscript an account of my family, my life, and the cruel usage I have very undeservedly undergone, with copies of the letters I have wrote on the occasion, of which are several to your Grace, whereby Posterity may know I have not been wanting either in industry, which the books I have published will justify, or in my application for preferment, which I so well deserve.

'If your Grace has any compassion for me, I humbly beg you will order notice to be left at Mr. Wither's, bookseller, in Fleet-street, when I may have the honour to wait on you, who am your Grace's most faithful and devoted servant, ARTHUR COLLINS.'

"Whilst I waited for his Grace's coming to St. James's, I spoke to the Duke of Portland, telling him I had three more sheets printed of the Life of the Earl of Clare that I had not delivered to him, but would bring them to his Grace the next morning; whereunto he said, it would be as well if I sent them, which I thought shewed a coldness, *and induced me not to send them till Friday morning.* I went in afterwards, with many that attended, to the King, who spoke first to the Duke of Portland, then to the Earl of Buckingham, the Duke of Grafton, and the Lord Delawarr, who stood together, and to Sir John Ligonier. The Marquis of Rockingham was the Lord of the Bed-chamber in waiting, and introduced two persons to kiss the King's hand. My modesty would not permit me to stand in the first rank; but I stood so as to be seen by the Lords, as also the King; but, having never had the honour of being introduced to his Majesty, was unknown to him.

"On departing out of the King's Bed-chamber, the Lord Viscount Gage spoke to me, asking whether I was on a new Edition of the Peerage. I told him, I had made collections towards it; but, there being so much to write, it was impossible, without some provision to enable me to keep a person to transcribe for me, to finish it in the manner I desired; and therefore, till that was done, I should think no further of it; and I told my Lord Delawarr the same, who said that I deserved to be provided for. I waited till half an hour after two, and the Duke of Newcastle not coming, and being told by the waiters it was then in vain to expect seeing of him, I left the Court, intending to dine with Mr. Perry (of Penshurst) in Berkeley-square, to whom I was always welcome; but, on my way there, being to pass Arundel-street, I resolved to call first on the Earl Granville, having ever had easy access to him. Being admitted to his Lordship, and making complaint how hard it was with me, telling him I had been at the King's Levee, and the answer I had given to my Lord Gage; he said, that he had often spoke for me, and would again; that he knew several Lords commiserated my condition; and that he hoped very soon to tell me of some provision being made for me, which he heartily wished. I must say, his Lordship was ever an encourager of Literature; and, on several occasions when I have been with him, has said to other Lords present at the same time, 'Here is Collins, who has served us, and we do nothing for him;' to which all the answer made was, 'that the Ministry ought to shew me more favour.' Taking leave of his Lordship, I went into Berkeley-square, and dined with Mr. Perry, his Lady, and Mr. Burnaby, who had been in foreign parts one of the King's Ministers; and, from the observation I made of him, he seemed to be a person of address and affable behaviour. Mr. Perry, before Mr. Burnaby came, asked my opinion of the way he intended to pursue in obtaining the Barony of Lisle, to which his Lady had pretence; and desired me to draw the case of the state of the Barony, which I promised to do. I took my leave of him about five o'clock; and in my return to my chambers in the Temple, I made it in my way to call at Newcastle House, in Lincoln's-inn-fields, where I delivered the letter before mentioned, went to my chambers, and staid there the whole evening, musing on what I should do the next morning, and looking over papers."

It is pleasing to add, that provision was at length made for this most able and indefatigable Writer; the King granting him a pension of 400l. *per annum*, which he enjoyed, however, but a few years.]

THOMAS DAVIES

A MAN of uncommon strength of mind, who prided himself on being through life a companion for his superiors, was born in or about the year 1712. In 1728 and 1729 he was at the University of Edinburgh, completing his education; and became, as Dr. Johnson used to say of him, "learned enough for a Clergyman."

Mr. Davies imbibed very early a taste for theatrical pursuits; and in 1736 his name occurs among the Dramatis Personæ of Lillo's celebrated tragedy of "Fatal Curiosity," at the Theatre in the Haymarket; where he was the original performer of young Wilmot; under the management of Henry Fielding.

In a short time he commenced Bookseller, in Duke's-court, opposite the church of St. Martin in the Fields; and afterwards in Round-court, near the Strand; but met with misfortunes in trade, which induced him to return to the stage; and on the 24th of January 1746, "Venice Preserved" was acted for his benefit at Covent-Garden Theatre; when, as the play-bill says, the part of Pierre was *attempted* by him. Not succeeding, probably, to his hopes on a London stage, he became an itinerant, and performed at York; where he married Miss Yarrow, daughter of an actor there, whose beauty was not more remarkable than her private character was ever unsullied and irreproachable. He also performed at Edinburgh (where he appears to have been the Manager of the Theatre) the characters of Romeo, Richard III. and Ranger.

He then went to Dublin; and, with his wife, performed several characters there.

In 1753 he came, with his wife, to Drury-lane Theatre; and, on Mr. Havard being taken ill, appeared first in the character of Stukely, in Moore's tragedy of "The Gamester." Here Mr. and Mrs. Davies remained several years, in good estimation with the Town, and played many characters, if not with excellence, at least with propriety and decency.

In his "Dramatic Miscellanies" he thus modestly speaks of his own performance on a particular occasion: "When sickness deprived the stage of this valuable man (Mr. Edward Berry), Mr. Garrick called the Writer of this Miscellany to represent the character of Gloster (in the tragedy of 'King Lear'); the candour of the audience gave him much more encouragement than he expected."

In the same entertaining Work he thus speaks of his wife : "Mrs. Davies, during Mrs. Cibber's illness, was invited to supply her place. She did not pretend to imitate that which was not to be attained by imitation, the action, voice, and manner of Mrs. Cibber. Mrs. Davies's figure, look, and deportment, were esteemed to be so correspondent with the idea of this amiable character (Cordelia in King Lear), that she was dismissed with no inconsiderable degree of approbation."

Churchill's indiscriminate satire, in the "Rosciad", endeavoured to fix some degree of ridicule on Mr. Davies's performance; but the pen of a Satirist is not entitled to implicit credit. It, however, had the ill effect, Dr. Johnson said, of driving this respectable performer from the stage.

In 1762, a few years before he finally quitted the Theatre, he resumed his former occupation of a Bookseller, in Russel-street, Covent Garden.

In 1772 he collected and republished, in three volumes, the beautiful Pastoral Poems, &c. of William Browne; who flourished in the reign of James I. and who was complimented with commendatory Verses by three of the best Pastoral Poets this nation has produced : Drayton, Jonson, and the unjustly contemned Wither.

He also re-published "The Poems of Sir John Davies; consisting of his Poem on the Immortality of the Soul; the Hymn of Astrea; and Orchestra, a Poem on Dancing.

In the same year he was the editor of "Miscellaneous and Fugitive Pieces [by the Author of The Rambler], 1773," in two volumes, 8vo; to which was afterwards added a third Volume. In these volumes, Dr. Johnson is the prominent feature; but we meet in them likewise with the names of Garrick, Colman, Cradock, Goldsmith, Francklin, Lloyd, and others. Dr. Johnson was for a short time displeased at the publication; and his behaviour on that occasion is thus described by Mrs. Piozzi : "When Davies printed the Fugitive Pieces without his (Dr. Johnson's) knowledge or consent, 'How,' said I, 'would Pope have raved, had he been served so!' 'We should never,' replied he, 'have heard the last on't, to be sure; but then Pope was a narrow man. I will, however,' added he, 'storm and bluster myself a little this time:' — so went up to London in all the wrath he could muster up. At his return, I asked how the affair ended. 'Why,' said he, 'I was a fierce fellow, and pretended to be very angry; and Thomas was a good-natured fellow, and pretended to be very sorry : so *there* the matter ended. I believe the dog loves me dearly. Mr. Thrale,' turning to my husband, 'What shall you and I do for Tom Davies? We will do something for him, to be sure.' "

In 1774 he published "The Works of Dr. John Eachard, late Master of Catharine Hall, Cambridge. [Dr. John Eachard, so well known from his witty detail of the causes of the *Contempt of the Clergy,* was the pleasantest controversial writer of the age in which he lived; and Mr. Davies preferred him to Swift, for the following reasons: "The celebrated Dean of St. Patrick's, says he, turns his pen too frequently into a scalping-knife, and makes his wit the executioner of his ill-nature. Not content to overcome his antagonist by the strength of his abilities and the force of his argument, Swift treats him as if he were not only the dullest, but the vilest of mankind. Eachard contents himself with hunting down the argument of his opponent, and rarely meddles with the man : he thinks it sufficient, if he can prove him a dull and affected, a foppish and pedantic, an ignorant and a foolish reasoner. He wishes not to render him hateful to the populace, or obnoxious to the government. He laughs in his antagonist's face at the very time he disarms him; then helps him to his sword again, and humorously rallies him for not knowing how to use it.]

In 1777, he was the Author of "The Characters of George the First, Queen Caroline, Sir Robert Walpole, Lord Hardwicke, Mr. Fox, and Mr. Pitt, reviewed. With Royal and Noble Anecdotes, and a Sketch of Lord Chesterfield's Characters.

In 1779 he published "Some Account of the Life and Writings of Massinger; prefixed to a new and improved Edition of his Works," in 4 volumes, 8vo.

A series of very curious Letters from Mr. Davies was inserted, by Mr. Malcolm, in "Letters between the Rev. James Granger, M. A. Rector of Shiplake, and many of the most eminent Men of his Time, 1805;" many of them highly characteristic both of Mr. Granger and Mr. Davies.

Not meeting with that success which his attention and abilities merited, Mr. Davies, in 1778, was under the disagreeable necessity of submitting to become a bankrupt; when, such was the regard entertained for him by his friends, that they readily consented to his re-establishment; and none, as he said himself, were more active to serve him, than those who had suffered most by his misfortunes. But all their efforts might possibly have been fruitless, if his great and good friend Dr. Johnson had not exerted all his interest in his behalf. He called upon all over whom he had any influence to assist Tom Davies; and prevailed on Mr. Sheridan, patentee of Drury-lane Theatre, to let him have a benefit; which he granted on the most liberal terms. This event took place May 27, 1778; when Mr. Davies made his last appearance on the stage, in the character of Fainall, in Congreve's comedy of "The Way of the World," and acquitted himself to the satisfaction of his friends and the publick.

In 1780, by a well-timed publication, "The Life of Mr. Garrick," in two volumes, which passed through four editions, he not only acquired considerable fame, but realized money.

He also published, "Dramatic Miscellanies, consisting of Critical Observations on several Plays of Shakspeare; with a Review of his principal Characters, and those of various eminent Writers, as represented by Mr. Garrick, and other celebrated Comedians. With Anecdotes of Dramatic Poets, Actors, &c. 1785." 3 vols. 8vo. A second edition appeared a few days only before his death.

Mr. Davies was also the writer of essays without number, in prose and verse, in the St. James's Chronicle, and some other of the public newspapers.

The Compiler of the present Volumes knew Mr. Davies well; and for several years passed many convivial hours in his company at a social meeting; where his lively sallies of pleasantry were certain to entertain his friends by harmless merriment. [In this Society Mr. Davies originally started the idea of writing the Life of Mr. Garrick; and, encouraged by their approbation, he frequently produced, at their dinners, a small portion of his intended work, which he would read to them with much complacency, and not a little to their general information.

This pleasant Association originated in occasional evening meetings of a few Booksellers, at the Devil Tavern, Temple Bar. That house, however, having been converted into private dwellings, a regular club was held, once a week, at the Grecian Coffee-house; where I recollect with no small satisfaction many happy hours that passed in rational and improving conversation.

After a trial of three or four years, the evening club was changed to a monthly dinner at *The Shakspeare;* and truly proud was *honest Campbell,* in producing his prime bottles to a Literary Society, whom he justly considered as conferring celebrity on his house, and to whom he constantly devoted the

Apollo Room.] The last time, however, that Davies visited his friends he wore the appearance of a spectre; and, sensible of his approching end, took a solemn valediction.

He died May 5, 1785, aged about 73; for, in the Postscript to the second edition of his "Dramatic Miscellanies," published 1785, he mentions a circumstance which occurred, he says, when he was in his 73rd year. He was buried, by his own desire, in the vault of St. Paul Covent Garden; and the following lines were written on the occasion :
"Here lies the Author, Actor, Thomas Davies;
Living, he shone a very *rara avis*.
The scenes he play'd Life's audience must commend,
He honour'd Garrick — Johnson was his friend."

JOHN-THEOPHILUS DESAGULIERS

JOHN-THEOPHILUS DESAGULIERS was born March 12, 1683. In 1716 he published a piece intituled "Fires improved; being a new Method of building Chimneys, so as to prevent their smoking." This was a translation from the French, and involved him in some dispute with Edmund Curll, whom he had employed as his publisher, and admitted to have a share in the book. Curll, in order to promote the sale, had puffed it off in a very gross manner; which induced Mr. Desaguliers to publish a Letter in a periodical paper called "The Town-Talk," then publishing by Sir Richard Steele, in which he informed the Publick, that, whenever his name hereafter "was or should be printed with that egregious flatterer Mr. Curll's, either in an advertisement or at the title-page of a book, except that of 'Fires improved,' he entirely disowned it." His merit had now attracted the notice of the Duke of Chandos, who made him his Chaplain, and presented him, about 1714, to the Living of Stanmore Parva, or Whitchurch (not *Edgware,* as stated in p. 81). In 1717 he went through a Course of his Lectures on Experimental Philosophy before King George I. at Hampton Court; with which his Majesty was so well pleased that he intended to have conferred upon him the valuable Rectory of

Much Munden in Hertfordshire; but that benefice was obtained for another person by the Earl of Sunderland, who prevailed with a friend to present him with a Living in Norfolk, the revenue of which, however, amounted only to 70*l*. a year. March 16, 1718, he accumulated the degrees of B. A. and LL. D. at Oxford. He had the honour of reading his Lectures before King George the Second, as well as the rest of the Royal Family; and exchanged the Living which he had in Norfolk for the Rectory of Little Warley in Essex, to which he was presented in 1727 by Sir John Tyrell, bart. He was likewise made Chaplain to Frederick Prince of Wales; and in 1738 was appointed Chaplain to Bowles's Regiment of Dragoons. When Channel-row, in which he had lived for some years, was ordered to be taken down to make way for the New Bridge at Westminster, Dr. Desaguliers removed to lodgings over the Great Piazza in Covent-garden, where he carried on his Lectures till his death. He is said to have been repeatedly consulted by Parliament upon the design of building that bridge; in the execution of which, Mr. Charles Labelye, who had been many years his assistant, was appointed a Supervisor. He likewise erected a Ventilator, at the desire of Parliament, in a room over the House of Commons. Dr. Desaguliers, who is styled by Dr. Priestley "an indefatigable Experimental Philosopher," died Feb. 29, 1743-4, at the Bedford Coffee-house, Covent-garden, where he had lodgings; and was buried March 6, in the Savoy. He translated into English, from the Latin, Gravesande's "Mathematical Elements of Natural Philosophy." This work was published by his son, John-Theophilus Desaguliers, in two vols. 4to. In Dr. Desagulier's character as a Divine we find only one publication by him, a single Sermon, in octavo, preached before the King in 1717, from Luke xiii. 5, "I tell you nay; but except you repent, you shall all likewise perish." It was a Thanksgiving Sermon; but on what particular occasion it was delivered we are not informed. — The following anecdote is recorded of his respect for the clerical character. Being invited to an illustrious company, one of whom, an officer, addicted to swearing in his discourse, at the period of every oath asked Dr. Desaguliers's pardon : the Doctor bore this levity for some time with great patience, but at length silenced the swearer with the following rebuke : "Sir, you have taken some pains to render me ridiculous, if possible, by your pointed apologies; now, Sir, I am to tell you, that if God Almighty does not hear you, I assure you I will never tell Him."

If credit is to be given to Mr. Cawthorn, Dr. Desaguliers was
in very necessitous circumstances at the time of his decease. In
the Poem intituled "The Vanity of Human Enjoyments," Mr.
Cawthorn laments his fate in these lines:
> "How poor, neglected Desaguliers fell!
> How he, who taught two gracious Kings to view
> All Boyle ennobled, and all Bacon knew,
> Died in a cell, without a friend to save,
> Without a guinea, and without a grave!"]

JAMES DODSLEY

M R. JAMES DODSLEY was the brother, the partner, and
successor in business, of the late ingenious Mr. Robert
Dodsley. James Dodsley was very early in life invited by his
brother Robert (who was 22 years older than himself) to assist
him in business. Their father kept the free-school at Mansfield,
Nottinghamshire; and, being very much respected, had also
many other scholars of neighbouring farmers and gentlemen.
He was a little deformed man; married a young woman of 17,
at the age of 75, and had a child by this union at 78. Besides
Robert and James, he had many other children. One son (named
Avery) lived with the late Sir George Savile, bart. and died in
his service. Another, Isaac, lived as gardener with Mr. Allen, at
Prior-park, and afterwards with Lord Weymouth, at Long Leate.
Isaac was 52 years in these families, and may justly be named
the father of the beautiful plantations at Prior-park and at Long
Leate. He retired from the latter situation at 78, and died in
his 81st year. — Mr. James Dodsley became an active and useful
partner to his brother; in conjunction with whom he published
many works of the first celebrity; "A Collection of Poems,"
"The Preceptor," "The Annual Register," &c. &c.

Robert quitted business in 1759; but James persevered in
acquiring wealth by the most honourable literary connexions. In
1782 he suggested to the Rockingham Administration the plan
of the tax on receipts; which, though troublesome to the trader,
has been productive of considerable revenue to the state. A few

years after (1788) he was nominated as a proper person to be
sheriff of London and Middlesex; in excuse for which, he
cheerfully paid the customary fine. It is worthy noticing, as a
literary anecdote, that he sold no less than 18,000 copies of
Mr. Burke's famous "Reflections on the French Revolution;"
with considerable advantage both to himself and to the Author,
to whom he made a very handsome compliment for the profits.
— His property (which was estimated to be about 70,000*l*.) he
gave principally to nephews and nieces, and their descendants;
to some of them 8000*l*. 3 per cents each, and to others 4 or 5000*l*.
each, in specific sums, or in higher funds: to each of his executors 1000*l*. These were, Mr. Thomas Tawney, of Brooke's-place,
Lambeth, who married a daughter of his brother Isaac; Mr.
John Walter, of Charing Cross (with whom he had been in habits
of friendship, Mr. Walter having served his apprenticeship with
his brother Robert); and Mr. George Nicol, his Majesty's bookseller, in Pall Mall. To his attorney, Mr. Webster, 1000*l*.; to Mr.
John Freeborn, who had been for several years his assistant in
business, 4000*l*.; to his maid-servant 500*l*.; to his coachman 500*l*.
and also his carriage and horses; to the poor of St. James's,
Westminster, 200*l*. 3 per cents; and to the Company of
Stationers, nearly 400*l*. — By a habit of secluding himself from
the world, Mr. James Dodsley (who certainly possessed a liberal
heart and a strong understanding) had acquired many peculiarities. He at one time announced an intention of quitting trade;
but, in less than a fortnight, repenting the resolution, again
advertised that he should continue in business, and re-solicited
the favour of his friends. For some years past, however, he kept
no public shop, but continued to be a large wholesale dealer in
books, of his own copy-right. Of these a part, to the amount of
several thousand pounds, was burnt by an accidental fire in a
warehouse which he had not prevailed on himself to insure; but
the loss of which he was philosopher enough to bear without the
least apparent emotion; and, in the presence of the writer of this
article, who dined with him before the fire was well extinguished,
sold, to a gentleman in company, the chance of the fragments of
waste-paper that might be saved, for a single hundred pounds.
This agreement was not fulfilled, but the whole remainder was
afterwards sold for 80 guineas. He kept a carriage many years;
but studiously wished that his friends should not know it; nor did
he ever use it on the Eastern side of Temple Bar. He purchased
some years since an estate, with a small house on it, between

Chislehurst and Bromley; on the house he expended an incredible sum, more than would have re-built one of twice the size, which afterwards he rarely visited, and at length let, with the estate, on a long lease, at a very low rent. — Though he often expressed his apprehension that the Law (if he should die intestate) would not dispose of his property as he could wish, he never could persuade himself to make a will till he was turned of 70; after which time he made four; the last of them Jan. 4, 1797, not long before his decease. He left every legacy clear of the tax, and appointed six residuary-legatees. — He was buried in St. James's church, Westminster; and in the chancel an open book of marble is inscribed,

"Sacred to the memory of JAMES DODSLEY,
many years an eminent bookseller in Pall Mall.
He died Feb. 19, 1797, aged 74.
His body lies buried in this church.
He was a man of a retired and contemplative turn of mind,
though engaged in a very extensive line of public business.
He was upright and liberal in all his dealings;
a friend to the afflicted in general,
and to the poor of this parish in particular."]

DR. ANDREW DUCAREL

ANDREW COLTEE DUCAREL was born in 1713, in Normandy; whence his father, who was descended from an antient family at Caen in that province, came to England, soon after the birth of his second son James, and resided at Greenwich. In 1729, being at that time an Eton scholar, he was three months under the care of Sir Hans Sloane, on account of an accident which deprived him of the sight of one eye.

In 1731 he was admitted a gentleman commoner of St. John's college, Oxford; June 1, 1738, proceeded LL. D.; Oct. 21, 1748, went out a grand compounder; became a member of the College of Doctors Commons in November 1743; and married, in 1749, Susanna, who survived him.

Though disappointed in his wishes of entering into holy

orders, he became intimately connected with the Church. He was elected commissary or official of the peculiar and exempt jurisdiction of the collegiate church or free chapel of St. Katharine, near the Tower of London, 1755; was appointed commissary and official of the city and diocese of Canterbury, by Archbishop Herring, in December, 1758; and of the sub-deanries of South Malling, Pagham, and Tarring, in Sussex, by Archbishop Secker, on the death of Dr. Dennis Clarke, in 1776.

He was elected F. A. S. Sept. 22, 1737; and was one of the first fellows of the Society nominated by the President and Council on its incorporation 1755. He was also elected, Aug. 29, 1760, member of the Society of Antiquaries at Cortona, on which occasion he sent them a Latin letter drawn up by his friend Mr. Morant. He was admitted F. R. S. Feb. 18, 1762; became an honorary fellow of the Society of Antiquaries of Cassel, by diploma, dated in November 1778; and of that of Edinburgh in 1781.

In 1755 he solicited the place of sub-librarian at the Museum, in the room of Mr. Empson; but it was pre-engaged.

The Doctor's first publication, though without his name, was "A Tour through Normandy, described in a Letter to a Friend, 1754," 4to. This tour through part of his native country was undertaken, in company with Dr. Bever, in the summer of 1752; and his account of it, considerably enlarged, was re-published under the title of "Anglo-Norman Antiquities considered, in a Tour through Part of Normandy, by Doctor Ducarel, illustrated with 27 Copper-plates, 1767," folio, inscribed to Bishop Lyttel-ton, president of the Society of Antiquaries. His Lordship had first remarked, 1742, the difference between the mode of archi-tecture used by the Normans in their buildings and that practised by the contemporary Saxons in England; and the Doctor's observations, actually made on the spot ten years afterward, confirmed the rules then laid down. This antient dependence of the English crown, with the many memorials in it by the English, was a favourite object of his contemplation. Its coinage was his next research; and he published "A Series of above 200 Anglo-Gallic, or Norman and Aquitaine Coins of the antient Kings of England, exhibited in 16 Copper-plates, and illustrated in 12 letters, addressed to the Society of Antiquaries of London, and several of its members; to which is added, a Map of the antient Dominions of the Kings of England in France, with some adjacent Countries, 1757," 4to. His portrait, engraved by Perry, from a painting by A. Soldi, 1746, was first prefixed to this work; which was the result of his acquaintance with M. de Boze, keeper of the French King's medals, and secretary of the Academy of Inscriptions and Belles Lettres; who published so many learned dissertations on antient coins and medals in their Memoirs, and a separate treatise on the coins of the prelates and barons of France, of which only two copies came to England, as presents from their author; one to Dr. Mead, purchased at his sale by Dr. Gifford; the other to Dr. Ducarel, at whose sale it was purchased by Mr. Gough.

Of the 527 coins in the 45 plates of this work the Doctor copied several into his own. He had besides a copy of that scarce book, "Figures des Monnoyes de France, 1619," 4to, by John Baptist Haultin, containing upwards of 500 French and other coins, in 126 wooden cuts. But the Doctor's copy had the addition of many MS notes, taken from a copy in the French King's library, containing the metals, weight, and dates of most of them. This is now in the British Museum.

In this undertaking the Doctor found himself seconded by Sir Charles Frederick, who engraved all the Aquitaine coins in his possession, in 36 quarto plates, but without any description or letter-press, and intended only for private use, being little known before their circulation on his decease, and that of his two numismatic friends before mentioned. "Sir Charles had desired Mr. North would take his papers concerning Aquitaine coins, and digest and fit them for the press. Mr. North waited on him, and they talked over the affair. He earnestly pressed it; but was desirous Mr. North's own piece on Henry the Third's Coins should first be published. Upon this Mr. North set about to finish it, till the unfortunate affair of Wormley happened (in which Mr. F. shewed himself his warm friend), which gave near two years delay to this work; during which time, a brother of the Society, who shall be nameless, came and told Mr. North, that Mr. F. had determined Mr. Folkes should have the management of them, and had put them into his hands for that purpose. This report quite damped his pleasing expectations; but he was in hopes that, through the Doctor's interposition, he might have that agreeable employ. Here the matter seems to have rested.

Dr. Ducarel had some view to forming a series of English medals, which, by admitting such as have been struck abroad relative to the history of this kingdom, he thought could be carried beyond the Conquest, provided the medals proved genuine. But when he engaged Francis Perry to engrave a series, of which the late Mr. Hollis gave the outline, he began no earlier than Henry VIII. and closed it with James I. in ten plates. Three supplemental ones were afterwards published of the same period. Mr. Hollis intended it should be more extensive, by taking in the Roman medals; he, however, assisted Perry in his own way. It was taken up by Mr. Snelling, who did not publish it in Mr. Hollis's life-time. — Mr. Snelling's being a posthumous publication, there is no letter-press to accompany his 33 plates, which reach from the Conquest to 1742. It will be easily seen that the medals of the first five kings are by Dassier.

Another work which the Doctor patronized was the "Series of antient Windows," engraved by Francis Perry, from the rude sketches of Aubrey, in his MS collections, from a transcript made by Mr. Ames of an abstract of Aubrey's four volumes of Collections, taken by Mr. Hutchins for his private use, from the larger work in the hands of Mr. Awnsham Churchill, of Hembury.

In 1760 he printed, for private use, in 4to, an account of his friend Browne Willis, read at the Society of Antiquaries that year. Of this Mr. Loveday, in a Letter to him, remarks, "It is really to be wished that every eminent member of the Antiquarian Society were on his decease as well accounted for." This and some few more may serve in lieu of the flattering eloges drawn up for the deceased members of the Academy of Sciences and Belles Lettres, printed at the expence of the respective bodies. A thick quarto volume of Dr. Willis's letters to Dr. Ducarel was in the hands of Mr. Gough; and is now in my possession.

A question being started by the Hon. Daines Barrington, concerning trees indigenous to Great Britain, in Phil. Trans. LIX. p. 5, and the chesnut, elm, lime and sycamore, box, abele, and yew, accounted non-indigenous; the Doctor undertook the defence of the first of these trees, and to prove it a native here; in which he was supported by his antiquarian friends Thorpe and Hasted, who, as Kentish men, seem to have thought themselves more particularly interested in the dispute. His and their letters on the subject were printed in Phil. Trans. LXI. art. 17, 18, 19; and Mr. Barrington, in the next article, gave up the controversy. If this defence was softened in the printing below what it was in its original state, we must extenuate the champion's severity by the goodness of his cause. He received great congratulations on his victory.

The Doctor's account of the early cultivation of botany in England, and more particularly of John Tradescant, a great promoter of that science, and of his monument and garden at Lambeth, appeared originally in Phil. Trans. vol. LXIII. p. 79; whence it was copied, in the "History of Lambeth Parish," with several improvements, communicated by the Doctor to Mr. Nichols.

Dr. Ducarel's Letter to Gerard Meerman, grand pensioner at the Hague, on the dispute concerning Corsellis, as the first printer in England, read at the Society of Antiquaries, 1760, and translated into Latin by Dr. Musgrave, with Mr. Meerman's answer, were published in the second volume of Meerman's "Origines Typographicæ, 1765;" and, with a second letter from Mr. Meerman, were given to the publick by Mr. Nichols, in a Supplement to his learned partner Mr. Bowyer's "Two Essays on the Origin of Painting, 1776."

When the new edition of Bishop Gibson's Codex was passing through the Clarendon press, in 1761, the Doctor collated the MS collections of Precedents annexed to it with the originals at Lambeth and elsewhere; in return for which, at his own desire, the delegates of the press presented him with two copies of the new edition handsomely bound.

From the time of Dr. Ducarel's appointment to be keeper of the Library at Lambeth, his pursuits took a different turn — to the ecclesiastical antiquities of this kingdom, and more particularly to those of the province of Canterbury, for which he was so well supplied with materials from that ample library.

In 1761 the Doctor circulated printed proposals for publishing a general repertory of the endowments of vicarages, for the service both of vicars and their parishioners, as nothing conduces so much to ascertain their mutual rights as antient original endowments. These are to be found in the registries of the bishop or dean and chapter of the diocese, or in the chartularies and register books of religious houses. Many of the former are lost, and the latter dispersed into various hands. He had proceeded so far as to set down, in alphabetical order, the name and date of every endowment in the registers of the see of Canterbury; and all such as he could discover in the public libraries, or in printed books. He therefore next solicited the like communications from other diocesans, or from possessors of antient records;

and subjoined a specimen of his method, and a list of the
endowments already discovered.

The Proposal for publishing the General Repertory of Endowments of Vicarages, originally circulated, with a specimen
annexed, in a single sheet, 4to, dated Dec. 3, 1761, was prefixed
(with a new date, Dec. 23, 1762) to "A Repertory of the
Endowments of Vicarages in the Diocese of Canterbury, 1763,"
4to, printed for the benefit of the charity-school at Canterbury;
of which I possess the Doctor's copy, with considerable additions
in MS. by him, which were all incorporated into a second
edition, in 8vo, 1782; to which were added, Endowments of
Vicarages in the Diocese of Rochester.

In a letter to Mr. Cole of Milton, 1757, he says, "I hope,
within this year, to have about twelve Dioceses ready for the
press; in another, to the Rev. Dr. Cox Macro, 1763, he tells
him he had eleven other Dioceses then ready; and in 1768 he
appears to have entertained thoughts of going to press with these
Collections.

He had a copy of the "Notitia Parochialis," formerly belonging to the Earl of Oxford, which he bought at T. Osborne's, and
presented to Lambeth Library; a particular and very interesting
account of the value of a very great number of small livings and
others in England, mostly signed by the rectors and vicars, 1705;
as an answer to some printed queries tacked, by order of Mr.
Harley, afterwards lord treasurer Oxford, at the bottom of a
brief sent that year for the repairs of the church of All Saints
in Oxford; six oblong volumes, and a seventh volume of index
to the rest. They contain a collection of private papers, and can
only be considered as designed for useful and certain information
(and not as legal evidence) of the state of small parishes at that
time, and many of them signed by the then incumbents.

In 1762 he was one of the Committee of the Society of Antiquaries for extracting papers from the minutes for press.

He drew up, 1763, an account of the MSS. in the Norfolk
Library belonging to the Royal Society, amounting to 563,
including 45 then first catalogued. On this occasion he was of a
committee with Lord Charles Cavendish and Dr. Birch.

In 1763 he was appointed by the Lords Commissioners of the
Treasury, at the head of whom Mr. Grenville then was, in conjunction with Sir Joseph Ayloffe, bart. and Mr. Astle, to digest
and methodize the records of the State Paper office at Whitehall,

and afterwards those in the Augmentation office. A calendar of
the records of the latter, in 2 volumes, folio, was purchased at
his sale by Mr. Cook, for the Bodleian Library.

In 1766, he communicated to the Society of Antiquaries a
paper on bezants; which Bishop Lyttelton, in a letter to him,
styled "curious and elaborate."

The share he took in the Rowleian discovery and controversy,
1771 and 1772, may be seen in the Gentleman's Magazine, vol.
LVI. pp. 361, 362. 461 — 464. 544 — 547. 580. 859.

In 1776 was printed, for private use, "A List of various
editions of the Bible, and Parts thereof, in English, from the year
1526 to 1776," in a single sheet, 8vo; and an improved edition,
1778, at the expence of the Archbishop of Canterbury. This
little tract owed its rise to a list of English Bibles copied from one
compiled by Mr. Ames, from 1526 to 1757, presented by Dr.
Gifford to the Lambeth Library. It was completed by Dr.
Ducarel, from his own observations, and the later discoveries of
his learned friends Dr. Percy bishop of Dromore and Mr. Tutet.
Mr. Nichols also, and Mr. Herbert, contributed not a few
articles from their own collections.

The account of Dr. Stukeley and his writings, prefixed to the
second volume of his Itinerary, published 1776, was drawn up
by Dr. Ducarel, who also prepared an epitaph for him.

The Doctor gave a MS abstract of the large history of the
Benedictine Abbey of Bec in Normandy, drawn up by Dom John
Bourget, monk of that house, and F. A. S. of London, to Mr.
Nichols; who printed it in 1779, 8vo, with an Appendix of
original deeds; and who likewise printed, in the same year, in 2
volumes, 8vo, "Some Account of the Alien Priories, and of such
Lands as they are known to have possessed in England and
Wales," collected by John Warburton, esq. Somerset herald, and
Dr. Ducarel; who did not, however, permit his name to be
mentioned; and considerably augmented by Mr. Gough and
some other learned friends of the publisher; to which was prefixed, a general description of the Seven Norman Cathedrals,
with very fine prints of them. Of this work a good analysis, with
a description of the plates, and some valuable notes, was given
by a learned correspondent of Mr. Urban in the Gentleman's
Magazine, vol. LVI. p. 747.

The Collection of Royal and Noble Wills, from the Conqueror
to Henry VII. printed by Mr. Nichols, 1780, was given to the
world in consequence of the suggestions of Dr. Ducarel; from

whose stores the far greater part of the materials was purchased at a pretty large price.

Of all the honours Dr. Ducarel enjoyed none gave him greater satisfaction than the commissariate of St. Katharine's*, a place to which he has done due honour in "The History of the Royal Hospital and Collegiate Church of St. Katharine, near the Tower of London, from its Foundation, in the Year 1273, to the present Time, 1782," 4to, adorned with seventeen plates. This history was originally compiled by the Doctor for the use of our present very amiable Queen, to whom a copy of it was presented in MS. a short time after her accession to the patronage of this collegiate church, the only ecclesiastical preferment in the gift of the Queen Consort of England. On a thorough repair of this curious old church, in 1778, an empty vault was discovered in the chancel, of a size that would hold two coffins and no more. This spot the Doctor claimed in virtue of his office, and has often pointed out to the writer of this article, and to many others of his friends, as a resting-place for his ashes and those of his lady. His own remains were accordingly there deposited.

Two additional plates to the History of St. Katharine's, representing the curious grotesque carvings under the old stalls there, were engraved a little before his death, at his own request, and given to the publick soon after, as a short Appendix to that History.

Of Croydon and Lambeth Palaces (the last remaining monuments of episcopal grandeur in or near the Metropolis) he has given particular Histories. That of Croydon appeared in 1783; and Lambeth in 1785, dedicated, by permission, to Archbishop Moore.

"Some Account of the Parish of Lambeth," published by the Editor of these Anecdotes in 1786, 4to, may be considered as no unsuitable Companion to the History of the Palace; and a valuable Appendix was published, by Mr. Denne, in 1795. Some Additions also to the History of Croydon were published in 1787.

Dr. Ducarel's memoirs of Archbishop Hutton and his family,

---

*St. Katharine's at the Tower, a royal hospital, or free chapel, founded by Queen Matilda in 1148, and refounded and enlarged by Philippa, queen of Edward III, was demolished at the end of 1825 for the building of St. Katharine's Dock, opened in 1828. [*Ed.*]

fairly written, were purchased at his sale, by the Rev. Dr. Lort, for the Hutton family.

His appointment to the place of librarian at Lambeth (to which a salary of 30*l*. per annum is annexed) took place under Archbishop Hutton, May 3, 1757; and the catalogues of that valuable collection are not a little benefited by his diligence and abilities. The Catalogue begun by Bishop Gibson, while librarian here, and continued by Dr. Wilkins with the greatest minuteness, was perfected by him to the time of Archbishop Cornwallis; a distinct catalogue made of the books of Archbishop Secker, who expended above 300*l*. in arranging and improving the MS library and printed books here; and another, in three volumes folio, of the pamphlets and tracts bound up by the direction of Archbishop Cornwallis. And in the library of MSS. the Catalogue begun by Dr. Wilkins, 720, and continued by succeeding librarians to No. 888, he extended to No. 1147, in 2 vols. Dr. Birch, who was an excellent judge of such merit, expresses his obligations to "the learned librarian, A. C. Ducarel; to whose knowledge, industry, and love of history and antiquity, the valuable library of MSS. of the archiepiscopal see of Canterbury is highly indebted for the order in which it is now arranged, and by whose obliging and communicative temper it is rendered generally useful." In this library are 13 large volumes of 1506 antient Charters, all originals, with many fine seals.

In 1757, he addressed to Archbishop Secker a letter concerning the first edition of Archbishop Parker's valuable book "De Antiquitate Britannicæ Ecclesiæ,"* now in the MS library at Lambeth, No. 959, giving an account of a great many Chartæ Antiquæ, MS notes, &c. &c. contained therein. This letter is printed at large in the Appendix to his History of Lambeth Palace.

He was engaged also in arranging and indexing above 30 volumes, folio, of leases, papers, &c.; and he could have greatly eased the Archbishop in dispatching and answering an infinite number of letters, and have been truly useful. Such was the Doctor's assiduity in whatever he undertook, that, besides the fair copy of the index by him taken of all the Lambeth registers, and the general index which he made to them, he reserved for

---

*This book is said to have been printed by John Day at a private press in Lambeth Palace, and to have been the first privately printed book issued in England. [*Ed.*]

himself another, which at his sale became the property of Mr. Gough. It contains, in 48 volumes, neatly bound, an account of every instrument relative to the see, province, and diocese of Canterbury, in the registers of all the Archbishops of Canterbury, from Pecham to Herring; and, together with a great variety of other materials amassed by the Doctor, may be justly styled a fund of ecclesiastical antiquities, for that province in particular, and for the kingdom at large. In this laborious undertaking he was materially assisted by the industry of his friend Mr. Rowe Mores; by Mr. Hall, his predecessor in the office of librarian, and by Mr. Pouncey, the very excellent Engraver, who for many years was his assistant as clerk and deputy-librarian, the latter of which posts he held under Dr. Ducarel's successor Dr. Lort.

On the death of Archbishop Secker the Doctor would have gladly held the office of secretary to his successor, "the income of which, after paying one-third to a deputy, would have made him ample amends for all the pains, trouble, and expence, he had been at many years in digesting the registers, in 68 volumes, folio."

The Doctor had an intention of publishing his Abstract of Archbishop Pecham's Register; and the rough draught of a Latin Title, with a Preface or Dedication to Archbishop Herring, 1755, together with a copy of the Abstract, and various notes by Mr. Mores, were afterwards in Mr. Gough's hands, by purchase at Mr. Mores' sale. Extracts from Pecham's register by Dr. Ducarel were bought at his sale by Dr. Lort.

"A volume of Miscellaneous Papers in Lambeth Library, digested by Dr. Ducarel," is among the bequests of Mr. Gough to the Bodleian Library.

The Doctor's great researches into antiquities occasioned his assistance to be courted on many publications, particularly that of Dr. Burton's "Monasticon Eboracense," which one cannot help regretting should be left incomplete, after the unwearied pains and application bestowed on it, so that he has been justly styled "one of our first men in monastic antiquities, and his first volume infinitely surpassing Sir William Dugdale's."

He also entered the lists for arranging Mr. Bridges's North-amptonshire papers with the Rev. Peter Whalley, of Courten hall, an excellent scholar, who was desired to produce some specimen of his talents in the way of Antiquity, at the county meeting, 1755; and with the Rev. Mr. Buckler, of All Souls college, a gentleman of abilities, and general erudition. A catalogue of the MSS. was sent him; but the general sense of the committee was in favour of Mr. Buckler: but at the meeting, on the ballot, Mr. Whalley had five voices, Mr. Buckler four, and Dr. Ducarel three, out of the thirteen who attended.

He had drawn up also an account of Doctors Commons, and, as an Appendix to it, complete lists of the different Chancellors of the several dioceses of this kingdom, as high as the registers go, in folio, which were so nearly ready for publication, that he repeatedly promised them with that express intention to Mr. Nichols; who, at the Doctor's request, caused complete indexes to be made to both; and, it is to be hoped, some learned Civilian will yet perfect and give them to the world. The materials for both these were among his collections in Mr. Gough's hands. Another work, which he intended for Mr. Nichols's press, and for which an index was in like manner made, was, "Testamenta Lambethana; being a complete List of all the Wills and Testaments recorded in the Archiespiscopal Register at Lambeth, from A. D. 1312 to A. D. 1636, extracted by Dr. Ducarel, F. R. and A. SS. Lambeth Librarian, &c. with a complete Index, A. D. 1759."

Among the other MSS. purchased by Mr. Gough were Dr. Ducarel's "Notes taken during his Tour in Holland, 1775."

For many years it was his custom to travel *incognito* in August with his friend Samuel Gale, esq. attended only by Dr. Ducarel's coachman and Mr. Gale's footman George Monk. Twenty miles was their usual stage on the first day, and every other day about fifteen. It was a rule, not to go out of their road to see any of their acquaintance. The coachman was directed to say, "it was *a job*; and that he did not know their names, but that they were civil gentlemen;" and the footman, "that he was a friend of the coachman's, who *gave him a cast*." They usually took up their quarters at an inn; and penetrated into the country for three or four miles round. After dinner, Mr. Gale smoked his pipe; whilst Dr. Ducarel took notes, which he regularly transcribed, and which after his death were purchased by Mr. Gough. They constantly took with them Camden's Britannia, and a set of maps. In Vertue's plate of London-bridge chapel, the figure measuring is Dr. Ducarel, that standing is Mr. Samuel Gale*.

*Views of the Chapel of Old London Bridge. Drawn, engraved, and published by G. Vertue. 1748. The Chapel of St. Thomas was built between 1384 and 1396 and was demolished 1831-32. [Ed.]

Dr. Ducarel closed a life of unremitted industry and application in antiquarian pursuits at his house at South Lambeth, May 29, 1785, soon after his return from a journey into Kent, where he had held a visitation for himself, and three different ones for his friend Archdeacon Backhouse. He was a stout, athletic man, and had a strong prepossession that he should live to a great age. He frequently told me (when partaking with him the social glass of wine he was fond of boasting to his particular friends) that "he had the stamina of a long life; and that, if he escaped any violent accident, or a stroke of the palsy, *he should take a peep into the next century.*" The immediate cause of the disorder which carried him off, was a sudden surprize on receiving, whilst at Canterbury, a letter informing him that Mrs. Ducarel was at the point of death. He hastened home, took to his bed, and died in three days. His lady survived him more than six years. He had appointed his old and intimate friends Mr. Fountaine and Mr. Tutet executors to his will; but, from some informality in the wording of it, both these gentlemen thought it prudent to decline the trust, which of course devolved upon his nephew, Gerard Gustavus Ducarel, esq. whom he had made his heir.

The Doctor had the happiness to enjoy the esteem of five successive Primates; and lived to be the oldest officer in the palace of Lambeth. His official attendance to the duties of Doctors Commons was uncommonly remarkable; and his attachment to the study of English Antiquities formed his principal amusement. His collection of books and MSS. in that particular line was valuable; and his indexes and catalogues so exact, as to render them highly convenient to himself and the friends he was desirous to oblige. All these, with a good collection of coins and medals, he gave, by his last will, to his nephew Gerard Gustavus, in the fond hope of their being preserved as *heir-looms* in his family. But they were all very soon consigned to the hammer of the auctioneer; and the greater part of the MSS. passed into the hands of Mr. Gough and Mr. Nichols.

In the latter part of his life he was too much immersed in professional engagements to enter into new attachments of friendship; but with those who were admitted to an intimacy he associated on the most liberal terms. Though he never ate meat till he was 14, nor drank wine till he was 18, yet it was a maxim which he religiously observed, that "he was an *old Oxonian,* and therefore never knew a man till he had drunk a bottle of wine with him." His entertainments were in the true style of the old English hospitality; and he was remarkably happy in assorting the company he not unfrequently invited to his table.

JOHN DUNTON

THIS eccentric Bookseller was born May 14, 1659, at Graff-ham in Huntingdonshire, where his father, John Dunton, fellow of Trinity college, Cambridge, was then rector. His mother, Lydia Dunton, was daughter of Mr. Daniel Carter, of Chesham; and died March 3, 1660. On the loss of his wife, Mr. Dunton went to Ireland, where he continued some years; and the son was placed, at a very early age, at the school of Mr. William Readings, at Dungrove, near Chesham.

In 1669 his father returned into England, obtained the rectory of Aston Clinton, where he married a second wife, and removed the son from school to his own immediate tuition, intending him for the Church. The acquirement of Latin he found easy; but the difficulty of Greek overcame all his resolutions. He made some little progress in logic, metaphysics, and morality; but at the age of fourteen was found too volatile for the Church; to the no small mortification of his father, who was himself the third John Dunton, in a lineal descent, that had been a minister. When nearly fifteen, to suit the peculiarity of his genius, he was apprenticed to Mr. Thomas Parkhurst, a respectable bookseller. In 1676 he lost his father; and, when his apprenticeship was nearly expired, made himself conspicuous in the great political dispute between the Tories and the Whigs. He, being a prime mover on the part of the Whig apprentices, and selected for their Treasurer, the Tories, to the number of 5000, presented an address to the King against the petitioning for parliaments. The dissenting party made their remonstrances to the former address, in another they presented to Sir Patience Ward, then lord mayor of London, who promised he would acquaint the King with their address; and then bid them return home, and mind the business of their respective masters.

By his own statement, his conduct during the seven years was not very regular; and at the expiration of the term 100 apprentices were invited to celebrate *the funeral*. He now entered on business as a bookseller on his own account; but, to avoid too large a rent, took only half a shop, a warehouse, and a fashionable chamber. "Printing," he says, "was the uppermost in my thoughts; and hackney authors began to ply me with specimens, as earnestly, and with as much passion and concern, as the watermen do passengers with oars and scullers. I had some acquaintance with this generation in my apprenticeship, and had never any warm affection for them; in regard I always thought their great concern lay more in how much a sheet, than in any generous respect they bore to the commonwealth of learning; and indeed the learning itself of these gentlemen lies very often in as little room as their honesty; though they all pretend to have studied you six or seven years in the Bodleian Library, to have turned over the Fathers, and to have read and digested the whole compass both of humane and ecclesiastic history: when, alas! they have never been able to understand a single page of Saint Cyprian, and cannot tell you whether the Fathers lived before or after Christ. And as for their honesty, it is very remarkable, they will either persuade you to go upon another man's copy, to steal his thought, or to abridge his book, which should have got him bread for his life-time. When you have engaged them upon some project or other, they will write you off three or four sheets perhaps, take up three or four pounds upon an urgent occasion, and you shall never hear of them more." — "The first copy I would venture to print, was written by the Reverend Mr. Doolittle, and intituled 'The Sufferings of Christ.' This book fully answered my end; for, exchanging it through the whole trade, it furnished my shop with all sorts of books saleable at that time; and it also brought me acquainted with those ingenious gentlemen, Mr. Waters, Mr. Shewel, Mr. Clark, Mr. Benson, Mr. Wells, and Mr. Sanders, who were then students under the care of Mr. Doolittle. There was a copy of Greek verses prefixed to this book, which occasioned a poetical duel between the two private Academies of Islington and Stepney; Mr. Wesley, then pupil under Mr. Veale, endeavouring to ridicule the Poem; with whom, and Mr. Kingston, his fellow student, I contracted a very intimate friendship. Mr. Wesley was much celebrated for his vein at poetry; though those that allow of no second rate in that art have endeavoured to lessen his reputation. — The second adventure I made in printing, was a copy written by Mr. Jay, rector of Chinner, intituled, 'Daniel in the Den; or, the Lord President's Imprisonment, and miraculous Deliverance.' It was dedicated to the Lord Shaftesbury, and published upon the occasion of his being acquitted by an ignoramus jury. This piece was well furnished with wit, and, being published at the critical time, sold well.

Books have their time of life as well as we;
They live by chance, but die by destiny.
Our fate is less severe, in this alone,
That books no resurrection have, we hope for one.

"This extraordinary success in my first attempts, gave me an ungovernable itch to be always intriguing that way. The next thing I printed was a Sermon preached by the Rev. Mr. John Shower, at the funeral of Madam Anne Barnardiston. The growing reputation of the author made the Sermon move very well. There have been three editions of it, two of my own printing, and a third by my worthy friend Mr. John Lawrence. When I was thus fixed in the trade, I resolved to make public a Collection of Funeral Discourses preached by my reverend father, Mr. John Dunton, intituled, 'The House of Weeping.' The success was well enough; but my chief design was to perpetuate my father's name, for whose memory I have always entertained a very great and just veneration."

Dunton's reputation grew with his circumstances; and, Aug. 3, 1682, he married Elizabeth, one of the daughters of Dr. Annesly, who at that time was a celebrated preacher among the Dissenters. He now opened a shop at the Black Raven in Princes-street; where he carried on business very prosperously, till the universal damp upon trade which was occasioned by the defeat of the Duke of Monmouth in the West; when, having 500*l.* owing him in New England, he determined, after much deliberation, to make a trip thither; and, after a long and tedious voyage of four months, and the loss of a venture of 500*l.* in another ship, which was cast-away, he arrived safe at Boston in March 1685-6; and opened a warehouse for the sale of the books which he had taken thither. Carrying with him powerful recommendations, and his books being of a class adapted to the Puritans, the success was equal to his wishes. His rivals in trade were but few; Mr. Usher, Mr. Philips, Mynheer Brunning, and Duncan Campbell, an industrious Scotchman, being then the only book-sellers in Boston; and Mr. Green the principal if not the only printer. He had taken with him a steady apprentice, Samuel Palmer, to whom he entrusted the whole charge of his business; which left him at leisure to make many pleasant excursions into the country.

He visited Harvard college particularly, and the town of Salem; where he opened another warehouse for his books. He also visited Wenham, an inland town; where he was most kindly received by Mr. Geery, the then minister of that place; whose character he thus delineates : "It were endless to enter on a detail of each faculty of learning Mr. Geery is master of, and therefore take his character in shorthand. The Philosopher is acute, ingenious, and subtle; the Divine curious, orthodox, and profound; the Man of a majestic air, without austerity or sourness; his aspect is masterly and great, yet not imperious or haughty. The Christian is devout, without moroseness, or starts of holy frenzy and enthusiasm; the Preacher is primitive, without the accessional colours of whining or cant; and methodical without intricacy or affectation; and, which crowns his character, he is a man of a public spirit, zealous for the conversion of the Indians, and of great hospitality to strangers. He gave us a noble dinner, and entertained us with such pleasant fruits as, I must own, Old England is a stranger to." — In a ramble to Ipswich he had an opportunity of seeing much of the customs of the Indians.

In the autumn he returned to London; and, being received by his wife and her father with all the marks of kindness and respect, expected nothing but a golden life of it for the future, though all his satisfactions were soon withered; for, being deeply entangled for a sister-in-law, he was not suffered to step over the threshold in ten months. Wearied with this confinement, he determined to take a trip to Holland, Flanders, Germany, &c.; and stayed four months at Amsterdam; whence he travelled to Cleves, Rhineberg, Dussledorp, Cologne, Mentz, &c.; and, returning through Rotterdam to London, Nov. 15, 1688, found his wife in health, and all her affairs in peace. On the day the Prince of Orange came to London, he again opened shop, at the Black Raven, opposite the Poultry Compter, where he traded ten years, with variety of successes and disappointments.

Of 600 books which he had printed, he had only to repent, he adds, of *seven*: "The second Spira," "The Post-boy robbed of his Mail," "The Voyage round the World," "The new Quevedo," "The Pastor's Legacy," "Heavenly Pastime," "The Hue and Cry after Conscience." These he heartily wished he had never seen, and advised all who had them to burn them. After confessing his errors in printing, he says, "As to bookselling and traffick, I dare stand the test, with the same allowance that every man under the same circumstance with me would wish to have, for the whole trading part of my life. Nay, I challenge all the Booksellers in London to prove I ever over-reached them or deceived them in any one instance. And when you come to that part of my life that relates to the *Auctions I made in Dublin*, you will find that in all the notes I made for Dublin, that I put the same price to every man. And would any Bookseller be at the pains to compare all my notes together (though I exchanged with all the trade), for every penny he finds charged more to himself than to other men, he shall have ten pounds reward, and a thousand thanks into the bargain, for rectifying a mistake I never designed." — In 1692, having been "put in possession of a considerable estate upon the decease of my cousin Carter, the Master and Assistants of the Company of Stationers began to think me sufficient to wear a Livery, and honoured me with the cloathing. My Livery-fine upon that occasion was twenty pounds, which I paid; and the year following, Mr. Harris (my old friend and partner), and about fifty more of the Livery-men, entered into a Friendly Society, and obliged ourselves to pay twenty shillings a man yearly to the Renter-warden, in regard that honour was usually once a year attended with costly entertainment to the whole Company.

"The first year I wore the Livery, Sir William Ashhurst being then Lord Mayor, I was invited by our Master and Wardens to dine with his Lordship. We went in a body from the Poultry church to Grocers-hall; where the entertainment was very generous, and a noble spoon he sent to our wives. To speak the truth, I do not think Sir William Ashhurst ever acted a little or a mean thing in his whole life. The world now smiled on me. I sailed with wind and tide; and had humble servants enough among the Booksellers, Stationers, Printers, and Binders; but especially my own relations, on every side, were all upon the very height of love and tenderness, and I was caressed almost out of my five senses. — And now, making a considerable figure in the Company of Stationers, the Right Hon. the Earl of Warrington did me the honour to send me a letter (the original of which I have still by me) in behalf of Mr. Humphreys, desiring all the interest I could make, to procure him the Clerk's place to the Company of Stationers. Upon my reading the Earl's letter, I did all that lay in my power to get Mr. Humphreys chosen Clerk, though by the majority of voices it was carried against him. However, the many civilities I received from the Company of Stationers, for the fifteen years I traded amongst them, do oblige me, out of mere gratitude, to draw the character of the most eminent of that profession in the three kingdoms." Here Mr. Dunton proceeds to characterize the principal Booksellers, Printers, Stationers, Bookbinders, &c. who were his contemporaries (as in a former part of the volume he had the several Authors with whom he had been connected in trade); several of whom have already been mentioned in the present work, and others shall be noticed in future pages.

In delineating the characters of others, Mr. Dunton has not forgot to describe his own *Projects;* "for I have been sufficiently convinced," he says, "that unless a man can either think or perform something out of the old beaten road, he will find nothing but what his forefathers have found before him. A Bookseller, if he is a man of any capacity and observation, can tell best what to go upon, and what has the best prospect of success. I remember Mr. Andrews, a learned and ingenious Scotsman of this age, has offered me several translations, and told me they would certainly sell; the substance of the book was so and so, and could not miss. He added, I had printed more than any other, and yet none had printed less. This was sharp enough, I confess; however, it is a difficult matter to attack a man in his own science. I have, it is true, been very plentifully loaded with the imputation of *Maggots,* &c. And what is the reason? Why, because I have usually started something that was new; whilst others, like footpads, ply only about the high-roads, and either abridge another man's book, or one way or other contrived the very life and soul out of the copy, which perhaps was the only subsistence of the first Proprietor. I once printed a book, I remember, under the title of *Maggots*; but it was written by a Dignitary of the Church of England. However, I am willing to submit myself, and to stand or fall by the impartial judgment of the Reader. My *first Project* was the 'Athenian Gazette.' As the Athenian Society had their first meeting in my brain — so it has been kept ever since religiously secret: but I will now oblige the Reader with a true discovery of the *Question-project,* and of the several persons that engaged in it.

"I had received a very flaming injury, which was so loaded with aggravations, that I could scarce get over it; my thoughts were constantly working upon it, and made me strangely uneasy: sometimes I thought to make application to some Divine, but how to conceal myself and the ungrateful wretch, was the difficulty. Whilst this perplexity remained upon me, I was one day walking over St. George's-fields, and Mr. Larkin and Mr. Harris were along with me, and on a sudden I made a stop, and said, 'Well, Sirs, I have a thought I'll not exchange for fifty guineas!' They smiled, and were very urgent with me to discover it; but they could not get it from me. The first rude hint of it, was no more than a confused idea of concealing the Querist, and answering his question. However, so soon as I came home, I managed it to some better purpose, brought it into form, and hammered out a title for it, which happened to be extremely lucky, and those who are well acquainted with the Grecian History may discover some peculiar beauties in it. However, the honest Reader that knows nothing of criticism may see the reason why this Project was intituled the 'Athenian Gazette,' if he only turns to Acts xvii. 21. When I had thus formed the design, I found that some assistance was absolutely necessary to carry it on, in regard the Project took in the whole compass of Learning, and the nature of it required dispatch. I had then some acquaintance with the ingenious Mr. Richard Sault; who turned Malebranche into English for me, and was admirably well skilled in the mathematicks; and over a glass of wine I unbosomed myself to him, and he very freely offered to become concerned. So soon as the design was well advertised, Mr. Sault and myself, without any more assistance, settled to it with great diligence (and Numbers 1.-2. were entirely of Mr. Sault's composure and mine). The Project being surprizing and unthought-of, we were immediately overloaded with letters; and sometimes I have found several hundreds for me at Mr. Smith's coffee-house in Stocksmarket, where we usually met to consult matters.

"The 'Athenian Gazette' made now such a noise in the world, and was so universally received, that we were obliged to look out after more members; and Mr. Sault, I remember, one evening came to me in great transport, and told me he had been in company with a gentleman, who was the greatest prodigy of learning he had ever met with; upon inquiry, we found it was the ingenious Dr. Norris, who very generously offered his assistance *gratis,* but refused to become a stated member of Athens. He was wonderfully useful in supplying hints; for, being universally read, and his memory very strong, there was nothing could be asked, but he could very easily say something to the purpose upon it.

"In a little time after, to oblige *Authority,* we altered the title of 'Athenian Gazette,' into 'Athenian Mercury.' The undertaking growing every week upon our hands, the impatience of our Querists, and the curiosity of their questions, which required a great deal of accuracy and care, did oblige us to adopt a third member of Athens; and the reverend Samuel Wesley being just come to town, all new from the University, and my acquaintance with him being very intimate, I easily prevailed with him to embark himself upon the same bottom, and in the same cause. With this new addition we found ourselves to be masters of the whole design, and thereupon we neither lessened nor increased our number.

"The success of Athens growing so very considerable, Mr. Brown and Mr. Pate began to ape our design in a paper they intituled the 'Lacedemonian Mercury,' which immediately interfered with us under a title, which, it is true, was pretty and pertinent enough. Upon this, I was resolved one way or other to blow them up, in regard, it was both ungenerous and unjust to interlope upon a man, where he has the sole right and property; for the children of the brain are as much ours, as those we beget in lawful wedlock. I first of all advertized, that all the questions answered in the 'Lacedemonian Mercury' should be answered over again in our 'Athenian Mercury,' with amendments, with the life of Tom Brown, the chief antagonist. This news startled them pretty much. At that time I was altogether unacquainted with Mr. Brown. However, one evening he comes to me, with all the civility imaginable, and desires to take a glass with me. I sent for my Athenian brethren, and we went to the Three Cranes, where we discoursed the matter with him at large : but, Mr. Sault being a gentleman of courage, and a little inclined to passion, was going to draw upon Mr. Brown, for an uncivil reflection; upon which Mr. Brown cried *peccavi,* and promised very faithfully that he would never meddle any more with the 'Lacedemonian Mercury;' and though they had not dropt it, yet the flaming wickedness, and the blasphemy that was in it, would have ruined the design.

"A little after this was published, 'The New Athenian Comedy,' containing, 'The Politicks, Œconomicks, Tacticks, Crypticks, Apocalypticks, Stypticks, Scepticks, Pneumaticks, Theologicks, Poeticks, Mathematicks, Sophisticks, Pragmaticks, Dogmaticks, of our most Learned Society.' This Play was a poor performance, writ, however, on purpose to expose us; but failed so far in the design of it, that it promoted ours. There was nothing of wit through the whole of it, and the reader may take notice that Mr. S———'s genius was quite run out towards the conclusion of the third act, and could not carry it an inch farther.

"The Earl of ——— was once pleased to frown upon the 'Athenian Mercury,' and forced us into silence; but, when men are pleased to make personal application (for the offence was only taken at a question that was sent us, of a father that had two daughters), it is a sign there is a sore place, else they would never wince for the matter; however Captain M———al procured us liberty to proceed, and had twenty-five guineas for that service. I have waded through these, and many other difficulties with this design; and nothing could discourage me, when my cause was so great and good.

"The 'Athenian Mercury' began at length to be so well approved, that Mr. *Gildon* thought it worth his while to write 'A History of the Athenian Society;' to which were prefixed several poems written by the chief Wits of the age (*viz.* Mr. Motteux, Mr. Foe, Mr. Richardson, &c. and in particular, Mr. *Tate* (now Poet Laureate), was pleased to honour us with a Poem directed to the Athenian Society. Mr. *Swift**, a country gentleman, sent an Ode to the Athenian Society; which, being an ingenious poem, was prefixed to the Fifth Supplement of the 'Athenian Mercury.' Many other persons did also rhime in the praise of our Questions. Our Athenian Project did not only obtain among the populace, but was well received by the politer sort of mankind. That great and learned Nobleman, the late Marquis of Halifax, was once pleased to tell me, that he constantly perused our Mercuries, and had received great satisfaction from very many of our Answers. The late Sir William Temple, a man of clear judgement, and wonderful penetration, was pleased to honour me with frequent letters and questions, very curious and uncommon; in particular, that about the *Talismans* was his. The Honourable Sir Thomas Pope Blount, when he resided in town, has very frequently sent for me to his chamber, and given me particular thanks for my Athenian Project; and the last visit I made him, he told me the Athenian Society was certainly the

---

*Afterwards the celebrated Dean.

most useful and informing design that had ever been set on foot in England. Sir William Hedges was pleased to tell me, he was so well pleased with the 'Athenian Mercuries,' that he would send several complete sets into the Indies, to his friends; and that he thought the publick, and himself in particular, so much obliged to me, that I should be always welcome to his house, and that he would serve me to his utmost with reference to my trade. I could mention many more honours that were done me, by Sir Peter Pett, and several others, whose learning and judgment the world has little reason to question.

"Our 'Athenian Mercuries' were continued till they swelled, at least, to twenty volumes folio; and then we took up, to give ourselves a little ease, and refreshment; for the labours and the travels of the mind are as expensive, and wear the spirits off as fast, as those of the body. However our Society was never formally dissolved.

"The old Athenian volumes, a while ago, growing quite out of print, a choice collection of the most valuable questions and answers, in three volumes, have lately been re-printed, and made publick, until the title of 'Athenian Oracle;' two of which I dedicated to the most illustrious and magnanimous Prince, James Duke of Ormond (Chancellor of the Universities of Oxford and Dublin), and Lord Lieutenant of Ireland.

"A *second Project* of mine, which was set on foot by the Old Athenians, and lately published by the New, is intituled, 'The Athenian Spy; or the Secret Letters of Platonic Courtship, between the Athenian Society, and the most ingenious Ladies in the Three Kingdoms; with the form of solemnizing Platonic Matrimony, invented by the Athenian Society.'

"A *third Project* of mine, for the promotion of Learning, was a Monthly Journal of Books printed in London, and beyond Sea; which was chiefly extracted out of 'The Universal Bibliotheque,' and 'Journal des Sçavans;' and it first appeared under the title of 'A Supplement to the Athenian Mercury,' but was afterwards called, 'The Complete Library.' This design was carried on about ten months, when Monsieur Lecrose interfered with me in a Monthly Journal, intituled 'The Works of the Learned;' upon which I dropped my own design, and joined with Lecrose's bookseller, in publishing 'The Works of the Learned.' But, Lecrose dying, it was discontinued; though the same design, under the same title, is yet on foot, and managed by several hands, one of which is the ingenious Mr. Ridpath.

"IV. *Another Project* (which I writ myself, and published a year ago) was intituled 'The Post Angel : or Universal Entertainment.'

"My *fifth Project* has been preparing for the press for these ten years, and is intituled, 'The New Practice of Piety. Writ in imitation of Dr. Brown's *Religio Medici:* or, a System of uncommon Thoughts, extracted from the Experience of Forty Years.'

"My *sixth Project* was, 'The Challenge, sent by a young Lady to Sir Thomas ———, intituled *The Female War*; wherein the present Dresses and Humours of the Fair Sex, are vigorously attacked by Men of Quality, and as bravely defended by several Ladies.'

"VII. My next *Project* was intituled, 'The Post-Boy robbed of his Mail; or, The Pacquet broke open, containing Five Hundred Letters that were taken from several Posts, discovering the Secrets of Men and Women of all Ranks and Qualities.' The Club of Gentlemen supposed to have been concerned in this frolick make remarks upon the Letters as they break them up. This Project obtained so well, that both volumes are now out of print.

"My *eighth Project* was a design to expose vice, intituled, 'The Night Walker; or, Evening Rambles in search after lewd Women; with the various Conferences held with them.' This Project was so well received, that I purposed to continue it monthly.

"IX. My last *Project* (amongst many that I shall leave unmentioned) was intituled 'The Merciful Assizes; or, a Panegyrick on the late Lord Jeffreys' hanging so many in the West.' You must know, Reader, in the book intituled 'The Bloody Assizes' (of which I sold above six thousand) the Lord Jeffreys is made a very cruel man : but in this new Project I (wholly) change the scene, and turn the Bloody Assizes into Merciful Assizes. But let none be surprized that I make Jeffreys the subject of a panegyrick; for there is a witty Author has defended the bloody Nero; and of late, a learned gentleman has published an Apology for the Failures of Dr. Walker; and with the same design that these gentlemen writ, do I venture to praise that *nonsuchman*, George Lord Jeffreys. This panegyrick was so well accepted, that my friend Mr. George Larkin was pleased to explain the Project by an ingenious Poem.

"Thus I have given a brief account of the Projects I formerly engaged in; and whether they give me the title of *Maggot*, or Promoter of Learning and Virtue, is left to the candour and judgment of the honest Reader."

THE ELSTOBS

MR. WILLIAM ELSTOB, and his learned Sister, being persons not generally known, though both of them exceedingly eminent in their way, a short account of them is here inserted, from the papers of the sister, who, about the year 1738, compiled a brief Narrative of her own and her brother's Life, and gave it in her own hand-writing to Mr. *George Ballard,* at whose request she drew it up. Dr. Nathanael Wetherell, the worthy master of University College, was so fortunate as to find the narrative among Mr. Ballard's MSS. in the Bodleian Library, and sent a transcript of it to Dr. Charles Lyttelton, Bishop of Carlisle, who communicated it to the late Rev. Dr. Samuel Pegge, and by him the following particulars were extracted.

William Elstob was born Jan. 1, 1673, at Newcastle upon Tyne. He was the son of *Ralph Elstob,* merchant in that place, who was descended from a very antient family in the bishoprick of Durham; as appears not only from their pedigree in the Herald's office, but from several writings now in the family, one of which is a grant from William de la More, master of the Knights Templars, to Adam d'Elnestob, in the year 1304, on condition of their paying 24s. to their house at Shotton, *et faciendo duos conventus ad curiam suam de Foxdene.*

It appears, by a note on the MS Life, that Mrs. Elstob had drawn up the pedigree of her family, very curiously, upon vellum; shewing, that, by the maternal side, the Elstobs were descended from the old kings or princes of Wales; in the middle there was a column, on the top of which stood King Brockmail, on one side the paternal, and on the other maternal descents. This was in the earl of Oxford's library.

William had the earliest part of his education at Newcastle, whence at about eleven years of age he removed to Eton, where he continued five years. From Eton, by the advice of an uncle, who was his guardian, he was placed at Catherine Hall in Cambridge, in a station below his birth and fortune. This, and the air not agreeing with his constitution, which was consumptive, was the occasion of his removal to Queen's College, Oxford, where he was a commoner, and continued till he was elected fellow of University College, by the friendship of Dr. Charlet, master of that college, Dr. Hudson, &c.

In 1702, he was by the Dean and Chapter of Canterbury presented to the united parishes of St. Swithin and St. Mary Bothaw, in London, where, after he had discharged the duty of a faithful and orthodox pastor, with great patience and resignation, after a long and lingering illness, he died March 3, 1714-15, and was buried in the chancel o St. Swithin's Church, London, under the communion-table.

Mr. Elstob was extremely well versed in the Saxon tongue; and, being then resident in college, the very learned Dr. Hickes solicited him to give a Latin translation of the Saxon Homily of Lupus, and prevailed. The original, with the Latin version, is inserted by the Doctor in his Epistolary Dissertation above-mentioned, p.99, seqq. The Epistle Dedicatory to Dr. Hickes, thereunto prefixed, is dated University College, v Id. or 9 August, 1701; Mr. Elstob being then joint tutor in the College with Dr. Clavering, late Bishop of Peterborough, and in possession of a transcript of the original Saxon made by Junius, to which he hath not only added the Latin version before-mentioned, but also many excellent notes. He styles it "the first fruits of his labours in the Saxon tongue."

Before Mr. Elstob left Oxford, he printed, with large additions, a neat edition (the fifth) of the celebrated Roger Ascham's Epistles; to which he subjoined the letters of John Sturmius, Hieron, Osorius, and others, to Ascham and other English gentlemen, Oxford, 1703, 8vo.

In 1709, his Latin version of the Saxon Homily on St. Gregory's Day, which he presented to his learned sister in a short Latin epistle, was printed at the end of her fine edition of the Saxon original.

Mr. Elstob published the larger Devotions which the Saxons made use of at that time in their own language, which from probable conjectures he fancies was the performance either of Ælfric archbishop of Canterbury, or of Wolfstan archbishop of York. And to shew the world that they did not contain any thing but what is pure and orthodox, he has obliged the publick with a faithful translation of them.

Mr. Elstob was particularly useful to his sister, in the great advances she made in literature, as likewise in her publications. This she testifies, both in her preface to the edition of the Saxon Homily, and in the MS Life of her brother. But concerning her, I must now subjoin some few Memoirs, and the rather, because, as she was living when Mr. Ballard published his "Memoirs of the learned Ladies of Great Britain, 1752," there is no account of her in that work. Mr. Ballard otherwise was well acquainted with her, corresponded with her, and had the highest esteem for her on account of her uncommon learning and accomplishments, and doubtless would have done all proper honour to her memory on that occasion.

She was born in the parish of St. Nicholas, in Newcastle upon Tyne, Sept. 29, 1683; so that she was ten years younger than her brother. Her mother, who was a great admirer of learning, especially in her own sex, observed the particular fondness which her daughter had for books, and omitted nothing that might tend to her improvement so long as she lived; but she was so unfortunate as to lose her mother when she was about eight years of age, and had just gone through her Accidence and Grammar. A stop was now put to her progress for a time, through a vulgar mistaken notion of her guardian, *that one Tongue was enough for a woman.* However, the force of natural inclination still carried her to improve her mind in the best manner she could; and, as her propensity was strong towards languages, she with much difficulty obtained leave to learn the French tongue. But her situation in this respect was happily much altered when she went to live with her brother, who, being impressed with more liberal sentiments concerning the education of women, very joyully assisted and encouraged her in her studies for the whole time he lived. Under his eye, she translated and published an "Essay on Glory," written in French by the celebrated Mademoiselle de Scudery. But what characterizes Mrs. Elstob most, she, as she intimates in her Dedication to the Saxon Homily, was the first English woman that had ever attempted that antient and obsolete language, and I suppose is also the last. But she was an excellent linguist in other respects, being not only mistress of her own and the Latin tongue, but also of seven other languages. And she owed all her skill in the learned tongues, except what may be ascribed to her own dili-

gence and application, to her brother. She was withal a good
Antiquary and Divine, as appears evidently from her works,
which I must now recite.

She published an English-Saxon Homily on the Birth-day,
that is, the Death-day, of St. Gregory, antiently used in the
English-Saxon church, giving an account of the Conversion of
the English from Paganism to Christianity, translated into modern English, with notes, &c. London, 1709. It is a pompous book,
in large octavo, with a fine frontispiece, headpieces, tailpieces,
and blooming letters. She dedicates her work, which was printed
by subscription, to Queen Anne. Mr. Thoresby, in the Ducatus
Leod. p. 129, gives notice of this intended publication, and there
styles her the *justly celebrated Saxon Nymph*. Her preface,
which is indeed an excellent and learned performance, was particularly serviceable to Mr. Ballard, who has made good use of
it, in evincing the advantages of the Anglo-Saxon literature, and
ingenuously acknowledges it.

In 1715, she printed "The Rudiments of Grammar for the
English-Saxon Tongue, first given in English; with an Apology
for the Study of Northern Antiquities, being very useful towards
the understanding our antient English Poets and other Writers,"
4to.

As the Life of her brother and of herself, written at the request
of Mr. Ballard, have been noticed above, they are omitted here.
Moreover ,she tells us in her own Life, that she had taken an
exact copy of the *Textus Roffensis* upon vellum, "now in the
library of that great and generous encourager of learning, the
late right honourable the earl of Oxford." Mr. Astle had in his
collection a MS volume, chiefly in her hand-writing, but partly
in that of her brother, intituled, "Collectanea quædam Anglo-
Saxonica, è Codd. MSS. hinc inde congesta." And in Dr.
Pegge's transcript of the *Textus Roffensis* there was the Saxon
alphabet on the reverse of the second folio signed *E. E.* which is
evidently her name. It appears also from a work of her brother's,
that she had joined with him in preparing and adorning an
edition of Gregory's Pastoral; a work which was probably intended to include both the original, and the Saxon version of it.
And she informs us herself, in her Life, that "she had transcribed
all the Hymns from an antient MS. belonging to the church of
Sarum."

Mrs. Elstob is described by Mr. Rowe Mores, as "the *in-
defessa comes* of her brother's studies, a female student in the

university." She was "a Northern lady of an antient family and a genteel fortune; but she pursued too much the drug called learning, and in that pursuit failed of being careful of any one thing necessary. In her latter years she was tutoress in the family of the Duke of Portland, where we have visited her in her sleeping-room at Bulstrode, surrounded with books and dirtiness, the usual appendages of folk of learning. But if any one desires to see her as she was, when she was the favourite of Dr. Hudson and the Oxonians, they may view her portraiture in the initial G. of The English-Saxon Homily on the Birth-day of St. Gregory. The countenance of St. Gregory in the Saxon G is taken from Mr. Thwaites, who published an edition of "Ephraim Syrus," Oxon. 1709; and both were engraved by Gribelin, though Michael Burghers was at that time engraver to the University."

In the Preface to the Anglo-Saxon Grammar, p. 11, she speaks of a work of larger extent, in which she was engaged, and which had *amply experienced Dr. Hickes's encouragement.* This was a Saxon *Homilarium,* or a collection of the English-Saxon Homilies of Ælfric, archbishop of Canterbury. It was a noble though unsuccessful enterprize, and indeed her most capital undertaking. Mr. Ballard gives the following account of it: "Dr. Hickes, well knowing the great use which those Homilies had been of, and still might be, to the Church of England, designed to publish, among other Saxon tracts, a volume of Saxon Homilies. But then he tells us, that though for want of further encouragement he could not carry on any one of those designs, yet it was no small pleasure to him, to see one of the most considerable of them attempted, with so much success, by Mrs. Elizabeth Elstob, "who," adds he, "with incredible industry hath furnished a Saxon *Homilarium,* or a collection of the English-Saxon Homilies of Ælfric, Archbishop of Canterbury, which she hath translated, and adorned with learned and useful notes, and for the printing of which she hath published proposals; and I cannot but wish that for her own sake, as well as for the advancement of the Septentrional learning, and for the honour of our English-Saxon ancestors, the service of the Church of England, the credit of our country, and the honour of her sex, that learned and most studious gentle-woman may find such encouragement as she and her great undertaking deserve." This work was begun printing in a very pompous folio at the Theatre in Oxford (and five or more of the Homilies were wrought off in a very beautiful manner), and was to have borne the following title: "The English-Saxon Homilies of Ælfric, Archbishop of Canterbury, who flourished in the latter end of the tenth Century, and the beginning of the eleventh. Being a Course of Sermons collected out of the Writings of the antient Latin Fathers, containing the Doctrines, &c. of the Church of England before the Norman Conquest, and shewing its Purity from many of those Popish Innovations and Corruptions which were afterwards introduced into the Church. Now first printed, and translated into the Language of the present Times, by Elizabeth Elstob."

This elogium of Mrs. Elstob, and her undertaking, by so great a man, and a person so well versed in the subject as Dr. Hickes, redounds infinitely to the lady's honour. The design, however, though so prosperously begun, and even so far advanced, proved abortive; for the work was never published, for want, I imagine, of encouragement. What is become of the MS. I have not at present learned.

But this excellent woman, notwithstanding her profound learning and masculine abilities, was very unfortunate in life. After the death of her brother, and the ill success of her studies, she was obliged to depend upon her friends for subsistence, but did not meet with that generosity she might reasonably expect; Bishop Smalridge being the only person from whom she received any relief. After being supported by his friendly hand for a while, she at last could not bear the thoughts of continuing a burthen to one who was not very opulent himself; and, being shocked with the cold respect of some, and the haughty scorn of others, she determined to retire to a place unknown, and to try to get her bread by teaching children to read and work; and she settled for that purpose at Evesham in Worcestershire. Here she led at first but an uncomfortable and penurious life; but, growing acquainted afterwards with the gentry of the town, her affairs mended, but still she scarcely had time to eat, much less for study. She became known after this to Mr. George Ballard, of Campden in Gloucestershire, who has so often been mentioned; and about the year 1733, Mrs. Capon, the wife of a clergyman of French extraction, who kept a private boarding-school at Stanton in that county, and was herself a person of literature, enquired of him after her, and, being informed of the place of her abode, made her a visit. Mrs. Capon, not being in circumstances to assist her herself, wrote a circular letter to her friends, in order to promote a subscription in her behalf. This letter, which was extremely well written, describing her merit, her extensive learning, her printed works, her ease and affluence till her brother's death, her multiplied distresses afterwards, and the meekness and patience with which she bore them, had the desired effect, and an annuity of twenty guineas was raised for her. This enabled her to keep an assistant, by which means she could again taste of that food of the mind from which she had been so long obliged to fast. A lady soon after shewed Mrs. Capon's letter to Queen Caroline; who, recollecting her name, on account of the Dedication before-mentioned, and delighted with the opportunity of taking such eminent merit into her protection, said, "she would allow her 20*l. per annum*; but," adds she, "as she is so proper to be mistress of a boarding-school for young ladies of a higher rank, I will, instead of an annual allowance, send her 100*l*. now, and repeat the same at the end of every five years." On the death of Queen Caroline, in 1737, a most unlucky event in appearance for poor Mrs. Elstob, she was seasonably recommended to the late Duchess dowager of Portland; and her Grace, to whose father, the Earl of Oxford, she had been well known, was pleased to appoint her governess to her children. This was in the year 1739; and from this period, the letters she wrote to Mr. Ballard, which are now in the Bodleian Library, are observed to have a more sprightly turn, and she seems to have been exceedingly happy in her situation. She died in an advanced age, in her Grace's service, May 30, 1756, and was buried at St. Margaret's Westminster.

HENRY FIELDING

AN Author of great eminence in writings of wit and humour, was born at Sharpham, near Glastonbury in Somersetshire, April 22, 1707. His father, Edmund, was the third son of John Fielding, Doctor in Divinity, and Canon of Salisbury, who was the fifth son of George Earl of Desmond, and brother to William third earl of Denbigh, nephew to Basil, the second Earl, and grandson to William, who was first raised to that peerage.

Edmund Fielding served in the wars under the Duke of Marl-borough, and died Lieutenant-general of his Majesty's forces, at London, in the year 1740, having had four wives. His first wife was Sarah, daughter of Sir Henry Gould, Knight, one of the Judges of the Court of King's Bench, and aunt to the late Sir Henry Gould, successively a Baron of the Exchequer, and a Justice in the Court of Common Pleas. By this lady, Lieutenant-general Fielding had two sons, Henry and Edmund, the last of whom, who was an officer in the marine service, departed this life without issue; and four daughters, Catharine, Ursula, Sarah, and Beatrix, who all died unmarried. The General, by his second wife, had six sons, George, James, Charles, John, Basil, and William. Of these, John, who in due course of time was raised to the honour of knighthood, was well known to the world as an active magistrate, and head of the Public Office in Bow-street, Covent-garden. It is greatly to the honour of Sir John Fielding's memory that he was a distinguished promoter of the Magdalen-house for penitent prostitutes, the Asylum for deserted young girls, and the Marine Society for fitting out indigent boys for the sea-service.

Henry Fielding received the first rudiments of his grammatical education at home, under the care of the Rev. Mr. Oliver, who was so far from gaining the affections of his pupil, that he is said to have been the original from which the humorous and striking portrait of parson Trulliber is drawn, in the Adventures of Joseph Andrews. From the tuition of Mr. Oliver, our author was removed to Eton-school, where he had the advantage of being early known to several young gentlemen, who afterwards ranked among the first people of the kingdom. These were Mr. Lyttelton, Mr. Fox, Mr. Pitt, Mr. Hanbury Williams, Mr. Winnington, and others, whose subsequent preferments and titles we need not specify. At this great seminary of education, Mr. Fielding gave distinguishing proofs of strong and peculiar parts; and, when he quitted the place, he was said to be uncommonly versed both in the Greek and Latin Classics; his acquaintance with, and his admiration of which, he retained through his whole life. From Eton he went to the University of Leyden, where he continued to shew an ardent thirst for knowledge. Here he studied the Civilians, with a remarkable application, for two years; but remittances failing him, he was obliged to return to London, when he was not 21 years of age. The fact was, that General Fielding, having a large family to provide for, found it impracticable to supply his eldest son in the manner that could be wished. Nominally his appointment was about 200*l.* a year; but, as he himself used to say, "any body might pay it that would." At the same time, he was sensible that his father's limited income could not afford very considerable disbursements; and therefore he never remitted of his filial piety, which his nearest relations agreed to be a shining part of his character. Mr. Fielding being thus unfortunately circumstanced, aggravated the evils of poverty by a strong propensity to extravagance and dissipation. Though under age, he found himself his own master, in a place where the temptations to pleasure were numerous, and the means of gratification easily attained. The brilliancy of his talents soon brought him into request with men of taste and literature; but it was not to men of taste and literature only that his acquaintance was confined. He united with the voluptuous, as well as with the learned and the witty, and plunged into excesses, the bad effects of which accompanied him all the remainder of his life.

In the pecuniary difficulties experienced by Mr. Fielding, the bent of his genius, and the readiness of his wit, naturally led him to write for the stage; in doing which he might have risen to eminence, had his situation granted him the leisure and reflection which are necessary to the due perfection of dramatic productions. As, for several years, he made a considerable figure by the number, at least, if not by the excellence of his plays, we shall take a connected view of him in this capacity, before we proceed to other parts of his life. His first comedy was intituled, "Love in several Masks," and was acted at the Theatre Royal in Drury-lane, in 1727-8, when he was only in the 21st year of his age. Though it immediately succeeded the long and crowded run of "The Provoked Husband," it met with a favourable reception; and considering, observes Mr. Murphy, that it was our author's first attempt, it had, no doubt, the marks of a promising genius. It probably derived no small advantage from it being represented by such actors and actresses as Mr. Wilks, Mr. Cibber, Mrs. Oldfield, and Mrs. Porter. — Mr. Fielding's next dramatic production, "The Temple Beau," was brought forwards in 1729 at Goodman's-fields. It was tolerably successful, and is allowed to contain a great deal of spirit and real humour. The character, however, of Wilding, is very inferior to that of Ranger, in Dr. Hoadly's "Suspicious Husband." — "The Temple Beau" was followed, in the same year, by a comedy of three acts, called

"The Author's Farce;" which contains a supposed rehearsal of another piece, intituled, "The Pleasures of the Town," which was principally designed to ridicule the prevailing fondness for the Italian singers. It was first acted at the little theatre in the Haymarket, with very considerable success; and in 1732 was revived at Drury-lane, after being revised and greatly altered. — In 1731, Mr. Fielding produced "The Lottery," a ballad farce, which is a lively and entertaining performance. It met with a good reception at Drury-lane, and still remains on the list of acting farces. This is especially the case near the time of drawing the state-lotteries, when the scene of the wheels in Guildhall gives great pleasure to the nightly residents of the upper regions of the theatre. — Five other productions came from our author's pen in the year 1731. These were, "The Coffee-house Politician," a comedy; "The Tragedy of Tragedies; or, the Life and Death of Tom Thumb the Great;" "The Letter Writers," a farce; "The Grub-street Opera," a ballad farce; and the "Modern Husband," a comedy.

In 1732, Mr. Fielding gave to the world four dramatic pieces, all of which were acted at Drury-lane. These were, "The Mock Doctor," a ballad farce; "The Covent Garden Tragedy," a burlesque; "The Debauchees," a comedy of three acts; and "The Miser," a comedy. The "Mock Doctor," with an exception to the songs, which are not very numerous, is taken from the "Médecin malgré lui" of Moliere. It is a very pleasant performance, and maintains its rank to this day, as one of the most constant and favourite after-pieces which the theatre affords. "The Covent Garden Tragedy" merits no attention, and little can be said in praise of the "Debauchees." Like the "Tartuff" of Moliere, and the "Non-Juror" of Cibber, its principal intention is to expose Monkish hypocrisy and villainy. The "Miser" may be considered as the most perfect comedy which our author has written; and it has maintained its ground upon the stage ever since it was first performed. Its excellency, however, chiefly belongs to Molière, from whom it is for the most part taken. Mr. Murphy justly observes, that it has the value of a copy from a great painter, by an eminent hand. — "The Intriguing Chambermaid," a ballad opera, acted at Drury-lane, and "Don Quixote in England," a comedy, represented at the new theatre in the Haymarket, were the productions of the year 1733. "The Intriguing Chambermaid," which still continues on the list of acting farces, is almost entirely borrowed from the "Dissipateur."

Its being one of the pieces in which Mrs. Clive appeared, contributed not a little to its acceptance and success. Notwithstanding the difficulty of sustaining a character so wonderfully drawn by Cervantes, the "Don Quixote in England" met with a favourable reception. — A farce, intituled, "An old Man taught Wisdom," and a comedy, called "The Universal Gallant," were produced in 1734. "The old Man taught Wisdom," say the writers of the Biographia Dramatica, "was acted with good success at Drury Lane Theatre, and continues on the acting list to this day. The characters are all *outré* to the greatest degree, and the piece is entirely devoid of even the shadow of a plot. Yet there is something laughable in it on the whole; and therefore, as it pleases the canaille, it is in general more frequently performed than many farces of an infinitely greater share of merit." "The universal Gallant" was condemned by the audience; and, we apprehend, not unjustly. — Our author was much happier in his next performance, which appeared at the Haymarket theatre in 1736. This was "Pasquin," a dramatic satire on the times : being the rehearsal of two plays, viz. a Comedy, called the "Election;" and a Tragedy, called "the Life and Death of Common Sense." Mr. Murphy is of opinion, that, if "Pasquin" were restored to the stage, it would perhaps be a more favourite entertainment with our audiences than the much admired "Rehearsal;" and that a more rational one it certainly would be, as it would undoubtedly be better understood. The "Pasquin" was followed, in 1737, by the "Historical Register," a production of a similar nature. These two pieces were the occasion of producing a great revolution in the state of the theatrical world; for, it was owing to some reflections thrown out in them on the ministry, that an Act of Parliament was passed for limiting the number of theatres, and submitting every new dramatic work to the inspection of the Lord Chamberlain, previously to its appearance on the stage. Besides the "Historical Register," Henry Fielding brought out, in 1737, three farces, "Eurydice," "Eurydice hissed," and "Tumble-down Dick." The first was condemned; the second was a sort of apology for it, and the third was a kind of a pantomime. It does not seem to have been acted till the year 1744. Our author abstained from writing for the stage from 1737 to 1742, when he produced at Drury-lane a farce, intituled, "Miss Lucy in Town," being a sequel to the "Virgin Unmasked." This piece was performed for some nights with applause : but, it being hinted that a particular man of quality was pointed at in one of the characters, an order was obtained, from the Lord Chamberlain, to forbid its farther representation. In the same year, Mr. Fielding, in conjunction with the Rev. Mr. Young, published "Plutus the God of Riches," being a translation from Aristophanes. This was printed as a specimen of a proposed complete version of all the comedies of Aristophanes, for which proposals were delivered : but the design was never carried into execution. The last of Henry Fielding's plays, which was brought upon the stage during his life, was "The Wedding Day," a comedy. It was acted at Drury-lane, in the spring of 1743, and struggled with difficulty through six nights. The profits of the house did not amount to fifty pounds.

Considering that our author was possessed of an admirable comic genius, it has been matter of enquiry whence it happened that he did not, on the whole, greatly succeed as a dramatic writer. The subject has particularly been attended to by Mr. Murphy; whose remarks are judicious and important, and constitute an essential part in the estimation of Henry Fielding's literary character. Notwithstanding the number of his plays and farces, he derived but small aids towards his subsistence from the treasurer of the theatre. Some of his pieces were condemned, and others sustained the run of only a few nights. If their ill reception was owing to the looseness with which several of them were disgraced, it redounds to the honour of the audience. The pecuniary disappointments which Mr. Fielding met with in this respect were nobly alleviated by the patronage of the late Duke of Richmond, the Duke of Bedford, John Duke of Argyle, the Duke of Roxborough, and many persons of distinguished rank and character. Among these, George Lord Lyttelton deserves especially to be mentioned; for, his friendship to our author softened the rigour of his misfortunes while he lived, and exerted itself towards his memory when he was no more, by taking pains to clear up imputations of a particular kind, which had been thrown out against him.

About six or seven years after Mr. Fielding had commenced his career as a writer for the stage, he fell in love with, and married, Charlotte, the daughter of Mr. Cradock, of Salisbury, a lady of great personal beauty, with a fortune of fifteen hundred pounds. Nearly about the same time his mother died; by which event he came into the possession of an estate at Stower in Dorsetshire, the value of which was something more than two hundred a year. To this estate, which, in conjunction with the fortune of his wife, whom he tenderly loved, might have secured him a decent independence, he determined to retire from the follies and intemperances of the town. But here another folly awaited him. The pride of family came upon him, and he began immediately to vie in splendour with the neighbouring country squires. He encumbered himself with a large retinue of servants; and, the turn of his mind leading him to a fondness for the delights of society and convivial mirth, he threw wide open the gates of hospitality, and, in less than three years, his whole patrimony was devoured by hounds, horses, and entertainments. In short, by a desire, as Shakspeare expresses it,

   — "Of shewing a more swelling port
   Than his faint means would grant continuance,"

he was brought back to the same unfortunate situation which he had before experienced; with this aggravating circumstance attending it, that he had no prospect of any such resources in future as those he had so indiscreetly lavished away. Henry Fielding was not, however, of a disposition to give himself up to despair. He determined to repair his broken fortunes by betaking himself to the study of the law. Accordingly, being then about thirty years of age, he was entered of the Temple; and his application, whilst he was a student there, was remarkably intense. Sometimes, indeed, the early taste he had taken of pleasure would return upon him, and conspire with his spirits and vivacity to carry him into the wild enjoyments of the town. Nevertheless, it was particular in him, that, amidst all his dissipations, nothing could suppress the thirst he had for knowledge, and the delight he felt in reading. This prevailed in him to such a degree, that he has frequently been known to retire late at night from a tavern to his chambers, and there read, and make extracts from, the most abstruse authors, for several hours before he went to bed. After the customary time of probation at the Temple, he was called to the bar; and it is allowed that he carried with him to Westminster-hall no incompetent share of legal learning. As long as his health permitted him, he attended, with punctual assiduity, both in term-time and on the Western circuit; and it is probable that he would have arisen to considerable eminence in the law, had not the progress of his success been stopped by repeated attacks of the gout. These came so frequently upon him, that it was impossible for him to be as constant at the bar as the laboriousness of his profession required.

Under the pressure of pain and adverse circumstances, Henry Fielding still found resources in his genius and abilities. His pen never lay idle; but was always producing, almost as it were extempore, a play, a farce, a pamphlet, or a news-paper. He was the author of a large number of fugitive political tracts, which had their value during the course of the incidents to which they related. The periodical paper, called "The Champion," owed its chief support to his talents; and, though his essays in that collection cannot now be precisely ascertained, they contributed not a little to his reputation at the time of their appearance. He did not write much poetry, and in what he did write he was not sufficiently attentive to the correctness of his versification. His poetical pieces, therefore, which are inserted in his "Miscellanies," published in 1743, have not found a place in the general edition of his works. Of some of his other productions, previously to the full display of his genius, it may not be amiss to give a short account. The "Essay on Conversation," as he himself informs us, was designed to ridicule one of the most pernicious evils that attends society, viz. pampering the gross appetites of selfishness and ill-nature, with the shame and disquietude of others; and to shew that true good-breeding consists in contributing to the satisfaction and happiness of all around us. This design is pursued with great good sense and acquaintance with the world. Our author's rules for the conduct of conversation are extremely judicious. The "Essay on the Knowledge of the Characters of Men" is principally levelled at hypocrisy, which vice it well exposes, with a view of guarding against it the honest, undesigning, and open-hearted man. In the "Journey from this World to the next" are many strokes of true humour. The characters introduced in it are well sustained; and the work affords an agreeable foretaste of that talent for the delineation of life and manners which Mr. Fielding afterwards so fully displayed. To the same praise is the "History of Jonathan Wild" entitled, with this exception, that the reading of it is rendered disagreeable by the low scenes of profligacy and vice with which it abounds. The representations may be just, and introduced with a laudable intention; but they are odious and disgusting.

Hitherto Henry Fielding had given only preludes to some great work, in which all the component parts of his genius were to be seen in their full and vigorous exertion; in which his imagination was to strike us by the most lively and just colouring, his wit to enliven by the happiest allusions, his invention to enrich with the greatest variety of character and incident, and his judgment to charm not only by the propriety and grace of particular parts, but by the order, harmony, and congruity of the whole. To this high excellence our author made strong approaches in his "History and Adventures of Joseph Andrews, and his friend Mr. Abraham Adams," which first appeared in the year 1742. "Joseph Andrews," as the preface to the work informs us, "was intended for an imitation of the style and manner of Cervantes:" and all who are acquainted with both writers will testify how delightfully Mr. Fielding has copied the humour, the gravity, and the fine ridicule of his Master. In this performance he was employed in the very province for which his talents were peculiarly formed; namely, the fabulous narration of some imagined action, which did occur, or might probably have occurred in human life. Nothing could more happily be conceived than the character of parson Adams: to whom we are attached, in the most endearing manner, by the humanity and benevolence of affection, the goodness of heart, and the zeal for virtue which come from him on all occasions. His excellent talents, his erudition, and his real acquirements in sacred and profane literature, together with his honesty, command our esteem and respect; while his simplicity and innocence in the ways of men provoke our smiles by the contrast they bear to his genuine and intellectual attainments. These circumstances conduce to make him in the highest manner the object of mirth; and, at the same time, the many ridiculous embarrassments to which he is liable do not degrade him in our estimation. To crown the whole, that habitual absence of mind, which is his predominant foible, and which never fails to give a tinge to whatever he is employed in, makes the honest clergyman almost a rival of the renowned Don Quixote. In fact, the adventures he is led into, in consequence of this infirmity, assume something of the romantic air which accompanies the Knight Errant; and the instances of his forgetfulness tend as strongly to excite our laughter as the mistakes of the Spanish hero. When Don Quixote imagines the barber's bason to be Mambrino's helmet, no reader ever found the situation to be more ridiculous and truly comic than parson Adams's travelling to London to sell a set of sermons, and actually snapping his fingers and taking two or three turns round the room in extacy, when introduced to a bookseller in order to make an immediate bargain, and then immediately after exclaiming, not being able to find these same sermons, "I

profess, I believe I left them behind me." There are many
touches in the conduct of this character which occasion exquisite
merriment; and it will not be found too bold an assertion to say,
that the celebrated description of an absent man, by La Bruyère,
is extremely short of that true and just resemblance to nature
with which our author has delineated the features of Adams.
While the former is carried to extravagance, though an agreeable
one, the latter has the fine lights and shades of probability. The
Rev. Mr. Young, a learned and much-esteemed friend of Mr.
Fielding's, sat for this picture. Mr. Young was remarkable for
his intimate acquaintance with the Greek writers, and was as
passionate an admirer of Æschylus as parson Adams is represented to have been. The overflowings of his benevolence were
likewise as strong, and his fits of reverie as frequent. Indeed,
they occured to him upon the most interesting occasions. Such
was the gentleman from whom the idea of parson Adams was
derived. How it is interwoven into the history of Joseph Andrews, and how sustained with unabating pleasantry to the conclusion, is universally felt and acknowledged. The whole work
indeed abounds with situations of the truly comic kind; and the
incidents and characters are unfolded with fine turns of surprise.
In short, it is one among the productions of invention which
will always continue in request.

At the time in which Joseph Andrews was published, Mr.
Fielding still continued in the practice of the law; but his
application to it was not uniform and steady. He pursued it by
starts, and after frequent intermissions; than which nothing can
be more fatal to success in the legal profession. His conduct,
however, though not free from blame, was not wholly without
excuse. Repeated shocks of illness disabled him from being so
assiduous in his attendance in the courts of justice as he would
otherwise have been. From business he derived few supplies, and
therefore his prospects grew every day more gloomy and melancholy. Besides the demands for expence which were created by
his valetudinarian habit of body, he had a family to maintain.
To these discouraging circumstances was added the long illness
of his wife, whom he tenderly loved; so that the measure of his
afflictions was well nigh full. To see her daily languishing and
withering away before his eyes was too much for a man of his
strong sensations. On this trying occasion, the fortitude with
which he had met all the other calamities of life deserted him;
and her death brought on such a vehemence of grief, that his

friends began to think him in danger of losing his reason. When, however, the first emotions of sorrow were abated, philosophy administered her aid; his resolution returned; and he began again to struggle with his fortune. When the Rebellion broke out in 1745, he engaged in a periodical paper, with the laudable and spirited design of rendering service to his country. This was called the "True Patriot," and it was not without its effect in exciting the sentiments of loyalty, and a love for the constitution in the breast of his countrymen. Mr. Addison, in his "Free-holder," had set a fine example in this species of composition, and in Mr. Fielding he had not an unworthy follower. In the "True Patriot" was displayed a solid knowledge of the British laws and government, together with occasional sallies of humour, which would have made no inconsiderable figure in the political works of the greatest wits among our author's predecessors. Another periodical paper, written by him, was the "Jacobite's Journal." It appeared in the beginning of the year 1748, and was calculated to discredit the shattered remains of an unsuccessful party; and, by a well applied raillery and ridicule, to bring the sentiments of the disaffected into contempt, with a view of effac-ing them not only from the conversation but from the minds of men.

By the time that Mr. Fielding had attained the age of forty-three, he had been so incessantly pursued by reiterated attacks of the gout, that he was rendered wholly incapable of continuing any longer in the practice of a barrister. He was obliged, there-fore, to accept of an office not a little unpopular, and which is liable to many injurious imputations, namely, that of an active magistrate in the commission of the peace for Middlesex. In this situation he gave strong evidence of his attention to the calls of duty. His solicitude to render himself an useful citizen, was manifested by the various tracts which he published, relative to several of the penal laws, and to the vices and mal-practices which those laws were intended to restrain.

It might have been expected that these various and pressing employments, united with the tortures of the gout, would have damped the vigour of Mr. Fielding's imagination; but this is not the case. His invention subsisted in its full activity, and he found leisure to amuse himself, and afterwards the publick, with the history of Tom Jones. This was the second grand epoch of our author's genius, when all his faculties were in perfect unison, and conspired to produce a complete work. It is observed, by Mr.

Murphy, that in the progress of Henry Fielding's talents there seem to have been three remarkable periods. The first was, when his genius broke forth at once with an effulgence superior to all the rays of light it had before emitted, like the sun in his morning glory, without the ardour and blaze which afterwards attended him; the second, when it was displayed with collected force, and a fulness of perfection, like the sun in meridian majesty, with all his highest warmth and splendour; and the third, when the same genius, grown more cool and temperate, still continued to cheer and enliven, but shewed, at the same time, that it was tending to its decline, like the same sun, abating from its ardour, but still gilding the western hemisphere. The history of Tom Jones is indeed a wonderful performance, whether we consider the fruitfulness of its invention, the admirable delineation and variety of its characters, the conduct of the story, or the winding up of the whole: nor is it surprising that it should have received the warmest encomiums, or that it should continue (and probably will always continue) to be one of the most popular novels that ever was produced. Mr. Murphy's copious and critical illustration of its merit is highly interesting. The work was dedicated to the Honourable George Lyttelton, (afterwards Lord Lyttelton,) by whose desire our author first thought of such a composition, who perused the manuscript when completed, and who gave it his entire approbation. Considering his religious dispositions, it is rather extraordinary that he should not make the objection which many virtuous minds have justly done to the looseness of Tom Jones's character. It should appear, however, that neither Mr. Lyttelton nor Mr. Fielding entertained any suspicion that the performance was blameable on this account, if we may judge from the language which the latter gentleman had used in his dedication. "From the name," says he, "of my patron, indeed, I hope my reader will be convinced, at his very entrance on this work, that he will find in the whole course of it nothing prejudicial to the cause of Religion and Virtue; nothing inconsistent with the strictest rules of decency, nor which can offend even the chastest eye in the perusal. On the contrary, I declare, that to recommend goodness and innocence hath been my sincere endeavour in this history. This honest purpose you have been pleased to think I have attained: and, to say the truth, it is likeliest to be attained in books of this kind; for, an example is a kind of picture, in which virtue becomes as it were an object of sight, and strikes us with an idea of that loveliness which Plato asserts there is in her naked charms."

From the period of the publication of Tom Jones, the vigour of our author's mind sunk, though by slow degrees, into a decline. "Amelia," which was published at the close of the year 1751, and which was dedicated to his great friend Ralph Allen, esq. has indeed the marks of genius, but of a genius beginning to fall into decay. Mr. Fielding does not appear in this performance to have lost the fertility of his invention, and his judgment seems to have been as strong as ever; but the warmth of his imagination is abated; and in his landscapes or his scenes of life he is no longer the colourist which he was before. The personages introduced in the work delight too much in narrative; and there are not in the characters those touches of singularity, those specific differences, which are so beautifully marked in our author's former productions. The humour, of course, loses here much of its high flavour and relish. Nevertheless, "Amelia" holds the same proportion to "Tom Jones," that the "Odyssey" of Homer bears, in Longinus's estimation, to the "Iliad." In various respects it breathes a fine vein of morality; many of the situations are affecting and tender; and, upon the whole, it is the Odyssey, the moral and pathetic work of Henry Fielding. "Amelia," in Mr. Murphy's edition of our author's writings, is printed from a copy corrected by his own hand. The exceptionable parts are retrenched, and the performance will be found less blameable than it was in its original state. While Mr. Fielding was planning and executing this piece, it ought not to be forgotten, that he was distracted by that multiplicity of avocations with which a public magistrate is surrounded; and that his constitution was labouring under attacks of the gout, which, of course, were severer than ever. Nevertheless, the activity of his mind was not to be subdued; for, no sooner was one literary pursuit ended than fresh game arose. He immediately engaged in a periodical paper, under the title of "The Covent Garden Journal, by Sir Alexander Drawcansir, Knight, Censor General of Great Britain." This paper was published twice in every week, viz. on Tuesday and Saturday; and it conduced so much to the entertainment of its readers, for a twelvemonth together, that there was a general regret when Mr. Fielding's bad state of health obliged him to discontinue the undertaking. There are in the collection various essays of such good sense and fine humour, that they would have been admired in the lucubrations of the "Tatler" and "Spectator." The choicest of them are preserved in the twelfth volume of our author's works. Soon after the "Covent Garden Journal" was dropped, Mr. Fielding's whole frame of body was so entirely shattered by continual inroads of complicated disorders, and the incessant fatigue of business in his office, that, by the advice of his physician, he set out for Lisbon, in hopes of profiting by the genial air of that climate. At this time a dropsy had risen to so great a height, that he was obliged to submit to repeated operations of tapping. However, notwithstanding his distressful situation, his imagination still continued to make strong efforts to display itself; and the last gleams of his wit and humour faintly sparkled in the account he left behind him of his voyage to Portugal. In about two months after his arrival at Lisbon, his strength became quite exhausted, and he yielded up his breath on the eighth day of October, 1754, and in the forty-eighth year of his age. Our author married a second wife, by whom he left four children, to whose education, Mr. Ralph Allen, in conjunction with their uncle, Sir John Fielding, largely contributed. One of them is now a barrister of considerable reputation, and an active police magistrate at Queen-square, Westminster.

We shall conclude the testimony to our author's literary excellence, with the concise and elegant encomium passed upon him by the late Mr. James Harris. This ingenious and learned gentleman, having treated of the absurd manner in which the plots of tragedies and comedies are often wound up, adds as follows: "A witty friend of mine, who was himself a dramatic writer, used pleasantly, though perhaps rather freely, *to damn the man who invented fifth acts*. So said the celebrated Henry Fielding, who was a respectable person both by education and birth, having been bred at Eton school and Leyden, and being lineally descended from an Earl of Denbigh. His Joseph Andrews and Tom Jones may be called master pieces in the comic epopee, which none since have equalled, though multitudes have imitated; and which he was peculiarly qualified to write in the manner he did, both from his life, his learning, and his genius. Had his life been less irregular, (for irregular it was, and spent in a promiscuous intercourse with persons of all ranks,) his pictures of human kind had neither been so various nor so natural. Had he possessed less of literature, he could not have infused such a spirit of classical elegance. Had his genius been less fertile of wit and humour, he could not have maintained that uninterrupted pleasantry, which never suffers his readers to feel fatigue*."

There are not so many little anecdotes preserved concerning Mr. Fielding as might perhaps have been expected considering the eccentricity of his disposition, and his talents for conversation. In the opinion of Lord Lyttelton, he had more wit and humour than Pope, Swift, and all the other wits of that time put together. But when our author died, the passion for collecting every trivial incident concerning literary men, or every expression uttered by them, had not taken place; or, at least, was far from being carried to the height which has lately been done.

THOMAS GAINSBOROUGH

M R. THOMAS GAINSBOROUGH, the justly-celebrated Painter, was born at Sudbury in Suffolk in 1727. His father, on his outset in life, was possessed of a decent competency; but a large family and a liberal heart soon lessened his wealth. The son very early discovered a propensity to Painting. Nature was his teacher, and the woods of Suffolk his academy, where he would pass in solitude his mornings, in making a sketch of an antiquated tree, a marshy brook, a few cattle, a shepherd and his flock, or any other accidental objects that were presented. — In the neighbourhood of his father was a very respectable Clergy-man, of the name of Coyte. With the sons of this gentleman young Gainsborough and his brothers passed much of their time, and from the instructions of the old man reaped some advantage. The Parson's garden having been plundered of a great quantity of wall-fruit, much pains was taken, but without effect, to dis-cover the thief. Young Gainsborough having, one Summer morning, risen at an early hour, and walked into the garden to make a sketch from an old elm, seated himself in an obscure corner, and had just taken out his chalk to begin, when he observed a fellow's head peeping over the wall of the garden, which was next the road, with an apparent intention of seeing if the coast was clear. He made a sketch, upon a rough board, of

---

*Harris's Philological Inquiries, pp. 163, 164.

the head of the man; and so accurate was the resemblance, that he was instantly known to be a man from a neighbouring village; and, upon a close enquiry, proved to be the fellow who had before robbed the garden. — From delineation he got to colouring; and, after printing several landscapes from the age of ten to twelve, he quitted Sudbury in his thirteenth year, and came to London, where he commenced Portrait-painter; and from that time never put his family to the least expence. The person at whose house he principally resided was a Silversmith of some taste; and from him, he was ever ready to confess, he derived great assistance. Mr. Gravelot the Engraver was also his patron, and got him introduced at the old Academy of the Arts in St. Martin's-lane. He was afterwards placed under the tuition of Mr. Hayman, with whom he did not long remain; but afterwards, for a short time, resided in Hatton-garden, and practised painting of portraits of a small size, and also pursued his favourite subject, Landscape. In or about the year 1747 he married a young lady, who possessed an annuity of 200*l.*; and then, retiring to Ipswich, lived in a house of which the rent was only 6*l.* a year. When Mr. Thicknesse was first appointed Lieutenant-governor of Landguard Fort, he found Mr. Gainsborough in this humble habitation. Both Mr. Thicknesse and his neighbours were at that time strangers to his genius; which they first discovered by a similar accident to that which had marked Gainsborough's first outset in life; for the young Painter, seeing a country fellow, with a *slouched* hat, looking wishfully over his garden-wall at some wind-fall pears, he caught up a bit of board, and painted him so inimitably well, that the board was shaped out, and the figure set upon a wall in a gentleman's garden at Ipswich, where it attracted the notice of Mr. Thicknesse, and induced many to speak to *that melancholy-looking figure.* - - Mr. Gainsborough about 1758 removed from Ipswich to Bath, where he began painting portraits at the low price of five guineas for a three-quarter canvas; and was soon so successful as to be encouraged to raise his price to eight guineas. (His last prices in London were forty guineas for a half, and one hundred for a full length.) In 1761, for the first time, he sent some of his works to the Exhibition in London. In 1774 he quitted Bath; and settled in London, in a part of the Duke of Schomberg's house in Pall Mall. In this situation, possessed of ample fame, and in the acquisition of a plentiful fortune, he was disturbed by a complaint in his neck, which was not much noticed upon the first attack, nor was it apprehended to be more than a swelling in the glands of the throat, which it was expected would subside in a short time; but it was soon discovered to be a cancer, which baffled the skill of the first medical professors. Finding the danger of his situation, he settled his affairs, and composed himself to meet the fatal moment, and expired Aug. 2, 1788. He was buried, according to his own request, in Kew Church-yard.

DAVID GARRICK

THIS excellent Actor, whose name will ever be held in respect by the admirers of theatrical representations, was the son of Peter Garrick, a captain in the army, who generally resided at Litchfield. He was born at Hereford, where his father was on a recruiting party, and baptized Feb. 20, 1716, as appears by the church register of the parish of All Souls in that city. His mother's maiden name was Clough, daughter to one of the vicars in Litchfield cathedral. At the age of ten years he was put under the care of Mr. Hunter, master of the grammar-school at Litch-field; and very early shewed his attachment to dramatic enter-tainments, having in the year 1727 represented the character of Serjeant Kite in the Recruiting Officer with great applause. From school he went to Lisbon, to visit his uncle; but stayed only a short time there before he returned to England; on which he went again to Mr. Hunter; and in 1735 became the pupil of Mr. Samuel Johnson, who about that time undertook to teach the classics to a certain number of young gentlemen. But even under this most able tutor, the vivacity of his character unfitted him for serious pursuits, and his attachment to the Drama prevailed over every other object. After a time, Mr. Johnson grew tired of teaching; and Mr. Garrick being desirous of a more active life, the tutor and pupil took the resolution to quit Litchfield, and try their fortunes in the Metropolis. They accordingly set out to-gether, on the 2d of March, 1736; and on the 9th of the same month, Mr. Garrick was entered of Lincoln's Inn, it being then intended that the Law should be his profession. Having had a recommendation from Mr. Walmsley to Mr. Colson, master of the school at Rochester, he, on the death of his uncle, about 1737, went directly thither, with a view to finish his education. In the company of so rational a philosopher as Mr. Colson, he was imperceptibly and gradually improved in the talent of thinking and reasoning; nor were the example and precepts of so wise a man vainly bestowed on a mind so acute as that of Garrick. His father died soon after, and was not long survived by his mother. He then engaged in the wine trade, in partnership with his brother, Peter Garrick; but this connexion lasting but a short time, he resolved to try his talents on the stage; and in the summer of 1741 went down to Ipswich, where he acted with great applause, under the name of Lyddal. The part which he first performed was that of Aboan, in the tragedy of Oroonoko. After a summer spent in the country, he determined to venture on the London stage. He had now essayed his powers, and considered himself as worthy to appear in a high form on any theatre; but it is generally said, that the then directors of Drury Lane and Covent Garden could not be induced to entertain the same sentiments. He was therefore obliged to accept the offer of Mr. Giffard, master of Goodman's Fields play-house, who engaged him; and he made his first appearance there on the 19th of October, 1741, with great success, in the character of Richard the Third. [It appears by Davies's "Life of Garrick," that the audience at first were totally at a loss whether to clap or hiss," &c.] This deserves to be insisted on, as it shews how little qualified people are to judge *of any thing* at first. Afterwards, when half a dozen people had thought proper to declare their approbation, then servility, fashion, &c. followed of course, and joined the cry. I know nothing of music; but it is certain that the merit of the Italian music, which, like their painting, is undoubtedly the best in the world, was not only not perceived in England at first (and in France not yet), but such people as Addison endeavoured publicly to decry it as bad.

The seeing a young man, in no more than his twenty-fourth year, reaching at one single step to that height of perfection which maturity of years and long practical experience had not been able to bestow on the then capital performers of the English stage, was a phænomenon which could not but become the object of universal speculation, and as universal admiration. The theatres towards the court-end of the town were on this occasion deserted, persons of all ranks flocking to Goodman's Fields, where Mr. Garrick continued to act till the close of the season, when, having very advantageous terms offered him for performing in Dublin during some part of the summer, he went over thither, where he found the same just homage paid to his merit, which he had received from his own countrymen. In the ensuing winter, however, he engaged himself to Mr. Fleetwood, manager of Drury Lane playhouse; in which theatre he continued till the year 1745, in the winter of which he again went over to Ireland, and continued there through the whole of that season, being joint manager with Mr. Sheridan in the direction and profits of the theatre royal in Smock Alley. From thence he returned to England, and was engaged for the season of 1746 with the late Mr. Rich, patentee of Covent Garden. This was his last performance as an hired actor; for in the close of that season, Mr. Fleetwood's patent for the management of Drury Lane being expired, and that gentleman having no inclination farther to pursue a design by which, from his want of acquaintance with the proper conduct of it, or some other reasons, he had already considerably impaired his fortune, Mr. Garrick, in conjunction with Mr. Lacy, purchased the property of that theatre, together with the renewal of the patent; and in the winter of 1747, opened it with the best part of Mr. Fleetwood's former company, and the great additional strength of Mr. Barry, Mrs. Pritchard, and Mrs. Cibber, from Covent Garden. In this station Mr. Garrick continued until the year 1776, with an interval of two years, from 1763 to 1765, which he devoted to travelling abroad; and, both by his conduct as a manager, and his unequalled merit as an actor, from year to year, added to the entertainment of the publick, which with an indefatigable assiduity he consulted. Nor were the publick by any means ungrateful in returns for that assiduity. By the warm and deserved encouragement which they gave him he was raised to that state of ease and affluence, to which it must be the wish of every honest heart to see superior excellence exalted. After his return from his travels, Mr. Garrick declined the performance of any new character; but continued to appear every season in some of his favourite parts until the year 1776; when, satisfied with the wealth he had acquired, and the fame which he had established, in familiarity with many of the most respectable persons of the kingdom, he retired to the enjoyment of repose from the fatigues of his profession, and quitted the stage on the 10th day of June, 1776, after performing the character of Don Felix, in Mrs. Centlivre's comedy of The Wonder. At this period the stone, a disorder to which he had been long subject, began to make such inroads on his constitution, that the happiness which he expected from retirement was often interrupted, and sometimes destroyed, by the violence of the pain he endured. He had been used to try the effects of quack medicines, to relieve him from the torments which he suffered, and it has been thought that his health received much injury from this injudicious mode of tampering with his malady. At Christmas 1778 he visited Earl Spencer at Althorpe, where he was taken ill, but recovered sufficiently to return to London, and died at his house in the Adelphi, after a few days illness, on the 20th of January, 1779. His body was interred with great funeral pomp, in Westminster Abbey, on the 1st of February following. Mr. Garrick in his person was low, yet well-shaped, and neatly proportioned; and, having added the qualifications of dancing and fencing to that natural gentility of manner which no art could bestow, but with which our great mother Nature endows many even from infancy, his deportment was constantly easy, natural, and engaging. His complexion was dark, and the features of his face, which were pleasingly regular, were animated by a full black eye, brilliant and penetrating. His voice was clear, melodious, and commanding; and, although it might not possess the strong overbearing powers of Mr. Mossop's, or the musical sweetness of Mr. Barry's, yet it appeared to have a much greater compass of variety than either; and, from Mr. Garrick's judicious manner of conducting it, enjoyed that articulation and piercing distinctness, which rendered it equally intelligible, even to the most distant parts of an audience, in the gentle whispers of murmuring love, the half-smothered accents of infelt passion, or the professed and sometimes awkward concealments of an aside speech in comedy, as in the rants of rage, the darings of despair, or all the open violence of tragical enthusiasm.

"Were it our office to record the failings of Mr. Garrick, we could only persuade ourselves to observe, that they were chiefly such as are overlooked in characters of less distinguished opulence and celebrity. We forbear therefore to violate his fame by a safe but ungenerous recapitulation of petty errors; adding only, in excuse for his well-known vanity, that perhaps no man who had been fed with such excess of praise, would have exhibited fewer marks of self-approbation. We hope, indeed, we may be forgiven, if we dwell longer on a singular inconsistence in his character, which has been often mentioned, but never fairly stated. He has been loudly praised for liberality, and as loudly censured on the score of avarice. Perhaps the alternate predominance of qualities, so opposite in their natures, may be thus accounted for. In any exigence that presented itself on a sudden, he was readily generous, because he knew benevolence was the most popular of virtues, and that the exertion of it would be expected from the possessor of a fortune extensive as his own. But this hasty impulse was occasionally blasted by intermediate reflection. During the interval that sometimes necessarily passed between the promise and the actual disbursement, the tedious process by which he had acquired a sum equal to that he was expected to part with, impressed itself forcibly on his imagination. It was not till then that his disposition inclined to parsimony. This ungraceful narrowness, this inglorious repentance, is often detected among those in whose thoughts their own gradual advance towards wealth is always uppermost; and the frequent occurrence of an idea, like this, to Mr. Garrick, will assist us in reconciling the contradictory tales of his deficiency and excess of bounty; for to deny that he was sometimes magnificent in his donations, would be to refuse his memory a tribute that can only be withheld at the expence of notoriety and truth. Such, however, was the fate of his pecuniary favours, that he often forfeited the gratitude due to them, through his backwardness in yielding what he had pledged himself to bestow, and did bestow at last. By some, indeed, he has been charged with raising hopes of relief, and finally disappointing them. This charge however, if true, can be imputed only to a stronger and less resistible operation of the cause already mentioned. In the mean time, his example serves to shew us how resolutely we ought to seize the moment that disposes our wavering natures to benevolence, as second thoughts are not always propitious to the interests of humanity. We may conclude by adding, that deliberation, so useful on many occasions, in respect to poetry and charity, exerted a fatal influence over Akenside and Garrick. It unstrung the lyre of the one, and contracted the heart of the other. Need I say that this paragraph was written by Mr. Steevens?

To Mr. Garrick's reputation as an actor, the concern of the publick at having lost him, bears a stronger testimony than panegyrick, in any other form, could supply. As to his particular *forte* or superior cast in acting, it would be perhaps as difficult to determine it, as it would be to describe minutely his several excellences in the very different parts in which he at different times thought proper to appear. Particular superiority was swallowed up in his universality; and should it even be contended, that there have been performers equal to him in their respective casts of playing, yet even *their* partizans must acknowledge, that there never existed any one performer that came near his excellence in so great a variety of parts. Every passion of the human breast seemed subjected to his powers of expression; even Time itself appeared to stand still, or advance, as he would have it. Of this no one can be ignorant who ever saw him in the several characters of Lear or Hamlet, Richard, Dorilas, Romeo, or Lusignan; in his Ranger, Bays, Drugger, Kitely, Brute, or Benedict. During the course of his management, the publick were much obliged to him for his indefatigable labour in the conduct of the theatre, and the pains he took to discover and gratify their taste: and, though the situation of a manager will perpetually be liable to attacks from disappointed authors and undeserving performers; yet, it is apparent, from the barrenness both of plays and players of merit for some years at the opposite theatre, that Mr. Garrick cannot have refused acceptance to many of either kind, that were any way deserving of the town's regard. In short, notwithstanding this is not the age of either dramatic or theatrical genius, the pains he took in rearing many tender plants, added several valuable performers to the English stage, whose first blossoms were far from promising so fair a fruit as they have since produced:— and among the several dramatic pieces which made their first appearance on the theatre in Drury Lane, there are very few, whose authors have not acknowledged themselves greatly indebted to Mr. Garrick for useful hints or advantageous alterations, to which their success has in great measure been owing. Add to this the revival of many pieces of the more early writers; pieces possessed of great merit, but which had, either through the neglect or ignorance of other managers, lain for a long time unemployed and unregarded. But there is one part of theatrical conduct which ought unquestionably to be recorded to Mr. Garrick's honour, since the cause of virtue and morality, and the formation of public manners, are very considerably dependent on it; and that is, the zeal with which he ever aimed to banish from the stage all those plays which carry with them an immoral tendency, and to prune from those which do not absolutely on the whole promote the interests of vice such scenes of licentiousness and libertinism as a redundancy of wit and too great liveliness of imagination have induced some of our comic writers to indulge themselves in, and to which the sympathetic disposition of an age of gallantry and intrigue had given a sanction. The purity of the English stage was certainly much more fully established during the administration of this theatrical minister than it had ever been during preceding managements : for what the publick taste had itself in some measure begun, he, by keeping that taste within its proper channel, and feeding it with a pure and untainted stream, seemed to have completed : and to have endeavoured as much as possible to adhere to the promise made in the prologue which was spoken at the first opening of that theatre under his direction,

"Bade scenic virtue form the rising age,
And Truth diffuse her radiance from the stage."

His superiority to all others in one branch of excellence, however, must not make us overlook the rank in which he is entitled to stand as to another; nor our remembrance of his having been the *first actor* living, induce us to forget that he was far from being the *last writer*. Notwithstanding the numberless and laborious avocations attending on his profession as an actor, and his station as a manager, yet still his active genius was perpetually bursting forth in various little productions both dramatic and poetical, whose merit cannot but make us regret his want of time for more extensive and important works. Of these he has publicly avowed himself the author of thirty-five, some of which are originals, and the rest translations or altera- tions from other authors, with a design to adapt them to the present taste of the publick. Besides these, Mr. Garrick was the author of an Ode on the death of Mr. Pelham, which, in less than six weeks, ran through four editions. The Prologues, Epilogues, and Songs, which he wrote, are almost innumerable, and possess a considerable degree of happy conception and execution. It would be in vain to attempt any enumeration of them; and it is less necessary, as we cannot doubt but some one of his surviving friends will take care to give a complete edition of his works, in such a manner as will do honour to his memory.

WILLIAM GED

WILLIAM GED, an ingenious artist, was a goldsmith in Edinburgh, and made his improvement in the art of printing in 1725. The invention was simply this. From any types of Greek or Roman, or any other character, he formed a plate for every page or sheet, of a book, from which he printed, instead of using a type for every letter, as is done in the common way. This was first practised, but on blocks of wood, by the Chinese and Japanese, and pursued in the first essays of Coster, Gutenberg, and Faust, the European inventors of the present art. "This improvement," says James Ged, is principally considerable in three most important articles; viz. "expence, correctness, beauty, and uniformity." But these improvements were controverted by Mr. Mores and others. In July 1729, William Ged entered into partnership with William Fenner, a London Stationer, who was to have half the profits, in consideration of his advancing all the money requisite. To supply this, Mr. John James, then an Architect at Greenwich (who built Sir Gregory Page's house, Bloomsbury Church, &c.) was taken into the scheme; and afterwards his brother, Mr. Thomas James, a Founder, and James Ged, the inventor's son. In 1730 these partners applied to the University of Cambridge for printing Bibles and Common Prayer Books by blocks instead of single types, and, in consequence, a lease was sealed to them April 23, 1731. In their attempt, they sunk a large sum of money, and finished only two Prayer-books; so that it was forced to be relinquished, and the lease was given up in 1738. Ged imputed his disappointment to the villainy of the pressmen and the ill-treatment of his partners (which he specifies at large), particularly Fenner, whom John James and he were advised to prosecute, but declined it. He returned to Scotland in 1733, and had no redress. He there, however, set about Sallust, which he printed at Edinburgh in 1736, 12mo. Fenner died insolvent in or before the year 1735; and his widow married Mr. Waugh, an Apothecary, who carried on the printing-business with her, and whom she survived. Her printing materials were sold in 1768. James Ged, wearied with disappointments, engaged in the Rebellion of 1745 as a Captain in Perth's regiment; and, being taken at Carlisle, was condemned, but, on his father's account, by Dr. Smith's interest with the Duke of Newcastle, was pardoned, and released in 1748. He afterwards worked for some time, as a journeyman, with Mr. Bettenham, and then commenced master; but, being unsuccessful, he went privately to Jamaica, where his younger brother William was settled as a reputable Printer. His tools, &c. he left to be shipped by a false friend, who most ungenerously detained them to try his skill himself. James Ged died the year after he left England; as did his brother in 1767. In the above pursuit Mr. Thomas James, who died in 1738, expended much of his fortune, and suffered in his proper business; "for the Printers," says Mr. Mores, "would not employ him, because the block-printing, had it succeeded, would have been prejudicial to theirs." Mr. William Ged died, in very indifferent circumstances, Oct. 19, 1749, after his utensils were sent for Leith to be shipped for London, to have joined with his son James as a Printer there. Thus ended his life and project; which, ingenious as it seemed, must," says Mr. Mores, "had it succeeded, have soon sunk under its own burthen," for reasons needless here to recapitulate. — [See the "Biographical Memoirs of William Ged, including a particular Account of his Progress in the Art of Block-printing," published by J. Nichols in 1781, 8vo.] — It is but justice, however, to add, that, since that period, the plan has been revived, first by my friend Mr. Alexander Tilloch, the learned Editor of "The Philosophical Magazine," who, without having known of Ged's plan, obtained a patent for a similar invention, which he afterwards relinquished. But the exertions of Mr. Andrew Wilson have been more successful; as he has been able to accomplish several very considerable *Stereotype* Editions.

RICHARD GOUGH

IN a Work indeed devoted to the commemoration of Literary Ornaments of the Eighteenth Century, and more particularly of those who were the intimate associates of Mr. BOWYER; it would be unpardonable to neglect the name of Mr. GOUGH; a name endeared also to my own feelings by every social and every grateful recollection. I shall here, therefore, enlarge the Memoirs which appeared in the Gentleman's Magazine, and were prefixed to the "Catalogue of his Library," originally formed on the basis of long and unreserved habits of intimacy, and from materials furnished by himself.

"RICHARD GOUGH was born Oct. 21, 1735, in a large house in Winchester-street, London, on the site of the Monastery of the Austin Friars, founded by Humfry de Bohun, Earl of Hereford and Essex, in the year 1253.

"He was the only son of Harry Gough, Esq. by Elizabeth his wife, daughter of Morgan Hynde, esq. of London; who, with two brothers, raised a fortune by the breweries in Long Acre and Portpool-lane; originating from some village in Dorsetshire, which themselves forgot; and, being Dissenters, were not registered."

Of his father Mr. Gough was proud, and justly proud; but I shall copy his own words:

"Harry Gough, esq. of Perry hall, was born April 2, 1681, whom the Editor of the new edition of Camden's Britannia justly "glories in calling father," was highly distinguished for his abilities by some excellent judges of their merit. He went, when only eleven years old, with Sir Richard Gough, his uncle, to China, kept all his accompts, and was called by the Chinese *Ami Whangi,* or the *white-haired boy.* In 1707 he commanded the ship Streatham; his younger brother Richard purser, 1709. He continued to command this ship till 1715; and with equal ability and integrity he acquired a decent competency, the result of many hardships and voyages in the service of the East-India Company, to which his whole life was devoted while he presided among their Directors, being elected one of them in 1731, if not sooner. Possessed of great application and great activity, one of his friends used to say, "if he would take the whole East-India Company on him, he must answer for it; for nobody would assist him, though they would contradict him." Nor was his duty in Parliament less attended to, while he represented the borough of Bramber, from 1734 to his death, and refused several offices from the then Chancellor of the Exchequer, Sir Robert Walpole, afterwards Earl of Orford, whose confidence he possessed. The long and late debates during the opposition to that Minister hurt his health; for he would often go to the House with a fit of the gout coming on. He purchased, 1717, of the wife of Sir Richard Shelley, one moiety of the Middlemore estate in Warwickshire (the other moiety of which he before possessed); which afterwards descended to his son and heir Richard, together with the property at Enfield, which he purchased in 1723, and from which, in compliment to him, an East-India ship took her name, in 1730.

At the very early age of eleven Richard Gough commenced a task that would have reflected credit on any period of life; which, by the indulgence of his Mother, appeared in print, under the title of "The History of the Bible, translated from the French, by R. G. Junior, 1746. London, printed [by James Waugh] in the year 1747." Of this curious Volume, consisting of 160 sheets in folio, no more than 25 copies were printed, as presents to a few particular Friends; and, when completed at the press, it is marked, by way of colophon, "*Done at twelve years and a half old.*"

Another juvenile work was, "The Customs of the Israelites; translated from the French of the Abbot Fleury, by R. G. 1750," 8vo. [This was also printed by Mr. Waugh; but not for sale.]

He had also fully prepared for the press, even to the title-page and preface, a work of infinite labour and research, under the title of "*Atlas Renovatus*; or, Geography modernized."

"On the death of his father, which happened July 13, 1751, Mr. Gough was admitted, in July 1752, fellow-commoner of Bene't college, Cambridge, where his relations Sir Henry Gough and his brother John had before studied under Dr. Mawson, afterwards successively Master of his College, and Bishop of Landaff, Chichester, and Ely. The College tutor, 1752, was Dr. John Barnardiston, afterwards Master.

"His private tutor was the Rev. John Cott, fellow of the College, son of the Town-clerk of Lynne, and afterwards rector of Braxted in Essex, where he died in 1781, having married a niece of the late Dr. Keene, Bishop of Chester.

"Under the immediate tuition of the three excellent Scholars before mentioned, Mr. Gough early imbibed a taste for Classical Literature and Antiquities; and it is not to be wondered at that his connexion with a College eminent for producing a succession of British Antiquaries inspired him with a strong propensity to the study of our National Antiquities. Here was first planned the BRITISH TOPOGRAPHY."

From Cambridge, July13—16, 1756, he visited Peterborough, Croyland, and Stamford. He continued these visits every year to various parts of the kingdom, taking notes, which, on his return, were digested into a form which furnished materials for the new edition of CAMDEN'S BRITANNIA, the result of twenty years excursions."

Mr. Gough was much respected and esteemed by the great Philanthropist JOHN HOWARD; who frequently pressed him to become his travelling companion. In 1767, particularly, he strongly endeavoured to persuade him to take a trip to Holland; assuring his mother that "he would take great care of the young voyager;" and in 1769 invited him as earnestly "to pass over to Calais, spend the winter at Geneva, and visit Italy in the Spring."

"Feb. 26, 1767, he was elected Fellow of the Society of Antiquaries of London; and, by the partiality of the late worthy President, Dr. Milles, Dean of Exeter," (his own words are here used) "was, on the death of Dr. Gregory Sharpe, Master of the Temple, nominated Director of the same Society, 1771; which office he held till Dec. 12, 1797, when he quitted the Society altogether.

"He was chosen Fellow of the Royal Society of London 1775; but quitted that Society also in 1795.

"He opened a correspondence with Mr. URBAN in 1767, with an account of the village of Aldfriston in Sussex, under the signature of D. H.; which signature he retained to the last, but not altogether uniformly; nor is another signature in some later volumes with the same letters to be mistaken for his. And on the death of his fellow-collegian Mr. Duncombe, in 1786, the department of the Review in that valuable Miscellany was, for the most part, committed to him. If he criticised with warmth and severity certain innovations attempted in Church and State, he wrote his sentiments with sincerity and impartiality — in the fullness of a heart deeply impressed with a sense of the excellence and happiness of the English Constitution both in Church and State.

"In 1768 he published, in one quarto volume, his "Anecdotes of British Topography;" re-printed in two of the same size in 1780; and left ready for a *third edition,* with many considerable additions.

"In 1773 he formed the design of a new edition of CAMDEN'S BRITANNIA, which he was seven years translating, and nine printing, and which was published in three volumes, folio, 1789."

This National Work was thus properly inscribed:

"To the Patron of Arts and Sciences, the Father of his People, GEORGE III. who has condescended to encourage Researches into Antiquity, this Work, the earliest general Account of his Kingdom, is humbly dedicated by his most dutiful Subject,   RICHARD GOUGH."

Of this valuable work it may not be superfluous to observe, that Mr. Gough translated it from the original, and supplied his additions, with so little interruption of the ordinary intercourse of life, that none of his family were aware that he was at any time engaged in so laborious an undertaking. The copy-right he gave (without any other consideration than a few copies for presents) to his old and worthy friend Mr. Thomas Payne; who defrayed the expence of engraving the copper-plates; and afterwards disposed of the whole of his interest in the work to Messrs. Robinsons.

"Having purchased the Collections of Mr. Thomas Martin, he put out an improved "History of Thetford, 1779," 4to; with plates from views taken by the then Captain Grose, who accompanied him in the snowy season of 1778.

"Having also purchased the plates of the Medals, Coins, and Great Seals, executed by the celebrated Simon, and first published by Vertue in 1753, he gave a new and enlarged edition of them in 1780.

"He assisted Mr. Nichols in the "Collection of Royal and Noble Wills, 1780;" to which he wrote the Preface, and compiled the Glossary.

In 1781 he was chosen an honorary member of the Society of Antiquaries at Edinburgh; and in 1785 of a similar Society at Perth.

"In 1786, he published the first volume of the SEPULCHRAL MONUMENTS OF GREAT BRITAIN, applied to illustrate the History of Families, Manners, Habits, and Arts, at the different Periods from the Norman Conquest to the Seventeenth Century. With Introductory Observations. Vol. I. Containing the First Four Centuries." This splendid Volume was published without the Author's name; about which, however, there was no secrecy, as the Plate of his Family Arms appears in the Title-page.

The Second Volume, published in 1796, and an Introduction to it in 1799, contained the Fifteenth Century; with which Mr. Gough thought proper to conclude his labours, instead of continuing the Work to the end of the Sixteenth Century, as was originally intended.

This truly magnificent work would alone have been sufficient to perpetuate his fame, and the credit of the Arts in England; where few works of superior splendour have before or since appeared. The independent master of an ample fortune, he was in all respects pre-eminently qualified for the labours of an Antiquary;

the pain of whose researches can but rarely meet an adequate remuneration. This magnificent work must long ago have convinced the world, that he possessed not only the most indefatigable perseverance, but an ardour which no expence could possibly deter.

"He drew up the History of the Society of Antiquaries of London, prefixed to the first volume of their Archaeologia, 1770.

"He assisted in the copious, well-digested, and accurate 'History of Leicestershire;' undertaken and conducted with a perseverance which would baffle common County Historians, by the same Friend; to whose benevolence, impartiality, and integrity, he is proud to bear this public testimony."

"Having purchased, at the sale of the late Matthew Duane, Esq. the Plates of the Coins of the Seleucidæ, Kings of Syria, in his Collection, engraved by Bartolozzi, he drew up an account of the several reigns under which they are arranged; with the Inscriptions remaining in honour of some of the Sovereigns, and particularly that discovered (in the late possession of Egypt by his Majesty's troops) in honour of Ptolemy Epiphanes, King of Egypt, connected with this period through Antiochus IV. or Epiphanes, King of Syria. This work was published in 4to, 1803.

"In the same year he was called upon by the express desire of his friend Mr. Manning, to assist in the publication of his 'History of Surrey,' in which William Bray, esq. of Shere, was a principal coadjutor, of which the first volume appeared in 1804; a second in 1810; and the third and last is now in the press.

"He counted some of the first Antiquaries of the Three Kingdoms among his Correspondents; but, having once incorporated their observations in his various publications, he guarded their correspondence from the impertinence of modern Editors.

"Of his own Notes, written in Printed Books, he had made the BRITISH MUSEUM the depository; though, like others of his friends, *he never attained to the honour of being one of the Trustees;* which, he has heard it observed, should be the *blue ribband of literary men,* and is now become an object of successful canvass.

"So unambitious was he of public honours, that, as he took no degree at Cambridge, and that University confers no honorary ones, he resisted the solicitations of many members of the Sister University, and of his old and valuable friend Dr. Pegge, to share his honours with him in 1791; though he felt real satisfaction in assisting at them, and retained to the last a grateful sense of the good wishes of that learned Seminary.

"In Politicks, he was, as his Father had been before him, a firm friend to the House of Brunswick, and a stranger to the mutability of his contemporaries. That independence which he gloried in possessing as his inheritance, and which he maintained by a due attention to his income, discovered itself in his opinions and his attachments. As he could not hastily form connexions, he may seem to have indulged strong aversions. But he could not accommodate himself to modern manners and opinions; and he had resources within himself, to make it less needful to seek them from without. And perhaps the greatest inconvenience arising from this disposition was the want of opportunities to serve his friends. But he saw enough of the general temper of mankind, to convince him that favours should not be too often asked; and that as to be too much under obligation is the worst of Bondage, so to confer obligations is the truest Liberty."

The account thus far given of Mr. GOUGH, the greatest part of which is literally from his own pen, it may now be allowable to enlarge.

One of the most prominent features in his character was an insatiable thirst for Literature; and particularly that branch of it in which he so eminently excelled, the study of our National Antiquities. Young as he was at the time of his Father's death, in 1751; not having then attained his 16th year; an only son, with the certainty of inheriting a plentiful fortune; his attention was principally turned to the improvement of his mind, and the foundation of a noble Library. Hence the pleasurable diversions of the age to him had little charms. The well-stored shop of *honest Tom Payne* at the Mews Gate, or the auction-rooms of the *two Sams,* Baker and Paterson, had beauties far transcending the alluring scenes of fashionable dissipation.

At Cambridge his studies were regular and severe; diverted only by occasional visits to the Metropolis; or by excursions to various parts of the kingdom.

His attentions, meanwhile, were not so entirely devoted to Literature, as to exclude him from social duties and the rational pleasures of life.

Aug. 18, 1774, soon after the death of his Mother, an event by which he came into possession of an excellent family residence at Enfield, with the large estate bequeathed to him in reversion by his Father, he added considerably to his other comforts, by marrying Anne, fourth daughter of Thomas Hall, esq. of Gold-

ings, Herts; a lady of distinguished merit; whose family was
equally respectable with his own; and who, after a long and
happy union, has to lament the loss of him whose object through
life was to increase her happiness.

Those only who have had the satisfaction of seeing Mr. Gough
in his domestic and familiar circle can properly appreciate his
merits. Though highly and deservedly distinguished as a scholar,
the pleasantry and the easy condescension of his convivial hours
still more endeared him, not only to his intimates, but even to
those with whom the forms and customs of the world rendered
it necessary that he should associate.

There was, however, another class of society to which, if
possible, he was still more dear — the poor and the afflicted, to
whom he was at all times a father, a protector, and a benefactor.

The faithful domestick, when unable to continue his services,
continued to receive his pay, in the shape of an annuity, with
additional comforts.

Greatly as the blessing of a long life is to be esteemed, the
circumstances which attend it are often of the most afflicting
nature; and amongst these, the loss of our earliest and most
valuable friends is not the least distressing. This observation is
not new; but it forcibly recurs, on recollecting the valuable
Friend who is the subject of this memoir.

During the period of more than thirty years, in which the
present Editor of the Gentleman's Magazine has had the melancholy satisfaction of recording the departure of numberless
Worthies with whom it has been his happiness and his pride
to have formed an intimacy, he never felt himself so inadequate
to the task. The loss of Mr. Gough was the loss of more than a
Brother — it was losing a part of himself.

For a long series of years he had experienced in Mr. Gough
the kind, disinterested friend; the prudent, judicious adviser; the
firm, unshaken patron. To him every material event in life was
confidentially imparted. In those that were prosperous, no man
more heartily rejoiced; in such as were less propitious, no man
more sincerely condoled, or more readily endeavoured to
alleviate.

The bright gem of intellect, though frequently clouded, had
intervals of its former splendour; and the frequent emanations of
benevolence displayed through a long and painful illness, whilst
they comforted and delighted those around him, added poig-
nancy to the regret they experienced for those bitter sufferings,

which threatened to overwhelm a noble mind with total imbecility; from which he was mercifully relieved, without any apparent struggle at the last, on the 20th of February 1809; and was buried on the 28th, in the church-yard of Wormley, Herts, in a vault built for that purpose, on the South side of the chancel, not far from the altar which for several years he had devoutly frequented.

His Library (with the exception of the valuable Department of British Topography bequeathed to the Bodleian Library), was sold, agreeably to his own direction, by Messrs. Leigh and Sotheby, in 20 days, beginning April 5, and ending April 28, 1810; and produced 3552*l*. 3*s*.

His Prints, Drawings, Coins, Medals, Seals, Painted Glass, Paintings, Pottery, Brass Monuments, Marble Fragments, Chinese and other Bronzes, Miniatures, and Miscellaneous Antiquities, were sold July 19, 1810, and the two following days; and produced 517*l*. 6*s*. 6*d*.

By his last will, Mr. Gough gave to the UNIVERSITY OF OXFORD all his printed Books and Manuscripts on Saxon and Northern Literature, "for the use of the Saxon Professor :" — all his "Manuscripts, printed Books and Pamphlets, Prints and Drawings, Maps, and Copper Plates, relating to British Topography (of which, in 1808, he had nearly printed a complete Catalogue); his interleaved Copies of the "British Topography," "Camden's Britannia," and the "Sepulchral Monuments of Great Britain," with all the Drawings relative to the latter Work; and all the Copper Plates of the "Monuments" and the "Topography." — And XIV Volumes of Drawings of Sepulchral and other Monuments in France." — All these he wills and desires may "be placed in the BODLEIAN LIBRARY, in a building adjoining to the Picture Gallery, known by the name of *The Antiquaries Closet*, erected for keeping Manuscripts, printed Books, and other Articles relating to British Topography; so that all together they may form one uniform Body of English Antiquities."

THOMAS GUY

" MR. GUY, in Lombard-street, makes an eminent figure in the Company of Stationers, having been chosen Sheriff of London, and paid the fine; and is now [1695] a Member of Parliament for Tamworth. He entertains a very sincere respect for English Liberty. He is a man of strong reason, and can talk very much to the purpose, upon any subject you will propose. He is truly charitable, of which his Alms-houses for the Poor are standing testimonies." *Dunton,* p. 281. — This generous Benefactor was the son of Thomas Guy, citizen and carpenter, who was by profession a lighterman and coal-dealer in Horseley-down, Southwark. He was bound apprentice, Sept. 2, 1660, for eight years, to Mr. John Clarke, Bookseller, in the porch of Mercers chapel; and, in 1668, having taken up his freedom, and been admitted a Liveryman of the Company, set up trade with a stock of about 200*l.* near Stocks Market, in the house which forms the angle between Cornhill and Lombard-street. The English Bibles being at that time very badly printed, Mr. Guy engaged with others in a scheme for printing them in Holland, and importing them; but, this being put a stop to, he contracted with the University of Oxford for their privilege of printing them; and, having been admitted into the Court of Assistants of the Stationers Company, he carried on a great Bible-trade for many years to considerable advantage. Thus he began to accumulate money, and his gains rested in his hands; for, being a single man, and very penurious, his expences were next to nothing. His custom was, to dine on his shop-counter, with no other table-cloth than an old newspaper; he was also as little nice in regard to his apparel. The bulk of his fortune, however, was acquired by purchasing seamen's tickets during Queen Anne's wars, and by South-sea stock in the memorable year 1720. To shew what great events spring from trivial causes, it may be observed, that the publick are indebted to a most trifling incident for the greatest part of his immense fortune's being applied to charitable uses. Mr. Guy had a maid-servant, whom he agreed to marry; and, preparatory to his nuptials, he had ordered the pavement before his door to be mended so far as to a particular stone which he marked. The maid, while her master was out, innocently looking on the paviours at work, saw a broken place they had not repaired, and mentioned it to them; but they told her that Mr. Guy had directed them not to go so far. "Well," says she, "do you mend it : tell him I bade you, and I know he will not be angry." It happened, however, that the poor girl presumed too much on her influence over her wary lover, with whom the charge of a few shillings extraordinary turned the scale entirely against her : for Guy, enraged to find his orders exceeded, renounced the matrimonial scheme, and built Hospitals in his old age. In 1707, he built and furnished three wards on the North side of the outer court of St. Thomas's Hospital in Southwark; and gave 100l. to it annually for eleven years preceding the erection of his own Hospital. Some time before his death, he erected the stately iron gate, with the large houses on each side, at the expence of about 3000l. Aug. 5, 1717, he offered to the Stationers Company, through the medium of his friend Mr. Richard Mount, 1000l. "to enable them to add 50l. a year, by quarterly payments, to the poor members and widows, in augmentation of the quarterly charity;" also 1100l. "to be paid quarterly to such charitable uses as he should appoint by his will, in writing;" and a further sum of 1500l. to have 75l. a year paid quarterly for another charitable purpose, to be appointed in like manner;" in default of such appointments the sum of 125l. to be paid annually by the Company of St. Thomas's Hospital.* And, no appointment having been made, the same is now regularly paid by the Hospital. He was 76 years of age when he formed the design of building the Hospital near St. Thomas's which bears his name. The charge of erecting this vast pile amounted to 18,793l. besides 219,499l. which he left to endow it : and he just lived to see it roofed in. He erected an alms-house with a library at Tamworth, in Staffordshire (the place of his mother's nativity, and which he represented in parliament), for 14 poor men and women; and for their pensions, as well as for the putting out of poor children apprentices, bequeathed 125l. a year. To Christ's Hospital he gave 400l. a year for ever : and the residue of his estate, amounting to about 80,000l. among those who could prove themselves in any degree related to him. He died Dec .17, 1724, in the 81st year of his age, after having dedicated to charitable purposes more than any one private person upon record in this kingdom.

---

*Demolished about 1865 to make room for S.E. Rly. The hospital was removed to Walworth and later to its present site opposite the Houses of Parliament. [Ed.]

WILLIAM HERBERT

M R. HERBERT indefatigably pursued his favourite study [the history of typography] till his death, which happened, from a dropsical complaint, March 15, 1795, in his 77th year. The various labours of this good man's life deserve the public acknowledgment. His career commenced in the service of the East India Company, as purser's clerk to three of their ships. That which was to take in a lading of pepper stopped at Tellicherry, and, before she had completed her lading, an alarm of six French men of war was given. The Governor demanded 30 men out of each ship, as he had power to do, for the defence of the place; and the ships sailed away without lights round the Lucadine Islands, and by Mount Delhi, to Bombay. After the alarm was over, they returned, and sent Mr. Herbert, in a miserable boat, full of bugs, and without change of linen, to demand their men, whom the Governor refused to give up, and he returned: but the ships having left their station, the boat could not find them; and the wind being against him, he was obliged to remain at Tellicherry, being engaged to return to his ship by the middle of July. He was obliged to undertake a journey over-land on the 16th of that month, with a Portuguese boy, who understood a little English, Portuguese, and *Parriar,* or *lingua Franca,* 12 sepoys, 8 porters, in all 20, besides himself and boy, and went round by sea to Calicut, before he ascended the heights, with two Bramins, who were bound by their *caste* to conduct him safe. The anxiety at not meeting the ships at the appointed time he did not recover from for a twelvemonth; though he rejoined them, Aug. 8, at Fort St. David, Fort St. George being in the hands of the French. At his return, having produced a number of plans of the several settlements, he received from his honourable masters 300*l.* These plans were afterwards incorporated into a publication by Bowles, printseller, near Mercers chapel. Mr. Herbert set up the business of a printseller and engraver of charts on London-bridge, and continued in it till the houses on the bridge were taken down. The first night he spent in his house on the bridge, he was witness to a dreadful fire in some part of London, on the banks of the Thames, which, with several other succeeding ones, suggested to him the thought of a floating fire-engine. He proposed it to Captain Hill, of the Royal Exchange Assurance, who told him, "there must be a fire every now and then, for the benefit of insurance." He published his proposal in the Gazetteer, and it was soon adopted. He retired with an easy fortune; though, by his first marriage, he had nearly forfeited his expectations to what his aunt received by marriage with Dr. Porter, the physician, and had at her own disposal; and which, by the persuasion of some common friends, she gave to Mr. Herbert. He married to his second wife a niece of the Rev. Mr. Newman, pastor of the meeting in Carter-lane; and to the third, a sister of Mr. Croshold of London, and daughter of John Croshold, mayor of Norwich (who, by Mary, second daughter of the late Thomas, and brother to Robert Masham, esq. of Stratton Strawless, co. Norfolk, had issue Alexander, who died student of Caius college, Cambridge, 1748, and three daughters, Mary, Philippa, married to Mr. Herbert, and Sarah, who died April 3, 1795, leaving her fortune to her sister Mrs. Herbert). — Robert Masham, esq. uncle Mr. Herbert, was the representative of that family settled at Stratton Strawless, in South Erpingham hundred, Norfolk, from the middle of the 14th century. (See Blomefield, III. 593, 4.) The plates of Sir Richard Atkins's "History of Gloucestershire" having escaped the fire which, in 1712-3, destroyed Mr. Bowyer's printing-office; and, except two or three, fallen into the hands of Mr. Herbert; he caused the lost ones to be supplied, and republished the work in 1768, correcting the literal errors, but not restoring to their proper place several particulars pointed out in the original errata. Great part of this second edition was also destroyed by fire. The active mind of Mr. Herbert did not stop here. After the death of Mr. Ames, and the dispersion of the materials which had been collected for the "History of Printing in Great Britain and Ireland," he stept forward to resume the subject. While he resided in Gulston-square, Whitechapel, his application to possess himself of every article of information that libraries or auctions could furnish him with, was intense. The encouragement he received from the collectors of *black letter* books, from his Majesty's library to the smallest library of an individual, he has gratefully acknowledged in the preface to his new edition of Mr. Ames's " Typographical Antiquities," in three volumes; the first in 1785; the second, 1786; the third, 1790; all the volumes paged in continuation. If there were not a limit assigned by a wise and kind Providence to human life and human proficiency, we should say that Mr. Herbert wore himself out by too close an application to his favourite pursuit. But who can say this of a man who had attained almost the verge of his 77th

year? Who can say this, who knows how little his faculties were
impaired by his long life? Who, that knew his integrity, simplicity, and modesty, and how punctually he fulfilled the relative,
social, and public duties required at his hands, can presume to
imagine he will lose the reward of a long and happy life?

THOMAS HOLLIS

THOMAS HOLLIS, of Corscombe, in the county of Dorset,
esq. was born in London, April 14, 1720. This nominal
birth-day Mr. Hollis ever afterwards, without regard to the
change of style, continued to observe. His great-grandfather
Thomas, of Rotherham in Yorkshire, a whitesmith by trade, and
Baptist by persuasion, settled in London during the Civil Wars,
and died there, in 1718, aged 84, leaving three sons, Thomas,
Nathaniel, and John. Of these the eldest, Thomas, a considerable
merchant, is chiefly memorable for his benefactions to New-
England, particularly to Harvard college in Cambridge (where
he founded a professorship, scholarships, &c.) to the amount of
near 5000*l.* in which his brothers were joint contributors, without any restriction in regard to religious sects. Thomas, the only
son of Nathaniel, died in 1735 (three years before his father),
leaving one son, the subject of this note, and of course the heir
to his father, and also to his great-uncle Thomas, who died in
1730. His mother was the daughter of Mr. Scott, of Wolverhampton, in whose family Mr. Hollis was nurtured in his infancy. The above account will rectify a mistake which has
prevailed, of his being a descendant of Denzil Lord Holles,
though his grandfather used to say, they were of one family,
which separated in the time of Henry VIII. He was educated at
the free-school of Newport in Shropshire, till he was about eight
or nine years of age (probably), by a Mr. or a Dr. Lee; and afterwards at St. Alban's, by Mr. Wood. In his 13th or 14th year
he was sent to Amsterdam, to learn the Dutch and French
languages, writing, accompts, &c.; stayed there about fifteen
months; and then returned to London to his father, with whom
he continued till his death, in 1735. After this he was some years

in the house of his cousin Timothy Hollis, esq. His guardian was Mr. John Hollister, then treasurer of Guy's Hospital; who, to give him a liberal education, suitable to the ample fortune he was to inherit, put him under the tuition of Professor Ward, whose picture, to preserve his memory, Mr. Hollis presented to the British Museum; and, in honour of his father and guardian, he caused to be inscribed round a valuable diamond ring, *Mnemosynon Patris Tutorisque.* From Dr. Jeremiah Hunt, Dr. Foster, and other eminent persons, he imbibed that ardent love of liberty, and freedom of sentiment, which strongly marked his character. He professed himself a Dissenter. In 1739-40 he went to chambers in Lincoln's-inn, being admitted as a law-student; but does not appear to have studied the law as a profession, though he resided there till July 19, 1748, when he set out on his travels for the first time, and passed through Holland, Austrian and French Netherlands, part of France, Switzerland, Savoy, and part of Italy, and returned through Provence, Brittany, &c. to Paris. His fellow traveller was Thomas Brand, esq. of The Hyde, in Essex, his particular friend and future heir. His second tour, which commenced July 16, 1750, was through Holland to Embden, Bremen, Hamburgh, the principal cities on the North and East side of Germany, the rest of Italy, Sicily and Malta, Lorrain, &c. The journals of both his tours are preserved, and would be a valuable acquisition to the publick. On his return home, finding he could not obtain a seat in Parliament in the disinterested manner he wished, without the smallest appearance of bribery, he began his collection of books and medals, "for the purpose of illustrating and upholding liberty, preserving the memory of its champions, to render tyranny and its abettors odious, to extend science and art, to keep alive the honour and estimation of their patrons and protectors, and to make the whole as useful as possible; abhorring all monopoly; and, if such should be the fitness of things, to propagate the same benevolent spirit to posterity." Among Mr. Hollis's noble benefactions to foreign libraries, none is more remarkable than that of two large collections of valuable books to the public library of Berne, which were presented anonymously, as by "an Englishman, a lover of liberty, his country, and its excellent constitution, as restored at the happy Revolution." Switzerland, Geneva, Venice, Leyden, Sweden, Russia, &c. shared his favours. His benefactions to Harvard college commenced in 1758, and were continued every succeeding year, to the amount in all of 1400*l*. Dr.

Jonathan Mayhew, pastor of the West-church in Boston, was
his confidential friend and correspondent, and partook largely
of his esteem and beneficence. But his liberality to individuals, as
well as to public societies, cannot here be specified. Mr. Hollis
purchased at Mr. Charles Stanhope's sale, June 3, 1760, an
original of Milton when a boy, painted by Cornelius Jansen. A
fire happening at his lodgings in Bedford-street, Jan. 23, 1761,
he calmly walked out, taking the picture only in his hand. The
fire, however, was happily got under without any loss. A new
edition of Toland's Life of Milton was published under his care
and direction, in 1761. He presented, Oct. 29, 1761, an original
portrait of Sir Isaac Newton, painted by Zeeman, 1726, to
Trinity College, Cambridge. All the Tracts that were published
against the Jesuits he collected in 1762, and sent to the public
library of Zurich, having been slighted, as he thought, by the
Curators of the British Museum. In April 1763, Mr. Hollis gave
the publick a new and accurate edition of Algernon Sydney's
Discourses on Government, on which the pains and expence he
bestowed are almost incredible. His patronising this edition, and
other works of the same kind, procured him, and no wonder, the
name and reputation of a Republican. "Roma Antica," by the
Abbate Venuti, though a posthumous work, owed its birth to
Mr. Hollis. In 1763 his friend Count Algarotti published his
"Saggio sopra l'Academia de Francia che è in Roma," with a
Dedication to Mr. Hollis, to his great surprize, as, when he could,
he always declined such compliments. The noble library, philosophical apparatus, &c. of Harvard college, being consumed by fire,
Jan. 24, 1764, Mr. Hollis immediately subscribed 200*l.* towards
repairing the loss. In this year Mr. Locke's two Treatises on Government, and in the next his Letters on Toleration, were published
separately, under the auspices of Mr. Hollis. In June he presented some Egyptian Antiquities, anonymously, to Count Caylus
at Paris. Dr. Wallis's Latin Grammar of the English Tongue was
reprinted at Mr. Hollis's desire, to promote the knowledge of
our language among foreigners. The elegant preface prefixed was
written, as has been already said, by Mr. William Bowyer,
who was ever desirous of forwarding Mr. Hollis's public-spirited
intentions. A fine collection of books, intended by Mr. Hollis for
Harvard college, being burnt, with his bookbinder's house, June
6, he immediately began collecting "a finer parcel." One of his
presents this year being consigned to the public library, "if any,"
at Bermuda; on Dr. Mayhew's replying that he believed there

was none, the Biographers of Mr. Hollis add, "Though Bp. Berkeley's project of establishing and endowing a college at Bermuda miscarried, yet, one would think, he did not bring back the collection of books he intended for that foundation." He certainly did not, but it does not appear that he ever was at Bermuda, or got nearer to it than Newport in Rhode-Island. There he resided, and there he left his books. A second magnificent present of books was made by our Patriot to Berne this year. His expences in books, virtù, presents, charity, &c. amounted in 1764 to about 800*l*. and were seldom much less. In this year he sent to Sydney college, Cambridge, where Cromwell was educated, an original portrait of him by Cooper, since etched by P. S. Lambourne and J. Bretherton. — Dr. Mayhew died of a nervous fever, July 9, aged 49, "overplied," as Mr. Hollis expresses it, in Miltonic phrase, "by public energies." For a drawing of him, by Cipriani, from a picture at Boston, Mr. Hollis paid 30 guineas. Dr. Andrew Elliot succeeded to his correspondence. In 1767 Mr. Hollis's projected re-publications of Andrew Marvell's Works, and of Milton's Prose Works, both proved abortive. For a frontispiece to the latter, Cipriani had drawn and etched Milton victorious over Salmasius. In August 1770, Mr. Hollis carried into execution a plan which he had formed five years before, of retiring into Dorsetshire, and of his situation there he gives the following account, from *Corscombe, Sept.* 24 : "Retreat is now become more and more acceptable to me. Where I shall dwell afterwards precisely, I do not know at present; but as near to this place as may be. It is called Urles, or Urles-farm; and is a most healthy, and, I think, beautiful spot; the very earth itself is sweet beyond a nosegay; but the house is bad, and a very old farm-house. I thank God, I am well; but I feel, in several ways, the effects of my late long most rigid plan : I rise from six to seven, and to bed from eleven to twelve; and the whole day, each to the other, passes in such a variety of transactions, some not personal and of scope, that I am often surprized at the recollection of them. That of which I am most chary, is my time; and people knowing the streightness of my apartment, and that I mean well under certain singularities, are cautious enough, in general, not to break in upon and consume it. The idea of singularity, by way of shield, I try by all means to hold out." Early in the afternoon of New Year's-day, 1774, Mr. Hollis was in a field at some distance from his place of residence at Corscombe, attended by only one workman, who was receiving his directions concerning a tree which had been lately felled. On a sudden, he put one of his fingers to his forehead, saying, "Richard, I believe the weather is going to change; I am extremely giddy." These words were scarcely off his lips, when he fell on his left side. The man sprang to his assistance, and, raising him up, administered what little relief he could. He was still sufficiently himself to say, "Lord have mercy upon me; Lord, have mercy upon me; receive my soul;" which were the last words he was able to pronounce. His lips moved afterwards, but no sound was formed, and he expired presently after. The following quaint character of this extraordinary man appeared in one of the public prints some years before his death, July 5, 1770: "Thomas Hollis is a man possessed of a large fortune; above the half of which he devotes to charities, to the encouragement of genius, and to the support and defence of liberty. His studious hours are devoted to the search of noble authors, hidden by the rust of time; and to do their virtues justice, by brightening their actions for the review of the publick. Wherever he meets the man of letters, he is sure to assist him; and, were I to describe in paint this illustrious citizen of the world, I would depict him leading by the hands Genius and distressed Virtue to the Temple of Reward." Mr. Hollis, in order to preserve the memory of those heroes and patriots for whom he had a veneration, called many of the farms and fields in his estate at Corscombe by their names; and by these names they are still distinguished. In the middle of one of these fields, not far from his house, he ordered his corpse to be deposited, in a grave ten feet deep, and that the field should be immediately plowed over, that no trace of his burial-place might remain. In the testamentary disposition of his fortune he shewed himself as much superior to common connexions as he affected to be through life; for, without the least regard to his natural relations, he bequeathed all his real, and the residue of his personal estate, to his dear friend and fellow-traveller, Thomas Brand, esq. of The Hide, in Essex, who took the name and arms of Hollis, and whose first application of his liberality was to solicit a seat in Parliament. — To the books which Mr. Hollis published, or procured to be published, before mentioned, may be added the following: "Nedham's Excellence of a Free State;" "Neville's Plato Redivivus" (a re-publication of Mr. Spence's edition); "Neville's Parliament of Ladies," and "Isle of Pines." — This note is preserved nearly as originally written. But it is proper to observe, that very copious "Memoirs of Mr.

Hollis" compiled by Archdeacon Blackburne, were printed, in
two splendid volumes, in 4to, 1780, with a considerable number
of copper-plates, by Bartolozzi, Basire, and other engravers of
eminence. In the frontispiece is introduced an admirable profile
of Mr. Hollis.

JOHN HOOLE

THE fondness of this benevolent Poet for literature shewed
itself when he was a boy, so as to make him a favourite with
his schoolmaster, while his harmless and gentle disposition caused
him to be beloved by his schoolfellows. He quitted school well
versed in the Latin and French languages, with a small portion
of the Greek. He was perfectly master of arithmetick, a most
excellent penman, and possessed a good talent in drawing; but
his knowledge of Italian was entirely his own acquiring after he
quitted school. His father, Mr. Samuel Hoole, who then carried
on a branch of the watch-making business (which, by the use of
some newly-invented engines, of his own construction, he had
rendered very profitable), wished to have brought him up in his
own trade, and actually began to teach him the use of his tools;
but to this way of life Nature had opposed an insuperable bar,
for John Hoole was so very short-sighted that he could not practise the trade without great inconvenience, nor, in some respects,
without danger, from the fragments of brass and steel to which
his eyes, by their near approach to his work, were exposed. He
was not, however, wanting in mechanical talents, for he not only
completed some pieces of work with his own hands, but, in
many respects, was assisting to his father in the machinery which
he constructed for Mr. Rich, the then proprietor of Covent-
garden theatre. Being prevented from exercising any mechanical
calling, he was placed in the service of the East-India Company,
in their Accomptants' office, under Mr. Hort, the chief accomp-
tant; of whose abilities, integrity, and kind treatment of the young
men under his care, he always spoke with respect. While in this
office, Mr. Hoole formed an intimate connexion with several
clerks in the Company's service of his own age, particularly Mr.

Peter Corbett, Mr. John Winter, Mr. Ranceford Tookey, and Mr. John Tristram; young men of good sense, but all singular or eccentric characters; and with them he spent many of his leisure hours. They used frequently to dine and sup together; but were never guilty of any such nocturnal revels as frequently disgrace the characters of young gentlemen. Their youthful parties were always entertaining, and often whimsically diverting. Mr. Hoole's principal amusement, however, was at the theatre, where he had free access behind the scenes, in virtue of his father's being machinist; but thence arose an inconvenience which his father had not foreseen; namely, that the son had begun to conceive a great relish for a theatrical life, so as to form serious thoughts of appearing on the stage : but his father having declared his entire disapprobation of such a measure, he would not indulge his propensity any farther than by privately amusing himself and his friends with the rehearsal of different plays. Mr. Hoole used to tell a story of a whimsical distress he was brought into by his short-sightedness, while performing the part of the Ghost in "Hamlet," at the Little Theatre in Lincoln's-inn-fields (now Spode's China warehouse); for, having almost finished his speech to young Hamlet, and coming near to the period when the Ghost descends, he was not able to discern the place where the trap-door would open, and, fearing either to miss the spot, and to be left standing on the stage, or of meeting with some accident, by the trap-door opening where he did not expect it, he protracted his speech as much as he could — "But soft — methinks I scent the morning air — brief let me be," &c. at the same time feeling about the stage with his foot for the trap-door, while his friend, who acted as prompter, in as great distress as himself, cried, in a whisper, "Here Jack, here Jack, a little more this way." He, however, luckily hit the right place, and descended with proper ghostly dignity. — Together with his attachment to poetry, Mr. John Hoole was not indifferent to the Loves and Graces; his heart was early susceptible of the tender passion. In 1757 he married Miss Susannah Smith, of Bishop Stortford, who was frequently called the handsome Quaker; and, in marriage with her, he formed a connexion with two very worthy families, the Smiths of Bishop Stortford, and the Etheredges of Buntingford; and through them he became acquainted with Mr. John Scott, of Amwell, by profession a Quaker, but a good poet, and author of many pleasing and well-known productions. He also received every testimony of regard from the Quakers in general;

for, though that society are averse to marriages with those of a different persuasion, yet no sect whatever could have refused their cordial friendship to a man of Mr. Hoole's disposition. During the early part of Mr. Hoole's marriage his appointments at the India-house were but slender. This, however, he supplied by his industry; and, at his leisure hours, laboured indefatigably in making out the invoices for the Company's outward-bound ships, and moreover employed himself in translating French publications relative to the transactions of that nation in India during the war of 1756, commonly called the Seven Years War. Upon Mr. Hoole's removal from the Accomptants-office to that of the Auditor of India Accompts, he not only enjoyed a more lucrative post than in his former station, but also the constant company of Mr. Oldmixon, the chief of that office, who, like himself, was a reader of the Italian language, and an admirer of poetry in general. It was probably at the instance of this gentleman that Mr. Hoole determined on writing his tragedy of "Cyrus;" and, that he might complete it without interruption, he, in the autumn of 1767, having obtained leave of absence from the India-house, suddenly disappeared from among his friends and acquaintance in London, till they began to be seriously alarmed about him, particularly his mother, who then lived in Moorfields with her youngest son and daughter. She was, however, at length relieved from her anxiety, by a letter from Mr. John Hoole to his brother, inviting him to his retreat, which proved to be a small house at the Thames side, at Wandsworth, in the neighbourhood of Mr. Oldmixon; and, upon Mr. Samuel Hoole's repairing thither, he found his brother in good health, who merrily acquainted him with the cause of his absconding. This rural retirement was so much to Mr. John Hoole's taste, that he continued in the house for several years, and took great pleasure in passing to and fro by water, having, at the same time, chambers in Clement's-inn. In September, 1770, Mr. Hoole had the misfortune to break the patella or knee-pan of his leg by a fall, in the dusk of the evening, down a flight of steps, which were then at the end of George's-court, Clerkenwell, but which, soon afterwards, as if it had been to save others from a like accident, were taken away, and the place made a gradual slope. This fracture, which is deemed by the faculty very difficult to treat, and very tedious in the cure, confined him to his bed in Clement's-inn for several months, during which time he was constantly and carefully attended by that

eminent surgeon Mr. Richard Grindall, who had a great friendship for him; and his long confinement was alleviated by frequent
visits from his numerous friends and acquaintance. As soon as
he was so far recovered as to be able to quit his chamber, he
removed to his mother's house in Moorfields, where a bed was
provided for him on the ground-floor, to save the necessity of
going up and down stairs, and two chairmen came regularly
every day, with what is called a boot-chair, having an extended
cavity at the bottom, to permit the leg being placed in a straight
posture; and thus he was conveyed to attend his duty at the
India-house. This fracture of the patella generally produces a
stiffness in the joint, which ever afterwards prevents the patient
from walking without difficulty; and this was a cause of great
anxiety on the part of Mr. Hoole. He did indeed, for some
time, experience that inconvenience, though not to so great a
degree as he expected. But, a few years afterward, he had the
misfortune (if it is to be so called) of breaking his knee-pan a
second time; and, after this second fracture was healed, he found
the joint became more flexible; and, consequently, he could walk
with more ease. The same accident befell him a third time, and
with the like success; for, the joint of his knee now allowed full
motion to the leg, by which means he walked, all the remainder
of his life, with great ease and vigour, and with little or no appearance of limping in his gait. — He died Aug. 2, 1803, in his
76th year. Mr. Hoole first displayed his poetical talents in an
elegy on the death of Mrs. Woffington, the celebrated actress.
He translated the works of Tasso, Ariosto, and Metastasio, if
not with congenial fervour of imagination, yet with correctness,
elegance, and taste. His Tasso's "Jerusalem delivered" has gone
through several editions. In 1767 he published "The Works of
Metastasio, translated from the Italian," 2 vols. 12mo. In 1773,
the first volume of a Translation of Ariosto's "Orlando Furioso,"
and, ten years after, he published it complete, in 5 vols. 8vo;
in 1791, the "Orlando" of Ariosto, reduced to 24 books, the
narrative connected, and the stories disposed, in a regular series,
2 vols. 8vo; and, 1792, a Translation of Tasso's "Rinaldo," in
1 vol. 8vo. He was the author of three dramatic pieces, the
tragedies of "Cyrus," "Timanthes," and "Cleonice, Princess of
Bythinia." The first two pieces were derived from Metastasio.
They were performed with tolerable success, particularly the
tragedy of "Cyrus," the fable of which is very interesting, and
which was animated by noble sentiments, well expressed. This

play had the advantage of being supported by the talents of Powell, in the zenith of his fame; by those of Smith, when he was a great favourite with the publick; and by those of Mrs. Yates, when she was in the maturity of beauty and theatrical repute. The tragedy of "Cleonice" was by no means so successful. Indeed, it fell a victim to the severity of Criticism, which has capriciously suffered many worse performances to enjoy a better fate. Mr. Hoole conducted himself very liberally on this occasion, by returning a considerable part of the money which he had received for the copy-right, alledging, that, as the piece was not successful on the stage, it could not be very profitable to the bookseller, and ought not to be a loss.

JACOB ILIVE

T. ILIVE was the father of Jacob, whom Mr. Rowe Mores thus describes: "Jacob Ilive was a printer, and the son of a printer; and had two brothers, Abraham and Isaac, who were both likewise printers. Abraham died at Oxford in 1777. Jacob applied himself to letter-cutting [1730], and carried on a foundery and a printing-house together: in the year 1734 he lived in Aldersgate-street, over against Aldersgate coffee-house. Afterwards, when Calasio was to be reprinted under the inspection of Mr. Romaine, or of Mr. Lutzena a Portuguese Jew, who corrected the Hebrew, as we ourselves did sometimes another part of the work, he removed to London House (the habitation of the late Dr. Rawlinson), where he was employed by the publishers of that work. In 1751 Mr. Ilive published a pretended translation of The Book of Jasher, said to have been made by one Alcuin of Britain. The Account given of the translation is full of glaring absurdities; but of the publication this we can say from the information of the only one who is capable of informing us, because the business was a secret between the two. Mr. Ilive in the night-time had constantly an Hebrew Bible before him (*sed qu. de hoc*) and cases in his closet. He produced the copy for Jasher, and it was composed in private, and the same worked off in the night-time in a private press-room. Mr. Ilive was an

expeditious compositor; he knew the letters by the touch." Rowe
Mores, Dissertation on Founders, p. 64.*

Ilive, who was somewhat disordered in his mind, was author
of several treatises on religious and other subjects. He published
in 1733 an Oration proving the plurality of worlds, that this
earth is hell, that the souls of men are apostate angels, and that
the fire to punish those confined to this world at the day of judgment will be immaterial, written in 1729, spoken at Joiners Hall
pursuant to the will of his mother, Elizabeth daughter of Thomas
James, a benefactor to Sion-college library, and descendant of
Dr. Thomas James librarian of the Bodleian. She was born 1689,
and died Aug. 29, 1733, and held the same singular opinions in
divinity as her son. He also published a second pamphlet,
called "A Dialogue between a Doctor of the Church of England
and Mr. Jacob Ilive, upon the subject of the Oration, 1733."
This strange Oration is highly praised in Holwell's third part of
interesting Events relating to Bengal. For publishing "Modest
Remarks on the late Bishop Sherlock's Sermons," he was confined
in Clerkenwell Bridewell from June 15, 1756, till June 10, 1758,
during which period he published "Reasons offered for the
Reformation of the House of Correction in Clerkenwell; shewing, 1. The present state of this gaol, the debauchery of the
prisoners, and the miserable condition they are in from the want
of a sufficiency of food, &c. 2. Proposals in what manner these
evils may be prevented for the future, humbly submitted to the
consideration of the magistrates and inhabitants of the County
of Middlesex. To which is prefixed a plan of the said prison
engraved on copper, with references describing the manner in
which this gaol should be altered for the purposes proposed,
with a calculation of the expence thereof. 1757;" 8vo; and "A
Scheme for the Employment of all Persons sent as disorderly to
the House of Correction in Clerkenwell; shewing, 1. that the profits of their labour will find them in a sufficiency of food; 2. pay
the keeper an annual salary; and 3. defray the other expences and
necessary repairs of the said gaol. The whole proving, that the
county by the execution of this scheme will soon save several
hundred pounds a year. 1759," 8vo. He projected also twelve
other *reforming* treatises; 1. of the city tythings, &c. 2. of the

---

*Mores also added that "he worked in a night-gown and swept his case
to pye with the sleeves." His father, Thomas Ilive, who worked in Aldersgate, was the first to print Hebrew books for Jews in England. (*Ed.*)

justices of the peace, &c. 3. of thief-takers, &c. 4. of sheriffs, &c. 5. of the office of chamberlain, &c. 6. a relation of his own examination of Hicks's-hall, July 13, 1757, on the subject of his plan for reforming the house of correction; 7. of the Saxon courts of justice, &c. 8. of the building the gaol of Newgate upon the proposed plan, &c. 9. of the orphans debt, &c. 10. of debts under five pounds, &c. 11. a scheme for the erection of county work-houses, &c. 12. of ecclesiastical affairs. The several titles are literally exhibited *at length* at the end of the above pamphlet. Neither of them has yet been published, and probably neither of them was ever finished."—"July 3, 1762, being Saturday, Mr. Jacob Ilive and others, having given notice to the several free-men of the Company of Stationers, to meet that day to choose master and wardens of the said company; the said Jacob Ilive was first chosen chairman, to conduct the business of the day. After standing on the upper table in the Hall, he thanked the freemen for the honour they had done him; laid before them several branches of the two charters; and proposed Mr. Chris-topher Norris, and some one else, to their choice for master; the former of whom was chosen. Then, in like manner, he proposed John Lenthall, esq. and John Wilcox, gent. with two others, for wardens. The choice fell on the said John Lenthall and John Wilcox. A committee was then appointed by the votes of the common-hall, to meet the first Tuesday in each month at the Horn Tavern in Doctors Commons, to enquire into the state of the Company, consisting of 21 persons; five of which, the master and wardens being of that number, were empowered to act as if the whole were present. July 6, being the first Tuesday in the month, the new-elected master came into the Hall about twelve, and was seated at the upper end of it. The Clerk of the Hall being sent for, he was desired to swear Mr. Norris into his office; but, upon his declining it, Mr. Ilive swore him in. A boy then offered himself to be bound; but, no warden being present, he was desired to stay till next month; when several others were bound, some freemen made, and others admitted on the livery; of whom, one at least has frequently polled on contested elections at Guildhall." [from a communication by Mr. Bowyer.]

JOSEPH JACKSON & THOMAS COTTRELL

IT is but common justice to mention in this place the names of Cottrell and Jackson, as Letter-founders who were trained up under the auspices, and pursued with commendable industry the steps, of their excellent instructor. Mr. Mores says, "Mr. Thomas Cottrell is in order *à primo proximus.* He was in the late Mr. Caslon's house, an apprentice to *dressing,* but not to *cutting.* This part he learned, as Mr. Moxon terms it, 'of his own genuine inclination.' He began in the year 1757, with a fount of English Roman;" [and afterwards cut a fount of Norman, intended (but not used) for Domesday-book]. "He lives in Nevil's-court, in Fetter-lane; obliging, good-natured, and friendly; rejecting nothing because it is out of the common way, and is expeditious in his performances." — Mr. Cottrell died in 1785, I am sorry to add, not in affluent circumstances, though to his profession of a Letter-founder were superadded that of a Doctor for the Tooth-ache, which he cured by burning the ear; and had also the honour of serving in the Troop of his Majesty's Life-guards.—"Mr. Joseph Jackson was in Mr. Caslon's house too, an apprentice to the whole art, into which he launched out for himself upon the same principle as did Mr. Cottrell; for, actuated by the same motives, they both flew off together. Mr. Jackson lives in Salisbury-court, in Fleet-street; he is obliging, and communicative, and his specimen will, *adjuvante Numine,* have place amongst the literate specimens of English letter-cutters." — Of Mr. Jackson Mr. Mores would have said more, if he had lived to witness the progress of his diligent exertions. He too, after cutting a variety of types for the Rolls of Parliament (a work which will ever reflect honour on the good taste and munificence of the present Reign), employed his talents on Domesday, and in a manner more successful than his fellow-labourer. I have much gratification in stating, that the two beautiful volumes of that valuable record were finished at the press in 1783, on a plan which I had the honour of projecting, and Mr. Jackson the skill to execute, under the title of "Domesday Book; sive Liber Censualium Willielmi Regis Angliæ, inter Archivis Regiis in Domo Capitulari Westmonasterii asservatus: Jubente Rege Augustissimo Georgio Tertio prelo mandatus. Londini, Typis J. Nichols, 1783." — To Mr. Jackson's Occidentals may also be added a beautiful Pica Greek, which he cut under the express direction of Mr. Bowyer, who used to say, "the types in common use were *no more Greek than they were English.*" And (under the direction of Joshua Steele, esq. the ingenious author of "Prosodia Rationalis, an Essay towards establishing the Melody and Measure of Speech,") Mr. Jackson augmented the number of *musical types,* by such as represent the emphasis and cadence of prose. *See Mores' Dissertation on Typographic Founders,* pp. 82, 83. 97. — Mr. Jackson, born in Old-street, Sept. 4, 1733, was the first child baptised in St. Luke's church; and received his education at a school in that neighbourhood, the gift of a Mr. Fuller; whence he was apprenticed to Mr. Caslon. Being exceedingly tractable in the common branches of the business, he had a great desire to learn the method of cutting the punches, which is in general kept profoundly secret; his master and master's father locking themselves in whenever they were at that branch of the business. This difficulty he surmounted by boring a hole through the wainscot, and observing them at different times, so as to form some idea of the mode in which the whole was performed; and applied himself at every opportunity to the finishing of a punch. When he had completed one to his own mind, he presented it to his master, expecting to be rewarded for his ingenuity : but the premium he received was a hard blow, with a threat that he should be sent to Bridewell if he again made a similar attempt. This circumstance being taken in dudgeon, his mother bought him what tools were necessary, and he improved himself at her house whenever he had an opportunity. He continued to work for his master, after he came out of his time, till a quarrel arose in the foundery about the price of work; and a memorial, which terminated in favour of the workmen, being sent to the elder Caslon (who was then in the commission of the peace, and had retired to Bethnal-green) young Jackson and Mr. Cottrell were discharged, as the supposed ringleaders. Compelled thus to seek employment, they united their slender stock in a partnership, and went on prosperously till, Jackson's mother dying, he entered, in 1759, on board the Minerva frigate, as armourer; and in May 1761 was removed, with Captain Alexander Hood, into the same situation in the Aurora; and proved somewhat successful, having about 40*l.* prize-money to receive at the Peace of 1763. During the time he was at sea, he was visited by a severe fit of sickness, in which he vowed, if he recovered, to lead in future a very penitent life; which promise he punctually fulfilled. On his return to London, he worked for some time under Mr. Cottrell; till, determining to adventure into business for himself, he was encouraged to do so by two Life-guardsmen, his fellow-workmen, who engaged to allow him a small pittance for subsistence, and to supply money for carrying on the trade, for two years. Taking a small house in Cock-lane, he soon satisfied his partners that the business would be productive before the time promised. When he had pursued his labours about six months, Mr. Bowyer accidentally calling to inspect some of his punches (for he had no specimen), approved them so much, that he promised to employ him; adding, "My father was the means of old Mr. Caslon riding in his coach: how do you know but I may be the means of your doing the same?" A short time after this, he put out a small specimen of one fount; which his young master carrying to Bethnal-green with an air of contempt, the good old Justice treated it otherwise; and desired his son "to take it home, and preserve it; and whenever he went to cuting again, to look well at it." It is but justice to the third William Caslon to add, that he always acknowledged the abilities of Jackson; and though rivals in an art which requires the greatest exertions of ingenuity, they lived in habits of reciprocal friendship. Business increasing rapidly, Mr. Jackson removed to Dorset-street, for a more capacious workshop; and about 1771 was applied to by the late Duke of Norfolk to make a mould to cast a hollow square. Telling the Duke that he thought this was practicable; his Grace observed, that he had applied to all the skilful mechanicks in London, Mr. Caslon not excepted, who declared it impossible. He soon convinced the Duke of his abilities; and in the course of three months producing what his Grace had been years in search of, was ever after held in great estimation by the Duke, who considered him as the first mechanick in the kingdom.—In 1762 he married Eliz. Tassell, originally a whinster in Spital-fields, a very worthy woman, and an excellent wife, who greatly contributed, by her care and industry, to his getting forward, on his first entering into business. She died Dec. 3, 1783, at the age of 49; and, in about six months after, he married Mary Pasham (the widow of a printer in Black Friars), who died Sept. 14, 1791, at the age of 52. Surviving the second of his wives but a few months, he died of a scarlet-fever, at his foundery, in Dorset-street, Salisbury-square, Jan. 14, 1792; and his remains were on the 23rd deposited, in the same grave with them both, in the front ground of the Spa-Fields Chapel, a neat oration being delivered on the occasion by the Rev. Mr. Towers; who preached also a funeral sermon on the 29th, at his meeting-house in Barbican, of which Mr. Jackson was one of the Deacons. By the death of this ingenious artist, and truly worthy man, the poor lost a most excellent benefactor, his own immediate connexions a steady friend, and the literary world a valuable coadjutor to their labours. To particularize the articles of his foundery which were more peculiarly superior, when all were excellent, would be unnecessary. Let it suffice to mention, as matters of difficulty and curiosity, the fac-simile types which he formed for Domesday Book, and for the Alexandrian New Testament; and, as a pattern of the most perfect symmetry, the types which printed the splendid edition of the Bible published by Mr. Macklin. Mr. Jackson had acquired some considerable property, the bulk of which, having left no child, he directed to be equally divided between fourteen nephews and nieces.—On his only apprentice, Mr. Vincent Figgins, the mantle of his predecessor has fallen. With an ample portion of his kind instructor's reputation he inherits a considerable share of his talents and his industry; and has distinguished himself by the many beautiful specimens he has produced, and particularly of Oriental types. And here I hope I shall not be accused of being ostentatiously vain, if I close this note with a P.S. which is subjoined at the particular request of the only person it could possibly offend. "I am greatly obliged to you for the very flattering mention of my name; but you have not done yourself the justice to record your own kindliness to me : that, on Mr. Jackson's death, finding I had not the means to purchase the Foundery, you encouraged me to make a beginning. You gave me large orders, and assisted me with the means of executing them; and, during a long and difficult struggle in pecuniary matters for fifteen years, you, my dear sir, never refused me your assistance : without which I must have given it up. Do mention this — that, as the first Mr. Bowyer was the means of establishing Mr. Caslon — his son, Mr. Jackson — it may be known, that Vincent Figgins owes his prosperity to Mr. Bowyer's successor."

THE JAMES FAMILY
PRINTERS AND LETTER FOUNDERS

MR. GEORGE JAMES was in this year (1724) appointed City Printer, in the room of Mr. Alderman Barber. Two of his brothers, John and Thomas, who distinguished themselves as letter-founders, will be noticed in a future page.— Harris James, originally a letter-founder, and related to this family, was formerly of Covent-Garden theatre, where he represented fops and footmen.

Thomas James, the father of George, who died in 1711, was thus characterized: "He is a man that reads much, knows his business very well, and is extremely obliging to his customers, and is something the better known for being husband to that she-state-politician Mrs. Elianor James." (Dunton, p. 334.)

This Mrs. Elianor James was a very extraordinary character, a mixture of benevolence and madness; an assertion that a perusal of the two following letters will fully justify.

1. "To the Lords Spiritual and Temporal assembled in Parliament.

"May it please your Lordships,

"I have read a Case that is before your Lordships, relating to one Dye; and I find he has been greatly baffled, and it appears to me that he is the injured person: and the consideration that he has been twenty years, and has borrowed two thousand pounds, which if he should lose, his children would be ruined; and these considerations moved me to humbly entreat your Lordships, for the love of justice, to consider the length of time, and the great charge, that right may take place, and that an end may be put to this suit: for justice is beautiful; and the God of justice bless your Lordships. My heart is wounded to think that England will be ruined if your Lordships don't stand in the gap: for what advantage can it be to England for Scotland to be united to it? Is the cruel usage wherewith they used the Episcopal churchmen there so soon forgot? Surely there is not a miracle wrought in them, that their natures should be changed: Therefore let England be England; and Scotland be as it is. And 'tis in your Lordships power to do good to the Church and Kingdom; for the King leaves it wholly to you, and to the House of Commons. Therefore so act, as you will answer before God, who has committed the Talent of power to your Trust; that you may employ it to his glory, and for the good of your country: and therefore give not the power out of your own hand: and God Almighty give your Lordships such wisdom, that you may be more than conquerors for the glory of God, and the good of the kingdom! Which that the Lord may grant, is the prayer of your humble servant, and souls' well-wisher,   ELIANOR JAMES."

2. "Mrs. James's Advice to all Printers in General.

"I have been in the element of Printing above forty years, and I have a great love for it, and am a well-wisher to all that lawfully move therein, and especially to you that are masters; therefore I would have you wise and just, and not willingly break the laws of God nor man, but that you would do by all men as you would desire they should do by you: and you cannot be ignorant of the great change in bringing up of servants in the art of printing; neither can you be insensible how remiss, provoking, and wasteful some servants are, especially when they are encouraged therein, by the unjust hope of getting away from their masters, and having over-work from other masters that have not had the charge and trouble of bringing them up, which is too frequently practised among you, to the ruin of the trade in general, and the spoiling of youth. For when a boy has served half his time, and has gained some experience in his trade, he presently begins to set up for conditions with his master; then he will not work unless he has so much for himself, and liberty to go where he pleases; which if his master denies, he then strives to vex his master, and waste his time and goods; and then when he beats him, away he runs with great complaints, when the master is all the while the sufferer; and it is no wonder to hear a boy that wants an honest principle to do his own duty, rail against and bely his master and mistress; for he thinks to excuse himself by blackening them. Now I would have this great evil prevented, and that you may easily do, if you will resolve to take no man's servant from him, and then a master may (as he ought) have the benefit of the latter part of his time, to make him amends for his trouble and charge, which is according to the will of God and good men. For if it should happen, that an apprentice by any trick should get away from his master, I would not have you give any encouragements, as money, but that he should serve the term of his indenture as an apprentice without; for giving him money makes him a journeyman before his time: for indeed, if there be any consideration, it ought to be given to the master that had the trouble and charge of bringing him up; and who will serve seven or eight years, if they can get off before? For besides, boys will have a thousand tricks to provoke their masters to anger, in trifling away their time, and flinging their houses into pie, except their masters will be under conditions to give them encouragements, and to give them that liberty to go where they will, and have money to spend, and this is to make the master the servant, and the boy the master; therefore, pray, brother, do not be guilty in destroying of youth, for it is the destruction of the trade. I desire you to take care not to bind any boy except he be above the age of fourteen, and the fewer the better. So I rest your sister and souls' well-wisher,

ELIANOR JAMES."

"Now to you, journeymen; you are my brothers, for my husband was a journeyman before he was a master, and therefore I wish you well: and take care that you are not guilty of any ill thing, as shewing servants ill examples, and giving bad counsels; for if you should, you would be like Judas, in betraying your master that employs you; for sober men, they scorn to be guilty of this crime; but for you of the worser sort, you are like devils, for you study how to do all manner of mischief to a good husband, for you hate them because they are better than yourself: had not you better imitate them, and pray to God to make you like them? For what benefit have you in starving your wives and children, and making yourselves sots only fit for hell? Pray, brothers, mend your faults, and pray to God to give you repentance, and to mend for the time to come, that you may be reconciled to God and man, which I heartily wish.

ELIANOR JAMES."

Mrs. James, at her death, was a generous benefactress to the church of St. Bene't, Paul's-wharf, where she gave some plate; and on a tablet in that church is this inscription:
"Anno 1710, Mrs. Elinor James, to prevent scandal, has thought fit to erect this table, to satisfy the world what she has given to her children since her husband's death." And then follow several sums, amounting to a few hundred pounds, with the dates annexed, which were divided between her daughters *Ilive* and *Saunders;* and a lease for 23 years, worth 26*l.* a year.

On another tablet: "Anno 1712. Mrs. Elinor James did, in her life-time, give to this parish of St. Benedict, Paul's-wharf, for the use of the Communion-table, a large basin furbelowed and gilt, weighing 55 oz.—a large dish, embossed and gilt, 40 oz. — a large salver, furbelowed and gilt, 41 oz. — a pair of embossed candlesticks and sockets, 30 oz. — a small dish, embossed and gilt, 7 oz. — a salver of 18 oz. and two others of 14 oz. each — one chalice, with a patten, 6 oz. — and two chalices without pattens; besides several other articles, and an embroidered valance for the pulpit."

In the Library of Sion College are portraits of the father and mother of Mr. George James; and of his great-grandfather; which Mr. Malcolm thus describes:

1. "Thomas James, S.T.P. 1627, æt. 57; first keeper of the Bodleian Library at Oxford. Given by his grandson's wife. A florid countenance, full face, and white beard. Dressed in a black gown, cap, and ruff.

2. "Thomas James, Typogs; presented by his wife; a half-length picture, seated in a chair, the legs and arms of which are spiral. He has a stern thin visage; his hair brown, and part grey, and a white beard. His dress is a loose white gown, over an embroidered coat; laced band and ruffles, and black cap.

3. "Elianora conjux Thomæ James;" a very good picture, whose features and eyes have a disordered and singular expression. Her hair is dark, and fancifully adorned with rich lace, which hangs over the shoulders in tasteful folds. Her gown is of red silk; and her hands are crossed on a book, the binding of which is most minutely finished, and very splendid. On a table open before her is a pamphlet, intituled, "A Vindication of the Church of England, by Mrs. James: in Answer to a Pamphlet, intituled, A new Test of the Church of England's Loyalty." Londinium Redevivum, vol. I. p. 34; vol. II. p. 471.

Mr. Thomas James had left his books by will to the use of the publick, and the president and fellows of Sion college wre indebted to his widow for giving them the preference: but Mr. Reading, in his Catalogue of that Library, observes that "Mrs. James, by virtue of a clause in her husband's will, claimed all the duplicates in his study. Accordingly some scores of folios, and some hundreds of smaller books, were returned. She insisted also that her husband's books, given *anno* 1711, might stand together in a distinct part of the Library; and was so far gratified, that the stalls were enlarged (*anno* 1720), and all the books digested anew, in order to print the foregoing Catalogue; which I hope will answer the utmost expectations of every Benefactor's

friends, since now all the world may read his name subjoined
to all the books which he has given."

WILLIAM LAW

OF Mr. William Law, the celebrated Mystick (whose name
frequently occurs in these volumes), I shall here give some
particulars, from Mr. Gibbon's "Memoirs of his own Life," and
other sources. — After stating that his Grandfather, Edward
Gibbon, esq. who lived at Putney in great hospitality, and died
in December 1736, at the age of 70, by his last Will (at the
expence of his Son Edward, to whose marriage he was not
reconciled) enriched his two Daughters, Catherine and Hester;
and that the former became the wife of Mr. Elliston, an East-
India Captain; he says, "A life of devotion and celibacy was
the choice of my Aunt, Mrs. Hester Gibbon, who, at the age of
85, still [1796] resides in a Hermitage at Cliffe in Northamptonshire, having long survived her spiritual guide and faithful companion, Mr. William Law, who, at an advanced age, about the
year 1761, died in her house. In our family he had left the
reputation of a worthy and eminently pious man, who believed
all that he professed, and practised all that he enjoined. The
character of a Nonjuror, which he maintained to the last, is a
sufficient evidence of his principles in Church and State; and
the sacrifice of interest to conscience will be always respectable.
His theological writings, which our domestic connexion has
tempted me to peruse, preserve an imperfect sort of life; and
I can pronounce with more confidence than knowledge on the
merits of the Author. His last compositions are darkly tinctured
by the incomprehensible visions of Jacob Behmen; and his Discourse on the absolute Unlawfulness of Stage-Entertainments is
sometimes quoted for a ridiculous intemperance of sentiment
and language: 'The Actors and Spectators must all be damned.
The Playhouse is the Porch of Hell, the place of the Devil's
abode, where he holds his filthy Court of Evil Spirits. A Play is
the Devil's triumph; a sacrifice performed to his glory, as much
as in the Heathen Temples of Bacchus or Venus,' &c. &c. But

these sallies of religious phrenzy must not extinguish the praise
that is due to Mr. William Law as a Wit and a Scholar. His
argument on topicks of less absurdity is specious and acute; his
manner is lively, his style forcible and clear; and, had not his
vigorous mind been clouded by enthusiasm, he might be ranked
with the most agreeable and ingenious Writers of the times.
While the Bangorian Controversy was a fashionable theme, he
entered the lists, on the subject of Christ's kingdom, and the
authority of the Priesthood. Against the 'Plain Account of the
Sacrament of the Lord's Supper,' he resumed the combat with
Bishop Hoadly, the object of Whig idolatry and Tory abhorrence; and, at every weapon of attack and defence, the Nonjuror, on the ground which is common to both, approves himself at least equal to the Prelate. On the appearance of the
'Fable of the Bees,' he drew his pen against the licentious doctrine, that private vices are public benefits; and Morality as
well as Religion must join in his applause. Mr. Law's master-
work, the "Serious Call," is still read as a popular and powerful book of devotion. His precepts are rigid, but they are founded
on the Gospel; his satire is sharp, but it is drawn from the
knowledge of human life; and many of his portraits are not
unworthy the pen of La Bruyère. If he finds a spark of piety in
his Reader's mind, he will soon kindle it to a flame; and a
Philosopher must allow that he exposes, with equal severity and
truth, the strange contradiction between the faith and practice of the Christian World. Under the names of Flavia and
Miranda, he has admirably described my two Aunts, the Heathen
and the Christian Sister." — "This, says Mr. Lemoine, "is the
character the famous Historian is compelled by the spirit of truth
to give to the piety and goodness of Mr. Law, the most original
Writer of his day." — " Many years since," adds another Correspondent, "I was acquainted with some of his admirers, from
whom I understood that Mr. Law was a bachelor all his life-
time; that in person he was a well-set man, and rather of a dark
complexion, though remarkably cheerful in his temper; and that
he was upwards of 70 years of age when he paid the debt of
Nature. From another person of veracity I have likewise heard,
that such was Mr. Law's love of privacy and a state of recollection, that it was very seldom indeed that he passed away more
than two hours in the company of any person whatever. With a
very small patrimony also, Mr. Law was remarkably charitable;
but it was principally confined to his poor neighbours, the manu-

facturers of wooden-ware in and about King's Cliffe, co. Northampton. In this benevolent disposition he was joined by the
two maiden Ladies with whom he resided at King's Cliffe. Their
object was, not to encourage the idle and dissolute, but to promote and facilitate the good intentions and endeavours of the
industrious; and sorry I am that I cannot recollect the particulars of some anecdotes of Mr. Law which I have heard from a
man of letters now no more. From him, if I mistake not, I
likewise heard, that Mr. Law gave the copies of all his works
intended for publication to his Bookseller; but that for some
one of them Messieurs Richardson and Urquhart insisted upon
his acceptance of 100 guineas. Your Correspondent might have
added to what he relates as the sallies of Mr. Law's frenzy, that
the latter, the better to understand his favourite author Jacob
Behmen, made himself master of the German language; a task
of no small labour and difficulty to a native of this country.
Whether the "Serious Call" be Mr. Law's master-piece, I have
some doubt. I should give the palm to his "Case of Reason
stated," in answer to "Christianity as old as the Creation." The
style and conclusions are almost as plain and convincing as any
of the deductions in common arithmetick; and at this present
time [1800], as the public mind is not quite cured of the predilection it has lately entertained for the French Goddess of
Reason; I presume a cheap edition of that work by Mr. Law
might effectually remove their propensity, as it exhibits Reason
not the *Empress* (as the French and English Free-thinkers have
displayed her), but too often "the blind tool and most abject
drudge of the passions." I cannot say that I ever saw a fair
statement of the religious tenets of the people, like Mr. Law,
attached to such writers as Jacob Behmen, but who have lately
been swept away by the fanciful followers of Emanuel Sweden-
borg, whose genuine origin in this country is impartially delineated in the "Rise and Dissolution of the Infidel Societies." — I
forgot to mention the opinion of Mr. John Wesley respecting
Mr. Law's literary abilities, *viz.* 'that his writings would remain
an everlasting testimony of the strength and purity of the English
language.' W. H. REID."

Thus far I had actually printed my account of Mr. Law
(founded on what had been said in Gent. Mag. vol. LXX.
pp. 720, 1038), when the kindness of a Friend pointed out to me
"A short Account of the Life and Writings of the late Rev.
William Law, A.M. Author of *The Serious Call to a Devout*

Life, and of many other not less valuable Works; with an Appendix, which contains Specimens of his Writings. By Richard Tighe, 1813;" from which I shall extract a few dates. Mr. Law was born at King's Cliffe in 1686; and was the second son of Mr. Thomas Law, grocer. He was educated at the Grammar-school either of Oakham or Uppingham; admitted a Student of Emanuel College, Cambridge, Jan. 7, 1705; B.A. 1708-9; Fellow 1711; M.A. 1712. Not chusing to take the oaths to King George I. he resigned his Fellowship in 1716. He was for some little time a Curate in London; and soon after went to reside at Putney with Mr. Gibbon, as Tutor to his son Edward, who was the historian's father. In 1717 he engaged in controversy, by writing in favour of the authority of the Christian Ministry in a National Church. Between that period and 1737 he published several Tracts, all in support of Religion in general, accompanied with the earnest recommendation of good morals. In 1727 he founded an Almshouse at King's Cliffe for two old women, either unmarried and helpless or widows; also a School for 14 girls; which in 1755 had an annual income of 54*l.*; improved in 1813 to 69*l.* Whilst standing at a door in London, he had a sealed paper, directed to him, delivered into his hands, containing a Bank-note for 1000*l.*; with which, it is supposed, those Charities were established. Mrs. Hester Gibbon (his Pupil's sister) and Mrs. Hutcheson (widow of Archibald Hutcheson, esq. of the Middle Temple), two excellent ladies, were introduced to each other's acquaintance by the means of Mr. Law; and, having formed the plan of retiring from the world to the exercise of charitable and religious duties, they took Mr. Law as their chaplain, instructor and almoner. At first they hired a house at Thrapston in Northamptonshire; but in 1740 they enabled Mr. Law to prepare for them a roomy house, near the church, at King's Cliffe. Mrs. Gibbon's annual income was nearly 1000*l.*; Mrs. Hutcheson's about 2000*l.;* and their bounty was extended to the poor of an extensive circle. In 1745 Mrs. Hutcheson founded a School at King's Cliffe for 18 boys, endowed with an annual income of 148*l.* Mr. Law died April 9, 1761; and his remains were placed in a new tomb, built by Mrs. Gibbon. Mrs. Hutcheson died in January, 1781, aged 91; and her remains were placed, by her particular desire, *at the feet of Mr. Law,* in a new tomb. Mrs. Gibbon died in June 1790, aged 86; and was buried with Mr. Law. Her property she gave by will to her nephew the historian, who long expected it, but not without apprehensions that his aunt would devise it to some of those friends with whom she had spent her life.

STEPHEN MARTIN LEAKE

STEPHEN MARTIN LEAKE, Esq. descended from a family of the *Martins* in Devonshire, was son of Stephen Martin, a naval officer in the reign of Queen Anne, and for some time senior captain, an elder brother of the Trinity House, in the commission of the peace for Middlesex, Essex, and Surrey, and deputy lieutenant of the Tower Hamlets. Captain Martin married Elizabeth, daughter and coheir of Captain Richard Hill, of Yarmouth in Norfolk, by Mary his wife. Christian, the other daughter and coheir of Captain Hill, married Sir John Leake, knight, rear-admiral of Great Britain, admiral and commander-in-chief of the Fleet, and one of the Lords Commissioners of the Admiralty in the above reign. Sir John Leake and Captain Martin being united in the closest friendship by this matrimonial connexion, and still more by 20 years service together in the fleet, and Sir John having lost his lady and their issue, to evince his regard for his brother-in-law, adopted him his heir; who, from affection and gratitude, obtained his Majesty's sign manual, authorizing him to assume the sirname and bear the arms of *Leake,* in addition to his own. Captain Martin Leake died Jan. 19, 1725-6, in the 70th year of his age; and Elizabeth his wife Sept. 14, 1723, aged 57. Their remains were deposited in a vault in the cemetery of Stepney in Middlesex, with those of Sir John Leake and his family.

Stephen Martin Leake, their only surviving son, having been educated at the school of Michael Maittaire, was admitted of the Middle Temple in 1723, and in the same year was sworn a younger brother of the Trinity House. He was appointed, in 1724, a deputy-lieutenant of the Tower Hamlets; in which station he afterwards distinguished himself by his exertions during the rebellion in 1745. On the revival of the order of the Bath, in 1725, he was one of the Esquires of the Earl of Sussex, Deputy Earl Marshal. He was elected F.S.A. March 2, 1726-7;

and in the same year was created Lancaster Herald; in 1729 constituted Norroy; in 1741 Clarenceux; and, by patent, December 19, 1754, appointed Garter. In all his situations in the College, Mr. Leake was a constant advocate for the rights and privileges of the office. He obtained, after much solicitation, a letter, in 1731, from the Duke of Norfolk to the Earl of Sussex, his Deputy Earl Marshal, requesting him to sign a warrant for Mr. Leake's obtaining a commission of Visitation; which letter, however, was not attended with success. In the same year he promoted a prosecution against one Shiels, a painter, who pretended to keep an office of arms in Dean's Court. The Court of Chivalry was opened with great solemnity, in the Painted Chamber, March 3, 1731-2, in relation to which he had taken a principal part.* In 1733 he appointed Francis Bassans, of Chester, his deputy, as Norroy, for Chester and North Wales; and about the same time asserted his right, as Norroy, to grant arms in North Wales; which right was claimed by Mr. Longeville, who had been constituted Gloucester King of Arms *partium Walliæ,* annexed to that of Bath King of Arms, at the revival of that order. He drew up a petition in January 1737-8, which was presented to the King in Council, for a new Charter, with the sole power of painting arms, &c.; which petition was referred to the Attorney and Solicitor General; but they making their report favourable to the Painters, it did not succeed. He printed, in 1744, "Reasons for granting Commissions to the Provincial Kings at Arms for visiting their Provinces. Dr. Cromwell Malone having, in 1747, proposed to establish a Registry for Dissenters, in the College of Arms, he had many meetings with the heads of the several denominations, and also of the Jews; and drew up articles of agreement, which were approved by all parties; proposals were printed and discussed, a seal made to affix to certificates, and the Registry was opened, Feb. 20, 1747-8; but it did not succeed, owing to a misunderstanding between the ministers and deputies of the congregations. A bill having been brought in by the Proctors in the Session of Parliament for 1748, for taking the number of the people, with their marriages and births, he solicited a claim in favour of the College; but the bill did not pass. He being fixed upon to abstract the fair Register Books belonging to the most noble

---

*St. Edward's, or the Painted Chamber, was one of the apartments of the old Palace of Westminster destroyed by fire in 1834 (*Ed.*)

Order of St. George, they were delivered to him by Dr. Booth, dean of Windsor, in 1755; and, by Dr. Booth's importunity, he continued it from the death of Queen Anne; an undertaking the more necessary, as it had been wholly omitted from the decease of her Majesty. Garter completed the whole within that year. This having been translated into Latin, was deposited in the Registrar's Office of the Order.

As Garter King of Arms, he was appointed, in 1769, as a Plenipotentiary, jointly with the Marquis of Granby, for investing Prince Ferdinand of Brunswick with the ensigns of the Order of St. George. For the execution of this duty he left England in September, attended by two of his sons; one an herald, the other his secretary. On the 44th of October his Highness received the habit and insignia, at his head-quarters of the camp of the allied army at Nordorf on the Lahne. And in 1764 he was joined in a like commission with Colonel David Graeme, as Plenipotentiary for the investiture of his Serene Highness the Duke of Mecklenburg Strelitz, her Majesty's brother; which ceremony was performed at Neu Strelitz, on the 4th of June.

Garter, in 1726, published his *"Nummi Britannici Historia, or Historical Account of British Money."* A second edition, with large additions, was printed in 1745, dedicated to the Duke of Norfolk. It is much to Mr. Leake's honour, that he was the first person who has written professedly upon the English coinage. From affectionate gratitude to Admiral Sir John Leake, and at the particular desire of his father, he had written a history of the life of that Admiral, prepared from a great collection of books and papers relating to the subject which were in his possession. This he published in 1750, in large octavo. Fifty copies only were printed, to be given to his friends : this book is therefore very scarce and difficult to be procured. Mr. Bowyer, in 1766, printed for him 50 copies of the Statutes of the Order of St. George, to enable him to supply each Knight at his Installation with one, as he was required to do officially. Garter, ever attentive to promote sciences, was constantly adding to his store of knowledge, but more particularly in what related to arms, descents, honours, precedence, the history of the College, and of the several persons who had been officers of arms, and on every other subject in any way connected with his office. He also wrote several original essays on some of these subjects. These multifarious collections are contained in upwards of fifty volumes, all in his own hand-writing; which MSS. with many others, he be-

queathed to his son, John Martin Leake, esq. to whom the
publick, through the medium of Mr. Noble, are indebted for
this particular narrative, and full detail.

This valuable Head of the College married Anne, youngest
daughter, and at length sole heiress, of Fletcher Pervall, esq. of
Downton, in the parish and county of Radnor, by Anne his wife,
daughter of Samuel Hoole of London, by whom he had nine
children, six sons and three daughters, all of whom survived him.
He died, at his seat at Mile-end, Middlesex, March 24, 1773, in
the 70th year of his age; and was buried in the chancel of Thorpe
Soken church in Essex, of which parish he was long impropria-
tor, and owner of the seat of Thorpe hall, and the estate belonging to it, inheriting them from his father. His widow died Jan.
29, 1782, in Hertfordshire, aged 86.*

Three of his sons were connected with the College of Arms.
His eldest son, Stephen Martin Leake, esq. was created Norfolk
Herald Extraordinary, Sept. 21, 1761. John Martin Leake, esq.
his second son, was constituted Chester Herald, by patent, Sept.
27, 1752; which post he surrendered, in 1791, by permission of
the Duke of Norfolk, to his youngest brother, George Martin
Leake, esq. now Chester Herald. John Martin Leake, esq. was
also appointed secretary to the Earl of Suffolk, as Earl Marshal,
Dec. 23, 1763; in which office he continued till his Lordship's
resignation, in 1765.

SIR ROGER L'ESTRANGE

IN August 1663, Roger L'Estrange, esq. (after more than
twenty years spent in serving the Royal cause, near six of
them in gaols, and almost four under sentence of death in Newgate), had interest sufficient to obtain an appointment to a new-
created office, under the title of "Surveyor of the Imprimery and
Printing-presses;" together with "the sole licensing of all ballads,

---

*His collections, comprising 75 volumes, were bought by the College of
Arms in 1834 from the executor of his son, George Martin Leake,
Chester Herald 1791-1834. (*Ed.*)

charts, printed portraictures, printed pictures, books, and papers;
except books concerning common law, affairs of state, heraldry,
titles of honours and arms, the office of Earl Marshal, books of
divinity, physick, philosophy, arts and sciences, and such as are
granted to his Majesty's peculiar printer; and except such books
as by a late act of parliament are otherwise appointed to be
licensed." He had also a grant of "all the sole privilege of writing, printing, and publishing, all Narratives, Advertisements,
Mercuries, Intelligencers, Diurnals, and other books of public
intelligence; and printing all Ballads, Plays, Maps, Charts, Portraictures, and Pictures, not previously printed; and all Briefs
for Collections, Playbills, Quacksalvers Bills, Custom and Excise
Bills, Post-office Bills, Creditors Bills and Tickets in England and
Wales; with power to search for and seize unlicensed and treasonable, schismatical and scandalous books and papers." (Bagford's Collections, in Harl. MSS. 5910, vol. II.) The first fruits
of this new appointment appeared in *The Intelligencer,* No. 1,
August 31, 1663. These papers succeeded *The Parliamentary
Intelligencer* and *Mercurius Publicus,* published in defence of the
Government against the *Mercurius Politicus*; and in exposing
literary frauds, L'Estrange demonstrated both spirit and impartiality. Sept. 14, he points out "that audacious and scandalous
pamphlet, intitled, The First, Second, and Third Volumes of
Farewell Sermons;" and calls on those whose *heads* and *names*
are set before the books, to undeceive the publick by disclaiming
the work; which, on the 23d, was unequivocally done by Dr.
Robert Manton.—On the 24th, the publick are warned against
"the petty cozenage of some of the booksellers, who had persuaded their customers that they could not afford *The Newes*
under twopence a sheet, which was never sold to them at above
a fourth part of the price." — Oct. 7, a libel was seized in the
press, affirming *in terminis,* "that the people may put their King
to death, &c." — Nov. 3, he complains of an imposition practised by Henry Eversden, bookseller in St. Paul's Churchyard, in
having surreptitiously obtained the insertion of an advertisement
in a former paper, of a book intituled "Dr. Thomas Peirce's
Reply to Mr. Serenus Cressy's Misadventures against his Sermon
before the King;" whereas it was never intended for an answer
to Mr. Cressy, but as an introduction to Dr. Sherman's "Discourse on the Infallibility of the Holy Scriptures;" and as such
only had been regularly licensed. — May 14, 1664, notice is
given " that it was the King's pleasure to continue the healing

of his people for the Evil during the month of May, and then to give over till Michaelmas." — July 20 was appointed for drawing a Lottery in the Banqueting-house, Whitehall.

"His Sacred Majesty," says the important Patentee, "having been lately and graciously pleased to grant and commit the privilege of publishing all intelligence, together with the survey and inspection of the Press*, to one and the same person; it may be good discretion, I suppose, for the person so intrusted, to begin (as his first step toward the work) with some considerations and advertisements, by way of preamble and introduction to the future order and settlement of the whole affair. First, as to the point of printed Intelligence, I do declare myself, (as I hope I may, in a matter left so absolutely indifferent, whether any or none) that, supposing the press in order, the people in their right wits, and news or no news to be the question, a public Mercury should never have my vote; because I think it makes the multitude too familiar with the actions and counsels of their superiors, too pragmatical and censorious, and gives them, not only an itch, but a kind of colourable right and licence to be meddling with the Government. All which (supposing as before supposed) does not yet hinder, but that in this juncture a paper of that quality may be both safe and expedient; truly, if I should say necessary, perhaps the case would bear it; for certainly there is not anything which at this instant more imports his Majesty's service and the publick, than to redeem the vulgar from their former mistakes and delusions, and to preserve them from the like for the time to come: to both which purposes the prudent management of a *Gazette* may contribute in a very high degree: for, besides that it is every body's money, and, in truth, a good part of most men's study and business, it is none of the worst ways of address to the genius and humour of the common people; whose affections are much capable of being tuned and wrought upon by convenient hints and touches, in a shape and air of a pamphlet, than by the strongest reasons and best notions imaginable, under any other and more sober form whatsoever. To which advantages of being popular and grateful, must be added, as none of the least, that it is likewise seasonable and worth the while were there no other use of it than only to detect and disappoint the malice of those scandalous and false reports, which

---

*L'Estrange first occurs in the Stationers' Books, in the character of a licenser, Oct. 30, 1663.

are daily contrived and bruited against the government. So that, upon the main, I perceive the thing requisite, and (for ought I can see yet) once a week may do the business, for I intend to utter my news by weight, and not by measure. Yet if I shall find, when my hand is in, and after the planting and securing of my correspondents, that the matter will fairly furnish more, without either uncertainty, repetition, or impertinence, I shall keep myself free to double at pleasure. One book a week may be expected however; to be published every Thursday, and finished upon the Tuesday night, leaving Wednesday entire for the printing it off. The way as to the vent, that has been found most beneficial to the master of the book, has been to cry and expose it about the streets, by mercuries and hawkers; but whether that way be so advisable in some other respects, may be a question: for, under countenance of that employment, is carried on the private trade of treasonous and seditious libels; nor, effectually, has any thing considerable been dispersed, against either Church or State, without the aid and privity of this sort of people. Wherefore, without ample assurance and security against this inconvenience, I shall adventure to steer another course."

"A word now to the second branch of my care and duty; that is, the survey and inspection of the press. I find it, in general, with the printers as with their neighbours, there are too many of the trade to live one by another*; but more particularly I find them clogged with three sorts of people, foreigners, persons not free of the trade, and separatists: which I offer, to the end that, when it shall be thought fit to retrench the number, the reformation may begin there. In the mean time, to prevent mischief (as far as in me lies), and for their encouragement that shall discover it, take these advertisements of encouragement to the discovery of unlawful printing: I. If any person can give notice, and make proof, of any printing press erected and being in any private place, hole, or corner, contrary to the tenor of the late act of parliament for the regulating of printing and printing presses; let him repair with such notice, and make proof thereof, to the surveyor of the press, at his office at the Gun in Ivy-lane, and he shall have forty shillings for his pains, with what assur-

---

*It appears by the Stationers' Books, May 12, 1663, that there were at that time 59 persons in and about London, exercising the trade of Master-printers.

ance of secrecy himself shall desire. II. If any such person as aforesaid shall discover to the said surveyor any seditious or unlawful book to be upon such a private press imprinting, and withal give his aid to the seizing of the copies and the offenders; his reward shall be five pounds. III. For the discovery and proof of any thing printing without authority or licence, although in any public house, ten shillings. IV. For the discovery and proof of any seditious or unlawful book to be sold or dispersed by any of the mercuries or hawkers, the informer shall have five shillings."

Agreeably to the hint in L'Estrange's Prospectus, on the Thursday following appeared the "Newes*, published for Satisfaction and Information of the People. With Privilege; No. 1, Sept. 3".   1663.

It is but justice to add, that these papers contained more information, more entertainment, and more advertisements of importance, than any succeeding paper whatever, previous to the golden age of letters which may be said to have commenced in the reign of Queen Anne.

BERNARD AND HENRY LINTOT

O F these very respectable Booksellers, Father and Son, the little that is known being principally through the dense and partial medium of "The Dunciad," I feel a peculiar pleasure, as a Brother of the Craft, in endeavouring to vindicate their memories.

"BARNABY† BERNARD LINTOTT, son of John Lintott, late of Horsham in Sussex, yeoman," was bound apprentice, at Stationers' Hall, to Thomas Lingard, Dec. 4, 1690; turned over to

---

*Thus "The Intelligencer" and "The Newes" continued to be published, the one on Monday, the other on Thursday, till the beginning of January 1665-6; when the publication of L'Estrange was superseded by *The Gazette.*

†This was the name under which he was bound apprentice; but he soon dropped *Barnaby*; and, after some years, wrote Lintot with a single *t* at the end.

John Harding 169. .; and made free, March 18, 1699. He soon after commenced business, as a Bookseller, at the sign of the Cross Keys, between the Temple Gates, where he was patronized by many of the most eminent Writers of a period which has been styled the Augustan age of English Literature.

The earliest Work published by him that at present occurs to recollection is a volume intituled *"Examen Miscellaneum*; consisting of Verse and Prose. London, printed for *B. L.* and sold by John Chantry, at the Pestle and Mortar, without Temple Bar. 1702." By a List of Books at the end of this Volume, it appears that Lintot published some of "Toland's Works;" and that he dealt largely in Law Books and Dramatic Writings. — He published some of Dryden's Poems singly; and several, afterwards, for Lady Chudleigh, Pope, Gray, Farquhar, Dr. King, Fenton, and Parnell.

In 1708 he was called on by the Company of Stationers, to take upon him their Livery.

In 1714 he reprinted his "Miscellanies;" and thus displayed the names of the several Writers. "Miscellaneous Poems and Translations by several Hands; particularly, 'The First Book of Statius his Thebais translated:' 'The Fable of Vertumnus and Pomona, from the Fourteenth Book of Ovid's Metamorphoses;' 'To a young Lady, with the Works of Voiture;' 'On Silence;' 'To the Author of a Poem intituled *Successio*;' 'The Rape of the Lock, an Heroi-comic Poem;' 'An Ode for Musick on St. Cecilia's Day;' 'Windsor Forest, to the Right Hon. George Lord Lansdown;' 'An Essay on Criticism.' — 'By Mr. Pope.' — The Second Edition. London; printed for Bernard Lintot between the Two Temple Gates in Fleet Street; and William Lewis, in Russel Street, Covent Garden, 1714." — I have given the full title of this volume for various reasons. It shews the estimation in which the name of Pope was held even at that early period. The name of that great Poet, it may be objected, is placed in the Title-page *ad captandum,* as if he were the actual Editor of the Work, an idea which he afterwards affected to discountenance. It is plain, however, that he must have consented to the publication of the several Poems above enumerated; a circumstance which the name of Mr. William Lewis (Pope's early friend) tends also to confirm. Nor had Pope any reason to be ashamed of the company in which he was introduced — Dryden — Bate — Swift — Gay — Broome — Southcote — Edmund Smith — Fenton — Betterton, &c. &c.

In the same year, 1714, Mr. Lintot entered into a very liberal agreement with Mr. Pope, for his Translation of Homer's Iliad; the printing of which was soon after begun by Mr. Bowyer, and diligently attended to by all parties. — Mr. Gay, in a Letter to Congreve, April 7, 1715, facetiously says, "Mr. Pope's Homer is retarded by the great rains that have fallen of late, which causes the sheets to be long a-drying. This gives Mr. Lintot great uneasiness; who is now endeavouring to engage the Curate of the Parish to pray for fair Weather, that his work may go on."

In 1715-16 we find Mr. Lintot pursuing his profession on the frozen River Thames:

"In this place *Bowyer* plies; there's *Lintot*'s stand."

Bernard Lintot* was appointed, with Jacob Tonson and William Taylor, by the Hon. Spencer Compton, then Speaker of the House of Commons, to be one of the Printers of the Votes; and so continued till 1727.

There does not appear to have been any altercation between the Bookseller and the Author during the whole period of the publication of the *Iliad* or *Odyssey,* which continued till 1725; but, from whatever cause it may have arisen, the friendship between Mr. Pope and his Publisher appears to have terminated with the conclusion of Homer.

In an *undated* Letter, addressed by Mr. Pope to the Earl of Burlington about that period, his description of his old friend *Bernard Lintot* is given with the most exquisite humour.

Perhaps Mr. Pope conceived that Lintot had risen *above his proper level;* for it appears that early in 1726, having, by successful exertions in business, acquired a decent competence, and made some additions to his paternal inheritance in Sussex, he was desirous of tracing the origin of his family; and for that purpose consulted Humphrey Wanley, who had then the custody of the Earl of Oxford's Heraldic MSS. and in whose Diary is the following memorandum: "Young Mr. Lintot the Bookseller came enquiring after *Arms,* as belonging to his father, mother, and other relations, who now, it seems, want to turn *gentlefolks.* I could find none of their names."

Mr. Pope, in a Letter to Mr. Pitt, on the subject of his Translation of Vida, July 23, 1726, says, "I received a letter from you

---

*Joshua Lintot had a similar appointment jointly with Jacob Tonson, Timothy Goodwin, and J. Roberts, 1708-1710.

with satisfaction; having long been desirous of any occasion of testifying my regard for you, and particularly of acknowledging the pleasure your version of Vida's Poetick had afforded me. I had it not indeed from your bookseller; but read it with eagerness, and think it both a correct and a spirited translation. I am pleased to have been (as you tell me) the occasion of your undertaking that work: that is some sort of merit; and, if I have any in me, it really consists in an earnest desire to promote and produce, as far as I can, that of others. But as to my being the publisher, or any way concerned in reviewing or recommending of "Lintot's Miscellany," it is what I never did in my life, though he (like the rest of his tribe) makes a very free use of my name. He has often reprinted my things, and so scurvily, that, finding he was doing so again, *I corrected the sheets as far as they went, of my own only*; and, being told by him that he had two or three copies of yours (which you also had formerly sent me, as he said, through his hands,) I obliged him to write for your consent before he made use of them. This was all: your second book he has just now delivered to me, the inscription of which to myself I will take care he shall leave out; and either return the rest of your verses to him, or not, as you shall like best. I am obliged to you, Sir, for expressing a much higher opinion of me than I know I deserve: the freedom with which you write is yet what obliges and pleases me more; and it is with sincerity that I say, I would rather be thought by every ingenuous man in the world, his servant, than his rival."

Mr. Pope had at this period undoubtedly conceived a very ill impression of his *quondam* Bookseller; and in 1727 vented his indignation without mercy in the "Dunciad." His principal *delinquency,* however, seems to have been, that he was a stout man, clumsily made, not a very considerable Scholar, and that he filled his shop with *rubric posts.* Against his benevolence and general moral character there is not even an insinuation.

Bernard Lintot appears to have soon after relinquished his business to his son Henry; and to have retired to Horsham in Sussex; for which county he was nominated High Sheriff in November 1735; an honour which he did not live to enjoy; as his death happened Feb. 3, 1735-6, at the age of 61. In the Newspapers of the day he was styled "Bernard Lintot, esq. of the Middle Temple, late an eminent Bookseller in Fleet-street."

Henry Lintot, his only son, was born about August 1709; was admitted to the freedom of the Company of Stationers, by patrimony, Sept. 1, 1730; obtained the Livery the same day*; and from that time their business was carried on in the joint names of Bernard and Henry; but the Father passed the principal part of his time in Sussex. — Two days after the death of Bernard, Henry was appointed High Sheriff for that county, where his residence was at Southwater, in the Rape of Bramber, about 4 miles from Horsham. — He married, first, Elizabeth, daughter of Sir John Aubrey, Bart. of Llantrythed in Glamorganshire, (whose mother was Margaret, daughter of Sir John Lowther, Bart.); by whom he had an only daughter and heiress, Catharine, who was married, Oct. 20, 1768, (with a fortune of 45,000*l.*) to Captain Henry Fletcher, at that time a Director of the East India Company. — Mr. Lintot married, secondly, Philadelphia ——, by whom he had no issue. He died in 1758; and his widow Jan. 31, 1763.

LINTOT AND HIS AUTHORS

MANY Months after the article on the LINTOTS was printed off, the unwearied researches of Mr. D'Israeli brought to light a small Memorandum-book of those enterprizing Booksellers, intituled, "Copies when purchased;" and, from this document, his "Quarrels of Authors" are illustrated by some very interesting particulars respecting Mr. Pope and other Writers. But the plan of his publication not admitting of *minutiæ* which may be pardonable in these desultory pages; I am tempted (by the permission of Mr. Nunn, the present Owner of the MS.) to enter more particularly into its Contents; and the rather, as a considerable number of Books enumerated were produced from Mr. Bowyer's press.

The period which, from conjecture, I had assigned for Lintot's commencing business is literally accurate; the earliest Copies which he purchased appearing to be three different Works of

---

*He obtained the patent of Law Printer about 1748; and in 1754 was elected into the Court of Assistants of his Company.

Toland, in 1701-2. In July he purchased "Love and Business; in a Collection of occasional Verse and Epistolary Prose, not hitherto published," and "A Discourse on Comedy, in reference to the English Stage. In Fourteen Letters. By George Farquhar." In November he bought a share in Cibber's "Last Shift;" employed Mr. Gildon as Editor of the "Examen Miscellaneum;" and from that period, till the time of his quitting business, he was a very considerable Purchaser, as the following List of his Copies (some of which were *old Works* bought from his Brethren of the Trade) may testify. For the sake of readier reference, I place them in alphabetical order.

	£	s.	d.
Mr. BAKER.			
1702-3, Jan. 13. Yeoman of Kent	32	5	0
1708, Dec. 10. Fine Ladies Airs, a Comedy	21	10	0

Oxford Act,   ⎱
Hampstead Heath, ⎰   no sum or date
Humours of the Age,   mentioned.

Mr. THOMAS BALLARD, Little Britain.

	£	s.	d.
1718-19. Bought of him a Fourth of a Half of the several Shares of all the Copies formerly belonging to Mr. Thomas Basset, deceased (except his Law Copies); *viz.* Heylin's Help to History, &c. &c. in all 133 Books : among which, Miege's Dictionary, 4to and 8vo; on every impression of which, the Author to have 10*s.* a sheet on each book for revising, and 100 books	45	0	0
HAMMOND BANKS.			
1714, Dec. 16. Dryden's Fresnoy's Art of Painting	20	0	0
BARFORD.			
1726, April 26. The Assembly, a Poem	15	15	0
Mr. BEDFORD.			
1711-12, Jan. 4. Divinity and Law	3	4	6
BETTERTON.			
1712, April 7. The Miller's Tale, with some Characters from Chaucer	5	7	6
Mr. BOHUN.			
1708, Jan. 26. Half of Institutio Legalis	10	1	6
1722, Dec. 18. Correcting Institutio	10	15	0
Mr. BOSVILE.			
1705-6, Jan. 23. A 30th Share of Vaughan's			

Reports	2	0	0

BOWYER.

1708-9, Jan. 13. Half Share of Lauderdale's Virgil	5	7	6

BREVAL.

1724, April 18. His "Remarks on several Parts of Europe." The Author one Guinea clear. The Bookseller one Guinea; and to be at the expence of paper, print, copper-plates; &c. The Copy to remain to the Bookseller.

BRIGHT.

1707, Oct. 3. Half Share of Lady's Visiting-day, by Burnaby	2	15	0

Mr. BROCKWEL.

1710, Dec. 12. ⎱ Annals K. G. Year 4 .... 1714, Dec. 11. ⎰	2	10	0

BROOME.

1726-7, Feb. 22. Miscellany Poems	35	0	0

Mr. DANIEL BROWN.

1701, Dec. 1. Seneca's Morals, A Twelfth Share ...	20	0	0
1718, April 11. Modern Cases, the Fifth of a Half	3	0	0
1719, May 5. A 20th Share in the Daily Courant	51	5	0

[This Share, and my own which I had originally, were given up to Mr. Buckley, when the Sale of the Paper did not pay the Expence.]

1729. Sold to him a Fourth part of a Half Share of Webb's Antiquities of Stonehenge.

Mr. BURNET.

1711, Jan. 27. Our Ancestors as wise as we	5	7	6
1712, Feb. 2. A Letter from a Trojan to the Grecians in Devereux Court	3	4	6

Mrs. CENTLIVRE.

1703, May 14. Paid Mrs. Knight for Love's Contrivance	10	0	0
1709, May 14. The Busy Body	10	0	0

Mr. CIBBER.

1701, Nov. 8. A Third of Love's last Shift	3	4	6
1705, Nov. 14. Perolla and Izadora	36	11	0
1707, Oct. 27. Double Gallant	16	2	6
—— Nov. 11. Lady's last Stake	32	5	0
—— Feb. 26. Venus and Adonis	5	7	6
1708, Oct. 9. Comical Lover	10	15	0
1712, Mar. 16. Cinna's Conspiracy	13	0	0

1718, Oct. 1.   The Nonjuror 105   0   0
        Myrtillo, a Pastoral,
        Rival Fools,   no price
        Heroick Daughter,   or date.
        Wit at several Weapons,
              COGGAN [FRANCIS].

1707, Dec. 4.   One Half of Love and a Bottle   2   3   0
              CONINGSBY.

1721, Nov. 9.   Fourth Share of Howard's Cookery 13 10   0
              CONSTABLE.

1730, June 8.   Reflections upon Accuracy of Style 5   5   0
        Mr. GEORGE CONYERS, Little Britain.
      Bought of him a Fourth Share of the several
      Law Copies and Trials belonging to Mr.
      Thomas Basset, deceased, being the same
      that were sold by auction to Mr. Basset
      by Mr. John Nicholson's Executors, and
      for the same sum; *viz.* Lex Mercatoria,
      &c. &c. in all 109 Books — besides several
      Tryals in Folio, &c. 33   0   0
             Captain COOK.

1711, Dec. 17.   Seventh Share of his Voyages,
      bought of Mr. Gosling 7   3   0
              Cox.

1709, July 30.   Lady Chudleigh's Defence 1   1   6
              CROSSE.

1719, June 10.   Practical Distiller 1   1   6
              CROXALL.

1714, Sept. 22.   An Ode to the King 12 18   0
              CRULL.

1705, Aug. 28.   Whitlock on Government 3 10   0
          CURLL and PEMBERTON.

1714-15, Mar. 4.   Half of Noy's Rights of the
      Crown 3   4   6
1715-16, Jan. 5.   Half Share of West on Treasons 4   6   0
              Mr. DAREY.

1705, Mar. 29.   Rights of the Church, Half 20   0   0
              Mr. DENNIS.

1703, Feb. 24.   Paid Mr. George Strahan, Book-
      seller, for Half Share of "Liberty asserted"... 7   3   0
1708, Nov. 10.   Appius and Virginia 21 10   0

		£	s	d
1711, April 25.	Essay on Public Spirit	2	12	6
—— Jan. 6.	Remarks on Pope's Essay	2	12	6

Mr. DIGBY.

		£	s	d
1713, June 10.	For translating Quintus Curtius ...	10	15	0
—— Dec. —.	Translating Wiquefort's Embassador	45	0	0
1718, Feb. 18.	Translating Raguenet's Description of the Monuments at Rome	5	5	0

D'URPHEY.

		£	s	d
1709, May 7.	The Modern Prophets.................. The Old Moon and the New.	6	9	0

Mr. DAVID EDWARDS.

		£	s	d
1716, Nov. 7.	Journals of Parliament	5	7	6

ELSUM.

		£	s	d
1710, Aug. 18.	His Book of Painting	4	0	0

Mr. FARQUHAR.

		£	s	d
1701, July 3.	Letters and Poems	3	4	6
1702, Dec. 22.	Twin Rivals	15	0	0
1705, Feb. 12.	Rsecruiting Officer..................	16	2	6
1706, Jan. 27.	Beaux Stratagem	30	0	0

Mr. FENTON.

		£	s	d
1716, Oct. 14.	Paid Mr. Fenton for his Micellanies	21	10	0
—— ——.	Paid more for the said Miscellanies	13	4	3

Rev. Mr. FIDDES.

		£	s	d
17—, ——.	Body of Divinity 252		10	0

FRANCIS.

		£	s	d
1727-8, July 4.	Maxims of Equity, with 750 Books of the said Copy 100		0	0

Mr. GAY.

		£	s	d
1713, May 12.	Wife of Bath	25	0	0
1714, Nov. 11.	Letter to a Lady	5	7	6
1715, Feb. 14.	The What d'ye call it..................	16	2	6
—— Dec. 22.	Trivia	43	0	0
—— ——.	Epistle to the Earl of Burlington...	10	15	0
1717, May 4.	Battle of the Frogs	16	2	6
—— Jan. 8.	Three Hours after Marriage	43	2	6
	Revival of the Wife of Bath	75	0	0
	[The Mohocks, a Farce, 2*l*. 10*s*. — Sold the Mohocks to him again.]			

		£234	10	0

		Mr. GILDON.	£	s.	d.

			£	s.	d.
1701, Nov. 15.	For Examen Miscellaneum		5	7	6

HARTE.

1726, Nov. 18.	Mr. Harte's Miscellaneous Poems...	30	0	0

JACOB.

1712, Dec. 6.	Court-keeper, a Half	16	2	6
1714, Dec. 11.	Accomplished Conveyancer, 3 vols.	105	0	0
1715, June 27.	Modern Justice	26	17	6
—— Jan. 7.	First Table to the Statutes	3	4	6
—— ———.	Clerk's Remembrancer, one Half ...	5	0	0
1716, March 29.	Grand Precedent, a Sixth part ...	2	0	0
—— ———.	Court-keeper's Companion, a Third	1	15	10
1717, Nov. 9.	Appendix to the Modern Justice......	5	5	0
1718, June 28.	Papers relating to Appeals............	1	11	6
1718, July 17.	Justice's Companion, a Fourth	1	6	3
—— Aug. 16.	Parish Officer, a Half	2	12	6
—— Oct. 11.	Laws of Appeals	10	10	0
—— Nov. 7.	Second Table to the Statutes	7	7	0
—— Jan. 3.	Militia Law	2	12	6
—— Mar. 11.	Lex Constitutionis	21	0	0
1719, April 18.	Paid for Additions and Corrections to the Modern Justice	4	4	0
—— Dec. 18.	For Additions to the Statute-Law common-placed	10	10	0
—— ———.	Lady's Law	7	7	0
1728, Feb. 26.	Additions to the Clerk's Remembrancer...	3	3	0
1728, Oct. 26.	Additions to the Appendix to the Modern Justice	2	2	0
1728, Nov. 23.	Additions to the Fifth Edition of Parish Officer	1	1	0
1731, April 7.	Additions to the Sixth Edition	1	1	0
—— April 22.	Additions to the Lady's Law	3	3	0

JAMES.

1728, June 7.	His Gardening..........................	70	0	0

JEAKE.

1726-7, Feb. 22. Charters of the Cinque Ports, by
Subscription; one Half Guinea the Author,
and one Half Guinea the Bookseller.

Mr. JOHNSON.

1712, Dec. 17.	Successful Pirate	10	15	0

1718-19, Jan. 10. The Masquerade 36 15 0

Mr. THOMAS JOHNSON, Schoolmaster.

1711, July 25. Decerpta ex Ovidii Fastis 5 7 6

1713, Feb. 1. Nouns and Verbs, Ovid's Metamorphoses, and Phædrus 13 0 0

JONES.

1712, May 30. Memoirs of Lives, Foreign and
Domestic, for the Year 1711 .... 3 15 0

Dr. KING.

1707-8, Feb. 18. Paid for Art of Cookery 32 5 0

1708-9, Feb. 16. Paid for First Part of Transactions* 5 0 0

Paid for his Art of Love 32 5 0

1709, June 23. Second Part of the Transactions ... 5 0 0

1709-10, March 4. Paid for the History of Cajamai 5 0 0

1710, Nov. 10. Paid for King's Gods................. 50 0 0

1712, July 1. Useful Miscellany, Part I.............. 1 1 6

Paid for the Useful Miscellany...... 3 0 0

KING.

1713-14, Feb. 4. Third Share of Geddes's Tracts
against Popery 3 6 0

KEILL.

1722, March 29. His Astronomy, English 100 0 0

Captain KILLEGREW

1718-19, Feb. 14. Chit-Chat 84 0 0

KNAPTON.

1709, March 8. Third Share of Fair Quaker of Deal 6 13 4

Rev. Mr. LAWRENCE.

1713-14, Feb. 4. The Clergyman's Recreation 5 7 6

1715-16, Mar. 15. The Gentleman's Recreation... 16 2 6

1717-18, Feb. 17. The Fruit-Garden Kalendar 36 15 0

Mr. LEIGH.

1704, March 30. For Half Copy of Toland's Letters
to Serena 10 0 0

Mr. STEPHEN LEWIS, of Merton College, Oxford.

1714-5, Feb. 1. Translation of Aristænetus's Letters 5 7 6

---

*Dr. King's banter on the Royal Society, under the title of "Useful
Transactions."

Mr. Lund.

1710, June 23. Heywood of Government	4	6	0

Mears.

1716, Mar. 29. A Sixth Share of the Supplement to the Accomplished Conveyancer	2	0	0

Mr. Morehead.

1711, Nov. 24. Transcribing Symbolum Mundi ...	3	0	0
1712, Sept. 11. Translating Part of Dupin	26	13	0
——— ———. Captain Stephens, another Part	2	14	0
—— Dec. 16. For Part of Quintus Curtius	1	0	0

Mr. Nutt.

1716, July 25. Half Share of an Impression of Nelson's Reports in Chancery, No. 1000 ...	2	13	9
—— ———. Half of the Impression of Manwood's Forest Laws, No. 1000	10	15	0
1717, Dec. 4. A Fourth of the Impression of Coke on Littleton; also a Fourth of the Impression of Natura Brevium, 1000 each	53	15	0

Mr. Oldisworth.

1709, July 25. Answer to the Rights, vol. 1	25	0	0
————————————vols. II & III	50	0	0
1711, May 7. Essay on Private Judgment............	15	1	0
—— May 12. Reasons for restoring the Whigs......	2	12	0

Oldmixon.

1715-16, Feb. 20. Index to Wiquefort's Embassador	7	0	0

Osborne.

1722, Aug. 2. A Twelfth Share of Sandford's Genealogical History, with the Copper-plates	7	15	0

Mr. Ozell.

1711, Nov. 18. ⎱ Translating Homer's Iliad, Books			
1712, June 4. ⎰ I, II, III	10	8	6
1713, April 29. Translating Moliere	37	12	6
Squire Trelooby [a Comedy; no price.]			

Paul.

1713-14, Jan. 28. Chancellor Egerton *v.* Coke	10	15	0

Pitt.

1726, Oct. 13. His Miscellaneous Poems	21	0	0

Mr. Playford.

1703, Nov. 8. For Half Share of "Different Widows"	1	10	0

Pointer.

1713, Dec. 23. Chronological History	10	15	0

Mr. POPE

1712, Feb. 19.	Statius, First Book .... }	16	2	6
	Vertumnus and Pomona .... }			
1712, Mar. 21.	First Edition of the Rape	7	0	0
1712, 9 April.	To a Lady presenting Voiture...... ⎫			
	Upon Silence .... ⎬	3	16	6
	To the Author of a Poem called ⎪			
	Successio .... ⎭			
1712, Feb. 23.	Windsor Forest	32	5	0
1713, July 23.	Ode on St. Cecilia's Day	15	0	0
1714, Feb. 20.	Additions to the Rape	15	0	0
—— Mar. 23.	Homer, vol. I 215		0	0
	650 Books on Royal Paper 176		0	0
1715, Feb. 1.	Temple of Fame	32	5	0
1715, April 31.	Key to the Lock......................	10	15	0
1716, 9 Feb.	Homer, vol. II 215		0	0
1716, May 7.	650 Royal Paper 150		0	0
—— July 17.	Essay on Criticism	15	0	0
1717, Aug. 9.	Homer, vol. III 215		0	0
1718, Jan. 6.	650 Royal Paper 150		0	0
—— Mar. 3.	Homer, vol. IV. 210		0	0
	650 Royal Paper.....................150		0	0
—— Oct. 17.	Homer, vol. V. 210		0	0
1719, April 6.	650 Royal Paper.....................150		0	0
1720, Feb. 26.	Homer, vol. VI. 210		0	0
1720, May 7.	650 Royal Paper 150		0	0
1721, Dec. 13.	Parnell's Poems.........................	15	0	0

Paid Mr. Pope for the Subscription-money
due on the Second Volume of his Homer;
and on his Fifth Volume, at the Agreement
for the said Fifth Volume. — (I had Mr.
Pope's Assignment for the Royal Paper
that were then left of his Homer) 840 0 0
    Copy-money for the Odyssey, Volumes
I. II. III.; and 750 of each Volume printed
on Royal Paper, 4to 615 6 0
    Copy-money for the Odyssey, Volumes IV.
V.; and 750 of each Volume, Royal 425 18 7½

£.4244 8 7½

RIDER.

1715-6, Feb. 21.   Roman Catholic System of Allegi-   £ s. d.
ance   5   5   0

Captain ROGERS.

1712, Oct. 25.   Rogers's Voyages, one Half   20   0   0
—— ———.   Paid Mr. Ridpath, for correcting
Rogers's Voyage, my Share.....................   5   0   0

ROPER.

1704, May 15.   Twelfth Share of Hist. of "Formosa"   0 15   0

N. ROWE, Esq.

1713, Dec. 12.   Jane Shore 50 15   0
1715, Apr. 27.   Jane Grey   75   5   0

SETTLE.

1711, Sept. 8.   The City Ramble 3 10   0

Dr. SEWEL.

1714-15, Mar. 10.   Paid Dr. Sewel, for translating
Part of Quintus Curtius, and *Part of
Lucretius* 6 19   9
And for writing Observations on the
Tragedy of Jane Shore   1   1   6

SHOREE.

1712, August 13.   Translation of Cornelius Nepos   5   0   0

SKINNER.

1726, May 13.   For an Impression of 1500 of the
Reports of Robert Skinner, Esq................350 15   0

SMITH [EDMUND.]

1705-6, March 11.   Phædra and Hippolytus   50   0   0

SMITH of Kendal.

1725, June 24.   Complete Body of Distilling   20   0   0
1729, Sept. 13.   Doctrine of Fermentation 6 10   0

SMITH [JAMES MOORE].

1726, Dec. 31.   The Rival Modes 105   0   0

SOMERVILE.

1727, July 14.   A Collection of Poems, &c.............   35 15   0

Sir RICHARD STEELE.

1703-4, June 11.   Lying Lovers 21 10   0

STEPHENS.

1711, Oct. 31.   His Sermon before the Irish Protestants residing at London   7   0   0

STRAHAN.

1703-4, Feb. 3.   Half of Mr. Dennis's Liberty
asserted   7   3   0

1704, April 14.	A Sixth of the History of "Formosa"	8 15 0
	Mr. Theobald.	
1713, May 22.	Plato's Phædon	5 7 6
	For *Æschylus's* Tragedies	1 1 6
	being part of Ten Guineas.	
1714, June 12.	La Motte's Homer.....................	3 4 6
1714, April 21.	*Articles signed by Mr. Theobald,	

to translate for B. Lintot the 24 Books of
Homer's Odyssey into English blank verse.
Also the four Tragedies of Sophocles, called
Œdipus Tyrannus, Œdipus Coloneus, Tra-
chiniæ, and Philoctetes, into English blank
verse, with Explanatory Notes to the twenty-
four Books of the Odyssey, and to the four
Tragedies. To receive, for translating every
450 Greek verses, with Explanatory Notes
thereon, the sum of............................ 2 10 0

To translate likewise the Satires and
Epistles of Horace into English rhyme. For
every 120 Latin lines so translated............ 1 1 6

These Articles to be performed, according
to the time specified, under the penalty of
50*l.* payable by either party's default.

Paid in hand 2 10 0

Dr. Tilly.

1711, Dec. 27.	Dr. Tilly's Sermons	32 5 0
1713, Jan. 2.	—— Devotions.......................	10 15 0

Mr. Toland.

1701, June 12.	Paid for Art of governing by Parties	20 0 0
—— ——.	For his Anglia Libera..................	10 15 0
	For his Vindicius Liberius.............	5 5 0
1702, ——.	Reasons for inviting over......... ⎱	no sum put
—— ——.	Paradoxes of State .... ⎰	down
1704, ——.	Letters to Serena.......................	10 0 0
1711-12, Feb. 15.	Letters against Popery............	5 7 6
1714, Feb. 11.	General Monk's Letters.............	10 15 0
1713, Sept. 17.	Dunkirk or Dover....................	5 7 6
1714, Oct. 28.	Naturalizing the Jews	10 15 0

---

*"This entry has a line drawn through it, as if the Agreement has not
been executed. Perhaps Lintot submitted to pay Theobald for *not doing*
the Odyssey, when Pope undertook it." D'Israeli.

—— Nov. 12. Art of Canvassing 5 7 6
1714, July 3. The Grand Mystery.................... 10 15 0
1713, Nov. 24. Art of Restoring...................... 10 0 0

TONSON.

1717, June 13. An Agreement about Pope's Works.
1718, Feb. 16. An Agreement to be equally con-
cerned in all Plays they should buy, Eighteen
Months following the above Date.
1721, Mar. 2. An Agreement about the VOTES.
Nov. 27. An Agreement about Vernon's Cases.
1722, Feb. 7. An Agreement for Mariamne......... 26 5 0
—— Mar. 1. His Agreement for the Half of Sir
R. Steele's Comedy that was to be published 25 0 0
—— Mar. 22. An Assignment of ½ of the Copy of
Busiris.
—— Oct. 10. For Liberty to print 1500 Grief-à-
la-Mode, and Tender Husband, the sum of 14 14 0
—— Oct. 24. A Copy of an Agreement for pur-
chasing 250 of the Duke of Buckingham's
Works — *afterwards jockeyed by Alderman
Barber and Tonson together.*
—— Oct. 26. An Assignment for the Half of the
Conscious Lovers, for 70 0 0
Half of the Copy of the Tender Husband.
1723, Feb. 24. Assignment of Half of Gay's Works,
reciprocally, being printed in Quarto.
The Tragedy of Mariamne, and
The Fatal Constancy.
1724, June 24. Agreement with Ward and Tonson
about Vernon's Cases, under a penalty of
300*l.*
1725, April 10. An Agreement about the Earl of
Macclesfield's Tryal.

Mr. TRAPP.

1710, Jan. 3. Prælectiones Poeticæ, Pars I. 20 0 0
Correcting a Book on the Lord's
Prayer 2 3 0

URRY.

1714, Dec. 17. To publish the Works of Chaucer.
Himself to have One Third; the College of
Christ Church at Oxford One Third: and
Bernard Lintot One Third (and he the said

Lintot to pay for paper, print, copper-plates,
and all incidental expences) of all the moneys
arising by the Subscription for the said Book.
WILKINSON.
1703, June 26.   Vice Reclaimed...................... 10 15   0
Bp. WILLIAMS.
Half of his Sermons at Boyle's Lectures... 21 10   0

SWIFT ON LINTOT

Verses designed to be prefixed before BERNARD LINTOT'S *New
Miscellany*, 1725.

"Some Colinæus praise, some Bleau;
Others account them but so so;
Some Plantin to the rest prefer,
And some esteem old Elzevir;
Others with Aldus* would besot us;
I, for my part, admire *Lintottus*.—
His character's beyond compare,
Like his own person, large and fair.
They print their names in letters small,
But LINTOT stands in capital:
Author and he with equal grace
Appear, and stare you in the face.
Stephens prints Heathen Greek, 'tis said,
Which some can't construe, some can't read.
But all that comes from Lintot's hand
Ev'n Rawlinson might understand.
Oft in an Aldus or a Plantin
A page is blotted, or leaf wanting:
Of Lintot's books this can't be said,
All fair, and not so much as read.
Their copy cost them not a penny
To Homer, Virgil, or to any;

---

*Printers, famous for having published fine editions of the Bible, and of
the Greek and Roman classics.

> They ne'er gave sixpence for two lines
> To them, their heirs, or their assigns :
> But Lintot is at vast expence,
> And pays prodigious dear for — sense.
> Their books are useful but to few,
> A scholar, or a wit or two :
> Lintot's for general use are fit;
> For some folks read, but all folks ———."

On a Miscellany of Poems. — To Bernard Lintot.

> "Ipsa varietate tentamus efficere ut alia aliis; quædam
> fortasse omnibus placeant."
>   Plin. *Epist.*

> "As when some skilful Cook, to please each Guest,
> Would in one Mixture comprehend a Feast,
> With due proportion and judicious care
> He fills his Dish with diff'rent sorts of Fare,
> Fishes and Fowl deliciously unite,
> To feast at once the Taste, the Smell, and Sight :

GEORGE LORD LYTTELTON

THIS excellent Nobleman, the eldest son of Sir Thomas Lyttelton of Hagley in Worcestershire, bart. was born in 1709*; and educated at Eton; where he was so much distinguished, that his exercises were recommended as models to his school-fellows.

From Eton Lyttelton went to Christ Church; where he retained the same reputation of superiority, and displayed his abilities to the publick in a Poem on Blenheim. He was a very early Writer, both in Verse and Prose. His "Progress of Love," and his "Persian Letters," were both written when he was very young.

---

*He was born at seven months, and thrown away by the nurse as a dead child, but upon closer inspection was found to be alive.

He stayed not long at Oxford; for in 1728 he began his travels, and visited France and Italy. When he returned, he obtained a seat in Parliament, for the borough of Oakhampton (on the death of Mr. Northmore), in 1735; and continued their Representative till he was made a Peer; and soon distinguished himself among the most eager opponents of Sir Robert Walpole, though his father, who was one of the Lords of the Admiralty, always voted with the Court. For many years the name of George Lyttelton was seen in every account of every debate in the House of Commons. He opposed the Standing Army; he opposed the Excise; he supported the motion for petitioning the King to remove Walpole.

The Prince of Wales, being (1737) driven from St. James's, kept a separate Court, and opened his arms to the Opponents of the Ministry. Mr. Lyttelton was made his Secretary, and was supposed to have great influence in the direction of his conduct. He persuaded his Master, whose business it was now to be popular, that he would advance his character by Patronage. Mallet was made under-secretary, and Thomson had a pension. For Thomson he always retained his kindness, and was able at last to place him at ease. Moore courted his favour by an apologetical poem, called "The Trial of Selim," for which he was paid with kind words, which, as is common, raised great hopes, that at last were disappointed. He now stood in the first rank of Opposition; and Pope, who was incited, it is not easy to say how, to increase the clamour against the Ministry, commended him among the other Patriots. This drew upon him the reproaches of Mr. Fox, who, in the House, imputed to him as a crime his intimacy with a Lampooner so unjust and licentious. Lyttelton supported his friend, and replied, "that he thought it an honour to be received into the familiarity of so great a Poet."

While he was thus conspicuous, he married (1741) Miss Lucy Fortescue, sister to Lord Fortescue, of Devonshire, by whom he had a son Thomas (afterwards the second Lord Lyttelton), and two daughters, and with whom he appears to have lived in the highest degree of connubial felicity. "But human pleasures are short; she died in childbed, about six years afterwards (1747), and he solaced his grief by writing a *long Poem to her memory*; without however condemning himself to perpetual solitude and sorrow; for soon after he sought to find the same happiness again, in a second marriage, with the daughter of Sir Robert

Rich (1749); but the experiment was unsuccessful."

But to return to his political life. After a long struggle, Walpole gave way, and honour and profit were distributed among his conquerors. Lyttelton was made (1744) one of the Lords of the Treasury; and from that time was engaged in supporting the schemes of the Ministry. Politicks did not, however, so much engage him, as to withhold his thoughts from things of more importance. He had, in the pride of juvenile confidence, with the help of corrupt conversation, entertained doubts of the truth of Christianity; but he thought the time now come when it was no longer fit to doubt or believe by chance, and applied himself seriously to the great question. His studies, being honest, ended in conviction. He found that Religion was true; and what he had learned he endeavoured to teach (1747), by "Observations on the Conversion and Apostleship of St. Paul;" a treatise to which, as Dr. Johnson remarks, "Infidelity has never been able to fabricate a specious answer." This Book his Father had the happiness of seeing, and expressed his pleasure in a letter which deserves to be inserted, and must have given to such a Son a pleasure more easily conceived than described: "I have read your Religious Treatise with infinite pleasure and satisfaction. The style is fine and clear, the arguments close, cogent, and irresistible. May the King of Kings, whose glorious cause you have so well defended, reward your pious labours; and grant that I may be found worthy, through the merits of Jesus Christ, to be an eye-witness of that happiness which I don't doubt he will bountifully bestow upon you! In the mean time, I shall never cease glorifying God, for having endowed you with such useful talents, and given me so good a son.

Your affectionate Father, THOMAS LYTTELTON."

A few years afterwards (1751), by the death of his Father, he inherited a Baronet's title, with a large estate, which, though perhaps he did not augment, he was careful to adorn, by a house of great elegance and expence, and by great attention to the decoration of his park. As he continued his exertions in Parliament, he was gradually advancing his claim to profit and preferment; and accordingly was made, in 1754, Cofferer and Privy-counsellor. This place he exchanged next year for the great office of Chancellor of the Exchequer; an office, however, that required some qualifications which he soon perceived himself to want.

The year after, his curiosity led him into Wales; of which he has given an account, perhaps rather with too much affectation of delight, to Archibald Bower, a man of whom he had conceived an opinion more favourable than he seems to have deserved, and whom, having once espoused his interest and fame, he never was persuaded to disown.

About this time he published his "Dialogues of the Dead," which were very eagerly read, though the production rather, as it seems, of leisure than of study, rather effusions than compositions.

When, in the latter part of the last Reign, the inauspicious commencement of the war made the dissolution of the Ministry unavoidable, Sir George Lyttelton, losing his employment with the rest, was recompensed with a Peerage (1757); and rested from political turbulence in the House of Lords.

His last literary production was, "The History of Henry the Second, 1764," elaborated by the researches and deliberations of twenty years, and published with the greatest anxiety. The story of this publication is remarkable. The whole Work was printed twice over, a great part of it three times, and many sheets four or five times. The Booksellers paid for the first impression; but the charges and repeated operations of the press were at the expence of the Author, whose ambitious accuracy, to my knowledge, cost him at least a thousand pounds. [The Work was originally published by Mr. Sandby; who died at Teddington in Middlesex, Nov. 2, 1799, in his 82nd year, deeply regretted by all who knew him. He was for many years a Bookseller of high eminence in Fleet-street; but exchanged that profession (about 1765) for the far more lucrative one of a Banker, in the old established firm of Snow and Denne, in the Strand.]

He began to print the Work in 1755. Three Volumes appeared in 1764, a second edition of them in 1767, a third edition in 1768, and the conclusion in 1771-2. Andrew Reid, a man not without considerable abilities, and not unacquainted with letters or with life, undertook to persuade the Noble Author, as he had persuaded himself, that he was master of the secret of punctuation; and, as fear begets credulity, he was employed, I know not at what price, to point the pages of "Henry the Second." The Book was at last pointed and printed, and sent into the world. His Lordship took money for his copy, of which, when he had paid the pointer, he probably gave the rest away; for he was very liberal to the indigent.

When Time brought the History to a third edition, Reid was either dead or discarded; and the superintendence of typography and punctuation was committed to a man originally a comb-maker, but then known by the style of Dr. Saunders [a Scotch LL.D.]. Something uncommon was probably expected, and something uncommon was at last done; for to the edition of Dr. Saunders is appended, what the world had hardly seen before, a list of errors of nineteen pages.

But to Politicks and Literature there must be an end. Lord Lyttelton had never the appearance of a strong or of a healthy man; he had a slender uncompacted frame, and a meagre face*: he lasted, however, above sixty years, and then was seized with his last illness.

His Lordship was buried at Hagley; and the following inscription is cut on the side of his Lady's monument:

"This unadorned stone was placed here
by the particular desire and express directions
of the late Right Honourable GEORGE Lord LYTTELTON,
who died August 22, 1773, aged 64."

JEREMIAH MARKLAND

JEREMIAH MARKLAND, one of the most learned and penetrating Critics of the eighteenth century, and not more valued for his universal reading, than beloved for the excellence of his heart, and primitive simplicity of manners, was one of the twelve children of the Rev. Ralph Markland, author of "The Art of Shooting flying;" and vicar of Childwall, Lancashire, a small preferment, in the gift of the Bishop of Chester. He was a very worthy man; whose life was strictly conformable to the doctrine he preached; and who was esteemed, by all who knew him, as an ornament to the Church, and a dignity to human nature. The time of his death is not known.

---

*"It is an anecdote no less remarkable than true, that Lord Lyttelton never could comprehend the commonest rules of Arithmetick." *R.C.*

Jeremiah was born Oct. 29*, 1693. "His father, in 1704, having already a great family of children, and likely to have more, got this boy to be admitted upon the foundation of Christ's Hospital in London, with a view of his being sent to the University with the usual exhibition of 30*l. per annum* for seven years; which view succeeded; and in the year 1710 he was admitted of St. Peter's College in Cambridge; and in 1717 was chosen fellow of the same College. It soon appeared to him that he never should be able to perform the duty of a Clergyman; the weakness of his lungs being such, that reading Lectures, only one hour in a day, disordered him greatly." *These are his own words.*

After having obtained the fellowship, Mr. Markland continued several years, as a tutor, at Peter-house.

He became first distinguished in the learned world by his "Epistola Critica ad eruditissimum virum Franciscum Hare, S. T. P. Decanum Vigorniensem; in quâ Horatii loca aliquot et aliorum veterum emendantur, Cantabr. 1723," 8vo; in which he gave many proofs of extensive erudition and critical sagacity. Bishop Hare would have provided for him, if he would have taken orders; but *non saxa nudis surdiora a navitis,* as Mr. Clarke observed in a letter to Mr. Bowyer.

He was at that time deeply engaged in notes and emendations on Propertius; and promised a new edition of the Thebaid and Achillaid of Statius. But he published only an edition of the *Sylvæ,* which appeared in 1728, under the title of "P. Papinii Statii Silvarum Libri quinque; ex vetustis Exemplaribus recensuit, et Notas atque Emendationes adjecit, Jer. Marklandus, Coll. S^{ti} Petri Cantabrig. Socius. Lond. 1728," 4to; for which he solicited the communications of the Learned. — The number of copies printed were 400, and 25 on large paper. — It being not convenient for him to pay Mr. Bowyer for printing the volume of Statius so soon as he himself had wished and intended, he insisted on adding the interest.

Some time before this he had begun, at Cambridge, an edition of part of Apuleius, of which seven sheets were printed off, from Morell's French edition; but, on Dr. Bentley's sending him a rude message concerning his having left out a line that was

---

*The Admission-book at Christ's Hospital says, "Oct. 18;" but the date above is from his own hand-writing. Possibly he was born on the 18th, and baptized on the 29th.

extant in one of the MSS. he stopped short, and went no farther. Part of the impression remained for many years at Cambridge in Mr. Bentham's warehouse; but Mr. Bowyer (who would have carried on the work) could never get a copy of it.

"After several years' residence at St. Peter's college, in 1728 he undertook the education of a young gentleman* in Hertfordshire, with whom he continued above two years at his house, and as long abroad in France†, Flanders, and Holland. Some time after their return into England, the gentleman married; and when his eldest son was about six years old, Mr. Markland undertook the care of his education, as he had done to the father, and was with him seven years." *This paragraph is again Mr. Markland's.*

After his return from France, Mr. Markland again took up his residence at Peter-house; and resumed his learned labours.

In 1740, Dr. John Davies, President of Queen's College, Cambridge, published his second edition, in folio, Greek and Latin, of the Dissertations of Maximus Tyrius; "cui accesserunt viri eruditissimi Jer. Marklandi Annotationes." This volume was printed by Mr. Bowyer, under the immediate superintendence of the very learned Professor Ward, and under the sanction of the Society for the Encouragement of Learning; who complained of the expence which Mr. Markland occasioned by his extreme nicety in correcting the proof sheets. In an address to the reader, prefixed to his Annotations, Mr. Markland demonstrated the truth of his discovery, that Maximus had himself published two editions of his work; a discovery sufficient in itself to immortalize the name of this eminent Critick.

In 1743 Mr. Markland resided at Twyford; where, in June, he talks of the gout as an old companion with him : and at this period of his life, if ambition had been his aim, he might have gratified it; there being positive proof, under his own hand, that he *twice* declined to offer himself a candidate for the Greek

---

*William Strode, esq. of Punsborn, Herts, who married Lady Anne, daughter of James Cecil fifth Earl of Salisbury.

†In 1774, he mentions "buying Fell's edition of the Greek Testament in France above 40 years ago." — "The life of scholars is generally sedentary, and therefore cannot contain many facts : he indeed was in France with Mr. Strode, particularly in Languedoc; but I know of nothing interesting on that head, though I have heard him relate a few laughable particulars." *Rev. E. Clarke to Mr. Nichols, Nov.* 10, 1777.

Professorship, a station where abilities like his would have been eminently displayed.

On the 28th of February, 1743-4, he calls himself "*a poor rustic;*" and tells Mr. Bowyer, "I suppose you have heard that the Greek Professor at Cambridge is dying. I am invited very kindly to accept of it by several friends, who have given me information, and advised me to be a Candidate; instead of going an hundred miles to take it, I would go two hundred the other way to avoid it. But this is *inter nos*," &c.

From 1744 to 1752 his residence was at Uckfield in Sussex, where he boarded in the house of the schoolmaster under whose care young Mr. Strode had been placed; and where he first formed an intimacy with the Rev. William Clarke; whose son Edward was placed under his private tuition.

In 1745 Mr. Markland published "Remarks on the Epistles of Cicero to Brutus, and of Brutus to Cicero: in a Letter to a Friend. With a Dissertation upon Four Orations ascribed to M. Tullius Cicero; *viz.* 1. Ad Quirites post Reditum; 2. Post Reditum in Senatu; 3. Pro Domo suâ, ad Pontifices; 4. De Haruspicum Responsis. To which are added, some Extracts out of the Notes of learned Men upon those Orations, and Observations on them, attempting to prove them all spurious and the works of some Sophist; 1745," 8vo.

In common with many learned and good men, whose memories will not be disgraced by mentioning this trifling circumstance, and amongst whom might be named the great Dr. Samuel Clarke, he sometimes was fond of relaxing from severer studies, by playing at Whist. It appears by a letter to Mr. Bowyer, dated Sept. 19, 1748, that he once won what, at that period, must have been esteemed a very large sum of money. He says, "The Paralytick you mention, to whose case that of Horace is applicable, *Mergas profundo fortior exsilit,* was formerly my acquaintance, and great benefactor; for I won an hundred pounds of him at Whist, and got it every farthing. The moral of the story, if I take it right, is, *Vexatio dat intellectum.*"

In June 1749, he was under considerable apprehension of danger from the illness of his young pupil Mr. Strode; and in the same year he says, "I have made another attack upon *Cicero de Oratore,* in which I fancy I have found out strange doings."

Feb. 27, 1749-50, Mr. Markland says, "I have lately had two letters from the Vice-chancellor (Dr. Keene, our Master), who wishes me to take the Greek Professorship, which is about to be vacant again. You, who know me, will not wonder that I have absolutely refused to be a Candidate for it. This, perhaps, is a secret at present; and therefore do not mention it to any body."

In the next month, he communicated some very judicious Remarks on an edition, then printing by Mr. Bowyer, of "Kuster de Verbo Medio," &c.

In a letter to Mr. Clarke, dated Uckfield, Sept. 2, 1751, he says, "Euripides goes on with success; at least I think so. I dare not say it to any body but yourself, that I have found out very many things in him which had escaped Scaliger. who seems to have read this Author with great attention; though, to humble my own vanity, I ought to add, that several of those of Scaliger had escaped me. — Many accidents concurring have determined me not to go to Brighthelmstone this week. The place is extremely full at present, so that there is some doubt of my being able to procure lodgings."*

In 1752, having completed the education of his amiable young pupil, he first began to seclude himself from the world. "By this time (*these are his own words*) being grown old, and having moreover long and painful annual fits of the gout, he was glad to find, what his inclination and infirmities, which made him unfit for the world, and for company, had for a long time led him to, a very private place of retirement near Dorking in Surrey." — In this pleasant and sequestered spot, he saw as little company as possibly he could; his walks were almost confined to the narrow limits of his garden; and he described himself, in 1755, to be "as much out of the way of hearing, as of getting. Of this last," he adds, "I have now no desire; the other I should be glad of." What first induced him to retire from the world is not known. It has been supposed to have proceeded from disappointment; but of what nature it is not easy to imagine. There is a traditionary report, that he once received a munificent proposal from Dr. Mead, to enable him to travel, on a most liberal plan, in pursuit of such literary matters as should appear eligible to himself; and that his retirement arose from a disgust his extreme delicacy occasioned him to take during the negotiation. He was certainly disinterested to an extreme; and money was never considered by him as a good, any farther

---

*Brighthelmstone was the ancient spelling of the town in Sussex now called Brighton. [*Ed.*]

than it enabled him to relieve the necessitous.

Aug. 31, 1755, he writes thus to Mr. Bowyer: "Dr. Burton breakfasted with me on Wednesday morning; I did not know before that he had been dangerously ill of a fever. He tells me that one Mr. Musgrave, of Corpus in Oxford; has been at Paris, to collate Euripides; and has put into the press at Oxford his Hippolytus, which he thinks will be out by Christmas. I understand there is to be no Latin version, which, I fear, will hurt the sale; and if he prints it without accents, in the modern fashion (which I forgot to ask him), it will hurt it still more, however skilful in other respects the work may be." — The work was published in 1756 under the title of "Euripidis Hippolytus, ex MSS. Bibliothecæ Regiæ Parisiensis emendatus. Variis Lectionibus et notis Editoris accessere viri clarissimi Jeremiæ Markland Emendationes." On the margin of his copy, Mr. Markland has written these words: "This title was put without my knowledge, and very contrary to my inclination. J. MARKLAND." — In this book also he has written several corrections on the Play, and on the Notes.

Mr. Markland assisted Mr. Bowyer in an edition of Seven Plays of Sophocles, 1758, by the notes which he communicated to him.

In 1760, Mr. Markland printed, in quarto, at the expence of his friend William Hall, esq. of the Temple, an excellent little treatise, under the title of "De Græcorum Quintâ Declinatione Imparisyllabicâ, et inde formatâ Latinorum Tertiâ, Quæstio Grammatica." No more than *forty copies* of this pamphlet having been printed, which were all given away, it was annexed, in 1763, to an admirable edition of the "Supplices Mulieres" of Euripides, in quarto, but without his name; the omission of which, Dr. Foster told him, occasioned the book not to have fair play. Why it was published anonymously, a letter from him to Mr. Bowyer will explain: "As to the compliments of Scholars, I believe you do not set any great value upon them, and I believe I set as little; to avoid which myself, and to excuse others the necessity of making them right or wrong, were two reasons why no name is put to this edition." (*April* 11.)

The following memorandum is taken from his own handwriting in a copy of that book:

"This was printed, at the expence of Dr. Heberden, A.D. 1763. There were only 250 copies printed, this kind of study being at that time greatly neglected in England. The writer of the Notes was then old and infirm; and having by him several things of the same sort, written many years before, he did not think it worth while to revise them; and was unwilling to leave them behind him, as they were, in many places not legible to any body but himself; for which reason he destroyed them. Probably it will be a long time (if ever) before this sort of Learning will revive in England; in which it is easy to foresee that there must be a disturbance in a few years, and all public disorders are enemies to this sort of literature."

The second edition of Mr. Foster's "Essay on the different Nature of Accent and Quality, 1763," 8vo, contains "Some Additions from the Papers of Dr. Taylor and Mr. Markland "

In 1765 Mr. Markland had a fresh opportunity of indulging his benevolence to the fullest extent — by *distressing himself*, to support the widow with whom he lodged, against the injustice and oppression of her son, who, taking the advantage of maternal weakness, persuaded her to assign over to him almost the whole of her little property. The consequence was a law-suit, which, after an enormous expence to Mr. Markland, was terminated against the widow. His whole fortune, after that event, was expended in relieving the distresses of this family. Whatever sums he could command were constantly disposed of for their support. Yet it was with difficulty he could be prevailed on to accept the pecuniary assistance which many of his friends were desirous of affording him. From Dr. Law, then master of Peter House, for whom he justly entertained the highest regard, and whose benevolence he repeatedly experienced, he not without hesitation accepted a present in August 1766; and in the same month refused a generous offer of Abp. Secker. In October that year he declined even entering into a correspondence with his old acquaintance Bp. Law, who wished to serve him.

His whole property, exclusive of the annual receipt from his fellowship, May 21, 1767, consisted of 500*l*. Three per Cent. Reduced Annuities.

In June 1767 he had a violent attack of St. Anthony's Fire; and in August was afflicted with the yellow jaundice. This disorder began with an excessive diarrhœa. "If this does not stop," says he, "it will soon carry off an old man. I am under no uneasiness, having made my Will." *Aug.* 5, 1767. On the receipt of a handsome sum from Dr. Barnard, he wrote thus to Mr. Bowyer: "I received yours this morning; together with that of Dr. Barnard, which I have not yet opened, nor shall: I mean as to the bill part; but this must not be mentioned for the world, for fear of giving offence. One thing you may mention as you please, that I am greatly satisfied with his not writing to me; it looks as if he did not like to be thanked; which to me is a sure mark of a noble mind." *July* 12, 1767.

Nov. 5, he says, "The book of debtor and creditor is quite needless to me, who have no accounts with any body but yourself; and know every farthing I owe, and every farthing due to me, as exactly as if it were set down in an hundred accountbooks. I deal in Hoare's notes for security. If they miscarry by the post, I have time to send up word, and stop payment: but a banknote, once lost, is lost for ever; or, if I could detect the stealer, his being hanged would be no satisfaction to me for the loss of the money, and would give a great deal of trouble. — I am glad you have got an horse. It would be an excellent thing for me; but am past it (being in my seventy-fifth year) as much as I am past country-dances."

In 1768, Mr. Markland condescended to accept from Mr. Strode an annuity of 100*l.* which, with the dividends arising from his fellowship, was from that time the whole of his income.

Fortunately for the world of letters, the notes on the two "Iphigeniæ," which Mr. Markland at one time intended to destroy, were preserved; and presented, in February 1768, "Doctissimo, et, quod longè præstantius est, Humanissimo Viro Wilhelmo Heberden, M.D. arbitratu ejus vel cremandæ, vel in publicum emittendæ post obitum scriptoris."

Dr. Heberden, whose generosity was unbounded, readily accepted the gift on Mr. Markland's own conditions; paid the whole expence of the printing, as he had before done that of the "Supplices Mulieres;" and in 1770 had secured a copy of it corrected for a *second* edition, though at that time it was intended that the *first* should not be published till after Mr. Markland's death.

He had then burnt all his notes, except those on the New Testament; and the disposal of his books became now to him a matter of serious concern. He wished them to be in the hands of the friend to whom he presented the greater part of them in his life-time, and the remainder at his death.

April 25, 1770, he tells Mr. Bowyer: "On Sunday I wrote to Dr. Heberden, to acquaint him, that, as you had some time since told me that he intended one of his sons for holy orders, I would, on demand, send him up a copy I had of Kuster's edition of the New Testament, with a large margin, on which I had written many things on the Evangelists and the Acts, which perhaps might be of use to the young man towards setting him up."

In the summer of the same year Mr. Bowyer, having determined to re-publish his "Conjectures on the New Testament," applied to his kind and learned friend Mr. Markland for assistance; who, July 30, says, "In mine to you yesterday, I expressed some unwillingness of having any thing printed which is written in the margin of my Greek Testament: I had not then thought of an obvious expedient, which has occurred since; viz. that my name may be concealed (the chief thing I aimed at); and at the end of each note, if any be made use of, may be put the letter *R*. This will answer the intent of each of us:" — Feb. 10, 1771: "The Notes in the two paper-books were written a long time before those in *the folio edition*." — May 20: "I shall send you the sheets on the New Testament by Friday's carrier: you will receive them that night, or the next morning. The reason of my sending them is, because, as I see you have taken a great deal of pains to transcribe into the margin out of the papers I sent last, it may save you, or Mr. Nichols, a good deal of trouble, if ever there should be occasion for a second edition. I have not had ability or inclination to read them: but I see the letter *R* often occurs. Curiosity (they say) is one of the last things which dies in a man: this prompted me to look for five or six places, which I find are mostly omitted here; which I do not wonder at, knowing the difficulty and the distraction of such an undertaking. You say you are afraid of me: you need not; for there is not a more quiet man in the world." — May 23: "With this you will receive the sheets on the New Testament; in some of which, viz. Acts xii, xxi, 3, &c. I could not forbear scribbling something, which perhaps you will not be able to read, owing to the weakness of my hand when I wrote it. I think that your undertaking is enough to distract even a younger man than yourself, and one who is perfectly at ease both in mind and body. Had I considered the difficulty of it sooner, I should have been against it. — I have sent a few pens, all I could find, to be cobbled by you at your leisure*; for I cannot meet with any like those of your emendation.

---

*Mr. Markland, for many years, used no pens but what were made or mended by Mr. Bowyer.

These will last my life. You may bring them with you, if you come after Midsummer." — July 18, "I have read over the articles marked with *R* as well as I could, without any fair copy, and by guess; and I have sent them, that there might be no more delay on my account; though you say in your last, "I am sorry that I undertook it." I should say so too, were you under any necessity of publishing it. But I suppose you are not, and am very sorry that you have such an unanswerable excuse to plead; a disorder, to which I believe all attention and application are hurtful, as perhaps they chiefly, joined to too much sitting-still, may have been the cause of it."

Mr. Markland's intended edition of the "Two Iphigeniæ," which had been printed in 1768, 8vo, with a view to posthumous publication, were given to the world in 1771, under the title of "Euripidis Dramata, Iphigenia in Aulide, et Iphigenia in Tauris, ad Codd. MSS. recensuit, et Notulas adjecit, Jer. Markland, Coll. D. Petri Cantabrigiensis Socius."

On this subject Mr. Markland shall speak for himself: "On the 5th of this month I received from Dr. Heberden a Bank note of 20*l.* with notice of some wine and chocolate he had sent me. In my letter of thanks, I took the opportunity of telling him, "I have for some time been in fear of your generosity; which was the reason of my being glad to put off the publication of Euripides till after my death, because I apprehended that you designed the whole advantage of the edition (for the printing of which you had already paid, beside the 50*l.* Bank note you had sent) should be mine; which I thought was unjust in me to take, and unreasonable. If you can be prevailed upon (which I greatly wish) to suffer the expence of the printing to be re-paid you out of the sale of the book, I will write to Mr. Bowyer immediately to re-print the first half-sheet, and to strike out the words *post obitum scriptoris,* and *dum in vivis erat,* and to advertise it forthwith under my name. If you have any objection, you need only to say that you had rather things should continue as they are." *June* 14, 1771. — In one of July 5 following, he says, "My great concern is, that the expence of printing may be paid whenever they are to be published. I do not care a straw about any thing after that, except to save trouble to others. You call it *pride* : I call it *justice*." — In another letter in this year, he mentions a work* as being in forwardness, under

---

*This work was completed, and possibly is still in being.

the title of "Quæstiones Venusinæ* ad Horatii Carmina," &c. having "got as far as Serm. I. 3. in the transcription."

In this year Mr. Markland was agreeably gratified by the news of Mr. Bowyer's proffered legacy, not so much on his own account, as that of his sister Catharine, who is some degree depended on him for support. For the amount of this legacy, or any part of it, Mr. Markland or his sister had permission to draw, whenever they thought proper.

Mr. Bowyer published the second edition of his "Conjectures," in 8vo, 1772; and meditated an 8vo edition of the sacred text as a companion to it, which, however, he did not live to accomplish. On the 13th of August this year, Mr. Markland writes to him: "The printing of the notes on the two little quartos next summer is a thing of so great uncertainty, both with regard to me and yourself, that I shall say nothing of it at present, as there is time enough to think of it: but any thoughts of coming to London, in my present circumstances, are death to, dear Sir, yours sincerely."

October 27, 1773, he says, "When you ask me a question in the *Res Nummaria,* you ask one who knows as little of that matter as if he were of the Royal Society. I never had the least inclination to study that part of Antiquity; of which I shall give you a surprizing instance, when I tell you, *that I have not read our Friend's account of the Antient Coins.* From some scraps of it, I perceive a prodigious shew of erudition; but whether it be exact or not, I am not a judge." — "My complaints are the same as yours, owing to the same cause, much sitting still. Forty years ago I drank nothing but water for several years; but Dr. Boerhaave told me that when I grew old I must come to wine, which I find to be true; so that now I have bid adieu to water and all its works; except chocolate, which with eggs and milk are my chief support: one bottle of wine serves me four or five days." — *Dec.* 3. "It is pleasant to observe how naturally a man returns to the point whence he set out, *viz.* milk, which is now the chief sustenance to me at 80 years old: not to mention other infirmities of infancy, among which I must very poetically mention one, *madidique infanti nasi.*"

For a considerable part of his life, he had been much afflicted with the gout, which he held to be "one of the greatest prolongers of mortality in Nature's store-room, as being so great

*See Horace, Od. iii. 4, ver. 9; Sat. ii. 1, ver. 35.

an absorbent of all other maladies."

He still, however, continued to commit his thoughts to writing; and Jan. 27, 1775, says, "Do not forget me if you meet with any folio edition of the New Testament, the paper of which will bear ink; Beza's (I have that) will not. I shall not write much upon it (I am too old), and yet I would not have every thing I can say lost. I did not think it reasonable to take your edition; that is, the meat out of your mouth. As far as I remember, Gregory's Oxford edition would answer my purpose. Perhaps you are better acquainted with it.

"What will become of us? For I foresee the American Petition will be rejected. I have feared it a long time. I have less reason to be concerned than you have, being much older; and yet I cannot forbear being uneasy for posthumous calamaties, which I foresee will be owing to the weakness of some, and the wickedness of others. The Provost of Eton* brought his son hither, a youth of about eleven years old. I told him, I was afraid he will see evil days in England; for that it seemed to be ripening apace. You, I believe, will laugh at all this, as appearances are different to different persons; and yet I think every man in England has reason to be uneasy at such a majority of Members of —— who will sell you to the best bidder; in which case you have only one way (and that a very disagreeable one) to help yourself.

In 1775 the "Supplices Mulieres," with the "Quæstio Grammatica," were re-printed in octavo, from a copy corrected by Mr. Markland, for the use of Eton-school.

"It amazes me when I consider what strange oversights have been made in the New Testament by men of the greatest learning and sagacity, in a book that has been read more than any book in the world. What can be the reason of it? They would not have done so in any other author. Reverence, perhaps, has got the better of common sense. I could send you instances which would astonish you. — Poor America! and poor England!" *Jan.* 29.

Feb. 5. "Dr. P.'s† wealth, you say, is confirmed by good authority. I am sorry for it, because I think a Christian priest, with no children, to die worth 30,000*l.* has a very *unscriptural* look. One news-paper says, that he left to twenty fellows of

---

*Dr. Barnard.

†Dr. Powell, Master of St. John's College, Cambridge.

the College, who were his contemporaries, 100*l.* each. This would have been very pretty and commendable, had it been done a fortnight before he was taken ill: otherwise it has the look of playing fast and loose, and seems to declare that, if he had never died, he never would have done any good with his riches."

On the 19th of October this year, this worthy man put his own mind at ease, by making the following concise disposition of his property: "My books and papers I leave to Dr. William Heberden of Pall Mall. Every thing else which belonged to me (all which together is scarcely worth mentioning) I leave to Mrs. Martha Rose of Milton; whom I believe to be one of the most worthy persons, and know to be one of the greatest objects of humanity and Christian compassion, I ever was acquainted with in a long life; whom therefore I make my sole Executrix."

He still continued to correspond as usual with Mr. Bowyer: Nov. 5, 1775, "The person* to whom you made the present of Kuster's Greek Testament, folio, not long ago, has often, to my knowledge, thought that there is no book in the world which he would not rather publish than the New Testament, because it is impossible to give an edition which would satisfy others and himself too. What can be done, says he, in cases where there is no Greek, no sense, contradiction, the negative wanting or abounding; and yet all the copies agreeing? Instances of all which, not yet given, are easily given, and any *one* of them would bring all the world upon his back! 'But have not all these things,' say you, 'been taken notice of long ago?' It is wonderful, and almost incredible to say, *They have not;* and the reason is not difficult to those who will consider the case of the great men who have written upon the New Testament. All this I believe to be true (you perhaps will not); but I have put no name, because of accidents: and I would not give a straw, to have every body think as I do.

An attack of the gout, attended with a fever, put an end to his existence in this world, July 7, 1776.

His excellent friend, Mr. Strode, (accompanied by the Writer of these Memoirs) went immediately to Milton Court, to give directions for the funeral; which was performed, strictly agreeably to his own request, in the church of Dorking. It was Mr. Strode's intention to have placed a *marble tablet* in the church; but, at the suggestion of Dr. Heberden, who wrote the epitaph,

*Mr. Markland himself.

a *brass plate* was very properly preferred; which has the following inscription :

"JEREMIAH MARKLAND, A. M.
was born the 29th of October, 1693;
educated in the School of Christ's Hospital, London; and elected Fellow of St. Peter's College, Cambridge. Unambitious of the rewards and honours which his abilities and application might have obtained for him in the learned professions, he chose to pass his life in a liberal retirement. His very accurate knowledge of the Greek and Latin languages was employed in correcting and explaining the best antient Authors, and more particularly in illustrating the Sacred Scriptures. To these rational pursuits he sacrificed every worldly view; contented with the inward pleasure resulting from such studies, and from the public and private assistance which they enabled him to communicate to others. But, above all, his uncommon learning confirmed in the highest degree his hopes of a happier life hereafter.
He died at Milton, in this parish,
the 7th day of July, 1776."

DR. RICHARD MEAD

THIS great Physician (whose abilities and eminence in his profession, united with his learning and fine taste for those arts which embellish and improve human life, long rendered him an ornament, not only to his own profession, but to the nation and age in which he lived) was born at Stepney, Middlesex, Aug. 11, 1673; and received the early part of his education under his father, Matthew Mead, a celebrated Nonconformist Divine; who, with the assistance of Mr. John Nesbitt, superintended the education of thirteen children. In 1688 he was placed under the care of Mr. Thomas Singleton; and in 1689 under Grævius at Utrecht. In 1692 he removed to Leyden*, where

---

*He was contemporary with Boerhaave, with whom he afterwards maintained the most friendly intercourse through life.

he attended for three years the lectures of Herman and Pitcairn, and applied himself most successfully to the study of physic. In company with Samuel, his eldest brother, David Polhill, esq. and Dr. Thomas Pellet, he visited Italy, and luckily discovered at Florence the Mensa Isiaca, which had been many years given over as lost. He took his degree of Doctor of Philosophy and Physic at Padua, Aug. 16, 1695; and passed some time afterwards at Naples and Rome. On his return, about Midsummer 1696, he settled in the very house where he was born, and practised in his profession there for seven years with success.

In 1702 he published his "Mechanical Account of Poisons." These Essays, however justly esteemed on their first appearance, did their Author still more honour in the edition he published of them more than forty years afterwards. He became fellow of the Royal Society in 1704, in 1706 was chosen one of their Council, and in 1717 a Vice-president. He was chosen physician to St. Thomas's Hospital, May 5th, 1703, when he removed from Stepney to Crutched Fryars; where having resided seven years, he removed into Austin Fryars; and about the same time was appointed by the Company of Surgeons to read the anatomical lectures in their hall. In the mean time, Dec. 4, 1707, he was honoured by the University of Oxford with the degree of Doctor of Physic by diploma. On the last illness of Queen Anne, he was called in to a consultation, and ventured to declare that "she could not hold out long." He opened his mind freely on this subject to his friend and protector Dr. Radcliffe, who made use of that friendship to excuse his own attendance. Radcliffe surviving the Queen but three months, Mead removed into *his* house, and resigned his office in St. Thomas's Hospital. Uninfluenced by prejudices of party, he was equally the intimate of Garth, Arbuthnot, and Freind. He was admitted Fellow of the College of Physicians April 9, 1716; and executed the office of Censor in 1716, 1719, and 1724. In 1719, on an alarm occasioned by the fatal plague at Marseilles, the Lords of the Regency directed Mr. Craggs, then Secretary of State, to apply to Dr. Mead, to give the best directions for preventing the importation of the plague, or stopping its progress. His opinion was approved, and quarantine directed to be performed. Of his "Discourse concerning Pestilential Contagion," no less than seven editions were printed by Mr. Bowyer in 1720; the eighth, which appeared in 1722, and again in 1743, was enlarged with many new observations, and translated into Latin by Professor

Ward, whose services to Dr. Mead, on occasion of the Harveian Oration in 1723, I have already mentioned in vol. I. p. 267. By order of the Prince of Wales, Dr. Mead assisted, Aug. 10, 1721, at the inoculation of some condemned criminals: the experiment succeeding, the two then young Princesses, Amelia and Caroline, were inoculated April 17, 1722, and had the distemper favourably. On the accession of their royal father to the throne, in 1727, Dr. Mead was appointed physician in ordinary to his Majesty, and had afterwards the satisfaction of seeing his two sons-in-law (Dr. Edward Wilmot and Dr. Frank Nicholls) his associates in the same station. Being desirous of retirement, he declined the presidentship of the College of Physicians, which was offered him Oct. 1, 1734; but was elected honorary member of that at Edinburgh, Oct. 6, 1745. Mr. Bowyer printed the improved edition of his "Account of Poisons" in 1744; his treatise "De Imperio Solis ac Lunæ," &c. in 1746; "De Morbis Biblicis" in 1749; and "Monita Medica" in 1750. This was the last, and perhaps the most useful of all his works* : with a candour and simplicity so characteristical of a great man, he freely communicates in it all the discoveries that his long practice and experience had opened to him with regard to different diseases and their several cures.

The world was deprived of this eminent physician Feb. 16, 1754; and on the 23rd he was buried in the Temple church, near his brother Samuel, a counsellor at law.

To Dr. Mead there is no monument in the Temple; but an honorary one was placed by his son in the North aile of Westminster Abbey. Over the tomb is the Doctor's bust; at his right hand a wreathed serpent, darting its sting, and on his left several books. Below the bust are his arms and crest.

The Doctor was twice married. By his first lady he had ten children (of whom three survived him; two daughters, married to Dr. Wilmot and Dr. Nicholls; and his son Richard, heir to his father's and uncle's fortunes). By the second lady, he had no issue. During almost half a century he was at the head of his profession; which brought him in one year upwards of seven thousand pounds, and between five and six for several years. The Clergy, and in general all men of learning, were welcome

---

*His "Medical Works" were collected and published in one volume, 4to, 1762.

to his advice; and his doors were open every morning to the
most indigent, whom he frequently assisted with money; so that,
notwithstanding his great gains, he did not die very rich. He
was a most generous patron of learning and learned men, in all
sciences, and in every country; by the peculiar magnificence of
his disposition, making the private gains of his profession answer
the end of a princely fortune, and valuing them only as they
enabled him to become more extensively useful, and thereby to
satisfy that greatness of mind which will transmit his name to
posterity with a lustre not inferior to that which attends the
most distinguished character of antiquity. To him the several
Counties of England, and our Colonies abroad, applied for the
choice of their physicians. No foreigner of any learning, taste,
or even curiosity, ever came to England without being introduced to Dr. Mead; and he was continually consulted by the
physicians of the Continent. His large and spacious house in
Great Ormond-street became a repository of all that was curious
in Nature or in Art, to which his extensive correspondence with
the Learned in all parts of Europe not a little contributed. The
King of Naples sent to request a collection of all his works;
presented him with the two first volumes of Sig. Bajardi, and
invited him to his own palace: and, through the hands of M. de
Boze, he frequently had the honour of exchanging presents with
the King of France. He built a gallery for his favourite furniture,
his pictures, and his antiquities. His library, as appears by the
printed catalogue of it, consisted of 6592 numbers, containing
upwards of 10,000 volumes, in which he spared no expence for
scarce and antient editions. It is remarkable that many of his
books sold for much more than they had cost him. His pictures
also were chosen with so much judgment, that they produced
3417*l*. 11*s*.; about six or seven hundred pounds more than he
gave for them. Nor did he make this great collection for his
own use only, but freely opened it to public inspection. Ingenious men were sure of finding at Dr. Mead's the best helps in all
their undertakings; and scarcely any thing curious appeared in
England but under his patronage. He constantly kept in pay a
great number of scholars and artists of all kinds, who were at
work for him, or for the publick. He was the friend of Pope,
of Halley, and of Newton; and placed their portraits in his
house, with those of Shakspeare and Milton, near the busts of
their great masters the antient Greeks and Romans.

Mr. Bowyer, who was intimately acquainted with Dr. Mead,

used to consult him as a physician; nor would the Doctor accept from him a fee. And not unfrequently having occasion for medical advice when Dr. Mead was unable to come to him, he generally received a friendly rebuke the next time he went to Ormond-street : "If I was not able to come to you," the good Doctor would say, "why could not you have sent for my son Wilmot?"

Mr. Bowyer was not inattentive to these kindnesses; and endeavoured to shew his gratitude by occasional literary presents. In a copy of Dr. Mead's Catalogue of Books, p. 240, occurs the following article : "Antiquæ Britannicæ Linguæ Dictionarium, per Thomam Davies; *interfoliat. cum notis MSS. Guil. Wotton.* Lond. 1632."

He never took a fee of any clergyman, but one, and that was Mr. Robert Leake, fellow of St. John's college, Cambridge; who, being fallen into a valetudinarian state, dabbled rather too much with the writings, and followed too closely some of the prescriptions, of the celebrated Dr. Cheyne. Being greatly emaciated in a course of time, by keeping too strictly to that gentleman's regimen, misapplying perhaps his rules, where the case required a different treatment, his friends advised him to apply to Dr. Mead; which he did, going directly to London, to wait on the Doctor, and telling him that "he had hitherto observed Cheyne's directions, as laid down in his printed books." Mead (a proud man, and passionate) immediately damned Cheyne and his regimen. "Follow my prescriptions," said he, "and I will set you up again." Mr. Leake submitted; and, beginning to find some benefit, he asked the Doctor every now and then, whether it might not be proper for him to follow at the same time such and such a prescription of Cheyne. Which Mead took ill. When the well-meaning patient was got pretty well again, he asked the Doctor what fees he desired or expected from him. "Sir," said the Physician, "I have never yet, in the whole of my practice, taken or demanded the least fee from any Clergyman; but, since you have been pleased, contrary to what I have met with in any other gentleman of your profession, to prescribe to me, rather than to follow my prescriptions, when you had committed the care of your recovery to my skill and trust, you must not take it amiss, nor will, I hope, think it unfair, if I demand ten guineas of you." The money, though not perhaps without some little reluctance, was paid down. The

Doctor at the same time told Leake, "You may come to me again before you quit London." He did so; and Mead returned to him six guineas out of the ten guineas which he had received.

CONYERS MIDDLETON

DR. CONYERS MIDDLETON, son of William Middleton, rector of Hinderwell in Yorkshire, was born at Richmond, in that county, on Dec. 27, 1683. His father, being possessed of an easy fortune besides his preferment in the Church, gave him a liberal education; and at seventeen years of age he was sent to Trinity college in Cambridge, of which in 1706 he was chosen fellow. In 1707 he commenced master of arts; and in two years after joined with several other fellows of his college in a petition to Dr. Moore, then bishop of Ely, as their visitor, against the celebrated Dr. Bentley, their master. In the early part of his life, he was not thought to possess any very extraordinary talents; and at the time he engaged in the controversy with Bentley, his attention was more devoted to musick than to study. This occasioned Bentley to call him in contempt *a fiddler*; and probably to this sarcasm the world may be indebted for the many excellent works he afterwards produced. However, he had no sooner joined in the proceedings against Bentley, than he withdrew himself from his jurisdiction, by marrying Mrs. Drake, daughter of Mr. Morris, of Oak-Morris in Kent, and widow of Counsellor Drake of Cambridge, a lady of ample fortune. After his marriage, he took a small rectory in the Isle of Ely, which was in the gift of his wife; but resigned it in little more than a year, probably because he thought it not worth keeping.

In October 1717, when King George I. visited the University of Cambridge, he was created, with several others, a doctor of divinity by mandate; and was the person who gave the first motion to that famous proceeding against Dr. Bentley, which made such a noise in the Nation. Bentley, whose office it was to perform the ceremony called *Creation,* made a new and extraordinary demand of four guineas from each of the Doctors, on pretence of a fee due to him as Divinity-Professor, over and above a broad piece, which had by custom been allowed as a present on this occasion. Upon this a warm dispute arose; the result of which was, that many of the Doctors, and Middleton among the rest, consented to pay the fee in question, upon condition that the money should be restored if it were not afterwards determined to be his right. It was determined against Bentley, but still he kept the money : upon which Middleton commenced an action against him for the recovery of his share of it. Bentley behaving with contumacy, and shewing all imaginable contempt to the authority of the University, was at first suspended from his degrees, and then degraded. He petitioned the King for relief from that sentence : upon which Middleton, by the advice of friends, thought it expedient to put the publick in possession of the whole affair. This occasioned him to publish, within the year 1719, the four following pieces : 1, "A full and impartial Account of all the late Proceedings in the University of Cambridge, against Dr. Bentley." 2, "A Second Part of the full and impartial Account, &c." 3, "Some Remarks upon a Pamphlet, intituled, "The Case of Dr. Bentley farther stated and vindicated, &c." The Author of the piece here remarked was the well-known Dr. Sykes; and he is treated here by Dr. Middleton with great contempt and severity : who seems, however, afterwards to have changed his opinion of him, and to have been upon very charitable terms with him: for, in his "Vindication of the Free Enquiry into the Miraculous Powers," which was published after his death, he appeals to his authority, and calls him "a very learned and judicious writer." The last tract is intituled, 4, "A true Account of the present State of Trinity College in Cambridge, under the oppressive Government of their Master Richard Bentley, late D.D." But this regards only the quarrel betwixt him and his College, and is employed in exposing his misdemeanors in the administration of College affairs. It seems to have been written in order to take off a suspicion which many then had, that the proceedings of the University against Dr. Bentley did not flow so much from any real demerit in the man, as from a certain spirit of resentment and opposition to the Court, the great promoter and manager of whose interest he was thought to be there; for, it must be remembered, that, in that part of his life, Dr. Middleton was a strong Tory; though, like Bishop Gooch and other considerable persons, his contemporaries in the University, he afterwards became a very zealous Whig.

But Middleton had not yet done with Bentley. The latter, in 1720, published, "Proposals for a new Edition of the Greek Testament, and Latin Version." Middleton, in 1721, published, 5, "Remarks, Paragraph by Paragraph, upon the Proposals, &c.;" and at setting out, "only desires his readers to believe, that they were not drawn from him by personal spleen or envy to the author of them, but by a serious conviction, that he had neither talents nor materials proper for the work he had undertaken." Middleton's motto to this piece was very happily chosen, and deserves to be transcribed. It is taken from an oration of Peter Burman, who, with a view of defending his brother critic against his adversaries, says, in a strain of irony, "Doctus criticus et adsuetus urere, secare, inclementer omnis generis libros tractare, apices, syllabas, voces, dictiones confodere, et stylo exigere, continebitne ille ab integro et intaminato divinæ sapientiæ monumento crudeles ungues?" Bentley defended his "Proposals" against these "Remarks," which, however, he did not ascribe to Middleton, but to Dr. Colbatch, a learned Fellow of his College, and Casuistical Professor of Divinity in the University. He very well knew the true author, but was resolved to dissemble it, for the double pleasure it would give him, of abusing Colbatch, and shewing his contempt of Middleton. He did, indeed, abuse Colbatch to that degree, that the Vice-chancellor and heads of the University, at a meeting in February 1721, pronounced his book to be a most scandalous and malicious libel, and resolved to inflict a proper censure upon the author, as soon as he should be discovered : for no names had yet appeared in the controversy. Middleton then published, with his name, an answer to Bentley's Defence, intituled, 6, "Some farther Remarks, Paragraph by Paragraph, upon Proposals lately published for a new Edition of a Greek and Latin Testament, by Richard Bentley, 1721." His motto, "Occupatus ille eruditione secularium literarum scripturas omnino sanctas ignoraverit, &c." These two pieces against Bentley are written with great acuteness and learning; and though the Critic affected greatly to despise them, yet they destroyed the credit of his Proposals so effectually, that his intended publication of the New Testament came to nothing.

Upon the great enlargement of the Public Library at Cambridge, by the addition of 30,000 volumes, which had been collected by Dr. Moore, late Bishop of Ely*, the erection of the new office of *Principal Librarian* was first voted, and then conferred upon Dr. Middleton; who drew up a plan for disposing of the books together in the new-projected building, intituled, "Bibliothecæ ordinandæ Methodus," which is printed among his Works.

After the decease of his first wife, he travelled through France into Italy, and arrived at Rome early in the year 1724. Much leisure, with an infirm state of health, was the cause of his journey to Italy; where, though his character and profession were well known, he was yet treated with particular respect by persons of the first distinction both in Church and State. The author of his Life in the "Biographia Britannica" relates, that, on his first coming there, he got himself introduced in his character of Principal Librarian to his Brother Librarian at the Vatican, who received him with great politeness; but, upon his mentioning Cambridge, said, he did not know before that there was any University in England of that name; and at the same time took notice, that he was no stranger to that of Oxford, for which he expressed a great esteem. Our new Librarian took some pains to convince his Brother not only of the real existence, but of the real dignity of his University of Cambridge. At last the Keeper of the Vatican acknowledged, that he had indeed heard of a celebrated School of that name in England, where youth were prepared for their admission at Oxford; and Dr. Middleton left him at present in that sentiment. But this unexpected indignity made him resolve to support his residence at Rome in such a manner, as should be a credit to his station at Cambridge; and accordingly he agreed to give 400*l. per annum* for a hotel, with all accommodations, fit for the reception of persons of the first rank in Rome; which, joined to his great fondness for antique curiosities, occasioned him to trespass a little upon his fortune. He returned through Paris towards the end of the year 1725, and arrived at Cambridge before Christmas.

In December 1731 Dr. Middleton was presented by Colonel King, Dr. Woodward's executor, to the professorship then recently founded by Dr. Woodward; and in July 1732 published

---

*"Which had been offered to the Earl of Oxford for 8000*l.* and were afterwards purchased for 6000 guineas, by King George I. and by him presented to the University."

his "Inauguration Speech." Reading lectures upon fossils, however, was not an employment suited to his taste, or to the turn of his studies; and he resigned it in 1734. The resignation, however, might probably be owing to his second marriage, as the professorship was tenable only by a single man. The salary certainly was an object to him.

In 1735 he published "A Dissertation concerning the Origin of Printing in England," of which I shall have occasion to speak further hereafter.

Soon after this, he married a second wife, Mary, a daughter of the Rev. Conyers Place, of Dorchester; and, upon her death, a third, Anne, daughter of John Powell, esq. of Boughroyd, near Radnor.

In 1741 came out his great work, "The History of the Life of M. Tullius Cicero," in two volumes, 4to, published by subscription, and dedicated to Lord Hervey, who was much the author's friend. Dr. Warton having asserted that in a little piece written by Lord Lyttelton in his youth, the "Observations on the Life of Tully," there is a more dispassionate and impartial character of the Orator, than in the panegyrical volumes of Middleton; the late Mr. Maty well observed, "that this is a controvertible proposition;" and adds, "As to the assertation, that Middleton saw the book *de Tribus Luminibus,* and availed himself much of it, I have been told by a gentleman who lived much with him at the time, that he did see it, but did not find it much to his purpose."

In December 1748 he published his "Free Inquiry into the Miraculous Powers which are supposed to have subsisted in the Christian Church from the earliest Ages, through several successive Centuries." Innumerable answerers now appeared against him; two of whom, Dodwell and Church, distinguished themselves with so much zeal, that they were each complimented by the University of Oxford with the degree of Doctor in Divinity. It does not appear that he originally intended to reply to any of them separately; for he was meditating a general answer to all the objections made against the Free Inquiry; but, being seized with illness, and imagining he might not be able to go through with it, he singled out Church and Dodwell, as the two most considerable of his adversaries, and employed himself in preparing a particular answer to them. This, however, he did not live to finish; but died, of a slow hectic fever and disorder in his liver, on the 28th of July, 1750, in the 67th year of his age, at Hildersham in Cambridgeshire, an estate of his own purchasing. His death happening about the same period with that of Mr. Gordon, the translator of Tacitus, Lord Boling-broke said to the late amiable Dr. Heberden, "Then there is the best Writer in England gone, and the worst!" A little before his death, he thought it prudent to accept of the small vicarage of Hascomb in Surrey, worth 50*l*. a year, from Sir John Frederick, bart. He published a great variety of tracts on various learned subjects, too many and too well known to need enumeration here; all which, except the Life of Cicero, were collected, and printed together, in four volumes, 4to, 1752.

Dr. Middleton superintended in his own house the education of two or three young gentlemen of rank, among whom was Thomas the second Lord Montfort (then Mr. Bromley), for whose father he purchased a valuable library, since dispersed by a bookseller's marked catalogue. From 1745 till his death, he had also under his tuition Mr. Robarts, nephew to the Earl of Radnor of that name, who generously continued the annual allowance to Dr. Middleton after the young gentleman was dead.

Besides the mezzotinto print of him, which is a very good likeness, a medal of him was cast and repaired by Giovanni Pozzo, at Rome, in 1724; which some years ago was copied in London by Mr. Stewart; and was afterwards engraved, as well as copied, at an easier expence, by Mr. Wedgwood.

EDWARD ROWE MORES

EDWARD-ROWE MORES, M.A. F.S.A. descended from an antient family, which had been seated from the beginning of the sixteenth century at Great Coxwell, in the county of Berks, and allied by his grandmother to that of Rowe, which had been settled at Higham-Bensted,* in Walthamstow, in the

---

*The seat of the Rowes from 1568, when it was purchased by Sir Thomas Rowe, lord mayor of London that year, who died 1570; and was buried in Hackney church, in a chapel built by him, as was also his son Sir Henry, lord mayor of London 1607, who died 1612, and his grandson Henry, all successively lords of the manor of Shaklewell.

county of Essex, ever since the middle of the same century, was born January 13, 1730, at Tunstall in Kent, where his father was rector near thirty years. He was educated at Merchant Taylors School; and admitted a commoner of Queen's college, Oxford, June 24, 1746. While he resided at that University he assisted in correcting an edition of Calasio's Concordance, 1746, intended by Jacob Ilive, a crazy printer, who afterwards associated with the Rev. William Romaine, and published this Concordance in 4 volumes folio, 1747.

Before he was 20, Mr. Mores published, in 4to, 1748, "Nomina et Insignia gentilitia Nobilium Equitumque sub Edvardo primo rege militantium;" the oldest treasure, as he styles it, of our Nobility after Domesday and the Black Book of the Exchequer. He had also printed, except notes and preface, a new edition, in 8vo, of Dionysius Halicarnassensis "de claris Rhetoribus," with vignettes engraved by Green, the few copies of which were sold after his death.

In 1752 he printed in half a sheet 4to, some corrections made by Junius in his own copy of his edition of Cædmon's Saxon Paraphrase of Genesis, and other parts of the Old Testament, Amsterdam. 1655; and in 1754 he engraved 15 of the drawings from the MS. in the Bodleian library. The title of these plates is, "Figuræ quædam antiquæ ex Cædmonis monachi paraphraseos in Genesim exemplari pervetusto in bibliothecâ Bodleianâ adservato delineatæ; ad Anglo-Saxonum mores, ritus, atque ædificia seculi, præcipuè decimi, illustranda in lucem editæ; anno Domini MDCCLIV." These plates were purchased by Mr. Gough; and by him have been bequeathed to the Bodleian Library.

In 1752 Mr. Mores was elected a member of the Society of Antiquaries; and two years after was one of a Committee for examining the Minute-books of that Society, with a view to select from thence papers proper for publication.

Being intended for orders by his father, he took the degrees of B.A. May 12, 1750; and M.A. Jan. 15, 1753; before which time he had formed considerable collections relative to the Antiquities, &c. of Oxford, and particularly to those of his own College, whose archives he arranged, and made large extracts from, with a view to its history. He had three plates of the Black Prince's apartments there, since pulled down, drawn and engraved by that very ingenious artist B. Green. Twenty-eight drawings at his expence, by the same hand, of antient gates, halls, &c. since ruined or taken down, were purchased by Mr. Gough; as also some collections for a history of Godstow Nunnery, by Mr. Mores, for which a plate of its ruins was engraved, and another of Iffley church.

His MSS. relative to his College, with his collections about All Souls College, fell after his death into the hands of Mr. Astle, who presented the former to Mr. Price of the Bodleian.

Mr. Mores appears to have assisted Mr. Bilson in his burlesque on the latter Society, published in a folio sheet, intituled, "Proposals for printing by subscription the History of the Mallardians," treating them as a set of stupid *bon vivans;* at least he may be presumed to have contributed the prints of a cat said to have been starved in their library, and of two antient grotesque busts carved on the South wall of the College, the plates of which were in his possession.

When Mr. Mores left the University, he went abroad, and is reported to have actually taken orders; but whether this tradition has any better foundation than his affectation of wearing his academical habit, and calling it that of a Dominican friar, we do not pretend to vouch. It has been said that he entered into deacon's orders in the Church of England, to exempt himself from serving civil offices; but it does not appear that he received ordination from the Bishop of London.

In the original warrant for letters of administration granted to his son, on his lying intestate, and in the bond given on that occasion (which I have seen in the Prerogative-office), he is styled *"The Reverend Edward-Rowe Mores,* late of the parish of Leyton, in the county of Essex, *Doctor in Divinity."* When, where, or how, he came by this degree, is extremely unaccountable; nor would this have been inserted, had I not been assured by a very intimate friend* of his, that Mr. Mores received the honorary title of D.D. in consequence of a literary favour which he had conferred on some foreign Roman Catholic Ecclesiastics, who wished to repay him by a pecuniary acknowledgment, which he politely declined accepting. Mr. Mores was as ambitious of singularity in Religion as in other pursuits; and if he could be said to be a member of any particular church, it was that of Erasmus, whom he endeavoured to imitate. He thought the Latin language peculiarly adapted to devotion, and wished,

---

*The Rev. William Ellis, M.A. and master of the grammar-school at Alford, Lincolnshire.

for the sake of *unity*, that it was universally in use. He composed a Creed in it, with a kind of Mass on the death of his wife, of which he printed a few copies, in his own house, under the disguised title of "Ordinale Quotidianum, 1685. Ordo Trigintalis;" beginning "Susannæ Mores," &c. Hymnus, "Cœlos vidimus," &c. Of his daughter's education he was particularly careful. From her earliest infancy he talked to her principally in Latin. The gentleman from whom I received this information dined with Mr. Mores when his daughter was not more than two years old. Among other articles they had soup, with which the child had soiled her lip. *Absterge labium,* said the father. The child understood the Latin, and wiped her *upper* lip. *Inferius,* said Mr. Mores, and she did as he meant she should. She was sent to Rouen, for education; but without the least view to her being a Roman Catholic: on the contrary, he was much displeased when he found she had been perverted. Two original letters to the Superior of the House under whose care she was placed, contain a sufficient refutation of the report of his being himself a member of the Church of Rome.

On his return to London, Mr. Mores resided some years in the Heralds' College, intending to have become a member of that Society, for which he was extremely well qualified, by his great knowledge and skill in heraldic matters.

In 1759 he circulated Queries for a Parochial History of Berkshire, but made no considerable progress.

He retired about 1760 to Low-Leyton; in which village he had resided some time before, and, while he was churchwarden there, considerably improved the church. Here, on an estate left him by his father, he built a whimsical house, called *Etlow Place,* on a plan, it is said, of one in France.

The Equitable Society for assurance on lives and survivorship by annuities of 100*l.* increasing to the survivors, in six classes of ages from 1 to 10 — 10 to 20 — 20 to 30 — 30 to 40 — 40 to 50 — 50 to the extremity of life, owes its existence to Mr. Mores. It had been first suggested and recommended in lectures in 1756, by Mr. James Dodson, mathematical master at Christ's Hospital, and author of "The Mathematical Repository," who had been refused admission into the Amicable Society on account of his age; but he dying, November 23, 1757, before his design was completed, except the plan of reimbursement to him and his 54 associates, Mr. Mores undertook to apply for a charter, in 1761; but, failing of success, he, with 16 more of the original subscribers, resolved to persevere in establishing their Society by deed. It was hereby provided that Mr. Mores should be perpetual director, with an annuity of 100*l*. He drew up and published, in 1765, "A short Account of the Society," in 8vo. (of which a seventh edition with additions was printed in 1767).

In the latter part of his life, Mr. Mores (who had long turned his thoughts to the subject of early Printing) began to correct the useful publication of Mr. Ames*. On the death of Mr. John James of Bartholomew Close (the last of the *old* race of letter-founders), in June 1772, Mr. Mores purchased all the curious parts of that immense collection of punches, matrices, and types, which had been accumulating from the days of Wynkyn de Worde to those of Mr. James. From these a large fund of entertainment would probably have been given to the curious, if the life of Mr. Mores had been prolonged. His intentions may be judged of from his valuable "Dissertation on Typographical Founders and Founderies;" and as no more than 80 copies of that pamphlet were printed, it will always be a typographical curiosity. The Editor of these Anecdotes bought the whole impression, at the sale of Mr. Mores' curiosities; and, after subjoining a small Appendix, gave it to the publick.†

Mr. Mores was a most indefatigable collector, and possessed great application in the early part of his life; but in the latter part gave himself up to habits of negligence and dissipation; which brought him to his end‡, by a mortification, in the 49th year of his age, at his house in Low Leyton, Nov. 28, 1778. His large collection of curious MSS. and his valuable library of books were sold by auction, by Mr. Paterson, in August following. Of the former, his "History and Antiquities of Tunstall in Kent" (the only papers that were completed for the press, and for which he had engraved a set of plates out of the many drawings taken at his expence) was purchased at the sale by Mr.

---

*Joseph Ames: *Typographical Antiquities,* first published in 1749. If, as Nichols thought, Mores intended a complete revision of Ames's work, he did not do so, and made only a few corrections. [*Ed.*]

†A new edition of the *Dissertation,* edited with an Introduction and Notes by Harry Carter & Christopher Ricks, was issued by the Oxford Bibliographical Society in 1961. [*Ed.*]

‡Mr. Mores died of a mortification in his leg, which he suffered to reach his vitals, sitting in an arm-chair, while the workmen passed through the room to repair the next. He would not admit physician or nurse; and scarcely his own mother, who constantly resided with him after she had lost an annuity of 100*l*.

Nichols, who printed it in 1780 as a specimen of Parochial Antiquities, which served to shew the ideas of this industrious Antiquary, and his endeavour to make even the minutest record subservient to the great plan of National History.

Several books of English Antiquities with his MS notes, and the most valuable part of such of the MSS. and scarce tracts as relate to our local antiquities, were purchased by Mr. Gough; and, by his bountiful bequest, now enrich the Antiquaries Closet in the Bodleian Library.

Mr. Astle purchased his Epitome of the Registers of the See of Canterbury, preserved in the Archiepiscopal Library at Lambeth, beginning with the first Register called Peckham, A.D. 1279, and ending with that of Archbishop Tenison in 1710; and his "Excerpta ex Registris Cur. Prærog. Cantuar." 3 vols. 8vo; vol. I. containing Extracts from Wills in the Prerogative-office, from 1385 to 1533; vol. II. extracts from 1533 to 1561; vol. III. extracts from 1592 to 1660. Mr. Astle had also his catalogue of the Rolls preserved in the Lambeth Library, made in the year 1758; his collections for the History and Antiquities of the City of Salisbury, containing several curious particulars and transcripts of records, &c. with some short Annals of the University of Oxford, from 1066 to 1310; and a MS. in Latin intituled "De Ælfrico Archiepiscopo Dorovernensi Commentarius. Auctore Edwardo-Rowe Mores, A.M. Soc. Antiq. Lond. Soc." This last MS. is in the hand-writing of Mr. Mores, and seems to have been intended for publication.

Mr. Mores married Susannah, daughter of Mr. Bridgman, an eminent grocer in Whitechapel, who was before his father-in-law by having married the widow of his father. By this lady, who died in 1767, and is buried in the church-yard at Walthamstow, he had a daughter, Sarah, who married, in 1774, Mr. John Davis, house-painter at Walthamstow, and died before her father; and a son, Edward Rowe, married, in 1779, to Miss Spence.

JOHN AND ZACHARIAH MUDGE

JOHN MUDGE was a very celebrated surgeon and physician, author of the Essay on the Method of grinding, polishing, &c. the great Speculum. He was a son of the Rev. Zachariah Mudge, Vicar of St. Andrew's, Plymouth, so honourably mentioned by Johnson, with whom both father and son maintained a close intimacy, vide Boswell's Life. John Mudge, the Surgeon, was consulted by Johnson for the cure of a dreadful complaint under which he laboured. In the latter part of his life he obtained a diploma from Scotland, and became a practising Physician. He was much beloved by all who knew him for his cheerfulness and urbanity, and respected for his intellectual genius. The watchmaker was his brother, his name Thomas. I knew them both intimately. Mudge was the author of an ingenious Essay on the Vis Vitæ, and a radical cure for a Catarrhous Cough, now very scarce. John Mudge was the father of Col. William Mudge, distinguished by his Maps of England, planned by order of the Ordnance."

Mr. Northcote, in his 'Memoirs of Sir Joshua Reynolds,' says, "In the autumn of the year 1762, Mr. Reynolds having impaired his health by incessant application to his profession, again paid a visit to his native country, accompanied by his friend Dr. Johnson, with whom he was entertained at the seats of several noblemen and gentlemen in the West of England. During their stay at Plymouth, they were the guests of Dr. John Mudge, who was then a Surgeon, and afterwards an eminent Physician of that town, a man whose virtues and various powers of mind, if described, would occupy a much larger space than I shall presume to give them in this short Memoir.

"Mr. Reynolds's friendship for the whole family, and the interest he took in whatever related to them, were of the liveliest kind. This acquaintance with the Mudges, both father and son, ought to be reckoned amongst the earliest of his literary connexions. Yet, though I refrain to give way to my own grateful and friendly feelings towards this family, I hope I shall be excused in recording the testimonies of two such good judges of human nature, as Burke and Johnson, upon this very subject. In a letter which the former wrote to Mr. Malone, in the year 1797, and which I here quote from its intimate connexion with the subject of my biography, he speaks of how much Sir Joshua 'owed to the writings and conversation of Johnson;' adding, that 'nothing shews more the greatness of Sir Joshua's parts, than his taking advantage of both, and making some application of them to his profession, when Johnson neither understood, nor desired to understand, any thing of painting, and had no distinct idea of its nomenclature, even in those parts which had got most into use in common life. But, though Johnson had done much to enlarge and strengthen his habit of thinking, Sir Joshua did not owe his first rudiments of speculation to him. He has always told me, that he owed his first disposition to generalize, and to view things in the abstract, to old Mr. Mudge, Prebendary of Exeter, and father to the celebrated mechanic of that name. I have myself, adds Mr. Burke, 'seen Mr. Mudge the clergyman at Sir Joshua's house. He was a learned and venerable old man; and, as I thought, very much conversant in the Platonic philosophy, and very fond of that method of philosophising. He had been originally a Dissenting minister, a description which at that time bred very considerable men, both among those who adhered to it, and those who left it. He had entirely cured himself of the unpleasant narrowness which in the early part of his life had distinguished those gentlemen, and was perfectly free from the ten times more dangerous enlargement which has been, since then, their general characteristic. Sir Joshua Reynolds had always a great love for the whole of that family, and took a great interest in whatever related to them.' — In addition to this, I shall insert, from the periodical Obituary of the day, a high eulogy bestowed upon the same individual by Johnson himself, on his demise, in the year 1769. He speaks of him as 'The Rev. Mr. Zachariah Mudge, Prebendary of Exeter, and Vicar of St. Andrew's in Plymouth; a man equally eminent for his virtues and abilities, and at once beloved as a companion, and reverenced as a pastor. He had that general curiosity to which no kind of knowledge is indifferent or superfluous, and that general benevolence by which no order of men is despised or hated. His principles, both of thought and action, were great and comprehensive. By a solicitous examination of objections, and judicious comparison of opposite arguments, he attained what inquiry never gives but to industry and perspicuity, a firm and unshaken settlement of conviction. But his grimness was without asperity; for, knowing with how much difficulty truth was sometimes found, he did not wonder that many missed it. The general course of his life was determined by his profession; he studied the sacred volumes in the original languages; with what diligence and success, his Notes upon the Psalms give sufficient evidence. He once endeavoured to add the knowledge of Arabic to that of Hebrew; but, finding his thoughts too much diverted from other studies, after some time desisted from his purpose. His discharge of parochial duties was exemplary. How his Sermons were composed, may be learned from the excellent volume which he has given to the publick; but how they were delivered, can be known only to those who heard them; for, as he appeared in the pulpit, words will not easily describe him. His delivery, though unconstrained, was not negligent; and, though forcible, was not turbulent; disdaining anxious nicety of emphasis and laboured artifice of action, it captivated the hearer by its natural dignity, it roused the sluggish, and fixed the volatile, and detained the mind upon the subject without directing it to the speaker. The grandeur and solemnity of the preacher did not intrude upon his general behaviour; at the table of his friends he was a companion communicative and attentive, of unaffected manners, of manly cheerfulness, wishing to please, and easy to be pleased. His acquaintance was universally solicited, and his presence obstructed no enjoyment which Religion did not forbid. Though studious, he was popular; though inflexible, he was candid; and though metaphysical, yet orthodox.' Such was the Obituary testimony of Johnson to the memory of a man equally and deservedly dear to himself and to Sir Joshua Reynolds! In addition to this, I have myself heard Sir Joshua declare, that the elder Mr. Mudge was, in his opinion, the wisest man he had ever met with in his life; and so great an admirer was he of the literary works of Mr. Mudge, that he had intended to have re-published his Sermons, which were out of print, and also to have written a sketch of his life and character. Pity it was not done by one who could have done it so well!"

JOHN MURRAY

MR. JOHN MURRAY, an active, well-informed, and successful Bookseller, was a native of Edinburgh; and for some time was an Officer in the Honourable Corps of Marines, under the patronage of Sir George Yonge, Bart. His first commencement as a Bookseller is thus given by himself, in a letter to his friend William Falconer, the ingenious Author of "The Shipwreck," who was then at Dover, and by whom some lines addressed to Mr. Murray were intended to have been prefixed to the third edition of that beautiful Poem; but were omitted amidst the hurry of the Author on leaving England for India.

Brompton, Kent, 16th Oct. 1768.
"DEAR WILL,

"Since I saw you, I have had the intention of embarking in a scheme that I think will prove successful, and in the progress of which I had an eye towards your participating. Mr. Sandby, Bookseller, opposite St. Dunstan's church, has entered into company with Snow and Denne, Bankers. I was introduced to this gentleman about a week ago, upon an advantageous offer of succeeding him in his old business; which, by the advice of my friends, I propose to accept. Now, although I have little reason to fear success by myself in this undertaking; yet I think so many additional advantages would accrue to us both, were your forces and mine joined, that I cannot help mentioning it to you, and making you the offer of entering into company. He resigns to me the lease of the house; the good-will ———; and I only take his bound stock, and fixtures, at a fair appraisement; which will not amount to much beyond 400*l.*; and which, if ever I mean to part with, cannot fail to bring in nearly the same sum. The shop has been long established in the Trade; it retains a good many old customers; and I am to be ushered immediately into public notice by the sale of a new Edition of *Lord Lyttelton's Dialogues;* and afterwards by a like Edition of his *History.* These Works I shall sell by commission, upon a certain profit, without risque; and Mr. Sandby has promised to continue to me, always, his good offices and recommendation. — These are the general outlines; and if you entertain a notion that the conjunction will suit you, advise me, and you shall be assumed upon equal terms; for I write to you before the affair is finally settled; not that I shall refuse it if you don't concur (for I am determined on the

trial by myself); but that I think it will still turn out better were
we joined; and this consideration alone prompts me to write to
you. Many Blockheads in the Trade are making fortunes; and
did we not succeed as well as they, I think it must be imputed
only to ourselves. . . . Consider what I have proposed; and send
me your answer soon. Be assured in the mean time, that I remain,
dear Sir,

      "Your affectionate and humble servant, JOHN McMURRAY.
"P.S.—My advisers and directors in this affair have been,
Thomas Cumming, esq. Mr. Archibald Paxton, Mr. Samuel
Paterson of Essex-house, and Messrs. J. and W. Richardson,
Printers. These, after deliberate reflection, have unanimously
thought I should accept of Mr. Sandby's offer."

    "No reason," my Friend Mr. A. Chalmers observes, "can be
assigned with more probability for Mr. Falconer's refusing this
liberal offer, than his appointment, immediately after, to the
pursership of the Aurora frigate, which was ordered to carry
out to India, Messrs. Vansittart, Scrafton, and Forde, as Super-
visors of the affairs of the Company. He was also promised the
office of Private Secretary to those Gentlemen, a situation from
which his friends conceived the hope that he might eventually
obtain lasting advantages. — *Dîs aliter visum.*"

    Mr. Murray, in the mean time, engaged in an old and well-
established trade; which, from his connexions in India and at
Edinburgh, he considerably extended. For a short period, as
might be expected, he was a Novice in the art and mystery of
Bookselling; but soon became a regular proficient; and under
his auspices many useful and elegant Works were offered to the
learned world. One of his earliest publications was the *"Bibliotheca Hoblyniana*; a Catalogue of the Library of Robert Hoblyn,
esq." which had been printed for John Quicke, esq. of Exeter,
in 1769 (only 250 copies, all on royal paper of one size).

    In several instances Mr. Murray was his own Publisher. It is
very common, and indeed almost proverbial, for Authors to
complain of their Booksellers (whether justly or otherwise I shall
not stop to enquire) — but, in the pamphlets to which I allude,
the Bookseller turns the tables. — In 1777, appeared, "A Letter to
W. Mason, M.A. Precentor of York, concerning his Edition of
Mr. Gray's Poems, and the Practices of Booksellers; by a Bookseller;" a warm expostulation respecting an action commenced
against him in the Court of Chancery by Mr. Mason, for printing
Mr. Gray's Poems, his (Mr. Mason's) property. In this case, Mr.

Murray (as appeared by the decision of the Lord Chancellor) had the wrong side of the argument. But in 1784 he had the vantage ground, in "An Author's Conduct to the Publick, stated in the behaviour of Dr. William Cullen, his Majesty's Physician at Edinburgh." In this instance Mr. Murray was the complainant, and on very just grounds. "Having upon hand 84 volumes of Dr. Cullen's "Fist Lines of the Practice of Physic," which would prove no better than waste paper if he was not permitted to complete them in sets; and being informed that it was not the Author's intention to sell the additional two volumes, then printing, separately, he expostulated with the Doctor on the subject, in two letters, dated in April and May 1784 (the first being unanswered), and desired to have the uew edition in exchange for the books he had, volume for volume, according to the usual custom of the Trade. In answer, at last, Dr. Cullen, after telling him 'shortly, that his reasoning is not at all satisfying, and his examples not at all in point,' peremptorily refused to give an indemnification. This, however, we cannot but think, with Mr. Murray, 'every rule of honesty and fair-dealing required;' and we must also, with him, be astonished at the Professor's making his circumstances partly an excuse ('his poverty, not his will'), when we are told, that, 'on a moderate computation, he has realized 2000*l.* by the sale of this work.' — Without entering into other particulars, in which his Majesty's Physician exhibits such specimens of shuffling and cutting as we should not have expected from a Professor of so liberal a Science, we shall only add an extract of a letter from his earlier bookseller, Mr. William Creech, of May 25, 1784, to shew the sentiments of his countrymen on this proceeding: 'Dr. Cullen has behaved in a strange manner to the publick, by with-holding the fourth volume from the purchasers of the three former, and obliging them to buy the whole book anew. . . . I am perfectly clear that the purchasers of the three former volumes have an undoubted ground of action against him. — I mean to publish a notice in the newspapers, with my name, stating the facts, and informing the publick, that the with-holding of the fourth volume is not owing to me, but to the Doctor himself.' — Professions, it seems, as well as trades, have their crafts. *Great is Diana of the Ephesians!*" — (*Gent. Mag.* vol. LIV. p. 926.)

Mr. Murray wrote more than the publick were in general aware of, and was an Author in various shapes. One of his most formidable pamphlets was against another of his Authors, intituled, "The Defence of Innes Munro, Esq. Captain in the late Seventy-third or Lord Macleod's Regiment of Highlanders, against a Charge of Plagiarism from the Works of Dr. William Thompson; with the original Papers on both Sides, 1790," 8vo. — The dispute is not worth reviving; but many of the Letters in it shew that Mr. Murray had obtained the style of Authorship.

Mr. Murray began, in 1780, a volume of annual intelligence, under the title of "The London Mercury;" and in January 1783 commenced "The English Review," with the assistance of a phalanx of able writers; amongst whom were Dr. Whitaker the Historian of Manchester, Gilbert Stuart, &c. &c.

Mr. Murray died Nov. 6, 1793; and was succeeded by a son, who has also been the Publisher of several other valuable works; and has particularly distinguished himself by giving to the critical world "The Quarterly Review," of which he is the sole Proprietor and Publisher. — The Editor of that popular publication is Mr. William Gifford, the Translator of Juvenal, and author of "The Baviad" and "Mæviad." The contributors to it are very generally believed to be among the leading political and literary characters of the age, and it has already reached a circulation little short of 6000. — Mr. Murray is now on the eve of removing to Albemarle-street, as successor to Mr. William Miller.

ROBERT MYLNE

THIS distinguished Architect was born in Edinburgh, Jan. 4, 1733-4. His father, Thomas Mylne, was an Architect at Edinburgh, and a Magistrate of that City; and it is known that his family had been Master Masons to the Kings of Scotland for many generations, till the union of the crowns. Robert Mylne travelled early in life, for improvement in his hereditary science, and resided several years in Italy (five of them at Rome), where he obtained prizes, and other distinctions, and became a member of the academies of Rome, Florence, and Bologna. He visited Naples, and viewed the interior of Sicily, never, either before or since, examined with the same accuracy. Viewing the remains of Antiquity with the eye of an Architect, he was enabled to explain several very obscure passages of Vitruvius from what he saw in Sicily. His curious memorials of that tour, with sketches and illustrations, he was busily employed in digesting for publication in 1774: they are still extant, and will, probably, at some future time, be given to the Publick. Having made a very complete tour of Europe, going by France, and returning by Switzerland and Holland, he found himself in London at the time when proposals were to be offered for a Bridge at Black-Friars. His proposals being accepted, the first stone was laid in 1761, and the Bridge was completed in 1765, for the very sum specified in his estimate, namely 153,000*l*. He presented, some time after, to the British Museum, a model of a part of the Bridge, exhibiting a plan for a centre frame, invented by himself, and never yet improved upon. It is still to be seen in that national repository. With Dr. Johnson he had some paper war, on the proposed form of the Arches, after which they became very intimate friends. In 1762 he was appointed Engineer to the New River Company, and in 1767 was chosen a Fellow of the Royal Society. By the Dean and Chapter of St. Paul's, he was entrusted with the care and preservation of that fabrick, where, by his suggestion, the noble Inscription to the honour of Sir Christopher Wren, ending *"Si monumentum requiras circumspice,"* was placed over the entrance of the Choir. Mr. Mylne died in his 79th year, May 5, 1811, at the New River Head, where he resided as Engineer to the Company; and by his own desire, was buried in St. Paul's Cathedral, near the tomb of his illustrious predecessor; and his funeral was attended by a select party of Relations, Friends, and Artists. Mr. Mylne married in 1770 Mary Home, a sister of Mrs. John Hunter, so distinguished by her poetical genius, and of Mr. Home, Surgeon, the successor, and in most points of eminence the rival, of John Hunter, his brother-in-law. By this marriage he had nine children, of whom only one son, his successor as Engineer to the New River Company, and four daughters, now survive. Mr. Mylne had peculiarities in his character; but they were chiefly connected with a high independence of spirit, and an inflexible sense of duty and justice. He loved his profession, but not the emoluments of it, and therefore, after all his distinguished employments, did not die rich. Those who knew him could not fail to respect his integrity, and admire his talents. — Whilst he was at Rome in 1757, a good portrait of him was painted by Brompton, which was engraved at Paris by Vangeliste in 1783, inscribed, "Robert Mylne, Architect, Engineer, Surveyor, ætat. xxiv. F.R.S."

JOHN NICHOLS AND DR. JOHNSON

THIS is not the proper place for introducing any regular Memoir of Dr. Johnson, nor, after the elaborate volumes of Mr. Boswell, is such a task necessary. My intimate acquaintance with that bright Luminary of Literature did not commence till he was advanced in years; but it happens to have fallen to my lot (and I confess that I am proud of it) to have been present at many interesting conversations in the latest periods of the life of this illustrious pattern of true piety.

In the progress of his "Lives of the Poets," I had the good fortune to conciliate his esteem, by several little services; though, at the same time, I was perpetually goading him to furnish the press with copy. Many of his short notes during the progress of that work are printed in the Gentleman's Magazine, vol. LV. pp. 5—9; and in one of his Letters to Mrs. Thrale he says, "I have finished the Life of Prior — and now a fig for Mr. Nichols!" Our friendship, however, did not cease with the termination of those volumes; and I hope I shall be excused the vanity of recording in these pages a few kind letters from Dr. Johnson; and some parts of his interesting conversation at a period when his accurate Biographer was absent from London.

Oct. 10, 1782.

1. "SIR,

"While I am at Brightelmston*, if you have any need of consulting me, Mr. Strahan will do us the favour to transmit our papers under his frank. I have looked often into your 'Anecdotes;' and you will hardly thank a lover of literary history for telling you, that he has been informed and gratified. I wish you would add your own discoveries and intelligence to those of Dr. Rawlinson, and undertake the Supplement to Wood. Think

---

*The former name of the town now called Brighton.

on it. I am, Sir, your humble servant, SAM. JOHNSON."

Oct. 28, 1782.

2. "DEAR SIR,

"What will the Booksellers give me for the new Edition [of the Lives of the Poets]? I know not what to ask. I would have 24 sets bound in plain calf, and figured with the number of the volumes. For the rest, they may please themselves. — I wish, Sir, you could obtain some fuller information of *Jortin, Markland,* and *Thirlby.* They were three Contemporaries of great learning."
— It was in consequence of this request that I drew up the account of Thirlby, in the Gentleman's Magazine for 1784, p. 260 (see vol. IV. p. 264); which having been shewn to Dr. Johnson in the state of a proof-sheet, he added to it nearly half of what is there printed. The Doctor's MS. is now before me, and begins with "What I can tell of Thirlby, I had from those who knew him; I never saw him in my life." The communication concludes with "This is what I can remember." I will take this opportunity also of adding, that, on my shewing Dr. Johnson Archdeacon Blackburne's "Remarks on the Life of Milton," which were published, in 8vo, 1780, he wrote on the margin of p. 14, "In the business of Lauder, I was deceived; partly by thinking the man too frantick to be fraudulent." "Of this quotation from the ["Literary] Magazine" [a *poetical scale,* supposed to have been Johnson's], I was not the author. I fancy it was put in after I had quitted that work; for I not only did not write it, but do not remember it."

Jan. 10, 1783.

3. "SIR,

"I am much obliged by your kind communication of your account of Hinckley. I knew Mr. Carte as one of the prebendaries of Lichfield, and for some time Surrogate of the Chancellor. Now I will put you in a way of shewing me more kindness. I have been confined by illness a long time; and sickness and solitude make tedious evenings. Come sometimes, and see, Sir, your humble servant, SAM. JOHNSON."

4. "*Feb.* 4, 1784, Mr. Johnson, having been for many [weeks] confined, is very cheerless; and wishes that Mr. Nichols would now and then bestow an hour upon him."

Lichfield, Oct. 20, 1784.

5. "Sir,

"When you were here, you were pleased, as I am told, to think my absence an inconvenience. I should certainly have been very glad to give so skilful a Lover of Antiquities any information about my native place, of which however I know not much, and have reason to believe that not much is known. — Though I have not given you any amusement, I have received amusement from you. At Ashbourne, where I had very little company, I had the luck to borrow 'Mr. Bowyer's Life,' a book so full of contemporary history, that a literary man must find some of his old friends. I thought that I could now and then have told you some hints worth your notice; and perhaps we may *talk a Life over.* I hope we shall be much together. You must now be to me what you were before, and what dear Mr. Allen was besides. He was taken unexpectedly away, but I think he was a very good man. I have made little progress in recovery. I am very weak, and very sleepless; but I live on, and hope. I am, Sir, Your most humble servant, Sam. Johnson."

After these invitations, my visits to him were of course more frequent; and his communications were more confidential.

"He seriously entertained the thought of translating *Thuanus:* and often talked to me on the subject. Once, in particular, when I was rather wishing that he would favour the world, and gratify his Sovereign, by a Life of Spenser (which he said that he would readily have done, had he been able to obtain any *new* materials for the purpose), he added, "I have been thinking again, Sir, of *Thuanus:* it would not be the laborious task which you have supposed it. I should have no trouble but that of dictation, which would be performed as speedily as an amanuensis could write. — He was earnestly invited, by his warm friend the late Mr. Alderman Cadell, to publish a volume of *Devotional Exercises;* but this (though he listened to the proposal with much complacency, and a large of money was offered for it by Mr. Cadell), he declined, from motives of the sincerest modesty. — When talking of a regular edition of his own Works, not long before his death, he said, "that he had power [from the booksellers], to print such an edition, if his health admitted it; but had no power to assign over any edition, unless he could add notes, and so alter them as to make them new Works; which his state of health forbade him to think of."

I had occasionally the pleasure of introducing to him some of my literary friends, who were ambitious of this honour. Amongst

these was the Rev. Samuel Badcock, well known for his eminent
talents; who soon afterwards thus noticed the visit: "How much
I am obliged to you for the favour you did me in introducing
me to Dr. Johnson! *Tantùm vidi Virgilium.* But to have seen
him, and to have received a testimony of respect from him, was
enough. I recollect all the conversation, and shall never forget
one of his expressions. — Speaking of Dr. Priestley (whose writings I saw he estimated at a low rate), he said, 'You have proved
him as deficient in *probity* as he is in learning.' — I called him
an '*Index-scholar;*' but he was not willing to allow him a claim
even to that merit. He said, that 'he borrowed from those who
had been borrowers themselves, and did not know that the
mistakes he adopted had been answered by others.' — I often
think of our short, but precious, visit to this great man. I shall
consider it as a kind of an *æra* in my life." — The Rev. William
Tooke, F.R.S. (the companion of my boyish days, and the steady
friend through a pilgrimage of sixty years, whose fame is established by many valuable publications) accompanied me one
day to Dr. Johnson's; and highly delighted they were with each
other's conversation — particularly after Mr. Tooke had mentioned that, amidst the progress which Literature was making
at St. Petersburgh, translations of "The Rambler," and of
"Blackstone's Commentaries," had been made into the Russian
language, by the especial command of the Empress. — I was
present also when Mr. Henderson the Tragedian was first introduced to Dr. Johnson; who received him with the greatest cordi-
ality; and, having occasion to mention a certain *Dramatic Writer,*
added, "I never did the man an injury: but he would read his
Tragedy to me!" — Speaking one day of a person for whom
he had a real friendship, but in whom vanity was somewhat too
predominant, he observed, that "Kelly was so fond of displaying
on his side-board the plate which he possessed, that he added to
it his spurs. For my part," said he, "I never was master of a
pair of spurs but once; and they are now at the bottom of
the Ocean. By the carelessness of Boswell's servant, they were
dropped from the end of the boat, on our return from the Isle
of Sky."

At the beginning of the Winter of 1783 the project was started
of establishing an evening club for his comfort; which was
accordingly begun early in the year 1784, at the *Essex Head,*
in Essex-street. To this club, founded, according to his own
words, "in frequency and parsimony," he gave a set of Rules, as

Ben Jonson did his *Leges Convivales* at the Devil Tavern; and prefixed this motto:

> "To-day deep thoughts with me resolve to drench
> In mirth, which after no repenting draws."   MILTON.

The club consisted of a select number of his friends, who entered very heartily into the scheme, for the pleasure of enjoying his conversation, and of contributing their quota to the general amusement. The names of the constant members at the time of Dr. Johnson's death were thus placed in the book, "on the rota of indispensable monthly attendance:" Dr. Johnson, *Dr. Horsley, *Dr. Brocklesby, Mr. Joddrell, *Mr. Cooke, *Mr. Ryland, *Mr. Paradise, *Dr. Burney, *Mr. Hoole, *Mr. Sastres, Mr. Allen, Hon. Mr. Barrington, Mr. Barry, Mr. Wyatt, *Mr. Nichols, Mr. Poore, *Mr. Wyndham, *Mr. Cruickshank, *Mr. Seward, Mr. Clarke, Mr. Murphy, Mr. Bowles, *Mr. Metcalfe, Mr. Boswell. The three last gentlemen had been introduced in the room of Dr. Scott, who was named, but never attended; of Mr. Tyers, who abdicated the club, Feb. 1, 1784; and of Mr. Strahan, who followed his example on the 26th of June. [Those whose names are thus * marked attended the Doctor's funeral. The others, by some mistake, were not invited.]

The following letter, which I received only seven days before his death, is one of the last that he ever wrote:

"*Dec.* 6, 1784. The late learned Mr. Swinton of Oxford, having one day remarked that one man, meaning, I suppose, no man but himself, could assign all the parts of the Antient Universal History to their proper authors; at the request of Sir Robert Chambers, or of myself, gave the account which I now transmit to you in his own hand, being willing that of so great a work the History should be known, and that each writer should receive his due proportion of praise from posterity. — I recommend to you to preserve this scrap of literary intelligence in Mr. Swinton's own hand, or to deposit it in the Museum, that the veracity of this account may never be doubted. I am, Sir,

Your most humble servant,   SAM. JOHNSON.

"Mr. Swinton: The History of the Carthaginians, Numidians, Mauritanians, Gætulians, Garamantes, Melano Gætulians, Nigritæ, Cyrenaica, Marmarica, the Regio Syrtica, Turks, Tartars, and Moguls, Indians, Chinese; Dissertation on the Peopling of America; Dissertation on the Independency of the

Arabs. — The Cosmogony, and a small part of the History immediately following, by Mr. Sale. — To the Birth of Abraham, chiefly by Mr. Shelvock. — History of the Jews, Gauls, and Spaniards; and Xenophon's Retreat; by Mr. Psalmanazar. — History of the Persians, and of the Constantinopolitan Empire, by Dr. Campbell. — History of the Romans, by Mr. Bower." The original of the above Letter, agreeably to Dr. Johnson's desire, is deposited in the British Museum. It was also printed, at the time it was sent, by the Doctor's express desire, in the Gentleman's Magazine, vol. LIV. p. 892. — The date of it will shew that, amidst the pangs of illness, the love of truth, and an attachment to the interests of Literature, were still predominant. His Letter, I may add, appeared in public, not only by his permission, but by his express desire. And it may be matter of some exultation to Mr. Urban, whom Dr. Johnson always acknowledged to have been one of his earliest patrons, that the Gentleman's Magazine should have been by him selected as the repository of perhaps the last scrap he ever dictated for the press.

On the following day, he said to me, "I may possibly live, or rather breathe, three days, or perhaps three weeks; but I find myself daily and gradually worse." His farther conversation on the subject of Mr. Cave and the Magazine, &c. is printed on page 86. — Before I quitted him he asked, whether any of the family of Faden the printer were living. Being told that the Geographer near Charing Cross was Faden's son, he said, after a short pause, "I borrowed a guinea of his father near thirty years ago; be so good as to take this, and pay it for me."

Whilst confined by his last illness, it was his regular practice to have the Church-service read to him, by some attentive and friendly Divine; and he occasionally requested me to join the small devotional assembly. The Rev. John Hoole performed this kind office in my presence for the last time, when, by his own desire, no more than the Litany was read; in which his responses were in the deep and sonorous voice which Mr. Boswell has occasionally noticed, and with the most profound devotion that can be imagined. His hearing not being quite perfect, he more than once interrupted Mr. Hoole, with 'Louder, my dear Sir, louder, I entreat you, or you pray in vain!' — and when the service was ended, he, with great earnestness, turned round to the mother of Mr. Hoole, who was present, saying, 'I thank you, Madam, very heartily, for your kindness in joining me in this solemn exercise. Live well, I conjure you; and you will not feel the compunction at the last, which I now feel.' So truly humble were the thoughts which this great and good man entertained of his own approaches to religious perfection. — He said at another time, speaking of the little fear he had of undergoing a chirurgical operation, 'I would give one of these legs for a year more of life, I mean comfortable life, not such as that which I now suffer;' — and lamented much his inability to read during his hours of restlessness, 'I used formerly,' he added, 'when sleepless in bed, *to read like a Turk.*'

During the whole time of my intimacy with him, he rarely permitted me to depart without some sententious advice. At the latest of these affecting interviews, I was gratified by his approbation of a Sonnet which I shewed him, addressed to Mr. Urban (printed in vol. LXV. p. ii); and his words at parting were, "Take care of your eternal salvation. Remember to observe the Sabbath. Let it never be a day of business, nor wholly a day of dissipation." He concluded his solemn farewell with, "Let my words have their due weight. They are the words of a dying man." — I never saw him more. — In the last five or six days of his life but few even of his most intimate friends were admitted. Every hour, that could be abstracted from his bodily pains and infirmities, was spent in prayer, and the warmest ejaculations; and in that pious, praise-worthy, and exemplary manner, he closed a long life, begun, continued, and ended in virtue.

He expired, on the 13th of December 1784, without a pang, in the 75th year of his age, to the loss of his intimate associates and the world, whose unremitting friend he had ever been. And I had the mournful satisfaction of joining the train of friends who paid the last tribute of gratitude and esteem at his grave in Westminster Abbey.

THOMAS OSBORNE

"OF Tom Osborne," says Mr. Dibdin*, "I have in vain endeavoured to collect some interesting biographical details. What I know of him shall be briefly stated. He was the most celebrated Bookseller of his day; and appears, from a series of his Catalogues in my possession, to have carried on a successful trade from the year 1738 to 1768. What fortune he amassed is not, I believe, very well known: his collections were truly valuable, for they consisted of the purchased libraries of the most eminent men of those times. In his stature he was short and thick; and, to his inferiors, generally spoke in an authoritative and insolent manner. [In the latter part of his life his manners were considerably softened; particularly to the young Booksellers who had occasion to frequent his shop in the pursuit of their orders. If they were so fortunate as to call whilst he was taking wine after his dinner, they were regularly called into the little parlour in Gray's Inn to take a glass with him. "Young man," he would say, "I have been in business more than 40 years, and am now worth more than 40,000*l*. Attend to your business; and you will be as rich as I am."] 'It has been confidently related,' says Boswell, 'that Johnson, one day, knocked Osborne down in his shop, with a folio, and put his foot upon his neck. The simple truth I had from Johnson himself. "Sir, he was impertinent to me, and I beat him. But it was not in his shop: it was in own chamber."

"Of Osborne's philological attainments, the meanest opinion must be formed, if we judge from his advertisements, which were sometimes inserted in the London Gazette, and drawn up in the most ridiculously vain and ostentatious style. He used to tell the publick, that he possessed 'all the pompous editions of Classicks and Lexicons.' I insert the two following advertisements, prefixed, the one to his Catalogue of 1748, the other to that of 1753, for the amusement of my bibliographical readers, and as a model for Messrs. Payne, White, Miller, Evans, Priestley, Cuthell, &c.

'This Catalogue being very large, and of consequence very expensive to the proprietor, he humbly requests, that, if it falls into the hands of any gentleman *gratis,* who chooses not himself to be a purchaser of any of the books contained in it, that

---

*Bibliomania, p. 470.

such gentleman will be pleased to recommend it to any other whom he thinks may be so, or to return it.'

"To his Catalogue of 1753 was added the following:

'To the Nobility and Gentry who please to favour me with their commands. It is hoped, as I intend to give no offence to any nobleman or gentleman, that do me the honour of being my customer, by putting a price on my Catalogue, by which means they may not receive it as usual — it is desired that such nobleman or gentleman as have not received it, would be pleased to send for it; and it's likewise requested of such gentlemen who do receive it, that, if they chuse not to purchase any of the books themselves, *they would recommend it to any bookish gentleman of their acquaintance, or to return it*; and the favour shall be acknowledged by, their most obedient and obliged,

T. OSBORNE*.'

"*The Harleian Collection of MSS.* was purchased by the Government for 10,000*l.* and is now deposited in the British Museum. The *Books* were disposed of to *Thomas Osborne,* of Gray's Inn, Bookseller; — to the irreparable loss, and I had almost said, the indelible disgrace, of the country. It is, indeed, for ever to be lamented, that a collection, so extensive, so various, so magnificent, and intrinsically valuable, should have become the property of one, who necessarily, from his situation in life, became a purchaser, only that he might be a vender, of the volumes. Osborne gave 13,000*l.* for the collection; a sum, which must excite the astonishment of the present age, when it is informed that Lord Oxford gave 18,000*l.* for the *Binding* only, of the least part of them. In the year 1743-4 appeared an account of this collection, under the following title, '*Catalogus Bibliothecæ Harleianæ,*' *&c.* in four volumes (the 5th not properly appertaining to it.) Dr. Johnson was employed by Osborne to write the Preface, which, says Boswell, 'he has done with an ability that cannot fail to impress all his readers with admiration of his philological attainments.' In my humble apprehension, the Preface is unworthy of the Doctor: it contains a few general philological reflections, expressed in a style sufficiently stately, but is divested of bibliographical anecdote and interest-

---

*M. Dibdin here attributes an anecdote to *Osborne,* in which the former edition of this Work had misled him. It was *Charles Marsh,* not *Osborne,* who made the *Rum* Bargain.

ing intelligence. The first two volumes are written in Latin by
Johnson; the third and fourth volumes, which are a repetition
of the two former, are composed in English by Oldys: and notwithstanding its defects, it is the best Catalogue of a large
Library of which we can boast. It should be in every good
collection."

"To the volumes was prefixed the following advertisement:
'As the curiosity of spectators, before the sale, may produce disorder in the disposition of the books, it is necessary to advertise
the publick, that there will be no admission into the Library
before the day of sale, which will be on Tuesday the 14th of
February, 1744.' It seems that Osborne had charged the sum of
5s. to each of his first two volumes, which was represented by
the Booksellers 'as an avaricious innovation;' and, in a paper
published in 'The Champion,' they, or their mercenaries, rea-
soned so justly as to allege, that, if Osborne could afford a very
large price for the library, he might therefore afford to *give
away* the Catalogue,' *Preface to* vol. iii. p. 1. To this charge
Osborne answered, that his Catalogue was drawn up with great
pains, and at a heavy expence; but, to obviate all objections,
"those," says he, "who have paid five shillings a volume, shall
be allowed, at any time within three months after the day of
sale, either to return them in exchange for books, or to send
them back, and receive their money." This, it must be confessed, was sufficiently liberal.

"Osborne was also accused of *rating his books at too high a
price.* To this the following was his reply, or rather Dr. Johnson's; for the style of the Doctor is sufficiently manifest: 'If,
therefore, I have set a high value upon books — if I have vainly
imagined Literature to be more fashionable than it really is, or
idly hoped to revive a taste well nigh extinguished, I know not
why I should be persecuted with clamour and invective, since
I shall only suffer by my mistake, and be obliged to keep those
books which I was in hopes of selling.' *Preface to the 3d volume.*
The fact was, that Osborne's charges were extremely moderate;
and the sale of the books was so very slow, that Johnson assured
Boswell, 'there was not much gained by the bargain.' Whoever
inspects Osborne's Catalogue of 1748 (four years after the
Harleian sale) will find in it many of the most valuable of Lord
Oxford's books; and among them, a copy of the Aldine Plato
of 1513, *struck off upon vellum,* marked at 21l. only: for this
identical copy Lord Oxford gave 100 guineas, as Dr. Mead

informed Dr. Askew; from the latter of whose collections it was purchased by Dr. Hunter, and is now in the Hunter Museum. There will also be found, in Osborne's Catalogue of 1748 and 1753, some of the scarcest books in English Literature, marked at two, or three, or four shillings, for which three times the number of *pounds* is now given."

SAMUEL PALMER

MR. PALMER had amused me with the belief that the design (for an edition of the Psalms, with Leusden's Latin Version in the opposite column) was set aside, either on account of its being found impracticable, or at least too difficult and dangerous. It appeared, however, that Mr. Palmer imposed upon me; and that he knew that the design was carried on in another printing-house, though with such privacy, that I never heard or dreamed of it, though I had been long acquainted with Mr. Bowyer, who was employed in the printing of it. So far from it was I, that I began to think Mr. Palmer had only invented that story, to divert me from printing my proposed edition, in order to set me upon another work, in which he was more immediately concerned, and expected greater credit, as well as present profit from. This was his *History of Printing,* which he had long promised to the world, but for which he was not at all qualified. However, he designed to have added a second part, relating to the practical part, which was more suited to his genius, and in which he designed to have given a full account of all that relates to that branch, from the letter-founding, to the most elegant way of printing, imposing, binding, &c. in which he had made considerable improvements of his own, besides those he had taken from foreign authors. But this second part, though but then as it were in embryo, met with such early and strenuous opposition, from the respective bodies of letter-founders, printers, and book-binders, under an ill-grounded apprehension that the discovery of the mystery of those arts, especially the two first, would render them cheap and contemptible (whereas the very reverse would have been the case, they appearing indeed the more curious and worthy our admiration, the better they are known) that he was forced to set it aside. But as to the first part, viz. the History of Printing, he met with the greatest encouragement, not only from them, but from a very great number of the Learned, who all engaged to subscribe largely to it; particularly the late Earls of Pembroke and Oxford, and the famous Doctor Mead, whose libraries were to furnish him with the noblest materials for the compiling of it, and did so accordingly. The misfortune was, that Mr. Palmer, knowing himself unequal to the task, had turned it over to one Papiat, a broken Irish bookseller then in London, of whom he had a great opinion, though still more unqualified for it than he, and only aimed at getting money from him, without ever doing any thing towards it, except amusing him with fair promises for near three quarters of a year. He had so long dallied with him, that they were come within three months of the time in which Mr. Palmer had engaged to produce a complete plan, and a number or two of the first part by way of specimen of the work, viz. the invention and improvement of it by John Faust at Mentz. And these were to be shewn at a grand meeting of learned men, of which Dr. Mead was President that year; and, being his singular friend and patron, was to have promoted a large subscription and payment, which Mr. Palmer stood in great need of at that time; whereas Papiat had got nothing ready but a few loose and imperfect extracts out of Chevalier, Le Caille, and some other French authors on the subject, but which could be of little or no use, because he frequently mistook them, and left blanks for the words which he did not understand. These, however, such as they were, Mr. Palmer brought to me; and earnestly pressed me that I would set aside all other things I might be then about, and try to produce the expected plan and specimen by the time promised, since he must be ruined both in credit and pocket if he disappointed his friends of it. It was well for him and me that the subject lay within so small a compass as the consulting of about twelve or fourteen principal authors; so that I easily fell upon a proper plan of the work, which I divided into three parts; the first of which was, to give an account of the invention of the art, and its first essays by Faust at Mentz, and of its improvement by fusile or metal types, varnish, ink, &c. by his son-in-law, Peter Schoeffer. The second was to contain its propagation, and farther improvement, through most parts of Europe, under the most celebrated Printers; and the third, an account of its introduction and progress into England. This, together with above one half of the first part, were happily finished, and produced by the time appointed; and met with more approbation and encouragement from his friends than I feared it would, being conscious how much better it might have turned out, would time have permitted it. And this I chiefly mention, not so much to excuse the defects of so horrid a performance, as because it hath given me since frequent occasion to observe how many much more considerable works have been spoiled, both at home and abroad, through the impatience of the subscribers; though this is far enough from being the only or even the greatest inconvenience that attends most of those kinds of subscriptions. As to Mr. Palmer, his circumstances were by this time so unaccountably low and unfortunate, considering the largeness and success of his business, and that he was himself a sober industrious man, and free from all extravagance, that he could not extricate himself by any other way, but by a Statute of Bankruptcy, which caused his History to go sluggishly on; so that, notwithstanding all the care and kind assistance of his good friend Dr. Mead, a stubborn distemper, which his misfortunes brought upon him, carried him off before the third part of it was finished. This defect, however, was happily supplied by the late noble Earl of Pembroke, who being informed by Mr. Pain the engraver, Mr. Palmer's brother-in-law, what condition the remainder was left in, and that I was the person who had wrote the former parts, sent for me, and, with his usual generosity, enjoined me to complete the work, according to the plan; and not only defrayed all the charges of it, even of the paper and printing, but furnished me with all necessary materials out of his own library; and, when the work was finished, his Lordship reserved only some few copies to himself, and gave the remainder of the impression to Mr. Palmer's widow, not without some farther tokens of his liberality."

To return to the edition of the Hebrew Psalter — the cause of Mr. Palmer's delay is thus related by Psalmanazar: "His Lordship had excepted against Mr. Palmer's Hebrew types, which were of Athias's font, and a little battered, and insisted upon his having a new set from Mr. Caslon, which greatly exceeded them in beauty. But Mr. Palmer was so deeply in debt to him, that he knew not how to procure it from him without ready money, which he was not able to spare. The Bishop likewise insisted upon having some Roman and Italic types cast with some distinguishing mark, to direct his readers to the Hebrew letters they were designed to answer, and these required a new set of punches and matrices before they could be cast; and that would have delayed the work, which Mr. Palmer was in haste to go about, that he might the sooner finger some of his Lordship's money. This put him upon such an unfair stratagem, as, when discovered, quite disgusted his Lordship against him; viz. representing Mr. Caslon as an idle, dilatory workman, who would in all probability make them wait several years for those few types, if ever he finished them. That he was indeed the only Artist that could supply him with those types; but that he hated work, and was not to be depended on; and therefore advised his Lordship to make shift with some sort which he could substitute, and would answer the same purpose, rather than run the risk of staying so long, and being perhaps disappointed. The Bishop, however, being resolved, if possible, to have the desired types, sent for Mr. Bowyer, and asked him whether he knew a letter-founder that could cast him such a set out of hand; who immediately recommended Mr. Caslon; and, being told what a sad and disadvantageous character he had heard of him, Mr. Bowyer not only assured his Lordship that it was a very false and unjust one, but engaged to get the above-mentioned types cast by him, and a new font of his Hebrew ones, in as short a time as the thing could possibly be done. Mr. Caslon was accordingly sent for by his Lordship; and having made him sensible of the time the new ones would require to be made ready for use, did produce them according to his promise, and the book was soon after put to the press. As soon as I had finished what I, and some of my friends as well as I, thought a sufficient confutation of the Bishop's performance, and in the same language, though not so florid and elegant Latin, I sent to desire one of my booksellers to enquire of Mr. Bowyer, whether the new types cast for his Lordship were still in his possession? and whether I might be permitted the use of them, in the answer I had prepared for the press? I was answered in the affirmative; but one bookseller took it into his head to ask at the same time, what number of copies his Lordship had caused to be printed of his Psalter? and was answered only five hundred; one half of which had been presented by his Lordship to his learned friends, both in and out of England, and most of the rest were still unsold, there being but few among the learned, that were curious in such matters; the performance having been disapproved by all that

had seen it. This news so cooled the booksellers' eagerness after
my answer, that, upon my coming to town, and their acquainting
me with the state of the case, I was quite discouraged from
printing it. For they concluded, from what Mr. Bowyer had
said, that it would be dangerous to print above three hundred
of mine, the charge of which being deducted, the profit, upon
a supposition that they were all sold, would be so small, that
they could not afford me above two or three guineas for my
copy (which would have made about seven or eight sheets of a
middling octavo) without being losers. This was their way of com-
puting the matter, against which having nothing to object, I
locked up my papers in my cabinet, where they have lain ever
since. They did indeed offer me better terms, and to print a
greater number of copies, if I would be at the trouble of printing
it in English, which they thought would be more universally
read, out of dislike to the Bishop; but, besides that I cared not
to be at the pains of Englishing it, I thought it beneath the
subject to print it in any other language but that in which his
was wrote; and so wholly declined it."

DR. JAMES PARSONS

D R. JAMES PARSONS was born at Barnstaple, Devonshire,
in March 1705. His father, who was the youngest of nine
sons of Colonel Parsons, and nearly related to the baronet of
that name, being appointed barrack-master at Bolton in Ireland,
removed with his family into that kingdom, soon after the birth
of his then only son James, who received at Dublin the early
part of his education, and, by the assistance of proper masters,
laid a considerable foundation of classical and other useful learning, which enabled him to become tutor to Lord Kingston.
Turning his attention to the study of medicine, he went afterwards to Paris; where (I now use his own words) "he followed
the most eminent professors in the several schools, as Astruc,
Dubois, Lemery, and others, attended the Anatomical Lectures
of the most famous [Hunaud and De Cat]; and Chemicals at
the King's Garden at St. Come. He followed the Physicians in

both hospitals of the Hotel Dieu and La Charité, and the Chemical Lectures and Demonstrations of Lemery and Boulduc; and in Botany, Jussieu.

Having finished these studies, his Professors gave him honourable attestations of his having followed them with diligence and industry, which entitled him to take the degrees of Doctor and Professor of the Art of Medicine, in any University in the dominions of France. Intending to return to England, he judged it unnecessary to take degrees in Paris, unless he had resolved to reside there; and as it was more expensive, he therefore went to the University of Rheims, in Champaign, where, by virtue of his attestations, he was immediately admitted to three examinations, as if he had finished his studies in that academy; and there was honoured with his degrees, June 11, 1736. In the July following he came to London, and was soon employed by Dr. James Douglas to assist him in his anatomical works, where in some time he began to practise physic.

He was elected a member of the Royal Society in 1740; and, after due examination, was admitted a Licentiate of the College of Physicians, April 1, 1751; paying college fees and bond stamps of different denominations to the amount of 41*l*. 2*s*. 8*d*. subject also to quarterage of 2*l*. *per annum*. In 1755 he paid a farther sum of 7*l*. which, with the quarterage-money already paid, made up the sum of 16*l*. in lieu of all future payments."

Thus far from Dr. Parsons's own MS.

On his arrival in London, by the recommendation of his Paris friends, Dr. Parsons was introduced to the acquaintance of Dr. Mead, Sir Hans Sloane, and Dr. James Douglas. This great Anatomist made use of his assistance, not only in his anatomical preparations, but also in his representations of morbid and other appearances, a list of several of which was in the hands of his friend Dr. Maty; who had prepared an Eloge on Dr. Parsons, which was never used; but which, by the favour of Mrs. Parsons, I was enabled to copy from the original manuscript.

In 1738, by the interest of his friend Dr. Douglas, he was appointed physician to the public Infirmary in St. Giles's. In 1739 he married, at the parish church of St. Andrew, Holborn, Miss Elizabeth Reynolds; by whom he had two sons and a daughter, who all died young. Dr. Parsons resided for many years in Red Lion-square, where he frequently enjoyed the company and conversation of Dr. Stukeley, Bp. Lyttelton, Mr. Henry Baker, Dr. Knight, and many other of the most distinguished members of the Royal and Antiquarian Societies, and of that of Arts, Manufactures, and Commerce; giving weekly an elegant dinner to a large but select party. He enjoyed also the literary correspondence of D'Argenville, Buffon, De Cat, Beccaria, Amb. Bertrand, Valltravers, Ascanius, Turberville Needham, Dr. Garden, and others of the most distinguished rank in science.

As a practitioner, he was judicious, careful, honest, and remarkably humane to the poor; as a friend, obliging and communicative; cheerful and decent in conversation; severe and strict in his morals, and attentive to fulfil with propriety all the various duties of life.

In 1769, he proposed to retire from business and from London, for the sake of his health; and, having disposed of most of his books and his fossils with that view, went to Bristol: but soon found it inconsistent with his happiness to forsake all the advantages which a long residence in the capital, and the many connexions he had formed, had rendered habitual to him. He therefore returned to his old house; and died in it, after a week's illness, April 4, 1770.

By his last will, dated in October 1766, he gave his whole property to Mrs. Parsons; and, in case of her death before him, to Miss Mary Reynolds, her only sister, "in recompence for her affectionate attention to him and to his wife, for a long course of years, in sickness and in health."

It was his particular request that he should not be buried till some change should appear in his corpse; a request which occasioned his being kept unburied 17 days, and even then scarce the slightest alteration was perceivable. He was buried at Hendon.

A portrait of Dr. Parsons, by Mr. Wilson, is now in the British Museum; another, by Wells, was in the hands of his widow, with a third unfinished; and one of his son James; also a family piece, in which the same son is introduced, with the Doctor and his lady, accompanied by her sister.

Among other portraits, Mrs. Parsons had fine ones of the illustrious Harvey, of Bp. Burnet, and of Dr. John Freind; a beautiful miniature of Dr. Stukeley; some good paintings by her husband's own hand, particularly the Rhinoceros, which he described in the Philosophical Transactions. She possessed also his MSS. and some capital printed books; a large folio volume, intituled, "Figuræ quædam Miscellaneæ quæ ad rem Anatomicam Historiamque Naturalem spectant; quas propriâ adumbravit manu Jacobus Parsons, M.D. S.S.R. Ant. &c." another, called, "Drawings of curious Fossils, Shells, &c. in Dr. Parsons's Collection, drawn by himself. I have been indulged with a sight of these valuable drawings. Amongst other curiosities, is an exact delineation of a human fœtus, which was the subject of an extraordinary imposture; the upper part being well made, and in good proportion, the lower extremities monstrous. It was inclosed in a glass case, and shewn at the Heathcock, Charing Cross, as "a surprizing young Mermaid, taken on the coast of Acapulco." This figure the Doctor drew; and caused the showman to be turned out of town.

Dr. Parson's library was sold by Mr. Paterson, June 7, &c. 1769, and his fossils June 22, &c. the same year; both under the title of "an eminent Physician, who, on account of his health, is retiring into the country."

His widow, Mrs. Elizabeth Parsons, died Aug. 8, 1786, aged 86; and was buried at Hendon.

ALEXANDER POPE

Editor's Note: There is no separate article on Pope in the *Literary Anecdotes*, but references to him are scattered here and there among the copious notes in the nine volumes. The most interesting are here gathered together.

MR. TYERS ON POPE

" "POPE, whilst living with his father at Chiswick, before he went to Binfield, took great delight in cock-fighting; and laid out all his school-boy money, and little perhaps it was, in buying fighting-cocks. From this passion, but surely not the play of a child, his mother had the dexterity to wean him." —

"This writer had an opportunity of viewing Pope's garden and grotto, and should have seen the Poet himself if he had been at home; for our Sibyl through his Elysian fields would have introduced us. An acquaintance, whom this Rhapsody converted into a friend, undertook to authenticate a trifling circumstance of Pope's being surprized by some Patrician company, whom he neither desired nor expected to see, and who broke in upon his privacy. To avoid them, he fled to his gardener, whom he directed to take him up in his arms, and convey him over his boundary, which he did, and escaped by this help from his intruding visitors; as Anchises did, by the strength of Æneas, from the flames of Troy." — "I was formerly told by a respectable intelligencer (who had the opinion from the noble Lord himself) that Lord Peterborough did not think his friend Pope so good nor so great a Poet as Dryden." — "At the desire of Queen Caroline, Pope kept back the long prose Letter of Lord Hervey, now inserted in his Works; for she became apprehensive it might make her Counsellor (so he is described — 'Now at the ear of Eve, familiar toad' —) insignificant in the public esteem, and at last in her own." — "As Sir C. H. Williams, a great wit and a great courtier, was coming down the Thames, with a well-known literary gentleman who lives upon its poetical banks, he pointed to Pope's house, where the Bard was lying in his shroud, and cried out, in the words of Falstaff,

'I am afraid of the gunpowder Percy, though he be dead.'

"Pope set himself a poetical task, to translate, on an average, so many lines a day — like the Navigator, who reckons his vessel will complete her voyage at a set time, if she continues to sail at so many knots an hour, unobstructed by storms or calms."

"Lyttelton (as yet without a title) asked Pope one morning, how he had slept during the night. 'I have not had a wink of sleep,' says our Poet; 'but I have fared as well, for I have translated forty lines of Homer.' Lyttelton (now ennobled) thinks the translation performed, not so much in the *manner* of Homer, nor agreeable to the *sense*, in all places, as might perhaps be desired."

"Mr. Spence's Dialogues on the Odyssey recommended him to Mr. Pope, and the amiableness of his disposition continued him in his intimacy to his death. His name is to his Will in 1743. He was at this time Professor of History, and had been Professor of Poetry, in Oxford; and he had travelled abroad with Lord Middlesex, and brought home with him materials for his Polymetis. He was so high in patronage, that is is pretty certain he might have obtained a Mitre, if his ambition had prompted him to solicit one. . . . Spence was content with his income of about 900*l.* a year, of which he directed a part to benevolence. In a state of personal debility, he fell into a piece of water in his garden at Byfleet, where he was drowned. . . . In criticism Mr. Spence took the candid side. He was an Addison, not a Zoilus or a Dennis. Mr. Pope admitted him into such familiarity of communication, that he prepared a large collection of literary anecdotes and remarks from his conversation. . . . Spence intended these papers for the press after his death; and conditionally parted with them to his Bookseller in Pall Mall. But his executors, armed with a discretionary power, consulted the posthumous honour of the Editor (for possibly the collection was not worthy of the great name their Friend bore in the world, whose last work ought not to have been his least), and continue it in manuscript, to be consulted, like the Sibylline papers of old Rome, only upon extraordinary occasions. . . . Christopher Pitt, the Translator of Virgil, (is it assuming too much to assert, his best Translator?) the contemporary of Spence at New College, writes of him in this handsome manner in 1728: 'Mr. Spence is the completest Scholar, either in solid or polite learning, for his years, that I ever knew. Besides, he is the sweetest-tempered gentleman breathing.' How much richer in knowledge must he have been! (for Learning, like money and snow, accumulates very fast); for he lived to 1768." — "No man ever had so many enemies as Pope, nor was so well able to defend himself against them. . . . What the Dunces wrote against him he collected; and, if I am not misinformed, they were intended to have been preserved in bundles in the Museum. Whether they are to be found, or why they are not there, let the curious in such researches examine. . . . Cleland and Savage were called upon (by Dedications and Prefaces) to appear for Pope, when he did not care to record his own appearance, and served in the double capacity of Friends and of Spies. Savage collected together all the anecdotes of the Heroes of the Dunciad, that make them ridiculous in the notes. His high birth, his distresses, and his merit, made Pope his benefactor for life; and he contributed an annuity of 20*l.* a-year towards his support; but Savage irrecoverably lost the good opinion of Pope by his unconquerable arrogance, and he had the art of chilling the liberality of his warmest patrons. His behaviour became so offen-

sive to our Poet, and so injurious to his spirits (for Hawkesworth
told me it preyed upon his health) that he was heartily glad
when he withdrew from London. . . . Savage would have been
forgot (for characters of ingratitude are not worth a memorial),
if his Friend, almost the only person he had not alienated himself from, and who (as Archbishop Laud says of himself) 'never
deserts till he is first forsaken,' had not embalmed his memory
in a master-piece of Biography." — "A new glaring meteor now
began to shoot up its head above the literary horizon. The name
of this Giant was *Warburton*. The appellation of *Colossus* is not
to be given any longer, it having made ill-blood between Dr.
Brown and our late eminent Oxford Professor. This extraordinary man rose, from being a practising Attorney at Newark, where
his father was Town-clerk, to be Lord Bishop of Gloucester.
Before he shook off the Lay-habit, he surveyed all the arguments for and against Revelation with great labour and impartiality, and wrote afterwards with sovereign contempt of Free-
thinkers and their cause; and yet, at one time, by the Orthodox
he was reckoned Heterodox. He offered to enlist himself into the
service of Pope, and was taken at his word. He introduced himself as Twickenham, with a 'Vindication of the Essay on Man'
in his hand, which Poem was known all over Europe by French
translations. His attempt was, to defend the system, and confute
Crousaz, a Professor in Switzerland. Crousaz, it was said, made
it tremble to its centre; but this Defender of Pope's ethical faith
endeavoured to prop it up. Dr. Middleton desires Warburton to
advise Pope to be content with his explanation, and defend it
with the arguments he has found out. The more this metaphysical Poem was surveyed, till the new Commentator appeared,
the more unsolid was its foundation thought to be. If Warburton
had not come at the right hour, the system would never have
been half so well understood. It could not have resisted the
shock of time, and the fashion of new opinions. This Champion
preserved Pope from the sentence of condemnation. Warburton
became master of the spirit of Pope, and the director of his
opinions, as long as he lived. He trusted him with writing Notes
on his Works, of which he gave him the profits, and the custody
of his fame. It became the wish of both, that they might go
down hand in hand to posterity. What is a little singular, Warburton, amongst his earliest friends, who were Pope's enemies,
had roughly and roundly asserted, that the Essay was collected
'from the worst passages of the worst Authors.' This was either

unknown to Pope, or forgot, or forgiven. . . . Richardson says, that he was privy to this Essay, from the first scratches, to the last laboured manuscript in printed characters, which Pope gave him, on account of his trouble in collation. But the Commentary made the Poem considered as pious and philosophical. Poetical, at least enough so, it had been generally allowed. Had the great Warburton changed his opinion, or was it altered by interest? No matter; perhaps he was right at last. . . . The Bishop of Carlisle [Dr. Law], in a preface to his late new edition of his translation of Abp. King's "Origin of Evil" (in opposition to Warburton, who, while on a visit at Cambridge, was ready to quarrel on the subject) asserts, that Bolingbroke extracted the scheme of *the best*, from the book of the Archbishop (whose manuscript Diary of his own life is said to be extant); and that Lord Bathurst told him, he had seen these collected notions in the hand-writing of that Lord, lying by the side of Pope, when he was writing the Essay on Man. . . . Pope refused a degree of Doctor of Laws from the University of Oxford, during a visit there, because they would not confer the same honour on his *new* Favourite, who, it must be confessed, was to them a *new man.*" — "I have seen it lately in print, that there have been several who have versified as well as Pope. It this is to be taken for granted, Mr. Hayley must be admitted of that small number. His last Poem of the 'Triumphs of Temper,' amongst its many happy incidents, contains an enlargement of Pope's 'Cave of Spleen,' and is full of energy and excellent poetry. He has augmented the number of rhymes, the paucity of which, in all Pope's Poetry, is astonishing." — "It was expected that Warburton would have written his Life, for he promised it; and that his executors would have published some of his posthumous pieces. What could give rise to the expectation of finding a satirical Life of Dean Swift, in manuscript, by Pope, is not yet, perhaps, too late to inquire into; for two of his noble executors are still living. The last letters that pass between our Poet and the Dean express the most serious and solemn veneration for each other." — "Warburton was entangled by late friendships, *et recentibus odiis.* His propect of elevation in the Church, where he was afterwards recompensed with a Mitre by the interest of Lord Chatham, made him every day too great for his subject. He did nothing on this occasion; but, thirty years afterwards, he assisted Ruffhead with some biographical materials; and revised the Life, as written by his *Locum-tenens,* sheet by sheet." —

"Pope's income, in the last flourishing years of his life, amounted to about 800*l.* a-year; a part of which he appropriated to charity. *Res parta labore, non relicta."*

"Mr. Lockman, whose laborious application obtained for him the *languages,* and who was a Translator for half a century, had once thoughts, as he said, of composing a treatise on *Literary Thefts.* If this offspring of the pen had not been one of the *post nati,* too much of this unoriginal Rhapsody must have found a place there. Lockman, though not praised by Pope, had a portion of his esteem. He dedicated a Translation of a Latin Oration, written by Porce the Jesuit, in praise of dramatic poetry, to him. Though Lockman was by no means the best Poet in England, *he was something more, and better;* he was one of the honestest men in it. Though called *the Lamb* among his first literary friends, he had the spirit to reply to a person who spoke rudely of his poetry, and who had a mark set upon him by Pope, 'Thank God! my name is not at full length in the Dunciad!' It were pity that he who composed so many Lives in the 'General Dictionary,' should not have one in the 'Biographia.' Thus much is due to one of the first acquaintances this Writer was blessed with." — "On reciting, in my younger days, the Universal Prayer before *Tacitus* Gordon (a person formerly much known and much talked of, but whose name will be hardly revived till it appears alphabetically in the new edition of the 'Biographia'), I remember I made a pause after these lines,

> 'That mercy I to others shew,
> That mercy shew to me!'

'It would have been well,' says he, 'if Pope had observed that conduct to others. Can he lay his hand upon his heart, and say that he has?' He used to say of Pope, 'that he was a good Poet, but a weak Reasoner.' — The publick applied the character in the last book of the Dunciad to that gentleman:

> 'Where Tindal dictates, and Silenus snores.'

If Gordon took this to himself, it accounted for what he said of Pope; for no man can talk of a foe as he does of a friend."

"Though Pope turned all he wrote into wit and into gold, yet it may be questioned whether Churchill, that able and intrepid Satirist (who, as somebody spoke of him, 'had the courage to write what others had not courage to think') did not demand

and obtain more money from the Booksellers. Churchill tried with his political friend [Wilkes], the popular uthor of the North Briton, 'how far the liberty of the press would carry him.' His Satires were as much read (the first day of publication was almost the sale of an edition), and he had as extensive a field to range in for sport, as Pope. His intention was, to fetch blood at every stroke; but his weapon was not so sharp as Pope's. His pen, like the sword of Michael the Archangel in Milton, mowed down whole ranks at a time, and inflicted wounds that never closed. The pen of Churchill wakened every character from repose, or that was basking in the sunshine of the Court, as Ithuriel did Satan by the touch of his spear. He consulted his companion (who for so many years *rode on the air of whirlwind*) on one of his pieces; who assured him, in alliterative epithets, that it must succeed, for it was *personal, political,* and *poetical.*' — 'This Writer does not care,' says a wounded friend, with one of the Satires in his hand, 'how wretched he makes some people for life, for the wanton gratification of a few hours!' Churchill's performances are superior to Whitehead's (though of his *Manners* Paul printed four thousand copies); but are not comparable to *London,* or to *The Vanity of Human Wishes.* Pope was alive to praise the merits of the first, and Churchill commended them both. The *Prophecy of Famine,* written with the furious spirit of Tyrtæus, might, at a former time, have set the two Nations, now good friends, together by the ears. But it was written at the only moment when it could find readers." — "Pope's 'Philosopher and Guide,' says Hurd, ' 'tis well known, stuck close to him, till another and brighter star (Warburton) had got the ascendant.' Lord Bolingbroke never forgave Pope, for leaving him, and becoming the pupil of Warburton. Pope afforded a handle, which his old Patron seized, to cast a revengeful dishonour upon his memory."

DR. JOHNSON'S ACCOUNT OF POPE'S AGREEMENT WITH BERNARD LINTOT

Dr. Johnson, in his admirable Life of Pope (vol. XI. p. 76), after having made himself master of the minutest facts, says, "He offered an English Iliad to the subscribers in six volumes quarto, for six guineas; a sum, according to the value of money at that time, by no means inconsiderable, and greater than I believe to have been ever asked before. His proposal, however, was very favourably received; and the patrons of literature were busy to recommend his undertaking, and promote his interest. — The greatness of the design, the popularity of the author, and the attention of the literary world, naturally raised such expectations of the future sale, that the booksellers made their offers with great eagerness; but the highest bidder was Bernard Lintot; who became proprietor on condition of supplying, at his own expence, all the copies which were to be delivered to subscribers, or presented to friends, and paying two hundred pounds for every volume. — The encouragement given to this translation, though report seems to have over-rated it, was such as the world has not often seen. The subscribers were five hundred and seventy-five. The copies for which subscriptions were given were six hundred and fifty-four. For these copies Pope had nothing to pay; he therefore received, including the two hundred pounds a volume, five thousand three hundred and twenty pounds four shillings without deduction, as the books were supplied by Lintot. — Of the quartos it was, I believe, stipulated that none should be printed but for the author, that the subscription might not be depreciated; but Lintot impressed the same pages upon a small folio, and paper perhaps a little thinner; and sold exactly at half the price, for half a guinea each volume, books so little inferior to the quartos, that, by a fraud of trade, those folios, being afterwards shortened by cutting away the top and bottom, were sold as copies printed for the subscribers. Lintot printed some on royal paper in folio for two guineas a volume; but of this experiment he repented, as his own son sold copies of the first volume with all their extent of margin for two shillings. It is unpleasant to relate that the bookseller, after all his hopes and all his liberality, was, by a very unjust and illegal action, defrauded of his profit. An edition of the English Iliad was printed in Holland in duodecimo, and imported clandestinely for the gratification of those who were impatient to read what they could not yet afford to buy. This fraud could only be counteracted by an edition equally cheap and more commodious; and Lintot was compelled to contract his folio at once into a duodecimo, and lose the advantage of an intermediate gradation. The notes, which in the Dutch copies were placed at the end of each book, as they had been in the large volumes, were now subjoined to the text in the same page, and are therefore more easily consulted. Of this edition the sale was doubtless very numerous; but indeed great numbers were necessary to produce considerable profit."

JOHN JORTIN'S ACCOUNT OF HOW HE ASSISTED POPE

"When I was a soph at Cambridge, Pope was about his translation of Homer's *Ilias,* and had published part of it. He employed some person (I know not who he was) to make extracts for him from Eustathius, which he inserted in his Notes. At that time there was no Latin translation of that Commentator. Alexander Politi (if I remember right) began that work some years afterwards, but never proceeded far in it. The person employed by Mr. Pope was not at leisure to go with the work; and Mr. Pope (by his bookseller I suppose) sent to Jefferies, a bookseller at Cambridge, to find out a student who would undertake the task. Jefferies applied to Dr. Thirlby, who was my tutor, and who pitched upon me. I would have declined the work, having (as I told my tutor) other studies to pursue, to fit me for taking my degree. But he, *qui quicquid volebat valdè volebat,* would not hear of any excuse; so I complied. I cannot recollect what Mr. Pope allowed for each book of Homer; I have a notion that it was three or four guineas. I took as much care as I could to perform the task to his satisfaction; but I was ashamed to desire my tutor to give himself the trouble of overlooking my operations; and he, who always used to think and speak too favourably of me, said that I did not want his help. He never perused one line of it before it was printed, nor perhaps afterwards. When I had gone through some books (I forget how many) Mr. Jefferies let us know that Mr. Pope had a friend to do the rest, and that we might give over. When I sent my papers to Jefferies, to be conveyed to Mr. Pope, I inserted, as I remember, some remarks on a passage, where Mr. Pope, in my opinion, had made a mistake; but as I was not directly employed by him, but by a bookseller, I did not inform him who I was, or set my name to my papers. When that part of Pope's Homer came out in which I had been concerned, I was eager, as it may be supposed, to see how things stood, and much pleased to find that he had not only used almost all my notes, but had hardly made any alteration in the expressions. I observed also, that in a subsequent edition, he corrected the place to which I had made objections. I was in hopes in those days (for I was young) that Mr. Pope would make inquiry about his *coadjutor,* and take some civil notice of him; but he did not, and I had no notion of obtruding myself upon him; I never saw his face." *Dr. Jortin, MS.* — ["So all Pope's coadjutors complain of him; probably they had some reason for thinking that he was too well paid, and they too poorly. As Jortin was confessedly a scholar, Pope's incuriosity or incivility is reprehensible. I once saw an *original* letter of Pope's, in which he fairly owned, that he did not understand Greek, which was probably very true. It was read at Dr. Rutherford's; and Dr. Warton, who mentions it, was one of the company. The person at first employed, perhaps, was Broome; the second friend, Fenton. The history of *making a book* is worth detailing, and one man's running away with all the credit." See a very curious letter by Mr. Robertson, Gent. Mag. 1792, p. 610. Translating Eustathius and Homer are two different things. See Gent. Mag. 1792, p. 608; 1793, p. 391, 392. So the Iliad and Odyssey are distinct translations. *T. F.*] — "The history of the notes has never been traced. Broome, in his preface to his Poems, declares himself the commentator *in part upon the Iliad;* and it appears from Fenton's letter, preserved in the Museum, that Broome was at first engaged in consulting Eustathius; but that after a time, whatever was the reason, he desisted : another man of Cambridge was then employed, who soon grew weary of the work; and a third was recommended by Thirlby, who is now discovered to have been *Jortin,* a man since well known to the learned world, who complained that Pope, having accepted and approved his performance, never testified any curiosity to see him. The terms which Fenton uses are very mercantile : 'I think at first sight that his performance is very commendable, and have sent word for him to finish the seventeenth book, and to send it, with his demands for his trouble. I have here inclosed the specimen: if the rest come before the return, I will keep them till I receive your order.' Broome then offered his service a second time, which was probably accepted, as they had afterwards a closer correspondence. Parnall contributed the Life of Homer, which Pope found so harsh, that he took great pains in correcting it; and by his own diligence, with such help as kindness or money could procure him, in somewhat more than five years he completed his version of the Iliad, with the notes. He began in 1712, his 25th year, and concluded it in 1718, his 30th year." *Dr. Johnson*. — The Rev. Brooke Bridges, sometime rector of Orlingbury in Northamptonshire, had an original letter of Pope to his uncle, the Rev. Ralph Bridges, then chaplain to Dr. Compton, bishop of London, and afterwards incumbent of South Weald in Essex; in which Pope plainly acknowledges his "own want of a critical understanding in the original beauties of Homer." But this was in 1708, when Pope prepared the first specimen of his Version for Tonson's Miscellanies. He was afterwards much obliged to this Mr. Bridges (whose mother was Mr. Trumbull's sister) for large corrections in his subsequent translation; which are still preserved in the British Museum.

DANIEL PRINCE

MANY years a very prominent Bookseller and Printer at Oxford. During the long period of his being manager of the University Press, many valuable publications of course passed under his superintendance. Those in which he most prided himself will be seen in the following list, which not long before his death he transmitted to me as a curiosity:

"Blackstone's Magna Carta," 1759, 4to.
"Marmora Oxoniensia," 1763, fol.
"Listeri Synopsis Conchyliorum," 1770, fol.
"Blackstone's Commentaries," 4 vols. 4to. 3 editions, 1770, &c.
"Kennicott's Hebrew Bible," 2 vols. fol. 1776.
"Ciceronis Opera," 10 vols. 4to. 1784.

"Bradley's Observations and Tables," all printed in 1788, [but not published for some years after.]

Mr. Prince married a sister of Dr. Hayes; and died in New College Lane, Oxford, June 6, 1796, in his 85th year.

In Mr. Urban's Obituary, it was very justly stated, that his loss would be severely felt by many persons who were the objects of his bounty, and by all those who had the happiness to enjoy his friendship. His communications to that Miscellany were frequent and curious. The Poetical Department in March 1796 was enriched by him with some valuable verses by Mr. Thomas Warton, on Miss Cotes and Miss Wilmot; and that in June by a political poem of Lord Hervey's, originally printed in the first edition of Dodsley's Poems, but withdrawn before publication, as it was supposed to be too personal for the time.

EXTRACTS FROM LETTERS OF DANIEL PRINCE TO RICHARD GOUGH AND JOHN NICHOLS

July 2, 1789. "Our two magnificent Prisons are now finished. The Castle is a noble style, in imitation of the best old work. The only very old buildings are, the Castle Tower, which is well preserved, and Castle Hill, and the Lady's Chapel, next to my house. It was well known at New College that the whole of the East end of their Chapel was ordered by Horne Bishop of Winchester (in the early part of Queen Elizabeth's time), to be completely hid, by plastering up the whole; and, in the operation, where any parts projected beyond their level, they cut all even. A few years since, a small opening was made, which presented such an elegant specimen, that the Society have now opened the whole, and purpose to have it restored, under the direction of Sir Joshua Reynolds and Mr. Wyatt. The images were all demolished. What remains is Gothic architecture, carried on to the ceiling, with the niches empty. The bottom row has good sculpture, of the Nativity, &c. the human figures about the scale of nine inches. It is found in general that the roofs of the buildings, of 350 or more years standing, decay very fast in the timber, by heat from the lead. New College is now new roofed, and much repaired, at the expense of 7000*l*. The Altar's restoration will cost 2000*l*. more. They are the best prepared as to cash for such a work of any Society here. The light blue tiles are used instead of lead. Magdelen College, and indeed All Souls, are expected soon to want the same renewal. — On Monday last, without any violence from the wind, the old Oak at Magdalen College fell *fortunately* into the meadow. Had it fallen towards the river, and the walk, it must have done much damage. The root was entirely gone to powder, so that it dropped by the weight of an arm. The age of it is reckoned to be full 600 years, as the Founder, when directing the site of the College, ordered the boundary to the North to be near the *great Oak*. It is mentioned by Evelyn; the people divert themselves in crowding in numbers in the inside of the trunk. — The colour of New College altar is blue and gold. It is opened with great care. — The only regard lately shewn to Antiquities here is in the publication of two pair of Prints; *viz*. one pair, about the size of a quarto page, of Friar Bacon's Study, from the North and South; one pair, of a much larger size, about double the former, of Bocardo. — We have lately purchased Dr. Vansittart's library, full of oddities, some probably which will suit the thirst of an English Historian. We will send you a Catalogue about Michaelmass. — Mr. Gutch proceeds apace with the *Fasti Oxon*. — Our Bodleian Library is putting into good order. It has been already one year in hand. Some one, two, or three of the Curators work at it daily, and several Assistants. The revenue from the tax on the Members of the University is about 460*l*. *per annum,* which has existed 12 years. This has increased the Library so much, that it must be attended to, and a new Catalogue put in hand. They have lately bought all the expensive foreign publications. A young man of this place is about making a Catalogue of all the singular books in this place, in the College Libraries as well as the Bodleian. — In about six weeks we shall publish Dean Aldrich's Architecture, which we expect will be pronounced to be an honour to the kingdom, for the elegant engravings of the Author and the Architecture, by Heath, and the beauty of the printing. It could not have been supported but from the bounty of so large a Society. The Duke of Portland subscribes for fifty copies.   DAN. PRINCE.

"*Sept*. 17. The work at New College goes on very slowly, for want of Mr. Wyatt. It is said he has declared he can restore its original fashion. The whole design at our Castle will be long before it is complete. The Keeper, or *Governor* as he is now styled, is an ingenious Architect and Mason; and contrives, for the good of the publick, and the prisoners themselves, that great part of the work shall be done by Convicts, several of whom, by their industry and manifest reformation, have obtained their release at the expiration of two instead of three years. My Wife and I were last week at Mr. Pusey's house at Pusey, that antient Danish-hold estate. Mr. Pusey, whose name was *Bouverie,* is making great improvements on that new-acquired estate, in well preserving, and *adding* (by modern sculpture and painting) to the memory of that antient grant.

"The venerable old Baronet in that neighbourhood, Sir Robert Throckmorton, near his 100th year, now quite blind, but in health, has done great things to preserve and restore Buckland (his parish) church. An excellent example to Roman Catholick gentry! Indeed, Sir Robert and Mr. Pusey seem to try who shall leave the best monuments behind them — I saw Professor White. He waits, with the publick, to hear Dr. Gabriel's tale.

"Mr. Gutch is far advanced with his Volume. His Index will be extremely useful. — Nothing new in our press, except a new 'Conic Sections' by our Mathematical Reader. — Next week I shall go to a lordship (now a barony to the Duke of Marl-borough) Wormleighton, in Warwickshire. The church, accord-ing to Dugdale, was built in temp. Henry VII.; has an antient pavement, and well-preserved arms in all the windows. The village was all new built at one time, with a noble manor-house, in which are two grand state-rooms. More than half the house has been lately taken down, to save repairs; but several large buildings remain; viz. stables, large barns for hay and carts, a very uncommon building for wool. All the buildings, except the church, with a grand gate-way, are in one style, neat stone-work, at the end of Queen Elizabeth; and some have the arms of James I. Not a plough is used in the whole lordship; all pasture; and the tenants are to this day preserved from taxes; Lord Spencer, the present possessor, paying the poor's tax, by giving a portion of land for their maintenance. The Vicar you may remember at Cambridge. His name is La Rocque. This must be a specimen of the old manner of life, except the change by the reform in the church, when the poor fell on the Lord, who used to be supported from Kenilworth. — When you next pass farther in the town than Mr. Deputy Nichols's, pray look on the best printed book from the Oxford press, *Aldrich's Architecture*.

"We have a young man in this place, his name is Curtis, who was an apprentice to me, who has hitherto only dealt in Books of Curiosities, in which he is greatly skilled, superior in many respects to De Bure, Ames, or his Continuator. He has been employed five or six years in the Bodleian Library, and since at Wadham, Queen's, and Balliol. He purposes to publish a Catalogue of little or not known books in Oxford, particularly in Merton, Balliol, and Oriel."

"*Feb.* 14, 1790. Mr. Malchior, of this place, has published, in most delicate aquatinta, a large print of Magdalen College old Bridge, which was taken down to make room for the new bridge. It is more like a drawing than any thing I have yet seen. We are now taking down the Physick-garden House and Library, *i.e.* the Botany Professor's House and Botanic Library, though both new buildings, to make room for the approach to the bridge from the town. — Magdalen College Chapel and Hall, must undergo the same expensive reparation as New College Chapel has done; and under Mr. Wyatt's direction also. There are fears that the roof of all Magdalen College old Quadrangle is in danger. The timber of these buildings, which was chestnut, is now wasting very fast, and perhaps have stood their time. I think I can promise Mr. Cooke will let you have a proof print of Dr. Aldrich, though he took off but very few. — The Letter to Earl Stanhope is said here to be by Mr. (Charles) Hawtrey, of Christ Church, now one of the Portionists of Bampton, Oxfordshire. — The Letter to the Delegates at Devizes is by Mr. George Huntingford, an incomparable Greek scholar, now just elected Warden of Winton College. — The pamphlets from Johnson's and Kearsley's shops are rubbish; and the Letter to Dr. Gabriel, *smartly abusive,* is not by Mr. Griffith, who is a man of too elegant manners to appear in that dress. In the pamphlet entitled, "Observations on the Case of the Protestant Dissenters," ascribed to the Dean of Canterbury, is an excellent picture of *Kippis, of his* own drawing. — In a few days will be published, from our press, a new edition, and enlarged to 4 volumes, of Toup's 'Emendationes in Suidam;' and now from Hesychius, J. Pollux, Harpocration, Moeris Atticista, Timæus, &c. and considerably from the late Mr. Tyrwhitt's MSS. — Work for the Germans; but I fear will not sell enough at home. — Mr. Gutch has almost finished his *Fasti*. Dr. Blayney will compleat his Samaritan Pentateuch next summer."

"*Aug.* 17. Mr. Gutch now proposes to publish his *Annals of the University* genuine from Ant. à Wood, as you see by his *Fasti*; which I suppose you have. This work is that which Wood wrote in English, and which was new modelled and published in Latin by Fell, much to the Author's dissatisfaction. It is happy the MS. was preserved, as well for Mr. Gutch as the Publick. The work is to be in two volumes quarto. — New College will be a noble restoration of that magnificent Chapel; the internal colour a *warm white*. Magdalen College Chapel is under the same repair in a less degree. The new and beautiful buildings from the hands of Mr. Wyatt are Christ Church Eastern Gate to Peckwater, where part of Canterbury stood; and Oriel new Library. Several repairs are in hand, at Merton-hall, St. Mary-hall, and Balliol College. The expensive appendix to the Bodleian is worth your visitation. A great order is now sent to Holland, to enrich it.

Oct. 5, 1793. "You know what a formidable and discerning body the Associated Booksellers in London are, with *General Cadell** at their head, to select a learned Editor for a work; and perhaps you have not heard that this Company have engaged Dr. Joseph Warton, late Master of Winchester school, to publish a new Edition of Pope's Works. Warburton, it is allowed, was not a proper Editor; but, *entre nous,* must we think Dr. Joseph Warton a proper one, because a good Scholar, a Poet, and a Critick? His 'Essay on the Writings of Pope' does not much recommend him, as we expect an Editor should like his Author's abilities. The Doctor never lived in London, where in young life much treasures are always to be collected. Some men are more worn at 70 than others are at 80. The boys at school saw it, and became unawed at his appearance. Did you ever see the first Edition of the 'Dunciad?' a small six-penny pamphlet, published in 1727, I think, but cannot depend on the year, though I was the apprentice trusted to go to the Author with the proofs in great secrecy. I had the wit to keep

---

*Thomas Cadell (1742-1802), the partner of and eventual successor to Andrew Millar. He became one of the most eminent booksellers in London [*Ed.*]

the sheets with some of his marks to correct; but have lately
lost them, in removing my rubbish from my old house and shop
to one of the Savillian houses near New College: a dwelling
very convenient for me — Direct to me, as usual, at Mr. Cooke's,
Bookseller.

"Magdalen College Chapel will be opened this month; New
College, more and more admired, before Christmass. — I will
get you all the Speeches in the Theatre to be had, but have not
begun to collect. The Governors discourage printing, or copies;
but I cannot see why; except it be to prevent inferior examples
appearing.

"*June* 4. You might fairly apply to me to get sheets wanted
to complete the Oxford Bible, folio, for Churches, in 1716; and
I hope they still may be had; for great care was taken to preserve
the waste of that book, and indeed of some few others of Basket's
printing, worth preserving.* — About the year 1762, all Basket's
stock, &c. was removed to London; and I have often procured
sheets of that Bible, and also of the beautiful octavo Common
Prayer Book, which were almost his only shining examples of
paper and print. Any Bookseller of long standing in Paternoster-
row — of which but few remain, yet Mr. Nichols may find
them — will tell you whether a room, or small warehouse, still
remains of Basket's books, where even waste sheets are still
preserved. This is all I can suggest at this late date, viz. 33 years,
from 1762 to 1795. I am not in the least habit of gain, farther
than the stocks, bridges, and roads, can give interest to a cripple
for his money. I can felicitate Messrs. —— when they are successful in insuring, and hope they are careful in playing small
game, lest an unlucky event happens. Have you seen a pamphlet printed here, said to be done by Professor Randolph, a list
of the early printed books in the Bodleian Library? It is in
Elmsly's shop. I am told Strabo may be next winter; but no
speedy prospect is seen."

---

*Thomas Basket, printer to the King and holder of the Bible patent, died
30 March, 1761. [*Ed.*]

ROBERT RAIKES

R OBERT RAIKES was of a very respectable family, and was born at Gloucester in the year 1735. His father was of the same business as himself, a printer, and conducted for many years, with much approbation, the Gloucester Journal. The education Mr. Raikes received was liberal, and calculated for his future designation in life. At a proper season he was initiated into his father's business, which he afterwards conducted with punctuality, diligence, and care. Several pieces, among which may be pointed out the Works of Dr. Tucker, Dean of Glou-cester, are such as will suffer nothing by any comparison with the productions of modern typography. The incidents of Mr. Raikes's life were few, and those not enough distinguished from the rest of the world to admit of a particular detail. It is sufficient to say, that in his business he was prosperous, and that his attention was not so wholly confined to it, but that he found time to turn his thoughts to subjects connected with the great interests of mankind and the welfare of society. By his means some consolation has been afforded to sorrow and impru-dence; some knowledge, and consequently happiness, to youth and inexperience.

The first object which demanded his notice, was the miser-able state of the County Bridewell within the City of Gloucester, which being part of the County gaol, the persons committed by the magistrate out of sessions for petty offences, associated, through necessity, with felons of the worst description, with little or no means of subsistence from labour; with little, if any, allowance from the County; without either meat, drink, or cloathing; dependent chiefly on the precarious charity of such as visited the prison, whether brought thither by business, curi-osity, or compassion. To relieve these miserable and forlorn wretches, and to render their situation supportable at least, Mr. Raikes employed both his pen, his influence, and his property, to procure them the necessaries of life; and finding that ignor-ance was generally the principal cause of those enormities which brought them to become objects of his notice, he determined, if possible, to procure them some moral and religious instruction. In this he succeeded, by means of bounties and encouragement, given to such of the prisoners as were able to read; and these, by being directed to proper books, improved both themselves and their fellow prisoners, and afforded great encouragement to persevere in the benevolent design. He then procured for them a supply of work, to preclude every excuse and temptation to idleness. Successful in this effort, he formed a more extensive plan of usefulness to society, which will transmit his name to posterity with those honours whch are due to the great bene-factors of mankind. This was the institution of Sunday schools, a plan which has been attended with the happiest effects. The thought was suggested by accident. "Some business," says Mr. Raikes, "leading me one morning into the suburbs of the city, where the lowest of the people (who are principally employed in the pin manufactory) chiefly reside, I was struck with concern on seeing a groupe of children, wretchedly ragged, at play in the street. An enquiry of a neighbour produced an account of the miserable state and deplorable profligacy of these infants, more especially on a Sunday, when left to their own direction." This information suggested an idea, "that it would be at least a harmless attempt, if it should be productive of no good, should some little plan be formed to check this deplorable profanation of the Sabbath." An agreement was soon after made with proper persons, to receive as many children on Sundays as should be sent, who were to be instructed in reading and in the Church catechism, at a certain rate. The Clergyman who was curate of the parish at the same time undertook to superintend the Schools, and examine the progress made. This happened about 1781, and the good consequences evidently appeared in the reformation and orderly behaviour of those who before were in every respect the opposite of decency or regularity. The effects were so apparent, that other parishes, in Gloucester and in various parts of the kingdom, adopted the scheme, which has by degrees become almost general, to the great advantage and comfort of the poor, and still more to the security and repose of the rich. Since the first institution, many thousands of children have been employed, to their own satisfaction, in acquiring such a portion of knowledge, as will render them useful to society, without encouraging any disposition unfavourable to themselves or the world. Where riot and disorder were formerly to be seen, decency and decorum are now to be found; industry has taken the place of idleness, and profaneness has been obliged to give way to devotion. It is certain, if any reformation of manners is to be hoped for, it must be from a continual attention to the education of youth. The benefits which have sprung up in con-sequence of Mr. Raikes's plan are too obvious to need a defence, were any person captious enough to cavil with an institution, which requires only to be observed to extort applause. Satisfied, that the rising generation will feel the influence of the benevolent intentions of Mr. Raikes, we have great satisfaction in joining our plaudit to those of the world at large; and without hesitation place him in the same form with those whose active benevolence entitles them to be looked up to with reverence and respect to the latest posterity.

He was for some years a member of the Court of Assistants of the Stationers Company; and died at Gloucester, April 5, 1811, aged 75.

JOHN RATCLIFFE

HAVING no knowledge whatever of this *black-letter* gentleman, I should have passed him over in silence, if Mr. Dibdin had not expected to find his name in *my Index*. That he may not be wholly disappointed in that respect, I shall borrow a few lines from his own ingenious work:

"In 1776 died John Ratcliffe, esq. of Bermondsey, a bibliomaniac of a very peculiar character. If he had contented himself with his former occupation, and frequented the butter and cheese, instead of the book, market — if he could have fancied himself in a brown peruke, and Russia apron, instead of an embroidered waistcoat, velvet breeches, and flowing periwig, he might, perhaps, have enjoyed greater longevity; but, infatuated by the *Caxtons* and *Wynkyn de Wordes* of the West and Fletewode collections, he fell into the snare; and the more he struggled to disentangle himself, the more certainly did he become a victim to the disease. The Catalogue was collected with great judgment and expense, during the last thirty years of his life: comprehending a large and most choice collection of the rare old English *black-letter,* in fine preservation, and in elegant bindings. The sale took place on March 27, 1776; although the *year* is unaccountably omitted by that renowned auctioneer the late Mr. Christie, who disposed of them. — If ever there was a *unique* collection, this was one — the very essence of Old Divin-

ity, Poetry, Romances, and Chronicles! The articles were only
1675 in number; but their intrinsic value amply compensated
for their paucity. — Of some particulars of Mr. Ratcliffe's life,
I had hoped to have found gleanings in Mr. Nichols's "Anecdotes of Bowyer;" but his name does not even appear in the
Index; being probably reserved for the second forth-coming
enlarged edition. Meanwhile, it may not be uninteresting to
remark that, like Magliabecchi,* he imbibed his love of reading
and collecting, from the accidental possession of scraps and
leaves of books. The fact is, Mr. Ratcliffe first kept a *chandler's
shop* in the Borough; and, as is the case with all retail traders,
had great quantities of old books brought to him to be purchased
at so much *per pound!* Hence arose his passion for collecting
the *black-letter,* as well as *Stilton cheeses;* and hence, by unwearied assiduity, and attention to business, he amassed a sufficiency to retire, and live, for the remainder of his days, upon
the luxury of *old English Literature!"*

When this note was thus far printed, I was favoured with the
following addition by an unknown correspondent:

"Mr. Ratcliffe lived in East-lane, Bermondsey; was a very
corpulent man, and his legs were remarkably thick, probably
from an anasarcous complaint. The writer of this remembers
him perfectly well; he was a very stately man, and, when he
walked, literally went a snail's pace. He was a Dissenter; and
every Sunday attended the meeting of Dr. Flaxman, in the
Lower Road at Deptford. He generally wore a fine coat, either
red or brown, with gold lace buttons, and a fine silk embroidered waistcoat, of scarlet, with gold lace, and a large and well-
powdered wig. With his hat in one hand, and a gold-headed
cane in the other, he marched royally along, and not unfrequently followed by a parcel of children, wondering who the
stately man could be. — A few years before his death, a fire
happened in the neighbourhood where he lived; and it became
necessary to remove part of his household furniture and books.
He was incapable of assisting himself; but he stood in the
street, lamenting and deploring the loss of his *Caxtons,* when a
sailor who lived within a door or two of him attempted to
console him: "Bless you, Sir, I have got them perfectly safe!"
While Ratcliffe was expressing his thanks, the sailor produced

---

*Antonio Magliabecchi (1633-1714) librarian to Cosmo III, Grand Duke
of Tuscany. [*Ed.*]

two of his fine curled periwigs, which he had saved from the
devouring element; and who had no idea that Ratcliffe could
make such a fuss for a few books." *Gent. Mag.* vol. LXXXII.

The following Letter is thus indorsed by Dr. Ducarel, to whom
it was addressed : "12 Oct. 1772, Mr. Ratcliffe (the great
Collector of old Black-letter Books in East-lane, Rotherhithe) —
about old English Herbals."

"DOCTOR,   *Thursday, 12 o'clock.*
"The eldest Herball I can at present think of is a thin
Folio, printed for Peter Treveris in Southwark, 1529 — another,
printed by Jhon. King, 1561. I have since found a book called
'The vertuose Boke of Distillacion,' by Jerom of Brunswick,
containing a large Herball, printed by Laurence Andrew, 1527.
— I will call on you Friday 23 Instant, when shall hope to discourse the matter over with you. I am, with utmost respect,
your most obedient servant,   J. RATCLIFFE."

"Mr. Ratcliffe used to give coffee and chocolate every Thursday morning to Book and Print Collectors. Dr. Askew, Messieurs
Beauclerck, Bull, Crofts, Samuel Gillam, West, &c. &c. used to
attend, when he would produce some of his late purchases. He
generally husbanded them, and only produced a few at one
time. He would exultingly say, 'There, there is a curiosity! —
what think you of that?' — though probably at the same time
he had more than two or three copies in his possession. When
some one or more of his visitants would say, 'Ah! if I could
be so fortunate to procure a copy, I should not mind the price!'
his answer was, 'he had almost despaired of ever meeting with
such a rarity; but if he should be so fortunate in his researches
to find another, they might depend," &c. He generally used
to spend whole days in the Booksellers' Warehouses; and, that
he might not lose time, would get them to procure him a steak
or chop. His house at Bermondsey was once on fire, and he ran
about the place like a mad-man, exclaiming, 'Oh! my Caxtons!
— Oh, my Caxtons!' His Housekeeper, thinking he meant his
wigs, said, 'Sir, I beg you will not be so uneasy about your wigs,
they are all safe.' — If his Catalogue had been arranged as
now, the Sale would have been double the extent; there were
many hundred most rare Black-letter Books and Tracts, un-
bound, with curious *cuts.* They were sold, I remember, in large
bundles, and were piled under the tables in the Auction-room

on which the other books were exposed to view, and were not seen but by the Booksellers who were the purchasers, *viz.* Chapman, Collins, &c. He always wrote on the first fly-leaf — *Perfect* — or otherwise, in Roman print, which he in general wrote neatly and expeditiously. — At the Fleetwood Sale I was a great purchaser, though not to a large amount; they were sent me from Paterson's by bags-full. Mr. Dodd purchased most of his curious articles at that sale. Garrick also attended. There was one curious Play that I think sold for 27 shillings, and was the only one Garrick did not possess, but he lifted up his hands and eyes with astonishment at the extravagant price, and I think was not the purchaser."

SAMUEL RICHARDSON

M R. SAMUEL RICHARDSON was born in 1689, in Derbyshire; but in what particular town has not been ascertained. "My father," he says, in a letter to a friend, "was a very honest man, descended of a family of middling note in the county of Surrey; but which, having for several generations a large number of children, the not-large possessions were split and divided, so that he and his brothers were put to trades; and the sisters were married to tradesmen. My mother was also a good woman, of a family not ungenteel; but whose father and mother died in her infancy, within half an hour of each other, in the London pestilence of 1665. — My father's business was that of a joiner, then more distinct from that of a carpenter than now it is with us. He was a good draughtsman, and understood architecture. His skill and ingenuity, and an understanding superior to his business, with his remarkable integrity of heart and manners, made him personally beloved by several persons of rank, among who were the Duke of Monmouth and the first Earl of Shaftesbury, both so noted in our English history; their known favour for him having, on the Duke's attempt on the Crown, subjected him to be looked upon with a jealous eye, notwithstanding he was noted for a quiet and inoffensive man, he thought proper, on the decollation of the first-named unhappy Nobleman, to quit his London business, and to retire to Derbyshire, though to his great detriment; and there I, and three other children out of nine, were born."

It appears, from his own statement, that from his earliest youth he had a love for letter-writing. When not eleven years old, he addressed a letter of reproof to a widow of near fifty, occasioned by her over-strained pretences to religious zeal. We find also that he was at the same time a general favourite with the ladies, both young and old.

His father intended him for the Church; "but," to use his own words, "while I was very young, some heavy losses having disabled him from supporting me as genteelly as he wished in an education proper for the sacred function, he left me to choose, at the age of fifteen or sixteen, a business, having been able to give me only school-learning."

Mr. Richardson, it is generally admitted, had no acquaintance with the learned languages but what an education in the grammar-school of Christ's Hospital afforded; his mind, like that of Shakespeare, being much more enriched by nature and observation.

In 1706 he was bound apprentice to Mr. John Wilde, a printer of some eminence in his day; whom, though a severe task-master, he served diligently for seven years. He afterwards worked as a journeyman and corrector of the press for about six years, when he, in 1719, took up his freedom, and commenced business on his own account, in a court in Fleet-street; and filled up his leisure hours by compiling Indexes for the Booksellers, and writing Prefaces, and what he calls *honest Dedications*.

Dissimilar as their geniuses may seem, when the witty and wicked Duke of Wharton (a kind of Lovelace), about the year 1723, fomented the spirit of opposition in the City, and became a member of the Wax-chandlers Company, Mr. Richardson, though his political principles were very different, was much connected with, and favoured by him; and printed six numbers of his "True Briton," published twice a week. Yet he exercised his own judgment, in peremptorily refusing to be concerned in such papers as he apprehended might endanger his own safety, and which accordingly did occasion the imprisonment and prosecution of those who were induced to print and publish them.

Through the interest of his excellent friend, the Right Honourable Arthur Onslow (whom he had frequently the honour of visiting at Ember Court), he was employed in printing the first edition of the "Journals of the House of Commons;" of which he completed XXVI Volumes. He also printed from 1736 to 1737 a newspaper called "The Daily Journal;" and in 1738 "The Daily Gazeteer."

His "Pamela," the first work in which he had an opportunity of displaying his original talents, was published in 1741; and arose out of a scheme proposed to him by two respectable Booksellers (Mr. Rivington and Mr. Osborne) of writing a volume of "Familiar Letters to and from several Persons upon Business and other Subjects;" which he performed with great readiness; and in the progress of it was soon led to expand his thoughts in the *two volumes* of the "History of Pamela;" which appear to have been written in three months. This first introduced him to the literary world; and never was a book of the kind more generally read and admired. It was even recommended from the pulpit, particularly by Dr. Slocock, of Christ Church, Surrey, who had a very high esteem for it, as well as for its Author. It is much to be regretted that his improved edition, in which much was altered, much omitted, and the whole new-modeled, has never yet been given to the publick, as the only reason which prevented it in his life-time, that there was an edition unsold, must long have ceased.

Highly as his reputation as an Author was raised by "Pamela," he acquired, and very justly, still higher fame, in 1747, by his "Clarissa," which was honoured with a Preface from the pen of the very learned Mr. Warburton.

His next and last grand work was with the professed view to describe *a good man;* which was at first intended for the title of his book; but which he changed to that of "Sir Charles Grandison," and published it in 1753.

Soon after the first appearance of these volumes he was under the disagreeable necessity of laying before the publick "The Case of Samuel Richardson, of London, Printer, on the Invasion of his Property in the History of Sir Charles Grandison, before publication, by certain Booksellers in Dublin;" which bears date Sept. 14, 1753. [He gave a strict charge, before he put the piece to press, to all his workmen and servants, as well in print (that it might the stronger impress them), as by word of mouth, to be on their guard against any out-door attacks. This was the substance of the printed caution which he gave to his workmen, on this occasion : 'A bookseller of Dublin has assured me, that he could get the sheets of any book from any printing-house in London, before publication. I hope I may depend upon the care and circumspection of my friends, compositors and press-men, that no sheets of the piece I am now putting to press be carried out of the house; nor any notice of its being at press. It is of great consequence to me. Let no stranger be admitted into any of the work-rooms. Once more, I hope I may rely on the integrity and care of all my workmen — And let all the proofs, revises, &c. be given to Mr. Tewley [his foreman] to take care of.' He had no reason to distrust their assurances; most of them being persons of experienced honesty; and was pleased with their declared abhorrence of so vile a treachery, and of all those who should attempt to corrupt them. Yet, to be still more secure, as he thought, he ordered the sheets, as they were printed off, to be deposited in a separate warehouse; the care of which was entrusted to one, on whom he had laid such obligations, as, if he is guilty, has made his perfidy a crime of the blackest nature. What then must be his surprise, when intelligence was sent him from Dublin, that copies of a considerable part of his work had been obtained by three different persons in that city; and that the sheets were actually in the press?]

The transaction, on the part of the Irish booksellers, was infamous in the extreme; for they actually published a cheap edition of nearly half the Work before the Author himself had published a single Volume in England. He afterwards sent his own Edition to be sold there at a cheap price; but the invaders of his property were determined to undersell him; and for what he did sell, he could not get the money. His friends in Dublin expressed great indignation at the behaviour of their country-men, and endeavoured to serve him in the matter. Many letters passed, but to little purpose. This affair seems to have vexed Richardson to the heart. His reputation was at the highest, the sale of his works sure, and he reasonably expected to reap the profit of it.

Nothwithstanding, however, those disappointments which people in business are liable to meet with, Mr. Richardson's assiduity and success was gradually increasing his fortune.

In the year 1755 he was engaged in building, in town and

in the country. In the country he removed from North End
to Parsons Green, where he fitted up a house. In town, he took
a range of old houses, eight in number, which he pulled down,
and built an extensive and commodious range of warehouses
and printing-offices. It was still in Salisbury-court, in the North-
west corner, and it is at present concealed by other houses from
common observation. The dwelling-house, it seems, was neither
so large nor so airy as the one he quitted; and, therefore, the
reader will not be so ready, probably, as Mr. Richardson seems
to have been, in accusing his wife of perverseness, in not liking
the new habitation so well as the old. "Every body," he says,
"is more pleased with what I have done, than my wife."

He purchased a moiety of the patent of Law-printer at Midsummer 1760, and carried on that department of business in
partnership with Miss Catherine Lintot. [After Mr. Richardson's
death, his widow and Miss Lintot were for some time joint
patentees.]

He now allowed himself some relaxation from business; and
only attended from time to time to his printing-offices in
London. He often regretted, that he had only females to whom
to transfer his business. However, he had taken in to assist
him a nephew, who relieved him from the more burdensome
cares of it, and who eventually succeeded him. He now had
leisure, had he had health, to enjoy his reputation, his prosperous circumstances, his children, and his friends; but, alas! leisure
purchased by severe application often comes too late to be
enjoyed; and in a worldly, as well as in a religious sense,
——— When we find
The key of life, it opens to the grave.
His nervous disorders increased upon him, and his valuable
life was at length terminated, by a stroke of an apoplexy, on the
4th of July, 1761, at the age of 72.

He was buried, by his own direction, near his first wife,
in the nave, near the pulpit of St. Bride's church.

Mr. Richardson was twice married. By his first wife, Martha
Wilde, daughter of Mr. Allington Wilde, printer (who died in
1731), in Clerkenwell, he had five sons and one daughter; who
all died young. His second wife (who survived him twelve years)
was Elizabeth, sister of the late Mr. James Leake, bookseller of
Bath. By her he had a son and five daughters. The son died
young; but four of the daughters survived him; viz. Mary,
married in 1757 to Mr. Philip Ditcher, esq. an eminent surgeon

of Bath; Martha, married in 1762 to Edward Bridgen, esq. F.R. and A. SS.; Anne, (who died unmarried); and Sarah, married to Mr. Crowther, surgeon, of Boswell-court.

His country retirement, first at North End near Hammersmith, and afterwards at Parsons Green, was generally filled with his friends of both sexes. He was regularly there from Saturday to Monday, and frequently at other times, but never so happy as when he made others so, being himself, in his narrower sphere, the *Grandison* he drew; his heart and hand ever open to distress.

In a MS. of the late Mr. Whiston the bookseller, which fell into the hands of one of my friends, was the following passage: "Mr. Samuel Richardson was a worthy man altogether. Being very liable to passion, he directed all his men, it is said, by letters; not trusting to reprove by words, which threw him into hastiness, and hurt him, who had always a tremor on his nerves." I have heard nearly the same account from some of his workmen. But this, I believe, was not the reason; though the fact was certainly true; it was rather for convenience, to avoid altercation, and going up into the printing office; and his principal assistant, Mr. Tewley, was remarkably deaf.

Richardson has been often compared to Rousseau; and Rousseau was one of his professed admirers. In his Letter to D'Alembert, speaking of English Romances, he says, "These, like the people, are either sublime or contemptible. There never has been written in any language a romance equal, or approaching to Clarissa." But the esteem was not reciprocal : Mr. Richardson was so much disgusted at some of the scenes, and the whole tendency of the "New Eloisa," that he secretly criticised the work (as he read it) in marginal notes; and thought, with many others, that this writer "taught the passions to move at the command of Vice." If this secret censure of Mr. Richardson's should be thought too severe or phlegmatic, let it be considered, that, admitting the tendency of Rousseau's principles to be better in the main than his more rigid readers allow, his system is too refined to be carried into execution in any age when the globe is not uniformly people with Philosophers.

Mr. Richardsons reputation is far from being confined to his own country. He has been read in many of the languages, and known to most of the Nations of Europe; and has been greatly admired, notwitstanding every dissimilitude of manners, or even disadvantage of translation. Several writers abroad, where no prepossesion in his favour could possibly take place, have expressed the high sense which they entertained of the merit of his works.

M. Diderot, in his Essay on Dramatic Poetry, p. 96, mentions Richardson particularly as a perfect master of that art: "How strong," says he, "how sensible, how pathetic, are his descriptions! his personages, though silent, are alive before me, and of those who speak, the actions are still more affecting than the words."

[Mr. Jones of Welwyn, in his MS. says, "Dr. Young tells me, that he has been long and intimately acquainted with Mr. Richardson; and has always had the highest esteem for him, on account of the many excellences, natural and moral, which he discerned in him. As the Doctor has had much free conversation with him, he is acquainted with many particulars relating to him, which are known to none, or to but very few, besides himself. — Mr. Richardson having not had the advantage of a complete education (as the situation and circumstances of his father* would not allow him to bestow it†) Dr. Young, to whom he was recounting the various difficulties he had passed through, asking him, 'How he came to be an author?' he answered, 'when I was about 12 years of age, I drew up a short character of a certain gentlewoman in the parish, who was reputed a great Saint, but I looked upon her to be a great hypocrite. The character, it seems, was so exactly drawn, that, when it came to be privately handed about amongst some select friends, every one could discern the features, and appropriate the picture to the true original, though no name was affixed to it. This little success at first setting out did, you will naturally suppose, tempt me at different times to employ my pen yet further in some trivial amusements or other for my own diversion, till at length, though many years after, I sat down to write in good earnest, going upon subjects that took my fancy most, and following the bent of my natural inclination, &c.' — Dr. Young made this pertinent and just observation, that this man, with the advantages only or chiefly of mere nature, improved by a very moderate progress in education, struck out at once, and of his own accord, into a new province of writing, and succeeded therein to admiration. Nay, what is more remarkable, and seldom seen in any other

*A farmer in Derbyshire.
†He was educated at Christ's Hospital.

writers, he both began and finished the plan on which he set out, leaving no room for any one after him to make it more complete, or even to come near him : and it is certain that not one of the various writers that soon after, and ever since, attempted to imitate him, have any way equalled him, or even come within a thousand paces of him. That kind of Romance was and is peculiarly his own, and seems like to continue so. 'I consider him,' said Dr. Young, 'as a truly great natural genius; as great and super-eminent in *his* way, as were Shakspeare and Milton in theirs. — Mr. Shotbolt tells me, that when Mr. Richardson came down to Welwyn, with the late Speaker Onslow, and other friends, to visit Dr. Young, he took up his quarters with Mr. Shotbolt, there being not room enough at the Doctor's; and that, getting up early, above five of the clock, he wrote two of the best letters in Sir Charles Grandison in one or two mornings before breakfast. Mr. Onslow had a high esteem for him; and not only might, but actually would have promoted him to some honourable and profitable station at Court; but the good man neither desired nor would accept of such posts, &c. being much better pleased with his own private way of living. — Mr. Richardson, besides his being a great genius, was a truly good man in all respects; in his family, in commerce, in conversation, and in every instance of conduct. Pious, virtuous, exemplary, benevolent, friendly, generous, and humane to an uncommon degree; glad of every opportunity of doing good offices to his fellow-creatures in distress, and relieving many without their knowledge. His chief delight was doing good. Highly revered and beloved by his domesticks, because of his happy temper and discreet conduct. Great tenderness towards his wife and children, and great condescension towards his servants. He was always very sedulous in business, and almost always employed in it; and dispatched a great deal by the prudence of his management.

THOMAS RYMER

MR. THOMAS RYMER, born in the North of England, and educated at the grammar-school of Northallerton, whence he was admitted a scholar at Sidney college, Cambridge, was an excellent Antiquary and Historian. On quitting the University, he became a member of Gray's-Inn; and succeeded Mr. Shadwell as Historiographer to King William III. Some of his pieces relating to our Constitution are very good; and his valuable collection of the "Fœdera," in 20 volumes, continued from his death by Mr. Sanderson, will be a lasting monument of his industry and abilities. It was abridged by Mr. Rapin in French in Le Clerc's Bibliothèque, and a translation of it by Stephen Whatley, was printed in 4 vols. 8vo. 1731. Mr. Rymer's first warrant (signed "Marie R." the King being then in Flanders), empowering him to search the Public Offices for this undertaking, is dated Aug. 26, 1693; was renewed by King William, April 12, 1694; and again by Queen Anne, May 3, 1707, when Mr. Sanderson was joined to him in the undertaking. — Mr. Rymer wrote "Edgar, or the English Monarch," an heroic tragedy, 1678; several poems and translations; and "A View of the Tragedies of the last Age," which occasioned those admirable remarks preserved in the preface to Mr. Colman's edition of Beaumont and Fletcher, and since by Dr. Johnson in his "Life of Dryden," p. 316. Some specimens of his poetry are preserved in the first volume of "Nichols's Select Collection of Miscellany Poems, 1780;" and he was the author of the Latin inscription on Mr. Waller's tomb at Beaconsfield. — Peter Le Neve, in a letter to the Earl of Oxford, says, "I am desired by Mr. Rymer, historiographer, to lay before your Lordship the circumstances of his affairs. — He was forced some years back to part with all his choice printed books, to subsist himself; and now, he says, he must be forced, for subsistence, to sell all his MS Collections to the best bidder, without your Lordship will be pleased to buy them for the Queen's Library. There are fifty volumes in folio, of public affairs, which he has collected but not printed. The price he asks is 500*l*.

These MSS. have since been placed in the British Museum, and form no inconsiderable addition to that invaluable repository of Legal and Antiquarian knowledge. Some other affecting instances of "the poverty of the Learned" may be seen in D'Israeli's "Curiosities of Literature," vol. I. p. 34. Mr. Rymer died Dec. 14, 1713, and was buried in the church of St. Clement Danes.

Proposals were published Jan. 28, 1728-9, by Jacob Tonson, "for completing the subscription to a new edition of Rymer's Fœdera in 17 vols. folio, of which 15 volumes are already printed, and the remaining 2 volumes will be finished before the 25th day of March next: — I. The Number printed are only 200 copies, of which 150 are already subscribed for. II. This work is printed with the utmost care; and, to make it as exact as the nature of it requires and the importance of it deserves, it hath been collated anew with the Records in the Tower, by Mr. Holmes; by which means many paragraphs and lines omitted in the former edition are with due care supplied and corrected in this, which is printed page for page with the first. III. The price to the Subscribers of the remaining 50 setts is 50 guineas for each sett in sheets, 10 guineas of which is to be paid at the time of subscribing, and the remaining 40 guineas upon delivery of the 17 volumes in sheets. The subscriptions are taken in by J. Tonson in the Strand; and will be closed the 10th day of March next at farthest, or sooner if completed before."]

JOHN SELDEN

JOHN SELDEN was descended from a good family, and born Dec. 16, 1584, at Salvington in Sussex; educated at Chichester free-school, and admitted of Hart-hall, Oxon. 1598; removed to Clifford's Inn in 1602, to study the law; admitted of the Inner Temple in May 1604; and drew up "A Treatise of the Civil Government of this Island" in 1606. His first friendships were with Sir Robert Cotton, Sir Henry Spelman, Camden, and Usher, all of them learned in antiquities; which was also Mr. Selden's favourite object. In 1610, he began to distinguish himself by publications in this way, and put out two pieces that year; "Jani Anglorum Facies altera;" and "Duello, or the Original of single Combat." In 1612 he published notes and illustrations on the first eighteen songs in Michael Drayton's "Poly-

Olbion," and the year after wrote verses in Greek, Latin, and English, upon Browne's "Britannia's Pastorals;" which, with divers poems prefixed to the works of other authors, occasioned Sir John Suckling to give him a place in his Session of the Poets. Pursuing such studies, Mr. Selden soon acquired superior eminence. Though not above 33 years of age, he had shewn himself a great philologist, antiquary, herald, and linguist; and his name was so wonderfully advanced, not only at home, but in foreign countries, that he was actually then become, what he was afterwards usually styled, the great dictator of learning to the English nation. In 1618, when he was in his 34th year, his "History of Tithes" was printed in 4to. in the preface to which he reproaches the clergy with ignorance and laziness, with having nothing to keep up their credit, but *beard,* title, and habit, their studies not reaching farther than the *breviary,* the *postils,* and *polyanthea*; in the work itself he endeavours to shew, that tithes are not due under Christianity by divine right, though he allows the clergy's title to them by the laws of the land. This book alarming the clergy, and offending king James I. it was suppressed, and the author forced to make public submission. He again offended that monarch in 1621 by an opinion he gave against the Crown, as counsel, in the House of Lords, and was committed into the custody of the sheriff of London; but was released in five weeks by the favour of the lord keeper Williams. He was chosen member for Lancaster that year; but neglected all public business to apply himself to study. In 1624 he was appointed by the Inner Temple reader at Lyon's Inn, but refused to accept that office. In 1625 he was chosen burgess for Great Bedwin, Wiltshire, and again in 1626, when he was an active manager against the duke of Buckingham. In 1627, he was counsel for Mr. Hampden, and in the third parliament of king Charles was again elected for Lancaster, and had a considerable hand in the Petition of Rights. After the prorogation in June, retiring to Wrest in Bedfordshire, he finished his Commentaries on the Arundelian marbles. In the next session he warmly opposed the court, and was committed to the Tower, and had his study sealed up, March 24, 1628. He was closely confined three months, but magnificently supported at the king's expence; and being afterwards allowed the use of such books as he desired, he proceeded in his studies. In Hilary Term, 1629, declining to give security for his good behaviour (as unwarrantable by law), he was committed to the King's Bench prison.

He was released at the latter end of the year, though it does not appear how; only that the parliament in 1646, ordered him 500*l.* for the losses he had sustained on that occasion. In 1630, he was again committed to custody, with the earls of Bedford and Clare, Sir Robert Cotton, and Mr. St. John, being accused of having dispersed a libel, intituled, "A Proposition for his Majesty's Service to bridle the Impertinency of Parliaments;" but it was proved, that Sir Robert Dudley, then living in the Duke of Tuscany's dominions, was the author. All these various imprisonments and tumults gave no interruption to his studies; but he proceeded, in his old way, to write and publish books. In 1640 he was chosen member of parliament for the University of Oxford; and though he was against the Court, yet in 1642 the King had thoughts of taking the seal from the lord keeper Littleton, and giving it to him. In 1643, he was appointed one of the lay-members to sit in the assembly of divines at Westminster, in which he frequently perplexed those divines with his vast learning. About this time he took the Covenant; and the same year, 1643, was by the parliament appointed keeper of the records in the Tower. In 1644, he was elected one of the 12 commissioners of the Admiralty; and the same year was nominated to the mastership of Trinity Hall in Cambridge, which he did not think proper to accept. In the beginning of 1653, his health began to decline; and he died on the 30th of November that year, at the Friary House in White Friars, where he had resided for some years, being possessed of it in the right of Elizabeth countess-dowager of Kent, who had appointed him executor of her will, having before, from the first of her widowhood, committed the management of her person and affairs to him. He was buried in the Temple church, where a monument was erected to him; and Abp. Usher preached his funeral sermon. He left a most valuable and curious library to his executors, Matthew Hale, John Vaughan, and Rowland Jewks, esqrs.; which they generously would have bestowed on the society of the Inner Temple, on condition of their providing a proper place to receive it, which they declining, it was given to the University of Oxford. Mr. Selden was immensely learned, and skilled in Hebrew and Oriental languages beyond any man: Grotius styles him "the glory of the English nation." He was knowing in all laws; human and divine, yet did not greatly trouble himself with the practice of law: he seldom or never appeared at the bar, but sometimes gave counsel in his chamber. A chronological list of his writings, as published by Dr. Wilkins, is printed in Mr. Bowyer's Miscellaneous Tracts, p. 39. — Granger mentions seven different prints of Mr. Selden. There is a medal of him, struck in the last century, by one of the Dassiers; I know not which, for it has not the artist's name; it was left without a reverse, and that of the medal of Wolfius added to it. This last has the initials of Dassier the father. — Selden had sent his library to Oxford in his life-time: but hearing that they had lent out a book without a sufficient caution, he sent for it back again. After his death, it continued some time at the Temple, where it suffered some diminution: at last, the executors thinking that they were executors of his will rather than his passions, generously and nobly sent the whole to Oxford.

In 1671, came out, under his name, "A Discourse of the Office of Lord Chancellor of England:" in 1675, "Joannis Seldeni Liber de Nummis;" but this latter was written, before he was born, by Alexander Sardo of Ferrara. In 1683, Dr. Adam Littleton published his English translation of "Jani Anglorum Facies altera;" with "The Original of Ecclesiastical Jurisdiction of Testaments," and "The Disposition or Administration of Intestate Goods." And "The TableTalk" was published by his amanuensis R. Milward in 1689. Some of these, however, were thought not genuine, and unworthy of Selden's learning and judgment.

ELKANAH SETTLE

THIS writer having been particularly noticed by Dr. Johnson, in his Life of Dryden, some memorials of him may perhaps be acceptable. He was the son of Joseph Settle, of Dunstable, in Bedfordshire; born in 1648; and in the 18th year of his age was entered commoner of Trinity College, Oxon, in 1665; but, quitting the University without taking any degree, came to London, where he applied himself to the study of poetry; in which he lived to make no inconsiderable figure. According to Gildon, he once possessed a good fortune, which he soon dissipated. In 1671 he published "Cambyses, a Tragedy;" and in 1673, "The Empress of Morocco, a Tragedy," written in rhyme; by the success of which Dryden seems to have had his quiet much disturbed. "It was so much applauded," says Dr. Johnson, "as to make him think his supremacy of reputation in some danger. Settle had not only been prosperous on the stage, but, in the confidence of success, had published his play, with sculptures and a preface of defiance. Here was one offence added to another; and, for the last blast of inflammation, it was acted at Whitehall by the Court-ladies. Dryden could not now repress those emotions, which he called indignation, and others jealousy; but wrote upon the play and dedication such criticism as malignant impatience could pour out in haste. Of Settle he gives this character: 'He's an animal of a most deplored understanding, without reading and conversation. His being is in a twilight of sense, and some glimmering of thought which he can never fashion into wit or English. His style is boisterous and rough-hewn, his rhyme incorrigibly lewd, and his numbers perpetually harsh and ill-sounding. The little talent which he has, is fancy. He sometimes labours with a thought; but, with the pudder he makes to bring it into the world, 'tis commonly still-born; so that, for want of learning and elocution, he will never be able to express any thing either naturally or justly.' This is not very decent; yet this is one of the pages in which criticism prevails over brutal fury. He proceeds: 'He has a heavy hand at fools, and a great felicity in writing nonsense for them. Fools they will be in spite of him. His King, his two Empresses, his Villain, and his Sub-villain, nay his Hero, have all a certain natural cast of the father — their folly was born and bred in them, and something of the Elkanah will be visible.' — Settle's is said to have been the first play embellished with sculptures; those ornaments seem to have given poor Dryden great disturbance. He tries however to ease his pain by venting his malice in a parody. — Such was the criticism to which the genius of Dryden could be reduced, between rage and terror; rage with little provocation, and terror with little danger. To see the highest minds thus levelled with the meanest, may produce some solace to the consciousness of weakness, and some mortification to the pride of wisdom.. But let it be remembered, that minds are not levelled in their powers but when they are first levelled in their desires. Dryden and Settle had both placed their happiness in the claps of multitudes. — Settle had afterwards an opportunity of taking his revenge on one of Dryden's Tragedies. In a quarto pamphlet of 95 pages, he wrote a vindication of his own lines; and, if he is forced to yield any thing, makes his reprisals upon his enemy. To say that his answer is equal to the censure, is no high commendation. To expose Dryden's method of analysing his expressions, he tries the same experiment upon the same description of the ships in *The Indian Emperor,* of which however he does not deny the excellence; but intends to shew, that by studied misconstruction every thing may be equally represented as ridiculous." — Settle continued to cultivate the Tragic Muse; but, finding the Nation divided between the opinions of Whig and Tory, thought proper to join the Whigs, who were then, though the minor, yet a powerful party; and in support of which he employed his talents as a writer. In 1680, the famous ceremony of Pope-burning on the 17th of November was entrusted to his management; and he seems to have been at that time much in the confidence of those who opposed Government. He published, "A Narrative, written by E. Settle; printed for the Author, and sold by Thomas Graves, June 7, 1683;" which was answered in "Remarks upon E. Settle's Narrative. Printed for the Author; and sold by Langley Curtis, at Sir Edmundbury Godfrey's Head, at Fleet-Bridge, July 6, 1683. Price 1s." Mr. Settle afterward changed sides, turned Tory, and wrote for that party with as much zeal as he had formerly shewn for the interest of the Whigs: by which we see that politicians and patriots were made of the same sort of stuff in those times as in the present. After his change, like most other converts, he became equally violent against those with whom he had before associated, and actually entered himself a trooper in King James's army at Hounslow-Heath. He also wrote an heroic poem on the Coronation of the high and mighty monarch James II. 1685; commenced journalist for the Court, and published weekly an essay in behalf of the administration; but was unfortunate in the change of his party; for, before he had derived any solid advantage from abandoning his old friends, the Revolution took place. He soon after, however, obtained the office of Poet to the City of London; and with it a pension for an annual panegyric to celebrate the annual festival of their Chief Magistrate.

"Settle, the Poet to my Lord-mayor's show,
    Shall Dryden, Cowley, and our Duke outgo,"
says Capt. Ayloffe, in the Cambridge Commencement; Select

Collection of Miscellany Poems, 1780, vol. III, p. 189.

His predecessors in this office were, George Peele, 1585; A Munday, 1605, 1611, 1614, 1615, 1616; Thomas Dekker, 1612; Thomas Middleton, gent. 1613, 1619, 1621, 1626; John Squire, 1620; John Webster, 1624; Thomas Heywood, 1631, 1632, 1633, 1637, 1638, 1639; John Taylor the water poet, 1634; Edm. Gayton, 1655; J. B. 1656; John Tatham, 1657—1664; Thomas Jordan, 1671—1684; and Matthew Taubman, 1685 —1689.

Settle's first production of this sort was, "The Triumphs of London, performed on Thursday, Oct. 29, 1691, for the Entertainment of the Right Honourable Sir Thomas Stamp Knt. Lord Mayor of the City of London; containing a true Description of the several Pageants, with the Speeches spoken in each Pageant. All set forth at the proper Costs and Charges of the worshipful Company of Drapers. By E.S.; London, 1691." This was followed by "The Triumphs, &c." for Sir John Fleet, Bart. at the cost of the Company of Grocers, 1692. Mr. Settle was Laureate also to Sir William Ashurst, 1693; Sir Thomas Lane, 1694; Sir John Houblon, 1695; Sir Thomas Abney, 1700; Sir William Gore, 1701; Sir William Duncombe, 1708; and probably to all the intermediate lord mayors, though I have not seen the titles of his poems. The pageants for Sir William Duncombe were not exhibited, on account of the death of Prince George of Denmark, which happened ten day before lord mayor's day.

The last splendid exhibition of his kind was in the year 1761, when His present Majesty honoured the City of London by a Royal Visit, in the mayoralty of Sir Samuel Fludyer, bart.

In the latter part of his life Mr. Settle was so reduced as to attend a booth in Bartholomew Fair, kept by Mrs. Minns and her daughter Mrs. Leigh, and received a salary from them for writing drolls, which generally were approved of. He also was obliged to appear in his old age as a performer in those wretched theatrical exhibitions; and in a farce called "St. George for England," acted a dragon inclosed in a case of green leather of his own invention. To this circumstance Dr. Young refers in the following lines of his Epistle to Mr. Pope:

"Poor Elkanah, all other changes past,
For bread in Smithfield dragons hiss'd at last,
Spit streams of fire to make the butchers gape,
And found his manners suited to his shape.

Such is the fate of talents misapply'd," &c.

Having lost his credit, he lived poor and despised, subject to all the miseries of the most abject state of indigence, and destitute of any advantageous and reputable connexion: but, in the end, he obtained admission into the foundation of the Charterhouse, as one of the pensioners, and died there, Feb. 12, 1723-4. Some months before his decease, he offered a play to the managers of the theatre-royal in Drury-lane, but he lived not to bring it on the stage; it was called "The Expulsion of the Danes from Britain." The writer of a periodical paper, called "The Briton," Feb. 19, 1724, speaks of him as then just dead; and adds, "he was a man of tall stature, red face, short black hair, lived in the city, and had a numerous poetical issue; but shared the misfortune of several other gentlemen to survive them all." Mr. Settle's dramatic works, from 1671 to 1718, are seventeen in number. He was author also of "Sacellum Honoris; a congratulatory Poem to the Right Honourable the Marquis of Tavistock, on his happy Return from Travel; by E. Settle, Feb. 8, 1699-1700." "A Poem of the Anniversary Birth-day of the incomparable Youth, Mr. Matthew Bluck, Son and Heir to the Worshipful Matthew Bluck, Esq. of Hunsdon House in Hartfordshire. By E. S. 1702." "Eusebia Triumphans; the Hanover Succession to the Imperial Crown of England; an heroic Poem, by Elkanah Settle, (Latin and English) 1703," folio; and "Honori Sacellum, a funeral Poem to the Memory of the Right Honourable Robert Lord Tamworth, 1714."

THOMAS STACKHOUSE

THOMAS STACKHOUSE, a learned and pious, but necessitous Divine, was sometime minister of the English Church at Amsterdam, and afterwards successively curate at Richmond, Ealing, and Finchley; in all which places (as will be seen presently) he was much respected. The earliest of his publications, or at least the first which brought him into general notice, was, 1. a famous treatise called "The Miseries and great Hardships of the Inferior Clergy in and about London; and a modest

Plea for their Rights and better Usage; in a Letter to a Right Reverend Prelate, 1722," 8vo. 2. "Memoirs of Bishop Atterbury, 1723," 8vo. 3. "A Funeral Sermon on the Death of Dr. Brady, 1726," 8vo. 4. "A Complete Body of Divinity," &c. 1729, folio. 5. "A fair State of the Controversy between Mr. Woolston and his Adversaries, 1730, 8vo. 6. "A Defence of the Christian Religion, from the several Objections of modern Antiscripturists, 1731, 8vo. Of this volume (a close octavo volume of 509 pages; with a Preface, in which an account is given of the several Antiscripturists referred to in the Work; from what rise and original they seem to have sprung; what Books they have successively published; what the design of these Books is, and what the character and abilities of their respective Authors) a competent judge says, "Our Author has stated the several arguments of the Antiscripturists in a full light, and generally in their own terms; has answered them with great compass of learning, and clearness of argument; so that the Book is likely to prove not only a *monument* of the poison which has been vomited from the press in this profane age, but a *repository* likewise of what the ablest men among us have at the same time done to defend our common Christianity from the rude attacks of Infidelity." (*Bower, Historia Literaria, vol. III. p.* 56.) 7. "Reflections on the Nature and Property of Languages, 1731," 8vo. 8. "The Book-binder, Book-printer, and Bookseller confuted; or, the Author's Vindication of himself from the Calumnies in a Paper industriously dispersed by one Edlin. By the Rev. Mr. Stackhouse, Curate of Finchley, 1732," 8vo. In this rare pamphlet (of which the only copy I have ever seen is in the Library of Mr. Bindley) Mr. Stackhouse very feelingly, but spiritedly, exemplifies in himself *the miseries of a poor Clergyman.* The brief matter of fact is, that, in May 1732, Mr. Wilford and Mr. Edlin, "when the success of *some certain things published weekly* set every little Bookseller's wits to work," wished to engage Mr. Stackhouse to write *something* which might be published weekly, but what it was they knew not." By Wilford he had been before employed to write "A Preface to Sir William Dawes's Works;" but "had taken umbrage at Wilford's palming upon the World *a Set of Prayers,* all taken from *other Authors,* merely to lengthen out Sir William's *Duties of the Closet,* and make the *third* volume swell." Edlin "he knew of old, as the merest Marplot that ever took the publication of any Work in hand." This precious pair appointed Stackhouse to meet them at the Castle Tavern in Paternoster Row (Booksellers at that time made all their bargains at a Tavern). Edlin was for reviving his "Roman History;" and, with heavy imprecations on Dr. Bundy, maintained, that, with a little brushing-up, *i.e.* infusing some life and spirit into Ozell's dull style, the thing would still do in a weekly manner." Wilford would by no means come into that design. His talk ran chiefly on *Devotional Tracts* and *Family Directors.* To compromise the matter, Mr. Stackhouse proposed "A New History of the Bible;" there being nothing of that kind considerable in the English language, and his own studies for some years, whilst writing his "Body of Divinity," having qualified him for such a work. Proposals were accordingly drawn up; but, a disagreement happening between Wilford and Edlin, Wilford gave up the undertaking; and Mr. Stackhouse was left, much against his will, in the power of Edlin; who "had printed Proposals; got credit for paper; brushed up his old battered letter; picked up a poor Compositor or two; sent [to Finchley] a few curious books, and began to be very clamorous for copy." Mr. Stackhouse had engaged to supply three sheets in a week, provided he were allowed to furnish 40 or 50 sheets before any part of it was published. He accordingly set to work, and completed the Introduction. But Edlin was impatient to begin; and "what mercy," says Stackhouse, "he intended to have of his poor Author, appeared in the very first sheet he sent me to correct, which was very near a *whole page* above the *standard stipulation*; insomuch that, had I submitted to this *encroachment,* I had lost, on the impression of the whole Book, between 40 and 50 pounds copy-money." This imposition led to a quarrel; which was compromised by Edlin's giving *ten copies of* the Book, in consideration of the *supernumerary lines,* "to be presented by Mr. Stackhouse to some Bishops who had thought favourably of some of his other writings." After the reconciliation, Edlin sent an instrument to be signed, binding Stackhouse, his heirs, &c. in a penalty of 50*l.* to *write well,* and finish the "History of the Bible" for him. But this Stackhouse resolutely declined. For compiling the Introduction, few books of any consequence had been wanted; but for the History itself Mr. Stackhouse required the ablest *Commentators* upon the whole, and *Reconcilers* and *Criticks* upon different texts of Scripture; but could obtain from his Employer none but Bp. Patrick; Edlin suggesting, "that the chief of his Subscribers lived in Southwark, Wapping, and Ratcliff High-

way; that they had no notion of Criticks and Commentators; that the work would be adapted to their capacity, and therefore the less Learning in it the better." When the *Introduction* was finished (of which *two Numbers* were published without acquainting the Author) the breach became incurable. — No copy was ready of the "History;" and Stackhouse was informed, that, if he did not care to write for Edlin, he had found out another that would. With some difficulty, *twelve guineas* were obtained for the *twelve sheets* of Introduction; Edlin engaged another Author; and Stackhouse, who was happy to escape out of the trammels of a Tyrant, engaged to pursue his "History" under the more auspicious patronage of Mr. Batley and Mr. Cox, booksellers of reputation; and the work was accordingly completed in two folio volumes; which afterwards successively passed through numerous and large editions. The main purport of Mr. Stackhouse's address to Mr. Edlin is, to shew on whose side the infraction of the *Agreement* lay. — "In my Advertisement," he says, "of Nov. 29, 1732, I charged you with a palpable fraud and imposition upon the Publick, in affixing my name to what I never wrote. I charged your author (be he who he will) with an incapacity to execute the work he had undertaken. The little specimen he had given us I called an *Hodge Podge,* because what should have been the *narrative* part, what the *notes,* and what the proper *matter* for *dissertations,* I found confusedly thrown together, without any method or order. And, that your Subscribers might hold their hands, and no longer part with their money for such vile trash, I assured them, that I had already made some progress in my *History of the Bible,* would publish it in a convenient space of time, and endeavour to finish it in such a manner, as to deserve a general encouragement."
— "There is one charge against me, I must own, that I cannot so easily get clear of; and that is, my being a *Curate, very poor, and* (as you would intimate) *much in debt.*
     Parcius ista viris tamen objicienda memento.
For, of all the Booksellers in London, this is a Charge against me which becomes your mouth the least. Any of your wealthy Neighbours in the Strand, such an one especially as by long dealing in Monopoly has worked himself up to the degree of a *plumb**, might boast of his riches with some decency, and be permitted to break jests upon a *Country Curate* with a better

---

*An allusion to Jacob Tonson, the bookseller.

pretext; but for you, who not long ago *was one of us,* have so lately emerged from the *Gulf of Despond,* and, for aught you know, may be speedily plunged in again, to stand on the *brink,* laughing and making yourself merry to see how we poor caitiffs are forced to paddle and swim for life, is a barbarous pastime, and a sure token of a depraved mind, ignorant and regardless of the issues of Providence. And therefore consider, my good friend, the uncertainty of all human affairs; and be not *high-minded,* but fear,

> Lest Fortune shew you, in the nick
> Of all your glories, a dog-trick.

I am a *Curate* indeed, as sure as you are no *Bookseller;* but then I have a firm persuasion (whatever your sentiments may be) that God rules and governs the World; that he appoints every man his condition in life; and will raise me to an higher station in the *Church,* when he shall think proper, or I deserve it. In the mean time I hold it my duty to *shine,* as well as I can, in the little *sphere* I move in, and in *whatsoever state I am therewith to be contented.* 'We are all but Actors' (says the wise Epictetus) 'of a certain part that is given us by the *Master of the Drama,* and not of our own choosing. He therefore that acts his part well (be he but a *slave* or a *beggar*) deserves as much the Master's commendation as he that acts the Prince.' How I have acquitted myself on the stage of life, it might be prudence and modesty for me to say nothing, had not your insults upon my poverty, and contempt of my low *station* and *office,* compelled me to *this* foolishness *of boasting.* For, though I am far from justifying myself before men, in things for which I am conscious I stand guilty in the sight of God, yet in the light wherein I am now exposed to the censure of mankind, *i.e.* as a *Writer,* and as a *Curate,* I think I can abide the test; and may adventure to say, that in the former capacity I have laboured more abundantly (and perhaps under more disadvantages) than the rest of my contemporaries. I have published more books, upon more different subjects, than any. Nor must I forget to thank the *Publick* for the favourable reception they have given them. And that in *the latter* I have always conducted myself in such a manner, as to gain the good-will and esteem of the people among whom I have lived, in so much that I have never yet officiated in any place, whether in *Amsterdam, Richmond,* or *Ealing,* where I had not an handsome contribution made me, in augmentation of my *annual* stipend. And, upon this occasion, I should be

ungrateful, not to commemorate the kindness and munificence
of the gentlemen and other inhabitants of the parish of *Finchley,*
who, not long ago, perceiving some difficulties wherein I was
involved, did each of them come in with their assisting hand,
so *readily,* so *voluntarily,* as even to prevent me the trouble of
a *blush."* — The new *Proposals* issued by Mr. Stackhouse were
these: "My design in the composition of this Work is, to divide
the whole into general periods and distinctions of time; each
of these periods to subdivide into sections; in each section to give
my Reader, not only a plain narrative of the matters contained
in the Old and New Testament, but to take notice of all controverted questions, as they occur; and illustrate, by proper Dissertations, such passages in Scripture as seem to give umbrage
to Infidelity: under the page, in notes, to explain difficult texts,
rectify mis-translations, and reconcile seeming contradictions:
at due distances, to shew the connexion between Sacred and
Prophane History; at the end, to annex exact Chronological
Tables; and all along to intersperse such Cuts and Maps as
shall be conducive to the advantage and decoration of the Work:
assuring the publick, that whatever skill in writing, or application to study, I am capable of, and whatever helps and assistance
from the Learned (whether antient or modern) I can have
recourse to, shall be employed in a task, which I now freely
take upon me; and wherein I could not but disagree with Mr.
Edlin, when I perceived that his sole aim (under the cover of
my name) was to palm upon his Subscribers any hasty composition; and wherein, I hope, I have neither offended mankind,
nor injured mine own honour, in refusing to be a confederate.
To make my Subscribers amends however for the interruption,
which has almost been unavoidable, the Conditions that I offer
are these: I. That the Book shall be printed in folio, in a very
neat and correct manner, and on the same character and paper
with the Proposals, whereof the first number shall be delivered
the first Saturday in February 1732-3. II. That four sheets
(stitched in blue paper) shall once every fortnight, on Saturday,
be delivered at the Subscribers' houses (or any other place which
they shall think fit to appoint) at the price of six-pence. III. That
a number of Books will be printed on royal paper, for such as
are willing to subscribe for them, at the rate of one shilling for
each Number. IV. That, as I find it necessary to throw the
Introduction into a quite different form, more congruous to the
whole Plan of the Work; to prevent persons, who have been

Subscribers on my account from being any way detrimented thereby, I have ordered my Publisher to give each person, who brings in the Old Introduction, and subscribes to my Book, the new Preface *gratis*. The Publick are desired to observe, that four sheets of original composition are as much as can be afforded for six-pence, and as much as can well be executed, with any care and exactness, in the space of a fortnight. Subscriptions for me are taken in by Mr. Ballard, at Paul's coffee-house, in St. Paul's church-yard; by T. Payne, bookseller, at the Crown in Paternoster-row; and by myself, or family, at Mr. Gauden's in King's-street, Bloomsbury." At length this capital work appeared, under the title of "A new History of the Bible, from the Beginning of the World, to the Establishment of Christianity, 1732, &c. &c." 2 vols. folio; and, at the time, was thus briefly characterized: "In the new History of the Bible, lately published, written by Mr. Thomas Stackhouse, is given a plain and easy narrative of the matters contained in the Holy Scriptures, from the beginning of the World, to the full establishment of Christianity: In the notes is digested the sense of the best Commentators, in order to explain the several difficult texts, rectify the Mis-translations, and reconcile the seeming Contradictions, that any where occur: In the objections, all the material exceptions which are made to the facts recorded in each period of history, are fairly stated and answered: And in the Dissertations, which attend each chapter, the most remarkable passages are illustrated, and the Prophane and Sacred History all along connected. The whole is adorned with proper Maps and Sculptures; and all matters referred to in Scriptural, Chronological, and Alphabetical Tables."

Our laborious Author received a small reward for his industry in 1733 when he was presented to the vicarage of Benham Valence, *alias* Beenham, Berks; where he died, and was buried in the parish church, as appears by a neat tablet, which preserves his memory.

Mr. Stackhouse deserved well of Literature — and had a hard fate as to worldly matters, as a very small vicarage was his only church-preferment. A portrait of him was engraved in 1743, by Vertue, from a painting by J. Woolaston.

GEORGE STEEVENS

THIS eminent Scholar and profoundly learned Commentator was the only son of George Steevens, esq. of Stepney,
many years an East-India Captain, and afterwards a Director
of the East India Company, who died in 1768. He was born
at Stepney, May 10, 1736*, and admitted of King's College,
Cambridge, about 1751 or 1752. But he is best known as editor
of Shakspeare's Plays, twenty of which he published 1766,
in four volumes, 8vo.

A year before the appearance of this edition, Dr. Johnson had
published an edition, with notes, in eight volumes, 8vo. A coali-
tion between these two editors having been negotiated, another
edition, known by the name of "Johnson and Steevens's Edition," made its appearance in 10 vols. 8vo. 1773.

It was reprinted by these gentlemen, in the same number
of volumes, five years after; and again, in 1785, under the care
of Isaac Reed, esq. of Staple-inn, who, at the request of his
friends Mr. Steevens and Dr. Farmer, undertook the office of
editor.

A fourth edition of his work, with great additions and
improvements, was published by Mr. Steevens in fifteen volumes, 8vo, 1793, which at the time was certainly the most
complete edition extant of Shakspeare's Plays. This work, which,
through the indefatigable exertions of the editor, was carried
through the press in the space of eighteen months, is enriched
with much novelty of remark, and contains the accumulated
result of his acute and critical observations, made during a long
course of reading, chiefly devoted to the illustration of his favourite Bard. The diligent editor has taken all possible pains to
render his work full, clear, and convenient; and whoever con-
siders the prolegomena and notes, joined to the elegance of the
typographical execution, will be of opinion that our immortal
Bard was edited in a manner worthy his fame.

But this talent at explaining and illustrating the difficulties
and beauties of Shakspeare was disgraced by the worst of foibles,
a severity of satire, which too strongly marked a malevolence of
heart, from which his best friends cannot vindicate the editor.
The severity of his satire has, in some instances, recoiled on

---

*"George, son of George Steevens, of Poplar, mariner, and Mary his
wife, baptized May 19, 1736, nine days old."

himself; and perhaps the retort courteous was never better played off against him than by our friend, honest and generous Tom Davies, in his vigorous character of *Master Stephen*. It would be happy for him could as much be said for him as for that unfortunate and worthy man on a similar occasion. But "Peace be to his soul, if God's good pleasure be!"

Mr. Steevens was a good classical scholar, and was remarkable for the brilliancy of his wit, and for his satirical talents. The latter he occasionally indulged in some excellent *jeux d'esprit,* which made their appearance in various periodical publications.

He died January 22, 1800, at his house at Hampstead, where he had lived several years in the most recluse and unsocial retirement; and was buried in the chapel at Poplar, where, in the North aile, there is a monument to his memory by Flaxman, of which an engraving, in an elegant outline, is given by the Rev. Daniel Lysons in the Supplementary Volume of his "Environs of London."

Underneath is the following inscription; the verses in which are from the pen of Mr. Hayley:

"In the middle aile of this chapel
lie the remains of George Steevens, esq.
who, after having cheerfully employed
a considerable portion of his life and fortune
in the illustration of Shakspeare,
expired at Hampstead the 22nd day of January 1800,
in his 64th year.

The following character of Mr. Steevens appeared in the Gentleman's Magazine for 1800:

"If, as Dr. Johnson has observed, the chief glory of every people arises from its authors; from those who have extended the boundaries of learning, and advanced the interests of science; it may be considered as an act of public duty, as well as of private friendship to attend, with the regret of the patriot as well as the sensibility of the friend, the closing scene of those men, whose superior genius has improved, extended, or adorned, the literature of their country. Mr. George Steevens may be said to have possessed a pre-eminent claim to this character; and, though he is known rather as a commentator than as an original writer, yet, when we consider the works which he illustrated, the learning, sagacity, taste, and general knowledge, which he brought to the task, and the success which crowned his labours, it would not only be an act of injustice, but a most glaring proof of obstinacy and ignorance, to refuse him a place among the first literary characters of the age in which we live. The early editors of Shakspeare looked to little more than verbal accuracy; and even Warburton consigned the sagacity of his mighty mind to the restoring certain readings, and explaining dubious passages. Johnson, who possessed more of the knowledge necessary to an editor of Shakspeare than those who had preceded him in that character, was found wanting; and his first edition of Shakspeare's Plays, which had been expected with much impatience, brought disappointment along with it. In a subsequent edition, he accepted the assistance of Mr. Steevens; and consented that the name of that gentleman should be in editorial conjunction with his own. Mr. Steevens possessed that knowledge which qualified him in a superior degree for the illustration of our divine Poet, and without which the utmost critical acumen would prove abortive . He had, in short, studied the age of Shakspeare, and had employed his persevering industry in becoming acquainted with the writings, manners, and laws, of that period, as well as the provincial peculiarities, whether of language or custom, which prevailed in different parts of the kingdom, but more particularly in those where Shakspeare passed the early years of his life. This store of knowledge he was continually increasing by the acquisition of the rare and obsolete publications of a former age, which he spared no expence to obtain; while his critical sagacity and acute observation were employed incessantly in calling forth the hidden meanings of our great dramatic Bard from their covert, and, consequently, enlarging the display of his beauties. This advantage is evident from his last edition of Shakspeare, which contains so large a portion of new, interesting, and accumulated illustration.

"It is to his own indefatigable industry, and the exertions of his printer, that we are indebted for the most perfect edition of our immortal Bard that ever came from the English press. In the preparation of it for the printer, he gave an instance of editorial activity and perseverance which is without example. To this work he devoted solely and exclusively of all other attentions a period of 18 months; and, during that time, he left his house every morning at one o'clock with the Hampstead patrole, and, proceeding without any consideration of the weather or the season, called up the compositor and woke all his devils :

"Him late from Hampstead journeying to his book
Aurora oft for Cephalus mistook;
What time he brush'd the dews with hasty pace,
To meet the printer's dev'let face to face."

"At the chambers of Mr. Reed, where he was allowed to admit himself, with a sheet of the Shakspeare letter-press ready for correction, and found a room prepared to receive him, there was every book which he might wish to consult; and on Mr. Reed's pillow he could apply, on any doubt or sudden suggestion, to a knowledge of English literature perhaps equal to his own. The nocturnal toil greatly accelerated the printing of the work; as, while the printers slept, the editor was awake: and thus, in less than 20 months, he completed his last splendid edition of Shakspeare, in 15 large 8vo volumes; and almost incredible labour, which proved the astonishing energy and persevering powers of his mind. That he contented himself with being a commentator, arose probably from the habits of his life, and his devotion to the name with which his own will descend to the latest posterity. It is probable that many of his *jeux-d'esprit* might be collected; but I am not acquainted with any single production of his pen but a poem of a few stanzas in Dodsley's Annual Register, under the title of "The Frantic Lover;" which is superior to any similar production in the English language. Mr. Steevens was a classical scholar of the first order. He was equally acquainted with the *Belles Lettres* of Europe. He had studied History, antient and modern, but particularly that of his own country. How far his knowledge of the sciences extended, I cannot tell, whether it was merely elementary or profound; but when any application was made to them in conversation, he always spoke of, and drew his comparisons from them with the easy familiarity of intimate acquaintance. He possessed a strong original genius and an abundant wit; his imagination was of every colour, and his sentiments were enlivened with the most brilliant expressions. With these qualities, I need not add that his colloquial powers surpassed those of other men. In argument he was uncommonly eloquent; and his eloquence was equally logical and animated. His descriptions were so true to nature, his figures were so finely sketched, of such curious selection, and so happily grouped, that I have sometimes considered him as a speaking Hogarth. He would frequently, in his sportive and almost boyish humours, condescend to a degree of ribaldry but little above

O'Keeffe: with him, however, it lost all its coarseness, and assumed the air of classical vivacity. He was indeed too apt to catch the ridiculous, both in character and things, and to indulge rather an indiscreet animation wherever he found it. It must be acknowledged, that he scattered his wit and his humour, his gibes and his jeers, too freely around him: and they were not lost for want of gathering. This disposition made him many enemies, and attached an opinion of malignity to his character which it did not in reality possess. But there are many who would rather receive a serious injury than be the object of a joke, or at least of such jokes as were uttered by Steevens, which were remembered by all who heard them, and repeated by all who remembered them. A characteristic *bon mot* is a kind of oral caricature, copies of which are multiplied by every tongue which utters it; and it is much less injurious or mortifying to be the object of a satirical work, which is seldom read but once, and is often thought of no more, than to be hitched into a sarcastic couplet, or condensed into a stinging epithet, which will be equally treasured up by good-humour or ill-nature, for the different purposes of mirth or resentment. Mr. Steevens loved what is called fun; a disposition which has, I fear, a tendency to mischief. It is a hobby horse, which, while it curvets and prances merely to frighten a timorous rider, will sometimes unintentionally throw him in the dirt. Some open charges of a malignant disposition have been made against him; and, in the Preface to the works of a distinguished literary character, he is accused, while in the habits of intimate friendship and daily intercourse with that gentleman, of writing calumniating paragraphs in the newspapers against him. But these paragraphs Mr. Steevens did not write; and the late Mr. Seward assured me, that Mr. Bicknell, the author of a poem, called "The Dying Negro," acknowledged to him, that he was the author of them. Mr. Steevens received the first part of his education at Kingston upon Thames; he went thence to Eton, and was afterwards a fellow-commoner of King's college, Cambridge. He also accepted a commission in the Essex militia on its first establishment. The latter years of his life he chiefly passed at Hampstead in unvisitable retirement, and seldom mixed with society but in bookseller's shops, or the Shakspeare Gallery, or the morning *converzazione* of Sir Joseph Banks. I have heard of his caprices, of the fickleness of his friendships, and the sudden transition of his regards. These, however, I cannot censure; for I know not his motives: nor shall I attempt to analyse his sensibilities. But, whatever may have been his failings, I do not fear contradiction when I assert, that George Steevens was a man of extraordinary talents, erudition, and attainments; and that he was an honour to the literature of his country. When Death, by one stroke, and in one moment, makes such a dispersion of knowledge and intellect — when such a man is carried to his grave — the mind can feel but one emotion: we consider the vanity of every thing beneath the sun — we perceive what shadows we are — and what shadows we pursue."   ETONIENSIS."

WILLIAM STRAHAN

THIS distinguished Printer was born at Edinburgh in April 1715; and was apprenticed there to the profession which he pursued through life. He came early to London, where his capacity, diligence, and probity, raised him to great eminence. The good humour and obliging disposition, which he owed to nature, he cultivated with care, and confirmed by habit. His sympathetic heart beat time to the joy or sorrow of his friends. His advice was always ready to direct youth, and his purse open to relieve indigence. Living in times not the purest in English annals, he escaped unsullied through the artifices of trade, and the corruption of politicks. In him a strong and natural sagacity, improved by an extensive knowledge of the world, served only to render respectable his unaffected simplicity of manners, and to make his truly Christian philanthropy more discerning and more useful. The uninterrupted health and happiness which accompanied him half a century in this capital, proves honesty to be the best policy, temperance the greatest luxury, and the essential duties of life its most agreeable amusement. In his elevated fortune none of his former acquaintance ever accused him of neglect. He attained prosperity without envy, enjoyed wealth without pride, and dispensed bounty without ostentation. His ample property he bestowed with the utmost good sense and propriety. After providing munificently for his widow and his children, his principal study seems to have been to mitigate the affliction of those who were more immediately dependant on his bounty; and to not a few who were under this description, who would otherwise have severely felt the drying up of so rich a fountain of benevolence, he gave liberal annuities for their lives; and, after the example of his old friend and neighbour Mr. Bowyer, bequeathed 1000*l*, to the Company of Stationers for charitable purposes. He had been Master of the Company in 1774.

[The following character of him is copied from "The Lounger," a periodical paper, published at Edinburgh, Aug. 20, 1785.

"The advantages and use of Biography have of late been so often mentioned, and are now so universally allowed, that it is needless for any modern author to set them forth. That department of writing, however, has been of late years so much cultivated, that it has fared with Biography as with every other art; it has lost much of its dignity in its commonness, and many lives have been presented to the publick, from which little instruction or amusement could be drawn. Individuals have been traced in minute and ordinary actions, from which no consequences could arise, but to the private circle of their own families and friends, and in the detail of which we saw no passion excited, no character developed, nothing that should distinguish them from those common occurrences,

'Which dully took their course, and were forgotten.'

Yet there are few even of those comparatively insignificant lives, in which men of a serious and thinking cast do not feel a certain degree of interest. A pensive mind can trace, in seemingly trivial incidents and common situations, something to feed reflection, and to foster thought; as the solitary Naturalist culls the trodden leaves, and discovers, in their form and texture, the principles of vegetative Nature. The motive, too, of the relater often helps out the unimportance of his relation; and to the ingenuous and susceptible, there is a feeling not unpleasant in allowing for the partiality of gratitude, and the tediousness of him who recounts his obligations. The virtuous connections of life and of the heart it is always pleasing to trace, even though the objects are neither new nor striking. Like those familiar paintings that shew the inside of cottages, and the exercise of village-duties, such narrations come home to the bosoms of the worthy, who feel the relationship of Virtue, and acknowledge her family wherever it is found. And, perhaps, there is a calmer and more placid delight in viewing her amidst these unimportant offices, than when we look up to her invested in the pomp of greatness, and the pride of power.

"I have been led to these reflections by an account with which a correspondent has furnished me of some particulars in the life of an individual, a native of this country, who died a few weeks ago in London, Mr. William Strahan, Printer to his Majesty. His title to be recorded in a work of this sort, my correspondent argues from a variety of considerations unnecessary to be repeated. One, which applies particularly to the public office of the Lounger, I will take the liberty to mention. He was the author of a paper in "The Mirror;" a work, in the train of which I am proud to walk, and am glad of an opportunity to plead my relation to it, by inserting the eloge (I take that word as custom has sanctified it, without adopting its abstract signification) of one of its writers.

"Mr. Strahan was born at Edinburgh in the year 1715. His father, who had a small appointment in the Customs, gave his son the education which every lad of decent rank then received in a country where the avenues to Learning were easy, and open to men of the most moderate circumstances. After having passed through the tuition of a grammar-school, he was put apprentice to a Printer; and, when a very young man, removed to a wider sphere in that line of business, and went to follow his trade in London. Sober, diligent, and attentive, while his emoluments were for some time very scanty, he contrived to live rather within than beyond his income; and though he married early, and without such a provision as prudence might have looked for in the establishment of a family, he continued to thrive, and to better his circumstances. This he would often mention as an encouragement to early matrimony; and used to say, that he never had a child born, that Providence did not send some increase of income to provide for the increase of his household. With sufficient vigour of mind, he had that happy flow of animal spirits, which is not easily discouraged by unpromising appearances. By him who can look with firmness upon difficulties, their conquest is already half achieved; but the man on whose heart and spirits they lie heavy, will scarcely be able to bear up against their pressure. The forecast of timid, or the disgust of too delicate minds, are very unfortunate attendants for men of business; who, to be successful, must often push improbabilities, and bear with mortifications.

"His abilities in his profession, accompanied with perfect integrity and unabating diligence, enabled him, after the first difficulties were overcome, to get on with rapid success. And he was one of the most flourishing men in the trade, when, in the year 1770, he purchased a share of the patent for King's Printer of Mr. Eyre, with whom he maintained the most cordial intimacy during all the rest of his life. Besides the emoluments arising from this appointment, as well as from a very extensive private business, he now drew largely from a field which required some degree of speculative sagacity to cultivate; I mean, that great literary property which he acquired by purchasing the copyrights of some of the most celebrated Authors of the time. In this his liberality kept equal pace with his prudence, and in some cases went perhaps rather beyond it. Never had such rewards been given to the labours of literary men, as now were received from him and his associates in those purchases of copyrights from Authors.

"Having now attained the first great object of business, wealth, Mr. Strahan looked with a very allowable ambition on the stations of political rank and eminence. Politicks had long occupied his active mind, which he had for many years pursued as his favourite amusement, by corresponding on that subject with some of the first characters of the age. Mr. Strahan's queries to Dr. Franklin in the year 1769, respecting the discontents of the Americans, published in the London Chronicle of 28th July, 1778, shew the just conception he entertained of the important consequences of that dispute, and his anxiety as a good subject to investigate, at that early period, the proper means by which their grievances might be removed, and a permanent harmony restored between the two countries. In the year 1775 he was elected a member of parliament for the borough of Malmesbury, in Wiltshire, with a very illustrious colleague, the Hon. C. J. Fox; and in the succeeding parliament for Wotton Bassett, in the same county. In this station, applying himself with that industry which was natural to him, he attended the House with a scrupulous punctuality, and was a useful member. His talents for business acquired the consideration to which they were entitled, and were not unnoticed by the Minister.

"In his political connections he was constant to the friends to whom he had been first attached. He was a steady supporter of that party who were turned out of administration in spring

1784, and lost his seat in the House of Commons by the dissolution of parliament with which that change was followed; a situation which he did not shew any desire to resume on the return of the new parliament.

"One motive for his not wishing a seat in the next parliament, was a feeling of some decline in his health, which had rather suffered from the long sittings and late hours with which the political warfare in the last had been attended. Though without any fixed disease, his strength was visibly declining; and though his spirits survived his strength, yet the vigour and activity of his mind were also considerably impaired. Both continued gradually to decline till his death, which happened on Saturday, the 9th of July, 1785, in the 71st year of his age.

"Endued with much natural sagacity, and an attentive observation of life, he owed his rise to that station of opulence and respect which he attained, rather to his own talents and exertion, than to any accidental occurrence of favourable or fortunate circumstances. His mind, though not deeply tinctured with learning, was not uninformed by letters. From a habit of attention to style, he had acquired a considerable portion of critical acuteness in the discernment of its beauties and defects. In one branch of writing himself excelled, I mean the epistolary, in which he had not only shewed the precision and clearness of business, but possessed a neatness, as well as fluency of expression, which I have known few letter-writers to surpass. Letter-writing was one of his favourite amusements; and among his correspondents were men of such eminence and talents as well repaid his endeavours to entertain them. One of these, as we have before mentioned, was the justly-celebrated Dr. Franklin, originally a Printer like Mr. Strahan, whose friendship and correspondence he continued to enjoy, notwithstanding the difference of their sentiments in political matters, which often afforded pleasantry, but never mixed any thing acrimonious in their letters. One of the latest he received from his illustrious and venerable friend, contained a humourous allegory of the state of politicks in Britain, drawn from the profession of Printing, of which, though the Doctor had quitted the exercise, he had not forgotten the terms.

"There are stations of acquired greatness, which make men proud to recall the lowness of that from which they rose. The native eminence of Franklin's mind was above concealing the humbleness of his origin. Those only who possess no intrinsic elevation are afraid to sully the honours to which accident has reared them, by the recollection of that obscurity when they spring.

"Of this recollection Mr. Strahan was rather proud than ashamed; and I have heard those who were disposed to censure him, blame it as a kind of ostentation in which he was weak enough to indulge. But methinks ' 'tis to consider too curiously, to consider it so.' There is a kind of reputation which we may laudably desire, and justly enjoy; and he who is sincere enough to forego the pride of ancestry and of birth, may, without much imputation of vanity, assume the merit of his own elevation.

"In that elevation he neither triumphed over the inferiority of those he had left below him, nor forgot the equality in which they had formerly stood. Of their inferiority he did not even remind them, by the ostentation of grandeur, or the parade of wealth. In his house there was none of that saucy train, none of that state or finery, with which the illiberal delight to confound and to dazzle those who may have formerly seen them in less enviable circumstances. No man was more mindful of, or more solicitous to oblige the acquaintance or companions of his early days. The advice which his experience, or the assistance which his purse could afford, he was ready to communicate; and at his table in London every Scotsman found an easy introduction, and every old acquaintance a cordial welcome. This was not merely a virtue of hospitality, or a duty of benevolence with him; he felt it warmly as a sentiment : and that paper in "The Mirror," of which I mentioned him as the author (the letter from London in the 94th number), was, I am persuaded, a genuine picture of his feelings on the recollection of those scenes in which his youth had been spent, and of those companions with which it had been associated.]

MR. JOSEPH STRUTT

IN tracing the studious man and the artist in his path through life, a reader can anticipate but little gratification. Follow him, ere yet the thread of life be unravelled, to his solitary apartment; there you behold him with his pen or pencil in his hand, his mental faculties deeply absorbed, and barred against extraneous objects; and your presence would be an infringement upon the flights of his imagination, now on the wing, and panting to bring home some novel idea. But when, through the medium of an Author's literary labours, an interest has really been excited, whether on account of new information communicated, of methodical classification of subjects treated, of satisfactory elucidations and perspicuity of style, or from the intrinsic merit of his researches exhibiting at once unwearied labour and capacious powers of intellect; then every the minutest circumstance relative to him is sought after with avidity; the knowledge of his birth-place, of his family-connexions, of his person and character, are then memoranda of high importance.

Such notices may perhaps be expected by a generous and enlightened publick, as due to the memory of Mr. Strutt; whose literary labours, as well as the productions of his pencil and graver, they have been pleased highly to appreciate. An assemblage of interesting facts relative to the history and usages of his native country, comprised in several volumes, chiefly occupied the hours of a life chequered by misfortune, early embittered by the loss of an amiable partner, and long tending towards the grave through the pressure of bodily affliction.

Mr. JOSEPH STRUTT, the youngest son of Thomas and Elizabeth Strutt, was born October 27, 1749, at Springfield in Essex. Here his father possessed some property, and carried on the profession of a miller, to which he had been brought up under Mr. John Ingold, of Woodham-Walter, in the same county.

This Thomas was son of Mr. Thomas Strutt, miller, of Chelmsford, by Elizabeth, one of the daughters of Robert Younge, gent. of Halsted, in Essex.

On the expiration of his apprenticeship, Thomas Strutt, in 1743, married Elizabeth Ingold, one of his master's daughters; and settled first at Danbury, and afterwards at Springfield, in both which places he possessed some property; and at the latter of which he resided when his son Joseph was born. By his wife he had four sons and one daughter; of whom John* and Joseph alone attained to years of maturity.

---

*John Strutt was their second son; and was born November 30, 1745. He became a surgeon, and acquired considerable eminence in his profession.

In about a year after the birth of his son Joseph, Mr. Thomas Strutt embarked on a voyage for Constantinople; probably recommended by the Faculty so to do for the benefit of his health. He had a favourable passage to Smyrna, where he stayed some time: he sailed thence to Constantinople, and returned to Smyrna; where it is supposed he caught the small-pox; he lived till the ship arrived at Plymouth, and died there, about June 1751, before his wife could arrive to bid him adieu for ever. On receiving the melancholy intelligence, Mrs. Strutt proceeded to Plymouth, and recovered her deceased husband's effects.

Thus, at the tender age of a year and a half, was Joseph Strutt bereaved of his parent. The care of his early tuition now devolved on his mother: and she, at a suitable time, placed him at the school at Chelmsford, where he attained the rudiments of boyish education, as reading, writing, and a scanty knowledge of grammar. The lessons of piety and of his duty to his Maker, were early instilled into him from his mother's lips: her example and precept went hand in hand to invite his imitation: and he seems to have retained to his latest breath the fondest regard for the counsels of this monitress of his youth.

At the age of fourteen, he was apprenticed by his mother to the unfortunate Mr. William Wynn Ryland, in 1764; and in 1770 became a student at the Royal Academy; where he had the gold and silver medals adjudged to him; the former for a painting in oil, and the latter for the best Academy-figure.

Having with fidelity accomplished the term of his servitude under Mr. Ryland, Mr. Strutt took up his residence in the family of his friend Mr. Thane. His future prospects, and the ardour of his imagination, on entering the world for himself, are best declared in his own words, in a letter which he wrote to his mother on that occasion; part of which is here extracted.

"I thank you, honoured Madam, for the joy you express at this your son's first-gained laurel; and also those our worthy friends for the interest they take in my welfare, as also for every obligation they have so generously laid upon me: and though I know it is not in my power to repay their kindness, yet I have a heart that, thoroughly sensible of all these favours, overflows with gratitude and acknowledgements, which I am sure will never be forgotten: nor can I deviate from that respect, which I owe to their good-will: I will at least strive to the utmost to

give my worthy benefactors no reason to think their pains
thrown away. If I should not be able to abound in riches, yet,
by GOD's help, I will strive to pluck that palm which the
greatest Artists of foregoing ages have done before me: I will
strive to leave my name behind me in the world, if not in the
splendour that some have, at least with some marks of assiduity
and study; which, I can assure you, shall never be wanting in
me. What! though the path to honour is rough, and hard to
gain, yet so it is ordained: the honour gained, comes so much
the sweeter for the trouble, and thoroughly repays the assiduity
and labour of the Artist. Who can bear to hear the names of
Raphael, Titian, Michael Angelo, &c the most famous of the
Italian masters, in the mouths of every one and not wish to be
like them? And, to be like them, we must study as they have
done, take such pains, and labour continually like them: the
which shall not be wanting on my side, I dare affirm: so that,
should I not succeed, I may rest contented, and say, I have done
my utmost. GOD has blessed me with a mind to undertake; and
I hope, with His help, to persevere firmly, and to reap the
pleasure of making a figure in the world, as well as they have
done. You, dear Madam, will excuse my vanity; you know me,
from my childish days, to have been a vain boy, always desirous to execute something to gain me praises from every one;
always scheming and imitating whatever I saw done by any
body. But I fear I shall tire you; so I will change the subject.
I propose coming down about April, in the time of vacation at
the Royal Academy."

In the summer of the year 1771, Mr. Strutt was first introduced to the British Museum. He was there employed to make
some drawings for a gentleman. The rich stores of Science and
of Art, which there arrested his notice, tended to give a new
bias to his vigorous imagination: he embraced in idea the grand
projects which his subsequent labours brought to maturity.

June 27, 1771, Mr. Strutt says, in a letter to a friend, "I
hope, and indeed every thing assures me, I shall soon be
settled: I am about a work at the Museum on my own account;
and only wait till that is completed, to come to Stratford. I have
consulted with some people who understand the nature of
such works; and they all give me great hopes of making a
tolerable profit of it: besides which, it will introduce me still
further in the world; which is of some consequence to one in my
situation."

In another letter, dated London, Aug. 21, 1773, he asys, "I would not only be a great Antiquary, but a refined Thinker: I would not only discover antiquities, but would, by explaining their use, render them useful. Such vast funds of knowledge lie hid in the antiquated remains of the earlier ages: these I would bring forth, and set in their true light."

In 1773, Mr. Strutt published his first literary production, the "Regal and Ecclesiastical Antiquities of England;" and in June 1774, the first volume of what he then called his "great work," viz. Manners and Customs of the English.

Of his unwearied diligence in the pursuit of this second work, his own words may afford the most satisfactory evidence. Jan. 29, 1774, he thus writes to a friend: "If you knew the whole extent of my business at this present moment, you would pity me: for, having so many things upon my head at once, I can scarcely find a leisure moment: what with engraving of plates, correcting and writing for the press, and making my drawings, my whole time, from the morning till nine or ten at night, is quite taken up."

In August, 1774, Mr. Strutt married his cousin, Anne Blower, daughter of Mr. Barwell Blower, of Bocking, in Essex, bays-maker. He then resided in Duke-street, opposite Portland-chapel.

In 1775, he published a second volume of his "Manners and Customs:" and in 1776, he added a third Volume to this work; though his first design was to have comprised the whole in two volumes.

In 1777, Mr. Strutt again claimed public patronage for a new work, the "Chronicle of England;" a volume of which then appeared: and in the subsequent year, he brought forward a second volume of this work. It was indeed his intention to have extended the Chronicle to six volumes; but the want of due encouragement compelled him to relinquish his design: and this work must be regarded as a complete performance merely as far as it goes.

On the 24th of August, 1778, Mrs. Strutt gave birth to a daughter: and on the 15th of the following month she was herself cut off in early life; for she had not completed her 24th year. To attempt to describe what her inconsolable Husband felt on the occasion, were a useless labour. His grief was poignant, and durable; for till his latest moments he fondly cherished the memory of his Wife. She was buried in the ground belonging to the parish of St. Mary-le-bone. By her, Mr. Strutt had three children; Joseph, born May 28, 1775; William, born March 7, 1777; and Anne, born (as before mentioned) Aug. 24, 1778. The young sons are now living; but the daughter died young.

April 5, 1780, died Mrs. Elizabeth Strutt; and her son John (as before noticed) on the 24th of May, 1784. — The loss of this affectionate parent occasioned another severe shock to the already wounded feelings of her son Joseph: and indeed she well deserved the warmest filial respect : she was a good mother, a steady friend, and a firm Christian. She was born September 23, 1727.

In 1785, Mr. Strutt published the first volume of his "Dictionary of Engravers;" and the second volume appeared in 1786.

As to the merits of Mr. Strutt's literary productions in general, the writer of this sketch is entirely incompetent to decide either on their magnitude or deficiency. Justice, however, demands an explanation, where ill-natured personal invective abuses a person, whose whole life was devoted to convey instruction or afford gratification to his fellow-men. A snarling criticism on one of his Plates, from the pen of the Commentator on Shakspeare (George Steevens), occurs in the Gentleman's Magazine, vol. LV. p. 606; and a severe attack on the whole Work in vol. LVI. p. 418.

In 1790, Mr. Strutt, being severely afflicted with an asthmatic complaint, quitted London; and finding the country-air highly beneficial, settled at Bacons-farm in Hertfordshire, about three miles beyond the town of Hertford, situated in a small parish called Bramfield. Here he resided upwards of five years; and here he engraved the greater part of the plates for the Pilgrim's Progress; which exhibit perhaps as fair a specimen of his talents as an artist as any that can be produced.

At the village of Tewin, not far distant from Mr. Strutt's residence, much of his leisure-time was spent in performing the best offices to his fellow-creatures : here, at his own expence, he established a little Sunday-school for the instruction of the villagers, old or young; himself presiding, and, aided only by his two sons, inculcating the earliest rudiments of learning and the grand fundamental principles of religion. He also extended his times of teaching to two opportunities in the week besides the Sunday. By this means, great decorum was soon visible in the personal conduct and manners of the villagers. Squirrel-hunting and other disorderly sports were no longer practised on the

Sunday; but sobriety and decency were manifest, and the church-duties attended to with evident delight. Lord and Lady Cowper seconded Mr. Strutt's endeavours to correct the morals of the poor; and in a short time a day-school was established, still retaining the Sunday-tuition.

In Tewin parish stands the venerable pile called Queenhoo-Hall; which Mr. Strutt made the scene of the incidents recorded in his Tale founded upon facts illustrative of the manners of the Fifteenth Century; which he did not live to finish.

Mr. Strutt designed to have fixed his residence entirely in the country; and for that purpose rented a house at Welwyn; the quondam abode of the celebrated Author of the Night-Thoughts: but, after occupying it for one year, he was under the necessity of returning to London, to prosecute his studies at the Museum. He finally quitted the country in 1795: and in this year, he began to collect materials for his work of the Dresses and Habits of the English; the first volume of which was published in 1796; and the second in 1799.

In 1801, Mr. Strutt published the last work which he lived to complete; namely Sports and Pastimes of the English: a performance which, from the novelty of the subject, attracted the notice and admiration of readers of almost every class.

After the publication of the "Sports," Mr. Strutt took seriously in hand to illustrate the usages of the *Fifteenth Century* under the form of a pleasant fiction, or tale: and early in 1802, he had assembled the larger part of his materials, and prepared a considerable portion of his manuscript for the press; so that a month's additional labour might perhaps have completed the whole: when a bookseller engaged him to undertake a new edition of his second Work, the "Manners and Customs". To this proposal Mr. Strutt acceded (but unfortunately, as it proved in the issue); and, consequently, the former intended work was laid aside, — never, alas! to be resumed. Accordingly, great preparations were made for this new edition; the arrangements of the subjects delineated on the miscellaneous plates were altered; — several new drawings were made; — and thirty plates engraved anew, among which some never had appeared before; the expence of all this sustained by himself: when Death put an end to all his labours; and the bookseller afterwards declined taking any concern to get the work completed by a competent hand; and it yet remains in the same unfinished state.

In the beginning of October this year, Mr. Strutt, then residing in Charles-street, Hatton-Garden, was confined to his chamber with his last illness; and on Saturday the 16th, at three o'clock in the morning, he expired, in the 53rd year of his age. On the Wednesday following, he was buried in St. Andrew's church-yard, Holborn.

Mr. Strutt had long been a sufferer from an asthmatic complaint; to such a degree indeed, that in the winter-time, in London, it was painful to him to venture out of doors. He was also often afflicted with severe fits of the stone. In his latter years he grew exceedingly corpulent; and his corpulency increased till his death.

Thus have we traced Mr. Joseph Strutt from his cradle to his grave. The calamities incident to man were indeed his portion on this earth; and these greatly augmented by unkindnesses where he least deserved to have met with them. He was charitable without ostentation; a sincere friend, without intentional guile; a dutiful son; a faithful and affectionate husband; a good father; a worthy man; and, above all, it is humbly hoped, a sincere Christian. His natural talents were great, but little cultivated by early education. The numerous works which he gave to the world as an author, and as an artist, prove that he employed his time to the best advantage. The many checks he met with in the pursuit of his labours (which it might have been invidious to have detailed here) would, if known, have excited astonishment that he executed what he did, and, considering all things, that he did them well.

JAMES TASSIE

IN 1775 was published *A Catalogue of Gems*, by James Tassie. This small 8vo volume was later enlarged and published in two quarto volumes, entitled *A Descriptive Catalogue of a General Collection of Ancient and Modern engraved Gems . . . taken from the most celebrated Cabinets in Europe; cast in coloured Pastes, white Enamel and Sulphur by James Tassie, Modeller.*

["This truly ingenious Modeller, whose history is intimately connected with a branch of the Fine Arts in Britain, was born in the neighbourhood of Glasgow, of obscure parents; and began his life as a country stone-mason, without the expectation of ever rising higher. Going to Glasgow on a fair-day, to enjoy himself with his companions, at the time when the Foulis's were attempting to establish an Academy for the Fine Arts in that city, he saw their collection of paintings, and felt an irresistable impulse to become a Painter. He removed to Glasgow; and in the Academy acquired a knowledge of drawing, which unfolded and improved his natural taste. He was frugal, industrious, and persevering; but he was poor, and was under the necessity of devoting himself to stone-cutting for his support: not without the hopes that he might one day be a Statuary if he could not be a Painter. Resorting to Dublin for employment, he became known to Dr. Quin, who was amusing himself in his leisure hours with endeavouring to imitate the precious stones in coloured paste, and take accurate impressions of the engravings that were on them. That art was known to the Antients; and many specimens from them are now in the cabinets of the curious. It seems to have been lost in the Middle Ages; was revived in Italy under Leo X. and the Medici Family at Florence; became more perfect in France under the Regency of the Duke of Orleans, by his labours and those of Homberg. By those whom they instructed as Assistants in the Laboratory it continued to be practised in Paris, and was carried to Rome. Their Art was kept a secret, and their Collections were small. It is owing to Quin and to Tassie that it has been carried to such high perfection in Britain, and attracted the attention of Europe. Dr. Quin, in looking out for an Assistant, soon discovered Tassie to be one in whom he could place perfect confidence. He was endowed with fine taste: he was modest and unassuming: he was patient; and possessed the highest integrity. The Doctor committed his laboratory and experiments to his care. The Associates were fully successful; and found themselves able to imitate all the gems, and take accurate impressions of the engravings. As the Doctor had followed the subject only for his amusement, when the Discovery was completed he encouraged Mr. Tassie to repair to London, and to devote himself to the preparation and sale of those pastes as his profession. In 1766 he arrived in the Capital. But he was diffident and modest to excess; very unfit to introduce himself to the attention of persons of rank and of affluence: besides, the number of engraved Gems in Britain was small; and those few were little noticed. He long struggled under difficulties which would have discouraged any one who was not possessed of the greatest patience, and the warmest attachment to the subject. He gradually emerged from obscurity; obtained competence; and, what to him was much more, he was able to increase his Collection, and add higher degrees of perfection to his Art. His name soon became respected, and the first Cabinets in Europe were open for his use; and he uniformly preserved the greatest attention to the exactness of the imitation and accuracy of the engraving, so that many of his Pastes were sold on the Continent by the fraudulent for real Gems. His fine taste led him to be peculiarly careful of the impression; and he uniformly destroyed those with which he was in the least dissatisfied. The Art has been practised of late by others; and many thousands of pastes have been sold as Tassie's, which he would have considered as injurious to his fame. Of the fame of others he was not envious; for he uniformly spoke with frankness in praise of those who executed them well, though they were endeavouring to rival himself. To the antient Engravings he added a numerous Collection of the most eminent modern ones; many of which approach in excellence of workmanship, if not in simplicity of design and chastity of expression, to the most celebrated of the antient. Many years before he died he executed a commission for the late Empress of Russia, consisting of about 15,000 different engravings (see the article GEM, in the "Encyclopædia Britannica"). At his death, in 1799, they amounted to near 20,000; a Collection of Engravings unequalled in the world. Every Lover of the Fine Arts must be sensible of the advantage of it for improvement in knowledge and in taste. The Collection of Feloix at Paris consisted of 1800 articles; and that of Dehn at Rome of 2500. For a number of years, Mr. Tassie practised the modelling of portraits in wax, which he afterwards moulded and cast in paste. By this the exact likeness of many eminent men of the present age will be transmitted to posterity as accurately as those of the philosophers and great men have been by the antient statuaries. In taking likenesses he was, in general, uncommonly happy; and it is remarkable, that he believed there was a certain kind of inspiration (like that mentioned by the Poets) necessary to give him full success. The writer of this article, in conversing with him repeatedly on the subject, always found him fully

persuaded of it. He mentioned many instances in which he had
been directed by it; and even some, in which, after he had
laboured in vain to realize his ideas on the wax, he had been
able, by a sudden flash of imagination, to please himself in the
likeness several days after he had last seen the original. — He
possessed also an uncommonly fine taste in Architecture, and
would have been eminent in that branch if he had followed it.]

DR. JOHN TAYLOR

THIS eminent Scholar was born at Shrewsbury, where his
father was a tradesman.

"He was baptized at St. Alkmund's church in Shrewsbury,
June 22, 1704, at which church his father John Taylor was
married to his mother Anne Jarvis, on the 21st September in
the preceding year.

"The father was, I apprehend, admitted to his freedom as a
'barber chirurgeon,' in the company of those artisans in Shrewsbury, on the 3rd of January 1694. I express this with some
doubt, because it is not always easy to distinguish the father of
our learned Civilian from another person of the same names
and trade, exactly a contemporary with him in our town. In
fact, another John Taylour (so the name is written in the
document immediately to be quoted) was admitted to his
freedom as 'a barber chirurgeon and periwig maker' in the same
Company, on the 23rd of January 1699. I conceive however
the former entry to refer to our Doctor's father, as he was
baptized (at St. Mary's) Oct. 11, 1670, and the age of 29
seems too far advanced for a person to take up his freedom.

"Though his occupation was humble, he was not without
some pretensions to pedigree, if his father, the Rev. John Taylor,
B. A. third master of Shrewsbury school, was, as there seems
reason to believe, son of Andrew Taylour, a younger brother of
the antient family of Tayleur of Rodington (now of Buntings-
dale) of which I find a John Tailour, son of Galfrid, as early as
1313. Andrew Taylour was admitted a scholar of Shrewsbury
school in 1588; the Doctor had an uncle of the same name.

"As to the manner in which Taylor's destiny came to soar above the *res angusta domi,* my grandfather, who was but four years his junior, used to relate that it was in consequence of his father being employed to dress the wigs, and trim the beard, of —— Owen of Cundover, esq. That gentleman was accustomed to converse with his barber concerning his family, and his future prospects for his children : to all which the old man used to answer cheerily, except as to his son *Jack,* whom, he said, he could not get to take to the business, or to handle either the razor or comb. Hence, Mr. Owen determined to give young Taylor a learned education, in which expence he was, however, I doubt not, assisted by one of the exhibitions established from our school to St. John's college in Cambridge. I have been told that Dr. Taylor used to complain confidentially to his intimate friends, of the scenes of riotous festivity, of which gratitude obliged him to partake at the house of his Patron; whose favour he is said to have at length forfeited by refusing to drink a Jacobite toast on his knees."

Young Taylor took the degree of B. A. at St. John's in 1727; M. A. 1731; S. T. B. 1738; was chosen fellow in 1730; and became D. D. in 1760.

One of the earliest, if not the first of his publications, was, "Oratio habita coram Academiâ Cantabrigiensi in Templo Beatæ Mariæ, die solenni Martyrii Caroli Primi Regis, A. D. 1730, à Joanne Taylor, A. M. Collegii D. Joannis Evangelistæ socio. Lond. *Typis Gul. Bowyer, Sen. et Jun.** 1730," 8vo. This was followed the same year by "The Music-speech at the Public Commencement in Cambridge, July 6, 1730. To which is added, An Ode, designed to have been set to Music on that Occasion."

"Mr. Taylor was appointed Librarian in March 1732 (an office he held but a short time), and was afterwards Registrar. Either whilst he was Librarian, or rather before, and perhaps after, he took great pains, as did some others, before Booksellers were obliged to be called in, in classing the noble present of George I. to the University, consisting of 30,000 volumes of the best books, besides MSS. formerly belonging to Bp. Moore. The Catalogue of the Bible class, which is so large as to form a moderate folio, is still preserved in his neat handwriting, and affords full proof of his industry and knowledge

---

*I have found no other title-page with the names of *the father and son.*

in that branch of learning in which he particularly excelled
and delighted. I have often heard him say, that he would
undertake to shew the Library to the best scholar in Europe,
or a girl of six years old. Even this dull and laborious employ
furnished him with some pleasant stories; for, among his many
other good qualities, that of telling a story well was too
remarkable to be entirely omitted here. He used to say, that,
throwing the books into heaps for general divisions, he saw
one whose title-page mentioned somewhat of *height,* and
another of *salt*; the first he cast among those of Mensuration,
the other to those of Chemistry or Cookery; that he was startled,
when he came to examine them, to find that the first was
"Longinus de Sublimitate," and the other "A Theological
Discourse on the Salt of the World, that good Christians ought
to be seasoned with." One day shewing the Library to the late
Lord B. who was recommended to him, but of whose understanding the reports were unfavourable, he began by producing
such articles as might be most likely to amuse such a person;
but, observing him very attentive, though silent, he ventured
to go a little farther, and at last, as the jewel to the whole, put
Beza's MS. of the Gospels into his Lordship's hands, and began
telling his story; but, in the midst of it, his Lordship broke
his long silence, by desiring to know whether they were then
in the county of Cambridge or Hertford. The Doctor added,
that he snatched the MS. from him, and was very glad when
it was in its proper place, as thinking it not unlikely but that
it might have got tossed out of the window the next minute."

In the year 1732 appeared the Proposals for his "Lysias;"
on which Mr. Clarke writes thus to Mr. Bowyer: "I am glad
Mr. Taylor has got into your press: it will make his Lysias
more correct. I hope you will not let him print too great a
number of copies. It will encourage a young Editor, to have
his first attempt rise upon his hands. I fancy you have got him
in the press for life, if he has any tolerable success there; he
is *too busy a man to be idle.*" It was published, under the title
of "Lysiæ Orationes et Fragmenta, Græcè et Latinè.

At the end of this volume were advertised, as just published,
"Proposals for printing by Subscription a new and correct
edition of Demosthenes and Æschines, by John Taylor, A.M.
Fellow of St. John's College, and Registrar of the University
of Cambridge.—N.B. On or before the 24th day of December
next will be published (and delivered to Subscribers if desired)

Oratio contra Leptinem, which begins the third volume of the above mentioned work." The Dedication to Lord Carteret, intended for the first volume (which Dr. Taylor did not live to publish) is dated Dec. 3, 1747; the third volume (published nine years before the second) 1748; and the second 1757.

Earl Granville, then Lord Carteret, had before this time instructed to Dr. Taylor's care the education of his grandson, Lord Viscount Weymouth, and Mr. Thynne; and, as the Doctor informs us, at the same time laid the plan, and suggested the methods, of their education. In consequence of this Nobleman's recommendation, "to lay out the rudiments of civil life, and of social duties; to inquire into the foundations of justice and equity; and to examine the principal obligations which arise from those several connections into which Providence has thought proper to distribute the human species," Dr. Taylor was led, as he says, to "the system of that people, who, without any invidious comparison, are allowed to have written the best comment upon the great volume of Nature." These researches afterwards produced his "Elements of the Civil Law," printed in 4to, 1755, and again in 1769 : and this latter work, it is well known, occasioned a learned, but peevish, preface to the third volume of the "Divine Legation."

Dr. Taylor was admitted an advocate in Doctors Commons, February 15, 1741; and in 1742, he published "Commentarius ad Legem Decemviralem de inope Debitore in partes dissecando."

In 1743 the learned world was gratified by the publication of "Orationes Duæ : una Demosthenis contra Midiam, altera Lycurgi contra Leocratem, Græcè et Latinè; recensuit, emendavit, notasque addidit Joannes Taylor, LL.D. Coll. D. Johan. Soc."

In the next year appeared, "Marmor Sandvicense, cum Commentario et Notis Johannis Taylori, LL.D." being a Dissertation on a Marble brought into England by Lord Sandwich in 1739; containing a most minute account of the receipts and disbursements of the three Athenian magistrates deputed by that people to celebrate the feast of Apollo at Delos, in the 101st Olympiad, or 374 before Christ, and is the oldest inscription whose date is known for certain.

"Lord Sandwich, on his return from his voyage round the Mediterranean in 1738 and 1739, brought home with him, among many other curiosities, a marble vase from Athens, with two figures in basso relievo, and a very long inscription, as yet undecyphered, on both sides of a piece of marble about two feet in height. This marble, as a mark of respect to the Society of which he had been a member, he presented to Trinity-college, Cambridge; and it is now preserved in their Library. The inscription on it has been, with wonderful sagacity, explained and illustrated by the late learned Dr. Taylor: who has made it legible, and intelligible by every reader of the Greek language. What so respectable a person says of the noble Earl, it would be injustice to his memory to withhold: 'Nolui certè meam opellam deesse, tali potissimùm viro hortante, cujus inter postremas laudes olim recensebitur, potuisse eum cum fructu, non solùm proprio, verùm etiam publico, peregrinari.' The circumstances under which his Lordship discovered this valuable relic are rather singular. 'He saw it,' he tells us, 'lying among some rubbish and lumber, in a sort of wood yard belonging to Niccolo Logotheti, the English Consul, of whom he begged it. The Consul could give no acount when or where it was found; otherwise than it had lain there a good while in his father's life-time. He set no sort of value on it, and wondered much that his Lordship would be at the trouble of carrying it away." [Preface to the Earl of Sandwich's "Voyage round the Mediterranean".]

Dr. Taylor succeeded Dr. Reynolds, as Chancellor of the Diocese of Lincoln, in April 1744; but did not then think proper to enter into holy orders.

In a letter to Mr. Bowyer, without date, but written probably in 1744, whilst Lord Carteret was Secretary of State, Mr. Clarke says, "if he (Dr. Taylor) still persists in not going into orders, though an Archbishop would persuade him to it, it is plain he is no great friend to the Church, though, as my Lord Halifax said when he kept Mr. Addison out of it, I believe it is the only injury he will ever do it. I heartily wish he may be more agreeably, he will scarce be more usefully employed. Supposing, which I am in hopes of, from his Grace's recommendation, that my Lord Carteret should make him one of the Under Secretaries, what will become of all the Orators of the ages past? Instead of publising the sentiments of antient Demagogues, his whole time will be engrossed in cooking up and concealing the many finesses of modern politicks. But, however, I should rejoice to see him so employed, and hope there is some prospect of it."

The fact is, the Doctor intended to be a Civilian; and, to

enable him to keep his fellowship, without going into orders, as all are obliged to do at St. John's, except two Physicians and two Civilians, he was nominated to a Faculty Fellowship on the Law line: but, continuing in College to superintend his edition of Demosthenes, he probably saw that, in order to make the figure he could wish in that profession, he should have devoted himself to the practice of it earlier; and the prospect of a valuable College-living becoming now near, he took orders, and the rectory of Lawford being vacant, he claimed it: this was a new case then, and has never happened since. It was thought by many of the Society at least hard, that a person should be excused all his time from reading prayers, preaching, and other Ecclesiastical duties in College and the University, which must be performed in person, or another paid for doing them; and then, when the reward of all this long service seems within reach, that another, who has not borne any part of the heat and burthen of the day, should step in before you, and carry off the prize. The Doctor was however so lucky, as he generally was, as to carry his point, but not without much difficulty. His friends indeed, who kept up the credit of the house for punning, said from the first, that the Doctor would certainly *go to Law for 't*."

His preferments, after he entered into orders, were, the rectory of Lawford in Essex, in April 1751; the Archdeaconry of Buckingham, 1753; the Residentiaryship of St. Paul's in July 1757, succeeding Dr. Terrick, who is said to have been raised to the See of Peterborough expressly to make the vacancy; and the office of Prolocutor to the Lower House of Convocation the same year. He was also Commissary of Lincoln and of Stowe; and was esteemed one of the most disinterested and amiable, as he was one of the most learned, of his profession.

Browne Willis, in a letter to Dr. Ducarel, 1757, expresses his expectation that Dr. Taylor was to have had Dr. Neve's great prebend of Lincoln.

After he had actually entered into the Church, he continued to dine in common with the Advocates in Doctors Commons four times every term with their unanimous consent, except on those days in which the learned Civilians transacted the business of their Society, of which he always had notice; and this he did to the end of his life.

He was for many years a valuable member both of the Royal and Antiquarian Societies, his name being distinguished in the publications of the former; and was appointed Director of the latter, April 23, 1759, and at the next meeting one of their Vice-presidents.

Dr. Taylor died, universally lamented and beloved, at his Residentiary-house, Amen-corner, April 4, 1766; and was buried in the vaults under St. Paul's, nearly under the Litany-desk, where there is an inscription on a marble slab, which merely enumerates his titles.

At the time of his death, though a very large number of the quarto edition of Demosthenes remained unsold, an octavo edition of that work was just finished at the University press*; and an "Appendix to Suidas" was begun, of which only four sheets were printed.

Having shewn the preceding part of this Memoir to the *Friend of Dr. Taylor* to whom I had before been so much obliged, I was favoured with the following particulars : "You have mentioned that Dr. Taylor was too busy a man to be idle. This is too shining a particular in the Doctor's temper and abilities not to be a little more insisted upon. If you called on him in College after dinner, you were sure to find him sitting at an old oval walnut-tree table entirely covered with books, in which, as the common expression runs, he seemed to be buried : you began to make apologies for disturbing a person so well employed; but he immediately told you to advance, taking care to disturb, as little as you could, the books on the floor; and called out, 'John, John, bring pipes and glasses;' and then fell to procuring a small space for the bottle just to stand on, but which could hardly ever be done without shoving off an equal quantity of the furniture at the other end; and he instantly appeared as cheerful, good-humoured, and *degagé*, as if he had not been at all engaged or interrupted. Suppose now you had staid as long as you would, and been entertained by him most agreeably, you took your leave, and got half-way down the stairs; but, recollecting somewhat that you had more to say to him, you go in again; the bottle and glasses were gone, the books had expanded themselves as to re-occupy the whole table, and he was just as much buried in them as when you first broke in on him. I never knew this convenient faculty to an equal degree in any other scholar. His voice to me, who

---

*The notes only were wanting. These were afterwards added, and the book published in 1769.

know nothing of music, appeared remarkably pleasing and harmonious, whether he talked or read English, Latin, or Greek prose, owing to his speaking through his lips much advanced, which always produces softness : this practice, or habit, I believe, he learned from a speaking-master, to whom he applied to correct some natural defect; for which purpose he always kept near him an ordinary small swing-glass, the use of which was unknown to his friends; but in preaching, which he was fond of, one might perceive a shrillness or sharpness that was not agreeable; perhaps he could not speak so loud as was required, and at the same time keep his lips advanced and near together, as he had learned to do for common conversation. He understood perfectly, as a gentleman and scholar, all that belongs to making a book handsome, as the choice of paper, types, and the disposition of text, version, and notes. He excelled in many small accomplishments. He loved and played well at cards; was fond of carving, which he did with much elegance; an agreeable practice, but which, notwithstanding what Lord Chesterfield says, some persons who have frequented good tables all their life-time cannot do, though they can blow their nose passing well. He always appeared handsomely in full dress as a Clergyman, was grand in his looks, yet affable, flowing, and polite. Latterly he grew too plump, with an appearance of doughy paleness, which occasioned uneasiness to those who loved him, whose number, I think, must be considerable. He wrote a large, fair, elegant hand; was a perfect master of Dr. Byrom's short-hand, which he looked upon as barely short of perfection, and which he taught to as many as chose to learn, for the benefit of his friend. He never made a blot in his writing : always, besides his Adversaria, kept a proper edition of most books for entering notes in their margin, as the Louvre Greek Testament in folio. These were what Dr. Askew was entitled to by his will, besides his common-place books, which, I think, in his open way of writing, for he never spared paper, amounted before he left College to forty volumes in folio; in those he had put down a vast variety of philological learning, without neglecting matters of pleasantry; and I should think it must be impossible, if one that knew his manner and short-hand had liberty to examine them, but that they must furnish an excellent *Tayloriana*. I do not remember that he had any ear for music; no more had the excellent Dr. Powell, late Master of St. John's, nor the justly celebrated Linnæus, nor the equally far-famed Moralist and Philologer Dr. Johnson, and a thousand others whose organs were in other respects happily formed and arranged. He was also of remarkable *sang-froid* in very trying cases. Once being got into a coach and four with some friends, for *a scheme* as we call it, the gentleman driver, the late Rev. Roger Mostyn, who was remarkably short-sighted, picked up the reins as he thought, but left those of the leaders below, who being smartly whipped to make them go off at an handsome rate, soon found that they were at liberty, and went off with a speed beyond what the rest of the party could desire. They proposed to the Doctor to jump out, who replied with the utmost coolness, 'Jump out! why jump out? have not I hired the coach to carry me?' This looks more like the language of *Jack Tar*, than of one bred in the softening shade of Academus' grove; yet I have little doubt of its being literally true, as he used much the same language to me when the fore-wheel of the post-chaise came off twice in one stage. He also told me himself, that when the last of the two earthquakes at London happened (I mean that at six in the morning), he was waked by it, and said, 'This is an earthquake!' turned himself, and went to sleep instantly. Yet nothing of this appeared in his common behaviour; but all was soft and placid. When we used to joke with him on the badness of his furniture, which consisted of the table aforesaid, and three or four ordinary chairs, and they always filled with books, he used to say that his room was better and more expensively furnished than any of ours; which was certainly true, as he sat in the midst of an excellent library, containing a very fine collection of philological, classical, and juridical books, which formed the proper furniture of a scholar's room, though I cannot say that it is the usual or fashionable furniture of the times.

"This fine and large collection he increased greatly after he got to London, as all those who know it in Amen-corner will bear me witness. This was the more necessary for him to do, as he no longer had the command of the well-furnished libraries of Cambridge; and, as it was his taste and passion to do so, he was enabled to gratify them by his goodly income, which, had he lived, would have been very sufficient, even though it had received no farther increase. His testamentary disposition of this valuable library gave me less satisfaction than any other act of his life. The general fault consisted in not keeping them together, thereby depriving his admirers of the suite and connexion of his

ideas, as he had put them down in different books, but with
references backwards and forwards. It is plain that he could
not be actuated by the low fears and policy of Cujacius, who, to
prevent this, ordered his books to be sold separately; because the
Doctor entrusted the complete set with Dr. Askew, where any
thing of this kind might be practised with more likelihood of
success and secrecy, than if deposited in a public library, where
every person that consulted them would know the use that was
made of them by others. He probably meant well, and thought
that the surest way of keeping them together for a long time
was to place them in his learned friend's princely collection. But
the futility of this provision quickly appeared; and it would
have been much the same whether the hammer had sounded
over them immediately on his death, or in the very few years
after, when it did. The folio Terentianus Maurus, Mediolani,
1497, which cost the Doctor four guineas out of the Harleian
Collection, and which, I dare say, long before he was in easy
circumstances, an hundred would not have got from him, was
purchased for twelve guineas by Dr. Hunter, and is for the
present at least safely lodged in that noble repository of curiosities of all kinds.* Nor do I much more approve of his disposal
of the other part; had he given one, two, or three sets of the
most useful Classics, with Dictionaries, &c. to the School,† this
would have remained a testimony of his gratitude, and been
very serviceable to the Masters, Scholars, and neighbourhood,
without any prejudice to the University, which is well supplied
with these writers. Not so with the many curious articles that
he had picked up singly at a great expence from foreign parts
as he could hear of them. These are not likely to be of much
service in the Country; but might probably have been looked
into in the University, which also would have been the proper
place for distant Literati to have inquired for them, where
access would be remarkably easy and agreeable. Upon this
occasion one can hardly help mentioning, that when he heard
of Dr. Newcome's death, whom he did not love (and, as
we hope his aversions were not many, they might be the
stronger) he inquired how he had disposed of his books; and
though the account was a very good one, he received it with an
air of contempt; upon which one of the company said, 'Then,

---

*Since consigned to the University of Glasgow.
†At Shrewsbury. He was born in the parish of St. Alkmond in that town.

Doctor, do you now take care to do better;' upon which he sunk into seriousness, and said softly, 'I wish I may!' He was silent in large companies, but fond of dealing out his entertainment and instruction before one, two, or three persons. He entertained his friends with an hospitality and generosity that bordered upon munificence, and enjoyed himself in the convivial hours.

"I could add much more about the Doctor; as, a defence of him against Reiske, and those who blame the order of his publications, from himself; some pleasant tales, for he was an excellent story-teller; also others of a contrary nature. But please to take notice, that whatever I say of him, I neither do it through adulation, or any bad motive; having never received the value of a Denarius, further than perhaps dining with him once or twice in Ave-Maria Lane, where he kept a noble table; the only fault of which was, that it was too open to all comers; some of which were the dullest companions possible. One of them, who, I think, had been a schoolmaster, was, of all men I ever met with, the stupidest; and this man used to go about, and declare to every body, that he made it a point frequently to call on the Doctor, and sit long with him, to prevent his being dull, &c.; whereas the Doctor's known character was, that no one knew how to employ his time better.

"It may be a means of prolonging some worthy man's days, to mention, that he shortened his own by a modesty or shyness that prevented him from making his case fully known, and submitting himself to the direction of a physician, though he was intimately acquainted with several of the most eminent in the profession. He one day mentioned to me with some peevishness, that he was costive; I asked him why he would not consult Dr. Heberden: he said, 'How can I do so? he will not take any thing.' I replied, 'that he would certainly give him the best advice out of friendship and regard; but that there were others to whom he might apply, who might not have the same delicacy.' The misfortune was, that he had applied to three, and smuggled a receipt for a purge from each, and used them all alternately, and almost without intermission, at least in a manner they never intended; I think there were 175 charged in the Apothecary's bill for the last year. This calamity had hardly happened had he lived in a family, I mean with friends and relations about him, and not servants only, as the former could never have consented to his treating himself in such a strange manner."

DR. TAYLOR ON THE PARIS BIBLE AT CAMBRIDGE

1. To the Earl of OXFORD.

"MY LORD,   Cambridge, Dec. 20, 1740.

"The following account, relating to the *Paris Bible* of 1464, will not, I presume, be disagreeable to your Lordship, as it serves to clear up a very great difficulty in the History of Printing; and as the fame of this rare and very curious edition, I very well remember to have heard, excited your Lordship's curiosity. It will be no longer a subject of wonder, that your Lordship's commissions over all Europe, for a copy of this Book, were returned without success; as your Lordship will be convinced, from the perusal of these papers, that it could not have happened otherwise.

"When the Library of the late Bp. Moore came to be better known; nothing, in that very valuable Collection, was more likely to astonish the curious, than a Book of the three first Paris Printers, with a date, which not only contradicted the best and most authentic accounts of the Settlement of the Press in that City, but, what is still more amazing, the express testimony of those very Printers themselves upon another occasion. For, my Lord, not only Naudé, in his Addition to the History of Lewis XI. and Chevillier, Library-keeper of the Sorbonne, in his Dissertation upon the Origin of Printing, have uncontestably fixed the date of the Paris press at 1470; but the Edition of the Epistles of Gasparinus Pergamensis, which was set out at Paris the same year, is a convincing proof that this art had not been exercised in that part of Europe before this date; as will appear from the colophon:—

'Ut Sol lumen, sic doctrinam fundis in orbem,
     Musarum nutrix, regia Parisius,
Hinc propè divinam, tu quam Germania novit,
     Artem scribendi, suscipe promerita

Primos ecce libros, quos hæc industria finxit
    Francorum in terris, ædibus atque tuis :
Michael, Udalricus, Martinusque magistri,
    Hos impresserunt; ac facient alios.'

"Thus stood the History of Printing, when the late Bishop
of Ely [Dr. Moore] procured a Vulgate Bible in folio, with a
colophon that spoke, and that in the name of Michael [Fri-
burger], Ulric [Gering], and Martin [Crantz], the printers, as
expressly for 1464, as any other testimony could do for 1470.
Your Lordship very well remembers, I transcribed it for your
Lordship's use a few years ago, at Mr. Morgan's instance; and
that it stands thus :

'Jam semi undecimus lustrum Francos Ludovicus
Rexerat, Ulricus, Martinus, itemque Michaël
Orti Teutoniâ hanc mihi composuere figuram.'

"The Owner of the Book, misled by a false chronology
(perhaps that of Chevillier, who dates the reign of Lewis XI.
from July 1460), ordered his Binder to mark his Copy on the
back with 1463. But as Lewis XI. began his reign, according
to the best accounts, one year later, viz. succeeding his father
Charles VII. July 1461, and crowned the August following,
the true date cannot be higher than January, or February, 1464.
About which time, therefore, we must suppose this Book to be
printed.

"There is another very material difficulty arising from this
date, besides the contradictory accounts mentioned above;
which I believe none of those have taken notice of, who yet
were very sensible of the other. And that is this. If we admit the
story of Faust's exposing his new-printed books to sale at Paris
(I cannot indeed admit of the whole upon account of some
notable absurdities in it), we can scarce allow him to bring
those books to market till 1463 : for he had finished them at his
press in Germany but in 1462; and that pretty late in the year:
viz. the eve of the Assumption (14 Aug). Now, if ours be a
true date, how shall we account for the surprize of the Paris
purchasers, which they are said to express at the exact similitude of so many Copies that Faust offered to sale, and at the
novelty of an Art, of which they had formed no idea (for so the
story runs), when they had the very same invention brought
home to them some time before, and actually exercised in their
own City at the same juncture? For, besides the time which
must be required in laying-in materials, and setting up a print-

ing-house; this very large Volume, consisting of 240 sheets, which was finished at press but at the beginning of the year 1464, must have required, when the invention was very young, and the press moved heavily, a considerable time longer than the compass of one year to bring it to perfection.

"Upon shewing this curiosity a little whole ago to Mr. Maurice Johnson, of Spalding, a gentleman exceedingly well versed in Antiquities, he almost immediately cried out, that there had been an erasement, and that in those two words which establish the date, *Semi,* my Lord, is a visible forgery, wrote with the hand in printing-ink, on a place that had been scratched with the knife; but, otherwise, no bad imitation of the type; and, except that it borders a little too close upon the following word, upon the whole is a very ingenious counterfeit. The other word, *Lustrum* (thus, *Lustru*), has undergone no alteration but in the last letter, which is very ill connected with the letter preceding, and in a quite different manner from any other part of the Book, where these two letters meet. Besides, my Lord, that part of the word, which remains in print, and untouched, betrays, upon comparison, and to a very ordinary attention, the imposture at the end of it.

"When Mr. Palmer wrote the History of Printing, and was led, by the nature of his subject, to consider the circumstances of Bp. Moore's, or the Cambridge Bible, he could by no means get over the difficulty of this colophon; but was forced to cut the knot, by saying, that, probably, the Gentleman at Cambridge, who transcribed for Mr. Maittaire, had mistaken the words, and wrote *semi Lustrum* instead of *tribus Lustris;* which is, surely, such an hallucination, as I can suppose no man guilty of, who transcribed, and that by way of evidence, three lines for a friend with his eyes open.

"However, my Lord, Mr. Palmer was not far from the mark; though, surely, his manner of accounting for the difficulty was the clumsiest of all conjectures; and what must, of necessity, have been exposed and confuted as often as the Book should be laid open. For I will venture to pronounce, that this is a copy of the edition of the Bible in 1476; which is what Mr. Palmer alluded to in his *tribus Lustris:* an edition pretty well known, and altogether reconcilable with the testimony of our Printers, and History of Printing; the colophon of which,

'Jam tribus undecimus Lustris Francos Ludovicus
Rexerat, Ulricus, Martinus, itemque Michaël,

Orti Teutoniâ, hanc mihi composuêre figuram,'
is, either through wantonness; or, perhaps, in affectation of
being thought to be the master of a singular copy; or, what
is still more likely, out of avarice, transferred into what it is at
present; and what has puzzled the most inquisitive for above
twenty years last past.

"But, my Lord, the colophon of 1476 consists in all of five
lines:
'Jam tribus undecimus Lustris Francos Ludovicus
Reverat, Ulricus, Martinus, itemque Michaël,
Orti Teutoniâ, hanc mihi composuêre figuram
Parisii arte suâ : me correctam vigilantèr
Vænalem in Vico Jacobi Solaureus offert.'
But as these two last lines might be easily spared, our imposter
was very willing to part with them; since the colophon, thus
reduced, must necessarily set his copy at a greater variance from
the known edition of 1476. Upon a close examination I found
they had been totally erased, and ordinary piece of illumination
drawn over the place for the better disguise. Across this part of
the page, as far as the opposite column, there has formerly been
a rent; whether a casual or designed one, I leave your Lordship to guess, when I add, that on the back of the leaf is pasted
(seemingly in a careless manner) a piece of pretty thick paper,
in order to look like restoring what had been torn asunder;
but withal so artfully contrived, that it should cloak all that
part of the leaf where the erasement has been made.

"Yet, my Lord, after all this artifice, the rasure is very plain
when the leaf is held up to the light; especially of those two
lines I mentioned, even through the thick paper; which, doubtless, has no other business there, than to come in aid to this
notable piece of forgery.

"Thus, my Lord, I hope I have satisfactorily accounted for
one of the great difficulties that have, for a long time, clogged
the Annals of the Press. That part of Literary History has been
employed for a considerable time in clearing its way, and getting
rid of spurious dates, that perplexed its evidences, partly by
fraud, and partly accident.

"Of the former sort I reckon, in some measure, the famous
Lauderdaile Bible in your Lordship's very valuable Collection;
a Cicero de Officiis of 1465, in the Library of Mr. Raymund
Kraafft, burgomaster of Ulm, mentioned by Schelhornius in his
Amœnitates Literariæ, tom. 3; which is altered into 1440. And,

lastly, a piece of Thomas Aquinas, printed by Faust and Schoeffer, *anno D'ni millesimo quadringentesimo septuagesimo-primo,* which being altered by the pen from *septuagesimo* into *quinquagesimo,* bears date before the æra of Printing. I question not but that time will make more discoveries of this sort; and that the *Decor Puellarum* of Nicholas Jenson in 1461; and *Franciscus Florius de Amore Camilli et Æmiliæ,* said to be printed at Tours in 1467, will be found in one of these two lists I have been speaking of*.

> "I am, my Lord, &c.   J. TAYLOR."

PHILIP THICKNESSE

PHILIP THICKNESSE, "a seventh son without a daughter between," was born at Farthinghoe, Aug. 10, 1719; and, for some time after the death of his father, was placed at Aynhoe school; but soon removed, with his mother, to London; and, by the favour of Dr. Robert Freind, he was admitted a *gratis* (not a King's) scholar at Westminster; where he did not long remain, but was placed, on liking, with Mr. Marmaduke Tisdall, an Apothecary: but, that profession not suiting his inclination, he was permitted, in 1735, to accompany General Oglethorpe to Georgia; whence Mr. Thicknesse returned in 1737; and, as he was one of the first of the Emigrants who had arrived in this country, was invited to attend the Trustees who had the management of that Colony. During this attendance he had the promise of an Ensigncy in a Regiment then raising, under Colonel Oglethorpe, for its defence; but, by speaking the truth respecting the affairs of Georgia too plainly, he lost the Colonel's favour. At this time, however, his two brothers, Thomas and Ralph, both Fellows of King's College, were in high favour with Sir Edward Walpole; and the younger of them had steadily engaged in the interest of the Hon. Thomas Townshend, then M. P. for the University. By the recommendation, therefore, of those two gentlemen to Sir Robert Walpole, Mr. Philip Thicknesse obtained a Lieutenancy in an Independent Company at

---

*See Ames's Historical Account of Printing in England, p. 438.

Jamaica, where, for a considerable time, he was engaged in a variety of skirmishes with the Runaway Negroes in the Mountains; till, tired of this desultory warfare, and not agreeing cordially with some of his brother officers; hearing also that there was a talk of raising two Regiments in England; he obtained from Governor Trelawny permission for six months absence; and sailed for England in the latter end of the year 1740, in the Greenwich man of war; and obtained, in January 1740-1, the post of Captain-Lieutenant in Brigadier Jeffries's Marine Regiment of Foot.

In 1742 he married Maria, the only daughter of Mr. John Lanove, of Southampton, a French Refugee; whose wife was the only daughter of Mr. Berenger, of the same country, and under the same circumstances; and who, when he died, left his money (about 10,000*l.*) to accumulate, interest-upon-interest, during Mr. Lanove's life; and at his death to be divided equally between his children, when they shall arrive at the age of 24. Under this will, Mr. Thicknesse expected, at a period which he thought might not be very distant, the reversion of 40,000*l.*; but he was grievously disappointed.

Early in 1744-5 he was sent up the Mediterranean, in the Ipswich, with Admiral Medley, as his Captain of Marines; and was a sufferer in a most tremendous storm, near the Land's End, Feb. 27, in which the Admiral's ship, with a large fleet under his convoy, sustained considerable damage.

Returning to England after about a year's absence, he represents "himself and his *forty-thousand-pounder,* as reduced by the Peace to short allowance; from between *two and three hundred* a year, to live upon barely *ninety-two.*" One part of this defalcation arose from the non-payment of an annuity of 50*l.* which the father-in-law had engaged to pay him; but which, by the obstinacy of a wife by whom he was governed, Mr. Lanove was persuaded to withhold. This produced a quarrel; and Mr. Thicknesse, packing up his wife and three children, set off in a common waggon for Romsey; whence the good old Lord Palmerston forwarded them to Bath in his coach and six. With this wife he *starved* for seven years. She brought him four children; but died early in 1749, as at the same time did two of her children, of the *Pelham Fever**, which had also nearly

*A malignant Fever, which had proved very fatal in the family of Mr. Pelham, at that time Prime Minister.

killed her husband. Mr. Lanove soon after died broken-hearted, having first burnt his will (a circumstance by which Mr. Thicknesse obtained about 5000*l.*); and the widow, whose mind was deranged, jumped out of her first-floor window, and impaled herself on the spikes, before her own door, in the High Street, Southampton.

Mr. Thicknesse married, secondly, Nov. 10, 1749, Elizabeth, eldest daughter of the Earl of Castlehaven, with whom he resided for some time at Acton. With this Lady he also received 5000*l.*; with part of which (1500*l.*) he purchased, in February 1753, the Lieutenant-governorship of Landguard Fort; and with that honourable situation he was highly delighted, till the beginning of March 1762; when an unfortunate dispute with Mr. Vernon, then Colonel of the Suffolk Militia (afterwards Lord Orwell, and Earl of Shipbrook) very seriously interrupted his comforts; a circumstance much aggravated by the death of his wife. [In consequence of this dispute, Mr. Thicknesse sent the Colonel a present of a *wooden gun.* This produced an action for a libel by way of *reply,* and constitutes a *new case* on the books; writing alone having, before this time, been usually considered as subject to this appellation. Mr. (afterwards Chief Justice) De Grey was Counsel for the Defendant; and expressed himself greatly astonished 'that the nephew of a renowned Commander, the Hero of Porto Bello, should bring an action against a Brother Officer on such a contemptible occasion;' and the laugh of the day was assuredly against him. But it was no laughing matter to his adversary; for Governor Thicknesse was confined for three months in the King's Bench prison; and fined in 300*l.* But his gaiety did not forsake him, for he had a painting of a gun placed above the door of his apartment (the same afterwards inhabited by Mr. Wilkes), which from that time received the appellation of the *Gun-room.* On his return to the country, the Colonel declined attending a public dinner until he learned that Governor Thicknesse was not to be there; and he was greatly discomposed on receiving a polite letter from Mrs. Thicknesse, intimating, 'that, if would be at the ball in the evening, she would meet him *as sure as a gun.*']

On the 27th of September following, he married a third wife, the daughter of Thomas Ford, Esq. an eminent Solicitor, and Clerk of the Arraigns; and the first years of this marriage glided smoothly away. During the winter they lived in the Governor's apartments at Land-guard Fort, where they received and returned the visits of the neighbouring Nobility and Gentry; and in the summer months they inhabited a pretty little place called Felixstow cottage (now in possession of Sir Samuel Fludyer, Bart.), at three miles distance; which was merely a fisherman's hut, converted by the taste of Mr. Thicknesse, and afterwards embellished by the pencil of his wife, into a charming little residence, where he amused himself in field sports and literary pursuits.

In the Spring of 1766, having then six children living (four by his former wives, and two by the third wife), he obtained permission to resign his Government to Captain Singleton, on advantageous terms; and retired into France, where he resided from May till October, and placed his daughter Elizabeth for education in a nunnery at Ardres. Joyce, the younger sister, was afterwards placed in another nunnery. He detailed the particulars of this journey, in the St. James's Chronicle, under the title of *A Wanderer;* and afterwards gave them to the Publick, much altered and enlarged, as "Observations on the Customs and Manners of the French Nation; in a Series of Letters, in which that Nation is vindicated from the Misrepresentations of some late Writers," alluding more especially to Dr. Smollett.

The Governor's abode, on his return to England, was at a pretty little villa near Welling, Herts; which an unexpected event soon induced him to relinquish. His father-in-law Mr. Ford died May 3, 1768; and a small estate in Wales, within two miles of Pont-y-Pool, having devolved on Mrs. Thicknesse, as heiress to her mother, it was determined to repair thither, as the spot was known to be beautiful and romantic; and the genius of the Governor soon converted it into a Paradise: but an incident soon occurred, which produced another change of situation. By the sudden death of his mother-in-law, Madam Lanove, Mr. Thicknesse considered himself entitled to 12,000*l*; and had always looked forward to that event, as a provision for his old age, as well as for his family. Accordingly, he immediately repaired to Bath, to complete the education of his children, and introduce them properly into the world: and, for that purpose, he purchased a house in the Crescent; and built *St. Catherine's Hermitage,* romantically situated on the swell of a hill, then about three quarters of a mile distant from Bath; intended as a quiet retreat, in which Mrs. Thicknesse could educate the children, uninterrupted by the cares and ceremonies of the world. But the prospects which he had indulged, of inheriting the Berenger property, were annihilated, first by a Decree against him in Chancery, and again by an unsuccessful Appeal to the House of Lords.

In 1775, therefore, "driven out of his own country," he tells us, "with eight children in his train," and imagining he could live any where cheaper than in England," he fixed upon Spain, and determined to remove thither. On the 20th of June he arrived at Calais, which he describes as "a sort of enlarged King's Bench prison, where the English fugitives live within *the Rules,* and the French inhabitants make it a rule to oppress and distress them." After visiting his two daughters, he proceeded to cross the Pyrenees. This excursion employed him till November 1776; and produced "A Year's Journey through France and Spain, 1777;" 2 vols. 8vo.

From this time Mr. Thicknesse appears to have been for a few years stationary at Bath.

His "New Prose Bath Guide" appeared in 1778; the "Valetudinarian's Bath Guide, or the Means of obtaining long Life and Health," in 1780; his "Letter to Dr. Falconer of Bath," and "Queries to Lord Audley," in 1782.

In the Autumn of 1782 he made a third excursion to the Continent, which produced in 1783, "Pere Pascal, a Monk of Montserrat, vindicated; in a Charge brought against him by a Noble Earl of Great Britain;" and, in 1784, "A Year's Journey through the Pais Bas, or Austrian Netherlands."

In 1784, Mr. Thicknesse erected a rustic monument to the memory of the unfortunate Chatterton; which was soon after inscribed with the name of one of his own daughters, snatched away in the prime of life.

In 1785, Mr. Thicknesse published "A Letter to the Earl of Coventry," 8vo; and in that year he commenced his correspondence with Mr. Urban, under the signature of *Polyxena;* which he continued, under that of *A Wanderer,* his own initials, and other designations, till nearly the day of his death.

In 1786, he gave a public testimonial of his veneration for Mr. Howard, *the Visitor of Prisons;* whose merits he had duly noticed in his "Journey through the Pais Bas;" and in 1787 paid a handsome tribute of respect to a gallant Naval Officer.

In 1787 he published his "Letter to Dr. James Makittrick Adair," 8vo; and, in 1788, "Memoirs of the Life and Paintings of Mr. Gainsborough;" and Two Volumes of "Memoirs and Anecdotes of Philip Thicknesse, late Governor of Land-guard

Fort; and, unfortunately, Father to George Touchet Baron Audley."

In the second volume, dated Dec. 25, 1788, Mr. Thicknesse again appears before the publick in the character of a man of great sensibility — in some instances very ill used — but no respector of persons; and at the end of it advertizes his *Hermitage near Bath,* for sale, on June 15, 1789.

In 1789 Mr. Thicknesse also published "Junius discovered" [in the person of Mr. Horne Tooke].

In the Autumn of 1789, happening to reside a few weeks in the neighbourhood of Hythe, and observing a deserted barn at Sandgate, a small village on the sea coast, he immediately purchased the barn, which he transformed into a convenient cottage, commanding a view of France; where, on a clear day, the steeples of Boulogne might be readily discovered by a good glass, while the hills around it were very clearly discernible to every common observer.

Early in 1790 he passed some weeks at his native village in Northamptonshire, where he received the challenge from Captain Crookshanks, which makes a considerable figure in the Third Volume of his Memoirs, dated "Sandgate Barn, April 1, 1791."

The daily sight of the Continent, in time, became infectious; and in 1791 he described himself as "preparing to do what he had intended the preceding Summer; to set out for Paris — a journey far preferable, to see *the wrangling there,* than staying to *wrangle here* with an old superannuated *Hero* [Crookshanks], and a mad *Doctor* [Makittrick]."

He accordingly visited Paris, at an early period of the French Revolutionary phrenzy; and continued some time at Calais, in the Hotel formerly belonging to the Duchess of Kingston; but in August again pursued his route, through Boulogne and Abbeville, to Paris.

Returning once more to Bath, he published, March 9, 1792, "A Letter to Charles Bonner, Esq. Deputy Comptroller of the Post-office; which was followed, in May, by "A Letter to Lady Audley;" which, with the exception of a Letter in the Magazine, dated July 30, 1792, was his latest publication.

Having let his house in the Crescent at Bath to a Lady of Quality, he set off for France, with the intention of passing through that country to Italy, where he proposed to stay two or three years. On the 18th of November he was at Boulogne, in

perfect health and remarkably good spirits; but on the following
day had not proceeded a single stage, to Samers, on the way
to Paris, before he complained to his wife, who was in the
carriage with him, of a sudden pain in his stomach; and (sooner
almost than she could express her concern) added, "I have a
pain in my head too," when he instantly expired.

Mr. Thicknesse was a man of probity and honour, whose
heart and purse were always open to the unfortunate. None
were his enemies, but those who were unworthy of being his
friends; for he was as severe in his censure of the infamous, as
he was friendly to virtue and merit.

THE TOOKE FAMILY

IN 1795 was published "Varieties of Literature," 2 vols. 8vo.;
which were followed the next year by two other large
Volumes, 8vo. of curious "Extracts from Foreign Literary
Journals, and original MSS. now first published." — For these
learned and amusing Compilations, which were favourably
received by the publick, and are now both out of print, the
readers were indebted to the Rev. William Tooke, F. R. S. —
[The family of *Toke, Tooke, Tuke, or Tucke,* as they have at
different times been variously spelt, are descended from Le
Sieur de Touque, called in some copies *Toc,* and in others
Touke, mentioned in the Battle-abbey Roll; having, among
others, attended William the Conqueror in his expedition hither,
and being present on his behalf in the memorable Battle of
Hastings. His descendant Robert de Tooke, who is the first
mentioned in the Pedigrees of this family, bore for his arms,
*Parted per chevron Sable and Argent three griffins heads erased
and counterchanged:* Crest, *a griffin's head erased, holding in
his beak a Tuck proper.* Motto, MILITIA MEA MULTIPLEX. He
was present with King Henry III. in 1264, at the battle of
Northampton. His great-grandson is called Tooke de Took, and
of West Cliffe, from whom descended, in the fifth generation,
John Tooke, of the manor of Bere, or Byers Court, in the parish
of West Cliffe; who lived in the reigns of Henry V. and VI.

and had three sons; of whom Thomas, the eldest, was of Bere; Ralph, the second, was ancestor of those of Cambridgeshire, Dorsetshire, and Hertfordshire; and John, the third, died without male issue.

Thomas Tooke, of Bere, married Joane, daughter of William Goldwell, Esq. of Godington (a manor within the parish of Great Chart, in Kent), whose heir-general she at length was. He married, secondly, Cecilia, daughter of Sir Robert Chicheley, niece to the Archbishop, by whom he had issue. By his first wife he had three sons; Ralph, who succeeded to the family estate at Bere, where his posterity remained till the latter end of the 17th century; Richard; who died s. p.; and John, the youngest, who had Godington by his father's will, where he afterwards resided, and had an augmentation of honour granted to his arms by King Henry VII. as a reward for his expedition in a message on which he was employed to the French King, being an additional coat of arms, *viz. Argent, on a chevron between three greyhounds' heads erased Sable, collared Or, three plates;* which coat the Tokes of Godington have ever since borne in the first quarter of their arms, placing the original arms of Tooke in the second place; in whose descendants, resident here, most of whom lie buried in the parish church, the seat at Godington continued, down to Nicholas Tooke, alias Toke, Esq. usually called Captain Toke; who "so industriously and elegantly cultivated and improved our English vines, that the wine pressed and extracted out of their grapes seems not only to parallel, but almost to out-rival that of France." He was Sheriff of Kent in 1663; and, dying in 1680, was buried in the chancel of the church, with his five wives. There is an anecdote of him in the family, that, at the age of 93, being left a widower, he walked from thence to London, to pay his addresses to a sixth wife; but, being taken ill, he presently died. His Portrait (which, with that of his fifth wife, Diana, daughter of the Earl of Winchelsea, and a series of fine portraits of the family, several of which are by Cornelius Janssen, and others equally good, is preserved in the Hall at Godington) well expresses the strength of his frame and constitution. In the windows of the staircase at Godington are collected all the family arms, quarterings, and mottoes, in painted glass, formerly dispersed throughout the house; which are numerous, and well preserved. Leaving no male issue by either of his wives, he devised Godington, with the rest of his estates, to his nephew and heir at law, Sir Nicholas Tooke, alias

Toke, of Wye (son of his next brother, Henry Toke, M. D. of Offham); who in 1701 raised a large vault for his family against the North Wall of the church of Great Chart, where several of an early date are recorded on flat stones, enriched with their figures, and shields of arms, in brass. By marriage with the daughter of John Cockman, M. D. the manor and Priory of Little Dunmow and the manor of Bernstow came to his family, and descended to John Tooke, Esq. who was High-sheriff of Essex in 1770.

George Tooke, Esq. of Popes married Anna Tooke, eldest daughter of Thomas Tooke, of Bere. He bore a very active part in the expedition against Cadiz in the year 1625; from whence returning, after various adventures, he passed the remainder of his days at Popes, where he wrote several pieces of prose and verse, of very considerable merit — "The Danaids," a Poem; "The Eagle Trusser's Elegy, a Poem; in honour of Prince Rupert;" the latter of which, though consisting of not more than 100 pages, sold for three guineas at the sale of the books of Mr. Stace, bookseller in Scotland Yard, in the year 1810. Mr. Greaves's learned account of the Pyramids of Egypt, 2 vols. 8vo. is dedicated to George Tooke, Esq. who was in long habits of intimacy with that profound scholar. Mr. Tooke, in taking leave of him when embarking in the expedition against Cadiz, concludes by saying, *Il faut quitter la plume, pour dormir sur le dur.* — George Tooke sold his portion of the manor of Wormley to Richard Woollaston, Esq. who was Gun-founder to Oliver Cromwell; and whose grandson Richard conveyed it to William Fellowes, Esq. whose eldest son Coulston Fellowes, Esq. was the possessor in 1727.

Richard Tuke, Gent. a branch of the original Kentish stock (though in this and other parts of the family the name *by depreciation* was called *Tuke*), was Tutor to the Duke of Norfolk and Lord Thomas Howard; and had arms assigned him by King Edward IV.; *viz. A fess dancetté between three Lions passant.*

His son, Bryan Tuke, Esq. was in 1508 appointed to the Patent-office of King's Bailiff and Verger of Sandwich, with the wages and fees of twelve pence sterling a day. He was for some time Secretary to Cardinal Wolsey; and in 1522 Secretary to the King for the French tongue; Treasurer of the King's Chamber; and Clerk of the Signet. In 1528 King Henry VIII. granted to Bryan Tooke, Esq. and his heirs, the manors of

Thorpe, Thorpe Hall, and East Lee, all in the parish of South-church, Essex; and in the same year was kuighted, and was sent Ambassador to France with Bishop Tunstall. In 1533, being then of Hatfield, he was Sheriff of Hertfordshire and Essex; and at the dissolution of the Abbey of Waltham Holy Cross, the King further gave him the manor of South Weald, and the Rectory, together with an estate called Boswells, for 883*l*. 6*s*. 8*d*. Sir Bryan Tooke married Grissel, daughter of Sir Edward Boughton, of Woolaston, and had three daughters; Elizabeth, wife of Sir Reginald Scot; Aleana, of John Maynard, of London; and Mary, of George Tuchet, Lord Audley. He had also three sons, Maximilian, who died young; Charles, and George. He was a man of learning. Leland highly commends him for his wonderful eloquence in the English language, "Anglicæ linguæ eloquentiâ mirificus;" and, in his "Encomia illustrium Virorum," celebrates him, in eight distinct little Latin Poems, as his Benefactor, and as a Patron of the Muses.

"Bale saith, that he wrote Observations on Chaucer; as also against Polydore Vergil, for injuring the English; of whom, still alive, he justly and generously demanded reparations; though since, his *unresponsable memory* can make us no *satisfaction*. Dying Oct. 26, 1536, he lyeth buried with Dame Grissel his wife (deceasing two years after him) under a fair tomb in the North Isle of the Quire of St. Margaret's in Lothbury." *Fuller's Worthies, Essex.*

Thomas Tuke, M. A. was presented by King James I. in 1617, to the Vicarage of St. Olave Jewry; but was sequestered March 16, 1642-3, plundered, and imprisoned, for his Loyalty. His son Thomas was also a hearty sufferer in the same cause: but had the honour of presenting a Bible and Common Prayer to Charles II. on his landing at Dover; and the zealous attachment of the family was acknowledged, at the Restoration, by such rewards as Royal hands tied down by promise and compositions could afford. The last-named gentleman, who inherited the family mansion of Bere Court, was the father of Dr. Thomas Tooke, whose education was first at St. Paul's school, under the learned Dr. Gale, and more especially under the care of Mr. Fox, to whom he owned many obligations, and to whose family he was a constant and generous benefactor. He was admitted in Bene't College, Cambridge, under the tuition of Dr. Cory, 12 Oct. 1685; B. A. 1689; and, the learned Dr. Spencer with the body having a just regard to his talents and improvement, he was chosen a Fellow 20 Nov. 1690, upon the cession of Mr. Jolland. He took the degree of M. A. 1693; having about that period been appointed Master of the ancient Grammar School at Bishops-Stortford, at a time when its reputation was quite in ruins, and had nothing to recommend it but the name of Leigh (father and son) not even yet out of mind; but he raised it to a great degree of fame, as the numbers sent by him to his own and other Colleges attested : and considerably increased the trade of the town by such a beneficial concourse. The gentlemen of Hertfordshire and Essex having, at his earnest request and intreaty, rebuilt the school, he took great pains to procure the sums necessary for completing it, from those who had been educated in that town. The new school stood in the High-street, with the West-front to the church-yard, consisting of three rooms, which, with the stair-case, made a square building, one of which was the Grammar-school, and took up the half of it, all the front to the street; the other two were a Library and Writing-school. These were upon arches, under which were a market and shops, the property of the parish. June 23, 1699, on his marriage with Anne one of the daughters of Richard Lydal, M. D. Warden of Merton College, Oxford, he resigned his Fellowship; and having, by honest application and industry, raised the school to great repute, and acquired a large fortune, he purchased, in 1701, the manor of Bumpstead Hall in Essex. He took the degree of D. D. in 1702; by which time the Library was well furnished by his diligence; as he continually added to it at his own expence, and procured a great number of valuable authors from gentlemen who had been his scholars. By his interest also and care, the gallery in the church for the use of the school was erected. He revived the annual School-feast, charging his estate with a yearly present to the Preacher on that occasion; and gave, by his will, 10*l.* for books to be added to the Library, and to the church a chalice of 20*l.* value. June 17, 1707, Dr. Tooke was presented by John Sandford, Esq. to the Rectory of Lamborn in that county; in 1712 he bought the advowson of Lamborn; and in the same year he purchased Manuden Hall in the same county from Mr. William Calvert. In 1713 he sold Bumpstead Hall, and bought the Manor of Priors, in the parish of Lamborn. He gave in his life-time 20*l.* to Bene't College, towards the increase of their Library, and providing an Oration in the Hall on the 29th of May; and, by his will, gave them in present the perpetual advowson of the

Rectory of Great Brackstead, which he had purchased some time before of the Duke of Norfolk; and the reversion of that of Lamborn, which they were not to have till 50 years after his death. And it was thought by his friends that he would have been a more considerable Benefactor to the Society, had they elected him their Master, or gratified him by the choice of his Friend Dean Moss.

Dr. Tooke died May 24, 1721, aged 54, after more than 30 years intent and successful labours; and was buried in Lamborn church.

Benjamin *Tucke* was born about 1642; and, after having served an apprenticeship to Mr. John Crooke, was admitted a Freeman and Liveryman of the Stationers Company in February 1665-6. He was for some years Steward, and afterwards Treasurer, of St. Bartholomew's Hospital; and died about 1716.

His son Benjamin Tooke was born about 1670, and admitted on the Livery in March 1694-5. He was the Bookseller of Swift and Pope, and is immortalized in their respective publications. He died in 1732, leaving a considerable estate to his brother Andrew; whose literary merit claims a niche in this repository.

Andrew Tooke, second son of the elder Benjamin, was born in 1673; educated at the Charter-house, and at Clare Hall, Cambridge; B. A. 1693; chosen Usher at the Charter-house 1695; M.A. 1697; Professor of Geometry at Gresham College, 1709, in the room of Dr. Hooke, Fellow of the Royal Society, who met in his apartment there till they left the College in 1710. He was chosen Head School-master at the Charter-house in 1728; and in 1729 he married the widow of Dr. Levett, Physician to the House; and in that year resigned his Professorship, attending solely to his school, till he was carried off by a dropsy, January 20, 1731, aged 58. He had taken Deacon's orders, and sometimes preached. He published "Synopsis Græcæ Linguæ, 1711." A correct Translation of Pomey's "Pantheon," the 10th edition, 1726, and many succeeding ones. A Translation of Puffendorf's "Whole Duty of Man according to the Law of Nature, 1716." A Latin Version of Bishop Gastrell's "Christian Institutes, 1718." Ovid's "Fasti," from the Delphin 4to edition. "An exact Copy of the Last Will and Testament of Sir Thomas Gresham, Knight, 1724." His Library was sold by auction in 1732. He was buried in the chapel at the Charter-house.

The Rev. William Tooke, after having received a liberal classical education, obtained, in 1771, letters of ordination, both as Deacon and Priest, from Dr. Terrick, then Bishop of London; and in the same year, when on the point of settling on the living of West Thurrock in Essex, at the solicitation of the Rev. John Duncombe, then Rector, he heard of the vacancy of the place of Minister of the English Church at Cronstadt, an Island in the Gulph of Finland, subject to Russia, and serving as the great Sea-port to that part of the Empire. This opened too flattering a prospect to his curious and inquisitive turn of mind, to be rejected. Accordingly, on application to the Russia Company, the Governor, George Nettleton, Esq. observing qualities in him that attracted his regard, took him amicably by the hand, and his election followed. Arriving at Cronstadt about the commencement of the shipping season, his Church, which had been shut up three years, since the decease of the Rev. Mr. Lewis, was now thronged with masters of vessels and their crews. Here he remained three years, during which time, by his frequent visits to St. Petersburg, he so conciliated the favour and friendship of the Merchants of whom the Factory there consisted, that they, upon the sudden and unexpected resignation of Dr. John Glen King in 1774, unanimously signed a letter of recommendation in his behalf to the Russia Company in London; in consequence of which Mr. Tooke was appointed Chaplain to the Factory at St. Petersburg.

In that Imperial Residence, besides his intimacy, arising no less from sentiments of affection than from the obligations of his pastoral office, with the families of his proper province, he enjoyed the favourable regards of many persons of distinction at the Court of the Empress. The Orlofs, the Gallitzins, the Narishkins, Prince Potemkin, the Princess Dashkof, Count Bouturlin, and several others, communicated with him on a friendly footing. But what he considered of no inferior consequence was the opportunity afforded him of forming and cultivating an acquaintance with persons eminent for their talents and science, Natives as well as Foreign Ambassadors and Travellers from all parts; for Petersburg was at that time what the Hague had formerly been, the principal resort of diplomatic characters. Among the Academicians he was particularly intimate with those Luminaries in Science, the Professors Euler, father and son, and Pallas, with Guldenstædt, Krafft, Lepechin; in converse with whom he was able to reap and to communicate much information, and to which his fluency in speaking the French language afforded him great facilities. With many of the Hierarchy of the orthodox Greek church he kept up a constant intercourse. Gabriel, the Metropolitan, had him frequently at his Palace, the Nefski Monastery; where he was often in company with Plato, Archbishop of Moscow; Eugenius, Archbishop of Kherson, who gave him his translation into Greek of the Poet Virgil; and Pamphilief, the Empress's Confessor, who presented him with his picture. On the invitation of Procopius, Bishop of Kargapol and Olonetz, he made a visit to that Prelate at his Palace on the banks of the Onega, at the Monastery of St. Alexander Svirskoi. At Berlin, in 1783, in consequence of letters of recommendation from Professor Euler, he was introduced to the celebrated M. Formey, Secrétaire perpetuel, and by him to the Members of the Royal Academy in that capital; where he likewise found Professor Burja, with whom he renewed the intimacy he had formerly enjoyed with that elegant scholar at Petersburg. At Konigsberg he had frequent conversations with that profound and eccentric Philosopher M. Kant.

In his situation at Petersburg, my Friend continued eighteen years; and during that period how he employed the hours of leisure allowed him from the duties of his Church, his "History of the Reign of Catherine II." his "View of the Russian Empire," and his "History of Russia," render it entirely needless to mention. In 1777 his friend Stephen Falconet (1716 — 1791), then employed in his grand work, the famous Colossal Equestrian Statue of Peter the Great, wishing to give some idea of his talents and genius as a Statuary to the English publick; Mr. Tooke was induced to favour his laudable ambition, by giving his Treatise on the Statue of Marcus Aurelius, and some other of his Essays and Letters that passed between him and M. Diderot, an English dress. This done, he transmitted to me the MS. which I printed and published accordingly. In 1782 Mr. Tooke was elected a Fellow of the Royal Society of London; a few years afterwards a Member of the Imperial Academy of Sciences, and the following year a Member of the Free Economical Society at St. Petersburg. Thus agreeably situated, surrounded by a society of friends and acquaintance, many of them now of a long standing, and enjoying the accommodations of elegant life, while as yet not meditating a return to his native country, in 1792 he received the unwelcome intelligence of the demise of a valued and honoured Relative; by which event, however, such an addition to his patrimony devolved to him, as enabled him to settle with suitable dignity in the country alone preferable, in his estimation, to that to which he now resolved to bid adieu.

As some of his Letters happen to lie now before me, which are descriptive of manners very different from our own, a few extracts from them will be found not destitute of interest. The date of the first I take up is St. Petersburg, October 5, 1771. "Several fires having lately happened in the town, by which not fewer than a hundred buildings of various descriptions have been destroyed, besides other property to a great amount; and some circumstances since occurring which excited a suspicion that the mischief was not imputable solely to accident, an Imperial ukase was issued, commanding that no person should be seen in the streets after 10 o'clock at night, without a lantern, excepting doctors, pastors, and midwives; wisely judging that persons of these professions were liable to be called for at any hour of the night, and not have time to make this provision. My friend Dr. H. having passed the evening at a merchant's house some distance from his own, at about 11 o'clock took his leave, and was proceeding to the door, when his host insisted on his taking with him a servant carrying a lantern before him, as the night was very dark. The Doctor for some time resisted the friendly importunity; but in vain. He must comply. Accordingly Daniela was called, and with the lantern in his hand marched before the Physician. They had not proceeded above a quarter of their way, when they were stopt by the *caraoulchik,* or watchman, who seized my friend, and told him 'he must go with him to the *boutka* or watchhouse.' 'And for what?' exclaimed the Doctor. 'No matter for what,' replied the guardian of the night; 'you must come along with me: I know what you are.' The Doctor, not conscious of any harm in what he had said or done, endeavoured to expostulate with the man. But to no purpose. In short, after being confined in the stinking *boutka* all night, he was in the morning taken to the police; where the accusation brought against him was: that he, being a Doctor, was found walking in the street after 10 o'clock *with* a lantern carried before him. — You will anticipate the sequel. He was discharged, paying his fees; and the law was explained to the comprehension of the vigilant watchman, to prevent his making similar mistakes for the future.

"Shortly after the breaking out of the French Revolution, an order was published that no three persons should be seen to stand talking together in the streets. Taking a walk one day, soon after the appearance of this ukase, about the time when people were returning from the Exchange, I met an acquaintance, of whom I naturally inquired concerning the news of the day; what the letters from England brought, &c. Presently we were joined by another; then again by another. As we stood thus conversing in one of the recesses of the bridge over the Neva, up comes a *Desatnick*, or constable, accosting us with, 'Come, gentlemen, march away, if you please.' 'No, brother,' answered I, 'we don't please to march away. We prefer staying here.' 'But you *must* go,' returned the officer. 'But that *must* will happen only when we please,' rejoined I. 'Have not you heard of the ukase?' said he. 'What ukase?' 'Why, the ukase that says no three persons are to be seen talking together in the streets.' 'Well; what is that to us? have not you learnt to count? how many are we here?' Upon this he counted, '*odin, dwa, tre, chetiré*,' one, two, three, four. 'Well; now you see the law does not relate to us: that says *three.*' 'Very true, gentlemen; I ask your pardon. I was mistaken. Tarry as long as you please.'

"Mildness and goodnature are conspicuous features in the character of the Empress. Something suddenly occurs to her mind that might prove advantageous to her subjects. An ukase is immediately issued; and at first all is bustle to put it in execution Perhaps in two months it is entirely gone by and forgot. She lately took it into her head that we were ruining ourselves by extravagant living. Accordingly sumptuary laws were to be framed. Among other articles of luxury, carriages were not omitted. The law declared that no person not being above the rank of a Brigadier should be permitted to have any gilding upon his carriage. Upon this, all the merchants sent their chariots and coaches to the coachmakers, to be painted of one colour. You would have thought all the members of the Factory were turned Quakers. My chariot, being a remarkably neat one, had an elegant gilt ogee round the borders, which I could not resolve upon effacing, as it was that bit of ornament which, according to the fashion, gave a relief to the pannels, and procured it the admiration with which it was honoured. My friends wondered at the audacity which could prompt me to contravene the Imperial mandate. They urged, 'that my family would be stopped in the public street; that the penalty was no less than a hundred ducats; in short, that I rendered myself obnoxious to inconveniences and humiliations which I ought to avoid.' I however gave their remonstrances to the wind. Being to dine one day at Baron Sutherland's, the *Maître de police* (the Lord Mayor) was among the guests. Sitting before dinner in the drawing-room, the Baron, in his jocose manner, said: *'Votre Excellence,* here is our Pastor, who drives about the town with gilding on his carriage in defiance of the ukase.' 'How is that?' said his Excellence. 'Of what rank are you?' 'That I should be glad to be informed of by your Excellence.' 'What rank do you bear in your own country, Mons. le Pasteur, are you above a brigadier?' 'A brigadier forsooth! I am out of sight of a Brigadier. A Brigadier would think it an honour to pull off his hat to me.' 'Oh, then,' returned his Excellence, 'wear as much gold upon your carriage as you please.' — You perceive from the several instances I have given you, that the mode of expounding the laws in this country is truly exemplary."

With the Lutheran, Calvinistic, and other Pastors of the Reformed Communions, Mr. Tooke kept up a regular intercourse, by alternate meetings at the houses of each other. But the most conspicuous and pleasant of all assemblies of this nature, was the annual dinner given by her Majesty to the Ministers of Religion of all denominations in the Imperial City, and which she was pleased to call her *Diner de Tolerance,* or Toleration Dinner. At this the Archbishop Gabriel presided in full costume, as, indeed, were all the guests. On his right usually sat Plato, when in attendance on the Court, and on his left the *Angliski pastor,* or English Pastor; the others *seniores priores.* Pamphilief, the Imperial Confessor, and a Hiero-monach, with a napkin under his arm, taking his rounds to see that the guests were well served. It was truly a sumptuous banquet, and not more sumptuous than harmonious, and even facetious. Provisions of the best; with the choicest wines, and a desert from the Imperial Gardens and Hot-houses. Oh! If all the controversies of the Christian Church had been argued over Burgundy and Champain, they would, indeed, have cost more Christian wine; but, if we may judge from these councils, infinitely less Christian blood. As the extract,

however, will not prove tedious, and as the memory of such
a liberal institution deserves to be perpetuated with honour, I
shall here insert his own account of one of these convivial
meetings, as I find it in a note at page 119 of the Life of
Catherine II. vol. iii. 4th edition: "Ivan Pamphilief, her
Majesty's Confessor, invited the Clergy of the several Communions in Petersburg to dine with him annually on the 6th
of January; who generally met in a company of fifteen or
sixteen different denominations, all in the several habits of their
Church. At these agreeable meetings, his Eminence Gabriel,
Metropolitan Archbishop of Novgorod and St. Petersburg, always presided. Pamphilief did the honours of the table, with
that hospitality and suavity of manners for which the Russians
are so celebrated among all who visit that country. When
wines of various sorts were served round upon a salver, the
beforementioned Metropolitan once observed, with a sensible
allusion to the occasion, 'These wines are all good: they differ
only in colour and flavour.' — The persons present at one of
these dinners, as an example of the rest, were: Gabriel, Metropolitan; Innocentius, Archbishop of Pscove and Riga; Eugenius,
Archbishop of Kherson, the famous Translator of Virgil into
Greek hexameter verse; Ivan Pamphilief: all Members of the
Holy Synod. Other Russian Clergy were, Procopius, Archimandrite, and Rector of the Gymnasium at the Nefski Monastir;
Antonius, Archimandrite; Basilius, Protopope; Andrew Sam-
borsky, Protopope of St. Sophia, formerly Chaplain to the
Embassy at London; Nectarius, Monk at the Greek Gymna-
sium; Sergius, Monk; Livitzi, Pope of the Imperial Chapel;
Basilius, Pope of the Annunciation; with several other Popes
and Monks. Lutheran Preachers: Joachim Christian Grott,
great grandson of the famous Hugo Grotius; Jeremiah Lewis
Hoffman; Emanuel Indrenius, Pastor of the Swedish Church;
John Henry Krogius, Pastor of the Finns Church; John
George Lampe, of St. Peter's Church; Thomas Roinbott, of
St. Anne's Church; Martin Luther Wolff, also of St. Peter's;
Daniel Zachert. Ministers of the Reformed: John David
Collins, Pastor of the German Reformed Church; N. Mans-
bendel, Pastor of the French; William Tooke, of the English
Church; M. Reuter, of the Dutch; and Christian Frederick
Gregor, Pastor of the Congregation of the Herrenhuyters, or
brethren of the Unitas Fratrum. Roman Catholic Clergy:
Sergius Krachinsky; Petrus Stankievitch; Hieronymus Beroal-

digen; Johannes de Ducla; Armenian Clergy: Marcarius Kos-
kumof; Stephenus Lorismilikof; Niketa Cherkesof.Bishops and
Priests from the Greek Islands, from Valakhia, Moldavia, and
the worthy Abbé Guadalupe, from Mexico. At the conclusion
of the repast, the Metropolitan usually said, with a loud voice,
either in Russ or Latin, 'Glory to God in the highest! — On
earth peace! — Goodwill toward men!' Which done, the rest
of the evening was spent in agreeable and pleasant conversation
over a dessert of exquisite fruit and the choicest wines. The
guests talked to one another in Russ, German, French, Italian,
&c. as it might happen to suit. But the general conversation
was carried on in Latin."

One passage from another of his Letters to me, as it happens
to lie open on my table, I cannot resist the temptation to communicate, though under no little dread of swelling this note
beyond all bounds of prolixity; for, were I to indulge the reader
and myself in this way as far as I chose, there would be no
end to it in view. "When it was in agitation at the Court of
Petersburg to establish a College of Jesuits in the province of
Mohilef in the year 1782, a project which the Empress from
political motives, which are elsewhere detailed more at large
[Life of Catherine II. vol. iii. p. 5], was desirous of bringing to
effect, she wrote to Pope Pius VI. expressing her wish to enter
upon a negotiation to that end. The Holy Father, in reply,
declared his willingness to accede to her Majesty's request, although the Society had been formally abolished by Clement
XIV. if means could be devised for absolving the Holy Chair
from a charge of inconsistency, which, in the minds of the
faithful, might appear to shake the infallibility of the Sovereign
Pontiff. In the mean time a fresh difficulty occurred. The
orthodox Greek faith being that established in Russia, a Nuncio
could not be dispatched thither from the Court of Rome. This
scruple was, however, soon got over by transmitting an order
to Archetti, Bishop of Chalcedon *in partibus infidelium,* then
legate *à latere* at Warsaw, to repair to Petersburg; [which he
accordingly did, and the event may be seen in the work above
referred to.] "Mr. Tooke happened accidentally to be walking
on the Custom-house quay while the baggage of the Prelate
was bringing on shore from the galliot. The Officers of the
Customs were proceeding in their duty, when all at once the
two Chaplains who attended on the part of the Bishop brought
out a crimson velvet case (one having it in his hands, and the

other bare-headed, solemnly marching before). This was not to be touched by the Officers. 'Well; do you open it.' It contained a large old rotten bone. 'What is this?' 'It is the thigh-bone of St. John the Baptist.' 'Well; what is it worth?' (Now it should be known, that every kind of goods, wares, or commodities, not severally specified in the tariff, must pay duty *ad valorem*.) 'Worth! I said before, it is the thigh-bone of St. John the Baptist.' 'Well; and I say again, what is it worth?' Worth! no value can be set upon it.' 'Well; if it is of no value, why do you take the pains to bring it with you?' 'It is not to be valued, because it is inestimable.' 'How then,' returned the Officer, 'are inestimable wares to be rated *ad valorem?*' This problem seemed for a moment to nonplus even the disciple of Loyola. 'It is a sacred relic.' Still the question recurred, 'Well: what is it worth?' The result was, that, in order to save time, it was for the present laid aside. Next came out a box, ornamented with pearls and precious stones. This was found to contain a lock of the Virgin Mary's hair [which my Friend till then had thought to have been a bright red, but he is now convinced it was only a dark brown]. To this succeeded a long list of holy trumpery. But the business of farther examination was happily terminated by an order from Court to pass the whole baggage of the Prelate without exacting the dues. But," adds my Friend, "those who have had affairs to transact at no other than an English Custom-house, will with difficulty conceive the patient simplicity, the complaisant humility, the respectful suavity, so natural to Russian subordinates, with which these interrogatories were prosecuted." And the result he draws from the little occurrence, of no moment perhaps in itself, is this: "that in all controversies with Papists, and with others who are previously determined to be in the right, the best method is to grant their postulate, and only ask what it is worth; thus would many a religious dispute be cut short.]

JOHN URRY'S "CHAUCER"

ABOUT the latter end of the year 1711, it was proposed to Mr. Urry, who was a native of Scotland, by some persons well acquainted with his qualifications (who, he thought, had a right to command him), to put out a new edition of Chaucer; which he was persuaded to undertake, though much against his inclination. This recommendation was, probably, from Dean Aldrich, who well knew the talents of his pupil. — Having undertaken the task, Mr. Urry proceeded on it with such great diligence, that he thought it prudent to apply for a patent for the exclusive right of printing the work; which he obtained, July 20, 1714; and on December 17 assigned it to Mr. Bernard Lintot, by whom Proposals for publishing the work were issued in January 1714-15. But the design was very soon retarded by Mr. Urry's death, which happened on the 19th of the following March. That this excellent critic was one of the wits of Christ Church may be inferred from *Rag Smith's* having addressed to him a ludicrous analysis of his Latin Ode on Dr. Pocock, preserved by Dr. Johnson in his "Lives of the English Poets," art. *Smith*. He was remarkable for his learning and industry, for great charity, constant integrity, and a peculiar happiness of being always agreeable to his private friends. His gratitude to the place of his education it was his intention to express by a legacy of 500*l*. towards the new building of Peckwater; and he often took occasion to tell his friends with what cheerfulness he went on with his work, as it would enable him the better to perform his pious and generous intention; which, though he did not live to accomplish, was in some measure performed by his executor, William Brome, esq. (his intimate friend and fellow-student at Christ Church), as appears by the following heads of an "Agreement, August 16, 1715, between William Brome, executor to Mr. Urry, the Dean and Chapter of Christ Church, Oxon, and Bernard Lintot, bookseller; reciting the Queen's licence to Urry, to print Chaucer for fourteen years, from July 25, 1714, assigned over by him to Lintot, December 17 following. Urry, dying soon after, left Brome executor. The agreement recites Urry's intention to apply part of the profits towards building Peckwater Quadrangle. Brome assigns his right to the Glossary and licence to Lintot for remainder of the term; the Dean and Chapter and Mr. Broome to deliver to Lintot a complete copy of Chaucer and Glossary, and to correct it, or get it corrected. Lintot to print 1250 copies, 250 on royal paper, and 1000 on demy, at his own charge, and to furnish a number of copies not exceeding 1500; and have one-third of the profit. If the subscribers did not amount to 1250, then the remainder to be sold, and the profits equally divided; the Dean and Chapter's share to be applied to finish Peckwater Quadrangle.

	l.	s.	d.
1000 copies small paper, at 30s.	1500	0	0
250 large, at 50s.	625	0	0
	2125	0	0
Lintot one-third	708	6	8
Remainder for Dean and Chapter and Mr. Brome	1416	13	4

Mr. Lintot in 1715 circulated *new* Proposals for the publication of Chaucer; to which the following paragraph in the Preface has allusion: "I must not leave this subject [the Glossary] without doing justice to that worthy gentleman whose name was mentioned in the last Proposals for this Edition, as having undertaken *a more useful and copious Glossary for the better understanding of this Poet.* Such a work, performed by a person of his extensive learning and uncommon knowledge in this particular study, would have fully answered that character. But, as we are deprived of the benefit of his labours in this kind (for what reasons I am not at this time satisfied), I would not have his reputation suffer by the imperfections of this performance; and therefore am bound to acquit him of having any hand in compiling this Glossary. The number of *Errata* needs no apology to such as are acquainted with works of this nature; especially if it be considered that my distance from the press could not, without very much retarding the work, allow me to revise the sheets more than once." — Mr. Brome, though he took care that the work was properly published, was not the actual Editor; for the gentleman who undertook that office says, "I was equally a stranger to Mr. Urry, and his undertaking, till some time after his death; when a person, whose commands I was in all duty bound to obey, put the works of Chaucer into my hands, with his instructions to assist in carrying on this edition, and to prepare matters for a Glossary to it. Mr. Thomas Ainsworth, of Christ Church, has been employed by Mr. Urry in transcribing part of the work for the press, and was therefore thought qualified to proceed in preparing the rest for my perusal. This gentleman likewise died, in August 1719, soon after the whole text of Chaucer was printed off. Had he lived, he could have given a fuller account of this work than is to be expected here, which, I am persuaded, he would not have declined; but, as he always had the greatest veneration for the memory of Mr. Urry, would have readily embraced such an opportunity of expressing it." — A very fair and full account of Urry's edition is to be seen in the modest and sensible preface prefixed to it by Mr. *Timothy Thomas**, upon whom the charge of publishing Chaucer devolved, or rather was imposed, after Mr. Urry's death. — [Mr. A. Chalmers possesses a large-paper copy of Urry's Chaucer, a present from Mr. Timothy Thomas, which has many MS corrections in his hand. Among others he says that Bishop Atterbury was the chief person who proposed to Urry to undertake an edition of Chaucer. Mr. Thomas adds, that the Bishop (then dean of Christ Church) "did by no means judge rightly of Mr. Urry's talents in this case; who, though in many respects a most worthy person, was not qualified for a work of this nature." Mr. Chalmers's copy is corrected throughout in the same hand, and the principal additions signed T.T.] — The strange licence in which Mr. Urry appears to have indulged himself, of lengthening and shortening Chaucer's words according to his own fancy, and even adding words of his own without giving his readers the least notice, has made the text of his edition by far the worst ever published.

GEORGE VERTUE

GEORGE VERTUE, an eminent engraver and diligent collector of Antiquities relative both to his Art and the History of England, and no less distinguished by the amiable sincerity and integrity of his heart, was born in the parish of St. Martin in the Fields, 1684. His parents, he says himself, were

---

*"I learn this from a MS note in an interleaved copy of Urry's Chaucer, presented to the British Museum by Mr. *William Thomas.*

more honest than opulent. After serving three or four years as part of an apprenticeship with a master who engraved arms on plate, and had the chief business in London, but who, being unfortunate, retired to France, his native country, Vertue entered into a seven years' engagement with Michael Vandergucht, engraving copper-plates for him, till, in 1709, having received instructions and advice from several Painters, he began business for himself, and passed the first year in drawing and engraving for booksellers. He was early in life distinguished by Mr. Prior; who, in his lines on Tom Britton, joins Vertue with Sir Godfrey Kneller. He was also introduced to many persons of taste and eminence; which gave a shining appearance to the morning of his fortune. His mother was left a widow, with several children. "I was the eldest," he says, "and then the only child that could help them; which added circumspection to my affairs then, as well as industry to the end of my life." At intervals he practised drawing and music; and studied the French, Italian, and Dutch languages. Lord Somers employed him to engrave a plate of Abp. Tillotson; which he performed admirably, and was nobly rewarded. In 1711 he was one of the first members of the Academy of Painting then established, of which Sir Godfrey Kneller was at the head; and he continued till the end of that year to engrave portraits from Kneller, Dahl, Richardson, Jervase, Gilson, and others. On the accession of the present Royal Family, he engraved an admirable likeness of the new King, from a painting by Kneller, of which many thousands were sold. It was shewn at Court; and followed by portraits of the Prince and Princess. He commenced his researches after the lives of British Artists so early as 1713; and soon found a Mæcenas in that munificent collector Robert Harley, the second earl of Oxford; and another patron in Heneage Finch, earl of Winchelsea; who, having been elected President of the Society of Antiquaries on their revival in 1717, appointed Mr. Vertue, who was a member, to be their Engraver. He continued to execute the Society's prints till his death; and the prices of some of his earliest performances for them were:

1718. Richard II. in Westminster Abbey, copper-plate included 21*l.*;

1719. Ulphus's Horn 2*l.*;

1721. Shrine of Edward the Confessor (the Society found the plate) 15*l.* 15s.;

Waltham Cross, including paper and working-off 5*l*.

He also engraved the Oxford Almanacks from 1723 to his death; and embellished them by views of public buildings and historic events. The visits he paid to most of the galleries of the Nobility, and to the Universities, in search of English portraits, suggested a design of engraving a great variety of them, as well as of historic prints. With Lord Colerane, one of his noble patrons, he visited Salisbury, Winchester, and Stonehenge; with Mr. Stephens the Historiographer, St. Alban's, Verulam, and Gorhambury; with the Earl of Oxford, after passing a week at Wimpole, to Stamford, Burleigh, Grantham, Lincoln, and Welbeck; and in 1728 he accompanied the Duke of Dorset to Knowle and Penshurst.

In 1730 appeared his twelve heads of celebrated Poets; and that he had taken some considerable pains respecting the authenticity of them, appears from the following letter :

"MR. CHRISTIAN, Pray inform my Lord Harley that I have on Thursday last seen the daughter of Milton the Poet. I carried with me two or three different prints of Milton's picture, which she immediately knew to be like her father; and told me her mother-in-law (if living in Cheshire) had two pictures of him, one when he was a school-boy, and the other when he was about twenty. She knows of no other picture of him, because she was several years in Ireland, both before and after his death. She was the youngest of Milton's daughters by his first wife, and was taught to read to her father several languages. Mr. Addison was desirous to see her once, and desired she would bring with her testimonials of being Milton's daughter; but, as soon as she came into the room, he told her she needed none, her face having much of the likeness of the pictures he had seen of him. For my part, I find the features of her face very much like the prints. I showed her the painting I have to engrave, which she believes not to be her father's picture, it being of a brown complexion, and black hair, and curled locks. On the contrary, he was of a fair complexion, a little red in his cheeks, and light brown lank hair.   GEO. VERTUE."

After this, he again visited Oxford, Gloucester, Burford, Ditchley, Blenheim, and Cambridge; and soon after published the portraits of King Charles I. and his loyal adherents; and was was employed three years by the Knaptons in illustrating Rapin.

The name of Mr. Vertue is enrolled in the list of the Gentlemen's Society at Spalding; and that he was an attentive corresponding member the following letter, addressed to Maurice Johnson, junior, esq. the Secretary of that Society, will testify.

"DEAR SIR, *London, July* 29, 1732.

"Your kind and obliging letter has much more than repaid the courtesy you intended me of a visit, which I could no ways expect but with your conveniency, when you had spare time on your hands. Though that may not happen so soon as I desire it, still your kind and friendly sentiments on those few things I have heretofore shewn you, encouraged me then to wish for an opportunity of hearing your opinion about some others lately come into my hands, and that I know not how long they may continue with me, they being marbles, Roman, with inscriptions, and two antique brass statues. Our Society has adjourned. Mr. West is gone to France. Messrs. Gale are out of town. But, in relation to your request, I wish this sketch [of Roger Bacon] may be of any use. The original, from which I drew that I have, is painted in oil-colours; upon a thick board; the ground blue, the habit of a dark or black; the whole picture not quite so big as the life. It is now at Knowle, the seat of the Duke of Dorset, in Kent. With this picture of Bacon is also, in the same gallery, many other learned men of early time in Europe: all probably collected early in Queen Elizabeth's time, by Thomas Sack-ville, afterwards Earl of Dorset, and Lord Treasurer before he died; a nobleman excellent for his great learning and other noble endowments. His picture I am now about to engrave; and that of his great-grandson, the right noble Duke of Dorset, now Lord-lieutenant of Ireland. — I have lately made a tour for a few days, and have seen Mr. Willis's Collection of English Coins; which are very perfect, and in great number; especially amongst his silver, he has a great many scarce pieces. And in my ramble have seen those admirable remains of the Arundel Collection of marbles, statues, busts, altars, bas-relievos, &c. now in the possession of the Lord Pomfret; with many other fine paintings, there and other places. — Mr. Folkes is in Norfolk. For his use I borrowed a small piece of gold, a coin of King James the First, from Mr. Willis; but still want one small piece more, to complete a plate of that King's coin that I am about, (that is) a quarter-piece of gold of King James, with

JACOB. D. G. ANG. SCOT. FR. HIB. REX. These pieces were coined in the very beginning of his reign. The whole and the half-piece, we have; but want the quarter. The other sceptre pieces have MAG. BRIT. FR. &c. which were struck the succeeding years of his reign. — Sir, wishing you all the pleasure of seeing daily improvement in your young Academists, that they may cultivate so fine and rare an opportunity, and distinguish themselves to the world in a virtuous and eminent degree, that we may both live to see it, that you may have the felicity of their grateful acknowledgments, is, dear Sir, the hearty wishes of your affectionate and obliged humble servant to command,

GEO. VERTUE."

In 1733 Mr. Beaupré Bell mentions Mr. Vertue as "having more business upon his hands than he could dispatch; and, being unacquainted with the abbreviations, &c. found on coins, not caring to engage in a work where he may probably err, though a greater price was proposed to him than any other engraver would demand." (Reliquiæ Galeanæ, p. 490.) — In 1734 he renewed his journeys through England, and accompanied Roger Gale to St. Alban's, Northampton, and Warwick; and in 1737 the Earl of Leicester carried him to Penshurst. His prices for portraits at that period may be partly learnt from his answer to a question from Dr. Z. Grey, July 19, 1737: "Mr. West is a gentleman so much my friend, that I can't forget easily any recommendation from him, and on his account (if it was not my own inclination) I should use every one civily. What you propose to have done I can't justly be certain as to the expence of engraving; because for octavo plates, the head only of any person, I have had different prices, as the difficulty or labour is more or less. The general prices I have had for such works, has been 10 guineas, 8 guineas, and 6 the lowest, from pictures, paintings being done — indeed, when from a print bigger or lesser than is already engraved, it may cost a fourth or fifth part less, or near thereabouts. In respect to a print, if it be any noted one, I can soon send you a certain answer, if you please to let me know your intention; and shall think it no trouble, if you please to direct a line as before to, Sir, your respectful servant. G. VERTUE."

At the end of this year he again visited Oxford; and thence went to Compton Verney, Warwick, Coventry, Birmingham, and Coleshill, to Mr. Sheldon's at Weston, to Blenheim, Beaconsfield, Windsor, and Eton. In 1738 he made a tour through Kent, Sussex, and Hampshire, visiting Rochester, Canterbury, Chichester, Portsmouth, Southampton, and Winchester; and then to Petworth, Goodwood, Stansted, and Cowdray, of which he made various sketches and notes. He next engaged with Mr. Knapton in engraving the Illustrious Heads; and in 1739 accompanied Lord Colerane to Walpole in Norfolk, who carried him to Wansted, Moulsham, Gosfield, St. Edmund's Bury, Sir Andrew Fountaine's, Houghton, and Lynn. — In 1740 he published Proposals for a very valuable series of historic prints; and copied, for the Earl of Oxford, Queen Elizabeth's Progress to Hunsdon, most exactly, in water-colours; and received for it a handsome present in plate. He was now at the summit of his humble wishes; but his happiness was suddenly dashed, by the loss of his noble friend the Earl, June 16, 1741. "Death," says he emphatically, "put an end to that life that had been the support, cherisher, and comfort of many, many others, who are left to lament — but none more heartily than Vertue!" So struck was the poor man with this signal misfortune, that for two years there is an *hiatus* in his history — he had not spirits ever to be minute. He revived in 1743, by the favour of the Duke of Norfolk; for whom he engraved the large plate of the Earl of Arundel and his family, and collected two volumes of the Works of Hollar. The Countess Dowager of Oxford alleviated to him the loss of her lord; their daughter the Duchess of Portland befriended him; as did the Duke of Portland and the Earl of Burlington; and he, for a very short time, found a Royal Patron in Frederick Prince of Wales; who died March 20, 1751, and whom Vertue most pathetically laments. He lost his friends; but his piety, mildness, and ingenuity, never forsook him. He laboured almost to the last, solicitous to leave a decent competence to a wife with whom he had lived many years in tender harmony.

HORACE WALPOLE

A Communication from George Hardinge to John Nichols

"DEAR SIR,   *Milbourne-House,* June 22.
"I was intimate with HORACE WALPOLE for several years.

When I became familiar with his effeminacy of manners, it was lost in his wit, ingenuity, and whimsical but entertaining fund of knowledge.

"Though he was elegant and polished, he was not, I think, *well-bred,* in the best view of that phrase. He demanded a full stretch of admiring homage to his *bons-mots,* and rather lectured in a series of prose epigrams, than conversed playfully and so as to put the hearer quite at his ease.

"In the course of his kind predilection for me, a peculiar incident occurred, which I shall never forget. He had invited me to his Elysium (of its kind) Strawberry Hill. On my arrival, I found a note. He was gone to Houghton upon a sudden call; but insisted that I should pass the day and sleep under his roof, and with keys of all his treasures. I did not, and could not, go to bed for many hours after midnight.

"Dr. Akenside had *no wit.* — Horace Walpole had infinitely *too much:* his prose epigrams were unremitted, and left the hearer no resting-place. He talked as he wrote; and one left him, at least I did, fatigued, though charmed with his enlivening sallies. They were a demand upon the animal spirits, which almost invaded *the liberty of the subject,* the liberty of being dull, or of lying fallow. When definitions are made even by such a man as Mr. Locke of the boundaries which divide Wit from Humour, he puzzles common readers, and perhaps in part himself. But living instances are the best of all definitions. Lord Chesterfield and Mr. Walpole had unexampled powers in *wit* — of *humour* they had no conception. Fielding and Addison were pre-eminent examples and models of *humour,* though in different branches of it. The mock heroic irony of Addison was a more elevated cast of the power than Fielding possessed, who was only at home in the *Farce of Nature.* Mr. Walpole has often told me that he himself had no enjoyment of *Tom Jones.* 'It *might* be *nature,*' he said, '*it might* be *humour;* but it was of a kind that could not interest *him.*' I pitied him, as I should pity a man who had not all his five senses. There was a degree of quaintness in Mr. Walpole's wit; but it was not unbecoming in *him,* for it seemed a part of *his* nature. Some of his friends were as effeminate in appearance and in manner as himself, and were as witty. Of these I remember two, Mr. Chute and Mr. George Montagu. But others had effeminacy alone to recommend them.

"In his taste for architecture and *vertû* there was both whim and foppery, but still with fancy and with genius.

"His little *jeux d'esprits* in prose (for he terribly failed in verse) are jewels, and perhaps above them all his papers in *The World.* When I say that he failed in verse, I must except that striking Play, *The Mysterious Mother,* which, in a very original vein, is full of dramatic genius and of picturesque effect. *The Castle of Otranto* is a model of its kind; and there is a wonderful grace in the language, which is neither too familiar nor too elevated. It seems inseparable from the characters, the scenery, and the incidents. The *Historic Doubts* are very entertaining and well-reasoned. His manner of relating a fact, or of describing a character, was quite his own. I never saw it equalled.

"His politics were as *illegible,* if I may use that phrase, as those of Dr. Akenside. His partiality for his father was amiable, but in the outrage of it absurd. He was for a time a zealot in the cause of Liberty. But in the course of time that spirit cooled, and at last it flamed in the fury of his aversion, just in its principle, to all the sanguinary horrors in France, and their champions here.

"His passion for *Mad. Deffand* was the most wonderful incident of his life; congenial talents and mutual vanity attached and connected them; but she was *too young for him,* though superannuated in years, and by others at least more admired than beloved. I lament, for his honour, that such a correspondence has been published.

"We are told, in your entertaining *"Anecdotes,"* that Warburton was the best Letter-writer of the age. In my judgment Horace Walpole was infinitely superior to him and all his contemporaries in that pleasing but equivocal talent. I had many of his Letters for several years; and have retained some of them, which are delightfully entertaining and clever. Letters, however, especially if written by men of the world, supply no test of the writer's genuine sentiments.

"I have great pleasure in sending you a copy of a Letter from him, which I think beautiful, in his best manner. The Letter also which accompanies it in my packet is not inferior to it; and you are welcome to both of them.

"Upon the subject of Grignan I will indulge a little egotism; it is the food of age, as music is that of love. Mr. Walpole and I agreed in our passion for Madame Sévigné; and when I made a little tour in 1776, that passion carried me to the Château de Grignan, where I passed a day or two, and at my own cost obtained, I think, four drawings of it, which he accepted most gracefully, and which he has done me the honour to make heir-looms at Strawberry Hill.

"Strawberry Hill, July 4, 1779.

"I have now received the drawings of Grignan, and know not how to express my satisfaction and gratitude but by a silly witticism that is like the studied quaintness of the last age. In short, they are so much more beautiful than I expected, that I am *not* surprized at *your* having surprized me by exceeding even what I expected from your well-known kindness to me. They are charmingly executed, and with great taste. I own too that Grignan is grander, and in a much finer situation, than I had imagined, as I concluded that the witchery of Madame de Sévigné's ideas and style had spread the same leaf-gold over *places* with which she gilded her *friends.* All that has appeared of *them* since the publication of her Letters has lowered them. A single letter of her daughter, that to Paulina with a description of the Duchess of Bourbon's toilette, is worthy of the mother. Paulina's own letters contain not a tittle worth reading; one just divines that she might have written well if she had had any thing to write about (which, however, would not have signified to her Grandmother). Coulanges was a silly good-humoured glutton, that flattered a rich widow for her dinners. His wife was sensible : but dry, and rather peevish at growing old. Unluckily nothing more has come to light of Mad. de Sévigné's son, whose short letters in the collection I am almost *profane* enough to prefer to his mother's; and which makes me astonished that she did not love his wit, so unaffected, and so congenial to her own, in preference to the eccentric and sophisticated reveries of her sublime and ill-humoured daughter. Grignan alone maintains its dignity, and shall be consecrated here among other monuments of that bewitching period, and amongst which one loves to lose one's self, and drink oblivion of an æra so very unlike; for the awkward bigots to despotism of our time have not Mad. de Sévigné's address, nor can paint

an Indian idol with an hundred hands as graceful as the Apollo
of the Belvidere. When will you come and accept my thanks?
will Wednesday next suit you? But do you know that I must ask
you not to leave your gown behind you, which indeed I never
knew you put on willingly, but to come in it. I shall want your
protection at Westminster Hall.

Yours, most cordially,   H. WALPOLE."

                                        "March 8, 1782.

"It is very pleasing to receive congratulation from a friend on
a friend's success — that success, however, is not so agreeable
as the universal esteem allowed to Mr. Conway's character,
which not only accompanies his triumph, but I believe contributed to it. To-day, I suppose, all but his character will be
reversed; for there must have been a miraculous change if the
Philistines do not bear as ample a testimony to their Dagon's
honour, as conviction does to that of a virtuous man. In truth,
I am far from desiring that the Opposition should prevail yet:
The Nation is not sufficiently changed, nor awakened enough,
and it is sure of having its feelings repeatedly attacked by more
woes; the blow will have more effect a little time hence: the
clamour must be loud enough to drown the huzzas of five hoarse
bodies, the Scotch, Tories, Clergy, Law, and Army; who would
soon croak, if new Ministers cannot do what the old have made
impossible; and, therefore, 'till general distress involves all in
complaint, and lays the cause undeniably at the right doors,
Victory will be but momentary, and the conquerors would soon
be rendered more unpopular than the vanquished; for, depend
upon it, the present Ministers would not be as decent and as
harmless an Opposition as the present. Their criminality must
be legally proved and stigmatized, or the pageant itself would
soon be restored to essence. Base money will pass till cried down.
I wish you may keep your promise of calling upon me better
than you have done. Remember, that though *you* have time
enough before you, *I* have not; and consequently must be more
impatient for our meeting than you are, as I am, dear Sir,
yours most sincerely,   H. WALPOLE."

["The following Letter, though flattering to me; and, though
somewhat severe upon the Asiatic adventurer, my unpopular
client, but whom I personally esteemed, is yet so witty, that I
half long to copy it, as a *jeu d'esprit*, for the public eye. G. H.]

"Berkeley Square, May 17, 1783.

"Though I shall not be fixed at Strawberry on this day fort-night, I will accept your offer, dear Sir, because my time is more at my disposal than yours, and you may not have any other day to bestow upon me later. I thank you for your second, which I shall read as carefully as I did the former. It is not your fault if you have not yet made Sir —— white as driven snow to me. Nature has providentially given us a powerful antidote to eloquence, or the criminal that has the best Advocate would escape. But, when Rhetoric and Logic stagger my Lords the Judges, in steps Prejudice, and, without one argument that will make a syllogism, confutes Messrs. Demosthenes, Tully, and Hardinge, and makes their Lordships see, as clearly as any old woman in England, that *belief* is a much better rule of *faith* than demonstration [a covered fling at Scripture!] This is just my case: I do believe, nay and I will believe, that no man ever went to India with honest intentions. If he returns with 100,000*l.* it is plain that I was in the right. But I have still a stronger proof. — My Lord Coke says, 'Set a thief to catch a thief.' My Lord A. says, 'Sir —— is a rogue:' *Ergo* —

"I cannot give so complete an answer to the rest of your note, as I trust I have done to your pleadings, because the latter is in print, and your note is MS. Now, unfortunately, I cannot read half of it; for, give me leave to say, that either your hand or my spectacles are so bad, that I generally guess at your meaning rather than decypher it, and this time the context has not served me well. You shall comment on it when I see you; till when, I am, as usually, much yours, 　　H. WALPOLE."

"Berkeley Square, April 18, 1782.

"I have great pleasure, dear Sir, in your preferment, and sincerely wish you joy. I have no doubt but your abilities will continue my satisfaction as long as I can be witness to their success. I did not expect to live to see the door opened to con-stitutional principles. That they have recovered their energy, is a proof of their excellence; and I hope that, as they have sur-mounted their enemies, they will not be ever betrayed by their friends.

"Yours heartily, 　　　　　H. WALPOLE."

"DEAR SIR,

"I have had a calf born, but it was ugly and from a *mésalli-*

ance. But I have two more cows whose times are out, and you shall know as soon as they are delivered. When I received your note, I concluded it was to tell me of Lady D's message. She told me she would ask you to-morrow evening; and she desired I would meet you. I shall not tell *you* what she said of you.

"I have just seen the Balloon too; and all the idea it gave me was one I have not had since I was at school — *football.*

"My gout, thank you, is dormant; the rest, such rest as there is, gives me no trouble.

"I send you a new Strawberry Edition, which you will find extraordinary, not only as a most accurate translation, but as a piece of genuine French not metaphysicked by La Harpe, by Thomas, &c. and with versions even of Milton into *poetry,* though in the *French* language. The Duc had had 100 copies, and I myself as many for presents : none will be sold, so their imaginary value will rise.

"I have seen over and over again Mr. Barratt's plans, and approve them exceedingly. The Gothic parts are classic; you must consider the whole as Gothic modernized in parts, not as what it is, — the reverse. Mr. Wyatt, if more employed in that style, will show as much taste and imagination as he does in Grecian. I shall visit *Lee* next summer.

"I remain, yours ever,   H. WALPOLE."

["The book that he gave to me was the Duc de Nivernois' translation of Mr. Walpole's Essay upon Garden Landscape. *Lee* was the seat of Mr. Barrett in East Kent, new built by Mr. Wyatt, and most admirably vindicated, as well as justly admired, by Mr. Walpole. This elegant Letter, I think, deserves publication. It is very good *badinage.* I was on a visit then to East Kent, very near Lee. G. H.]

HUMFREY WANLEY ON
BAGFORD'S COLLECTION

"To the honored Sir HANS SLOANE, at Gresham College in Bishopsgate-street; present*.

Duke-street, York-buildings, May 6, 1707.

"SIR,

"I remember that some time ago, I have heard you and several other gentlemen speak of Mr. Bagford's design of giving the world a new History of Printing, viz. of the Original of the Art, and of the Progress of it throughout Europe, &c. Since then, I have seen Mr. Bagford's Collection, of which I thought an account would not be unacceptable to you; but, since my business will not presently permit me to wait on you in person, I take the liberty of sending this with my humble services to you.

"His Collection consists chiefly of *title-pages,* and other *fragments,* put together into books; many of them in some sort of order and method, and others not. *Ex. gr.*

"In one Volume, there are Specimens of *Letters* of all sorts, as well those used in foreign countreys as in England.

"In another, are Titles and Fragments of *Almanacks,* from A.D. 1537 downwards; with Titles of *Bibles, Law-books,* &c. printed by the *Company of Stationers* in *London.*

"In other Volumes, are the Titles of Books of all kinds printed by the *London Printers,* disposed into some sort of order; viz. as to the subject of the Book, or dwelling-place of the Printer.

"In others, are Title-pages of Books printed in *Oxford* and *Cambridge.*

"In others, Title-pages of those printed in *Scotland* and *Ireland.*

"Title-pages and Frontispieces, with other Specimens of the Works of our *English Engravers.*

"Titles of Books printed by *Roman-Catholicks, Presbyterians, Quakers,* by other *Sectaries,* by *Seditious Persons,* &c.

"Cuts of *Monuments, Tombs, Funerals,* &c. in *England.*

"Cuts of the same in Foreign Parts, with Cuts of the manner of *executing Criminals.*

"Cuts, with some Drawings of Habits of divers Nations, of several Trades, of *Utensils, Weapons, Fountains,* or *Wells,* with

---

*Mus. Brit. Bibl. Sloan. 4065.   Plut. XXVIII F.

other Prints useful in *Joiners'* and *Masons' Work.*

"Cuts of Figures in different postures, as *writing, reading, meditation,* with all the *Utensils* used in writing, &c. during some ages. Cuts of *Schools.* The *Heads* of some *Arithmeticians; Alphabets;* Specimens of *Knot-work,* and some *Great-text* and other Letters. Specimens of *Letter-graving. Heads* of Writing-masters, *Dutch, French, English.* Specimens of Letters engraven in *small;* as also of *short-hand,* &c. Heads of *short-hand* Writers, and Specimens of their Works; and many other things.

"*Title-pages* of *Books,* and *Printers' Devices;* printing in the *Spanish Netherlands, Spain,* and *Portugal;* Titles of Books published by *English Catholicks,* Alphabets of *Plantine Letter,* &c.

"*Title-pages, Alphabets,* and *Printers' Devices;* used at *Basil, Zurick,* and other places in *Switzerland.*

"The like for the *United Netherlands.*

"The like for *France.*

"The like for *Germany;* with some others of *Poland, Switzerland, Denmark, Bohemia,* and *France.*

"The like for *Italy;* with some others of Geneva, Sicily, &c.

"Collection of *Acts of Parliament, Ordonances, Proclamations,* &c. *regulating Printing;* with many other Papers.

"*Proposals* for printing particular Books.

"Catalogues of Books, relating to Painting, Printing, &c. Specimens of Paper differently coloured, *Marks* on the outsides of Reams of Paper; with *Orders, Cases, Reasons,* &c. relating to the *Manufacturer.*

"Old *Prints* or *Cuts* from A.D. 1467; with the *Effigies* and *Devices* of many Printers, *foreigners* and *English;* with other *Cuts* and Specimens of *Paper,* &c. [Amongst these are, rebuses, many devices, marks, vignettes, and signs, used in England by the earliest Printers at the beginnings and ends of their books. — At the ends of Caxton's, W and C in capitals, between the figure of 7, with half the figure of 8, thus (ꟗ), which was used in those days for 4; and this was to denote that he did not begin to print before 1474. — *Winken de Worde* used Caxton's device, with the addition of the sign *Sagittarius,* and a greyhound supporting the Arabic figures of 7 and 4, marked *ut supra,* with W. C.; over that the sun and stars in chief; the Golden Sun being the sign he lived at in Fleet-street, and the cognisance and badge of the House of York, &c. This sign was continued by *Whitchurch,* and others who succeeded in the printing-house, &c. &c. R. PYNSON, HENRY PEPWELL, &c. —

"My friend Mr. John Barber made City Printer March 22, 1708-9. He was admitted to be Printer to the Honourable City of London; for which he then paid for fees twelve guineas to the Lord Mayor, and six to the Chamberlain. His fee is 6l. a year, for two suits of cloth; the one for summer, the other for winter." *Harl. MSS.* 5910. *Collect. de Arte Typograph. è Collectione Bagford, Pars III.*]

"Collection of *Epitaphs* of the *Printers* in *Basel; Life* of *John Froben;* Catalogues of Books, &c.

"Collections relating to the Lives of the *Engravers* of divers countreys.

"*Titles* of Books printed in most parts of Europe before the year 1500.

"Collection of *Patents* for printing *Law Books,* &c.

"Some German Cards.

"With many other Volumes of Collections of the kinds above mentioned, though not so well sorted.

"And these Title-pages of Books are really useful upon many accounts; viz. as being authentic and exact; whereas, in most Catalogues, the Titles are abbreviated, and otherways imperfect. Besides, these Titles informed me of many Books I had never heard of before; and from them I have been enabled to enquire for several Books, some of which I have since procured, to my great satisfaction. And it is my opinion, that there are but few curious men, but, upon the view of this Collection, will own they have met with many *pieces,* in their several ways, which they knew not of before. And thus we see, that a single leaf of paper, though not valuable in itself, when come to be part of a Collection, may be of good use many ways; as either in respect of the *matter* it treats of, in respect of the *mark of the paper, of the date, printer's name, country, title, faculty, &c.*

"Mr. Bagford has also a very plentiful Collection of the Titles of Books remarkable and curious, which he has taken from the Books themselves. And when they are of such sorts as now are seldome to be seen complete, he has made such observations, as that the several Editions shall be certainly known, though your Book be imperfect at beginning and end.

"Mr. Bagford also says, that though his Collection is not put into exact order, that nevertheless his Book or *History of Printing* shall be drawn up with that regularity, as shall answer any Gentleman's desire and expectation.

"I hope you will excuse the trouble of this; and continue to

believe that I am, most sincerely,
>   Honored Sir,
> Your most humble and most obliged servant,
>   HUMFREY WANLEY."

BISHOP WARBURTON

THIS very learned Prelate was descended from an antient and respectable family at Orley hall in Cheshire, of which Sir Peter Warburton, the present baronet, is at the head.

William Warburton, the grandfather of our Bishop, distinguished himself as a royalist in the civil wars of the seventeenth century. He married Frances, daughter of Robert Awfield, of Etson in Nottinghamshire; and settled at Shelton, about six miles from Newark, where he practised the law, and was coroner for the county till his death.

Mr. William Warburton had three sons; the second of whom, George Warburton, was an attorney, and town-clerk of Newark; where he was much esteemed for integrity; and married, about the year 1696, Elizabeth, daughter of William Hobman, an alderman of the same town; by whom he had five children; George, William, Mary, Elizabeth, and Frances. He died about 1706; and his eldest son died young.

WILLIAM WARBURTON was born at Newark, Dec. 24, 1698; and was put to school there under Mr. Twells, whose son afterwards married his sister Elizabeth; but he had the chief part of his education under Mr. Weston and Mr. Wright, at Okeham; where he continued till 1714; when his cousin, Mr. William Warburton, being made head-master of the public grammar-school at Newark, he returned to his native place, and was for a short time under the tuition of that learned and respectable person.

His original destination was to the same profession as that of his father and grandfather; and he was accordingly articled, in 1714, as a clerk, to Mr. Kirke, an attorney at East Markham in Nottinghamshire; with whom he continued till April 1719.

From the expiration of his clerkship to the time of his entering into holy orders, his actual pursuits in life are involved in an obscurity which would be of no consequence in the memoirs of any ordinary man. But, in the history of so gigantic a Scholar, the mode of passing his early years becomes an object of no common interest.

It has been generally supposed, and there seems no occasion to doubt it, that he was regularly admitted in one of the Courts at Westminster; and that, for a short time at least, he practised as an attorney on his own account. Certain it is, that he very early returned to his family at Newark; and, the bent of his genius having long before appeared in a passionate love of reading, he had here an opportunity of giving way to his favourite inclination, under the immediate advice and assistance of his relation, the master of Newark school; who, besides his classical merit, which was great, had that of being an excellent Divine, and a truly learned as well as good man; and "employed all the time he could spare in instructing him, and used to set up very late at night with him to assist him in his studies."

The success which he met with as a man of business was probably not great. It was certainly not sufficient to induce him to devote the rest of his life to it : and it is probable that his want of encouragement might tempt him to turn his thoughts towards a profession in which his literary acquisitions might be more valuable, and in which he might more easily pursue the bent of his inclination. He appears to have brought from school more learning than was requisite for a practising Lawyer. This might rather impede than forward his progress; as it has been generally observed, that an attention to literary concerns, and the bustle of an attorney's office, with only a moderate share of business, are wholly incompatible. It is therefore no wonder that he preferred retirement to noise, and relinquished what advantages he might expect from continuing to follow the Law. "His love of letters continually growing stronger, and the seriousness of his temper, and purity of his morals, concurring with his unappeasable thirst of knowledge, determined him to quit that profession for the Church."

In 1723 he took deacon's orders; and his first printed work, consisting of Translations from Cæsar, Cicero, Pliny, Claudian, and others, appeared, under the title of "Miscellaneous Translations in Prose and Verse, from Roman Poets, Orators, and Historians," 12mo, was in that year addressed to Sir Robert Sutton, and seems to have laid the foundation of his first ecclesiastical preferment; for in 1726, being then in priest's orders, he obtained, by the recommendation of his patron, the small vicarage of Gryesly in Nottinghamshire.

About Christmas 1726 he came to London; and, while there, with that ardent thirst of knowledge which was his characteristic quality, became intimately acquainted with several literary characters; and, amongst others, with Mr. Theobald, to whom he communicated some notes on Shakspeare, which afterwards appeared in that Critic's edition of our great Dramatic Poet.*

On the 25th of April, 1728, by the interest of Sir Robert Sutton, he had the honour to be put upon the King's List of Masters of Arts, created at Cambridge, on his Majesty's visit to that University.

In June, the same year, he was presented by Sir Robert Sutton to the valuable rectory of Burnt (otherwise Brand) Broughton, Lincolnshire, but in the neighbourhood of Newark, where he fixed himself, accompanied by his mother and his sisters; and spent a considerable part of the prime of life, from 1728 to 1746 in a studious retirement, devoted entirely to letters; usually sitting up a great part of the night in study; and there planned, and in part executed, some of his most important works; but several years elapsed, after obtaining this preferment, before he appeared again in the world as a writer.

It was in this season of early discipline, while his mind was opening to many literary projects, that he conceived an idea, which he was long pleased with, of giving a new edition of Velleius Paterculus, a plan of which he printed in the "Bibliotheque Britannique, ou Histoire des Ouvrages des Savans de la Grande Bretagne, à la Haye, &c. 1736." But the design never was completed. Dr. Middleton, in a letter, dated April 9, 1737, returns him thanks for his letters, as well as the Journal, "which," says he, "came to my hands soon after the date of my last. I had before seen the force of your critical genius very successfully employed on Shakspeare, but did not know you had ever tried it on the Latin authors. I am pleased with several of your emendations, and transcribed them into the margin of my editions, though not equally with them all. It is a laudable and liberal amusement, to try now and then in our reading the

---

*Lewis Theobald (d. 1744), the Shakespearean critic, whom Pope satirised in the *Dunciad*. (*Ed.*)

success of a conjecture; but, in the present state of the generality of the old writers, it can hardly be thought a study fit to employ a life upon; at least not worthy, I am sure, of your talents and industry, which, instead of trifling on words, seem calculated rather to correct the opinions and manners of the world." These sentiments of his friend appear to have had their due weight; for, from that time, the intended edition was laid aside, and never afterwards resumed.

It was in the same year, 1736, that this colossal Writer may be said to have emerged from the obscurity of a private life into the notice of the world.

The first publication which rendered him afterwards famous now appeared, under the title of "The Alliance between Church and State."

The "Alliance" was much talked of at Court; and Bp. Hare, on whom that work had impressed the highest ideas of Mr. Warburton's merit, took the favourable opportunity of noticing him to the Queen; and the recommendation was very favourably received; but the sudden illness and death of her Majesty, Nov. 20, 1737, put an end to the friendly negotiation.

At the end of the "Alliance" was announced the scheme of Mr. Warburton's *magnum opus,* in which he had at this time made a considerable progress; and of which the first volume was published in January 1737-8, under the title of "The Divine Legation of Moses demonstrated on the Principles of a Religious Deist, from the Omission of the Doctrine of a future State of Rewards and Punishments in the Jewish Dispensation. In Six Books. By William Warburton, M. A. Author of The Alliance between Church and State." This volume, which was introduced by a long Dedication to the *Freethinkers,* met with a reception which neither the subject, nor the manner in which it was treated, seemed to authorize. It was, as the Author afterwards observed, fallen upon in so outrageous and brutal a manner, as had been scarcely pardonable, had it been "The Divine Legation of Mahomet;" and so many unhandsome reflections on it appeared in "The Weekly Miscellany," that, in less than two months, he was constrained to defend himself, in "A Vindication of the Author of the Divine Legation of Moses, from the Aspersions of the Country Clergyman's Letter in the Weekly Miscellany of February 24, 1737-8," 8vo.

After publishing the "Vindication," he applied himself with great industry to compose the *second volume* of his work, notwithstanding the clamours which had been raised, and now grew louder, against the *first*.

Mr. Warburton's extraordinary merit had now attracted the notice of the Heir-apparent to the Crown, in whose immediate service we find him, in June 1738, when he published "Faith working by Charity to Christian Edification."

His reputation was now rising every day; and, to exalt it as high as it could be carried, he had about this time the good fortune to render a service to Mr. Pope, by means of which he acquired an ascendancy over that great Poet, which will astonish those who observe the air of superiority which, until this connexion, had been shewed in all his friendships even with the greatest men of the age.

The "Essay on Man" had been now published some years; and it is universally supposed that the Author had, in the composition of it, adopted the philosophy of Lord Bolingbroke, whom on this occasion he had followed as his Guide, without understanding the tendency of his principles. In 1738, M. de Crousaz* wrote some remarks on it, accusing the author of Spinosism and Naturalism; which falling into Mr. Warburton's hands, he published a Defence of the *first* Epistle, and soon after of the other *three*. The opinion which Mr. Pope conceived of these Defences, as well as of their learned and highly respectable Author, will be best seen in his own Letters.

Early in June 1741 he was at Twickenham; and in the middle of that month accompanied Mr. Pope in a country ramble, taking Oxford in their way, where they parted; Mr. Pope, after one day's stay, going Westward; and Mr. Warburton, who stayed a day after him, to visit Dr. Conybeare then dean of Christ Church, returning to London. On *that day* the Vice-chancellor, Dr. Leigh, sent a message to his lodgings, to enquire whether a Doctor's degree in Divinity would be acceptable to him; to which unasked and unsought compliment such an answer was returned as so civil a message deserved. About the same time, Mr. Pope had the like offer made him of a Doctor's degree in Law; which he seemed disposed to accept, until he learned that some impediment had been thrown in the way of his friend's receiving the compliment intended for him by the Vice-chancellor. He then absolutely refused that pro-

---

*Crousaz was a professor of Switzerland, eminent for his treatise of Logick, and his *Examen de Pyrrhonisme*.

posed to himself. [In a letter to Mr. Warburton, dated Aug. 12, 1741, Mr. Pope says, "I have received some chagrin at the delay of your Degree at Oxon. As for mine, I will die before I receive one, in an art I am ignorant of, at a place where there remains any scruple of bestowing one on you, in a science of which you are so great a master. In short, I will be *doctored* with you, or not at all. I am sure, wherever honour is not conferred on the deserving, there can be none given to the undeserving; no more from the hands of Priests, than of Princes.]

Both the degrees were therefore laid aside; and the University of Oxford lost some reputation by the conduct of this business, being thus deprived of the honour of two names, which certainly would have reflected credit on the Society in which they were to have been enrolled.

Mr. Pope's affection for Mr. Warburton was of service to him in more respects than merely increasing his fame. He introduced and warmly recommended him to most of his friends; and particularly to Ralph Allen, esq. which laid the foundation of his fortune.

In consequence of this introduction, we find Mr. Warburton domesticated at Mr. Allen's seat, at Widcombe, near Bath, in November 1741, where he continued for more than six weeks; and returned to London, with Mr. Pope, through Oxford.

"The Divine Legation" had so rapid a sale that a *third edition* of the *first* volume was published early in 1742; as was also a *second* edition of the *second* volume; the whole corrected and enlarged; and the plan of the work announced, "to be concluded in Nine Books." In this edition he introduced some reflexions on the Leaders of the sect of Methodists, then rising into public notice. [In a letter to Mr. Desmaizeaux, Mr. Warburton says, "I have seen Whitefield's Journal; and he appears to me to be as mad as ever George Fox the Quaker was. These are very fit Missionaries, you will say, to propagate the Christian faith amongst Infidels. There is another of them, one Wesley, who came over from the same mission. He told a friend of mine, that he had lived most deliciously the last summer in Georgia, sleeping under trees, and feeding on boiled maize, sauced with the ashes of oak leaves; that he will return thither, and then will cast off his English dress, and wear a dyed skin, like the savages, the better to ingratiate himself with them."]

In June 1742 a new edition appeared of Mr. Pope's "Ethic Epistles," with the Commentary of Mr. Warburton; who at this period had the entire confidence of Mr. Pope, and had concerted with him the plan of the Fourth Book of the *Dunciad*. [The three first Books were published in 1729; the fourth in 1742. The variations between the *first* and the *complete* Edition are pointed out in the great Body of English Poetry printed under the immediate superintendance of Dr. Johnson.]

In 1742 Mr. Warburton new-modeled the Letters which he had written in vindication of Mr. Pope; and published them under the title of "A Critical and Philosophical Commentary on Mr. Pope's Essay on Man; in which is contained a Vindication of the said Essay from the Misrepresentations of Mr. de Resnel, the French Translator, and of Mr. de Crousaz, Professor of Philosophy and Mathematics, in the Academy of Lausanne, the Commentator."

In the autumn of 1742 Mr. Warburton renewed his visit to Mr. Allen at Widcombe; and printed a Sermon which had been preached at the Abbey Church of Bath on the 24th of October, for the benefit of the General Infirmary. To this Sermon, which was published at the request of the Governors, was added, "A Short Account of the Nature, Rise, and Progress, of the General Infirmary at Bath."

In the same year he printed a "Dissertation on the Origin of the Books of Chivalry" at the end of Jarvis's Preface to a Translation of Don Quixote; on which Mr. Pope, Dec. 28, 1742, observes, "I never read a thing with more pleasure than an additional sheet to Jervas's Preface to Don Quixote. Before I got over two paragraphs, I cried out, *Aut Erasmus, aut Diabolus!* I knew you as certainly as the Antients did the Gods, by the first pace and the very gait. I have not a moment to express myself in, but could not omit this which delighted me so greatly. — My Law-suit with Lintot is at an end. — Adieu! Believe no man can be more yours. Call me by any title you will, but a *Doctor of Oxford; Sit tibi cura mei, sit tibi cura tui.*"

Mr. Pope's attention to the interest of his friend did not rest in matters which were in his own power; he recommended him to some who were more able to assist him : in particular, he obtained a promise from Lord Granville; which ended, however, in nothing effectual.

Mr. Pope appears also to have been very solicitous to bring Lord Bolingbroke and Mr. Warburton together; and the meeting accordingly took place; but, we are told by Dr. Warton, they soon parted in mutual disgust with each other.

About the same time, at Mr. Pope's request, Mr. Warburton corrected the "Essay on Homer," as it now stands in the last edition; and published the first *complete edition* of "The Dunciad," in which *Theobald* gave way to *Cibber;* and also complete editions of "The Essay on Man," and "The Essay on Criticism;" with his own Commentary and Notes, which was the last service he rendered Mr. Pope in his life-time; who, from the specimens which he had now had of his friend's abilities, it may be presumed, determined to commit to his care the future publication and property of his works.

After a lingering and tedious illness, the event of which had been long foreseen, this great Poet died on the 30th of May, 1744; and, by his will, dated the 12th of the preceding December, bequeathed to Mr. Warburton one half of his library, and the property of all such of his Works already printed as he had not otherwise disposed of or alienated, and all the profits which should arise from any edition to be printed after his death; but at the same time directed that they should be published without any future alterations.

The first thing which he published after Mr. Pope's death was a small but very neat edition of "The Dunciad."

In 1744 his assistance to Dr. Zachary Grey was handsomely acknowledged in that learned Editor's Preface to Hudibras; but a literary warfare commenced soon after between the two learned Criticks.

"The Divine Legation of Moses" had now been published some time, and various answers and objections to it having started up from different quarters, Mr Warburton in 1744 turned his attention to these attacks on his favourite work, and defended himself in a manner which, if it did not prove him to be possessed of much humility or diffidence, at least demonstrated that he knew how to wield the weapons of controversy with the hand of a master.

His first defence appeared under the title of "Remarks on several Occasional Reflections in answer to the Rev. Dr. Middleton, Dr. Pococke (Bishop of Meath), the Master of the Charter-House (Nicholas Mann), Dr. Richard Grey, and others; serving to explain and justify divers Passages in the Divine Legation objected to by those learned Writers. To which is added, A general Review of the Argument of the Divine Legation, as far as it is yet advanced: wherein is considered the Relation the several Parts bear to each other, and the whole. Together with an Appendix, in Answer to a late Pamphlet, intituled, *An Examination of Mr. Warburton's Second Proposition*," 8vo.

This was followed, next year, by "Remarks on several Occasional Reflections; in Answer to the Rev. Doctors Stebbing and Sykes; serving to explain and justify the two Dissertations in The Divine Legation, concerning the Command to Abraham to offer up his Son, and the Nature of the Jewish Theocracy, objected to by those learned Writers. Part II. and last;" 8vo. Both these answers are couched in those high terms of confident superiority which marked almost every performance that fell from his pen during the remainder of his life.

Sept. 5, 1745, Mr. Warburton more closely cemented his friendship with Mr. Allen, by a marriage with his favourite niece Miss Gertrude Tucker; and Prior Park, the splendid seat of Mr. Allen, became from that time his principal residence, and ultimately his own property.

In 1747 his famous edition of Shakspeare was issued from the press; a work for which Mr. Tonson paid him 500*l.*; but which, he says, "the publick at this time of day had never been troubled with, but for the conduct of the two last editors [Theobald and Hanmer], and the persuasion of dear Mr. Pope. He was desirous I should should give a new edition of this Poet, as he thought it might contribute to put a stop to a prevailing folly of altering the text of celebrated Authors, without talents or judgment.

[At the sale of the effects of Mr. Jacob Tonson, bookseller, in 1767, one hundred and forty copies of Mr. Pope's edition of Shakspeare, in six volumes 4to (for which the original subscribers paid six guineas) were disposed of at sixteen shillings (only) per sett. Seven hundred and fifty of that edition had then been printed. — On the contrary, Sir Thomas Hanmer's Edition, printed in 1744, which was first sold for three guineas, had arisen to ten before it was re-printed!]

In 1749, a very extraordinary attack was made on the moral character of Mr. Pope, from a quarter whence it could be the least expected. His "Guide, Philosopher, and Friend," Lord Bolingbroke, published a book which he had formerly lent Mr. Pope in MS. The Preface to this work, written by Mr. Mallett, contained an accusation of Mr. Pope's having clandestinely printed an edition of his Lordship's performance without his leave or knowledge.

A Defence of the Poet soon after made its appearance, which

was universally ascribed to Mr. Warburton, and was afterwards owned by him. It was called, "A Letter to the Editor of the Letters on the Spirit of Patriotism, the Idea of a Patriot King, and the State of the Parties, &c. occasioned by the Editor's Advertisement*," &c. which soon after produced an abusive pamphlet, under the title of "A Familiar Epistle to the most impudent Man living;" a performance, as hath been truly observed, couched in language bad enough to disgrace even gaols and garrets.

In 1751 Mr. Warburton published the first complete edition of Mr. Pope's Works, with his own notes, in nine octavo volumes, handsomely printed by Mr. Bowyer.

At this advanced period of Mr. Warburton's life that preferment which his abilities might have claimed, and which had hitherto been withheld, seemed to be approaching towards him.

Very early in April 1753 he was promoted to a prebendal stall in the cathedral of Gloucester; and had reason to expect that he should be farther promoted to the Deanry of Bristol, then shortly expected to be vacant.

In September 1754 Mr. Warburton was appointed one of his Majesty's Chaplains in ordinary; and in that year he published a second volume of "Sermons at Lincoln's Inn."

In resigning his prebend at Gloucester, he was presented, in March 1755, to a stall at Durham, on the death of Dr. Mangey. This preferment was given him by Bp. Trevor, at the request of Mr. Murray, then Attorney General.

About the same time the degree of Doctor of Divinity was conferred on him by Dr. Herring, then archbishop of Canterbury; and, a new impression of "The Divine Legation" having been called for, he printed a fourth edition of the first part of it, corrected and enlarged, divided into two volumes, with a dedication to the Earl of Hardwicke.

In 1759 Dr. Warburton obtained the Royal Licence for the sole printing and vending the Works of the late Alexander Pope, esq.

At the latter end of this year Dr. Warburton received the honour, so justly due to his merit, of being dignified with the mitre. He was promoted, Dec. 22, to the bishoprick of Gloucester; consecrated on the 20th of January 1760; and on the

---

*Re-printed in the Appendix to Ruffhead's Life of Pope.

30th of the same month preached before the House of Lords on the occasion of that Anniversary.

It is a melancholy reflection, that a life spent in the constant pursuit of knowledge frequently terminates in the loss of those powers, the cultivation and improvement of which are attended to with too strict and unabated a degree of ardour. This was in some degree the misfortune of Dr. Warburton. Like Swift and the great Duke of Marlborough, he gradually sunk into a situation in which it was a fatigue to him to enter into general conversation. This melancholy habit was aggravated by the loss of his son and only child, a very promising young gentleman, who died of a consumption, July 18, 1775, in his 19th year.

He continued, however, both to correspond and to converse occasionally with a few old and valuable friends, in whose company, even to the last, his mental faculties were exerted in their wonted force; and at such times he would appear cheerful for several hours, and on the departure of his friends retreat as it were within himself.

After thus languishing for some time in a melancholy state of inertness of mind, he died at Gloucester, June 7, 1779.

JOSIAH WEDGWOOD

JOSIAH WEDGWOOD, ESQ. was elected Fellow of the Royal Society 1783, and of the Antiquarian Society 1786. [To his indefatigable labours is owing the establishment of a manufacture that has opened a new scene of extensive commerce, before unknown to this or any other Country. It is unnecessary to say that this alludes to the Pottery of Staffordshire, which, by the united efforts of Mr. Wedgwood and his late partner Mr. Bentley, has been carried to a degree of perfection, both in the line of utility and ornament, that leaves all works, antient or modern, far behind. But, though this improvement of the manufacture in which he was bred, and which had been the employment of his family for several generations, occupied much of Mr. Wedgwood's time, he was frequently employed in planning designs that will for ever record the greatness of his mind; for, however the practicability of uniting the Eastern and Western Coasts of this Kingdom, by means of Inland Navigation, may have been shewn by Yarranton and others; yet it remained for Mr. Wedgwood to propose such measures for uniting the Duke of Bridgewater's Canal with the navigable part of the River Trent (in executing which he was happy in the assistance of the late ingenious Mr. Brindley, whom he never mentioned but with respect) as first fully carried the great plan into execution, and thus enabled the Manufacturers of the inland part of that county and its neighbourhood to obtain, from the distant shores of Devonshire, Dorsetshire, and Kent, those materials of which the Staffordshire Ware is composed; affording, at the same time, a ready conveyance of the manufacture to distant counties; and thus not only to rival, but undersell, at foreign markets, a commodity which has proved, and must continue to prove, of infinite advantage to these Kingdoms; as the ware, when formed, owes its value almost wholly to the labour of the honest and industrious poor, who in Mr. Wedgwood lost a kind master and generous benefactor. Still farther to promote the interest and benefit of his neighbourhood, Mr. Wedgwood planned and carried into execution a Turnpike-road, ten miles in length, through that part of Staffordshire called *The Pottery;* thus opening another source of traffick, if, by frost or other impediment, the carriage by water should be interrupted. Having given this imperfect sketch of his public life, let us consider him in his private capacity; wherein, whether he is regarded as a husband, a father, a master, or a friend, his conduct will be found most exemplary. — Such is the account given by an old and valuable friend, who knew him long and intimately. Another friend adds, "Mr. Wedgwood was the younger son of a Potter, but derived little or no property from his father, whose possessions consisted chiefly of a small entailed estate, which descended to the eldest son. He was the maker of his own fortune; and his Country has been benefited in a proportion not to be calculated. His many discoveries of new species of Earthenwares and Porcelains, his studied forms and chaste style of decoration, and the correctness and judgment with which all his works were executed under his own eye, and by Artists, for the most part, of his own forming, have turned the current in this branch of commerce; for, before his time, England imported the finer Earthen-wares; but, for more than twenty years past, she has exported them to a very great annual amount, the whole of which is drawn from the Earth, and from the industry of the inhabitants; while the national taste has been improved, and its reputation raised in foreign countries. His inventions have prodigiously increased the number of persons employed in the Potteries, and in the traffick and transport of their materials from distant parts of the Kingdom: and this class of Manufacturers is also indebted to him for much mechanical contrivance and arrangement in their operations; his private manufactory having had, for 30 years and upwards, all the efficacy of a public work of experiment. Neither was he unknown in the walks of Philosophy. His communications to the Royal Society shew a mind enlightened by science, and contributed to procure him the esteem of scientific men at home and throughout Europe. His invention of a thermometer for measuring the higher degrees of heat employed in the various arts is of the highest importance to their promotion, and will add celebrity to his name. At an early period of his life, seeing the impossibility of extending the manufactory he was engaged in on the spot which gave him birth without the advantages of inland navigation, he was the proposer of the Grand Trunk Canal, and the chief agent in obtaining the Act of Parliament for making it, against the prejudices of the Landed Interest, which at that time stood very high, and but just before had been with great difficulty overcome in another quarter by all the powerful influence of a Noble Duke, whose Canal was at that time but lately finished. The Grand Trunk Canal is 90 miles in length, uniting the Rivers Trent and Mersey; and Branches have since been made from it to the Severn, to Oxford, and to many other parts; and it will also have a communication with the Grand Junction Canal from Braunston to Brentford. Having acquired a large fortune, his purse was always open to the calls of Charity, and to the support of every Institution for the public good. To his relations, friends, and neighbours, he was endeared by his many private virtues; and his loss will be deeply and long deplored by all who had the pleasure of knowing him intimately, and by the numerous objects to whom his benevolence was extended: and he will be regretted by his Country as the able and zealous Supporter of her commerce, and the steady Patron of every valuable interest of society." He died at Etruria in Staffordshire, Jan. 3, 1795, aged 64.]

THE WESLEYS

THE elder SAMUEL WESLEY, whose labours on Job gave occasion to this memoir, was born at Winterborn Whitchurch in Dorsetshire, where his father (John Wesley) was vicar. He was educated, first at the free-school at Dorchester, and then in a private academy among the Dissenters, whom he soon left, and was admitted a servitor, at the age of 18, of Exeter college, Oxford, 1684. He proceeded B. A. 1688; and, taking orders, was rector of South Ormesby, co. Lincoln; and afterwards obtained the rectory of Epworth, in the Isle of Axholme, in the same county. He was chaplain also to the Marquis of Normanby, afterwards Duke of Buckingham, who recommended him for an Irish Bishoprick.

John Dunton, who was nearly related to Mr. Wesley by marriage, and who in other parts of his multifarious writings enters deeply into their family squabbles, gives him the following character:

"Mr. Wesley had an early inclination to poetry; but he usually writ too fast to write well. Two hundred couplets a day are too many by two-thirds, to be well-furnished with all the beauties and the graces of that art. He writ very much for me both in verse and prose, though I shall not name over the titles, in regard I am altogether as unwilling to see my name at the bottom of them, as Mr. Wesley would be to subscribe his own. Mr. Wesley had read much, and is well-skilled in the languages. He is generous and good-humoured, and caresses his friend with a great deal of passion, so long as his circumstances are any thing in order, and then he drops him; and I challenge the rector of Epworth (for he is not yet *my Lord,* nor *his Grace*) to prove I injure him in this character; for that he was once glad of my friendship, none can question that reads the following letter (of which I have the original still by me):

Epworth, July the 24th, 97.

'DEAR BROTHER,

"It has been neither unkindness to you, with whom I have traded and been justly used for many years, much less unthankfulness to Mr. Rogers, for I shall own by obligations to that good man while I live, which has made me so long neglect answering your several letters; but the hurry of a remove, and my extraordinary business, being obliged to preach the Visita-

tion Sermon at Gainsborough at the Bishop's coming thither,
which is but just over. — Besides, I would fain have sent you an
Elegy, as well as an *Epitaph,* but cannot get one to my mind,
and therefore you must be content with half your desire; and
if you please to accept this epitaph it is at your service, and I
hope it will come before you need another *Epithalamium**. I
am

    'Your obliged friend and brother,   S. WESLEY.'

"I could be very maggotty in the character of this conforming
Dissenter (for so this letter shews him to be); but, except he
farther provokes me, I bid him farewell till we meet in Heaven,
and there I hope we shall renew our friendship, for (human
frailties excepted) I believe Sam Wesley a pious man. I shall
only add that the giving this true character of Parson Wesley
is all the satisfaction I ever desire for his dropping an old friend.
I shall leave him to struggle through life, and to make the best
of it. But, alas!

He loves too much the Heliconian strand,
Whose stream's unfurnish'd with the golden sand.

"I do not speak this out of prejudice to Mr. Wesley; for to
forgive a slight (or undeserved slander, invented by S——t. to
revenge the discovery I made of his wh-m, and whispered
about by a reverend brother) is so easy to me, it is scarce a
virtue. But this rhiming circumstance of Mr. Wesley, is what I
learn from the poem called 'The Reformation of Manners,'
where are these words:

"Wesley with pen and poverty beset,
And Blackmore vers'd in physick as in wit;
Tho' this of Jesus, that of Job may sing,
One bawdy play will twice their profits bring:
And had not both caress'd the flatter'd Crown,
This had no knighthood seen, nor that no gown."

Mr. Wesley was a very voluminous author; having published,
besides other things, "Maggots, or Poems on several Subjects,
1685," 8vo; "The Life of Christ, an heroic Poem, 1693," folio;
dedicated to the Queen, reprinted with large additions and corrections in 1697; "Elegies on Queen Mary and Archbishop
Tillotson, 1695," folio; "A Sermon preached before the Society

---

*These were articles in which Dunton traded, and regularly sold them
ready made.

for Reformation of Manners, 1698," 8vo; "A Letter concerning the Education of the Dissenters in their private Academies, 1703," and "A Defence of it," 12mo; "The History of the Old and New Testament attempted in Verse, and adorned with Three hundred and Thirty Sculptures, engraved by J. Sturt," 3 vols. 12mo, 1704, addressed to Queen Anne in a Poetical Dedication, "A Treatise on the Sacrament;" and "Dissertationes in Librum Jobi;" for which last, proposals were circulated in 1729, and which was finished after his death, and published by his son Samuel, 1736. Mr. Wesley had collated all the copies he could meet with of the original, and the Greek and other versions and editions; and after his labours and his library had been burnt with his house (which it seems had suffered the like fate once before, about the year 1707) he resumed the task in the decline of life, oppressed with gout and palsy through long habit of study. Among other assistances, he particularly acknowledges that of his three sons, and his friend Maurice Johnson.

Mr. Pope, in a letter to Dr. Swift, April 12, 1730, says, "I shall think it a kindness done myself if you can propagate Mr. Wesley's subscription for his Commentary on Job among your Divines (Bishops excepted, of whom there is no hope) and among such as are believers or readers of Scripture. Even the curious may find something to please them, if they scorn to be edified. It has been the labour of eight years of this learned man's life; I call him what he is, a learned man, and I engage you will approve his prose more than you formerly could his poetry. Lord Bolingbroke is a favourer of it, and allows you to do your best to serve an old Tory, and a sufferer for the Church of England, though you are a Whig, as I am."

His poetry, which is far from being excellent, incurred the censure of Garth; but he made ample amends for it by the goodness of his life. He died April 25, 1735, and left an exceedingly numerous family of children; four of whom are not unknown in the annals of English literature;

1. Samuel; of whom presently.

2. and 3. John and Charles Wesley, the two celebrated founders of the sect of Methodists; the former admitted at Lincoln college, the others at Brazen-nose college. [Charles Wesley was born at Epworth in 1708, admitted a scholar at Westminster in 1721; and elected to Oxford in 1726.]

4. Mrs. Mehetabel Wright, authoress of several Poems printed in the Sixth Volume of the "Poetical Calendar."

SAMUEL WESLEY, the eldest son, was first a scholar, and afterwards nearly 20 years usher of Westminster School; whence, in 1711, he was elected as a king's scholar to Christ Church, Oxford. He was author of two excellent Poems, called "The Battle of the Sexes," and "The Prisons opened;" and of another, called "The Parish Priest," a poem upon a Clergyman lately deceased, a very dutiful and striking Eulogy on his wife's father; which are all printed among his poems, and several humourous tales, in 4to, 1736, and after his death in 12mo, 1743. He was a member of the Philosophical Society at Spalding; and gave to their Museum an amulet that had touched the heads of the three Kings of Cologne, whose names were in black letters within. He died Nov. 6, 1739, aged 49, being at that time head-master of Tiverton-school; but never presented to any ecclesiastical benefice. He was buried in the church-yard at Tiverton; and his epitaph may be seen at the end of his life, prefixed to his Poems, 1743.

Thus far the history of the Wesleys is nearly the same as in the former edition of these Anecdotes; which I should have enlarged by further researches, had not the following most satisfactory account of the whole family been transmitted to me by the late excellent scholar and critic, the Rev. Samuel Badcock, in a letter dated from South Molton, Dec. 5, 1782; and, as an abridgment would be an injury to the publick, as well as to my late worthy friend and correspondent, it is here preserved entire; and the rather as it produced some good-tempered corrections from the late Rev. John Wesley, which shall also be preserved.

"Mr. Samuel Wesley, of Epworth, was the grandson of Mr. Bartholomew Wesley, who was ejected by the Act of Uniformity (in the year 1662) from the living of Charmouth in Dorsetshire. He practised physick after his ejectment; but the death of his son John Wesley so affected him, that he did not survive him long. This John Wesley (of whom see a very minute account in Calamy's Continuation or Supplement to the Abridgement of Baxter's Life, vol. I. p. 437—445) was ejected by the same rigorous act from the living of Whitchurch, near Blandford. Samuel Wesley (the son of John) was sent to the University; there he imbibed all the orthodoxy of the High Church, and forgot the Nonconformity of his ancestors. He was the author of several large works; the merit of which was by no means thought proportionable to their bulk. An heroic poem, called

'The Life of Christ,' excited the ridicule of the wits, particularly of Garth, in his Dispensary, and Swift in his Battle of the Books.

"Mr. Samuel Wesley the elder published a poetical version of the Old and New Testament; and at a very advanced age a voluminous work in Latin on the book of Job. This last work was presented to Queen Caroline by Mr. John Wesley (the celebrated father of the Methodists), who, in a letter to his brother Samuel, acknowledges the very courteous reception he was honoured with from her Majesty, who gave him *bows* and *smiles* — but *nothing for his poor father!* The work was never held in any estimation by the learned. The engravings seem to have been the first rude efforts of an untutored boy. Nothing can be conceived more execrable.

"Old Samuel Wesley married a woman of extraordinary abilities. She was one of the daughters of Dr. Samuel Annesley, a celebrated Nonconformist minister. Her letters to her children bear the marks of sublime piety and great sense; particularly one to her eldest son, on the principles of natural religion, which was some time in the possession of Dr. Priestley, with many others equally sensible and curious. This excellent pair had a very numerous offspring. Samuel Wesley, first an usher at Westminster-school, and afterwards head-master of Blundell's school at Tiverton, was the eldest; Charles, the Methodist preacher, was, if I have not been misinformed, the youngest.

"Samuel was a man of wit and learning: a High Churchman and a noted Jacobite. Sir Robert Walpole was the principal object of his political satires; many of which remain unpublished, on account of their treasonable tendency; for, in the rage of Jacobitism, he was not scrupulous in the selection of characters, but poured out the very dregs of it on Royalty itself. He, however, published enough to render himself obnoxious to the Ministry; so that little was left him but that penitence which, arising from mortification, only vents itself in abuse. Time, however, had so far gotten the better of his fury against Sir Robert, as to change the satirist into the suppliant. I have seen a copy of verses addressed to the great Minister in behalf of his poor and aged parent. But I have seen something much better. I have in my possession a letter of this *poor and aged parent* addressed to his son Samuel, in which he gratefully acknowledges his filial duty in terms so affecting, that I am at a loss which to admire most, the gratitude of the parent, or the affection and generosity of the child. It was written when the good old man was nearly fourscore, and so weakened by a palsy as to be incapable of directing a pen, unless with his left hand. I preserve it as a curious memorial of what will make Wesley applauded when his wit is forgotten.

"Mrs. Wesley lived long enough to deplore the extravagances of her two sons, John and Charles. She considered them as under *strong delusions to believe a lie;* and states her objections to their enthusiastic principles (particularly in the matter of *Assurance*) with great strength of argument, in a correspondence with their brother Samuel. He too exerted his best powers to reclaim them from their wanderings: but in vain! *'The extravagant* and *erring spirit'* could not be reduced to *'its own confine.'* It had burst its bonds asunder, and ran violently down the steep!

"Samuel Wesley married a woman of the name of Berry. Her father was a clergyman of the Established Church, and rector of Watton in Norfolk. Her grandfather was a Nonconformist minister; and after his ejectment from East Down in the North of Devonshire, resided at Barnstaple, where some of his descendants continue to live in reputation. — Samuel Wesley left an only daughter, who married a Mr. Earle, an apothecary at the last-mentioned place. They had an only daughter, who married a gentleman of the name of Mansel. She died in travail for her first child.

"JOHN WESLEY, the Methodist, was born about the beginning of the 18th century. Dr. Priestley had in his possession a letter from Mrs. Wesley to her son Samuel Wesley, who was at that time a scholar on the foundation at Westminster. She begins the letter with lamenting the great loss the family had sustained by a fire that had happened a few days before at the parsonage at Epworth, by which they were all driven to great necessity. The house was burnt to the ground, and few things of value could be saved, the flames spread so rapidly. She thanks God that no lives were lost, though for some time they gave up *poor Jacky* (as she expresses herself); for his father had twice attempted to rescue the child, but was beaten back by the flames. Finding all his efforts abortive, he 'resigned him to Divine Providence.' But parental tenderness prevailed over human fears, and Mr. Wesley once more attempted to save his child. By some means, equally unexpected and unaccountable, the boy got round to a window in the front of the house, and was taken out — I think by one man's leaping on the shoulders of another, and thus getting within his reach.

Immediately on his rescue from this most perilous situation the roof fell in. This extraordinary incident explains a certain device in some of the earlier prints of John Wesley, *viz.* a house in flames, with this motto from the prophet, 'Is he not a brand plucked out of the burning?' Many have supposed this device to be merely emblematical of his spiritual deliverance. But from this circumstance you must be convinced that it hath a primary as well as a secondary meaning. It is real as well as allusive. — This fire happened when John was about six years old; and, if I recollect right, in the year 1707.

"I need not expatiate on the abilities of this singular man. They are certainly wonderful! In the early part of life he discovered an elegant turn for poetry; and some of his gayer pieces in this line are proofs of a lively fancy, and a fine classical taste: I have seen some translations from the Latin poets, done by him at college, which have great merit. I once had an opportunity, by the favour of his niece, of inspecting some curious original papers, which throw great light on his genius and character. He had early a very strong impression (like Count Zinzendorf) of his designation to some extraordinary work. This impression received additional force from some domestic incidents; all which his active fancy turned to his own account. His wonderful preservation, already noticed, naturally tended to cherish the idea of his being designed by Providence to accomplish some purpose or other that was out of the ordinary course of human events. There were some strange *phænomena* perceived at the parsonage at Epworth, and some uncommon noises heard there from time to time, which he was very curious in examining into, and very particular in relating. I have little doubt that he considered himself as the chief object of this *wonderful* visitation. Indeed, *Samuel* Wesley's credulity was in some degree affected by it, since he collected all the evidences that tended to confirm the story, arranged them with scrupulous exactness, in a MS. consisting of several sheets, and which is still in being. I know not what became of the Ghost of Epworth; unless, considered as the prelude to the *noise* Mr. John Wesley made on a more ample stage, it ceased to speak when he began to act.

"The dawn of Mr. Wesley's public mission was clouded with Mysticism——that species of it which affects silence and solitude; a certain inexplicable introversion of the mind, which abstracts the passions from all sensible objects, and, as the

French Quietists express it, perfects itself by an absorption of the will and intellect, and all the faculties into the Deity. In this "palpable obscure" the excellent Fenelon lost himself when he forsook the shades of Pindus to wander in quest of "pure love" with Madam Guyon! Mr. Wesley pursued for a while the same *ignis fatuus* with Mr. William Law and the *Ghost* of De Renty——A state, however, so torpid and ignoble ill suited the active genius of this singular man. His elastic mind gained strength by compression; thence *bursting glorious,* he passed (as he himself somewhere says) 'the immense chasm upborne on an eagle's wings.'

"His system of Divinity, indeed, was relaxed; or rather, I would say, it was made more commodious for general use. The speculations of the Mystics were too abstracted and too much sublimated for the conceptions of the gross herd of mankind. Refined maxims, that have little connexion with the general sentiments and habits of the human race, were not calculated to make proselytes by the common engines of hope and fear. The million could neither be amused nor alarmed by principles in which the heart could feel no interest. A few minds of a peculiar texture might possibly take a fancy to them. But Mr. Wesley's business was with minds of every composition; and though the Poet says,

Oderunt hilarem tristes, tristemque jocosi;

yet he employed himself to search for some common band, by which dispositions the most heterogeneous, and sects the most discordant, might have a centre of union. He studied mankind beyond the walls of his college; and the fellow of Lincoln became, in a certain sense, a man of the world. His penetration is wonderfully acute; and his dexterity in debate hath been so long known, that it is almost become proverbial. He was ever more attentive to reason and prudence than his great rival, George Whitefield. He was more calm in his address; more candid in his sentiments; and more reasonable in his doctrines. He had all Whitefield's zeal and perseverance, with double his understanding, and ten times more learning and science. Though prudence was his Pole-star, yet imagination was frequently his card. He gave it all the play that was necessary to establish the credit of his mission.

"Mr. John Wesley's prudence hath been frequently imputed to some sinister motives; and what appeared to his friends as 'the wisdom of the serpent,' was pronounced by his enemies to

be 'the craft of the wicked one.' The zealots of the second
house of Methodism speak this with a full mouth. I was at
Bristol some years since, when the Hon. Mr. Shirley, by the
order of my Lady Huntingdon, called him to a public account
for certain expressions which he had uttered in some charge to
his clergy, which savoured too much of the Popish doctrine of
the merit of good works. Various speculations were formed as
to the manner in which Mr. Wesley would evade the charge.
Few conjectured right; but all seemed to agree in one thing; and
that was, that he would somehow or other baffle his antagonist:
and baffle him he did; as Mr. Shirley afterwards confessed in a
very lamentable pamphlet, which he published on this redoubted
controversy. In the crisis of the dispute, I heard a celebrated
preacher, who was one of Whitefield's successors, express his
suspicion of the event; 'for,' says he, 'I know him of old: he
is an eel; take him where you will, he will slip through your
fingers.'

"A poem, intituled 'Religious Discourse,'* and published by
him in one of his earlier collections, was pointed out to me,
by his own niece, as a very striking delineation of his disposition
and character. She said, her father regarded it in the same unfavourable light. I have some doubt of this; for I have the
orginal copy now before me, with marginal corrections (chiefly
verbal) in the hand-writing of Samuel Wesley. Had he thoroughly disapproved of it, he would have drawn his pen across
the whole. His correction of particular passages was a tacit
acknowledgement of his approbation of the rest.

"At the beginning of the poem are these lines:
'But who must talk? not the mere formal sage
Who speaks the obsequious echo of the age,
To Christian lives who brings the Gospel down,
A Gospel moderniz'd by ——!'

"On this hiatus Samuel Wesley notes in the margin —
'If T——n, too hard.' —— Tillotson was undoubtedly meant.
He was equally the object of dislike to Methodists and High-
churchmen. His Theology was too rational for the former; and
his Politicks were too moderate for the latter. The wonder
is not that John Wesley should have shewn an inclination to

---

*This Poem was not written by any of the Mr. Wesleys, but by the late
learned and mystic Mr. John Gambold.

insult the memory of a sober Divine; but the wonder is, that
Samuel Wesley should have been disposed to shew lenity to a
Low-churchman, and a Whig of the Revolution : especially
when it is considered that he himself hath made this same
renowned and amiable Prelate the object of bitter satire, both in
his 'Parish Priest,' and in a poem 'to the memory of Dr. South.'
In the former his name is mentioned, and very invidiously
contrasted with Stillingfleet's; in the latter he is plainly alluded
to, as a secret abettor of 'Socinus and his followers;'

> 'And yields up points their favour to engage,
> Transcribing *Episcopius* by the page.'

"The Archbishop hath been also charged with too free a
use of the *Fratres Poloni,* the great Codex of the Socinians;
though he never condescended to acknowledge the obligation
to such obscure writers; for who ever heard of Schlichtingius,
Pscipcovius, or Wolzogenius? In the oblivion into which they
were sunk, he might fancy himself to be secure from detection.
Or possibly he might think that whatever he could glean from
their works, that had any intrinsic value in it, should be left
to itself, to make its own way in the world, well knowing that
it could receive no assistance or recommendation from the
Brethren of Poland.

"But to return from this digression to the characteristic
Poem of our sagacious and wary Apostle.

"There are passages in it which might give occasion to Mr.
John Wesley's enemies to represent him as a man of more art
than integrity; and perhaps it would puzzle the most subtle of
his Proselytes to reconcile his maxims with that "child-like and
dove-like simplicity" which he teaches, and they profess. As
the poem is very curious, and but little known, I think you
will be pleased with a few extracts from it :

> 'To the pert Reas'ner, if you speak at all,
> Speak what within his cognizance may fall,
> Expose not Truths divine to Reason's rack,
> Give him his own belov'd ideas back.
> *Your* notions, till they *look like his,* dilute;
> Blind he must be, but save him from dispute.
> But when we are turn'd of Reason's noon-tide glare,
> And things begin to shew us what they are,

More free to such your true conceptions tell,
Yet graft them on the arts where they excel.
If sprightly sentiments detain their taste,
If paths of various learning they have trac'd,
If their cool judgement longs, yet fears, to fix,
Fire, erudition, hesitation mix.'

"It is this accommodating method which hath brought on
Mr. Wesley the opprobrium of Jesuitism. I hope his ends were
Catholic and disinterested; though I must acknowledge, that
such means have the suspicious complexion of selfish and
sectarian cunning.

'To positive adepts, *insidious* yield,
To gain the conquest, *seem* to quit the field.
Large in your grants—Be their opinion shewn,
Approve, amend, and *wind it to your own.*'
"The following lines have spirit and humour in them :

'There are who watch to adore the dawn of Grace,
And pamper the young proselyte with praise.
Kind, humble souls ! they with a right good-will
Admire his progress — till he stands stock-still !
So fond, so smooth, so loving and so civil,
They praise the cred'lous saint into a devil ?'

"Sectaries and enthusiasts of all descriptions have frequent
opportunities of contemplating characters of this unsteady make.
A religion that is founded more on passion than judgment;
which applies its criteria to certain feelings which have no
fixed principle in the understanding; a religion which consists of
singularities that are beyond the habits of common life and
general custom, will be ever subject to ridiculous and untoward
vicissitudes.
"Dr. Warburton hath been thought profane in the ridicule
he hath so repeatedly thrown on Mr. Wesley's account of
'the pains and throws of the second birth.' He considered the
whole as a compound of credulity and imposture. The learned
Bishop was not always delicate in the choice of his allusions. If
his ideas were gross, he never gave himself the trouble to
refine them down by the niceties of expression. As he thought,
so he writ; and seemed to imagine, that to polish a rugged
sentiment was to weaken its force. "The Devil," says he,
"acted as mid-wife to Mr. Wesley's new-born babes." In

another part of his book, he takes occasion, from a concession
of the Arch-Methodist, to declare, that 'Mr. William Law
begat Methodism, and Count Zinzendorff rocked the cradle.'
He allows Whitefield little credit; calls him 'the madder of
the two:' but, considering him in a very inferior light to Mr.
Wesley, almost passes him by unnoticed. Whatever good and
laudable intentions the Bishop might have had; or how zealous
soever he might have been to support the interest of sober
Religion against the insults and encroachments of Fanaticism;
yet, I think, it is pretty generally allowed that he was not perfectly
happy in the means he chose to effect his good purposes. There
is much acute reasoning, and much poignant and sprightly
wit, in his 'Doctrine of Grace;' but there is in it too much
levity for a grave Bishop, and too much abuse for a candid
Christian. If the subject was not unworthy of his pen, he
should not have given such a representation of it as to make
it look as if it was. Who begat, or who midwived, or who
nursed *Methodism,* is a point I shall leave to the determination
of others. Mr. Wesley's own account of this matter is seen
to a better advantage in his poem, than in Bp. Warburton's
extracts from his Journals. Excuse this quotation; it shall be
the last.

'But, lest, reform'd from all extremer ill,
They should but civilize old Nature still;
The loftier charms and energy display
Of Virtue model'd by the Godhead's ray;
The lineaments divine, Perfection's plan,
The baseness and the dignity of man.
Commences now the agonizing strife,
Previous to Nature's death and second life.
Struck by their own inclement piercing eye,
Their feeble virtues blush, despair, and die.
They view the scheme that mimic Nature made,
A fancy'd goodness, and Religion's shade.
With angry scorn they now reject the whole,
Unchang'd the heart, undeified the soul,
Till indignation sleeps away to faith,
And God's own power and peace take root in sacred wrath.'

"Particular instances may be adduced, that in a detached
view might render Mr. Wesley's understanding a very problem-

atical thing. But an impartial and wise judge will not determine by a few particulars, but by the result of the whole. Mr. Wesley had a very important end in view; and it required a great degree of sagacity, as well as resolution, to plan and pursue the means that were necessary to effect it. These means considered in their joint dependance and operation were extraordinary, and called for an equal share of enthusiasm to actuate, and wisdom to superintend. Such schemes of reformation as were so extensive and complicated as his, were not the transient visions of an overheated fancy, but the deep projects of a subtle mind, and called for the most determined efforts of a warm, resolute, and yet cautious spirit.

"In one of Mr. Wesley's earlier publications, intituled, 'An Earnest Appeal to Men of Reason and Religion,' he, in the strongest language, disavows all pecuniary motives; and calls on posterity to vindicate his disinterestedness in one of the boldest apostrophes I ever read: 'Money must needs pass through my hands,' says he; 'but I will take care (God being my helper) that the Mammon of unrighteousness shall only pass through; it shall not rest there. None of the accursed thing shall be found in my tents, when the Lord calleth me hence. And hear ye this, all you who have discovered the treasures which I am to leave behind me; if I leave behind me ten pounds (above my debts and the little arrears of my fellowship) you and all mankind bear witness against me, that I lived and died a thief and a robber.' I doubt not but his pride, and something better than his pride, will prevent the stigma.

"At the age of fourscore, Mr. Wesley is still active and cheerful. His activity indeed hath always kept him in spirits, and prevented those fits of languor and despondency which generally overtake the indolent. He is an excellent companion; and, in spite of censure, I believe he is an honest man. The jealousy of the Tabernacle hath joined with the zeal of a higher house, to detract from the purity of his character; but the *arrow that flew in darkness* only recoiled on those who sent it.

"Mr. Wesley, after receiving the sacrament this last summer at the cathedral of Exeter, was invited by the Bishop* to dine at the Palace. There were some who thought his Lordship

*Dr. John Ross.

might have spared the compliment; but others considered it as only another proof, added to the many he hath already given, of his amiable courtesy, candour, and good-sense. How far he relaxed his zeal or his dignity by his condescension, may be a point to be canvassed by the scrupulous; but the wise and the good of every communion will settle it in a moment.

"The discourse at the table turned on a variety of literary topicks. At that time the publick was amused by the controversy about Rowley's Poems. Mr. Wesley said, that he had made enquiries about Chatterton; and, from the information he could gather, he could scarcely believe him equal to such a complicated and ingenious piece of fraud. The subject introduced the name of Mr. Jacob Bryant. Mr. Canon Moore asked him, if he had ever read that gentleman's "Analysis." He said, he had not only read the two first volumes, but had actually abridged them. Mr. Moore lent him the third volume, which he intended to abridge likewise. These are instances of uncommon assiduity, as well as singular curiosity, in this "transcendant man," as Bishop Warburton denominated him, in a vein of mingled satire and irony; but posterity may, perhaps, apply the epithet to him without a jest.

"I could with pleasure enlarge on this subject; but I write in great haste, and have only time to add, that there was a sister of the Wesleys, called Mehetabel, who married a gentleman of the name of Wright. I have seen some good pieces of hers both in prose and verse. She was unfortunate both before and after marriage; as was another of her sisters, who married the famous Wesley Hall of Salisbury, who had the honour of being Mr. Madan's precursor in the great mission of Thelypthora! I am, dear sir, yours, &c.   S. Badcock."

The preceding Letter was first printed in the "Bibliotheca Topographica Britannica," No. XX.; and, having afterwards been fully noticed by Mr. Maty, in his "'New Review," it produced the following Remarks from Mr. John Wesley:

"1. A day or two ago the Review fell into my hands, which contains a letter from the Rev. Mr. Badcock. I have not the pleasure of knowing this gentleman; but I esteem him for his useful and ingenious publications; and I think it my duty to inform both him and the publick better, of some points wherein they have been misinformed.

"2. He says, 'Mr. Samuel Wesley, of Epworth, in Lincolnshire, *was sent* to the University.' This is not accurate. He was educated for some years at a Dissenting academy, from which he then privately retired, and entered himself at Exeter college, in Oxford. — 'His heroic poem, the Life of Christ, excited the ridicule of the wits.' His own account of it was, 'the cuts are good; the notes pretty good; the verses so so.' — 'At a very advanced age he published a Latin work on the book of Job, which was never held in any estimation by the learned.' I doubt that. It certainly contains immense learning; but of a kind which I do not admire.

"3. 'He married a woman of extraordinary abilities, the daughter of Dr. Samuel Annesley.' (Dr. Annesley and the then Earl of Anglesea were brothers' sons.) — 'Samuel, his eldest son, was a noted Jacobite.' Nay, he was no more a Jacobite than he was a Turk. And what amends can Mr. Badcock, or Mr. Maty, make, for publishing this egregious falsehood? — ' Many of his political satires remain unpublished, on account of their treasonable tendency.' Here is a double mistake. For, 1. He never published any thing political, whether satirical or not. 2. He never wrote any thing of a treasonable tendency; he sacredly avoided it. — 'In his rage of Jacobitism, he poured out the very dregs of it on Royalty itself.' No, never. He never wrote, much less published, one line against the King. I speak it from personal knowledge, having often heard him say, 'If it reflects on the King, it is none of mine.' His constant practice may be learn from those lines, in "The Battle of the Sexes,"

'Forgive the voice that useful fiction sings,
   Not impious tales of deities impure;
Not faults of breathless Queens, or living Kings,
   In open treason, or in veil obscure.'

'Time, however, changed the satirist against Sir Robert, into an humble suppliant.' Nay, I do not believe, he ever wrote a line to Sir Robert, either in verse or prose.

"4. 'Mrs. Wesley lived long enough to deplore the extravagance of her two sons, John and Charles; considering them as *under strong delusions to believe a lie.*' By vile misrepresentations she was deceived for a time. But she no sooner heard them speak for themselves, than she was thoroughly convinced they were in no delusion; but spoke *the words of truth and soberness.* She afterwards lived *with me* several years, and died rejoicing and praising God.

"5. I was born in June 1708, and was between six and

seven years old, when I was left alone in my father's house, being then all in flames, till I was taken out of the nursery window, by a man strangely standing on the shoulders of another. Those words in the picture, *Is not this a brand plucked out of the burning?* chiefly allude to this.

"6. 'He had early a very strong impression of his designation to some extraordinary work.' Indeed not I: I never said so. I never thought so: I am guiltless in this matter. The strongest impression I had till I was three or four and twenty was, *Inter sylvas Academi quærere verum:* — and afterwards (while I was my father's curate), to save my own soul, and those that heard me. When I returned to Oxford, it was my full resolve to live and die there; the reasons for which I gave in a long letter to my father, since printed in one of my Journals. In this purpose I continued, till Dr. Burton, one of the trustees for Georgia, pressed me to go over with General Oglethorpe (who is still alive, and well knows the whole transaction), in order to preach to the Indians. With great difficulty I was prevailed upon to go, and spend upwards of two years abroad. At my return, I was more than ever determined to lay my bones at Oxford. But I was insensibly led, without any previous plan or design, to preach, first in many of the churches in London, then in more public places; afterwards in Bristol, Kingswood, Newcastle, and throughout Great Britain and Ireland. Therefore all that Mr. Badcock adds, of the incidents that 'gave an additional force,' to an impression that never existed, is very ingenious; yet is in truth a castle in the air.

"7. It is true, that for a while I admired the mystic writers. But I dropped them, even before I went to Georgia; long before I knew or suspected any such thing as justification by faith. Therefore all that follows, of my 'making my system of divinity more commodious for general use;' and of 'employing myself to search for some common bond, whereby the most dissonant sects might have a centre of union,' having no foundation to stand upon, falls to the ground at once. I had quite other work while I was at Oxford, being fully engaged, partly with my pupils, and partly with my little offices, being Greek lecturer, and moderator of both the classes.

"8. 'His dexterity in debate has been so long known, that it is almost become proverbial.' It has been my first care, for many years, to see that my cause was good: and never, either in jest or earnest, to defend the wrong side of a question. And

shame on me if I cannot defend the right, after so much
practice, and after having been so early accustomed to separate
truth from falsehood, how artfully soever they were twisted
together!

"9. If the poem on Religious Discourse 'delineates the
disposition and character of the author,' it does not delineate
mine; for I was not the author, but Mr. John Gambold. What
becomes then of that good-natured remark? — 'The wonder is
not, that John Wesley should have shewn an inclination to
insult the memory of a sober Divine; but that Samuel Wesley
should have been disposed to shew lenity to a Whig of the
Revolution.' Mistake upon mistake! 1. Those marginal notes
were not wrote by Samuel, but Charles Wesley. He told me
so this very day. 2. Both my father and all his sons have
always praised God for the happy Revolution. ——— I let
Bishop Warburton alone. He is gone to rest! I well hope, in
Abraham's bosom.

"10. 'Mr. Wesley had a very important end in view' ———
What end, but to save sinners? What other end could I
possibly have in view? or can have at this day? — 'Deep
projects of a subtle mind.' Nay, I am not subtle, but the
veriest fool under the sun, if I have any earthly project at all
now! For what do I want which this world can give? And,
after the labour of fourscore years,

> No foot of land do I possess,
> No cottage in the wilderness:
> A poor, way-faring man,
> I dwell awhile in tents below,
> Or gladly wander to and fro,
> Till I my Canaan gain."

The preceding Letter from Mr. Wesley, transplanted into
the Magazine, was thus answered:

"MR. URBAN,   South Molton, May 10, 1785.
"As Mr. John Wesley hath done me the honour of publicly
noticing my paper respecting his family, I think it a piece of
civility due to him, to notice his strictures in return.

"I am pleased that any 'publications' of mine should be
esteemed 'ingenious and useful,' by a man so well qualified
to judge of their merits. For his acquaintance with my name, as
the author of the publications which I suppose he had in his
eye, I am indebted to certain writers, who took the liberty of

proclaiming it in pamphlets, letters, reviews, and advertisements, with the *very generous* intention (for they are all *benevolent* men) of injuring its credit. The attempt, however, hath operated contrary to their wishes; and, if I needed a testimony, Mr. Wesley's would serve instead of a thousand.

"My paper was drawn up in great haste; but it was drawn up under the impression of sentiments not hastily adopted. An opinion of Mr. Wesley's great abilities, and an esteem for qualities which he possesses of still greater account, have long been familiar to my mind. I have been conversant with his writings from my earliest youth; and, though never his disciple, have been always his admirer.

"I have already informed the publick by what means I became acquainted with some papers which relate to the more secret history of his family. Had they been papers of a *merely* family or personal concern, I would never have communicated any account of them to the publick. Had they tended to fix any reproach on the private characters of individuals, I would have suppressed them : and I was not conscious of doing an injury to the memory of Mr. Samuel Wesley when I called him a *Jacobite*. I called him, indeed, by a title which in politicks I abhor: but I have learnt to separate *political* from *moral* character; and have no doubt but a Jacobite may be as good a man, and as perfect a Christian, as even a Whig or a Presbyterian. I judge of no man merely by his opinions or prejudices; nor at all times would I judge of him by any improper bias, or influence, that they may give to his conduct. If I know the cause, I can account for the effect; and if I can excuse the former, surely I cannot want an apology for the latter.

"There are certain fundamental principles of conduct, in which all good men, with all their prejudices and partialities, are united. They are the common bands of society: the universal laws, which are independent of custom or country, sects and parties; and may be said to know no distinction between 'Greek or Jew; Scythian, barbarian, bond or free.'

"I have now given my *creed of charity;* which, for a *Calvinist,* as I have been denominated, is somewhat free: and I would risk the credit of any orthodoxy rather than recal it.

"I esteem Mr. Wesley for the zeal he hath discovered in vindicating his brother from the imputation of Jacobitism; but, till I am convinced, I cannot retract: and my conviction of

Mr. Samuel Wesley's antipatny to the House of Brunswick is founded on evidence too strong to be overcome by mere general assertions to the contrary.

"However, if there be an error in my account, let *me* be wholly answerable for it. Mr. Wesley should not have coupled Mr. Maty's name with mine; especially in such uncivil language. If I cannot prove what I have advanced, let the blame rest on my own head alone : he is guiltless.

"And, were I convinced that I had been guilty of a false accusation, no man would be more ready to acknowledge it. But as I cannot, in justice to my own persuasions, revoke what I have written, it is certainly due, both to the publick and to myself, to give some reason for what I have asserted.

"I would first, in general, observe, that when I called Mr. Samuel Wesley 'a *noted* Jacobite,' I only echoed back the voice of popular fame. His brother cannot be ignorant that he always bore this character; and his greatest friends, and most intimate associates in this part of the kingdom, made no scruple of applying to him a title, to which, I really believe, he had no dislike.

"His daughter often assured me, that he was strongly attached to the exiled family; and she once shewed me a small print of the Pretender, which, *she said,* had been presented to her father, and which he esteemed as a sort of a precious memorial. A late excellent and ever-honoured friend of mine, who was the pupil of Mr. Samuel Wesley, and who in his earlier days had imbibed a tincture from politicks of the same colour and quality (though his maturer wisdom dictated far different sentiments), frequently called his old master a Jacobite; and appeared to entertain no conception, that any one would question his right to an appellation, to which that good man affixed no moral turpitude or infamy, though a genuine '*Whig of the Revolution.*'

"Other pupils of Mr. Wesley have confirmed to me this account of his political principles; but my conviction hath not arisen from general or vague report, even though backed by the authority I have mentioned; but from evidence more particular and more decisive.

"Mr. Wesley says, in his Remarks on my paper, that 'he [*viz.* Samuel Wesley] never published any thing political, whether satirical or not.' — 'He never wrote any thing of a treasonable tendency; he sacredly avoided it.' — 'He never *wrote,* much less published, *one line against the King.'*

"Had Mr. Wesley read the poems which Mrs. Earle, his brother's only child, put into my hands, he never could have expressed himself in such unqualified language. Amid a number which I once possessed, I can at present only lay my hands on one, entitled 'The Regency.' It was written by Mr. Samuel Wesley, purposely with a view to raise a laugh at the expence of the King [George the First] in the choice which he made of the persons who were intrusted with the prerogative while he visited Hanover. — I will transcribe a few verses of this witty and sarcastic poem; and let our readers judge how far the author '*sacredly* avoided' what had a 'treasonable *tendency.'*

'As soon as the wind it came fairly about,
That kept the King in, and his enemies out;
He determin'd no longer his confinement to bear,
And thus to the Duchess his mind did declare.

Quoth he 'My dear *Kenny**, I've been tir'd a long while,
With living obscure in this poor little Isle;
And, now Spain and Pretender have no more mines to spring,
I'm resolv'd to go home, and live like a King.'

Quoth Kenny 'Great sir! I approve your design,' &c.

And so Kenny ludicrously runs over the list of the Regents; estimates their several qualifications; and, by exposing them obliquely, laughs at the King himself.
    "Of the Duke of Argyle she is made to say:

'And had not the stars been equally strong,
To keep him in the right, and you in the wrong,
It might have induc'd him such schemes to pursue,
As had made him be lov'd — full as little as you.'

    "After lashing the Lords of the Regency all round, the
        Duchess says, in the conclusion,

---

*The Duchess of Kendal, the King's favourite mistress.

'On the whole, I'll be hang'd, if all over the realm,
There are thirteen such fools to be put at the helm :
So for this time be easy, nor have jealous thought,
They ha'n't sense to sell you, nor are worth being bought.'

' 'Tis for that (quoth the King in very bad French)
I chose them for my Regents, and you for my Wench :
And neither, I'm sure, will my trust e'er betray;
For the Devil won't take you, if I turn you away.'

"Let these lines be glossed over by any art or refinement whatever, yet they can never be accommodated to that reverence which Mr. Wesley would acknowledge to be due to *the Lord's anointed,* let him be who he may.

"I cannot produce the poem Mr. Samuel Wesley addressed to Sir Robert Walpole in behalf of his father. I have only a general recollection of it; but a recollection sufficient to make me assert with confidence, that such a poem did really exist : and I particularly remember, that he intreated the great Statesman not to permit any prejudices, that he might have imbibed against himself, to stand in the way of his beneficence to his father.

"But I will not any farther urge a circumstance, of which I am utterly incapable of producing the proof that may be required to establish it.

"I was not acquainted with the later periods of Mrs. Wesley's life : I only spoke of what I knew. Her letters breathe a spirit of rational and enlightened piety; and she frequently deplored, in very pathetic language, the departure of her two sons from the simplicity of Christian faith, and their innovations on the order and decorum of the established worship. She adopted, it seems, very different sentiments of their principles and conduct several years before her death. To whatever society of Christians she united herself, I doubt not but she was an honour to them; and wonder not that a life, that had been so singularly pious and exemplary, should close, as Mr. Wesley says his mother's did, with a hope full of immortality.

"Her Letters to her daughter on the first Principles of Religion, together with some other curious papers, I communicated some years ago to Dr. Priestley; and when he expressed a desire to transcribe them, I saved him the trouble, by freely making him a present of the originals. One of the most valuable (and which, in a letter to me, he calls *'uncommonly curious'*) he hath unfortunately lost. I took no copy of it myself, so that I am afraid it is irrecoverable.

"It is a kind of presumption to publish speculations about the state of another person's mind, and the different steps by which it acquires certain principles and habits; especially at a time when that person may speak for himself, and call all that you have advanced the fiction of your own imagination. And it would be the height of insolence and obstinacy to persevere in maintaining what he, who hath the best right to contradict it, positively disavows. *'For what man knoweth the things of a man, save the spirit of a man, which is in him?'*

" 'Therefore,' (says Mr. Wesley) 'all that Mr. Badcock adds, of the incidents that *gave an additional force* to an impression that never existed, is very ingenious; yet it in truth a castle in the air.'

"Let my conjectures then be the mere dream of fancy. I will not dispute for what I cannot prove, nor have even a wish to maintain. I might have been deceived, when I talked of Mr. Wesley's enthusiastic impressions and prophetic notices. But, when I spoke of his admirable talents, his extraordinary exertions, his honest zeal, and his generous superiority to the world and its possessions, I am sure I was not deceived; I *built no castle in the air,* but raised a humble pillar to his fame on that ground where posterity will erect a nobler and more lasting monument. SAM. BADCOCK."

Mr. Wesley thus rejoined :

City Road, Dec. 24, 1785.

"MR. URBAN,

"This morning a friend sent me the Gentleman's Magazine for last May, wherein I find another letter concerning my eldest brother. I am obliged to Mr. Badcock for the candid manner wherein he writes; and wish to follow his pattern, in considering the reasons which he urges in defence of what he wrote before. — 1. Mr. Badcock says, 'His brother cannot be ignorant, that he always bore the character of a Jacobite; a title to which I really believe he had no dislike.' Most of those who gave him this title did not distinguish between a *Jacobite* and a *Tory;* whereby I mean, 'one that believes God, not the People, to be the origin of all Civil Power.' In this sense he was a *Tory;* so was my Father; so am I. But I am no more a *Jacobite* than I am a Turk; neither was my Brother. I have heard him over and over disclaim that character.

"2. 'But his own daughter affirmed it.' Very likely she might; and doubtless she thought him such. Nor is this any wonder, considering how young she was when her father died, especially if she did not know the difference between a Tory and a Jacobite; which may likewise have been the case with Mr. Badcock's friends, if not with Mr. Badcock himself.

"3. 'Mr. Wesley says, He never published any thing political.' This is strictly true. — 'He never wrote, much less published, *one line* against the King.' He never *published one*. But I believe he did write those verses, intituled, *The Regency;* and therein, 'by obliquely exposing the Regents, exposed the King himself.' In this my Brother and I differed in our judgments; I thought, exposing the King's ministers was one way of exposing the King himself. My Brother thought otherwise; and therefore, without scruple, exposed Sir Robert Walpole, and all other evil ministers. Of his writing to Sir Robert I never heard before, and cannot easily believe it now.

"4. From the moment that my mother heard my brother and me answer for ourselves, she was ashamed of having paid any regard to the vile misrepresentations which had been made to her after our return from Georgia. She then fully approved both our principles and practice; and soon after removed to my house, and gladly attended all our ministrations, till her spirit returned to God.   JOHN WESLEY."

This extraordinary man was born at Epworth in 1703; and was entered a scholar of the Charter-house about 1713, where he continued for seven years, under the instruction of the celebrated Dr. Walker and Mr. Andrew Tooke, author of "The Pantheon," and contemporary with Dr. Kenrick Prescot, late master of Catharine-hall, Cambridge. Being elected off to Lincoln college, Oxford, he became there a fellow about 1725; took the degree of M. A. in 1726; and was joint tutor with the late rector, Dr. Hutchins. During his residence there, he was equally distinguished by application and abilities, and laid up those large and varied stories of knowledge which he directed, during his long life, to the best purposes. But what chiefly characterised him, even at the early age of 26, was piety. By reading the works of the famous William Law, he, his brother Charles, and a few young friends, entered into that strict course of life which marks their sect at the present day. They received the sacrament every week; observed all the fasts of the church; visited prisons; rose at four o'clock, and partook of no amusements. From the exact method in which they disposed of each hour, they acquired the nick-name of *Methodists,* and are the only people who take to themselves a term first given in reproach. The ridicule and contempt which this singular conduct produced, John and Charles Wesley were well qualified to bear. They were neither to be intimidated by danger, affected by interest, nor deterred by disgrace. But their honest zeal did not stop here. In 1735 they embarked for Georgia, in order to convert the Indians; but returned to England in 1737, when the charges of enthusiasm, bigotry, and fanaticism, were urged with so much bitterness, and examined with so little candour, that they were forbidden to preach any more in the churches. This gave rise to field-preaching, in which George Whitefield was first; with whom the Wesleys had cordial friendship, though they separated their congregations on some differences in sentiments. John Wesley embraced the mild and general views of Arminius, which, it must be confessed, are more benevolent in their nature, and practical in their tendency, than Calvin's. His abhorrence of the doctrine and the man occasioned long, bitter, and useless controversy; though he never treated his opponents with the ill-breeding and abuse that he received from them. He now appeared as a zealous reformer, and the great leader of a set no way differing in essentials from the Church of England. His peculiar opinions were, justification by faith, and Christian perfection; of which it may be remarked, the former is to be found in our own Articles, and the latter, however he might enforce its possibility, he always disclaimed having attained himself. In 1738 he visited, at Hernhuth in Germany, Count Zinzendorff, the chief of the Moravians. In the following year we find him again in England, and, with his brother Charles, at the head of the Methodists. He preached his first *field sermon* at Bristol, on the 2d of April 1738, from which time his disciples have continued to increase. In 1741 a serious altercation took place between him and Mr. Whitefield. In 1744, attempting to preach at a public inn at Taunton, he was regularly silenced by the magistrates. Though he remained the rest of his days nearer home, he travelled through every part of England, Scotland, and Ireland, establishing congregations in each kingdom. In 1750 he married a lady, from whom he afterwards parted, and she died in 1781 : by her he had no children. This separation, from whatever motives it originated, we have heard some of his followers say, was the only blot in his character. Others have observed on this head, that nothing could be more effectually disappointed than ambition or avarice in an union with John Wesley. In 1755 he published "Serious Thoughts on the Earthquake at Lisbon;" and in 1771 seems first to have commenced politician, by publishing "Thoughts on Public Affairs;" which was followed by "Thoughts on Slavery, 1774;" "An Address to the Colonies, 1775;" "Observa- on Liberty, 1776." His other writings it is not very easy to enumerate. Few men have written so voluminously; divinity, devotional and controversial, history, philosophy, medicine, politicks, poetry, &c. &c. were all, at different times, the subjects of his pen; and whatever may be the opinions held of his divinity, it is impossible to deny him the merit of having done infinite good to the lower class of people. Abilities he unques- tionably possessed, and a fluency which was highly acceptable, and well accommodated to his hearers. He had been gradually declining for about three years : yet he still rose at four o'clock, and preached, travelled, and wrote, as usual. He preached at Leatherhead Feb. 23, 1791. On the 28th the first symptoms of his approaching dissolution appeared. The four succeeding days he spent in praising the God of his mercies; and departed on the morning of March 2, to receive the reward of a life spent in bringing "glory to God in the highest, and peace and good-will to men."

His remains, after lying in his Tabernacle in a kind of state, dressed in the gown and cassock, band, &c. which he usually wore, and on his head the old clerical cap, a Bible in one hand, and a white handkerchief in the other, were, agreeably to his own directions, and after the manner of the interment of the late Mr. Whitefield, deposited in a piece of ground near his chapel at the Foundery, Moorfields, on the morning of the 9th of March, in the plainest manner consistent with decency, amidst the tears and sighs of an innumerable company of his friends and admirers, who all appeared in deep mourning on the occasion. A sermon, previously to the funeral, was preached by Thomas Whitehead, M.D. (one of the physicians to the London hospital), accompanied with suitable Hymns, &c. And on the 13th, the different chapels in his connexion in London were hung with black.

Where much good is done, we should not mark every little

excess. The great point in which Mr. Wesley's name and mission will be honoured is this: he directed his labours towards those who had no instructor; to the highways and hedges; to the mines in Cornwall, and to the colliers in Kingswood. These unhappy creatures married and buried among themselves, and often committed murders with impunity, before the Methodists sprang up. By the humane and active endeavours of him and his brother Charles, a sense of decency, morals, and religion, was introduced into the lowest classes of mankind; the ignorant were instructed, the wretched relieved; and the abandoned reclaimed. He met with great opposition from many of the Clergy; and unhandsome treatment from the Magistrates, who frequently would refuse to check or punish a lawless mob, that often assembled to insult or abuse him. He was, however, one of the few characters who outlived enmity and prejudice; and received, in his latter years, every mark of respect from every denomination. — The political sentiments of popular men are of importance to the State. John Wesley was a strenuous advocate for Monarchy; and all his followers in America were firmly Royal. Those of Mr. Whitefield declared in favour of Independence. His personal influence was greater than, perhaps, that of any other private gentleman in any country. It was computed that in 1791 there were in the three kingdoms 80,000 members of this society. He visited them alternately; travelled 8000 miles every year; preached three or four times constantly in one day; rose at four, and employed all his time in reading, writing, attending the sick, and arranging the various parts of this numerous body of people. — Amongst his virtues, forgiveness to his enemies, and liberality to the poor, were most remarkable: he has been known to receive into even his confidence those who have basely injured him; they have not only subsisted again on his bounty, but shared in his affection. — All the profit of his literary labours, all that he received, or could collect (and it amounted to an immense sum, for he was his own printer and bookseller), was devoted to charitable purposes. Yet, with such opportunities of enriching himself, it was doubtful whether the sale of the books would pay all his debts. His travelling expences were defrayed by the societies which he visited.

The superintendency of his various chapels and societies he committed, about the year 1784, by a deed enrolled in Chancery (in trust for support of his preachers and their poor families), to an hundred travelling preachers, then in various parts of these

kingdoms; and among the number was the Rev. Dr. Coke, at
that time in America, whose mission was supposed to have
increased the converts in the West India Islands, and other parts
of America, to near 50,000, after the conclusion of the war,
and founder, in 1789, of a college in South Carolina, called
Wesley college.

On a review of the character of this extraordinary man, it
appears that, though he was endowed with eminent talents, he
was more distinguished by their use than even by their possession. Though his taste was classic, and his manners elegant, he
sacrificed that society in which he was particularly calculated to
shine; gave up those preferments which his abilities must have
obtained, and devoted a long life in practising and enforcing
the plainest duties. Instead of being "an ornament to literature,"
he was a blessing to his fellow creatures; instead of "the genius
of the age," he was the servant of God!

[John Wesley's Chapel, opened 1778, still stands on the east
side of the City Road. His house, next to it, restored after bomb
damage, is now a Wesley Museum. In front of the chapel is the
statue of Wesley, erected in 1891, and in a yard at the back is
his grave. (*Ed.*)]

REV. GEORGE WHITEFIELD

"I WAS born," he says, "in Gloucestershire, in the month
of December 1714, at the Bell-inn; and can truly say I
was froward from my mother's womb. I was so brutish as to
hate instruction, and used purposely to shun all opportunities of
receiving it. I can date some very early acts of uncleanness.
Lying, filthy talking, and foolish jesting, I was much addicted
to. Sometimes I used to curse, if not swear. Stealing from my
mother I thought no theft at all, and used to make no scruple
of taking money out of her pocket before she was up. I have
frequently betrayed my trust; and have more than once spent
money I took in the house, in buying fruit, tarts, &c. to satisfy
my sensual appetites. Numbers of Sabbaths have I broken, and
generally used to behave myself very irreverently in God's Sanc-

tuary. Much money have I spent in Plays, and in the common entertainments of the age. Cards, and reading Romances, were my heart's delight. Often have I joined with others in playing roguish tricks; but was generally, if not always, happily detected. For this I have often since, and do now, bless and praise God. It would be endless to recount the sins and offences of my younger days — they are more in number than the hairs of my head. My heart would fail me at the remembrance of them, was I not assured that my Redeemer liveth, ever to make intercession for me. However the young man in the Gospel might boast how he had kept the Commandments from his youth, with shame and confusion of face I confess that I have broken them all from my youth. Whatever foreseen fitness for salvation others may talk of, and glory in, I disclaim any such thing — if I trace myself from my cradle to my manhood, I can see nothing in me but a fitness to be damned; and if the Almighty had not prevented me by his grace, and wrought most powerfully upon my soul, quickening me by his free spirit when dead in trespasses and sins, I had now either been sitting in darkness, and in the shadow of death, or condemned, as the due reward of my crimes, to be for ever lifting up my eyes in torments. But such was the free grace of God to me, that though corruption worked so strongly in my soul, and produced such early and bitter fruits, yet I can recollect very early movings of the blessed Spirit upon my heart, sufficient to satisfy me that God loved me with an everlasting love, and separated me, even from my mother's womb, for the work for which he afterwards was pleased to call me. I had early some convictions of sin; and once, I remember, when some persons (as they frequently did) made it their business to teaze me, I immediately retired to my room, and, kneeling down, with many tears, prayed over that Psalm wherein David so often repeats these words, *But in the name of the Lord I will destroy them.* I was always fond of being a Clergyman, used frequently to imitate the Minister's reading prayers, &c. Part of the money I used to steal from my parent I gave to the poor; and some books I privately took from others (for which I have since restored four-fold), I remember, were books of devotion. My mother was very careful of my education, and always kept me in my tender years from intermeddling in the least with the public business. About the 10th year of my age, it pleased God to permit my mother to marry a second time. It proved what the world call *an unhappy match;* but

God over-ruled it for good. When I was about twelve, I was placed at a school called St. Mary de Crypt in Gloucester, the last grammar -school I ever went to. Having a good elocution and memory, I was remarked for making speeches before the Corporation at their annual visitation.But I cannot say I felt any dawnings of God upon my soul for a year or two, saving that I laid out some of the money that was given me on one of the aforementioned occasions, in buying Ken's Manual for Winchester Scholars, a book that had much affected me when my brother used to read it in my mother's troubles, and which, for some time after I bought it, was of great benefit to my soul. During the time of my being at school, I was very fond of reading Plays; and have kept from school for days together, to prepare myself for acting them. My master, seeing how mine and my schoolfellows vein run, composed something of this kind for us himself, and caused me to dress myself in girl's cloaths (which I had often done) to act a part before the Corporation. The remembrance of this has often covered me with confusion of face, and I hope will do so even to the end of my life. Before I was 15, having, as I thought, made a sufficient progress in the Classicks, and, at the bottom, longing to be set at liberty from the confinement of a school, I one day told my mother, 'since her circumstances would not permit her to give me an University education, more learning I thought would spoil me for a tradesman, and therefore I judged it best not to learn Latin any longer.' She at first refused to consent; but my corruptions soon got the better of her good-nature. Hereupon, for some time, I went to learn to write only. But, my mother's circumstances being much on the decline, and being tractable that way, I from time to time began to assist her occasionally in the public-house, till at length I put on my blue apron and my snuffers, washed mops, cleaned rooms, and, in one word, became a professed and common drawer. Nothwithstanding I was thus employed in a large inn, and had sometimes the care of the whole house upon my hands, yet I composed two or three Sermons, and dedicated one of them, in particular, to my elder brother. One time, I remember, I was very much pressed to self-examination, and found myself very unwilling to look into my heart. Frequently I read the Bible when sitting up at night. Seeing the boys go by to school, has often cut me to the heart. And a dear youth (now with God) would often come intreating me, when serving at the bar, to go to Oxford.

My general answer was, *I wish I could*. After I had continued about a year in this servile employment, my mother was obliged to leave the inn. My brother, who had been bred up for the business, married, whereupon all was made over to him; and I being accustomed to the house, it was judged best that I should continue there as an assistant. But it happened that my sister-in-law and I could by no means agree; and therefore, after continuing a long while under a great burden of mind, I at length resolved (thinking my absence would make all things easy) to go away. Accordingly, by the advice of my brother, and consent of my mother, I went to see my elder brother, then settled at Bristol. Here God was pleased to give me great sensible devotion, and fill me with such unspeakable raptures, particularly once in St. John's church, that I was carried out beyond myself. I felt great hungerings and thirstings after the blessed Sacrament; and wrote many letters to my mother, telling her I would never go into the public employment again. Thomas à Kempis was my great delight, and I was always impatient till the bell rung to call me to tread the courts of the Lord's house. But in the midst of these illuminations, something secretly whispered, *This would not last*. And indeed it so happened. For (oh that I could write in tears of blood!) when I left Bristol (as I did in about two months), and returned to Gloucester, I changed my devotion with my place. Alas! all my fervour went off; and I had no inclination to go to church, or draw nigh unto God. However, I had so much Religion left as to persist in my resolution not to live in the inn; and therefore my mother gave me leave, though she had but a little income, to have a bed upon the ground, and live at her house, till Providence should point out a place for me. Having now, as I thought, nothing to do, it was a proper season for Satan to tempt me. Much of my time I spent in reading Plays, and in sauntering from place to place. I was careful to adorn my body, but took little pains to deck and beautify my soul. Evil communications with my old school-fellows soon corrupted my good-manners. By seeing their evil practices, all sense of Religion gradually wore off my mind, and I at length fell into a secret sin, the dismal effects of which I have felt, and groaned under ever since. Having lived thus for some considerable time, a young student, who was once my schoolfellow, and then a servitor of Pembroke college, Oxford, came to pay my mother a visit. Amongst other conversation, he told her how he had discharged all College expences that quarter, and received a penny. Upon that my mother immediately cried out, 'This will do for my son.' Then turning to me, she said, "Will you go to Oxford, George?" I replied, *With all my heart.* Whereupon, having the same friends that this young student had, my mother, without delay, waited on them. They promised their interest, to get me a Servitor's place in the same College. She then applied to my old master, who much approved of my coming to school again. In about a week I went and entered myself, and spared no pains to go forward in my book. God was pleased to give me his blessing, and I learned much faster than I did before. But all this while I continued in sin; and at length got acquainted with such a set of debauched, abandoned, atheistical youths, that if God, by his free, un-merited, and especial grace, had not delivered me out of their hands, I should long since have sat in the scorner's chair. By keeping company with them, my thoughts of Religion grew more and more like theirs. I went to public service only to make sport, and walk out. I took pleasure in their lewd conversation. I began to reason as they did, and was in a fair way of being as infamous as the worst of them. But (oh stupendous love!) God even here stopped me, when running on in a full career to Hell. For just as I was upon the brink of ruin, he gave me such a distaste of their principles and practices, that I discovered them to my master, who soon put a stop to their proceedings. Being thus delivered out of the snares of the Devil, I began to be more and more serious, and felt the spirit of God at different times working powerfully and convincingly upon my soul. One day in parti-cular, as I was coming down stairs, and overheard my friends speaking well of me, God so deeply convicted me of hypocrisy, that though I had formed frequent but ineffectual resolutions before, yet I had then power given me over my secret and darling sin. Notwithstanding, some time after being overtaken in liquor (as I have been twice or thrice in my life-time), Satan gained his usual advantage over me again; an experimental proof to my poor soul, how that wicked one makes use of intemperate men as machines to work them up to just what he pleases." — Thus far in Mr. Whitefield's own words. When admitted a servitor at Pembroke college, he very soon distin-guished himself by the austerities of his devotion, and acquired considerable eminence in some religious assemblies in Oxford; "lying whole days and weeks prostrate on the ground in silent or vocal prayer; leaving off the eating of fruits; choosing the worst sort of food, though his place furnished him with variety, thinking it unbecoming a penitent to have his hair powdered; wearing woollen gloves, a patched gown, and dirty shoes," to contract a habit of humility. At the age of 21, the fame of Mr. Whitefield's piety recommended him so much to Dr. Benson, the then Bp. of Gloucester, that he made him a voluntary offer of ordination, which Mr. Whitefield at last thought proper to accept; and was accordingly ordained, June 10, 1736. On the following Sunday he preached his first Sermon, at Gloucester, in the church where he had been baptized, "on the Necessity and Benefit of Religious Society;" and in the week following, on his return to Oxford, took the degree of B. A.; and, immediately after this regular admission into the ministry, applied himself to the most extraordinary, the most indefatigable duties of his character; and was invited to preach in most of the large churches in London, till, in December 1737, having at length made himself universally known, he embarked for America, where the tenets of Methodism began to spread very fast under his friends the Wesleys; and first determined upon the institution of the Orphan-house at Georgia, which he afterwards effected. He returned to London, after visiting Ireland, in December 1738; and in January 1739 was ordained priest by Bp. Benson; after which time, the churches not being sufficiently capacious, he preached daily wherever he thought there would be a likelihood of making proselytes; in *prisons, fields,* and *open streets;* in church-yards; on Kennington Common, and in Moorfields; and particularly to the colliers of Kingswood, on Hannam Mount, near Bristol. In August 1739 he went a second time to Georgia; and preached incessantly in various parts of the American Continent. On his return to England, in March 1741, he found that "the Moravians had made inroads upon the societies; and that Mr. John Wesley had been prevailed on to preach and print in favour of perfection and universal redemption." He preached, however, *once,* but no more, at the *Foundery,* a place which his friend John Wesley had procured during his absence; and "to have heard the weeping between him and Mr. Charles Wesley, after prayer, would have melted any heart." From this time a separation of these sectarian leaders took place; and a *Tabernacle* was erected by the friends of Mr. Whitefield, near the Foundery; which "he disliked, as it looked like erecting altar against altar." After this he visited many parts of Essex; and preached, on a common near Braintree, to near 10,000 persons. In this year he also visited Scotland; and was particularly noticed by many persons of considerable distinction. In October, he travelled from Edinburgh to Abergavenny; where he married Mrs. Jones, a widow lady, and from that time till August 1744 continued in England. The next four years were passed in America; whence, after stopping at the Bermuda Islands, he returned to England, in July 1748, after an absence of four years; but found his congregation of the Tabernacle sadly scattered, and his own pecuniary affairs in a very deranged state. But his congregation was soon recruited; and a very unexpected incident occurred. The pious and benevolent Countess of Huntingdon, having expressed a desire to see him at her house at Chelsea as soon as he came on shore; he went, and, having preached twice, the Countess informed him, that several of the Nobility desired to see him. In a few days, the Earl of Chesterfield, and a whole circle of persons of fashion, attended; and, having heard him once, they desired to hear him again. "I therefore preached again," he says, "in the evening; and went home never more surprized in my life. All behaved quite well, and were in some degree affected. The Earl of Chesterfield thanked me; and said, 'Sir, I will not tell you, what I shall tell others, how I approve of you;' or words to that purpose. At last Lord Bolingbroke came to hear; sat like an Archbishop; and was pleased to say, I had 'done great justice to the Divine Attributes in my discourse.' Soon afterwards her Ladyship removed to town; where I preached generally twice a week to very brilliant audiences." In October that year he visited Scotland for the third time. In 1750 he went to Ashby-de-la-Zouch, to wait on the Countess of Huntingdon, who had been ill; and, in his way thither, had "a most comfortable interview, at Northampton, with Dr. Doddridge, Mr. Hervey, and two pious Clergymen of the Church of England, both known to the learned world by their valuable writings." After a long course of peregrination, his fortune increased, as his fame extended among his followers; and, after preaching for a short time in Long Acre chapel, where "he met all sorts of opposition and difficulties," he began, May 10, 1750, to build a new Chapel at Tottenhamcourt-road; which he opened on the 7th of November; and continued during that winter to preach commonly in it about fifteen times in every week; and here, and at the Tabernacle near Moorfields, with the help of some assistants, he continued for several years, attended by very crowded congregations, and quitting the kingdom only occasionally. Besides the Tabernacle and Chapel already mentioned, by being chaplain to the Countess of Huntingdon, he was connected with two other religious meetings, one the celebrated Chapel at Bath, which he opened in July 1765, and the other at Tunbridge, chiefly erected under that Lady's patronage. America, however, which always engaged much of his attention, was destined to close his eyes; and he died at Newberry, about 40 miles from Boston in New England, Sept. 30, 1769.

JOHN WILKES

JOHN WILKES was born Oct. 17, 1727. His father, Israel Wilkes, lived in the true style of ancient English hospitality; to which both he and his wife (Sarah, the daughter of John Heaton, esq.) were always remarkably attentive. Their coach was regularly drawn by six horses; and their house was much frequented, particularly by many characters of distinguished rank in the commercial and learned world. To this circumstance, and the unbounded indulgence of his parents, John Wilkes was indebted for that literary turn of mind by which he was very early distinguished.

Israel Wilkes had three sons; Israel*, John, and Heaton. He had also two daughters.

John, the second son, after having imbibed the first scholastic rudiments at Hertford, was placed under a private tutor, Mr. Leeson, a Dissenting Clergyman, who resided in the Vicarage-house at Aylesbury; and by whom he was afterwards attended to the University of Leyden. When he had completed his studies, he made a tour through the Dutch Provinces, the Austrian Netherlands, and part of Germany.

Mr. Wilkes was elected F. R. S. in April 1749; and in October married —— Mead, heiress to the Meads of Buckinghamshire.

---

*Many years a Merchant in London. He was elected F. R. S. in 1760; but afterwards settled at New York, where he died, Nov. 25, 1805, æt. 83.

By that lady he had an only daughter, Mary, born August 5, 1750; and soon after, from a total dissimilarity of sentiment, Mr. Wilkes and his wife agreed to live separately.

He was appointed High Sheriff for Buckinghamshire in February 1754. In that situation he made his first essay in municipal and provincial interests; and evinced his qualifications, acquired by study and attention to the duties of a Magistrate, as well as the politeness of a Gentleman.

In the same year, on the 14th of April, he unsuccessfully offered himself as a candidate to represent the Borough of Berwick: but was elected for Aylesbury, July 6, 1757; and in that year, on the first raising of the Buckinghamshire Militia, he was appointed Lieutenant-colonel.

In 1761 he was again elected Member for Aylesbury; wrote several Political Essays in the St. James's Chronicle; made an unsuccessful application for the Embassy at Constantinople; and was also disappointed in not obtaining the office of Governor of Canada, the Treaty of Peace not then taking place.

March 9, 1762, he published "Observations on the Papers relative to the Rupture of Spain, laid before both Houses of Parliament on Friday, Jan. 29, 1762, by his Majesty's Command;" and in June, on the resignation of Sir Francis Dashwood, Mr. Wilkes succeeded him as Colonel. The "North Briton" was begun on the 2d of that month; and, Oct. 5, he fought a duel with Earl Talbot at Bagshot, of which the particulars were given by himself, in a Letter to Earl Temple.

In No. XXI. Oct. 13, appeared a Letter, with Mr. Wilkes's name, to Dr. Burton, Master of Winchester School, relative to a son of the Earl of Bute.

In March 1763, he prefixed to a new edition of Ben Jonson's Tragedy, "The Fall of Mortimer," an ironical Dedication to the Earl of Bute; and published "A Peep into Futurity."

The North Briton, No. XLV. April 23, produced the General Warrant by which Mr. Wilkes was committed to the Tower on the 30th. May 4, he was dismissed from the Buckinghamshire Militia; and on the 6th he obtained an important verdict, which determined the illegality of General Warrants; and, erecting a printing-press immediately after in his own house, he published the Proceedings of Administration, with all the original papers. The North Briton also again made its appearance.

On the 7th of July a verdict was obtained against the King's Messenger by Mr. Wilkes's Journeymen Printers, who had been illegally taken into custody.

Mr. Wilkes now retired to Paris; where in consequence of a challenge from Captain John Forbes, Aug. 15, he was put under arrest by the Marshals of France; but, as soon as he was at liberty, proceeded to wait for his Challenger at Menin.

On his return to England, he published, Nov. 12, the North Briton, No. XLVI.; and on the 15th attended in his place as a Member of the House of Commons; when it was resolved,* that the North Briton should be burnt by the common hangman. On the following day, on account of what had passed in the House, he fought a duel with Samuel Marshal, esq.; and received a dangerous wound from a pistol-bullet.

Dec. 6, he obtained a verdict of 4000*l.* against Robert Wood, esq. one of the Under Secretaries of State.

On the 16th, Dr. Heberden and Mr. Cæsar Hawkins were ordered to attend him, to observe the progress of his cure; but he declined their assistance: yet, in justification of the characters of Dr. Brocklesby and Mr. Graves, the Surgeon who extracted the ball, he sent for Dr. Duncan, one of his Majesty's Physicians in ordinary, and Mr. Middleton, one of the Serjeant-surgeons; and went next week to Paris, whence, Jan. 14, 1764, he certified to the Speaker, that he was confined to his room, and could not risk a journey back.

Jan. 19, he was expelled the House of Commons, for writing and printing the North Briton, No. XLV; on the 21st he was convicted in the Court of King's Bench, for re-publishing that obnoxious number with notes, and for printing the "Essay on Woman."

On the 5th of August, he was outlawed; and, retiring to Paris, he printed "A Letter to the worthy Electors of Aylesbury, in the County of Bucks, Oct. 22, 1764;" and also "A Letter to a Member of the Club in St. Alban's Street, from Mr. Wilkes at Paris, 1764," 8vo. — On the first of November his outlawry was confirmed; and at that period he was again in treaty for the Embassy at Constantinople; but was again disappointed.

From December 1764 till September 1765, he employed in visiting Lyons, Turin, Parma, Florence, Rome, Naples, Marseilles, and Geneva; and, on his return to England, addressed a Letter, Nov. 1, 1766, to the Duke of Grafton, then Prime

---

*At the same time a prosecution was ordered against him in the House of Lords, for printing the "Essay on Woman."

Minister; and a second, written from Paris, Dec. 12, to the same Nobleman.

"A complete Collection of the genuine Papers, Letters, &c. in the Case of John Wilkes, Esq. late Member for Aylesbury, in the County of Bucks; à Paris, chez J. W. Imprimeur, Rue du Colombier, Faubourg St. Germain, à l'Hotel de Saxe, avec Approbation et Privilege," appeared in 1767.

After having been in exile four years, Mr. Wilkes sent a sub-missive Letter to the King, March 4, 1768; which was deli-vered by his servant at the Queen's House. About the same time he published "Animadversions on Sir John Cust's Speech, Feb. 8, to the Ten Oxford Gentlemen, for Bribery;" and announced "A History of England, from the Revolution to the Accession of the Brunswick Line, by John Wilkes; dedicated to the Free-holders of Middlesex;" of which he published the "Introduc-tion," but proceeded no farther.

On the 10th of March, he offered himself a Candidate to represent the City of London; and was elected on the 16th by shew of hands, with loud applause; but (there being seven Candidates) proved unsuccessful on the poll, though he had 1247 votes.

He wrote a short Letter to the Solicitor and Deputy-solicitor of the Treasury, March 22; pledging his honour as a Gentle-man, to appear in the Court of King's Bench the ensuing Term; which he did on the 20th of April, when Lord Mansfield and the rest of the Judges agreed that they had no power to commit him on his voluntary appearance; and he retired from the Court unmolested.

March 28, he was elected one of the Knights of the Shire for the County of Middlesex; and on the 5th of September was served with a *Capias utlegatum,* and committed to the King's Bench; the affidavit amending the information, by substituting *tenor* for *purport.* The illegality of his Outlawry was argued, May 7, in the Court of King's Bench; the case opened by Serjeant Glynn; answered by Mr. Thurlow; and adjourned to the next Term; when it was reversed, as illegal. But the two verdicts obtained against him, for re-publishing the North Briton, No. XLV, and printing and publishing the "Essay on Woman," were unanimously confirmed. For the first, he was sentenced to pay a fine of 500*l.*; and (having already been two months in confinement) to a farther imprisonment of ten months; and, for the second, to pay a like fine, suffer twelve months imprisonment, and to find two securities for his good behaviour for seven years, of 500*l*. each, and himself 1000*l*.

Oct. 28, being Mr. Wilkes's birth-day, a mob called for illuminations, and broke windows, in the principal streets; but were soon dispersed.

Nov. 1, he published "A Letter on the Public Conduct of Mr. Wilkes;" and, on the 28th, again solicited the Royal clemency, in a Petition presented by his friend Sir Joseph Mawbey.

Jan. 2, 1769, he was elected Alderman of the Ward of Farringdon Without, by a great majority; Mr. Bromwich, an eminent Paper-maker on Ludgate-hill, having declined the poll. From a mistake in closing the books before the time agreed on, this return was declared void; but, at a new election, on the 27th of the same month, there being no other candidate, Mr. Wilkes was declared duly chosen; yet his elegibility was for some time disputed in the Court of Aldermen.

On the 14th of the same month Mrs. Mead died; and her daughter, the wife of Mr. Wilkes, came into the possession of a considerable fortune, the reversion of which was secured to her only daughter.

Jan. 31, 1769, and again on Feb. 1, he was brought up before the House of Commons, in support of his own Petition; which being declared frivolous, he was expelled the House, Feb. 3, and a new writ issued. On this occasion he published, "A Letter to the Right Hon. George Grenville, occasioned by his Publication of the Speech he made in the House of Commons on the Motion for expelling Mr. Wilkes, Friday, Feb. 3, 1769. To which is added, a Letter on the Public Conduct of Mr. Wilkes; first published Nov. 1, 1768; with an Appendix, 1769."

The re-election of Mr. Wilkes was recommended, at a meeting of the Freeholders, by James Townsend and John Sawbridge, Esqrs. both Members of Parliament, and both alike strangers to *him*; and he was, on Feb. 19, re-elected without opposition.

On the 27th he was again voted incapacitated; and again re-elected March 16, though Mr. Dingley, who had never been proposed, entered a protest against the election. On the 3rd of March, with great parade, he was made a Free Mason. Being a third time expelled the House of Commons, March

17, he published an Address to the Electors. A new election succeeded, April 13; when he was opposed by Col. Henry Lawes Luttrell, who had 296 votes, and Serjeant Whitaker 5. Mr. Wilkes had 1147; but the next day his election was once more declared null and void; and, the following day, Col. Luttrell was reported to be duly elected. Mr. Wilkes circulated a counter-address, which was answered by Mr. Luttrell; whose election, though petitioned against by the Freeholders, was confirmed by the House, May 8.

April 20, Mr. Wilkes was brought by *Habeas Corpus* to Lord Mansfield's chambers, discharged his bail, and paid his first fine.

In July he was invited to become a candidate for Westminster; but declined, conceiving himself to be the legal Member for the County.

The Supporters of the Bill of Rights, Oct. 20, sent him 300*l.* being one quarter's allowance from that Society to him whilst a Prisoner in the King's Bench.

About this time appeared "A complete Collection of the genuine Papers, Letters, &c. in the Case of John Wilkes, Esq. elected Knight of the Shire for the County of Middlesex, March 28, 1768. *Berlin,* 1769; *avec Approbation et Privilege*; with a Portrait of Mr. Wilkes." This was followed by a genuine publication (from himself) of "Letters between the Duke of Grafton, the Earls of Halifax, Egremont, Temple, and Talbot, Baron Bottetourt, Right Hon. Bilson Legge, Right Hon. Sir John Cust, Bart. Mr. Charles Churchill, Monsieur Voltaire, the Abbé Winckelmann, &c. &c. and John Wilkes, Esq. with Explantory Notes. Vol. I. 1769." — Frequent references are made to a *second* volume; which he never found leisure or inclination to publish. — "Some Notes by Mr. Wilkes on a few Passages of the late Mr. Churchill's Works," were also published this year.

He now brought an action in the Common Pleas, against Lord Halifax, one of the Secretaries of State (Lord Egremont, the other Secretary, being dead) for false imprisonment and the seizure of his papers; and, Nov. 11, he obtained a verdict of 4000*l.*

April 18, 1770, he published another Address to the Freeholders of Middlesex; having been discharged from his imprisonment in the King's Bench the day before; and been sworn-in Alderman the 24th, notwithstanding the opinion of the Crown

Counsel against his election.

On the 31st of October, a public meeting was held in Westminster for the purpose of impeaching Lord North, at which Mr. Wilkes presided.

On the 13th of February 1771, he visited King's Lynn, where he was presented with the freedom of that antient Corporation; and was next morning presented with an occasional Poem by Sir William Browne, bound in morocco.

In March 1771, he, as Sitting Alderman, discharged Wheble and Miller, two Printers committed by the House of Commons: which House he was thrice ordered to attend; but declined, and wrote to the Speaker (Sir Fletcher Norton): but the Lord Mayor (Crosby) and Alderman Oliver, who attended the House, were both committed to the Tower.

About this time appeared "The Controversial Letters of John Wilkes, Esq. the Rev. John Horne, and their principal Adherents; with a Supplement, containing material anonymous Pieces, &c. 1771."

Mr. Wilkes was this year chosen Sheriff, July 3, with Mr. Alderman Bull; and opened the galleries at the Old Bailey; but could not prevail on the Lord Mayor to follow his example in not giving French wine at his entertainments.

In April 1772, the City of London presented him with a rich silver cup, embossed with the assassination of Julius Cæsar; and the two Sheriffs, Wilkes and Bull, published a joint address to the Livery.

On Michaelmas day, on the election of Lord Mayor, Mr. Wilkes and Mr. Townsend were returned to the Court of Aldermen by the Livery. After a tedious poll, the shew was confirmed; and Mr. Townsend was chosen by the Aldermen.

In this year, by the particular request of the Author (with whom, if not personally acquainted, he undoubtedly had a frequent epistolary correspondence, which after his death was found carefully preserved), he was a very useful assistant to Mr. Henry-Samson Woodfall, in the re-publication of Junius's Letters.

In April 1773, the Sheriffs of London (Oliver and Lewes), on receiving the Speaker's Letter for a call of the House, returned Mr. Wilkes one of the Representatives of the County of Middlesex; and at Michaelmas his friend Bull was elected Lord Mayor.

Being again returned for Middlesex, he attended, on a call

of the House, Feb. 5, 1774, to be sworn, and take his seat; but was refused, a certificate from the Clerk of the Crown having been denied him.

About the same time William Temple, Esq. left him a legacy of 300*l.* "for his strenuous exertions in the Cause of Liberty, and his glorious and noble defence of the English Constitution, against a Series of despotic Tyrants and wicked Ministers."

He was elected Lord Mayor, Oct. 5, 1774; and, having been re-chosen one of the Representatives for the County of Middlesex Oct. 28, he took his seat in the House of Commons, unmolested, Dec. 2; and was afterwards a frequent Speaker in that Assembly.

April 20, 1775, as Lord Mayor, he presented to the King, from the City of London, a spirited Remonstrance; and, on the 14th of July, a Petition.

After having several times unsuccessfully stood candidate for the Chamberlainship of London, he obtained that honourable and lucrative office, Dec. 1, 1779. His attention was now diverted from the storms of party to the calmer and more useful duties of his office; and from that time he discontinued a collection of diurnal publications, which he had been in the habit of carefully preserving.

That he was by no means, however, insensible to the calls of active public duty, we may infer from the services rendered by his vigilant and spirited conduct during the Riots in 1780; for which he received the thanks of the Privy Council.

In 1784, he withdrew occasionally to a small house at Kensington Gore, where he built an aviary, cultivated an elegant little garden, and amused himself in the study of natural history. Nor was he unmindful of literary pursuits; for, in the recess of 1785, he began to print a handsome and complete Edition of his "Speeches in Parliament;" a volume which is now, from its extreme rarity, a great bibliographical curiosity.

This was followed, in 1786, by a single Speech in defence of Mr. Hastings; on which he justly prided himself; it being, perhaps, the ablest exculpation of that gentleman which has appeared in print.

In 1787, on the death of Mr. Thomas Thorpe, he selected the Editor of these Volumes as his Deputy for the South side of the Ward of Farringdon Without; and, on St. Thomas's day that year, received the unanimous thanks of his numerous

Constituents, for his judicious and impartial conduct.

In 1788 he paid his new Deputy the compliment of publishing from his press, to present to particular friends, a beautiful edition of the Poems of Catullus, which, like the Glasgow Horace, is immaculate, not a stop misplaced or omitted*. The Edition principally followed was that of Padua, 1737.

In 1788, he availed himself of the short recess which, in the latter months of the Summer, the routine of office in the City of London permits to its Officers, by retiring to Sandham Cottage, in the Isle of Wight; which he highly improved, embellished, and adorned with, classical inscriptions. In this peaceful retreat he passed many of his pleasantest hours, free from the distraction of parties, or cares of office; and, amid the pleasures of the surrounding scenery, a well-chosen Library, and a few intelligent friends, he experienced a more solid delight, than when hailed by the rabble as "Patron of expiring Liberty."

Pursuing his literary labours, Mr. Wilkes next distinguished himself by an admirable Edition of Theophrastus, in the same bold type which had been used in Mr. Bowyer's correct and beautiful Edition of the Greek Testament in Quarto. This Volume, like the Catullus, was intended only for presents.

In 1790 Mr. Wilkes exchanged his residence from Princescourt to Grosvenor-square; where he resided with his daughter, during the winter months, till his death: constantly walking to Guildhall every day when his duty required his attendance, in which he was strictly diligent and perfectly regular.

In 1790, with my good friends Elmsly and Robson, I visited him at Sandham Cottage; a pleasure which I gladly repeated in the Summer of the following year, and occasionally afterwards as often as business would permit.

In January 1792, at a dinner in Grosvenor-square, where I met Dr. Warton and a few other select literary friends, Mr. Wilkes produced some specimens of his version of Anacreon; and strongly recommended Dr. Warton to engage with him jointly in a new Edition of Pope's Works; which the Doctor soon after undertook, and completed, singly.

Dec. 14, 1792, he addressed his Ward, in an admirable Speech, on the Constitution of the Country.

---

*The allusion is to the edition of the works of Horace printed at Glasgow by Robert and Andrew Foulis in 1744. [*Ed.*]

His latest publication was, "A Supplement to the Miscellaneous Works of Mr. Gibbon, 1796," 4to; which, though without his name, and not printed for sale, was avowed in the presents which he made of it to his friends.

Having entered his 71st year, Mr. Wilkes died, Dec. 6, 1797; and was buried in Grosvenor chapel.

To the various merits of Mr. Wilkes impartial Posterity will do ample justice. A Patriot in the truest sense of the word, his exertions and intrepidity added legal security to the liberties of Englishmen. As a Magistrate, his conduct was manly and exemplary. As Chamberlain, his regularity of attendance and superior merit were generally acknowledged. Patience and candour distinguished his decisions in the many causes which came daily under his cognizance in that office; and, whenever called on to deliver the sentiments of the Corporation to distinguished public characters, dignity and classical elegance were his peculiar characteristics. — In the literary world he will be remembered by his elegant editions of a Latin Poet and a Greek Moralist.

Full of wit, easy in his conversation, elegant in his manners, and happy in a retentive memory, his company was a perpetual treat to his friends. It may be added also, that, though his income was handsome, his liberality kept equal pace with it.

BROWNE WILLIS

B ROWNE WILLIS, esq. LL.D. was born Sept. 14, 1682, at St. Mary Blandford, in the county of Dorset. He was grandson of Dr. Thomas Willis, the most celebrated physician of his time, and the eldest son of Thomas Willis, esq. of Bletchley, in the county of Bucks. His mother was daughter of Robert Browne, esq. of Frampton, in Dorsetshire. He had the first part of his education under Mr. Abraham Freestone at Bechampton; whence he was sent to Westminster school; and at the age of seventeen was admitted a gentleman commoner of Christ Church college, Oxon, under the tuition of Edward Wells, D.D. the famous Geographer.

When he left Oxford, he lived for three years under the tuition of Dr. William Wotton.

In 1702 he proved a considerable benefactor to Fenny Stratford, by reviving the market of that town; and between the years 1704 and 1707 he contributed very largely towards the repairing and beautifying Bletchley church.

In 1705 he was chosen member of parliament for the town of Buckingham, in the room of Sir Richard Temple, bart. who had made his election for the county of Bucks; and, during the short time he was in parliament, he was a constant attendant, and generally upon committees.

In 1707 he married Catherine, daughter of Daniel Elliot, esq. of a very antient family in Cornwall, with whom he had a fortune of 8000*l.* and by whom he had a numerous issue. She died October 2, 1724, aged 34, and was buried at Bletchley.

In 1717-18, the Society of Antiquaries being revived, Mr. Willis became an active member of it.

Aug. 23, 1720, the degree of M.A. was conferred on him, by diploma, by the University of Oxford.

At his solicitation, and in concurrence with his cousin, Dr. Martin Benson, afterwards Bishop of Gloucester, rector of Fenny-Stratford, a subscription was raised for building the beautiful chapel of St. Martin's in that parish; which was begun in 1724, and consecrated by Dr. Richard Reynolds, bishop of Lincoln, May 27, 1730.

A dreadful fire having destroyed above 50 houses, and the church, at Stoney-Stratford, May 19, 1746, Mr. Willis, besides collecting money among his friends for the benefit of the unhappy sufferers, repaired, at his own expence, the tower of the church; and afterwards gave a lottery-ticket towards the rebuilding of that church, which came up a prize.

In 1741 he presented the University of Oxford with his fine cabinet of English coins, at that time looked upon as the most complete collection in England, and which he had been upwards of forty years in collecting; but the University thinking it too much for him, who had then a large family, to give the gold ones, purchased them for 150 guineas, which were paid to Mr. Willis for 167 English gold coins, at the rate of four guineas per ounce weight; and even in this way the gold coins were a considerable benefaction. This cabinet Mr. Willis annually visited upon the 19th of October, being St. Frideswide's day, and never failed making some addition to it. He also gave some MSS. to the Bodleian Library, together with a picture of his grandfather, Dr. Thomas Willis. — In 1749 he was honoured by the University with the degree of LL.D. by diploma.

In 1752 he laid out 200*l*. towards the repairs of the fine tower at Buckingham church; and was, upon every occasion, a great friend to that town.

In 1756, Bow Brickhill church, which had been disused near 150 years, was restored and repaired by the generosity of Dr. Willis.

In 1757, he erected, in Christ Church, Oxford, a handsome monument for Dr. Iles, canon of that cathedral, to whom his grandfather was an exhibitioner; and in 1759 he prevailed upon University College to do the same in Bechampton church for their great benefactor Sir Simon Benet, bart. above 100 years after his death; he also, at his own expence, placed a square marble stone over him, on account of his benefactions at Bechampton, Buckingham, Stoney-Stratford, &c.

Dr. Willis died at Whaddon Hall, Feb. 5, 1760; and was buried in Fenny-Stratford chapel, Feb. 11.

I am indebted for great part of this memoir to the "Account of Mr. Willis," which was read before the Society of Antiquaries in 1760, by Dr. Ducarel, who thus sums up the character of his friend: "This learned Society, of which he was one of the first revivers, and one of the most industrious members, can bear me witness, that he was indefatigable in his researches; for his works were of the most laborious kind. But what enabled him, besides his unwearied diligence, to bring them to perfection, was, his being blessed with a most excellent memory. He had laid so good a foundation of learning, that though he had chiefly conversed with records, and other matters of antiquity, which are not apt to form a polite style, yet he expressed himself, in all his compositions, in an easy and genteel manner. He was, indeed, one of the first who placed our ecclesiastical history and antiquities upon a firm basis, by grounding them upon records and registers; which, in the main, are unexceptionable authorities. During the course of his long life, he had visited every Cathedral in England and Wales, except Carlisle; which journeys he used to call his *pilgrimages*. In his friendships, none more sincere and hearty; always communicative, and ever ready to assist every studious and inquisitive person. This occasioned an acquaintance and connexion between him and all his learned contemporaries. For his mother, the University of Oxford, he always expressed the most awful respect and the warmest esteem. As to his piety and moral qualifications, he was strictly religious, without any mixture of superstition or enthusiasm, and quite exemplary in this respect : and of this, his many public works, in building, repairing, and beautifying of churches, are so many standing evidences. He was charitable to the poor and needy; just and upright towards all men. In a word, no one ever deserved better of the Society of Antiquaries; if industry and an incessant application, throughout a long life, to the investigating the antiquities of this national church and state, is deserving of their countenance."

To this well-drawn character I shall take the liberty to annex a sportive sally of a female pen, the late Miss Talbot, who, in an unprinted letter to a lady of first-rate quality (dated from the rectory-house of St. James's parish, Jan. 2, 1738-9) very humorously characterizes Mr. Willis.

["You know Browne Willis, or at least it is not my fault that you do not; for when at any time some of his oddities have peculiarly struck my fancy, I have writ you whole volumes about him. However, that you may not be forced to recollect how I have formerly tired you, I will repeat, that, with one of the honestest hearts in the world, he has one of the oddest heads that ever dropped out of the moon. Extremely well versed in coins, he knows hardly any thing of mankind; and you may judge what kind of education such an one is likely to give to four girls, who have had no female directress to polish their behaviour, or any other habitation than a great rambling mansion-house in a country village. As, by his little knowledge of the world, he has ruined a fine estate, that was, when he first had it 2000*l. per annum*; his present circumstances oblige him to an odd-headed kind of frugality, that shews itself in the slovenliness of his dress, and makes him think London much too extravagant an abode for his daughters; at the same time that his zeal for Antiquities makes him think an old copper farthing very cheaply bought for a guinea, and any journey properly undertaken that will bring him so some old Cathedral on the Saint's day to which it was dedicated. As, if you confine the natural growth of a tree, it will shoot out in a wrong place — in spite of his expensiveness, he appears saving in almost every article of life that people would expect him otherwise in; and, in spite of his frugality, his fortune, I believe, grows worse and worse every day. I have told you before, that he is the dirtiest creature in the world; so much so, that it is quite disagreeable to sit by him at table: yet he makes one suit of clothes serve him at least two years; and then his great coat has been transmitted down, I believe, from generation to generation, ever since Noah. One Sunday he was quite a beau. The bishop of Gloucester is his idol; and if Mr. Willis were Pope, St. Martin, as he calls him, would not wait a minute for canonization. To honour last Sunday as it deserved, after having run about all the morning to all the St. George's churches whose difference of hours permitted him, he came to dine with us in a tie-wig, that exceeds indeed all description. 'Tis a tie-wig (the very colour of it is inexpressible) that he has had, he says, these nine years; and of late it has lain by at his barber's, never to be put on but once a year, in honour of the Bishop of Gloucester's [Benson] birth-day."]

"Browne Willis (wrote the Rev. John Kynaston) was indeed an original. I met with him at Mr. Cartwright's, at Aynhoe, in Northamptonshire, in 1753, where I was at that time chaplain to the family, and curate of the parish. Browne came here on a visit of a week that summer. He looked for all the world like an old portrait of the æra of Queen Elizabeth, that had walked down out of its frame. He was, too truly, the very dirty figure Miss Talbot describes him to be; which, with the antiquity of his dress, rendered him infinitely formidable to all the children in the parish. He often called upon me at the parsonage house, when I happened not to dine in the family; having a great, and, as it seemed, a very favourite point to carry, which was no less than to persuade me to follow his example, and to turn all my thoughts and studies to *venerable Antiquity;* he deemed *that* the *summum bonum,* the height of all human felicity. I used to entertain Mr. and Mrs. Cartwright highly, by detailing to them Browne's arguments to debauch me from the pursuit of polite literature, and such studies as were most agreeable to my turn and taste; and by parceling out every morning after prayers (we had daily prayers at eleven in the church) the progress Browne had made the day before in the arts of seduction. I amused him with such answers as I thought best suited to his hobby-horse, till I found he was going to leave us; and then, by a stroke or two of spirited raillery, lost his warm heart and his advice for ever. My egging him on served us, however, for a week's excellent entertainment, amid the dullness and sameness of a country situation. He represented me, at parting, to Mr. Cartwright, as one incorrigible, and lost beyond all hopes of recovery to every thing truly valuable in learning, by having unfortunately let slip that I preferred, and feared I ever should prefer, one page of Livy or Tacitus, Sallust or Cæsar, to all the Monkish writers (with Bede at the head of them)."

Mr. Cole tells us: "Mr. Willis never mentioned the adored town of Buckingham without the addition of *county-town*. His person and dress were so singular, that, though a gentleman of 1000*l. per annum,* he has often been taken for a beggar. An old leathern girdle or belt always surrounded the two or three coats he wore, and over them an old blue cloak. — He wrote the worst hand of any man in England — such as he could with difficulty read himself; and what no one, except his old correspondents, could decypher. — His boots, which he almost always appeared in, were not the least singular part of his dress. I suppose it will not be falsity to say they were forty years old; patched and vamped up at various times. They are all in wrinkles, and don't come up above half way of his legs. He was often called in the neighbourhood, *Old Wrinkle Boots.* The chariot of Mr. Willis was so singular that from it he was called himself, *The old Chariot.* It was his wedding chariot, and had his arms on brass plates about it, not unlike a coffin, and painted black. — He was as remarkable probably for his love to the walls and structures of churches, as for his variance with the clergy in his neighbourhood. He built, by subscription, the chapel at Fenny-Stratford; repaired Bletchley church very elegantly, at a great expence; repaired Bow Brickill church, desecrated and not used for a century; and added greatly to the height of Buckingham church tower. — He was not well pleased with any one who in talking of, or with him, did not call him *Squire.* — I wrote these notes when I was out of humour with him for some of his tricks. God rest his soul, and forgive us all. Amen!"

HENRY SAMPSON WOODFALL
& WILLIAM WOODFALL

HENRY WOODFALL, Senior, was the first, I believe, of a name which has now for almost a century been conspicuous in the annals of Typography. That the more immediate subject of this note was a man of wit and humour, is evident from the famous old ballad of *Darby and Joan*, which he wrote when an apprentice to the printer of that name. At the age of 40 he commenced master, at the suggestion, and under the auspices, of Mr. Pope, who had distinguished his abilities as a scholar whilst a journeyman in the employment of the then printer to this admired author. Of his personal history I know little farther, except that he carried on a considerable business with reputation; and had two sons; Henry, a printer, in Paternoster-row; and George, a bookseller at Charing Cross, both of whom I well remember. Henry Woodfall, esq. was master of the Stationers Company in 1766, the year when I became a freeman. He was an old member of the Common Council; and died, wealthy and respected, in 1769; leaving a son, Henry-Samson Woodfall, whose memory will always be dear to Literature, and whose name will descend to posterity as long as the English language exists. He was born at the sign of the Rose and ¡Crown, in Little-Britain, on the 21st of June, 1739, O. S. Under the fostering attentions of his grandfather Mr. H. S. Woodfall received the first rudiments of his education; and, before he had attained his fifth year, had the hononr of receiving from Pope half a crown, for reading to him, with much fluency, a page of Homer in the Greek language. Mr. H. S. Woodfall was afterwards sent to a respectable school at Twickenham, kept by Mr. Clarke, under whose tuition he made considerable proficiency in the Classics. At the age of little more than 11 years he was removed to St. Paul's; and, on examination, though found qualified from his acquirements to have been placed on the seventh (next to the highest) form, yet, from his juvenile appearance, was only admitted to the fifth. On leaving St. Paul's, he was taken apprentice by his father; and, on attaining the age of 19, had committed to his charge the business of editing and printing the Public Advertiser, though his name did not appear to the paper till the 17th of November 1760. From this period till the beginning of November 1793 he continued uninterruptedly in the exercise of the laborious functions which a daily newspaper necessarily requires, more especially where the joint duties of editor and printer devolve on the same person, as in the case of Mr. Woodfall. During the course of so long a period, when parties ran extremely high, and particularly from the beginning of the year 1769, when the celebrated Letters of *Junius** first appeared under that signature, it is not surprizing that a printer should have occasionally got into some difficulties; and this Mr. Woodfall, after he had retired from business, used to speak of not unpleasantly, and apparently with satisfaction; not with exultation, as acting in opposition to the then Administration, but as having passed through the perils to which he had been subjected, in publishing the party effusions of the most able writers of the day, without any serious inconvenience to the comforts he then enjoyed. The punishments consequent upon his political transgressions formed, he said, a kind of anti-climax of retribution : that he had been *fined* by the House of Lords; *confined* by the House of Commons: *fined and confined* by the Court of King's Bench; and *indicted* at the Old Bailey. In the conduct of the Public Advertiser, however, he was strictly impartial; and, notwithstanding the great and deserved popularity of Junius, yet, by a reference to his Papers of that day, it will be seen that as many very able letters on the ministerial side of the question were admitted as on that of the opposition, and without any other preference than priority of receipt, or than the temporary nature of the subject would demand. With regard to the line of conduct he had adopted respecting his paper, in a pecuniary point of view, it was always most scrupulously honourable and correct; and, though frequently offered money to suppress certain articles of intelligence, not pleasant to the particular individual, yet never could he be prevailed upon to forego what he deemed to be his duty to the publick, for any consideration of such a kind, however much to his personal advantage. Mr. Woodfall succeeded his father, as a printer, in Paternoster-row, in the year 1769 : and, on being offered the Common Councilship vacant by the death of his father, declined it, on the ground, as he jokingly said, that it was his duty to *record* great actions, not to *perform* them. Mr. Woodfall retired from business on the destruction of his printing-office by fire in December 1793, having parted with the Public

---

*These letters first appeared on 21 Jan. 1769, and the famous letter to the King on 19 Dec. of that same year (*Ed.*)

Advertiser in the preceding November. This paper was originally published under the title of "The London Daily Post, and General Advertiser," so far back as the year 1726; which was altered to that of the "General Advertiser" only, March 12, 1743-4, and took the name of "The Public Advertiser," Dec. 1, 1752. The paper was discontinued about two years after Mr. Woodfall parted with it. Mr. Woodfall was Master of the Stationers Company in the year 1797, of which he had been a liveryman upwards of 45 years. He resided at Chelsea during the last 12 years of his life, occasionally visiting his old and numerous acquaintance, by whom he was highly respected for his good humour and social qualities. He had lived much in intimacy with Garrick and Colman, Smollet, (Leonidas) Glover, Goldsmith, Hawkesworth, Bonnel Thornton, and other wits of his day, by whose labours the Public Advertiser rose to a very high reputation, as the depository of literary humour, criticism, and information. In Mr. Woodfall's time the newspapers were more devoted to the interests of general literature than at present; and it was not unusual with men of the first talents to send their thoughts on subjects of manners, morals, and other domestic and instructive topicks, which have been ill exchanged for the violence of party declamation. It remains only to add, that, in many cases, Mr. Woodfall acted as a liberal patron of early genius; and there are some gentlemen now living who are willing to confess their obligations to the kind encouragement he held out. He retired from active life, to enjoy the *"otium cum dignitate"* among a select circle of friends, who highly esteemed him for his amiable and inoffensive manners, and greatly regret his loss. His tomb in Chelsea church-yard is thus inscribed:

"Sacred
to the memory of
Henry-Samson Woodfall, esq.
many years an eminent printer in London,
who departed this life Dec. 12, 1805,
aged 66;
a gentleman
of a liberal mind and education;
the associate and patron of
many distinguished literary characters
of the last age;
exemplary in the discharge of his duty of
husband, father, and friend."

Of William Woodfall, the younger brother of Henry-Samson, it is difficult to speak without sensations of the deepest regret. Of this truly ingenious person it will be universally recollected that he made himself so eminently useful by the employment of his talents as a journalist, and by the character and distinction which his reports of the parliamentary debates acquired, that the publick will desire to possess the history of a person who so long, so zealously, and so largely, contributed to their information. He was early placed by his father under Mr. Richard Baldwin, of Paternoster-row, to learn the art of bookselling; from whose house he went back to his father's office, and assisted in the printing and editing of "The Public Advertiser." He became so warm an amateur of the drama, that, to gratify his *penchant* for the stage, he made an excursion into Scotland, and performed several times for his amusement in the company of a Mr. Fisher. He used to relate many pleasant anecdotes of this jaunt, the most fortunate event of which, however, because it constituted the future happiness of his life, was his marriage with a most amiable woman, with whom he returned to the Metropolis about 1772, and engaged himself as editor of "The London Packet." From this he was called by the proprietors of "The Morning Chronicle" to the double station of printer and editor, which he filled with much credit to himself until the year 1789, when he commenced a paper called "The Diary" on his own account. His memory was uncommonly retentive; and, were it not for this quality, he would probably have risen to affluence in a world upon which he entered with a competence, and left in very humble circumstances. Aided and incited, however, by this advantage, he explored a path hitherto unknown, and commenced a career of great but unprofitable labour, the fatiguing and difficult task of giving a report of the Debates in the two Houses of Parliament on the night of the proceeding. In this line he attained the highest degree of celebrity, as well for the fidelity of his report, as the quantity and rapidity of his execution. Before his time a very short sketch of the Debate was all that the newspapers attempted to give on the same night, and the more detailed reports were deferred to some subsequent day. Without taking a note to assist his memory, without the use of an amanuensis to ease his labour, he has been known to write sixteen columns after having sat in a crowded gallery for as many hours without an interval of rest. He took pride in this exertion, which brought him more praise than profit. It wore down his constitution, which was naturally good; and when other papers, by the division of labour, produced the same length of details with an earlier publication, he yielded the contest, and suffered his "Diary" to expire. After that time he employed his talents in various publications. In 1784 he was invited to Dublin, to report the debates upon the Commercial Propositions; at which time, so great was his fame, crowds followed him through the streets, eager to catch a glimpse of a man whom they considered as endowed with supernatural powers. One striking circumstance on this particular point I can identify : Mr. Woodfall presented me, from Dublin, with an early copy of this Report; which, at his suggestion, I printed as a separate pamphlet, and advertised for sale; but not more than *three* copies were ever called for. Mr. Woodfall possessed all the virtues of private life that endear a man to society, and was particularly distinguished for his literary talents. In 1793, he sought to be appointed Remembrancer of the City, an office for which he was peculiarly qualified : but private friendships and superior interest prevailed. Mr. Woodfall was also devoted to the *belles lettres;* and, as such, was the intimate friend of Garrick, Goldsmith, Savage, and all the other members of the old Literary School, of which he was one of the very few remaining disciples. He was so passionately fond of theatrical representations, as never to have missed the first performance of a new piece for at least 40 years; and the publick had so good an opinion of his taste, that his criticisms were decisive of the fall or fortune of the piece and the performer. Unfortunately for himself and his family, he placed all his hopes on the most precarious species of property, and became the proprietor of a news-paper, which his talents raised to eminence; but the talents of no individual could secure it a permanent station upon that eminence. The paper fell, and with it fell his hopes. Though disappointed, he was not to be diverted from his favourite pursuits. He was constant in his attendance at the bar of the House of Lords, which he visited so lately as July 27, 1803. Although he was far advanced in life, he was active, animated, and in full possession of his mental faculties, without the appearance of any considerable waste of his physical strength. To a large family, entirely dependent upon his industry, his death was therefore an unexpected, deplorable, and afflicting event. As, however, the circle of his acquaintance was as wide as the circle of polished life; as he was known by almost every man of rank, fortune, and literary acquirements in England;

and as he was loved by many of them, and respected by all; it is hoped that their regard for the man will not be buried in his grave, but that it will survive, and shew itself in acts of kindness to his sorely-afflicted family. He died, after a week's illness, in his 58th year, in Queen-street, Westminster, August 1, 1803; and his remains were interred on the 6th, in St. Margaret's church-yard, Westminster.

EDWARD WORTLEY-MONTAGUE

EDWARD WORTLEY-MONTAGUE* was the only son of a gentleman who bore the same names (who had been an intimate of all the great men, whether literary or political, in the reign of Queen Anne) by Lady Mary, one of the daughters of Evelyn Pierrepoint Duke of Kingston, a lady whose writings have long been the subject of public admiration. He was born in October 1713; and in the early part of his life seems, though he afterwards lost her favour, to have been the object of his mother's tenderest regard. In 1716, he accompanied her on his father's embassy to Constantinople, and is thus mentioned in one of her letters: "I thank God I have not at all suffered in my health, nor (what is dearer to me) in that of my child, by all my fatigues." Again: "If I survive my journey, you shall hear from me again. I can say with great truth, in the words of Moneses, 'I have long learnt to hold myself as nothing;' but, when I think of the fatigues my poor infant must suffer, I have all a mother's fondness in my eyes, and all her tender passions in my heart."

During young Montague's continuance at Constantinople, in 1718-19, it was his fortune to be the first of the English nation on whom the practice of inoculation for the small-pox was tried; a bold experiment, in which the fond mother was as successful as she could hope, and millions have had reason, in consequence of it, to resound her praises; though the practice is now in a great measure superseded by the equally safe and much milder use of vaccination.

---

*This Article was compiled for the "History of Leicestershire."

In 1719, Mr. Montague's parents returned to England; and he was placed at Westminster school, where the eccentricity of his disposition was first exhibited. From this learned seminary he thought proper, at an early age, to run away; and Mr. Forster* was requested to use every possible means for the discovery of the fugitive. Every expedient was tried; and every expedient failed of success. The purlieus of Covent Garden were searched in vain. Even the circuit of St. Giles's was paced by the friends and relatives of the family. Advertisements, hand-bills, all proved inefficacious — the prodigal was not to be found. At last mere accident effected what studied design could not accomplish. The accident was this: Mr. Forster had some business to transact with the Captain of an India ship which was moored at Blackwall. He set out for that place, attended by one of the domestics of old Mr. Wortley-Montague. Scarcely had they entered Blackwall, before the voice of a fisherman's boy arrested their attention. They were accustomed to the voice. They conceived it to be very like that of young Montague. They dispatched a sailor after him, under the pretence of a desire to purchase some of the fish he had in his basket. The sailor executed his commission, and returned with the boy. They were confirmed in their suspicions. It was indeed young Montague, with a basket of plaice, flounders, and other small fish, upon his head. When he found himself discovered, he laid down his basket, and ran away. The basket, however, being soon owned, the habitation of young Montague was quickly found out. He had been bound, by regular indentures of apprenticeship, to a poor, but very industrious fisherman; and, on enquiry, it appeared that he had, for more than one year, served his master most faithfully. He cried his fish with an audible voice. He made his bargains with shrewdness, and he returned the purchase-money with rectitude. He was brought home, and again placed in Westminster school; from which, in a very little time, he again ran away.

The second flight was managed more artfully than the first. He took an effectual method to elude for many years the search of his friends. He bound himself to the master of a vessel which sailed for Oporto. This man was a Quaker. What is not always

---

*This gentleman was afterwards better known to the publick as chaplain to the Duchess of Kingston, whose champion he was in a literary dispute between her Grace and Mr. Foote.

the case, his religious persuasion gave a turn of morality to his actions; he was strictly conscientious. There was a mixture of the parent and of the master in his treatment of young Montague. He found him, as he supposed, a poor, deserted, friendless boy; he cloathed him decently, fed him regularly, and made a sea-life as comfortable to him as the nature of it would admit. This treatment made very little impression on the mind of young Montague; he was either incapable of gratitude, or the few generous feelings he had were borne down by the wayward humour of his fancy, which, always feeble, and constantly roving, impelled him for ever to change the present scene. As soon as the vessel reached Oporto, Montague decamped. Not a syllable of the language did he know; yet he ventured a considerable distance up the country. It was the vintage season. He offered himself as an assistant in any capacity; was tried, and found very useful. For two or three years did he continue in the interior parts of Portugal; and probably would never have emerged from the situation in which his fancy had placed him, had not the following incident led to a discovery of his parentage.

Young Montague was ordered to drive some asses to the Factory. This task was allotted him on account of some business which was to be transacted in the English language. Montague, not dreaming of a discovery, set out with his group of dull companions. The English Consul knew him; and his old master the Quaker being there with his vessel, the discovery was complete. The asses were consigned to another (although perhaps not a better) driver. Montague was brought home; when Mr. Forster interposed. He exercised the milder offices of humanity. He pleaded for the prodigal in the true spirit of beneficence; and called up all the father in the bosom of old Montague, who received his son with joy equal to that of the father in the Gospel. A private tutor was employed, to recover those rudiments of learning which a life of dissipation and vulgarity might have obscured; and Mr. Forster was desired to complete his education. Forster acquitted himself ably in this department. But young Montague, who seemed born to frustrate every honourable effort that could be made in his favour, ran away a third time, and entered as a foremast-man on board a ship bound for the Mediterranean. This provoked old Montague beyond endurance. He now talked of for ever disclaiming a son whom it would never be possible to reclaim. Forster offered to take on himself the trouble of bringing back the graceless wanderer. The father at last consented; and the business was accomplished.

Young Montague being returned once more, it was proposed that he should go abroad for a few years. Forster engaged to accompany him. Young Montague agreed. A stipend was allotted for his support; and the West Indies was chosen as the place of retreat. Thither Mr. Forster accompanied Montague. There he renewed his classical studies; and there he continued for some years; when he was sent for by his father; and, on his return to England, had an appointment in some public office; though of what nature does not now appear. It may be presumed, however, that the irregularities of his past life had been forgotten; for in 1747 he was elected one of the knights of the shire for the county of Huntingdon. In his senatorial capacity he does not appear to have in any way particularly distinguished himself.

His expences far exceeding his income, this inconsiderate young man soon became deeply involved in debt; and, about the latter end of the year 1751, once more quitted his native kingdom.

His first excursion was to Paris, where he again appeared before the world, in a light if not disreputable, yet certainly not free from suspicion. In that gay and dissipated Metropolis he became acquainted with a person then resident there, who charged him with offences for which he became cognizable to the criminal jurisdiction of the kingdom of France. His own account of the accusation against him, as stated by himself, shall be given in his own words:

"Abraham Payba, a Jew, under the name of James Roberts, in his complaint, dated the 25th of October 1751, gives an account of his leaving England with Miss Rose, intending to make the Tour both of France and Italy, being provided with bills for considerable sums upon the Bank of England, and several eminent Bankers in London. He then sets forth, that, coming to lodge at the Hotel d'Orleans, he was greatly surprized by my pretending to visit him, as he had no manner of acquaintance with me. That next day he set out for the country; from whence returning on the 23rd of September, he found a card from me inviting him to dine, which he was polite enough to comply with; and that at my lodging he dined with a large company of English. That I forced him to drink (till I perceived he was fuddled) of several sorts of wines and other liquors during dinner, which was not over till about six in the evening, when the company retired to my apartments to drink coffee. That after this all the company went away, excepting Mr. Taafe, my lord Southwell, and myself; and that Mr. Taafe took a pair of dice, and, throwing them upon the table, asked, Who would play? That the complainant Roberts at first excused himself, because he had no more than two crowns about him; upon which the other said, that he had no occasion for money, for he might play upon his word of honour. That he (Roberts) still excused himself, alledging that he had occasion for all his money for a journey on which he was to set out on the Wednesday following: but that Mr. Taafe, Lord Southwell, and I, insisted so strongly on his playing, that, being flustered with wine, and not knowing what he did, he at last yielded; and that, taking advantage of his situation, we made him lose in less than an hour 870 Louis d'or; that is, 400 to Mr. Taafe, 350 to Lord Southwell, and 120 to me; and that we then suffered him to go about his business. That next day Mr. Taafe sent him a card inviting him to supper, but he excused himself; and on Sunday the 26th of September he received a letter from the same gentleman, desiring him to send the 400 Louis d'or he had won of him; and that he (Roberts) wrote him in answer, that he would pay him a visit on the Tuesday following: but that, on the 27th of September, between eleven and twelve at night, Mr. Taafe, lord Southwell, and I, knocked with great violence, menaces, and imprecations, at his gate; where getting admittance, we informed him, that if he did not give to each of us a draft for the several sums we had won of him, we would carry him instantly to the Bastile, the Archers, with the Governor of the Bastile, waiting below for that purpose. That we told him, it was a maxim in France, that all gaming debts should be paid in 24 hours after they were contracted; and at the same time we threatened to cut him across the face with our swords, if he should refuse to give us the drafts we demanded. That, being intimidated with our menaces, and ignorant of the customs of France, he gave us drafts for our several sums upon Mr. Watters the younger, banker in Paris, though he had no money of his in his hands. That the complainant, well knowing that the drafts would be refused, and thinking his life in danger, resolved next day, being the 28th, to set out for Lyons. That there, and since his return to Paris, he understood that Mr. Taafe, lord Southwell, and I, on the very day of his leaving Paris, came early to his lodging, where meeting only with Miss Rose and her sister, Mr.

Taafe persuaded the former to leave the complainant, and to go with him to the Hotel de Perou, promising to send her over to England in a short time. After this, that he searched all the trunks, portmanteaus, and drawers, belonging to the complainant, from whence he took out in one bag 400 Louis d'or, and out of another to the value of 300 Louis, in French and Portuguese silver; from another bag 1200 livres in crown pieces, a pair of brilliant diamond buckles for which the complainant paid 8020 livres to the Sieur Pierre, and his own picture set round with diamonds to the amount of 1200 livres, besides the value of the picture, which cost him ten Louis to the Sieur Marolle; a shirt buckle, set with diamonds, rubies, and emeralds, which cost him 650 livres to the Sieur Pierre; laces to the amount of 3000 livres; seven or eight women's robes or gowns valued at 4000 livres; two brilliant diamond rings; several gold snuff boxes; a travelling chest, containing his plate and china, and divers other effects, which he cannot call to mind; all which Mr. Taafe packed up in one box, and by the help of his footman carried in a coach (which waited for him at the corner of the street of the Little Augustines) to his own apartment. That afterwards Mr. Taafe carried Miss Rose and her sister in another coach to his lodging, where they remained three days, and then sent them to London under the care of one of his friends."

Such is the account Mr. Montague gave of the charge exhibited against him. The consequence of it to himself cannot be more fully described than in his own words: "On Sunday the 31st of October 1751, when it was near one in the morning, as I was undressed and going to bed, with that security which ought to attend innocence, I heard a person enter my room; and upon turning round, and seeing a man whom I did not know, I asked him calmly what he wanted? His answer was, that I must put on my clothes. I began to expostulate upon the motives of his appearance, when a commissary instantly entered the room, with a pretty numerous attendance; and told me with great gravity, that he was come, by virtue of a warrant for my imprisonment, to carry me to the Grand Chatelet. I requested him again and again to inform me of the crime laid to my charge; but all his answer was, that I must follow him. I begged him to give me leave to write to lord Albemarle, the English ambassador; promising to obey the warrant, if his Excellency was not pleased to answer for my forthcoming. But the commissary refused me the use of pen and ink; though he consented that I should send a verbal message to his Excellency; telling me at the same time, that he would not wait the return of the messenger, because his orders were to carry me instantly to prison. As resistance under such circumstances must have been unavailing, and might have been blameable, I obeyed the warrant by following the commissary, after ordering one of my domesticks to inform my lord Albemarle of the treatment I underwent. I was carried to the Chatelet, where the jailors, hardened by their profession, and brutal for their profit, fastened upon me, as upon one of those guilty objects whom they lock up to be reserved for public punishment; and, though neither my looks nor my behaviour betrayed the least symptom of guilt, yet I was treated as a condemned criminal. I was thrown into prison, and committed to a set of wretches who have no character of humanity but its form.

"My residence (to speak in the gaol dialect) was in the *secret,* which is no other than the dungeon of the prison, where all the furniture was a wretched matress, and a crazy chair. The weather was cold, and I called for a fire; but I was told I could have none. I was thirsty, and called for some wine and water, or even a draught of water by itself, but was denied it. All the favour I could obtain was, a promise to be waited on in the morning; and then was left by myself, under a hundred locks and bolts, with a bit of candle, after finding that the words of my gaolers were few, their commands peremptory, and their favours unattainable. After a few moments of solitary reflection, I perceived myself shut up in a dungeon destined for the vilest malefactors; the walls were scrawled over with their vows and prayers to Heaven, before they were carried to the gibbet or the wheel. Amongst other notable inscriptions, I found one with the following note underneath; viz. 'These verses were written by the priest who was burned and hanged, in the year 1717, for stealing a chalice of the holy sacrament.' At the same time I observed the floors were studded with iron staples, either to secure the prisoners, or to prevent the effects of their despair. I must own that the survey of my dreadful situation, deprived of the common comforts of life, even fire and water, must have got the better of conscience itself, irreproachable as mine was, and of all trust in the equity of my judges, had I not wrapped myself up in innocence, whose portion is fortitude, and whose virtue is tranquillity." In this dismal dungeon he continued until the 2d of November, when he was carried before a magistrate, and

underwent an examination, by which he understood the heads
of the charges against him; "and which," he adds, "I answered
in a manner that ought to have cleared my own innocence from
suspicion, and to have covered my antagonist with confusion."
This effect, however, appears not to have been produced. Proceedings were carried on for some time; and the decision at first
was in favour of Mr. Montague and Mr. Taafe. ["By a sentence
of the Lieutenant-criminal at Paris, made on the 25th January,
1752, both these gentlemen (who, with the complainant, were
the only persons engaged in this transaction then in France, the
rest having fled) were discharged from the complaints and accusa-
tions brought against them by the said James Roberts; and it
was directed, that their names should be erased and blotted out
of the gaol-books, and the clerks of the court be compelled to
do the same; which being done, they should be fully and
authentically discharged and acquitted thereof : That the said
James Roberts should be condemned to make reparation of
honour to the said Montague and Taafe, in the presence of
twelve such persons as they should chuse, and in such place
as they should appoint : That he should then and there declare,
that it was falsely and wickedly that he imagined, contrived,
and devised against them a calumnious accusation; that he
allowed them to be men of honour and probity, incapable of,
and unstained with, the facts injuriously and calumniously inserted in his complaint. Of which reparation an act should be
drawn up, in form of the verbal process, by the first notary
required to do it; and of this act a copy should be deposited
in the office of the recorder criminal of the Chatelet, and another
copy should be delivered by the said recorder or register to
each of the said Montague and Taafe : That the said Roberts
should be condemned to pay 10,000 livres, in damage and
interest, to each of the said Montague and Taafe, by way of
civil reparation. And by the same decree, the defendants Montague and Taafe were permitted to print and publish the
proceedings; and the said Roberts was condemned to pay all
the costs. From this sentence Roberts appealed to the High
Court of La Tournelle at Paris; where, on the 14th June 1752,
the judgment against him was reversed, the parties definitively
were dismissed the court, Roberts's name erased the gaol registers,
and costs compensated. From this sentence Montague and
Taafe, in their turn, appealed; but whether with any effect is
not at present recollected : it is most probable this disgraceful

business was here suffered to terminate."] *Mr. Seward, in the European Magazine, vol. XXIV. p.* 131.

In the Parliament which assembled in 1754, Mr. Montague was returned for Bossiney; and in 1759, he gave to the publick his "Reflections on the Rise and Fall of the antient Republics, adapted to the present State of Great Britain;" 8vo.

This Work, which is written with spirit, contains a concise and elegant relation of the Grecian, Roman, and Carthaginian stories, interspersed with occasional allusions to the then state of this Country, whose constitution the author appears to have studied, and which he has set off to considerable advantage.

Whether Mr. Montague received any immediate pecuniary advantage from his father, in consequence of this publication, as it hath been asserted, we know not; but it is certain that it could not influence him in making his will.

Mr. Wortley* died the 22d of January 1761, at the advanced age of 80 years; and by his will, made in the year 1755, bequeathed to his son an annuity of 1000*l.* a-year, to be paid him during the joint lives of himself and his mother, lady Mary; and after her death an annuity of 2000*l.* a-year, during the joint lives of himself and his sister, lady Bute. By the same will, he empowered Mr. Montague to make a settlement on any woman he might marry, not exceeding 800*l.* a-year; and to any son of such marriage he devised a considerable estate in the West Riding of Yorkshire.

The death of his father having secured him independence, Mr. Wortley-Montague seems immediately to have availed himself of it; and, possessing very accommodating principles, with a fine constitution for travelling, he once more took leave of his native country, and passed the remainder of his life entirely in foreign parts.

In the Parliament, however, which assembled in November 1761, he was, during his absence, again elected for Bossiney; and on the 21st of August 1762 lady Mary Wortley-Montague died, leaving her son only *one guinea;* "his father having," as she expressed it, "amply provided for him."

By these accidents, a vast fortune came to the late Earl of Bute, who married the daughter: nevertheless, this generous Nobleman ceded to his brother-in-law much more than he could

---

*It appears by his will that he did not use the name of Montague.

have possibly obtained, and even more than he could have claimed, by litigation.

In 1762 we find him at Turin; whence he wrote two letters to the earl of Macclesfield, which were read at the Royal Society, Nov. 25; and afterwards published in a quarto pamphlet, intituled, "Observations upon a supposed antique Bust at Turin."

His next peregrination was into the East, where he was accompanied by Nathanael Davison, esq.; and continued there nearly three years.

In September 1765 he was performing quarantine at Venice; where he was met by Mr. Sharpe, whose description of him shall be here given : ["One of the most curious sights we saw amongst these curiosities was the famous Mr. Montague, who was performing quarantine at the Lazaretto. All the English made a point of paying him their compliments in that place; and he seemed not a little pleased with their attention. It may be supposed that visitors are not suffered to approach the person of any who is performing quarantine : they are divided by a passage of about seven or eight feet wide. Mr. Montague was just arrived from the East. He had travelled through the Holy Land, Egypt, Armenia, and with the Old and New Testament in his hands for his direction, which he told us had proved unerring guides —he had particularly taken the road of the Israelites through the Wilderness, and had observed that part of the Red Sea through which they passed. He had visited Mount Sinai; and flattered himself he had been on the very part of the rock where Moses spake face to face with God Almighty. His beard reached down to his breast, being of two years and a half growth; and the dress of his head was Armenian. He was in the most enthusiastic raptures with Arabia and the Arabs. His bed was the ground; his food rice; his beverage water; his luxury a pipe and coffee. His purpose was, to return once more amongst that virtuous people; whose morals and hospitality, he said, were such, that, were you to drop your cloak in the highway, you would find it there six months afterwards, an Arab being too honest a man to pick up what he knows belongs to another; and, were you to offer money for the provision you meet with, he would ask you, with concern, why you had so mean an opinion of his benevolence, as to suppose him capable of accepting a gratification?"] From Abbé Winkelman's Letters, dated in the same year, we learn an anecdote, not calculated to eraze any unfavourable opinion which may have been entertained of Mr. Montague: "At Alexandria," says the Abbé, "he got acquainted with the Danish Consul, who had a very handsome wife. Under various pretences, he engaged the husband to go to Holland. Some time after, he shewed a feigned letter, mentioning the Consul's death, and married his wife, whom he now carries with him into Syria. Not long after, the Danish resident at Constantinople received from the Texel advice of the supposed dead Consul; so that Montague is not safe in any of the Grand Seignior's dominions."

His relation of the journey from Cairo in Egypt to the Written Mountains in the Deserts of Sinai, in a letter dated from Pisa, Dec. 2, 1765, was read before the Royal Society March 13, 1766, and published in their Transactions. In the same learned repository may also be found his "New Observations on what is called Pompey's Pillar in Egypt."

He is said also to have published (but I know not where) an "Explication of the Causes of Earthquakes." He had certainly great natural abilities, and a great share of acquired knowledge.

In 1766, he was about to return to the East; and in 1768 it was stated in the public papers, that he had been received with uncommon respect at Constantinople, after passing through Salonica, and viewing the Islands in the Archipelago.

In the beginning of the year 1773 he was at Rosetta in Egypt; which he quitted in June, and was at the Lazaretto off Leghorn in the same month. From that place he went to Venice, where he stayed above two years; during which time (in April 1774) he meditated a voyage to Mecca and Medina; but this probably never took place; or at least had not in September 1775, on the 25th of which month the learned Physician, to whom various Letters from him are addressed, thus writes to him: "In your voyage to Mecca and Medina I most sincerely wish you health, and every gratification your curiosity can expect. I shall be very glad to see your portrait. I have more than once visited that representing you near the Written Mountains. If we cannot, on account of distance, see our friends, it is no small satisfaction to see their representation. I most heartily coincide with you in your opinion of the activity and abilities of Lord Sandwich as First Lord of the Admiralty. Mr. Clark is sent home with Omai*;

---

*A native of Tahiti brought to London by Captain Furneaux and received by the King. [Ed.]

who is now so far acquainted with this country, that not long since, and without any person to attend him, he hired a horse, and rode to visit Baron Dimsdale, by whom he was inoculated, at Hertford. Mr. Mason, whom the King sent three years ago to the Cape of Good Hope to collect plants and seeds for the garden at Kew, is returned with many new acquisitions. He travelled near 900 miles to the North of the Cape, and has seen more of the interior of Africa than has been hitherto visited by Europeans."

During his residence at Venice, Mr. Wortley-Montague was visited by the Duke of Hamilton and Dr. Moore, who has preserved some curious particulars of his personal character and habits of life. ["Hearing that Mr. Montague resided at Venice, the Duke of Hamilton has had the curiosity to wait on that extraordinary man. He met his Grace at the stair-head, and led us through some apartments furnished in the Venetian manner, into an inner room, quite in a different style. There were no chairs; but he desired us to seat ourselves on a sopha, whilst he placed himself on a cushion on the floor, with his legs crossed in the Turkish fashion. A young black slave sat by him; and a venerable old man, with a long beard, served us with coffee. After this collation, some aromatic gums were brought, and burnt in a little silver vessel. Mr. Montague held his nose over the steam for some minutes, and snuffed up the perfume with peculiar satisfaction: he afterwards endeavoured to collect the smoke with his hands, spreading and rubbing it carefully along his beard, which hung in hoary ringlets to his girdle. This manner of perfuming the beard seems more cleanly, and rather an improvement upon that used by the Jews in antient times.— We had a great deal of conversation with this venerable-looking person, who is to the last degree acute, communicative, and entertaining, and in whose discourse and manners are blended the vivacity of a Frenchman with the gravity of a Turk. We found him, however, wonderfully prejudiced in favour of the Turkish characters and manners, which he thinks infinitely preferable to the European. or those of any other nation. He describes the Turks in general as a people of great sense and integrity; the most hospitable, generous, and the happiest of mankind. He talks of returning as soon as possible to Ægypt, which he paints as a perfect Paradise, and thinks, that had it not been otherwise ordered for wise purposes, of which it does not become us to judge, the Children of Israel would certainly have chosen to remain where they were, and have endeavoured to drive the Egyptians to the land of Canaan.]

At this period he had become enamoured of the dress and manners of Arabia, to which he conformed to the end of his life. As he sat in his Armenian dress, squat, after the Eastern fashion, to regale himself with smoking tobacco, and drinking coffee, he has been heard to say, not unfrequently, "that he had long since drunk his full share of wine and strong liquors; and that he had never once been guilty of a small folly in the whole course of his life."

At Venice also he was visited by Mr. Romney, the celebrated Painter; as we learn by the following extract from his elegant Biographer, Mr. Hayley: "After a busy residence of some months at Rome, Romney indulged himself with a survey of Venice; and he chanced to meet there an eccentric character of his own country, with whose singularities he was highly entertained. The learned and fanciful traveller, Wortley-Montague, after his rambles in Asia, was at this time living in Venice with the manners, the habit, and the magnificence of a Turk. Romney painted an admirable head of him in his Eastern garb, and in such a style of art, as clearly proves that the Painter had studied intensely, and successfully, the celebrated colourists of the Venetian school: indeed, his head of Montague might easily be mistaken for a Venetian picture. It was a favourite work of the Artist; and he long retained it as a study for his own use; but, after permitting a small print to be taken from it, as a decoration to Seward's Anecdotes, he presented the original to a friend. He had painted a large copy from it; which, with other exquisite portraits by the same master, is ranked among the choicest modern ornaments of that magnificent and interesting old mansion, Warwick castle. Romney was so captivated with the extensive knowledge, the lively spirit, and the fascinating conversation of Wortley-Montague, and that extraordinary traveller was so pleased with the manual and mental energy of the Artist, that it is probable their acquaintance might have led to the production of many pictures, had not their brief intimacy ended by a fatal mischance which terminated all the projects of Montague. While Romney was with him, he happened, in eating a small bird, to wound his throat with a bone: the accident produced inflammation; and in the course of a few days occasioned his death. Such was the fate of this singular man, who had escaped from the manifold perils of roving through the deserts of the East."

Of the accident which occasioned the death of this extraordinary person, there can be little doubt; but there appears to be some error in the circumstance of Mr. Romney's being present at the accident, as Mr. Montague survived it a considerable time.

Mr. Romney, after passing some time at Parma, and making a circuitous route through Turin, Lyons, and Paris, reached London in the beginning of June 1775. Mr. Montague's will was dated in that year, Nov. 28; and he lived till the 29th of April, 1776.

It has been suggested by a friend who had good means of information, that he had actually an intention to have returned to this country; that he had engaged his passage for Marseilles; that effectual measures were taken to satisfy the claims of his creditors, and extricate him from the immense debt which he had principally contracted by gaming when he had the prospect of succeeding to a very opulent fortune; and his affairs were finally so settled, that he might have passed here in ease the remainder of his life; which, from the vigour of his constitution, and salubrity of his regimen, promised to have been a long one. — He had scarcely a single vice — *for he is dead.* That he had virtues to counterbalance his failings, Omniscience will discover, when weighing them in the scale of merit.

His remains lie under a plain slab, in the cloister of the Hermitants at Padua, inscribed,

"Edvardi Vorthleyi Montague Cineres."

And immediately beneath is engraved the figure of a small fish.

By his will, made at Venice, Nov. 28, 1775, and proved in London Aug. 6, 1776, he appointed lord Sandwich and Robert Palmer esquire his executors; directing them, out of his estates in Leicestershire and Yorkshire, to raise money sufficient to purchase an annuity of 400*l.* for the support of his reputed son *Fortunatus,* otherwise *Massoud,* a Black, as he describes him, then living with him, of the age of 13 years, and whose education, he directs shall be in some country place in England, where he should be taught arithmetick, and to write English. He forbids his being taught Latin or Greek, or his residing in London, or either of the Universities of Oxford or Cambridge. He also provides for his son, Edward Wortley-Montague, then in the

East Indies; and gives a legacy to his daughter Mary, then a nun in the convent of the Ursulines at Rome. His books and manuscripts (except those in Turkish and Arabic, which he bequeathed to Fortunatus) he disposed of to his son Edward; and, from the legacies which he bequeathed, appears to have been in affluent, or at least in good circumstances.

THE SACRED TOUCH

THE late learned Mr. Anstis, in the 26th page of a MS discourse on Coronations, which he left at his death un-finished, hath these words, 'The miraculous gift in curing this distemper [the King's-evil] by the Royal Touch of our Kings, as well as of the French King's, is undeniable;' and in p. 49, taking notice of his having convinced a Surgeon of the antiquity of our Kings touching by several citations from our records, he adds, 'That he [the Surgeon] published these citations, and therefore I refer you [i. e. his son, the present Garter, to whom the Discourse is addressed] to that pamphlet.' I passed some days with him at Mortlake about twenty-six years ago, when a pam-phlet, wrote by a surgeon, about the King's-evil, was advertised in the newspaper, and had a good deal of discourse with him on the subject; and, by what was then said, I am persuaded that Mr. Becket's Enquiry into the Antiquity and Efficacy of Touching for the King's-evil, printed in octavo, 1722 (according to the booksellers' style, who begin their year even before Christ-mas), was the pamphlet in question: but I never saw it, and had entirely forgot the name of the surgeon; when, having Mr. Anstis's Discourse above mentioned before me, and consulting a learned gentleman (who had studied and practised physick above forty years, and transcribed my note for the press) about the name of the surgeon referred to by Mr. Anstis, it was either by his opinion, or my own inadvertence, that I put down Tooker for the name of that surgeon. I have endeavoured to find out this pamphlet, but in vain; the present Mr. Anstis had neither that nor any other treatise on the subject in his library. Whoever hath it, may observe by the records cited in it (especially if the accounts of the Household in 6th of Edward I. which there is scarce a man in England, besides Mr. Anstis, hath ever looked into, be cited for the cure of 182 persons of the King's-evil by that Prince) whether the author be the surgeon to whose book he refers. After all, whether the surgeon's name be Tooker, or Becket, or any other, is a matter of very little consequence.

Dr. Plot, in his Natural History of Oxfordshire, c. 10, § 125, Plate 16, N⁰ 5, gives a drawing of the Touch-piece supposed to be given by Edward the Confessor. The ribbon, he says, was white.

Mr. Barrington has preserved an anecdote, which he heard from an old man who was witness in a cause with respect to this supposed miraculous power of Healing. "He had, by his evidence, fixed the time of a fact, by Queen Anne's having been at Oxford, and touched him, whilst a child, for the evil: when he had finished his evidence, I had an opportunity of asking him whether he was really cured? Upon which he answered, with a significant smile, that he believed himself to have never had a complaint that deserved to be considered as the Evil; but that his parents were poor, *and had no objection to the bit of gold.*" The learned and honourable Writer very properly observes on this occasion, "that this piece of gold, which was given to those who were touched, accounts for the great resort upon this occasion, and the supposed afterwards miraculous cures." — Fabian Philips, in his Treatise on Purveyance, p. 257, asserts, "that the angels issued by the Kings of England on these occasions amounted to a charge of three thousand pounds *per annum;* and Queen Elizabeth was so tired of touching those who desired to be cured for the Evil, that in Gloucestershire during one of her progresses, she told those who were pressing on her, that 'God only could relieve them from their complaints.' By a Proclamation, March 25, 1616, it appears that the Kings of England would not permit such patients to approach them during the summer; and, by another proclamation, June 18, 1626, it is ordered, that no one shall apply for this purpose, who does not bring a proper certificate that he was never touched before; a regulation which undoubtedly arose from some supposed patients, who had attempted to receive the bit of gold more than once. — Sir Kenelm Digby informed Mons. Monconys, that, if the person had lost the piece of gold, the complaint immediately returned. — Gemelli (the famous Traveller) gives an account of 1600 persons being presented for this purpose to Louis XIV. on Easter

Sunday, 1686. The words used were, *Le Roy te touche, Dieu te guerisse.* Every Frenchman received 15 sous, and every Foreigner 30. *Observations on the Statutes,* 1775, p. 107, 108.

Since the above was first printed, my old friend the Rev. William Bickerstaffe sent me a copy of the original Proclamation; which, to use his own words, "in print and enframed, is yet preserved in St. Martin's church vestry in Leicester, of which the late Historian Carte's father was vicar; which faculty in the Stewart Family the said Carte in his History of England having asserted, suffered the loss of his annual subsidy from the Chamber of London."

"At the Court of Whitehall, 9th of January 1683.
Present, the King's Most Excellent Majesty; Lord Keeper, Lord Privy Seal, Duke of Ormond, Duke of Beaufort, Earl of Oxford, Earl of Huntingdon, Earl of Bridgewater, Earl of Peterborow, Earl of Chesterfield, Earl of Clarendon, Earl of Bathe, Earl of Craven, Earl of Nottingham, Earl of Rochester, Lord Bishop of London, Mr. Secretary Jenkins, Mr. Chancellor of the Duchy, Lord Chief Justice Jeffryes, Mr. Godolphin. Whereas, by the grace and blessing of God, the Kings and Queens of this Realm, by many ages past, have had the happiness, by their sacred touch, and invocation of the name of God, to cure those, who are afflicted with the disease called the King's-evil; and his Majesty in no less measure than any of his Royal Predecessors, having had good success therein; and, in his most gracious and pious disposition, being as ready and willing as any King or Queen of this Realm ever was, in any thing to relieve the distresses and necessities of his good subjects; yet, in his princely wisdom, foreseeing that in this (as in all other things) order is to be observed, and fit times are necessary to be appointed for the performing of this great work of charity, his Majesty was therefore this day pleased to declare in Council his Royal will and pleasure to be, That (in regard heretofore the usual times of presenting such persons for this purpose have been prefixed by his Royal Predecessors) the times of public healings shall from henceforth be from the Feast of All-Saints, commonly called Alhallow-tide, till a week before Christmas; and after Christmas until the first day of March, and then to cease till the Passion-week, being times most convenient, both for the temperature of the season, and in respect of contagion, which may happen in this near access to his Majesty's sacred Person. And when his

Majesty shall at any time think fit to go any progress, he will be pleased to appoint such other times for healing as shall be most convenient. And his Majesty doth hereby accordingly order and command, that, from the time of publishing this his Majesty's order, none presume to repair to his Majesty's Court to be healed of the said disease, but only at or within the times for that purpose hereby appointed as aforesaid : And his Majesty was farther pleased to order, that all such as shall hereafter come or repair to the Court for this purpose, shall bring with them certificates, under the hands and seals of the parson, vicar, or minister, and of both or one of the churchwardens of the respective parishes where they dwell, and from whence they come, testifying, according to the truth, that they have not, at any time before, been touched by his Majesty, to the intent to be healed of their disease. And all ministers and churchwardens are hereby required to be very careful to examine into the truth, before they give such certificates, and also to keep a register of all certificates they shall from time to time give. And, to the end that all his Majesty's loving subjects may the better take knowledge of this his Majesty's command, his Majesty was pleased to direct, that this Order be read publicly in all parish-churches, and then be affixt to some conspicuous place there; and for that end the same be printed, and a convenient number of copies sent to the Most Reverend Father in God the Lord Archbishop of Canterbury, and the Lord Archbishop of York, who are to take care that the same be delivered to all parishes within their respective provinces. LOYD.

"London, printed by the Assigns of John Bill deceased, and by Henry Hills, Printers to the King's most excellent Majesty."

In "The London Gazette," No 1893, from Monday, January the 7th, to Thursday January the 10th, 1683-4, is the following advertisement; viz. *"Adenochoiradelogia;* or, an Anatomick-Chyrurgical Treatise of Glandules and Strumaes, or King's-evil-swellings. Together with the Royal Gift of Healing or Cure thereof, by contact or imposition of Hands, performed for above 640 years by our Kings of England, continued with their admirable Effects and miraculous Events; and concluded with many wonderful Examples of Cures by their Sacred Touch; all which are succinctly described by John Browne, one of his Majesty's Chyrurgeons in ordinary, and Chyrurgeon of his Majesty's Hospital; published with His Majesty's Royal Approbation :

Together with the Testimony of many eminent Doctors and Chyrurgeons. Sold by Samuel Lowndes, over against Exeter-Change in the Strand." To this volume is prefixed a head of the Author, by R. White, not enumerated by Mr. Granger, on which is written, "Johannes Browne, Regis Britannici, nec non Nosocomii sui Chirurgus Ordinarius;" with a picturesque View of the Sovereign's performing the Ceremony; and by this publication it appears, that from May 1660 to April 1682 no less than 92,107 persons had been touched by the King.

The Form of "Prayers at the Healing," an Office which is omitted in Dr. Nichols's "Supplement to the Commentary on the Book of Common Prayer, 1711," was originally printed singly, and re-printed among the Additions to L'Estrange's "Alliance of Divine Offices," folio. The whole Form is also preserved by Bp. Kennett, in his "Register," p. 731; with a remark, that "he thinks this was the only Office changed by King James II. and performed by his own Priests;" and "that it was restored by Queen Anne, with very little correction." Mr. Thomas Fuller, in his "Appeal of injured Innocence," hath recorded, from Dr. Heylin, the Form of the Service at the Healing of the King's-evil by King Charles I. with no difference in the Form but in the Collect; for which see Bp. Kennett's Register.

Dr. Ducarel informed me, that being, in 1746, on a visit to the Rev. Mr. Bush, then vicar of Wadhurst in Sussex, he was shewn, in the Register-book of that parish, the following entry:

"We, the minister and church-wardens of the parish of Wadhurst, in the county of Sussex, do hereby certify, that Mr. Nicholas Barham of this parish, aged about 24 years, is afflicted (as we are credibly informed) with the disease commonly called the King's-evil; and (to the best of our knowledge) hath not heretofore been touched by his Majesty for the said disease. In testimony whereof we have hereunto set our hands and seals, this 23rd day of March, 1684.

> JOHN SMITH, Vicar.
>
> ROBERT LONGLY, } Church-wardens.
> THOMAS YONGE, }

Registered *per me*, JOHN SMITH."

The London Gazette, No 2180, from Thursday Oct. 7 to Monday Oct. 11, 1686, contains this advertisement:

"White-hall, Oct. 8, His Majesty is graciously pleased to appoint to heal weekly for the Evil upon Fridays; and hath commanded his Physicians and Chirurgeons to attend at the office appointed for that purpose in the Meuse, upon Thursdays in the afternoon, to give out tickets. Hereof all ministers of parishes are required to take notice, and to be careful to register the certificates they grant, in a book kept for that purpose."

Ridiculous as this mode of cure may appear, there was a regular form of service in the Book of Common Prayer for the occasion. It may be seen in those printed in Queen Anne's reign, and, I believe, in them only. I have looked over many editions of former reigns without being able to find it. The service is short; but certainly implies a belief in the cure.

It appears by the Newspapers of the time that on the 30th of March, 1714, *two hundred* persons were touched by Queen Anne. Amongst these was the famous *Samuel Johnson;* who was sent by the advice of Sir John Floyer, then a physician at Lichfield; and who many years afterwards, being asked if he could remember Queen Anne, said, "he had a confused, but somehow a sort of solemn recollection of a lady in diamonds, and a long black hood."

The following ingenious remarks on this subject were communicated to me, in 1781, by the learned and very ingenious Dr. Aikin. "Though the superstitious notions respecting the cure of the King's-evil by the touch of our English kings are probably at present entirely eradicated, it is still a curious and not uninstructive object of enquiry, by what means they were so long supported, and by what kind of evidence they have been able to gain credit even in the dawning of a more enlightened period. The testimony of Richard Wiseman, Serjeant-Surgeon to King Charles I. has been alleged as one of the strongest and most unexceptionable in favour of the Touch. He was a man of the greatest eminence in his profession; and his Works (collected in a folio volume, intituled, "Several Chirurgical Treatises, by Richard Wiseman, Serjeant-Chirurgeon, 1676") bear all the marks of an honest and upright disposition in their author. On the subject of the Royal Touch he delivers himself in the following strong and unequivocal terms : 'I myself have been a frequent eye-witness of many hundreds of cures performed by his Majesty's touch alone, without any assistance of Chirurgery; and those many of them such as had tired out the endeavours of able Chirurgeons before they came thither. It were endless to recite what I myself have seen, and what I have received acknowledgments of by letter, not only from the several parts of the Nation, but also from Ireland, Scotland, Jersey, and Guernsey.' The question which will naturally arise upon this passage is, Did Wiseman really believe what he asserted, or was he knowingly promoting an imposture? Both suppositions have their difficulties, yet both are in some degree probable. His warm attachment to the Royal Family and early prejudices might in some measure make his faith preponderate against his judgment; and, on the other hand, certain passages in his treatise necessarily shew a consciousness of collusion and fraudulent pretensions. It was his business, as Serjeant-surgeon, to select such afflicted objects as were proper to be presented for the Royal Touch. In the history of the disease, relating its various states and appearances, he says, 'Those which we present to his Majesty are chiefly such as have this kind of tumour about the *musculus mastoideus,* or neck, with whatever other circumstances they are accompanied; nor are we difficult in admitting the thick-chapped upper lip, and eyes affected with a *lippitudo;* in other cases we give our judgment more warily.' Here is a selection of the slightest cases, and a manifest doubt expressed concerning the success in more inveterate ones. A little below, observing that the *strumae* will often be suppurated or resolved unexpectedly from accidental ferments, he says, 'In case of the King's touch, the resolution doth often happen where our endeavours have signified nothing; yea, the very *gummata;* insomuch that I am cautious of predicting concerning them (though they appear never so bad), till 14 days be over.' From this we learn, that the Touch was by no means infallible, and that the pretence of its succeeding was not given up till a fortnight had passed without any change for the better. Indeed it appears very plain that the worst kind of cases were seldom or never offered the Touch; for in no disease does Wiseman produce more observations from his practice of difficult and dangerous chirurgical treatment, and in not one of these did he call in the assistance of the Royal Hand. It was indeed proposed in a single instance, but under such circumstances as furnish a stronger proof of imposture, than any thing hitherto related. A young gentlewoman had an obstinate scrophulous tumour in the right side of the neck, under the maxilla. Wiseman applied a large caustic to it, brought it to suppuration, treated it with escharotics, and cured it. 'About a year after,' he says, 'I saw her again in town, and felt a small gland of the bigness of a lupin, lying lower on that side of the neck. I would have persuaded her to admit of a resolvent emplaster, and to be touched; but she did not, as she said, believe it to be the King's-evil.' Here, after allowing his patient to undergo a course of very severe surgery, he is willing to trust the relics of the disease to the Royal Touch, assisted by a resolving plaster; but the complaint was now too trifling to engage her attention. Surely the greatest opponent of the touch will not place it in a more contemptible light!"

HISTORY OF THE ORIGIN OF PAMPHLETS

(*From a Dissertation, signed W. O.* [WILLIAM OLDYS, Esq.] *annexed to* MORGAN's Phœnix Britannicus, 1732," 4to.)

THE derivation of the word *Pamphlet* may be found in *Minshew's* "Guide to Tongues," fol. 1627; in the Preface to "Icon Libellorem;" Skinner's Etym. Ling. Angl. fol. 1671; and Spelman's Glossary.

The word *Pamphlet*, or *little* paper book, imports no reproachful character, any more than the word *great* book; signifies a pasquil, as little as it does a panegyric of itself : is neither good nor bad, learned nor illiterate, true nor false, serious nor jocular, of its own naked meaning or construction; but is either of them, according as the subject makes the distinction. Thus, of scurrilous and abusive pamphlets, to be burned in 1647, we read in Rushworth; and by the name of *Pamphlet* is the Encomium of Queen Emma called in Holinshed.

As for the antiquity of pamphlets, it is not only questionable, whether the Art of Printing should set a bound to it, but even the adoption of the name itself, which yet I take to be more modern than that Art; for I look upon them as the eldest offspring of paper, and to claim the rights of primogeniture even of bound volumes, however they may be shorter-lived, and the younger brother has so much outgrown the elder; inasmuch as

arguments do now, and more especially did in the minority of
our erudition, not only so much more rarely require a larger
compass than pamphlets will comprise; but these being of a
more ready and facil, more decent and simple form, suitable
to the character of the more artless ages, they seem to have been
preferred by our modest ancestry for the communication of
their sentiments, before book-writing became a trade: and
lucre, or vanity let in deluges of digressory learning, to swell
up unwieldy folios. Thus I find, not a little to the honour of
our subject, no less a person than the renowned King Ælfred,
collecting his sage precepts and divine sentences, with his own
Royal hand, into "quaternions of leaves stitched together;"
which he would enlarge with additional quaternions, as occasion
offered: yet seemed he to keep his collection so much within
the limits of a pamphlet size (however bound together at last),
that he called it by the name of his handbook, because he made
it his constant companion, and had it at hand wherever he was.

It is so difficult to recover even any of our first books or
volumes, which were printed by William Caxton, though it is
certain he set forth near half a hundred of them in folio, that
it were a wonder if his pamphlets should not be quite lost. There
are more extant of his successor Wynkin de Worde's printing
in this lesser form, whereof, as great rarities, I have seen both
in quarto and octavo, though holding no comparison probably
with those of his also, which are destroyed. But it was the
irruption of the grand controversy between the Church of Rome,
and the first opposers thereof, which seems to have laid the
great foundation of this kind of writing, and to have given
great credit to it at the same time, as well by the many eminent
authors it produced in Church and State, as the successful
detection and defeat thereby befalling those religious impostures,
which had so universally enslaved the minds of men.

The first single pamphlet that made a stir in London was
intituled "Simon Fish's Supplication of Beggars," 12mo, 1524,
B. L. It was written by an Attorney of Gray's Inn, while in
Germany, whither he was obliged to fly for having acted a part
in a play, which is no where named, that incensed Cardinal
Wolsey, and caused an inquiry after him. By interest with the
Lady Anne Bullen he caused it to be put in the King's hand,
which pleased him much, but was severely censured by the
bigoted chancellor Sir Thomas More, in his answer, called "The
Supplication of Souls," published without date. Fox and Burnet

both speak of this circumstance, and hint that it very early widened the breach opening between the Catholics and Protestants, and should be placed in the front of English prohibited books.

King James I. in 1611, published a royal pamphlet, which he thought so much above human patronage, that he dedicated it to JESUS CHRIST. It is a controversial piece written against Conrad Vorstius, in quarto. Montaigne observes in his "Défense de Senèque et de Plutarque," that nothing could excel the ingenuity and spirit contained in the numerous tracts published at the æra of the Reformation, the names and titles of which are now mostly forgotten.

The civil wars of Charles I. and the Parliament party produced an innumerable quantity of these paper lanthorns, as a Wit of that time called them, which, while they illuminated the multitude, did not always escape the flames themselves.

At this time might be mentioned the restless John Lilburne and the endless William Prynne, who wrote in earnest, for both bled in the cause. There are near a hundred pamphlets written by and concerning the first of these authors. But, the labours of the last being unparalleled, I may here not improperly observe, that, during the forty-two years he was a writer, he published above a hundred and sixty pamphlets, besides several thick bound volumes in quarto and folio, all said to be gathered into about forty tomes, and extant in Lincoln's-Inn Library. I think the printed catalogue of his writings extends not their whole number beyond one hundred and sixty-eight different pieces; but Anthony Wood to above one hundred and fourscore; who also computes, he must needs have composed at the rate of a sheet every day, from the time that he came to man's estate. That Author's character of him is drawn from his avowed enemies, even Papists, as Cressy, or personal antagonists, as Heylin, &c. But I cannot well omit what one sprightly Pamphleteer intimates, among other things, of him, to this purpose: "That Nature makes ever the dullest beast most laborious, and the greatest feeders: that though he had read and swallowed much, yet for want of rumination he concocted little: that to return things unaltered was a symptom of a feeble stomach; and as an error in the first concoction derives itself to the others, and nourishing up a prevalescent humour, begets at last a disease; even so, his judgment, being once deputrid, turned all his reading into bilious or putrid humours, which, being perpetually increased by his insatiate gluttony of books, did miserably foment and heighten his malady of writing." Another of his Draughtsmen has, among other humorous touches, as follows: "This is the *William,* whose passion is *the Conqueror.* The error of whose judgment, and unpardonable instability, is to be imputed to the loss of his two biasses; for if a bowl's deviation from the jack is occasioned hereby, much more a rational creature's, *à fortiori."* Neither will I omit what the Translator of the ingenious Father *Bartoli's* "Huomo di Lettere" says in his praise, where he calls him *Pater Patriæ,* for giving us a Dædalian clue in the blackest night of tyranny: farther adding, "Your numerous and nervous large and learned volumes (which who can reckon?) have been so successful in the refutation of errors, reformation of vice, regulation of disorders, restauration of Parliaments and laws, that I must, in justice, join you with the renowned General MONK, as the two worthiest subjects of all honour; for, if his generosity speaks him *Herculem Anglorum,* your erudition proclaims you *Alcidem Literarum,* &c."

This particular notice of our most voluminous Pamphleteer will lead us to a general review of the numerous produce of the press, during that turbulent series aforesaid, wherein he was such a fruitful instrument, to impregnate the same and promote the licentious superfœtation thereof. For by the grand collection of Pamphlets, which was made by Tomlinson the bookseller,* from the latter end of the year 1640 to the beginning of 1660, it appears, there were published in that space near thirty thousand several tracts: and that these were not the complete issue of that period, there is good presumption, and, I believe, proofs in being: notwithstanding, it is enriched with near a hundred manuscripts, which no body then (being written on the side of the Royalists) would venture to put in print; the whole, however, for it is yet undispersed, is progressionally and uniformly bound, in upwards of two thousand volumes, of all sizes. The catalogue, which was taken by Marmaduke Foster, the auctioneer, consists of twelve volumes in folio; wherein every piece has such a punctual register and reference, that the smallest even of a single leaf, may be readily repaired to thereby. They were collected, no doubt, with great assiduity and expence, and

---

*The name is wrongly given. It should read George Thomason (c. 1602-1666). [*Ed.*]

not preserved, in those troublesome times, without great danger and difficulty; the books being often shifted from place to place out of the Army's reach. And so scarce were many of these tracts, even at their first publication, that King Charles I. is reported to have given ten pounds for only reading one of them over, which he could no where else procure, at the owner's house, in St. Paul's Church-yard.

By the munificence of his present Majesty the British Museum was some years since enriched with this most valuable collection of 30,000 tracts, bound in 2000 volumes; 100, chiefly on the King's side, were printed, but never published.* The whole was intended for Charles the First's use, carried about England as the Parliament-army marched, kept in the collector's warehouses disguised as tables covered with canvas, and lodged last at Oxford under the care of Dr. Barlow till he was made Bishop of Lincoln. They were offered to the library at Oxford, and at length bought for Charles II. by his stationer Samuel Mearne, whose widow was afterwards obliged to dispose of them by leave of the said King 1684; but, it is believed, they continued unsold till his present Majesty bought them of Mearne's representatives. In a printed paper it is said the collector refused 4000*l.* for them.

Out of this immense collection Rushworth furnished himself with authorities; and, if the spirit of party was not so prevalent among them, we might still look them over with profit; but they are too much spoiled by the canting divinity of the times, which suits not the present age. Yet we have not been totally wanting in taste for these ephemerous productions, or of purchasers at an extravagant price, as Lord Somers, who gave more than 500*l.* for Tom Britton the smallcoal man's collection in this way; and Anthony Collins, whose collection afterwards produced above 1800*l.*; encouragement sufficient to induce other collectors to gather what the squalls of fate and chance may throw up.

Several tracts have been reprinted which heretofore were scarce, and both the originals and copies have fallen into equal neglect and disregard; as the topographical pamphlets of John Norden the surveyor, which, before they were reprinted, often sold for forty shillings a-piece. And some of Bale's tracts, as that of Anne Askew; more especially, "the Examination of Sir

---

*Now known as the Thomason Tracts. They were presented to the British Museum by George III in 1762. [*Ed.*]

John Oldcastle," which I have known to sell for three guineas, though gleaned by Fox into his Book of Martyrs. "The Expedition of the Duke of Somerset into Scotland" also has been sold for four guineas, though totally inserted in Holinshed. These, and some other personal narratives I could name, are as notorious as the advancement of Jordano Bruno's little book, called "Spaccio della Bestia Triomfante," to near thirty pounds, at the auction of Mr. Charles Bernard's books, serjeant-surgeon to her late Majesty; or of the uncastrated Holinshed, to near forty-five pounds, some years after. Though, when the former came to be known in English, it would sometimes pass off for so many pence; and the deficiencies of the latter, to be supplied out of Auditor Jett's library, it would not always rise to so many shillings, that is to say, above its ordinary estimation; plainly demonstrating, that unreasonable value arose not from any rich mines of knowledge, which the scarce part would communicate, from nothing intrinsically curious or instructive in it; nor even any material use to be made of it; but merely from the empty property of its singularity, and being, as the contending purchasers fondly apprehended, no where else recoverable.

Pamphlets have been the terror of oppression. Thus Philip the Second's wicked employment, treacherous desertion, and barbarous persecution of his secretary Antonio Perez, upbraids him, out of that Author's *Librillo,* through all Europe to this day. Mary Queen of Scots has not yet got clear of "Buchanan's Detection." Robert Earl of Leicester cannot shake off "Father Parsons's Green-coat." George Duke of Buckingham will not speedily outstrip "Dr. Eglisham's Fore-runner of Revenge." Nor was Oliver Cromwell far from *killing* himself, at the pamphlet which argued it to be *no Murder,* lest it should persuade others to think so, and he perish by ignobler hands than his own.*

In this manner did some take the liberty of calling these personages to account for their misdeeds, even whilst they were living. And with regard to that most memorable Usurper last mentioned, thus was a celebrated Writer of ours for immortalizing his name after his death: "When we fix any infamy on deceased persons, it should not be done out of any hatred to the dead, but out of love and charity to the living; that the curses, which only remain in men's thoughts, and dare not

---

Killing no Murder, by Will Allen (alias Col. Titus), 1657.

come forth against tyrants (because they are tyrants) while they are so, may at last be for ever settled and engraven upon their memory, to deter all others from the like wickedness; which, else, in the time of their foolish prosperity, the flattery of their own hearts and of other men's tongues would not suffer them to perceive. — The mischief of Tyranny is too great, even in the shortest time that it can continue : it is endless and insupportable, if the example be to reign too. — If it were possible to cut Tyrants out of all history, and to extinguish their very names, I am of opinion, that it ought to be done; but, since they have left behind them too deep wounds to be ever closed up without a scar, at least let us set such a mark upon their memory, that men of the same wicked inclinations may be no less affrighted with their lasting ignominy, than inticed by their momentary glories." How little soever these sentiments may be thought to need any corroboration, I flatter myself the following reply of our late excellent Queen Mary ought not here to be forgotten : When some of her courtiers would have incensed her against Monsieur Jurieu, who in his Answer to Father Maimburgh, that he might the better justify the Reformation in Scotland, made a very black representation of their Queen Mary : "Is it not a shame," said one of the company, "that this man, without any consideration for your royal person, should dare to throw such infamous calumnies upon a Queen from whom your Royal Highness is descended?" — "Not at all," replied this ingenuous Princess; "for is it not enough that by fulsom praises Kings be lulled asleep all their lives, but must flattery accompany them to their graves? How shall then Princes fear the judgment of posterity, if historians were not allowed to speak truth after their death?"

Thus much for the topics and arguments arising from those examples and authorities, which have occurred as most observable, upon this sudden recollection, to illustrate my present subject. What remains to be said of Pamphlets will more especially regard the present undertaking, to make a select revival of them; the approbation whereof may be grounded on these considerations :

First, the regard we owe to the preservation of good writings in general, and to their separation from the bad : but more in particular to these. For, if the reprinting of good old Books is commendable, much more is that of good old Pamphlets; they being, not to mention the greater ease of the expence, really more in want of such justice, to remove that mean opinion which some, unread therein, have more indistinctly entertained of them all, because many indeed are but meanly written; though the proportion is not greater than in books : and for those Pamphlets which really are well written (as abundance sufficient for any such undertaking have been, by the ablest pens, upon the most emergent points, however they daily perish in the common wreck, for want of a helping hand,) they cannot be denied a just claim to this care.

Secondly, because they stand in greater need of such care, than writings better secured by their bulk and bindings do. Many good old family books are descended to us, whose backs and sides our careful grandsires buffed and bossed and boarded against the teeth of time, or more devouring ignorance, and whose leaves they guarded with brass, nay silver clasps, against the assaults of worm and weather. But these defenceless conduits of advertisement are so much more obnoxious, by reason of their nakedness and debility, to all destructive casualties, that it is more rare and difficult, for want of a proper asylum, to meet with some tracts which have not been printed ten years, than with many books which are now more than ten times their age.

Thirdly, as being the liveliest pictures of their times. Pamphlets have this considerable advantage, that, springing usually from some immediate occasion, they are copied more directly from the life; so likelier to bear a resemblance, than any more extended draughts taken by a remoter light. But being therefore a kind of reading *à la mode,* and the events, their sources, so suddenly giving way to every fresh current of affairs, it is no wonder if these little maps of them are, in like manner, overborne, and become as transient as they : and yet, whenever the political wheel rolls into any of its former tracts, or present occurrences tally with those of past times, doubtless what was then advanced for the public good, might now be conducive thereto : whereas the disorders of former times revive, and the remedies which were prescribed against them are to seek; many, as well pleasant as profitable, being lost merely for want of revival.

Fourthly, the truest images of their authors. For, Pamphlets running so often upon new, particular, and unprecedented subjects, the writers have less opportunity to commit, and their writings are less liable to admit, such foul and frequent practices of plagiary, as books of matter more various, and bulk more voluminous, too often exhibit. Besides, the Author, being more vigorously prompted to application by the expediency of bringing forth his work opportunely, "is urged to strike out the images of his mind at a heat, in the most natural form and symmetry, in the most significant circumstances at once; seldom allowing leisure for the writer to doat upon, or dream over his work: neither to disguise it with the conceptions of other men, nor to deform it with chimæras of his own." Hence are they preferred by many criticks, to discover the genuine abilities of an Author, before his more dilatory and accumulated productions.

These, besides many other arguments which might be deduced from the commodious brevity, the vast choice, or variety of well-written Pamphlets, more particularly their regretted dispersion, consumption, and obscurity, but, above all, the many surprizing scenes to be unfolded and brought in view, by select and public collections, from the rich but disregarded store, are in my opinion sufficient recommendations to the encouragement of such a revival. What few attempts have hitherto been made seen either of a short-sighted nature, or of one too unbounded. Thus Edward Husband circumscribes himself to the Speeches and Ordinances of Parliament in a few years of King Charles I.; as the collections in King Charles II. and King William's reigns contain only some state-tracts of those times. And for John Dunton's collection, it might have succeeded better, had he not been for rambling into foreign, or heavy and unaffecting subjects. But the undertaking most likely to succeed is one wholly unconfined as to time, and only confined to matter domestically applicable; provided the undertaker chuses judiciously his materials. And certainly the publick might soon be obliged with a very valuable collection, if, in those particulars whereof the collector's own store should be deficient, he were supplied by such possessors of these curiosities, as have a relish for the project: which may be farther rendered a covenient receptacle for the restoration of what is not only rare and remarkable, but pertinent and seasonable.

And such, among others, are the advantages promised us by the present PHŒNIX; which, if it ever grows into a volume, and is accommodated with a compleat Index, I cannot help fancying we shall imagine ourselves led into new and untrodden paths; into regions of neglected but notable intelligence, which, having lain long dormant, and widely remote from ordinary observation, will look like a sudden resurrection of characters and descriptions, schemes and discoveries; or rather a kind of re-creation of them in the land of literature: so that it may yield the best comment upon past times, and become the grand expositor of many incidents, which general historians are either wholly ignorant of, or very superficially mention.   W.O.

ON THE FIRST PRINTED POLYGLOTTS

THE first Polyglott work was printed at Genoa in 1516, by Peter Paul Porrus, who undertook to print the Penta-glott Psalter of Augustin Justinian, Bishop of Nebo. It was in Hebrew, Arabic Chaldaic, and Greek, with the Latin Versions, Glosses, and Scholia, which last made the eighth column, in folio. The Arabic was the first that ever was printed: and this the first piece of the Bible that ever appeared in so many languages.

In 1518, John Potken published the Psalter, in Hebrew, Greek, Latin, and Æthiopic, [or Chaldaic, as he, with some others, called it,] at Cologne: but the name of the Printer is no where to be found throughout the book. It has no Preface properly so called: but from an Address of Potken to the studious Reader, which is printed on the last page of the Psalter, we are informed, that, while his earnest zeal for Christianity, and for the Roman See, made him extremely desirous of learning foreign languages, especially what he calls the Chaldee, for which he was destitute of any proper master; some Æthiopian Fryars happened to be at Rome (as he expresses it) *peregrinationis causâ,* to whom he eagerly applied; and that from his intercourse with them, he had acquired such a knowledge of their language, as to make him believe he might undertake an edition of the Æthiopic Psalter; which was actually published at Rome nearly five years before the date of his Polyglott performance. At the end of the above-mentioned address, he promised to perform something in the Arabic, if he should meet with sufficient encouragement.

The famous Bible of Cardinal Ximenes, commonly called the Complutensian, consists of six large folio volumes; having the Hebrew, Latin, and Greek, in three distinct columns, and the Chaldee paraphrase, with a Latin interpretation, at the bottom of the page, the margin being filled with the Hebrew and Chaldee radicals. It was begun in 1502, finished in 1517, but not published till 1522. A more particular account of it may be seen in Le Long, in Maittaire, and in De Bure; and an essay expressly on the subject by Mr. De Missey.

In 1546 appeared, at Constantinople, "Pentateuchus Hebræo-Chaldæo-Persico-Arabicus," in three columns; the Hebrew text in the middle: on the right-hand the Persic version of R. Jacob fil. Joseph; and on the left the Chaldee paraphrase of Onkelos: at the top is the Arabic paraphrase of Saadias, and at the bottom the commentary of Rasi. The whole is printed in Hebrew characters with points, the middle column on a larger size than the others. At the end of Genesis appears, "Absolutus est liber Geneseos in domo Eliezeris Berab Gerson Soncinatis."

In 1547 was published, from the same press, "Pentateuchus Hebraicus, Hispanicus, & Barbaro-Græcus." This edition was also printed in three columns: the Hebrew Text in the middle; the old Spanish version on the right hand; and on the left, the modern Greek, as used by the Caraïtes at Constantinople, who do not understand Hebrew. The Spanish is designed for the Refugee Spanish Jews. At the head and bottom of the pages are the Targum and the Commentary, as in the former editions.

The Royal or Spanish Polyglott was printed at Antwerp, by Christopher Plantinus, 1569—1572, by authority of Philip II. King of Spain, in Hebrew, Greek, Latin, and Chaldee, under the direction of Arias Montanus, in eight volumes, folio; containing, besides the whole of the Complutensian edition, a Chaldee paraphrase on part of the Old Testament, which Cardinal Ximenes had deposited in the theological library at Complutum, having particular reasons for not publishing it. The New Testament had the Syriac version, and the Latin translation of Santes Pagninus as reformed by Arias Montanus. This work was also enriched with various Grammars and Dictionaries of the several languages it consists of.

In 1586 a Polyglott Bible was published at Heidelberg, in two volumes, folio; printed in four columns, Hebrew, Greek, and two Latin versions, viz. St. Jerome's and those of Pagninus; with the notes of Vatablus; and in the margin are the idioms, and the radices of all the difficult words. Two other dates have been seen to this edition, *viz.* 1599 and 1616: but Le Long, after an attentive comparison, declares them to be only different copies of the same impression; but that some of them have the Greek Testament with the addition of the Latin version of Arias Montanus.

In 1596, Jacobus Lucius printed an edition, in Greek, Latin, and German, at Hamburg, in four volumes, folio, "Studio Davidis Wolderi;" the Greek from the Venice edition of 1518; the Latin versions those of St. Jerome and Pagninus.

In 1599, Elias Hutterus published one at Noremberg, in six languages; four of them, the Hebrew, Chaldee, Greek, and Latin, printed from the Antwerp edition: the fifth was the German version of Luther: and the sixth the Sclavonic version of Wittemberg. This Bible was never completed, and goes no farther than the book of Ruth.

The next work of this kind was, "Biblia Sacra Polyglotta, studio Guy Michaelis Le Jay. Parisiis, apud Antonium Vitré, 1628, & ann. seqq. ad 1645," in ten volumes, very large folio. This edition, which is extremely magnificent, contains all that is in those of Ximenes and Plantinus, with the addition of the Syriac and Arabic version.

This was soon followed by "Biblia Sacra Polyglotta, complectentia textus originales, Hebraïc. Chaldaïc. & Græc. Pentateuchum Samaritanum, & Versiones Antiquas, cum apparatu, appendicibus & annotationibus; studio & operâ Briani Walton. Londini 1657, & ann. seqq." in four volumes. To which was added, "Lexicon Heptaglotton, Hebraïcum, Chaldaïcum, Syraïcum, Samaritanum, Æthiopicum, Arabicum, & Persicum, digestum & evulgatum ab Edmundo Castello, 1686," in two volumes more. This may properly be called a new edition of Le Jay, with improvements; no pains having been spared in making it as perfect as possible: the whole was revised with great care, and accurately corrected; and it is justly considered as the most useful of all the Polyglotts, though Le Jay's is the handsomest. [This Polyglott was published by subscription, and was probably the first book ever printed in that manner in England. Of the books so published in this country, Minshieu's Dictionary in eleven languages may, perhaps, more properly be called the earliest, though not strictly within the modern idea of a *subscription*.] Dr. Walton's edition was supposed by Mr.

Palmer to have been printed from sheets surreptitiously obtained from the press at Paris; and to have been published with improvements so soon after, as to reduce M. Le Jay almost to want, after having expended above £5000. sterling to complete his work. But Mr. Palmer mistook the date of Le Jay's Polyglott (which he makes to be 1657), and then formed his conclusion of the sheets being sent into England from Paris; and met with a correspondent, it seems, that encouraged his error. Le Jay's Polyglott was published, in ten volumes, MDCXLV : the English Polyglott, in six volumes, not till MDCLVII, twelve years after the other. [Dr. Walton got leave to import paper, duty free, in 1652; began the work 1653; and published it 1657. It is surprising he could get through six such volumes in four years; though certainly many printers were employed on it; among others, Mr. Thomas Dawks, of Low Leyton, maternal grandfather to William Bowyer.] It is said indeed that the English put out proposals for a cheaper and better edition, soon after Le Jay's was published, which might in some measure hinder the sale of it. But other causes concurred. The enormous size of the book rendered it inconvenient for use : and the price deterred purchasers. And farther, the refusal of Le Jay to publish it under Richelieu's name, though that Minister, after the example of Cardinal Ximenes, had offered to print it at his own expence, damped the sale. — The English Polyglott, in return, made but little way in France.

THE AUTHOR OF *ΕΙΚΩΝ ΒΑΣΙΛΙΚΗ*

A S many tracts have been written to prove that King Charles could not be the Author of *ΕΙΚΩΝ ΒΑΣΙΛΙΚΗ* and still more to confirm his title to that book; I will transcribe an epitome of the controversy; and add such new testimonies as have occurred to me from the MSS. of Mr. Bowyer.

[On one side it is said, that in the year 1686, when the Earl of Anglesea's books were selling by auction, this book presented itself among others. The bidders being cold, the company had time to turn over the leaves; and there they found a declaration under his Lordship's own hand, that King Charles the Second and the Duke of York both assured him that it was not of the King's own compiling, but made by Dr. Gauden, Bishop of Exon. This made a noise; and Dr. Walker being questioned about it, as known to be very intimate with Gauden, he owned that the Bishop had imparted to him the plan in the beginning, and several chapters actually composed; and that he, on the other hand, had disapproved the imposing in such a manner on the publick; and in his treatise, intituled, "A True Account of the Author, &c." Dr. Walker says, "I know and believe the book was written by Dr. Gauden, except the sixteenth and twenty-fourth chapters, which were written by Dr. Duppa." Gauden delivered the MS. to Walker, who carried it to the press. A merchant of London, of the name of North, a man of good credit, married the Bishop's son's lady's sister; and, after young Gauden's death, his papers came into North's hands, being his brother-in-law. There he found one packet relating entirely to *ΕΙΚΩΝ ΒΑΣΙΛΙΚΗ*, containing, among other things, original letters, and a narrative written by Dr. Gauden's own wife. Bishop Burnet says, that, as he had once an occasion to quote this book, when in conference with King Charles the Second and the Duke of York, in 1673, they both declared that their Father never wrote it, but that it was written by Gauden, whom they rewarded with a Bishoprick. To this evidence has been opposed, the public testimony of both Charles II. and James II. to the contrary, under the great seal, in the patent to Mr. Royston, for printing all the works of King Charles I. And though it is highly probable that neither of these Princes were likely to know any thing of the contents of patents, this circumstance deserves at least as much credit as a private memorandum, unattested, purporting it to be written with a view that it could not answer: "I assert this," says Lord Anglesea, "to undeceive others:" but, if his intention had been "to undeceive others," why did he leave his declaration in the privacy of his study, on a single leaf, that might be obliterated or torn out; where indeed it was known to exist but by accident, the slow sale of the books affording time to the company to turn over the leaves? why did he not authenticate his declaration by proper witnesses, and publish it to the world; or leave it in some trusty hand, with a charge to publish it at some more convenient season? As to Gauden's pretensions to this book, they are easily to be accounted for, supposing them to be ill-founded. After the death of Dr. Bryan Duppa, Bishop

of Winchester, Gauden, presuming on the favour of some
persons at Court, solicited, with great eagerness, for the vacant
See, though he had openly abjured the whole Episcopal Order,
and was said to have advised King Charles II. by letter to
suppress it in Scotland. To strengthen his claim to this favour,
he is said to have whispered among his friends, and attempted,
without witness or credit, to persuade the King and his brother
the Duke of York, that their father was obliged to him for the
credit which he derived from *ΕΙΚΩΝ ΒΑΣΙΛΙΚΗ*: but this was
15 years after the death of Charles I. nor was any person then
living who could give evidence concerning the book. It is,
however, urged, that Dr. Walker, at the age of 70, and 40
years after the King's death, appeared in defence of this fiction :
but must Walker's evidence in favour of Gauden be deemed
indisputable, as has been insinuated, merely because Gauden
was his preceptor, and afterwards his intimate? This surely
is rather a reason why it ought to be suspected. Besides, Walker's
evidence is defective, and, in some instances, scarce consistent;
for, though he says Dr. Gauden shewed him the plan, and
several chapters actually composed, yet he does not say that
they were in the Doctor's hand; and he afterwards expresses
himself doubtfully, whether he read any part of the manuscript,
or only saw it with the title of the chapters; though surely, if
Gauden shewed him some part, actually composed, as his own
work, he could not have mortified him with such coldness and
want of curiosity as not to read it : besides, for what other
purpose was it shewn? and how could Walker be supposed
to live at this time in the house with Gauden, and know so
much, without knowing more? As to the evidence of Mr.
North and Mrs. Gauden, it can stand for little, if the following
positive evidence in favour of the book be considered : M. de la
Pla, minister of Finchingfield, in a letter to Dr. Goodall, informs
him, that William Allen, a man of repute and veracity, who
had been many years a servant to Gauden, declared, that
Gauden told him he had borrowed the book; and that, being
obliged to return it in a certain time, he sate up in his chamber
one whole night to transcribe it, Allen himself sitting up with
him, to make up his fire, and snuff his candles. It is also recorded
by Sir William Dugdale, who was perfectly acquainted with
the transactions of his own times, that these meditations had
been begun by his Majesty at Oxford, long before he went
thence to the Scots, under the title of *Suspiria Regalia;* and

that the manuscript itself, in the King's own hand-writing, being lost at Naseby, was restored to him at Hampton Court, by Major Huntingdon, who had obtained it from Fairfax. That Mr. Thomas Herbert, (afterwards Sir Thomas, the Traveller,) who waited on his Majesty in his bed-chamber in the Isle of Wight, and William Levet, a Page of the back-stairs, frequently saw it there, read several parts of it, and saw the King divers times writing farther on in that very copy which Bishop Duppa, by his Majesty's direction, sent to Mr. Royston, a bookseller, at the Angel in Ivy-lane, on the 23rd of December 1648, who made such expedition, that the impression was finished before the 30th of January, on which his Majesty died. Lastly, it is improbable that, if this book had been the work of Gauden, King Charles II. would have expressed himself with so little esteem and affection, when he heard of his death. "I doubt not," said he, "it will be easy to find a more worthy person to fill his place."

John Gauden was born at Mayland in Essex; made Dean of Bocking and Master of the Temple, in the beginning of the reign of Charles I.; Bishop of Exeter in 1660; and translated to Worcester two years after, which See he enjoyed but four months, dying at his Palace there, Sept. 20, 1662, aged 57. — A portrait of him is given by Dr. Nash, in which his character is strongly marked, though by a bad artist, and taken from a bad bust, placed over his grave in the Cathedral church at Worcester.] "Mr. Royston, who first printed the book (writes Mr. Bowyer), informed Sir William Dugdale, that, about the beginning of October 1648, he was sent to by the King, to prepare all things ready for the printing some papers, which he purposed shortly after to convey to him; and which was this very copy, brought to him the 23rd of December next following by Mr. Edward Symmons. Mr. Edward Symmons, who conveyed both the copies (viz. that written by Mr. Odart and that by the King) to the press, declared upon his death-bed, that is was the King's work, and assured several of his friends at Fowey, when he sent them some of the books, that he had printed them from the King's own copy.

There were seventeen editions printed of the book in 1648, without the Prayers; and twelve more in 1649, in which year there were at least six editions with the Prayers. These were first printed by Dugard, who was Milton's intimate friend, and happened to be taken printing an edition of the King's book.

Milton used his interest to bring him off, which he effected by
the means of Bradshaw, but upon this condition, that Dugard
should add Pamela's prayer to the aforesaid book he was
printing, as an atonement for his fault, they designing thereby
to bring a scandal upon the book, and blast the reputation of its
authority. To the same purpose Dr. Bernard, who (as well as
Gill) was Physician to Hills, Oliver's Printer, and told him this
story; adding, ' that he had often heard Bradshaw and Milton
laugh at their inserting this prayer out of Sir Philip Sydney's
Arcadia.' These Prayers are said in their title to have been
' delivered to Dr. Juxon,' &c. If so, they must have been
handed to the press by the King's enemies; for Dr. Juxon
and all his papers were immediately seized upon the King's
death; even the minutest scraps were examined, the King's
cloaths, cabinets, and boxes, were rifled. They were first printed
at Dugard's press, and afterwards were quickly translated to Mr.
Royston's, for every thing that was supposed to come from the
King quickened the sale of the impression. Mrs. Fotherly, of
Rickmansworth in Hertfordshire, daughter of Sir Ralph Whit-
field, first Serjeant-at-law to King Charles I. and grand-daughter
to Sir Henry Spelman, declared to Mr. Wagstaffe, that within
two days after the King's death, she saw, in a Spanish leather
case, three of these prayers, said to be delivered to the Bishop
of London at his death, from whom they were taken away by
the Officers of the Army; and it was from one of those Officers,
in whose custody they then were, that she had the favour to
see them; and that the person who shewed her those prayers,
shewed her also the George with the Queen's picture in it,
and two seals which were the King's. Three of the prayers therefore were the King's, the other added by the publisher."
W. BOWYER.

Dr. John Burton, in an Appendix to "The Genuineness of
Lord Clarendon's History," &c. has given some remarks on the
grounds upon which the King's title to this book was called in
question; which he concludes by observing, that, "considering
only the characters of the persons, and abstracting from the
proofs of the facts, the account which ascribes the honour of
the performance to Dr. Gauden appears on the face of the
thing altogether incredible, and that in favour of King Charles
will at least appear probable. But, when all the evidences on
both sides of the question are stated in a fair light, the point
will be at once determined, the King's right will be for ever

established : even prejudiced men may at last receive conviction, and be ashamed of their own credulity, and the impudence
of the astonishing accusation."

Dr. Nash has collected the principal arguments on each side
of this curious question; and finds reason to conclude, from
some observations of Bishop Warburton, and the whole of the
evidence both external and internal, that Gauden was not the
author of the book in question. "As he had the character of a
proud, ambitious man," says Dr. Nash, "he might be tempted
to encourage, if not invent this forgery, which tended so much
to gain him interest at Court. The only similitude I could find
between the Eik*wn* Basilikè and Gauden's other works consists
in the quaint Greek title, which, perhaps, might not be given
to the former by the King, or whoever wrote the book, but
by the Publisher to humour the false taste of the times."

Mr. Granger observes, "Whoever examines the writings of
the King and the Divine, will find that Charles could no more
descend to write like Gauden, than Gauden could rise to the
purity and dignity of Charles." But, after all, it may be observed,
that, in the volume of "King Charles's Works," there are some
other pieces which have since been proved not to have been
writen by him.*

[Mr. Hume says, "With regard to the genuineness of the production, it is not easy for an Historian to fix any opinion which
will be entirely to his own satisfaction. The proofs brought to
evince that this work is or is not the King's, are so convincing,
that, if an impartial Reader peruses any one side apart, he will
think it impossible that arguments could be produced sufficient
to counter-balance so strong an evidence : and when he compares
both sides, he will be some time at a loss to fix any determination.
Should an absolute suspense of judgment be found difficult or
disagreeable in so interesting a question, I must confess that I
much incline to give the preference to the arguments of the
Royalists. The testimonies which prove that performance to be
the King's, are more numerous, certain, and direct, than those
on the other side. This is the case, even if we consider the
external evidence; but when we weigh the internal, derived

---

*For the best account of the various editions of this work see *A New
Bibliography of the Eikon Basilike . . . with a note on the authorship*
by Francis F. Madan; Oxford Bibliographical Soc. Pubs. N.S. Vol 3,
1949. [*Ed.*]

from the style and composition, there is no manner of comparison. These meditations resemble, in elegance, purity, neatness, and simplicity, the genius of those performances, which we know with certainty to have flowed from the Royal pen : but are so unlike the bombast, perplexed, rhetorical, and corrupt style of Dr. Gauden, to whom they are ascribed, that no human testimony seems sufficient to convince us that he was the author. Yet all the evidences, which would rob the King of that honour, tend to prove that Dr. Gauden had the merit of writing so fine a performance, and the infamy of imposing it on the world for the King's. It is not easy to conceive the general compassion excited towards the King, by the publishing, at so critical a juncture, a work so full of piety, meekness, and humanity."]

REMARKS ON STEPHENS'S THESAURUS*

"THE old impressions of this great and valuable work, particularly that of Lyons 1573, being exceeding scarce, the publick is highly obliged to those learned gentlemen who have furnished us with a new edition, larger and more accurate than any of the preceding ones. We have the more reason to glory in the success of this noble and magnificent undertaking, which does honour to our age and nation, as several attempts of this nature have been heretofore made, and unhappily miscarried; particularly by Charles and Henry Stephens, by our own celebrated countryman Milton, by the Society of Baliol college in Oxford, and by Dr. Kuster, the excellent Editor of Suidas and Aristophanes.

This stately performance, after a very eloquent Dedication to his present Majesty, is introduced by a large Epistolary Preface, inscribed to the most ingenious Dr. John Hollings; containing a distinct and exact Account of the most considerable

---

*Robert Ainsworth (1660-1743), the author of this article was himself a lexicographer, his chief work being *Thesaurus Linguæ Latinæ Compendiarius,* 1736. He was a schoolmaster, first at Bolton, Lancashire, and later at Bethnal Green, London. [*Ed.*]

Latin Dictionaries which have appeared since the restoration of Learning, together with some Memoirs of the Compilers of them. Our readers will be pleased to see them as they stand in succession, and observe their principal characters; and the rather, as this is a piece of literary history, which has hitherto lain almost altogether uncultivated.

The first book of this kind that is mentioned, is the "Catholicon" of John Balbus, frequently styled Joannes de Janua, or Januensis, from his country, being a Genoese. It was one of the first fruits of the press after the invention of the typographical art, being imprinted at Mentz in 1460. This original impression consisted of 373 leaves, without either signatures of numeration of the pages, neither of which were then in use. The character was rude in comparison of later types, but extremely polite if we consider the time of its appearance, in the very infancy of printing; when we have far greater cause to admire so vast and disproportioned a production of it, than to animadvert upon its imperfections. Each side was divided into two equal columns, either of which contained precisely sixty-six lines, with a margin and interval sufficiently spacious; the paper large and strong, but otherwise not beautiful. The Author of this antient Lexicon bestowed many years in compiling of it, and finished it, as he tells us himself at the conclusion of his manuscript, on the nones of March, 1286. He was a man well versed in the liberal arts and sciences; of the order of Preaching Friars, and remarkable for his extraordinary sanctity.

There cannot indeed a great deal be said in commendation of this work, nor must the erudition of it be placed in competition with those of a more modern date; but, with respect to the age it was wrote in, it has not merited the contempt which Erasmus and some others have thrown on it. It led the way to those which afterwards outran it; and it should be remembered in its favour, that invention is at once a more difficult and a nobler instance of genius than improvement. It was for a long while the sole fountain from whence the Schools derived their knowledge in the Latin tongue : so that it is not to be wondered at, if a great many of the Literati exercised themselves in enlarging and embellishing it, and succeeding Glossographers imagined they ought to be intirely submitted to, and even applauded, wherever they could alledge the authority of the Catholicon in behalf of their opinions.

The pious Collector of it shewed a peculiar regard to such words as occurred in the sacred Scriptures, or especially related to them, and was careful to the utmost of his ability to discover, and even exhaust, the sense of them; an example of this we have under INTERPRES, where he has not only denoted the general meaning of it, but illustrated it by a short history of the several translations of the Old Testament out of the Hebrew into Greek, and out of either into Latin. "First by the Seventy, next by Aquila, a third and fourth by Theodotion and Symmachus; a fifth that was anonymous, and called the Vulgar Interpretation; besides a sixth and a seventh that were found by Origen, the last of which was of the Psalms only; and both which with immense labour and diligence he collated with all the preceding ones. The versions out of Greek into Latin were almost innumerable, as St. Augustine observes; for in the Western primitive Church, almost every man that got a Greek Bible into his hands, and was ever so little versed in that language, turned it into his own. St. Jerome, who was skilled in all the three tongues, was the only translator of the Scriptures from the Hebrew into the Latin immediately; his translation is very justly esteemed, not only for the elegance and perspicuity of it, but likewise for its strictness and fidelity."

Our Author was beholden to Papias for what he has said here in the explanation of this word; from whom, as well as Hugutius, he owns himself to have transcribed a great many articles.

All that I shall say farther of the Catholicon is that although the edition of 1460 has neither Faustus's Colophon, nor the mark of a Calf's Horn in the paper, which Naudæus and some others have fancied to be a certain criterion for distinguishing the books which he printed, yet there is not the least reason to doubt its being the work of that incomparable artist. Nor is there any foundation for Trithemius's opinion, which the reputation of his great knowledge in antiquity has imposed on many, of an edition of it antienter than this we are speaking of, printed upon wooden blocks, before fusile separate types, which this is undeniably done on, were invented. The blocks for this pretended original impression must be some years preparing; and it is not to be imagined that, amidst the plenty of manuscripts then extant, the copies done off them could be so quickly disposed of, as to encourage or require the undertaking another almost immediately after the first was wrought off; for that must

here be the case, considering there is an interval but of
ten years, at the most, between the date of our edition and the
very first offspring of the press. There cannot be a more improbable supposition; and indeed this prodigy of Trithemius's has
never yet been found in the most copious libraries, or occurred
to the most industrious enquiries of the Learned. But though
the editions of this work did not succeed one another so swiftly
in the primordial dawn of typography, as this Critick and his
followers contend for, yet, in truth, it passed through several
before the conclusion of that age, which was of all others the
most propitious to learning. As, for instance, in the year 1483;
there was an impression of it finished at Venice, corrected and
amended by the care, and at the expence, of Herman Liechtenstein. Four years after, *viz.* in 1487, another was completed
by the same person, and in the same city. The fourth edition
of it was likewise at Venice, 1495, under the revisal of Boneti
Locatelli. At the beginning of the fifth century, Petrus Ægidius,
a man of great eminence in the canon and civil laws, very
much enlarged it, and printed it at Lyons in 1506, a second
time in 1514, and lastly in 1520.

Our Editors, having occasion (as we have seen in their
account of the Catholicon) to make mention of Papias and
Hugutius, as writers to whom the compiler of it has professed
himself greatly indebted, have given us a brief history of them
as authors, and settled the times in which they flourished. It not
being possiblé for us to go through the subject now, we shall
close this article for the present with an abstract of it.

Papias was by nation a Lombard. We know not when he was
born, but he was undoubtedly more antient than Joannes
Januensis, as appears by this latter's copying from him. It is
surprising that any one should degrade him so low as the
age of the Catholicon; and even Trithemius, Platina, Cornel à
Beughem, and Jac. Phil. Bergomensis, are mistaken, in imagining him to be but one hundred years earlier; he was two at
the least, as we are assured by Caspar Barthius in his Adversaria,
who therein agrees with the Chronicon Albericum MS. where
it is noted, that in the year 1053, being the 13th of the
Emperor Henry, the son of Coñrad, Papias set forth his book,
intituled, ELEMENTARIUM DOCTRINÆ ERUDIMENTUM.

He was a man admirably versed in prophane literature, as
celebrated a grammarian as any of his time, a complete master
in the Greek and Latin tongues, and perfectly acquainted with

the Scriptures, and the Works of the Fathers. He wrote a great many things both on divine and human subjects. Trithemius had seen only three, *viz.* "De Ordine Dicendi," "De Linguæ Latinæ Vocabulis," and "Epistolæ ad diversos." The second is that he is most known by. Scaliger indeed undervalues it extremely; he treats it as ignominiously as Erasmus does the Catholicon, and calls it *futile opus*; but others extol it as much, and set it out for a rich repository of learning : Barthius in particular expatiates in the praises of it. Perhaps it will be speaking the truth of it to say, that it was enriched with the spoils of all that had preceded it. It had several impressions; one at Milan in 1476, and four following ones at Venice, *annis* 1485, 1487, 1491, and 1496.

Hugutius, whom the Catholicon transcribed also, was a Pisan by birth, and Bishop of Ferrara. A man of conspicuous figure about the year 1196. I suppose the first preferment the Pope conferred on him was the coadjutorship of a monastery, in the library of which he met with Papias, and out of him in a great measure composed his Glossary, or Book of Derivations. Boccatius gives him a good character in his "Genealogy of the Gods." Whether he wrote the "Treatise of Animals" that is usually ascribed to him is uncertain, as there were others of his name contemporary with him famous for learning; particularly one, promoted to the purple 1191, who was reckoned the greatest Civilian and Canonist of that age. His Vocabulary has never been printed, and the manuscript copies of it lie hid only in a few collections. He has recorded his own name and country in the Preface of it, after the odd manner of those times. "If any one asks," says he, "who was the author or doer of this work, it may be answered, God. If it be demanded who was the instrument in performing of it, it may be replied, Hugutius of Pisa." He died about the year 1212.

Our Editors apologize for insisting upon these things so largely. The Latin tongue had afterwards otherguise patrons to glory in than those they have now mentioned; but it is the established fate of Literature to grow up to maturity by slow degrees, from the most inconsiderable originals : and they wonder very justly at the ungrateful severity of Erasmus, and some other philologers, towards these primitive nurses, who first took care of the language in the very infancy of its reviction. If it received from them a stronger nourishment, and under their tutelage advanced to perfection, that cannot excuse their deriding or calumniating those who administered their best assistance at its new birth, and preserved it from perishing, till it was provided with more able guardians.

"To that weak and abject state of the Latin tongue, which our former article on this subject was employed in giving an account of, we may refer Joannes de Garlandia an Englishman, who lived in the reign of Harold the Dane, and made some considerable figure about the year 1040. He shone, not only in the character of a grammarian, but likewise of a chemist, a mathematician, and divine. His "Synonyma et Equivoca, or Book of Synonymous and Equivocal Terms," passed through the press at Cologne so soon as 1490; and was again printed at London, in quarto, by Richard Pynson 1496. This edition, as I judge by the title of it, was improved, not only by Galfridus's Exposition on the Synonyma, but by digesting the Equivoca into an alphabetical order; which circumstance seems to have been otherwise in the original.

It may suffice (to keep up the Series) barely to mention here a few others of the same inferior class with the foregoing writers. Such as, Simon de Janua, author of a Physical Lexicon; Marchesinus of Reggio, also near Modena, of the order of Minor Friars, who composed a Dictionary of the words used in the Scripture and Liturgies; it was, I presume, something of the same nature with Pasor's Lexicon of the New Testament, which we have now : its first appearance in print was at Mentz 1470. Nic. Jenson printed it next at Venice, in quarto, 1479. It had other editions elsewhere. I pass over Gemma Gemmarum, with other Vocabularies of like value; but Nestor Dionysius of Novaria, a Minorite, must not be entirely omitted; he flourished just upon the turn of Learning's fortune, when Letters began to shine, and one might sensibly discern their progress towards that meridian splendour they soon after rose to. He awoke, as it were, just time enough to discover and laugh at the blind dreams of those that preceded him, though at the same time he appeared to such as followed him not very sprightly or clear-sighted himself. His Dictionary was first published in 1488*. It was reprinted at Paris 1496; and at Venice that same year, by Phil. Pinzius; and afterwards in 1502 and 1507; and revised by Johan. Tacuinus.

Our Editors are at length come to a more auspicious period,

---

*1483, Milan. [Ed.]

when the Roman language had happily recovered its pristine lustre. They have now such men to celebrate as Erasmus, Valla, Longolius, and Linacre, with many others of like fame and ability; who were accurate grammarians, elegant translators of the most valuable Greek authors, and masters of all the purity and beauty of the Latin tongue. But their immediate concern is with those only who have distinguished themselves in the Republick of Letters under the character of Lexicographers.

The first taken notice of by them is Johannes Tortellius, a native of Arezzo in Tuscany; he was a favourite with two Popes. He was sub-dean and chamberlain to Eugenius the IVth, and afterwards the chief confident of Nicholas the Vth, his library-keeper, and an intimate companion of his studies. He was highly esteemed for his great knowledge and acquaintance with the Greek and Latin literature, and equally beloved for the engaging qualifications of a sweet disposition and venerable behaviour. Laurentius Valla, who was himself a most excellent grammarian, had an entire friendship for him, and paid such a deference to his opinion and judgment, that he dedicated to him his books "De Latinâ Elegantiâ." He was universally commended for his grammatical exactness in writing, as well as for the perfection of his style. His Dictionary is divided into two parts; the first, which is very short, treats of the invention, number, figure, pronunciation, and joining of the letters of the alphabet. The second, which is much longer, contains an alphabetical catalogue of Latin words, chiefly derived from the Greeks; of which (says Bayle) he teaches, or endeavours to teach, the orthography. This work was printed at Tarvis, 1477*. Its second impression was at Vicenza 1480. It had three editions afterwards at Venice, in the years 1493, 1495, 1504; and another at Vicenza again 1508, &c. Besides this great undertaking, our author wrote several Epistles, which were published. He likewise translated the Life of Athanasius by order of Pope Eugenius, and turned Appian's Hisory into Latin, *verbatim*. Vossius thinks it was he, who, under the title of Archpresbyter of Arezza, compiled the Memors of St. Zenobius.

With Tortellius, our Editors join Junianus Maius, a Neapolitan; not merely because they were contemporary, but as they had

---

Editio princeps Venice 1471, another edition appearing in Rome the same year. [*Ed.*]

nearly the same taste and bias in their studies. He wrote, besides Epistles and some other things, "De priscorum verborum proprietate." Trithemius gives him a very advantageous character; he extols both his genius and his elocution; and celebrates his skill in philology, divinity, philosophy, and rhetorick. He was indefatigable in investigating and noting the peculiar force and significancy of certain words and phrases. His Dictionary, under the above-mentioned title, was inscribed to Henry de Lunguard, an Archbishop, and Confessor to Ferdinand King of Naples. He tells that Prelate, in the Preface of it, "That he may in that book see what the antient and modern Grammarians have written of the power and virtue of words, in separate pieces, collected and digested into a regular method. He intimates as though the work were not originally begun by him, but that he had found a plan and part of a superstructure raised by some other hand, which, at a mighty expence of labour and contrivance, he had new-modelled and completed; retrenching what he saw superfluous in the first design, and enlarging it in other instances where he perceived it to be scanty and deficient : making considerable additions to it, not only from Laurentius Valla and Tortellius, but also from Servius, Donatus, Porphyrion, Acron (those approved Commentators on Horace, Terence, and Virgil); together with Macrobius, Aulus Gellius, Strabo, Nonius Marcellus, &c. He complains of its being hastened out of his hands by some people's eagerness, before he could methodize it so accurately as he desired, or enrich it with that affluence of words which he intended to collect from Pliny, Vitruvius, Columella, Celsus, and Varro." There were four impressions of this book in folio; the first at Naples 1475. The two following ones at Tarvisa* in 1477 and 1480. The last again at Naples, 1490.

After Maius follows Johnnes Reuchlinus or Capnio, a German, born of honest and genteel parents, on the 28th of December 1454. He was exceedingly well versed in the Hebrew, Greek, and Latin tongues; and happily promoted the restoration of them in his own country. Erasmus styles him the Phœnix of those three languages. He was sent ambassador from the Palatine Court to Rome, where he closely attended the Hebrew Lectures of Abdias a Jew, and the Greek ones of Argyrophylus. This latter observing his eager thirst after the Grecian Literature,

---

*i.e. Treviso. [*Ed.*] There was also an edition printed at Venice, 1482.

enquired whence he came, and being told he was of Germany, and not entirely ignorant of that Learning which he was a professor of, he desired him to read and interpret a paragraph or two of Thucydides; which when Reuchlin immediately did, pronouncing it aright, and translating it not only justly but elegantly, Argyrophylus cried out in a kind of transport and amaze, "Our banishment has transported Greece over the Alpine mountains." This excellent person had the felicity to be loved by princes, and applauded by all the Literati: his talents for negotiating their most arduous affairs with expedition and success recommended him to the former, and the praises of the latter were a tribute he deserved for his unwearied endeavours to promote their fame and interest.

He was the author of a Latin Dictionary, which some have highly commended; but, to speak impartially, as that tongue was not quite refined and reduced to its sterling purity at the time he compiled it, he admitted a great many foreign and even barbarous terms to creep in, that have much debased and undervalued it: for which reason, as well as because the succeeding age produced much better performances of the same kind, this has for a long while been of little or no value, and almost entirely forgotten: Reuchlin was but very young when it came out of his hands, and he presented it to the learned world as the *primitiæ* of his studies. Melchior Adam (in his Life) suggests as if he undertook it at the instance of the younger Amerbachs*, about the time of their setting-up for themselves: that is not improbable; there were none readier to excite or employ men of letters than those illustrious brothers. But our Editors think him mistaken in supposing it was first printed by them in folio at Basel; they are positive it was by their father, a man of incomparable learning and virtue†. There were prefixed to it some small grammatical and orthographical pieces, *viz.* a little tract of Guarinus Veronensis of the true writing of Diphthongs; a Dialogue on the Art of Pointing; a Discourse of Accent, &c. Indeed the whole book is much in the same way and character with these Prolegomena. The Printer of it tells us in the Preface, "That all the terms relating to Divinity, and both Canon and Civil Law, are clearly explained in it: that great regard has

---

*See Mr. De Missy's very curious Anecdote of Bruno and Basil Amerbach's Polyglott Psalter, in "The Origin of Printing," p. 126.
†Printed by John Amerbach, Basle, 1478.

been had to the orthography of them: that the diphthongs are rightly expressed; and the proper syllables duly accented." I do not find it had ever any more than one impression.

Nicolaus Perottus succeeds Reuchlin. He was of a noble family, and became Archbishop of Siponto. He was a person of extraordinary ingenuity and great reading; and not undeservedly accounted, after Tortellias, the chief restorer and support of the Roman tongue. He studied the Greek learning at Rome with indefatigable industry, under the munificent patronage of Cardinal Bessarion, a true Mæcenas of Literature. While he was a very young man he translated Polybius so elegantly into Latin, that the interpreters of that time never mentioned him but with the highest encomiums. It is true, there were some few who were envious of his reputation, and endeavoured to diminish it; but their very detraction involved in it the most delicate compliment: they pretended, the Version he published was not his own, but a very antient one he had somehow surreptitiously obtained, and, concealing the true author, unjustly assumed to himself the honour of it: but how glorious to him was the ground of their defamation! It was no other than this: Thucydides, Diodorus Siculus, Plutarch, and Appian, had been severally translated by the most excellent modern hands, who had strove to surpass one another in their performances; but this of Polybius, it seems, so far transcended them all in purity of diction, in equality and sweetness of style, that it could not be the product of any inferior to the Augustan age. All the writers that take any notice of him have agreed in extolling his singular abilities in the Greek and Latin languages, the idioms of which he could so entirely transmute one into another, that he erased all mark of their primitive character. The beauty of his Polybius likewise is universally acknowledged, but the fidelity of it is not so unquestionable: we must confess, he is accused by Casaubon and Huetius of taking very unjustifiable liberties with that writer, and deviating vastly from his original in a multitude of instances. Be that as it will; the world was highly obliged to him for his curious and useful collection of the purest and most genuine Latin. His large and elaborate Commentaries on Martial, which he intituled "Cornucopia," were of unspeakable service to young scholars, for whose benefit he wrote them: he has therein laid open the treasures of the Latin tongue; explained the nature and genius of it; shewn the peculiar signification of its words, and crowned all with so copious an index of them, that it might well serve for a Lexicon of that language, as it really did for a long while after.

Perottus entered upon this work at the importunate request of Pomponius Fortunatus; but having finished it he laid it by, nor would he allow it to be printed during his life, on account of the obscenity and filthiness of several passages of the Author he illustrated. But, having lent the manuscript to many who had requested the favour of consulting it, some ungrateful plagiary had stole its principal beauties, and decked a meaner offspring of his own with them, after the decease of their true parent. This obliged the friends of Perottus, who were concerned for the honour of his memory, to publish this posthumous piece, that the learned might no longer attribute to others what they were indebted only to him for.

Our Editors have not ascertained the date of the first edition of it: it was some time between 1482 and 1486, and not in 1470, as Du Cange supposed*. In less than ten years, *viz.* 1492, it was printed again in folio at Venice. Its next impression was by Aldus Manutius, in 1499. The year following there came forth an edition of it at Paris, printed by Gering and Rembolt. This was indeed a most beautiful one, and very carefully corrected by Joannes Pompeius Cornianus. But the noblest of all was that of Aldus, at Venice, 1513. This, besides the most diligent emendations, was enriched by the edition of Varro, Festus, and Nonius Marcellus; which last was in this edition of it exceedingly improved and enlarged by J. Jucundus, a man of infinite erudition, whom Scaliger respected as his master, and was used to style a library of all the antient and modern arts and sciences. After this the most learned Valentinus Curio published an accurate edition of our author and his associates, Varro, &c. at Basel, annis 1526 and 1532. Besides all these, the "Cornucopia" had several other impressions, *viz.* in 1504. At Paris, in 1506. In 1521 at Basel; and again in 1536. In short, all the Literati of that age admired and commended these Commentaries of the renowned Perotti.

The business of Lexicons was about this time indeed so mightily in vogue, that, as our Editors observe, some of the greatest rank and capacity in philology and criticism thought it no diminution of their dignity to employ themselves in amending,

---

*Venice 1489, 1490, 1492, 1494. [*Ed.*]
In omnes divinos libros notationes. Rome, 1553.

enriching, and embellishing the labours of others in that way; and this they did with a care and application equal to any they bestowed on the most valued authors of antiquity. Not one of the moderns had more respect paid him of this sort than our Perotti; first of all, by Ludovicus Odaxius; then by Polydore Vergil, who was at the pains of collating the first impression of the "Cornucopia" with an authentic copy in the Duke of Urbino's library, by which he minutely corrected all the errata of it: after him, as we have seen, the modeling, augmenting, and adorning it, was undertaken by no meaner hands than those of Cornianus, the most excellent Aldus, and that rich treasury of knowledge Valentinus Curio. It would be super-fluous to add here the testimonies of Gesner, Ludovicus Vives, Trithemius, and others, in honour of this noble work: Paulus Jovius supposed its intrinsic merit and serviceableness would render it immortal; and our Editors remark he judged rightly, as it has been taken into the composition of every subsequent Dictionary.

After this exalted character of Perotti, it is some displeasure to descend to that of Calepin, who follows him in the list of Lexicographers. Ambrosius Calepinus was a native of Calepio near Bergamo, and of the order of Augustin Friars. He lived to a great age, and died at Bergamo, anno 1510, where some say he was born, and where he lies buried in the Augustin Church, without any monument to distinguish him. He left the world no legacy but his Dictionary; which has, indeed, more by good fortune than any merit, sufficiently aggrandized his memory. Erasmus, Ludovicus Vives, Borrichius, Scioppius, Hieronimus Magius, and other very competent judges, all concur with our Editors in speaking very contemptibly of him. They represent him as not ashamed of transcribing from Perotti what Perotti was ashamed to publish; as incapable of supplying the deficien-cies of those authors, whose labours he only injudiciously heaped together; as a person altogether ignorant of Greek, and scare tinctured with human learning. They characterise his Dictionary as meanly, and load it with the most disgraceful epithets. It is jejune and sterile; barbarous and fulsome; dry, inaccurate, and throughout erroneous: and, after all the amend-ments and improvements of better hands than the first com-piler's, it remains an insipid performance, and worse than any that preceded it.

But, after all this accumulation of disgrace, our ingenious

Editor has picked up a single testimony in Calepin's favour; but seems to wonder how it could drop from the pen of the celebrated Jacobus Philippus, after he had read that Writer's Dedication of his Dictionary to the Senate and People of Bergamo, and his Poetical Address to the Work itself, at the beginning of it. Philippus says of him, "that he was of a sweet disposition and behaviour." And as for his book, he calls it "a great and valuable collection of the lucubrations of innumerable learned men, gathered with prodigious labour and industry, and sorted with the nicest accuracy and judgment." He is pleased likewise to style the Epistle the author prefixed to it, a very learned and elegant thing. Perhaps Philippus would have passed a less favourable judgment on Calepin's performance, if he had not been his countryman; of the same age and order with himself; and at the same time his most dear and intimate companion.

It is surprizing that a work so mean and despicable should surmount such an universal contempt, pass through such a number of editions, and employ the pains of so many learned men to revise, enlarge, and adorn it, as this of Calepin did. It grew under every posthumous impression; and such vast additions were made to it by a variety of hands, after the author's decease, that, though it still retained his name, it soon became a quite different thing from what he left it. There were but two editions of it in his life-time. The first was at Reggio in Lombardy, in 1502, in folio, upon a very fine letter. It is become extremely scarce. Our Editors have seen it (which is what few can boast of), and have inserted in their Preface the "Allocutio ad Librum" which is prefixed to it, and which does not appear in any of the following editions. As that has nothing but its rarity to recommend it, I chuse to omit it here; and observe, that the pages in this first edition were not numbered, but we know they amounted to fifty-five signatures, of four sheets each. The second edition was printed at Venice in 1509, by Liechtenstein : neither Gesner, nor the diligent and inquisitive Borrichius, who saw this, had ever lighted upon the former one. Our Editors have set down the dates of eighteen editions more that this Dictionary has passed through since the death of Calepin; and suppose several others might be discovered, if it were worth an enquiry.

Amongst the many contributors to the fame, as much as to the materials of this Lexicon, one of the most eminent was

Johnnes Passeratius, Regius Professor in the University of Paris. Our Editors have collected a great many encomiums on him, celebrating the politeness of his genius, the purity of his style, and the elegance of his writings : the most accomplished wits of his own time were ever ambitious of praising him; always excepting the ill-natured Scaliger, who treats him opprobriously. He was certainly a man of the justest taste, and of a nice discernment, but too difficult to please, very seldom approving the the works of others.

He died at Paris, 1602, in the sixty-eighth year of his age, and was buried in the church of the Dominicans, under a monument erected to his memory by Jo. Jac. Memmius, who styles him his dearest preceptor. This was probably some near relation of the most noble Henricus Memmius, who had been always Passeratius's bountiful patron, and at whose recommendation he was promoted to be Regius Professor of Eloquence in the University of Paris. His death was universally lamented; the Literati covered his hearse with their panegyricks : the truth is, in that age they were very liberal of them, they spoke of nobody indifferently; if they did not utterly degrade a man, they were sure to extol him above measure; there was rather too much of the Gascon in their compliments. "Our Passeratius was no less than the last of the Roman writers; the chief of all the grammarians and rhetoricians of his age; the principal pillar of the Parisian academy; the glory of polite learning; the Phœnix of Eloquence, and another Varro." The additions to Calepin's Dictionary generally ascribed to him were so superficial and indigested, so unworthy of, and unsuitable to, the account here given of his great abilities and erudition, that our Editors most readily assent to the opinion of very competent judges, that he had really no hand in that Lexicon at all; and that the imputing a share of it to him was only a trick and knavish device of the booksellers, who had the copy-right, to enhance the reputation of their book, and promote the sale of it. This memorable writer, however, left several genuine pieces behind him that justify his character. There are some beautiful poems of his extant in the third tome of the " Delitiæ Gallicæ;" but his most valuable work is a Treatise "of the Exchange and Affinity of Letters," printed at Paris 1606, in 8vo.

Our learned Editors observe very justly, that it would be endless to write particularly of all Calepin's benefactors : of Jac. Montanus, Paul Manutius, Laur. Chifletius, Lud. de la

Cerda, Conrad Gesnerus, Budæus, Ascensius, &c. all which were one way or other concerned in new-moulding or enlarging his Dictionary; for what we have now under that named is a great superstructure raised indeed by their hands, in which he had very little concern besides that of laying the foundation. But though they excuse themselves the task of pointing out these gentlemen's merit, they have allowed Gesner the liberty of setting for his own, and commending himself. And he tells us, "that he had corrected the impression of Calepin set forth at Basel in 1544, in innumerable places: that he had transplanted into it the four thousand words, which the last Venetian edition had been enriched with from the most approved authors: and which had been reckoned the chief ornaments of it; and had taken a peculiar care of what related to the Prosody; revising the whole for that purpose, and nicely distinguishing the quantities of the syllables in all the principal terms. That he had selected the proper names, which till then had been promiscuously dispersed throughout the work, and ranged them in a separate alphabet; adding to them as many others as he could find in the latest poetical dictionaries."

The next Lexicographer in order is Marius Nizolius, author of "Thesaurum Ciceronianum; or, Observations on Cicero, alphabetically digested." Printed Basel, 1530; afterwards at Venice, 1535, folio; and again there, 1541; with the addition of several words collected from Cicero after Nizolius by Zanchius. Hervagius published it again in 1548, with very great improvements by Cælius Secundus Curio; and a second time at Frankfort 1568. It had after these so many editions, that it would be tiresome to enumerate them. Our Editors have marked that of Lyons, 1608, folio, and that of Geneva, 1612, 4to, as the most correct and copious. At length this work, which at first sprung from Cicero alone, and was confined to him only, became more universal, and grew up to be in all respects a complete Lexicon. The finishing hand was set to it by M. Ludovicus Lucius, Professor in the University of Basel, who, in 1613, published it there in two volumes in folio, under the title of "Latinæ Linguæ Thesaurum bipartitum, &c. or, a Treatise of the Latin tongue, in two Parts: the first consisting of Nizolius's Collections from Cicero only; the second, extracted from several other Authors, containing and copiously explaining the Terms made use of by the most approved Orators, Historians, Lawyers, Physicians, and Poets; with Rules for expressing them grammatically." Much of this latter part was undoubtedly borrowed from Stephens.

To return to Nizolius; our Editors observe, that, whether through his own modesty or ill-fortune, it happens that we have hardly any memoirs of him, and that very few particulars relating to him have been handed down to posterity. It appears indeed that he was happy in the friendship of some very considerable persons, whose bounty relieved the domestic poverty he seems by his own expressions to have laboured under.

Our Editors take notice of a book of his, "De veris Principiis et verâ Ratione Philosophandi, &c. printed at Parma, 1553." He likewise translated Galen's "Explanation of the obsolete Words in Hippocrates," which was published with the Works of Galen 1550. The "Thesaurum Ciceronianum" was his masterpiece; but even that is now in no esteem with the Learned, who think it never was answerable to the time and pains he professes to have expended in the composing of it.

The last of all those that precede the immortal Stephens in the rank of Lexicographers is Basilius Zanchius of Bergamo. He has a title to this character, both as he contributed to Nizolius's Observations on Cicero, and as he added a great collection of words to Calepin, gathered from some of the best and purest authors. He was a canon of the order of Lateran, and resided for almost the whole of his life at Rome, beloved and honoured by the Literati of that city, which at that time were more than ordinarily numerous and eminent. He wrote "Observations on all the Books of Scripture," which were printed in 8vo at Cologne 1602; and "Questions on the four Books of Kings, and two of Chronicles," which he extracted chiefly from the works of Theodoret: likewise a "Treasury of Latin Epithets," and some sacred Poems very much esteemed, especially the "Hortus Sophiæ," in heroic verse, inscribed to Cardinal Bembo. He was made Keeper of the Vatican Library; filled that post with dignity and applause; and died at Rome in 1560.

The name of STEPHENS is greatly reverenced in the Republick of Letters, and with good reason; since to this family it is indebted for the most correct and beautiful impressions of the best Authors, the antient Greek ones particularly.

HENRY STEPHENS, the first distinguished person of his name, was a Frenchman, and one of the best printers of his time. He died in 1520, and left three sons behind him, who carried the art of printing to perfection; and were, two of them at least, very extraordinary men, exclusively of their professional merit.

ROBERT, his second son, was born at Paris in 1503; and applied so severely to letters in his youth, that he acquired a perfect knowledge in the Latin, Greek, and Hebrew tongues. His father dying, as we have said, in 1520, his mother was married the year after to Simon de Colines, in Latin Colinæus; who by this means came into the possession of Henry Stephens's printing-house, carried on the business till his death, in 1547, and is well known for the neatness and beauty of his Italic character. In 1522, when he was nineteen years of age, he was charged with the management of his father-in-law's press; and the same year came out, under his inspection, a New Testament in Latin, which gave such offence to the Paris Divines, that they threatened to have it burned, and him banished. He appears to have married, and to have set up for himself, soon after; for there are books of his printing dated so early as 1526. He married Perrette, the daughter of Badius, a printer; who was a learned woman, and understood Latin well. She had, indeed, more occasion for this accomplishment than wives usually have: for Robert Stephens had always in his house ten or twelve correctors of his press, who, being learned men of different nations, spoke nothing but Latin; from whence there was a necessity that his domestics should know something of the language. He resolved from the beginning to print nothing but good books: he only used the Roman characters at first, but afterwards employed the Italic. His mark was a tree branched, and a man looking upon it, with these words, *noli altum sapere,* to which he sometimes added *sed time.* In some of his first editions, he did not use figures and catch-words, as thinking them of little importance. In 1539, Francis I. named him his printer; and ordered a new set of letters to be founded, and antient manuscripts to be sought after, for him. The aversion which the Doctors of the Sorbonne had conceived against him, on account of the Latin New Testament in 1522, revived in 1532, when he printed his great Latin Bible: Francis protected him: but this king dying in 1547, he saw plainly that there was no more good to be done at Paris; and therefore, after sustaining the efforts of his enemies till 1552, he withdrew from thence to Geneva. It has been pretended by some that Robert Stephens carried with him not only the types of the royal press, but also the matrices, or moulds, those types were cast in: but this cannot be true, not only because no mention was made of any such thing for above sixty years after, but because none of the Stephens's afterwards ever used these types : and if Robert was burned in effigy at Paris, as Beza in the Icones relates, it was not for this, but for his embracing Calvinism at Geneva, of which he was suspected before he left Paris. He lived in intimacy at Geneva with Calvin, Beza, Rivet, and others, whose works he printed, and died there Sept. 7, 1559. This eminent artist was so exact and solicitous after perfection, that, in a noble contempt of gain, he used to expose his proofs to public view, with offer of a reward to those who should discover any faults; so that it is no wonder his impressions should be as correct as beautiful. He was, like the rest of his family, not only a printer, but a writer; his "Thesaurus Linguæ Latinæ" is a work of immense learning, as well as labour; and he published also in 1552, when he went to Geneva, a Latin piece, in answer to the Paris Divines, who had abused his Latin editions of the Old and New Testament, which shews his parts as well as learning. He left his substance, which was very considerable, to such of his children as should come to Geneva, exclusively of the rest. He had a daughter who understood Latin well, which she had learned by hearing it talked in her father's family; and three sons, Henry, Robert, and Francis. But, before we take any notice of these, we must say a word or two of his brothers, Francis and Charles.

Francis, older than himself, we know no more of, than that he worked jointly with his father-in-law Colinæus, after Robert had left him; and that he died at Paris about the year 1550. Charles, his younger brother, though more considerable than Francis, was yet inferior to himself both as a printer and a scholar; nevertheless, Charles wrote and printed many useful and valuable works. He was born about the year 1504, and became so perfectly skilled in Greek and Latin literature, that Lazarus de Baif took him for preceptor to his son Anthony, and afterwards carried him with him into Germany. He studied physic, and took a doctor's degree at Paris; but this did not hinder him from following the profession of his father, and being printer to the king. In the mean time, he was more of an author than a printer; having written upwards of thirty works upon various subjects. He died at Paris in 1564, leaving behind him a very learned daughter.

HENRY, ROBERT, and FRANCIS, the sons of Robert, make the third generation of the Stephens's, and were all printers. It is necessary to be somewhat particular about HENRY. He was born at Paris in 1528; and, being most carefully educated by his father, became the most learned of all his learned family. He was particularly skilled in the Greek language, which he conceived a fondness for from his infancy, studied afterwards under Turnebus and the best masters, and became at length so perfect in, as to pass for the best Grecian in Europe, after the death of Budæus. He had also a strong passion for poetry, while he was yet a child, which he cultivated all his life, and gave in his tenderest years so many proofs of uncommon abilities, that he has always been ranked among the *célèbres enfants*. He had a violent propensity to astrology in the younger part of his life, and procured a master in that way; but soon perceived the vanity of it, and laid it aside. It seems to have been about the year 1546, when his father took him into business: yet, before he could think of fixing, he resolved to travel into foreign countries, to examine libraries, and to connect himself with learned men. He went into Italy in 1547, and stayed there two years; and returned to Paris in 1549, when he subjoined some Greek verses, made in his youth, to a folio edition of the New Testament in Greek, which his father had just finished. In 1550, he went over to England; and in 1551 to Flanders, where he learned the Spanish tongue of the Spaniards, who then possessed those countries, as he had before learned the Italian in Italy. On his return to Paris, he found his father preparing to leave France: we do not know whether he accompanied him to Geneva; but, if he did, it is certain that he returned immediately after to Paris, and set up a printing-house. In 1554, he went to Rome, visiting his father at Geneva as he went, and the year after to Naples; and returned to Paris, by the way of Venice, in 1556. This was upon business committed to him by the government. Then he sat down to printing in good earnest, and never left off till he had given the world the most beautiful and correct editions of all the antient Greek and other valuable writers. He called himself at first printer of Paris; but, in 1558, took the title of printer to Ulric Fugger, a very rich German, who allowed him a considerable pension. He was at Geneva in 1558, to see his father, who died the year after; and he married in 1560. Henry III. of France was very fond of Stephens, sent him to Switzerland in search of manuscripts, and gave him a pension. He took him to court, and made him great promises: but the troubles, which accompanied the latter part of this king's reign, not only occasioned Stephens to be disappointed, but made his situation in France so dangerous, that he thought it but prudent to remove, as his father had done before him, to Geneva. Notwithstanding all his excellent labours, and the infinite obligations due to him from the publick, he is said to have become poor in his old age; the cause of which is thus related by several authors. Stephens had been at vast expence, as well as labour, in compiling and printing his "Thesaurus Linguæ Græcæ:" so much, in short, that, without proper reimbursements from the publick, he and his family must be inevitably ruined. These reimbursements, however, were never made; for his servant, John Scapula, extracted from this treasure, what he thought would be most necessary, and of greatest use, to the generality of students, and published a Lexicon in 4to, under his own name, which has since been enlarged and printed often in folio. By this act of treachery he destroyed the sale, though he could not destroy the credit of the Thesaurus; and, though he ruined his master, left him the glory of a work, which was then pronounced by Scaliger, and has ever been judged by all learned men, most excellent. He died in 1598, leaving a son PAUL and two daughters; one of which, named FLORENCE, had espoused the learned Isaac Casaubon in April 1586. He was the most learned printer that had then been, or perhaps ever will be : all his Greek authors are most correctly printed; and the Latin versions which he gave to some of them are, as Casaubon and Huetius have said, very faithful. The chief authors of antiquity printed by him are Anacreon, Æschylus, Maximus Tyrius, Diodorus Siculus, Pindar, Xenophon, Thucydides, Herodotus, Sophocles, Diogenes Laertius, Plutarch, Plato, Apollonius Rhodius, Æschines, Lysias, Callimachus, Theocritus, Herodian, Dionysius Halicarnassensis, Dion. Cassius, Isocrates, Appian, Xiphilin, &c. He did not meddle so much with Latin authors, although he printed some of them; as Horace and Virgil, which he illustrated with notes and a commentary of his own; Tully's Familiar Epistles, and the Epistles and Panegyric of the younger Pliny. But he was not content with printing the works of others: he wrote also a great many things himself. His "Thesaurus Græcæ Linguæ" has been already mentioned : another piece, which made him very famous, was his "Introduction à l'Apologie pour Herodote." This ran through many editions, and is a very severe satire upon popery and its professors.

PAUL STEPHENS, the son of Henry, though inferior to his father, was yet well skilled in the Greek and Latin tongues. His father was more solicitous about his being instructed in these, than in the art of printing. He carried on the business of a printer for some time at Geneva; but his press had greatly degenerated from the beauty of that at Paris, and he afterwards sold his types to Chouet, a printer. He died at Geneva in 1627, aged 60, leaving a son Anthony, who was the last printer of the Stephens's.

ANTHONY, quitting the religion of his father for that of his ancestors, quitted also Geneva, and returned to Paris, the place of their original. Here he was some time printer to the king; but, managing his affairs ill, he was obliged to give all up, and to have recourse to an hospital, where he died in extreme misery and blindness in 1674, aged eighty years. Such was the end of the illustrious family of STEPHENS, after it had flourished for five generations; and had done great honour to itself, by doing incredible service to the Republick of Letters.

Three editions of the Thesaurus were published by Robert Stephens; in 1531, 1536, and 1543. Two others were undertaken whilst he was living: one of them in 1545 by Theodosius Trebellius, intituled, "Promptuarium Linguæ Latinæ;" another in 1551 by Marius Nizolius; and a third, increased in bulk but not in value, by Philip Tinghius, a native of Florence, in four volumes, Lugd. Bat. 1579. The "Commentarii Latinæ Linguæ," by Stephen Doletus, [Etienne Dolet] an able French printer, 2 volumes in 4to, which are founded on the Thesaurus, was published in 1545.

Cælius Secundus Curio, an Italian, born in 1503, being persecuted for his religious sentiments, was driven to Basel, where he settled, was for more than two-and-twenty years a very celebrated orator, and died in 1569. He employed himself for a considerable time in correcting a work which came out in 1576, long after his death, under the title of "Thesaurus Linguæ Latinæ, sive Forum Romanum," in three volumes, folio.

Marcus Frid. Windelinus, published a "Medulla Latinitatis."

John Fungerus Frisius compiled a "Dictionarium Latino-Germanicum," which has passed through two or more editions.

M. Martinius, J. Norwegus Hessus, and John Gerard Vossius, are all commended by the editors of Robert Stephens, for their skill in etymology.

Robert Constantinus and Josephus Laurentius are also mentioned in very high terms, for their abilities in explaining the *Voces abstrusiores;* and G. Matthias Kœnigius, for having collected, in his "Gazophylacium Latinitatis," a great number of words which were to be met with in no preceding collection.

Peter Dasypodius was compiler of a Dictionary in common use in Germany; Morell, Gaudinus, and Petrus Danetus, were the Lexicographers of France : those of our own country, the following summary by Mr. Ainsworth will faithfully explain.

"Promptorium parvulorum sive clericorum," printed by Richard Pynson in the year MCCCCXCIX, in folio, is the first book of this sort I have ever met with. This consisteth only of one part, which exhibiteth the English words before the Latin, being destitute both of the Latin and historical parts. But these defects were in part supplied by

"Ortus vocabulorum, alphabetico ordine ferè omnia, quæ in Catholico, Breviloquio, Cornucopia, Gemmâ Vocabulorum, atque Medullâ Grammaticæ ponuntur, cum Vernaculæ Linguæ Anglicanæ expositione, continens," printed by Wynkyn de Worde in the year MDXXVI, in quarto. This is compiled in two distinct alphabetical parts, in the former of which the Latin words are placed before their explications in English, in the latter the English words are put before the Latin. The declensions and genders of Latin nouns, as well as the conjugations and preterperfect tenses of the verbs, are set down very particularly, both in the Dictionary before mentioned, and in the English part of this work. [First edition, 1500 (*Ed.*)]

The "Vulgaria Roberti Whitintoni Lichfeldiensis" printed in MDXXV, "Vulgaria Stanbrigi" in MDXXIX, and "Vocabula Magistri Stanbrigii" in MDXXXI, scarcely deserve to be mentioned in this place, being rather a sort of Vocabularies than Dictionaries of the Latin and English tongues.

Thomas Elyot also obliged our countrymen with the publication of a Latin and English Dictionary, printed at London in the year MDXLII, in folio, with the title of "Bibliothecæ Eliotæ," which seems to be much more copious than any of the former. This author was born of a knightly family in Suffolk, received part of his education at Oxford, then travelled beyond the seas, and on his return was introduced at Court. King Henry VIII. finding him to be a person of good parts, conferred the honour of knighthood upon him, and employed him in certain embassies beyond the seas, particularly to Rome about the divorce of Queen Katharine, and afterwards to the Emperor Charles V. during which last his great friend and crony Sir Thomas More was beheaded. He died in March MDXLVI, and was buried at Carleton in the county of Cambridge. But the Editors of the late edition of Stephens's Latin Thesaurus, for what reason I know not, say that Elyot was *primus qui has literas inter nos professus est.*

Thomas Cooper, being sensible of several defects in the Dictionary published by Sir Thomas Elyot, took no small pains in improving it; for, besides giving a much fuller acount of the different senses of the Latin words, "he added 33,000 words and phrases : the materials, for the most part, being taken from Robert Stephens's Thesaurus, and John Frisius's Latin and German Dictionary," saith Anthony Wood in the second edition of his "Athenæ Oxonienses" in MDCCXXI. This work passed through several editions; the first was at London in MDLII, which still retained the name of Elyot; but it was afterwards reprinted with large improvements in MDLXV, with the title of "Thesaurus Linguæ Romanæ et Britannicæ," &c. and again in MDLXXVIII, as also in MDLXXXIV, which last is esteemed the best. It may not be amiss to observe, that both Elyot's and Cooper's Dictionaries want the English part proper to assist younger scholars in translating English into Latin, though they have the historical and poetical part. This reverend author was born at Oxford, and afterwards elected into a fellowship of Magdalen College there. Queen Elizabeth had so great an esteem for him, on account of the service he had done to learning by the publication of this useful work, that she promoted him to the deanry of Gloucester in MDLXIX; to the bishoprick of Lincoln in MDLXX; and to that of Winchester in MDLXXXIV, where he ended his days 29 April MDXCIV.

Barret's "Alvearie," or quadruple Dictionary in English, Latin, Greek, and French, was printed at London in the year MDLXXX, in folio. The author of this work having been employed several years in the instruction of youth, and observing the Latin Dictionaries of his times to be very defective in giving proper assistance to younger students, chiefly for translating English into Latin, made a large collection both of words and phrases out of the classic authors to supply their defects in this particular, with a design to publish them to the world; but, being prevented by death, this work was afterwards published by a friend of the Author. As this hath gone through but one impression, so far as I can find, I need say no more of it, than that it seemeth to be a valuable performance for those times.

Thomas Thomasius, who was for some years printer to the University of Cambridge, and died 9 Aug. MDLXXXV, published also a Latin and English Dictionary, in quarto; which met with so favourable a reception, that it "underwent five impressions in the space of eight years, and bore in all fourteen impressions," say the editors of the last edition of Stephens's Thesaurus. I have not been able to procure a sight of the first edition of Thomasius, and therefore can neither determine the precise time of its first appearance in the world, nor ascertain the number of its parts when first published; but that some distinct parts were added to the following editions, will evidently appear by a recital of part of the title to the tenth edition thereof in MDCXV, printed by Legat, who succeeded him as printer to the said University; "Huic etiam (præter Dictionarium historicum et poeticum, ad prophanas historias, poëtarumque fabulas intelligendas valdè necessarium) novissimè accessit utilissimus de ponderum, mensurarum, et monetarum veterum reductione ad ea, quæ sunt Anglis jam in usu, tractatus. Decima editio superioribus, cum Græcarum dictionum, tum earundem primitivorum adjectione, multò auctior. Cui demum adjectum est supplementum, authore Ph. Hollando, med. doctore, nova aliquot dictionum millia complectens; unà cum novo Anglo-Latino dictionario." Hence we may observe, that how imperfect soever the former editions of this book were, yet this consisted of the three chief parts, into which most of the Latin and English dictionaries published since that time have been divided.

Philemon Holland, who made the said Supplement to Thomasius's Dictionary, was born at Chelmsford towards the latter end of the reign of King Edward VI.; educated in Trinity College, Cambridge; was afterwards, for about twenty years, master of the free-school at Coventry, after that practised physick in the same county, and departed this life 9 Feb. MDCXXXVI. This supplement is printed distinctly from the other parts of that book, and called Paralipomena, as containing such Latin words as the Doctor had gleaned from classic and other Latin authors, and were omitted by Thomasius.

John Rider, born at Carrington in Cheshire, educated in Jesus College Oxford, for some time minister of St. Magdalen Bermondsey in Southwark, then rector of Winwick in Lancashire, and promoted to the bishoprick of Killaloe in Ireland in the year MDCXII, where he continued to his death, which was in MDCXXXII, published a Dictionary, English and Latin, and Latin and English, at Oxford, in MDLXXXIX, in a large thick quarto. This, saith A. Wood, "was the first Dictionary that had the English before the Latin, epitomizing the learnedest and choicest

Dictionaries that were then extant, and was beheld as the best
that was then in use; but that part of it which had the Latin
before the English was swallowed up by the greater attempts
of Francis Holyoake." But that Mr. Wood was mistaken in this
case, if he means that Rider's Dictionary was the first which
consists of an English and Latin part, as well of the Latin and
the English, plainly appeareth by what is said before in my
account of the Promptorium, as well as of the "Ortus Vocabulorum," though, so far as I can find, Rider's was the first Latin
Dictionary in which the English part was placed at the beginning
of the book before the Latin part.

Francis Holyoake, who was born at Nether Whitacre in Warwickshire, educated at Queen's College at Oxford, afterwards
kept a school in his own country, and was made rector of
Southam there in MDCIV, took considerable pains in revising,
correcting, and augmenting what Rider had published, especially
with regard to the etymological part: this was first printed at
London in MDCVI, in quarto, and was afterwards reprinted
several times with enlargements. He died 12 Nov. MDCXXXII.

Thomas Holyoake, his son, who was born at Stony Thorp,
near Southam before mentioned, educated in Queen's College
Oxford, was rector of Whitnash in Warwickshire, and prebendary of the collegiate church of Wolverhampton in Staffordshire,
made very large additions to the Dictionary published by his
father, with a design to print them in a new edition; but dying
10 June MDCLXXV, the same was published by his son Charles,
of the Inner Temple, London, in a large and well-printed folio,
in MDCLXXVII.

Nicholas Gray likewise made some additions to Rider, which
were several times printed at London, saith A. Wood; but the
same author owneth himself at a loss as to the time of its first
publication, and adds, "that a second or third edition of Holyoake's coming out prevented, as it is said, the farther publication
of it." This gentleman was born in London, elected student of
Christ Church, Oxford, from Westminster School, in the year
MDCVI, and was afterwards the first master of the Charterhouse
School in London; but, after some years, marrying, against the
statutes of that house, the governors thereof discharged him from
that employment, by presenting him to the benefice of Castle
Camps in Cambridgeshire. In January MDCXXIV he was admitted
chief master of Merchant Taylors School in London, and in
MDCXXXI chief master of Eton, out of which he was expelled in

the time of the Civil Wars; but, being restored on the return of King Charles II. he died at Eton towards the close of the year MDCLX, and was buried in the Chapel there.

Christopher Wase, fellow of King's College in Cambridge, and afterwards superior beadle of law in Oxford, published likewise a Latin Dictionary, the second edition of which was printed in MDCLXXV. This is a compendium of Calepin; but "done with so much judgment," saith Dr. Littleton in his Latin Preface to his Dictionary, "that one can hardly find anything in it which savoureth of barbarism." However, it seemeth to be rather designed for the use of those who have made some proficiency in the Latin tongue, than for such as are only beginning to learn that language.

Francis Gouldman, who was educated in Christ's College in Cambridge, was for some time rector of South Okendon in Essex, and died in MDCLXXXIX, published also a Latin Dictionary in quarto, in MDCLXIV, which was afterwards reprinted several times, and the Cambridge edition in MDCLXXIV much enlarged by William Robertson*. But Gouldman's design, according to the account of Dr. Littleton, his successor in this sort of learning, was "rather to make new editions than to correct the former mistakes," or to throw out the many barbarous Latin words which had crept into the dictionaries then extant. For this reason,

Dr. Adam Littleton undertook to reform it; whose "greatest aim," as he tells the English reader in his Preface, "was to carry the purity of the Latin tongue throughout, and not to take things or words upon trust, so as to transcribe others mistakes." This was first published in quarto in London in MDCLXXVIII, and hath met with such a general approbation, that the sixth edition thereof was published but a few months ago. He was a minister's son, of an antient and genteel family at Westcot in Worcestershire, elected student of Christ Church in Oxford in MDCXLVII, was some time an usher in Westminster School, and in MDCLVIII became second master of the same. After the Restoration he was chaplain to King Charles II. rector of Chelsea, and subdean of Westminster. He died in the beginning of July MDCXCIV, and was buried in Chelsea church.

The Cambridge Dictionary in quarto, printed in MDCXCIII, with the title of "Linguæ Romanæ Dictionarium luculentum

---

*It was still further enlarged in 1678 by Dr. Scattergood.

novum," is an improvement of Littleton, made by several persons whose names have been concealed from public knowledge. What plan the editors of this have proceeded upon may be learnt by their own preface; in which, after a grateful acknowledgment of the great assistance they had by the extraordinary pains of the reverend and learned Dr. Littleton as to the English Latin part, they principally set forth, that they have inserted several whole classes of words, which had been either omitted before, or were very lately introduced into our language; and that they have been more exact, more distinct and full, in noting the various significations of verbs and nouns; that in the Latin *classic* they began their collection by a careful perusal of several authors, as Lucretius, Terence, Cæsar, Phædrus, Gratian, Petronius, &c. some of whom, they observed, had scarce been named, or if sometimes quoted, often so very little, and sometimes to very bad purposes, in dictionaries of the same volume with theirs; that the second edition of Robert Stephens's Latin Thesaurus lay always before them, and was constantly consulted by them; that they likewise used a manuscript collection in three large folios, digested into an alphabetical order, made by Mr. John Milton out of all the best and purest Roman authors; and farther, that the complete *indices* generally annexed to the Dauphin editions of most of the Roman writers had been very serviceable to them; that they had retrenched many far-fetched *etymons* in former Dictionaries, had given a larger account of the construction of verbs, had rejected all words and phrases, whose authors were either not to be found, or, when found, appeared in so barbarous and uncouth a dress as made them very unfit company for Tully, Cæsar, &c. And, finally, had distinguished the poetical Latin words by a flower † placed before them. Thus far they. Those who are desirous to have a more particular account of the difference between this Dictionary and that published by Dr. Littleton, as to the English and Latin part, may satisfy their curiosity by the comparison of a few sheets of each; but it is very manifest that these editors have made very large and useful improvements in the letters L, M, N, O, and P, in the Latin classical part, and augmented or corrected what had been done by Littleton (though neither in so large nor careful a manner as under the aforesaid letters) in most of the other parts of the work. The improvements made under the aforesaid letters, as also a large part of their title, as well as the preface, have been inserted in the several editions of Littleton (except the last, which hath a new preface, and that been otherwise somewhat altered) printed since the publication of this work at Cambridge; but the other parts of Littleton in general remain as they were when first published.

Elisha Coles published also a Latin and English dictionary in the year MDCLXXVII, designed chiefly for the use of scholars of a lower class. He hath indeed considerably enlarged the English Latin part, which containeth many more English words and phrases than any Latin Dictionary published before his time. But not a few of those words are now entirely obsolete, many of them interpreted in a wrong sense, and worse translated into Latin. And the Latin-English part is very defective, both with regard to the several senses of the Latin words, and the citation of the Roman writers proper to fix their authority. This work, however, being not half the price of Dr. Littleton's, hath gone through twelve impressions; the first whereof was printed in a small quarto, and all the following in octavo. The author of this work was born in Northamptonshire, entered into Magdalen college in Oxford in the year MDCLVIII, taught the languages to foreigners in the parish of Covent Garden in London, and was afterwards for some time an usher in Merchant Taylors School: after which, on some default, being obliged to quit that employment, he went into Ireland, where he continued till his death; but of the precise time thereof I have not been able to get any certain information.   R. AINSWORTH."

THE BOOKSELLERS OF LITTLE BRITAIN

THE following observations, by the Hon. Roger North, on the booksellers of Little Britain (of whom Mr. Edward Ballard, who died Jan. 2, 1796, at the very advanced age of 88, was the last genuine representative) will not, it is hoped, be here misplaced.

"Mr. Robert Scott, of Little Britain, was in his time the greatest librarian in Europe; for, besides his stock in England, he had warehouses at Frankfort, Paris, and other places, and dealt by factors. After he was grown old, and much worn by multiplicity of business, he began to think of his ease, and to leave off : hereupon he contracted with one Mr. Mills, of St. Paul's church-yard, near 10,000*l*. deep, and articled not to open his shop any more. But Mills, with his auctioneering, atlases, and projects, failed; whereby poor Scott lost above half his means. But he held to his contract of not opening his shop; and, when he was in London (for he had a country-house), passed most of his time at his house amongst the rest of his books; and his reading (for he was no mean scholar) was the chief entertainment of his time. He was not only a very great bookseller, but a very conscientious good man; and, when he threw up his trade, Europe had no small loss of him. — Little Britain was, in the middle of the last century, a plentiful and learned emporium of learned authors; and men went thither as to a market. This drew to the place a mighty trade, the rather because the shops were spacious, and the Learned gladly resorted to them, where they seldom failed to meet with agreeable conversation; and the Booksellers themselves were knowing and conversible men, with whom, for the sake of bookish knowledge, the greatest wits were pleased to converse; and we may judge the time as well spent there, as (in latter days) either in taverns or coffee-houses, though the latter has carried off the spare time of most people. But now this emporium is vanished, and the trade contracted into the hands of two or three persons, who, to make good their monopoly, ransack not only their neighbours of the trade, that are scattered about town, but all over England; aye, and beyond-sea too; and send abroad their circulators, and in that manner get into their hands all that is valuable. The rest of the trade are content to take their refuse, with which, and the first scum of the press, they furnish one side of a shop, which serves for the sign of a bookseller, rather than a real one; but, instead of selling, deal as factors, and procure what the country divines and gentry send for, of whom each one has his book-factor; and, when wanting any thing, writes to his bookseller, and pays his bill; and it is wretched to consider what pick-pocket work, with help of the press, these demi-booksellers make; they crack their brains to find out selling subjects, and keep hire-lings in garrets, on hard meat, to write and correct by the great; so puff up an octavo to a sufficient thickness, and there is six shillings current for an hour and a half's reading, and perhaps never to be read or looked upon after. One that would go higher, must take his fortune at blank walls and corners of streets, or repair to the sign of Bateman, Innys, and one or two more, where there are best choice and better pennyworths."

Of Bateman, who lived in Little Britain, and dealt principally in old books, John Dunton says, "There are very few booksellers in England (if any) that understand books better than Mr. Bateman, nor does his diligence and industry come short of his knowledge. He is a man of great reputation and honesty, and is the son of that famous Bateman who got an Alderman's estate by bookselling." Swift, in a letter to Stella, Jan. 6, 1710-11, says, "I went to Bateman's the bookseller, and laid out eight and forty shillings for books. I bought three little volumes of Lucian in French for our Stella." It was said that Bateman never would suffer any person whatever to look into one book in his shop; and, when asked a reason for it, would say, "I suppose you may be a physician or an author, and want some recipe or quotation; and, if you buy it, I will engage it to be perfect before you leave me, but not after; as I have suffered by leaves being torn out, and the books returned, to my very great loss and prejudice."